Haynes
THE BOOK ®

Peugeo

Service a   al

Mark Coombs

Roscommon County Library

3 0001 00273219 8

D0295037

Roscommon County Library Service

LEABHARLANN CHONTAE ROSCOMAIN

WITHDRAWN FROM STOCK

This book should be returned not later than the last date shown below. It may be renewed if not requested by another borrower.

Books are on loan for 14 days from the date of issue.

420 259
629
28722

DATE DUE	DATE DUE	DATE DUE	DATE DUE

COUNTY LIBRARY SERVICE ROSCOMMON

Models covered
Peugeot 406 front-wheel-drive Salo   (3394-312)
with normally-aspirated four-cylinde   ed editions;

1580 cc, 1761 cc, & 1998 cc petrol engi
1905 cc & 2088 cc turbo diesel engines

Does not cover 1998 cc (petrol) Turbo or 2946

© Haynes Publishing 1997

A book in the **Haynes Service and Repair Manual Series**

ABCDE
FGHIJ
KLMNO
PQ

Printed by **J H Haynes & Co Ltd**, Sparkford, Nr Yeovil, **Somerset BA22 7JJ, England**

Haynes Publishing
Sparkford, Nr Yeovil, Somerset BA22 7JJ, England

Haynes North America, Inc
861 Lawrence Drive, Newbury Park, California 91320, USA

Editions Haynes S.A.
Tour Aurore - La Défense 2, 18 Place des Reflets, 92975 PARIS LA DEFENSE Cedex, France

Haynes Publishing Nordiska AB
Box 1504, 751 45 UPPSALA, Sweden

ISBN **1 85960 394 7**

British Library Cataloguing in Publication Data
A catalogue record for this book is available from the British Library.

All rights reserved. No part of this book may be reproduced or transmitted in any form or by any means, electronic or mechanical, including photocopying, recording or by any information storage or retrieval system, without permission in writing from the copyright holder.

Contents

LIVING WITH YOUR PEUGEOT 406

MAINTENANCE

Routine maintenance and servicing

COUNTY LIBRARY SERVICE ROSCOMMON

42G289
629
28722

Roscommon County Library Service

Contents

REPAIRS & OVERHAUL

Engine and associated systems

Transmission

Brakes and suspension

Body equipment

Wiring diagrams

REFERENCE

Index

The Peugeot 406 Saloon was introduced into the UK in early 1996. At its launch, the 406 was offered with a choice of 1.6 (1580 cc - not available in the UK), 1.8 (1761 cc) and 2.0 litre (1998 cc) petrol engines or a 1.9 litre (1905 cc) turbo diesel engine.

The engines fitted to the 406 range are all versions of the well-proven units which have appeared in many Peugeot/Citroën vehicles over the years. The petrol engines are from the XU engine series, and are of four-cylinder overhead camshaft design; the 1.6 litre engine is a SOHC 8-valve unit and the 1.8 and 2.0 litre engines are DOHC 16-valve units. The diesel engine is from the XUD engine series, and is a SOHC 8-valve unit.

The engine is mounted transversely at the front of vehicle, with the transmission mounted on its left-hand end. All engines are fitted with a manual transmission as standard (an automatic transmission option was introduced at a later date on some engines).

All models have fully-independent front and rear suspension arrangements incorporating shock absorbers and coil springs.

A wide range of standard and optional equipment is available within the range to suit most tastes, including central locking, electric windows and an electric sunroof. An air conditioning system was available as an option on certain models.

In the summer of 1996, a 2.1 litre (2088 cc) turbo diesel engine was introduced into the range (a 2.0 litre petrol turbo model was also introduced, but is not covered by this manual). The new engine is a 12-valve version of the XUD engine which has also been used in other Peugeot/Citroën vehicles.

In early 1997, Peugeot introduced an Estate model, and also introduced the V6 petrol engine (not covered by this manual) into the range. Apart from this, only minor detail changes have been made to the vehicle.

Provided that regular servicing is carried out in accordance with the manufacturer's recommendations, the vehicle should prove reliable and very economical. The engine compartment is well-designed, and most of the items requiring frequent attention are easily accessible.

Peugeot 406 Saloon

Peugeot 406 Estate

The Peugeot 406 Team

Haynes manuals are produced by dedicated and enthusiastic people working in close co-operation. The team responsible for the creation of this book included:

Authors	Mark Coombs John S Mead
Sub-editor	Sophie Yar
Editor & Page Make-up	Bob Jex
Workshop manager	Paul Buckland
Photo Scans	John Martin Steve Tanswell
Cover illustration & Line Art	Roger Healing
Wiring diagrams	Matthew Marke

We hope the book will help you to get the maximum enjoyment from your car. By carrying out routine maintenance as described you will ensure your car's reliability and preserve its resale value.

Your Peugeot 406 manual

The aim of this manual is to help you get the best value from your vehicle. It can do so in several ways. It can help you decide what work must be done (even should you choose to get it done by a garage). It will also provide information on routine maintenance and servicing, and give a logical course of action and diagnosis when random faults occur. However, it is hoped that you will use the manual by tackling the work yourself. On simpler jobs it may even be quicker than booking the car into a garage and going there twice, to leave and collect it. Perhaps most important, a lot of money can be saved by avoiding the costs a garage must charge to cover its labour and overheads.

The manual has drawings and descriptions to show the function of the various components so that their layout can be understood. Tasks are described and photographed in a clear step-by-step sequence.

Acknowledgements

Thanks are due to Champion Spark Plug, who supplied the illustrations showing spark plug conditions. Duckhams Oils provided lubrication data. Thanks are also due to Sykes-Pickavant Limited, who provided some of the workshop tools, and to all those people at Sparkford who helped in the production of this manual.

We take great pride in the accuracy of information given in this manual, but vehicle manufacturers make alterations and design changes during the production run of a particular vehicle of which they do not inform us. No liability can be accepted by the authors or publishers for loss, damage or injury caused by any errors in, or omissions from, the information given.

Working on your car can be dangerous. This page shows just some of the potential risks and hazards, with the aim of creating a safety-conscious attitude.

General hazards

Scalding

• Don't remove the radiator or expansion tank cap while the engine is hot.
• Engine oil, automatic transmission fluid or power steering fluid may also be dangerously hot if the engine has recently been running.

Burning

• Beware of burns from the exhaust system and from any part of the engine. Brake discs and drums can also be extremely hot immediately after use.

Crushing

• When working under or near a raised vehicle, always supplement the jack with axle stands, or use drive-on ramps. *Never venture under a car which is only supported by a jack.*
• Take care if loosening or tightening high-torque nuts when the vehicle is on stands. Initial loosening and final tightening should be done with the wheels on the ground.

Fire

• Fuel is highly flammable; fuel vapour is explosive.
• Don't let fuel spill onto a hot engine.
• Do not smoke or allow naked lights (including pilot lights) anywhere near a vehicle being worked on. Also beware of creating sparks (electrically or by use of tools).
• Fuel vapour is heavier than air, so don't work on the fuel system with the vehicle over an inspection pit.
• Another cause of fire is an electrical overload or short-circuit. Take care when repairing or modifying the vehicle wiring.
• Keep a fire extinguisher handy, of a type suitable for use on fuel and electrical fires.

Electric shock

• Ignition HT voltage can be dangerous, especially to people with heart problems or a pacemaker. Don't work on or near the ignition system with the engine running or the ignition switched on.

• Mains voltage is also dangerous. Make sure that any mains-operated equipment is correctly earthed. Mains power points should be protected by a residual current device (RCD) circuit breaker.

Fume or gas intoxication

• Exhaust fumes are poisonous; they often contain carbon monoxide, which is rapidly fatal if inhaled. Never run the engine in a confined space such as a garage with the doors shut.

• Fuel vapour is also poisonous, as are the vapours from some cleaning solvents and paint thinners.

Poisonous or irritant substances

• Avoid skin contact with battery acid and with any fuel, fluid or lubricant, especially antifreeze, brake hydraulic fluid and Diesel fuel. Don't syphon them by mouth. If such a substance is swallowed or gets into the eyes, seek medical advice.
• Prolonged contact with used engine oil can cause skin cancer. Wear gloves or use a barrier cream if necessary. Change out of oil-soaked clothes and do not keep oily rags in your pocket.
• Air conditioning refrigerant forms a poisonous gas if exposed to a naked flame (including a cigarette). It can also cause skin burns on contact.

Asbestos

• Asbestos dust can cause cancer if inhaled or swallowed. Asbestos may be found in gaskets and in brake and clutch linings. When dealing with such components it is safest to assume that they contain asbestos.

Special hazards

Hydrofluoric acid

• This extremely corrosive acid is formed when certain types of synthetic rubber, found in some O-rings, oil seals, fuel hoses etc, are exposed to temperatures above 400°C. The rubber changes into a charred or sticky substance containing the acid. *Once formed, the acid remains dangerous for years. If it gets onto the skin, it may be necessary to amputate the limb concerned.*
• When dealing with a vehicle which has suffered a fire, or with components salvaged from such a vehicle, wear protective gloves and discard them after use.

The battery

• Batteries contain sulphuric acid, which attacks clothing, eyes and skin. Take care when topping-up or carrying the battery.
• The hydrogen gas given off by the battery is highly explosive. Never cause a spark or allow a naked light nearby. Be careful when connecting and disconnecting battery chargers or jump leads.

Air bags

• Air bags can cause injury if they go off accidentally. Take care when removing the steering wheel and/or facia. Special storage instructions may apply.

Diesel injection equipment

• Diesel injection pumps supply fuel at very high pressure. Take care when working on the fuel injectors and fuel pipes.

⚠ *Warning: Never expose the hands, face or any other part of the body to injector spray; the fuel can penetrate the skin with potentially fatal results.*

Remember...

DO

• Do use eye protection when using power tools, and when working under the vehicle.
• Do wear gloves or use barrier cream to protect your hands when necessary.
• Do get someone to check periodically that all is well when working alone on the vehicle.
• Do keep loose clothing and long hair well out of the way of moving mechanical parts.
• Do remove rings, wristwatch etc, before working on the vehicle – especially the electrical system.
• Do ensure that any lifting or jacking equipment has a safe working load rating adequate for the job.

DON'T

• Don't attempt to lift a heavy component which may be beyond your capability – get assistance.
• Don't rush to finish a job, or take unverified short cuts.
• Don't use ill-fitting tools which may slip and cause injury.
• Don't leave tools or parts lying around where someone can trip over them. Mop up oil and fuel spills at once.
• Don't allow children or pets to play in or near a vehicle being worked on.

The following pages are intended to help in dealing with common roadside emergencies and breakdowns. You will find more detailed fault finding information at the back of the manual, and repair information in the main chapters.

If your car won't start and the starter motor doesn't turn

- ☐ If it's a model with automatic transmission, make sure the selector is in 'P' or 'N'.
- ☐ Open the bonnet and make sure that the battery terminals are clean and tight.
- ☐ Switch on the headlights and try to start the engine. If the headlights go very dim when you're trying to start, the battery is probably flat. Get out of trouble by jump starting (see next page) using a friend's car.

If your car won't start even though the starter motor turns as normal

- ☐ Is there fuel in the tank?
- ☐ Is there moisture on electrical components under the bonnet? Switch off the ignition, then wipe off any obvious dampness with a dry cloth. Spray a water-repellent aerosol product (WD-40 or equivalent) on ignition and fuel system electrical connectors like those shown in the photos. Pay special attention to the ignition coil wiring connector and HT leads. (Note that diesel engines don't normally suffer from damp.)

A Remove the plastic cover and check the condition and security of the battery connections.

B Check that the fuel/ignition system (as applicable) wiring connectors are securely connected (2.0 litre petrol model shown).

C Check that the alternator wiring connectors are securely connected.

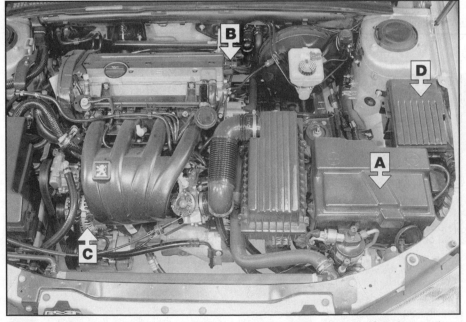

D Check that all fuses are still in good condition and none have blown.

Check that electrical connections are secure (with the ignition switched off) and spray them with a water-dispersant spray like WD-40 if you suspect a problem due to damp.

Jump starting

HAYNES HiNT *Jump starting will get you out of trouble, but you must correct whatever made the battery go flat in the first place. There are three possibilities:*

1) *The battery has been drained by repeated attempts to start, or by leaving the lights on.*
2) *The charging system is not working properly (alternator drivebelt slack or broken, alternator wiring fault or alternator itself faulty).*
3) *The battery itself is at fault (electrolyte low, or battery worn out).*

When jump-starting a car using a booster battery, observe the following precautions:

✔ Before connecting the booster battery, make sure that the ignition is switched off.

✔ Ensure that all electrical equipment (lights, heater, wipers, etc) is switched off.

✔ Take note of any special precautions printed on the battery case.

✔ Make sure that the booster battery is the same voltage as the discharged one in the vehicle.

✔ If the battery is being jump-started from the battery in another vehicle, the two vehicles MUST NOT TOUCH each other.

✔ Make sure that the transmission is in neutral (or PARK, in the case of automatic transmission).

1 Connect one end of the red jump lead to the positive (+) terminal of the flat battery

2 Connect the other end of the red lead to the positive (+) terminal of the booster battery

3 Connect one end of the black jump lead to the negative (-) terminal of the booster battery

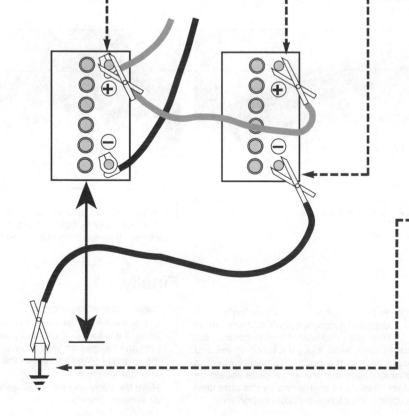

4 Connect the other end of the black jump lead to a bolt or bracket on the engine block, well away from the battery, on the vehicle to be started

5 Make sure that the jump leads will not come into contact with the fan, drivebelts or other moving parts of the engine

6 Start the engine using the booster battery, then with the engine running at idle speed, disconnect the jump leads in the reverse order of connection

Wheel changing

Some of the details shown here will vary according to model. For instance, the location of the spare wheel and jack is not the same on all cars. However, the basic principles apply to all vehicles.

 Warning: Do not change a wheel in a situation where you risk being hit by other traffic. On busy roads, try to stop in a lay-by or a gateway. Be wary of passing traffic while changing the wheel – it is easy to become distracted by the job in hand.

Preparation

☐ When a puncture occurs, stop as soon as it is safe to do so.
☐ Park on firm level ground, if possible, and well out of the way of other traffic.
☐ Use hazard warning lights if necessary.

☐ If you have one, use a warning triangle to alert other drivers of your presence.
☐ Apply the handbrake and engage first or reverse gear (or Park on models with automatic transmission).

☐ Chock the wheel diagonally opposite the one being removed – a couple of large stones will do for this.
☐ If the ground is soft, use a flat piece of wood to spread the load under the jack.

Changing the wheel

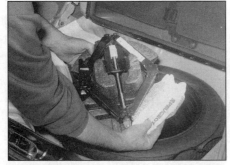

1 The spare wheel and tools are stored in the boot. Lift up the carpet/rear family seat (as applicable) and remove the tool kit and jack from the centre of the spare wheel. Unscrew the retainer and remove the spare wheel.

2 Remove the wheel trim/hub cap (as applicable). On models where anti-theft wheel bolts are fitted, pull off the plastic cover then unscrew the anti-theft bolt using the special socket provided.

3 With the vehicle on the ground, slacken each wheel bolt by half a turn.

4 Make sure the jack is located on firm ground, and engage the jack head correctly with the sill.

5 Raise the jack until the wheel is raised clear of the ground.

6 Unscrew the wheel bolts and remove the wheel. Fit the spare wheel and screw in the bolts. Lightly tighten the bolts with the wheelbrace then lower the car to the ground.

7 Securely tighten the wheel bolts in a diagonal sequence then refit the wheel trim/hub cap/wheel bolt covers (as applicable). Stow the punctured wheel and tools back in the boot, and secure them in position. Note that the wheel bolts should be slackened and retightened to the specified torque at the earliest possible opportunity.

Finally...

☐ Remove the wheel chocks.
☐ Check the tyre pressure on the wheel just fitted. If it is low, or if you don't have a pressure gauge with you, drive slowly to the nearest garage and inflate the tyre to the right pressure.
☐ Have the damaged tyre or wheel repaired as soon as possible.

Identifying leaks

Puddles on the garage floor or drive, or obvious wetness under the bonnet or underneath the car, suggest a leak that needs investigating. It can sometimes be difficult to decide where the leak is coming from, especially if the engine bay is very dirty already. Leaking oil or fluid can also be blown rearwards by the passage of air under the car, giving a false impression of where the problem lies.

⚠️ **Warning: Most automotive oils and fluids are poisonous. Wash them off skin, and change out of contaminated clothing, without delay.**

> **HAYNES HINT** *The smell of a fluid leaking from the car may provide a clue to what's leaking. Some fluids are distinctively coloured. It may help to clean the car and to park it over some clean paper as an aid to locating the source of the leak. Remember that some leaks may only occur while the engine is running.*

Sump oil

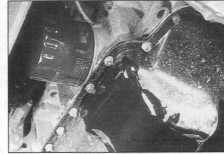

Engine oil may leak from the drain plug...

Oil from filter

...or from the base of the oil filter.

Gearbox oil

Gearbox oil can leak from the seals at the inboard ends of the driveshafts.

Antifreeze

Leaking antifreeze often leaves a crystalline deposit like this.

Brake fluid

A leak occurring at a wheel is almost certainly brake fluid.

Power steering fluid

Power steering fluid may leak from the pipe connectors on the steering rack.

Towing

When all else fails, you may find yourself having to get a tow home – or of course you may be helping somebody else. Long-distance recovery should only be done by a garage or breakdown service. For shorter distances, DIY towing using another car is easy enough, but observe the following points:

☐ Use a proper tow-rope – they are not expensive. The vehicle being towed must display an 'ON TOW' sign in its rear window.

☐ Always turn the ignition key to the 'on' position when the vehicle is being towed, so that the steering lock is released, and so that the direction indicator and brake lights will work.

☐ The towing eye is supplied in the vehicle toolkit which is stored in the luggage compartment with the spare wheel (see *"Wheel changing"*). To fit the eye, unclip the access cover from the relevant bumper and screw the eye firmly into position

☐ Before being towed, release the handbrake and select neutral on the transmission.

☐ Note that greater-than-usual pedal pressure will be required to operate the brakes, since the vacuum servo unit is only operational with the engine running.

☐ On models with power steering, greater-than-usual steering effort will also be required.

☐ The driver of the car being towed must

keep the tow-rope taut at all times to avoid snatching.

☐ Make sure that both drivers know the route before setting off.

☐ Only drive at moderate speeds and keep the distance towed to a minimum. Drive smoothly and allow plenty of time for slowing down at junctions.

Caution: On models with automatic transmission, do not tow the car at speeds in excess of 45 mph (75 kmh) or for a distance of greater than 60 miles (100 km). If towing speed/distance are to exceed these limits, then the car must be towed with its front wheels off the ground.

Introduction

There are some very simple checks which need only take a few minutes to carry out, but which could save you a lot of inconvenience and expense.

These "Weekly checks" require no great skill or special tools, and the small amount of time they take to perform could prove to be very well spent, for example;

☐ Keeping an eye on tyre condition and pressures, will not only help to stop them wearing out prematurely, but could also save your life.

☐ Many breakdowns are caused by electrical problems. Battery-related faults are particularly common, and a quick check on a regular basis will often prevent the majority of these.

☐ If your car develops a brake fluid leak, the first time you might know about it is when your brakes don't work properly. Checking the level regularly will give advance warning of this kind of problem.

☐ If the oil or coolant levels run low, the cost of repairing any engine damage will be far greater than fixing the leak, for example.

Underbonnet check points

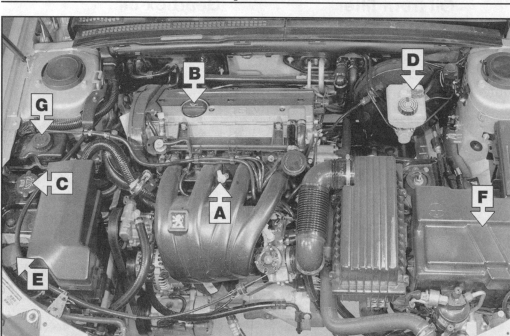

◀ 2.0 litre petrol (1.8 litre similar)

A *Engine oil level dipstick*
B *Engine oil filler cap*
C *Coolant expansion tank*
D *Brake fluid reservoir*
E *Screen washer fluid reservoir*
F *Battery*
G *Power steering fluid reservoir*

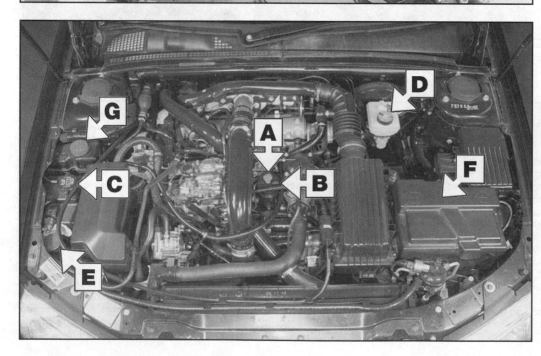

◀ 1.9 litre diesel

A *Engine oil level dipstick*
B *Engine oil filler cap*
C *Coolant expansion tank*
D *Brake fluid reservoir*
E *Screen washer fluid reservoir*
F *Battery*
G *Power steering fluid reservoir*

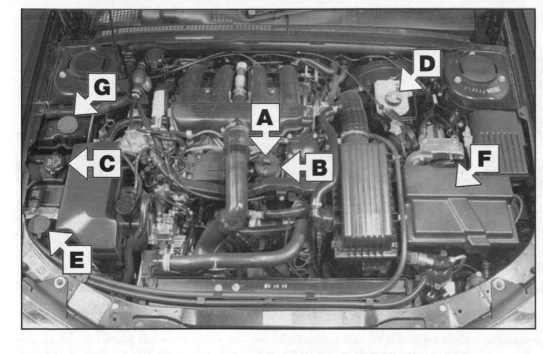

A *Engine oil level dipstick*
B *Engine oil filler cap*
C *Coolant expansion tank*
D *Brake fluid reservoir*
E *Screen washer fluid reservoir*
F *Battery*
G *Power steering fluid reservoir*

Engine oil level

Before you start

✔ Make sure that your car is on level ground.
✔ Check the oil level before the car is driven, or at least 5 minutes after the engine has been switched off.

 If the oil level is checked immediately after driving the vehicle, some of the oil will remain in the upper engine components, resulting in an inaccurate reading on the dipstick!

The correct oil

Modern engines place great demands on their oil. It is very important that the correct oil for your car is used (See "Lubricants, fluids and tyre pressures").

Car care

● If you have to add oil frequently, you should check whether you have any oil leaks. Place some clean paper under the car overnight, and check for stains in the morning. If there are no leaks, the engine may be burning oil *(see "Fault finding")*.

● Always maintain the level between the upper and lower dipstick marks (see photo 3). If the level is too low severe engine damage may occur. Oil seal failure may result if the engine is overfilled by adding too much oil.

1 The dipstick is located at the front of the engine (see *"Underbonnet check points"* for exact location); the dipstick end is brightly coloured for easy identification. Withdraw the dipstick.

2 Using a clean rag or paper towel remove all oil from the dipstick. Insert the clean dipstick into the tube as far as it will go, then withdraw it again.

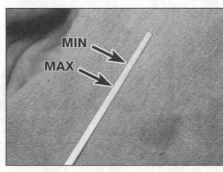

3 Note the oil level on the end of the dipstick, which should be between the upper ("MAX") mark and lower ("MIN") mark. Approximately 1.0 litre of oil will raise the level from the lower mark to the upper mark.

4 Oil is added through the filler cap. Unscrew the cap and top-up the level; a funnel may help to reduce spillage. Add the oil slowly, checking the level on the dipstick often. Don't overfill (see *"Car care" left*).

Coolant level

Warning: DO NOT attempt to remove the expansion tank pressure cap when the engine is hot, as there is a very great risk of scalding. Do not leave open containers of coolant about, as it is poisonous.

Car care

● Adding coolant should not be necessary on a regular basis. If frequent topping-up is required, it is likely there is a leak. Check the radiator, all hoses and joint faces for signs of staining or wetness, and rectify as necessary.

● It is important that antifreeze is used in the cooling system all year round, not just during the winter months. Don't top-up with water alone, as the antifreeze will become too diluted.

1 The coolant level must be checked with the engine cold. Remove the pressure cap (see Warning) from the expansion tank which is located on the right-hand side of the engine compartment.

2 The coolant level should be between the MAX and MIN marks on the expansion tank neck insert. The MIN mark is the thin bar at the base of the neck and the MAX mark is the slot approximately halfway up the neck.

3 If topping-up is necessary, remove the expansion tank cap and add a mixture of water and antifreeze to the expansion tank until the coolant level is between the level marks. Once the level is correct, securely refit the cap.

Brake fluid level

Warning:
● *Brake fluid can harm your eyes and will damage painted surfaces, so use extreme caution when handling and pouring it.*
● *Do not use fluid that has been standing open for some time, as it absorbs moisture from the air, which can cause a dangerous loss of braking effectiveness.*

HAYNES HiNT
● *Make sure that your car is on level ground.*
● *The fluid level in the reservoir will drop slightly as the brake pads wear down, but the fluid level must never be allowed to drop below the "MIN" mark.*

Safety first!

● If the reservoir requires repeated topping-up this is an indication of a fluid leak somewhere in the system, which should be investigated immediately.
● If a leak is suspected, the car should not be driven until the braking system has been checked. Never take any risks where brakes are concerned.

1 The upper (MAX) and lower (DANGER) fluid level markings are on the side of the reservoir, which is located in the left-hand rear corner of the engine compartment. The fluid level must always be kept between these two marks.

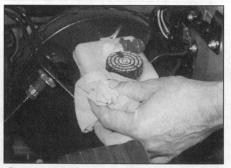

2 If topping-up is necessary, first wipe clean the area around the filler cap with a clean cloth, then unscrew the cap and remove it along with the rubber diaphragm.

3 Carefully add fluid, avoiding spilling it on the surrounding paintwork. Use only the specified hydraulic fluid. After filling the correct level, refit the cap and diaphragm and tighten it securely. Wipe off any spilt fluid.

Power steering fluid level

Before you start:
✔ Park the vehicle on level ground.
✔ Set the steering wheel straight-ahead.
✔ The engine should be turned off.

HAYNES HiNT *For the check to be accurate, the steering must not be turned once the engine has been stopped.*

Safety first!
● The need for frequent topping-up indicates a leak, which should be investigated immediately.

1 The power steering fluid level is checked in the fluid reservoir on the right-hand side of the engine compartment. With the engine cold, wipe clean the area around the reservoir cap.

2 Unscrew the reservoir cap, and check the fluid level is between the upper (MAXI) and lower (MINI) level indicators which are visible inside the reservoir.

3 Top-up the reservoir with the specified type of the fluid. Once the level is between the level marks, securely refit the reservoir cap. Do not overfill the reservoir.

Washer fluid level

Screenwash additives not only keep the winscreen clean during foul weather, they also prevent the washer system freezing in cold weather - which is when you are likely to need it most. Don't top up using plain water as the screenwash will become too diluted, and will freeze during cold weather. *On no account use coolant antifreeze in the washer system - this could discolour or damage paintwork.*

1 The washer fluid reservoir is located in the right-hand front corner of the engine compartment. To check the fluid level, remove the filler cap whilst holding a finger over the cap hole. The tube attached to the cap has level markings on it, and the fluid level can be clearly be seen through the clear tube.

2 If topping-up is necessary, add water and a screenwash additive in the quantities recommended on the bottle.

Tyre condition and pressure

It is very important that tyres are in good condition, and at the correct pressure - having a tyre failure at any speed is highly dangerous. Tyre wear is influenced by driving style - harsh braking and acceleration, or fast cornering, will all produce more rapid tyre wear. As a general rule, the front tyres wear out faster than the rears. Interchanging the tyres from front to rear ("rotating" the tyres) may result in more even wear. However, if this is completely effective, you may have the expense of replacing all four tyres at once! Remove any nails or stones embedded in the tread before they penetrate the tyre to cause deflation. If removal of a nail does reveal that the tyre has been punctured, refit the nail so that its point of penetration is marked. Then immediately change the wheel, and have the tyre repaired by a tyre dealer.

Regularly check the tyres for damage in the form of cuts or bulges, especially in the sidewalls. Periodically remove the wheels, and clean any dirt or mud from the inside and outside surfaces. Examine the wheel rims for signs of rusting, corrosion or other damage. Light alloy wheels are easily damaged by "kerbing" whilst parking; steel wheels may also become dented or buckled. A new wheel is very often the only way to overcome severe damage.

New tyres should be balanced when they are fitted, but it may become necessary to re-balance them as they wear, or if the balance weights fitted to the wheel rim should fall off. Unbalanced tyres will wear more quickly, as will the steering and suspension components. Wheel imbalance is normally signified by vibration, particularly at a certain speed (typically around 50 mph). If this vibration is felt only through the steering, then it is likely that just the front wheels need balancing. If, however, the vibration is felt through the whole car, the rear wheels could be out of balance. Wheel balancing should be carried out by a tyre dealer or garage.

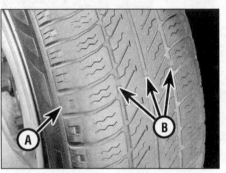

1 Tread Depth - visual check
The original tyres have tread wear safety bands (B), which will appear when the tread depth reaches approximately 1.6 mm. The band positions are indicated by a triangular mark on the tyre sidewall (A).

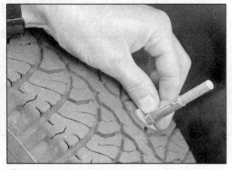

2 Tread Depth - manual check
Alternatively, tread wear can be monitored with a simple, inexpensive device known as a tread depth indicator gauge.

3 Tyre Pressure Check
Check the tyre pressures regularly with the tyres cold. Do not adjust the tyre pressures immediately after the vehicle has been used, or an inaccurate setting will result.

Tyre tread wear patterns

Shoulder Wear

Underinflation (wear on both sides)
Under-inflation will cause overheating of the tyre, because the tyre will flex too much, and the tread will not sit correctly on the road surface. This will cause a loss of grip and excessive wear, not to mention the danger of sudden tyre failure due to heat build-up.
Check and adjust pressures
Incorrect wheel camber (wear on one side)
Repair or renew suspension parts
Hard cornering
Reduce speed!

Centre Wear

Overinflation
Over-inflation will cause rapid wear of the centre part of the tyre tread, coupled with reduced grip, harsher ride, and the danger of shock damage occurring in the tyre casing.
Check and adjust pressures

If you sometimes have to inflate your car's tyres to the higher pressures specified for maximum load or sustained high speed, don't forget to reduce the pressures to normal afterwards.

Uneven Wear

Front tyres may wear unevenly as a result of wheel misalignment. Most tyre dealers and garages can check and adjust the wheel alignment (or "tracking") for a modest charge.
Incorrect camber or castor
Repair or renew suspension parts
Malfunctioning suspension
Repair or renew suspension parts
Unbalanced wheel
Balance tyres
Incorrect toe setting
Adjust front wheel alignment
Note: *The feathered edge of the tread which typifies toe wear is best checked by feel.*

Wiper blades

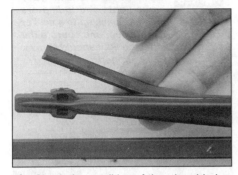

1 Check the condition of the wiper blades: if they are cracked or show signs of deterioration, or if the glass swept area is smeared, renew them. For maximum clarity of vision, wiper blades should be renewed annually.

2 To remove a windscreen wiper blade, lift the arm locking clip then raise the wiper arm slightly away from the screen.

3 Disengage the blade from the wiper arm and remove it from the vehicle, taking care not to allow the arm to damage the windscreen.

Battery

Caution: Before carrying out any work on the vehicle battery, read the precautions given in "Safety first" at the start of this manual.

✔ Make sure that the battery tray is in good condition, and that the clamp is tight. Corrosion on the tray, retaining clamp and the battery itself can be removed with a solution of water and baking soda. Thoroughly rinse all cleaned areas with water. Any metal parts damaged by corrosion should be covered with a zinc-based primer, then painted.

✔ Periodically (approximately every three months), check the charge condition of the battery as described in Chapter 5A.

✔ If the battery is flat, and you need to jump start your vehicle, see *Roadside Repairs*.

1 Remove the plastic cover to gain access to the battery, which is located at the front left-hand corner of the engine compartment. The exterior of the battery should be inspected periodically for damage such as a cracked case or cover.

2 Check the battery lead clamps for tightness to ensure good electrical connections, and check the leads for signs of damage.

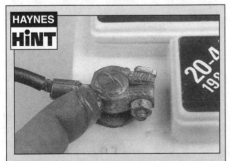

HAYNES HiNT

Battery corrosion can be kept to a minimum by applying a layer of petroleum jelly to the clamps and terminals after they are reconnected.

3 If corrosion (white, fluffy deposits) is evident, remove the cables from the battery terminals, clean them with a small wire brush, then refit them. Automotive stores sell a tool for cleaning the battery post . . .

4 . . . as well as the battery cable clamps

Bulbs and fuses

✔ Check all external lights and the horn. Refer to the appropriate Sections of Chapter 12 for details if any of the circuits are found to be inoperative.

✔ Visually check all accessible wiring connectors, harnesses and retaining clips for security, and for signs of chafing or damage.

 If you need to check your brake lights and indicators unaided, back up to a wall or garage door and operate the lights. The reflected light should show if they are working properly.

1 If a single indicator light, stop-light, sidelight or headlight has failed, it is likely that a bulb has blown, and will need to be replaced. Refer to Chapter 12 for details. If both stop-lights have failed, it is possible that the switch has failed (see Chapter 9).

2 If more than one indicator light or tail light has failed, it is likely that either a fuse has blown or that there is a fault in the circuit (see Chapter 12). The fuses are located behind in the driver's compartment fusebox, behind the cover on the driver's side lower facia panel, and also in the engine compartment fusebox.

3 To replace a blown fuse, simply pull it out and fit a new fuse of the correct rating (see Chapter 12). If the fuse blows again, it is important that you find out why - a complete checking procedure is given in Chapter 12.

Lubricants and fluids

Engine (petrol)	Multigrade engine oil to specification ACEA A2/96 or API SG *(Duckhams QS, QXR, Hypergrade Plus, Hypergrade, or 10W-40 Motor Oil)*
Engine (diesel)	Multigrade engine oil to specification ACEA B2/96 or API CD *(Duckhams QS, QXR, Hypergrade Plus, Diesel, Hypergrade, or 10W-40 Motor Oil)*
Cooling system	Procor 3000 antifreeze *(Duckhams Antifreeze and Summer Coolant)*
Manual transmission	SAE 75W-80W gear oil to API GL5 specification *(Duckhams Hypoid PT 75W-80W)*
Automatic transmission	ESSO LT 71141 Automatic Transmission Fluid only
Braking and clutch system	Hydraulic fluid to DOT 4 *(Duckhams Universal Brake & Clutch Fluid)*
Power steering	Automatic Transmission Fluid Dexron IID *(Duckhams Unimatic)*

Choosing your engine oil

Oils perform vital tasks in all engines. The higher the engine's performance, the greater the demand on lubricants to minimise wear as well as optimise power and economy. Duckhams tailors lubricants to the highest technical standards, meeting and exceeding the demands of all modern engines.

HOW ENGINE OIL WORKS

• Beating friction

Without oil, the surfaces inside your engine which rub together will heat, fuse and quickly cause engine seizure. Oil, and its special additives, forms a molecular barrier between moving parts, to stop wear and minimise heat build-up.

• Cooling hot spots

Oil cools parts that the engine's water-based coolant cannot reach, bathing the combustion chamber and pistons, where temperatures may exceed 1000°C. The oil assists in transferring the heat to the engine cooling system. Heat in the oil is also lost by air flow over the sump, and via any auxiliary oil cooler.

• Cleaning the inner engine

Oil washes away combustion by-products (mainly carbon) on pistons and cylinders, transporting them to the oil filter, and holding the smallest particles in suspension until they are flushed out by an oil change. Duckhams oils undergo extensive tests in the laboratory, and on the road.

Note: It is antisocial and illegal to dump oil down the drain. To find the location of your local oil recycling bank, call this number free.

Engine oil types

Mineral oils are the "traditional" oils, generally suited to older engines and cars not used in harsh conditions. *Duckhams Hypergrade Plus* and *Hypergrade* are well suited for use in most popular family cars.
Diesel oils such as *Duckhams Diesel* are specially formulated for Diesel engines, including turbocharged models and 4x4s.
Synthetic oils are the state-of-the-art in lubricants, offering ultimate protection, but at a fairly high price. One such is *Duckhams QS*, for use in ultra-high performance engines.
Semi-synthetic oils offer high performance engine protection, but at less cost than full synthetic oils. *Duckhams QXR* is an ideal choice for hot hatches and hard-driven cars.

For help with technical queries on lubricants, call Duckhams Oils on 0181 290 8207

Tyre pressures

Note 1: *The tyre pressures for each specific vehicle are given on a label attached to the rear edge of the driver's door. On models with a space-saver spare wheel, a separate pressure is given for the spare tyre, and care must be taken not to misread the sticker; the space-saver wheel is inflated to a lot higher pressure than the standard tyres (typically 60 psi). On models with a space-saver spare wheel, note that the spare is for temporary use only; whilst the spare is fitted, the vehicle should not be driven at speeds in excess of 50 mph (80 kmh).*
Note 2: *Pressures on the sticker apply to original-equipment tyres listed, and may vary if any other make or type of tyre is fitted; check with the tyre manufacturer or supplier for correct pressures if necessary.*
Note 3: *Tyre pressures must always be checked with the tyres cold to ensure accuracy.*

Saloon models (typical)	Front (psi)	Rear (psi)
185/70 R14 tyres, 195/65 R15 tyres	33	33
205/60 R15 tyres	35	35
Estate models (typical)		
185/70 R14 tyres	35	36
195/65 R15 tyres	33	35
205/60 R15 tyres	35	35

Notes

Chapter 1 Part A:
Routine maintenance & servicing - petrol models

Contents

Degrees of difficulty

Easy, suitable for novice with little experience	**Fairly easy,** suitable for beginner with some experience	**Fairly difficult,** suitable for competent DIY mechanic	**Difficult,** suitable for experienced DIY mechanic	**Very difficult,** suitable for expert DIY or professional

Lubricants and fluids
Refer to *"Weekly checks"*

Capacities

Engine oil (including oil filter)
1.6 engine .... 4.75 litres
1.8 litre engine:
    Models with air conditioning .... 4.25 litres
    Models without air conditioning .... 4.75 litres
2.0 litre engine .... 4.25 litres

Cooling system
All engines (approximate) .... 8.0 litres

Transmission
Manual transmission (approximate) .... 2.0 litres
Automatic transmission:
    Drain and refill .... 3.0 litres
    Total capacity (including torque converter) .... 8.3 litres

Fuel tank .... 70 litres

Engine
Oil filter .... Champion F118
Auxiliary drivebelt tension (for use with Peugeot electronic tool - see text):
    New belt .... 120 SEEM units
    Used belt .... 90 SEEM units

Cooling system
Antifreeze mixture:
    50% antifreeze .... Protection down to -37°C (5°F)
    55% antifreeze .... Protection down to -45°C (-22°F)
Note: *Refer to antifreeze manufacturer for latest recommendations.*

Fuel system
Air filter element .... Champion type not available at time of writing
Fuel filter .... Champion type not available at time of writing

Ignition system
Spark plugs:
    Type .... Champion RC10YCC
    Electrode gap* .... 0.9 mm
The spark plug gap quoted is that recommended by Champion for their specified plug listed above. If spark plugs of any other type are to be fitted, refer to their manufacturer's recommendations.

Brakes
Brake pad friction material minimum thickness .... 2.0 mm
Brake shoe friction material minimum thickness .... 1.5 mm

Tyre pressures
See end of *"Weekly checks"*

Torque wrench settings

	Nm	lbf ft
Auxiliary drivebelt tensioner pulley assembly retaining bolts (models without air conditioning):		
1.6 and 1.8 litre engines	30	22
2.0 litre engines	20	15
Auxiliary drivebelt automatic tensioner assembly retaining bolts (models with air conditioning)	20	15
Manual transmission filler/level plug	20	15
Roadwheel bolts	90	66

The maintenance intervals in this manual are provided with the assumption that you, not the dealer, will be carrying out the work. These are the minimum maintenance intervals recommended by us for vehicles driven daily. If you wish to keep your vehicle in peak condition at all times, you may wish to perform some of these procedures more often. We encourage frequent maintenance, because it enhances the efficiency, performance and resale value of your vehicle.

When the vehicle is new, it should be serviced by a factory-authorised dealer service department, in order to preserve the factory warranty.

Weekly, or every 250 miles (400 km)
- [ ] Refer to *"Weekly checks"*

Every 9000 miles (15 000 km) or 12 months - whichever comes first
- [ ] Renew the engine oil and filter (Section 3)
- [ ] Check the automatic transmission fluid level, and top up if necessary (Section 4)
- [ ] Check all underbonnet components and hoses for fluid leaks (Section 5)
- [ ] Renew the pollen filter (where fitted) (Section 6)
- [ ] Check the operation of the clutch (Section 7)
- [ ] Check the condition of the driveshaft rubber gaiters (Section 8)
- [ ] Check the steering and suspension components for condition and security (Section 9)
- [ ] Lubricate all hinges and locks (Section 10)

Every 18 000 miles (30 000 km)
In addition to all the items listed above, carry out the following:
- [ ] Check the condition of the front brake pads, and renew if necessary (Section 11)
- [ ] Check the condition of the rear brake pads and renew if necessary - rear disc brake models (Section 12)
- [ ] Check the operation of the handbrake (Section 13)
- [ ] Carry out a road test (Section 14)

Every 36 000 miles (60 000 km)
In addition to all the items listed above, carry out the following:
- [ ] Renew the spark plugs (Section 15)
- [ ] Renew the air filter (Section 16)
- [ ] Renew the fuel filter (Section 17)
- [ ] Check the condition of the auxiliary drivebelt, and renew if necessary (Section 18)
- [ ] Check the manual transmission oil level, and top-up if necessary (Section 19)
- [ ] Check the condition of the rear brake shoes and renew if necessary - rear drum brake models (Section 20)

Every 36 000 miles (60 000 km) or 2 years, whichever comes first
In addition to all the items listed above, carry out the following:
- [ ] Renew the brake fluid (Section 21)

Every 72 000 miles (120 000 km)
In addition to all the items listed above, carry out the following:
- [ ] Renew the timing belt (Section 22)

Note: It is strongly recommended that the timing belt renewal interval is halved to 36 000 miles (60 000 km) on vehicles which are subjected to intensive use, ie. mainly short journeys or a lot of stop-start driving. The actual belt renewal interval is therefore very much up to the individual owner, but bear in mind that severe engine damage will result if the belt breaks.

Every 72 000 miles (120 000 km) or 2 years, whichever comes first
In addition to all the items listed above, carry out the following:
- [ ] Renew the coolant (Section 23)

1A

Roscommon County Library Service
WITHDRAWN FROM STOCK
COUNTY LIBRARY SERVICE ROSCOMMON
420289

Underbonnet view of a 2.0 litre 16-valve model

1 Engine oil filler cap
2 Engine oil level dipstick
3 Battery
4 Brake fluid reservoir
5 Radiator
6 Coolant expansion tank
7 Suspension strut upper mounting
8 Air filter housing
9 Power steering pump
10 Air conditioning compressor
11 Alternator
12 Power steering fluid reservoir
13 Washer fluid reservoir
14 Fuse/relay box
15 Thermostat housing
16 Throttle housing

Front underbody view

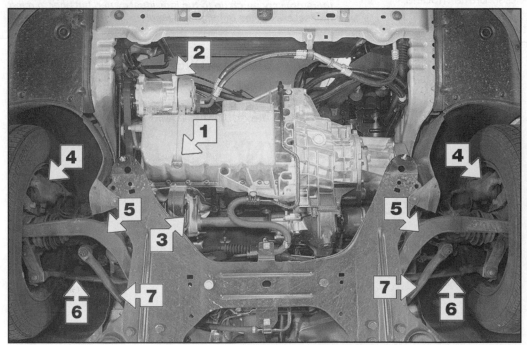

1 Engine oil drain plug
2 Air conditioning compressor
3 Driveshaft intermediate bearing
4 Brake caliper
5 Front suspension lower arm
6 Track rod
7 Front suspension anti-roll bar

Rear underbody view

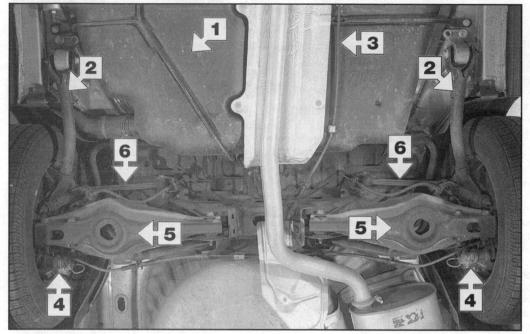

1 Fuel tank
2 Rear suspension leading arm
3 Handbrake cable
4 Brake caliper
5 Rear suspension lower arm
6 Rear suspension track arm

Maintenance procedures

1 General information

1 This Chapter is designed to help the home mechanic maintain his/her vehicle for safety, economy, long life and peak performance.

2 The Chapter contains a master maintenance schedule, followed by Sections dealing specifically with each task in the schedule. Visual checks, adjustments, component renewal and other helpful items are included. Refer to the accompanying illustrations of the engine compartment and the underside of the vehicle for the locations of the various components.

3 Servicing your vehicle in accordance with the mileage/time maintenance schedule and the following Sections will provide a planned maintenance programme, which should result in a long and reliable service life. This is a comprehensive plan, so maintaining some items but not others at the specified service intervals, will not produce the same results.

4 As you service your vehicle, you will discover that many of the procedures can - and should - be grouped together, because of the particular procedure being performed, or because of the proximity of two otherwise-unrelated components to one another. For example, if the vehicle is raised for any reason, the exhaust can be inspected at the same time as the suspension and steering components.

5 The first step in this maintenance programme is to prepare yourself before the actual work begins. Read through all the Sections relevant to the work to be carried out, then make a list and gather all the parts and tools required. If a problem is encountered, seek advice from a parts specialist, or a dealer service department.

2 Intensive maintenance

1 If, from the time the vehicle is new, the routine maintenance schedule is followed closely, and frequent checks are made of fluid levels and high-wear items, as suggested throughout this manual, the engine will be kept in relatively good running condition, and the need for additional work will be minimised.

2 It is possible that there will be times when the engine is running poorly due to the lack of regular maintenance. This is even more likely if a used vehicle, which has not received regular and frequent maintenance checks, is purchased. In such cases, additional work may need to be carried out, outside of the regular maintenance intervals.

3 If engine wear is suspected, a compression test (refer to Chapter 2A) will provide valuable information regarding the overall performance of the main internal components. Such a test can be used as a basis to decide on the extent of the work to be carried out. If, for example, a compression test indicates serious internal engine wear, conventional maintenance as described in this Chapter will not greatly improve the performance of the engine, and may prove a waste of time and money, unless extensive overhaul work is carried out first.

4 The following series of operations are those often required to improve the performance of a generally poor-running engine:

Primary operations

a) Clean, inspect and test the battery (refer to "Weekly checks").
b) Check all the engine-related fluids (refer to "Weekly checks").
c) Check the condition and tension of the auxiliary drivebelt (Section 18).
d) Renew the spark plugs (Section 15).
e) Check the condition of the air filter, and renew if necessary (Section 16).
f) Renew the fuel filter (Section 17).
g) Check the condition of all hoses, and check for fluid leaks (Section 5).

5 If these operations do not prove effective, carry out the following secondary operations:

Secondary operations

All items listed under "Primary operations", plus the following:

a) Check the charging system (refer to Chapter 5A).
b) Check the ignition system (refer to Chapter 5B).
c) Check the fuel system (refer to Chapter 4A).
d) Renew the ignition HT leads - where fitted (Section 15).

1A

3 Engine oil and filter renewal

Note: *A suitable square-section wrench may be required to undo the sump drain plug on some models. These wrenches can be obtained from most motor factors or your Peugeot dealer.*

1 Frequent oil and filter changes are the most important preventative maintenance procedures which can be undertaken by the DIY owner. As engine oil ages, it becomes diluted and contaminated, which leads to premature engine wear.

2 Before starting this procedure, gather together all the necessary tools and materials. Also make sure that you have plenty of clean rags and newspapers handy, to mop up any spills. Ideally, the engine oil should be warm, as it will drain better, and more built-up sludge will be removed with it. Take care, however, not to touch the exhaust or any other hot parts of the engine when working under the vehicle. To avoid any possibility of scalding, and to protect yourself from possible skin irritants and other harmful contaminants in used engine oils, it is advisable to wear gloves when carrying out this work. Access to the underside of the vehicle will be greatly improved if it can be raised on a lift, driven onto ramps, or jacked up and supported on axle stands. Whichever method is chosen, make sure that the vehicle remains level, or if it is at an angle, that the drain plug is at the lowest point. Where fitted, remove the splash guard from under the engine.

3 Slacken the drain plug about half a turn; on some models, a square-section wrench may be needed to slacken the plug. Position the draining container under the drain plug, then remove the plug completely. If possible, try to keep the plug pressed into the sump while unscrewing it by hand the last couple of turns **(see Haynes Hint)**. Recover the sealing ring from the drain plug.

HAYNES HiNT

As the drain plug releases from the threads, move it away sharply so the stream of oil issuing from the sump runs into the container, not up your sleeve!

3.7 Using an oil filter removal tool to slacken the oil filter

4 Allow some time for the old oil to drain, noting that it may be necessary to reposition the container as the oil flow slows to a trickle.

5 After all the oil has drained, wipe off the drain plug with a clean rag, and fit a new sealing washer. Clean the area around the drain plug opening, and refit the plug. Tighten the plug securely.

6 If the filter is also to be renewed, move the container into position under the oil filter, which is located on the front side of the cylinder block.

7 Using an oil filter removal tool if necessary, slacken the filter initially, then unscrew it by hand the rest of the way **(see illustration)**. Empty the oil in the old filter into the container.

8 Use a clean rag to remove all oil, dirt and sludge from the filter sealing area on the engine. Check the old filter to make sure that the rubber sealing ring hasn't stuck to the engine. If it has, carefully remove it.

9 Apply a light coating of clean engine oil to the sealing ring on the new filter, then screw it into position on the engine **(see illustration)**. Tighten the filter firmly by hand only - **do not** use any tools. Where necessary, refit the splash guard under the engine.

10 Remove the old oil and all tools from under the car, then lower the car to the ground (if applicable).

11 Remove the dipstick, then unscrew the oil filler cap from the cylinder head cover, or from the top of the filler tube on the front side of the cylinder block, as applicable. Fill the engine, using the correct grade and type of oil (*see "Weekly checks"*). An oil can spout or funnel may help to reduce spillage. Pour in half the specified quantity of oil first, then wait a few minutes for the oil to fall to the sump. Continue adding oil a small quantity at a time until the level is up to the lower mark on the

OIL CARE
FOLLOW THE CODE

OIL BANK LINE
0800 66 33 66

Note: It is antisocial and illegal to dump oil down the drain. To find the location of your local oil recycling bank, call this number free.

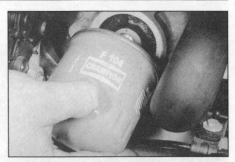

3.9 Apply clean engine oil to the new filter, then screw it into position and tighten it by hand only

dipstick. Adding approximately 1.0 litre will bring the level up to the upper mark on the dipstick. Refit the filler cap.

12 Start the engine and run it for a few minutes; check for leaks around the oil filter seal and the sump drain plug. Note that there may be a delay of a few seconds before the oil pressure warning light goes out when the engine is first started, as the oil circulates through the engine oil galleries and the new oil filter (where fitted) before the pressure builds up.

13 Switch off the engine, and wait a few minutes for the oil to settle in the sump once more. With the new oil circulated and the filter completely full, recheck the level on the dipstick, and add more oil as necessary.

14 Dispose of the used engine oil safely, with reference to *"General Repair Procedures"*.

4 Automatic transmission fluid level check

1 Take the vehicle on a short journey, to warm the transmission up to normal operating temperature, then park the vehicle on level ground. The fluid level is checked using the dipstick located at the front of the engine compartment, directly in front of the engine/transmission unit **(see illustration)**. The dipstick top is brightly-coloured for easy identification.

2 With the engine idling and the handbrake and footbrake firmly applied, move the selector lever through all the gear positions

4.1 Withdrawing the automatic transmission dipstick

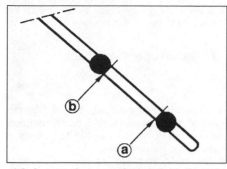

4.2 Automatic transmission fluid dipstick lower (a) and upper (b) fluid level markings

then return it to the "P" (Park) position. With the selector lever in the "P" (Park) position, withdraw the dipstick from the tube, and wipe all the fluid from its end with a clean rag or paper towel. Insert the clean dipstick back into the tube as far as it will go, then withdraw it once more. Note the fluid level on the end of the dipstick; it should be between the upper and lower marks **(see illustration)**.

3 If topping-up is necessary, add the required quantity of the specified fluid to the transmission via the dipstick tube. Use a funnel with a fine-mesh gauze, to avoid spillage, and to ensure that no foreign matter enters the transmission. **Note:** *Never overfill the transmission so that the fluid level is above the upper mark.*

4 After topping-up, take the vehicle on a short run to distribute the fresh fluid, then recheck the level again, topping-up if necessary.

5 Always maintain the level between the two dipstick marks. If the level is allowed to fall below the lower mark, fluid starvation may result, which could lead to severe transmission damage.

6 Frequent need for topping-up indicates that there is a leak, which should be found and corrected before it becomes serious.

5 Hose and fluid leak check

⚠️ **Warning: Refer to the safety information given in "Safety First" and Chapter 3 before disturbing any of the cooling system components.**

1 Carefully check the radiator and heater coolant hoses along their entire length. Renew any hose which is cracked, swollen or which shows signs of deterioration. Cracks will show up better if the hose is squeezed. Pay close attention to the clips that secure the hoses to the cooling system components. Hose clips that have been over-tightened can pinch and puncture hoses, resulting in cooling system leaks.

2 Inspect all the cooling system components (hoses, joint faces etc.) for leaks. Where any

A leak in the cooling system will usually show-up as white- or rust-coloured deposits on the area adjoining the leak

problems of this nature are found on system components, renew the component or gasket with reference to Chapter 3 **(see Haynes Hint).**

Fuel

⚠️ **Warning: Refer to the safety information given in "Safety First" and Chapter 4 before disturbing any of the fuel system components.**

3 Petrol leaks are difficult to pinpoint, unless the leakage is significant and hence easily visible. Fuel tends to evaporate quickly once it comes into contact with air, especially in a hot engine bay. Small drips can disappear before you get a chance to identify the point of leakage. If you suspect that there is a fuel leak from the area of the engine bay, leave the vehicle overnight then start the engine from cold, with the bonnet open. Metal components tend to shrink when they are cold, and rubber seals and hoses tend to harden, so any leaks will be more apparent whilst the engine is warming up from a cold start.

4 Check all fuel lines at their connections to the fuel rail, fuel pressure regulator and fuel filter. Examine each rubber fuel hose along its length for splits or cracks. Check for leakage from the crimped joints between rubber and metal fuel lines. Examine the unions between the metal fuel lines and the fuel filter housing. Also check the area around the fuel injectors for signs of O-ring leakage.

5 To identify fuel leaks between the fuel tank and the engine bay, the vehicle should raised and securely supported on axle stands. Inspect the petrol tank and filler neck for punctures, cracks and other damage. The connection between the filler neck and tank is especially critical. Sometimes a rubber filler neck or connecting hose will leak due to loose retaining clamps or deteriorated rubber.

6 Carefully check all rubber hoses and metal fuel lines leading away from the petrol tank. Check for loose connections, deteriorated hoses, kinked lines, and other damage. Pay particular attention to the vent pipes and hoses, which often loop up around the filler neck and can become blocked or kinked,

making tank filling difficult. Follow the fuel supply and return lines to the front of the vehicle, carefully inspecting them all the way for signs of damage or corrosion. Renew damaged sections as necessary.

Engine oil

7 Inspect the area around the camshaft cover, cylinder head, oil filter and sump joint faces. Bear in mind that, over a period of time, some very slight seepage from these areas is to be expected - what you are really looking for is any indication of a serious leak caused by gasket failure. Engine oil seeping from the base of the timing belt cover or the transmission bellhousing may be an indication of crankshaft or transmission input shaft oil seal failure. Should a leak be found, renew the failed gasket or oil seal by referring to the appropriate Chapters in this manual.

Automatic transmission fluid

8 Where applicable, check the hoses leading to the transmission fluid cooler at the front of the engine bay for leakage. Look for deterioration caused by corrosion and damage from grounding, or debris thrown up from the road surface. Automatic transmission fluid is a thin oil and is usually red in colour.

Power assisted steering (PAS) fluid

9 Examine the hose running between the fluid reservoir and the power steering pump, and the return hose running from the steering rack to the fluid reservoir. Also examine the high pressure supply hose between the pump and the steering rack.

10 Where applicable, check the hoses leading to the PAS fluid cooler at the front of the engine bay. Look for deterioration caused by corrosion and damage from grounding, or debris thrown up from the road surface.

11 Pay particular attention to crimped unions, and the area surrounding the hoses that are secured with adjustable worm drive clips. Like automatic transmission fluid, PAS fluid is a thin oil, and is usually red in colour.

Air conditioning refrigerant

⚠️ **Warning: Refer to the safety information given in "Safety First" and Chapter 3, regarding the dangers of disturbing any of the air conditioning system components.**

12 The air conditioning system is filled with a liquid refrigerant, which is retained under high pressure. If the air conditioning system is opened and depressurised without the aid of specialised equipment, the refrigerant will immediately turn into gas and escape into the atmosphere. If the liquid comes into contact with your skin, it can cause severe frostbite. In addition, the refrigerant contains substances which are environmentally damaging; for this reason, it should not be allowed to escape into the atmosphere.

13 Any suspected air conditioning system

1A

leaks should be immediately referred to a Peugeot dealer or air conditioning specialist. Leakage will be shown up as a steady drop in the level of refrigerant in the system.

14 Note that water may drip from the condenser drain pipe, underneath the car, immediately after the air conditioning system has been in use. This is normal, and should not be cause for concern.

Brake fluid

⚠️ **Warning: Refer to the safety information given in "Safety First" and Chapter 9, regarding the dangers of handling brake fluid.**

15 With reference to Chapter 9, examine the area surrounding the brake pipe unions at the master cylinder for signs of leakage. Check the area around the base of fluid reservoir, for signs of leakage caused by seal failure. Also examine the brake pipe unions at the ABS hydraulic unit.

16 If fluid loss is evident, but the leak cannot be pinpointed in the engine bay, the brake calipers and underbody brake lines should be carefully checked with the vehicle raised and supported on axle stands. Leakage of fluid from the braking system is a serious fault that must be rectified immediately.

17 Brake/clutch hydraulic fluid is a toxic substance with a watery consistency. New fluid is almost colourless, but it becomes darker with age and use.

Unidentified fluid leaks

18 If there are signs that a fluid of some description is leaking from the vehicle, but you cannot identify the type of fluid or its exact origin, park the vehicle overnight and slide a large piece of card underneath it. Providing that the card is positioned in roughly the right location, even the smallest leak will show up on the card. Not only will this help you to pinpoint the exact location of the leak, it should be easier to identify the fluid from its colour. Bear in mind, though, that the leak may only be occurring when the engine is running!

Vacuum hoses

19 Although the braking system is hydraulically-operated, the brake servo unit amplifies the effort you apply at the brake pedal, by making use of the vacuum in the inlet manifold, generated by the engine. Vacuum is ported to the servo by means of a large-bore hose. Any leaks that develop in this hose will reduce the effectiveness of the braking system.

20 In addition, many of the underbonnet components, particularly the emission control components, are driven by vacuum supplied from the inlet manifold via narrow-bore hoses. A leak in a vacuum hose means that air is being drawn into the hose (rather than escaping from it) and this makes leakage very difficult to detect. One method is to use an old length of vacuum hose as a kind of stethoscope - hold one end close to (but not in!) your ear and use the other end to probe the area around the suspected leak. When the end of the hose is directly over a vacuum leak, a hissing sound will be heard clearly through the hose. Care must be taken to avoid contacting hot or moving components, as the engine must be running, when testing in this manner. Renew any vacuum hoses that are found to be defective.

6 Pollen filter renewal
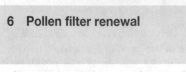

1 Operate the windscreen wipers and switch off the ignition so the wiper arms stop at the top of their travel.

2 Unscrew the retaining nut then unclip and remove the passenger side plastic inlet vent cover from the base of the windscreen **(see illustration)**.

3 Unclip the passenger side inlet vent panel and remove the panel from beneath the windscreen to gain access to the pollen filter **(see illustration)**.

4 Ease the pollen filter out of its housing and remove it from the vehicle **(see illustrations)**.

5 Wipe clean the housing then install the new filter, making sure it is clipped securely in position.

6 Clip the vent panel into position, making sure it is correctly engaged with the driver's side panel, then refit the vent cover and retaining nut.

7 Switch the ignition back on and return the wiper arm to the at rest position.

7 Clutch operation check
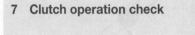

1 All petrol engine models covered by this manual are equipped with a cable-operated, self-adjusting clutch mechanism which is virtually maintenance-free.

2 The only maintenance necessary is to check that the clutch pedal moves smoothly and easily through its full travel, and that the clutch itself functions correctly, with no trace of slip or drag.

3 If any problems are experienced, refer to Chapter 6 for further details.

8 Driveshaft gaiter check
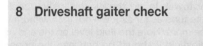

1 With the vehicle raised and securely supported on axle stands, turn the steering to full left or right lock, then slowly rotate the roadwheel. Inspect the outer constant velocity (CV) joint rubber gaiters, squeezing the gaiters to open out the folds **(see illustration)**. Check for signs of cracking, splits or deterioration of the rubber, which may allow the grease to escape, or water and grit to enter. Also check the security and condition of the retaining clips. Repeat these checks on the inner CV

6.2 Undo the retaining nut and remove the passenger side plastic inlet vent cover . . .

6.3 . . . then unclip the inlet vent panel from the vehicle

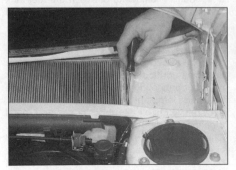

6.4a Carefully ease the pollen filter out from its housing . . .

6.4b . . . and remove it from the vehicle

8.1 Checking a driveshaft gaiter for damage

9.2 Checking a steering gear gaiter for damage

9.4 Check for wear in the hub bearings by grasping the wheel and trying to rock it

joints. If any damage or deterioration is found, the gaiters should be renewed (Chapter 8).

2 At the same time, check the general condition of the CV joints themselves by first holding the driveshaft and attempting to rotate the wheel. Repeat this check whilst holding the inner joint and attempting to rotate the driveshaft. Any appreciable movement indicates wear in the CV joints, wear in the driveshaft splines, or a loose driveshaft retaining nut.

9 Steering and suspension component check

Front suspension and steering check

1 Raise the front of the vehicle, and securely support it on axle stands.

2 Visually inspect the balljoint dust covers and the steering rack-and-pinion gaiters for splits, chafing or deterioration **(see illustration)**. Any wear of these components will cause loss of lubricant, together with dirt and water entry, resulting in rapid deterioration of the balljoints or steering gear.

3 Check the power steering fluid hoses for chafing or deterioration, and the pipe and hose unions for fluid leaks. Also check for signs of fluid leakage under pressure from the steering gear rubber gaiters, which would indicate failed fluid seals within the steering gear.

4 Grasp the roadwheel at the 12 o'clock and 6 o'clock positions, and try to rock it **(see illustration)**. Very slight free play may be felt, but if the movement is appreciable, further investigation is necessary to determine the source. Continue rocking the wheel while an assistant depresses the footbrake. If the movement is now eliminated or significantly reduced, it is likely that the hub bearings are at fault. If the free play is still evident with the footbrake depressed, then there is wear in the suspension joints or mountings.

5 Now grasp the wheel at the 9 o'clock and 3 o'clock positions, and try to rock it as before. Any movement felt now may again be caused by wear in the hub bearings or the steering track-rod balljoints. If the inner or outer balljoint is worn, the visual movement will be obvious.

6 Using a large screwdriver or flat bar, check for wear in the suspension mounting bushes by levering between the relevant suspension component and its attachment point. Some movement is to be expected as the mountings are made of rubber, but excessive wear should be obvious. Also check the condition of any visible rubber bushes, looking for splits, cracks or contamination of the rubber.

7 With the car standing on its wheels, have an assistant turn the steering wheel back and forth about an eighth of a turn each way. There should be very little, if any, lost movement between the steering wheel and roadwheels. If this is not the case, closely observe the joints and mountings previously described, but in addition, check the steering column universal joints for wear, and the rack-and-pinion steering gear itself.

Suspension strut/ shock absorber check

8 Check for any signs of fluid leakage around the suspension strut/shock absorber body, or from the rubber gaiter around the piston rod. Should any fluid be noticed, the suspension strut/shock absorber is defective internally, and should be renewed. **Note:** *Suspension struts/shock absorbers should always be renewed in pairs on the same axle, or the handling of the vehicle will be impaired.*

9 The efficiency of the suspension strut/shock absorber may be checked by bouncing the vehicle at each corner. Generally speaking, the body will return to its normal position and stop after being depressed. If it rises and returns on a rebound, the suspension strut/shock absorber is probably suspect. Examine also the suspension strut/shock absorber upper and lower mountings for any signs of wear.

10 Hinge and lock lubrication

1 Lubricate the hinges of the bonnet, doors and tailgate with a light general-purpose oil. Similarly, lubricate all latches, locks and lock strikers. At the same time, check the security and operation of all the locks, adjusting them if necessary (see Chapter 11).

2 Lightly lubricate the bonnet release mechanism and cable with a suitable grease.

1A

11 Front brake pad check

1 Firmly apply the handbrake, then jack up the front of the car and support it securely on axle stands. Remove the front roadwheels.
2 For a comprehensive check, the brake pads should be removed and cleaned. The operation of the caliper can then also be checked, and the condition of the brake disc itself can be fully examined on both sides. Refer to Chapter 9 for further information **(see Haynes Hint)**.
3 If any pad's friction material is worn to the specified thickness or less, *all four pads must be renewed as a set.*

12 Rear brake pad check

1 Chock the front wheels, then jack up the rear of the vehicle and support it on axle stands. Remove the rear roadwheels.
2 For a quick check, the thickness of friction material remaining on each brake pad can be measured through the top of the caliper body.

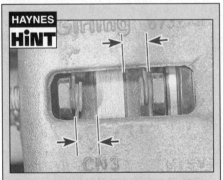

For a quick check, the thickness of the friction material on each brake pad can be measured through the aperture in the caliper body

If any pad's friction material is worn to the specified thickness or less, all four pads must be renewed as a set.
3 For a comprehensive check, the brake pads should be removed and cleaned. This will permit the operation of the caliper to be checked, and the condition of the brake disc itself can be fully examined on both sides. Refer to Chapter 9 for further information.
4 If any pad's friction material is worn to the specified thickness or less, *all four pads must be renewed as a set.*

13 Handbrake check

1 Check and, if necessary, adjust the handbrake (see Chapter 9). Check that the handbrake cables are free to move easily and lubricate all exposed linkages/ cable pivots.

14 Road test

Instruments and electrical equipment

1 Check the operation of all instruments and electrical equipment.
2 Make sure all instruments read correctly, and switch on all electrical equipment in turn, to check that it functions properly.

Steering and suspension

3 Check for any abnormalities in the steering, suspension, handling or road "feel".
4 Drive the vehicle, and check that there are no unusual vibrations or noises.
5 Check that the steering feels positive, with no excessive "sloppiness", or roughness, and check for any suspension noises when cornering and driving over bumps.

Drivetrain

6 Check the performance of the engine, clutch (where applicable), gearbox/ transmission and driveshafts.
7 Listen for any unusual noises from the engine, clutch and gearbox/transmission.
8 Make sure that the engine runs smoothly when idling, and that there is no hesitation when accelerating.
9 Check that, where applicable, the clutch action is smooth and progressive, that the drive is taken up smoothly, and that the pedal travel is not excessive. Also listen for any noises when the clutch pedal is depressed.
10 On manual gearbox models, check that all gears can be engaged smoothly without noise, and that the gear lever action is not abnormally vague or "notchy".
11 On automatic transmission models, make sure that all gearchanges occur smoothly, without snatching, and without an increase in engine speed between changes. Check that all the gear positions can be selected with the vehicle at rest. If any problems are found, they should be referred to a Peugeot dealer.

Check the operation and performance of the braking system

12 Make sure that the vehicle does not pull to one side when braking, and that the wheels do not lock prematurely when braking hard.
13 Check that there is no vibration through the steering when braking.
14 Check that the handbrake operates correctly without excessive movement of the lever, and that it holds the vehicle stationary on a slope.
15 Test the operation of the brake servo unit as follows. With the engine off, depress the footbrake four or five times to exhaust the vacuum. Hold the brake pedal depressed, then start the engine. As the engine starts, there should be a noticeable "give" in the brake pedal as vacuum builds up. Allow the engine to run for at least two minutes, and then switch it off. If the brake pedal is depressed now, it should be possible to detect a hiss from the servo as the pedal is depressed. After about four or five applications, no further hissing should be heard, and the pedal should feel much harder.

Every 36 000 miles

15 Spark plug renewal and ignition system check

Spark plug renewal

1 The correct functioning of the spark plugs is vital for the correct running and efficiency of the engine. It is essential that the plugs fitted are appropriate for the engine (a suitable type is specified at the beginning of this Chapter). If this type is used, and the engine is in good condition, the spark plugs should not need attention between scheduled replacement intervals. Spark plug cleaning is rarely necessary, and should not be attempted unless specialised equipment is available, as damage can easily be caused to the firing ends.
2 On 1.8 and 2.0 litre models, to gain access to the spark plugs, the ignition coil unit fitted in the centre of the cylinder head cover must first be removed. Disconnect the wiring connector at the left-hand end of the coil unit, then undo the six retaining bolts and lift the coil unit upwards, off the spark plugs and from its location in the cylinder head cover **(see illustration)**.

15.2 Ignition coil unit wiring connector (arrowed) - 1.8 and 2.0 litre models

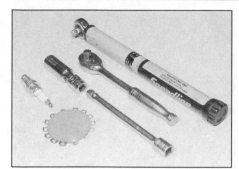

15.6 Tools required for spark plug removal, gap adjustment and refitting

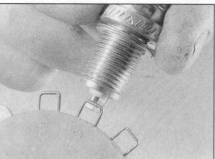

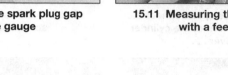

15.10 Measuring the spark plug gap with a wire gauge

15.11 Measuring the spark plug gap with a feeler blade

3 On certain models, to improve access to some of the plugs, it may be necessary to remove the air inlet ducting (refer to Chapter 4A for further information).

4 On 1.6 litre models, if the marks on the original-equipment spark plug (HT) leads cannot be seen, mark the leads 1 to 4, corresponding to the cylinder the lead serves (No 1 cylinder is at the transmission end of the engine). Pull the leads from the plugs by gripping the end fitting, not the lead, otherwise the lead connection may be fractured.

5 It is advisable to remove the dirt from the spark plug recesses, using a clean brush, vacuum cleaner or compressed air before removing the plugs, to prevent dirt dropping into the cylinders.

6 Unscrew the plugs using a spark plug spanner, suitable box spanner, or a deep socket and extension bar (see illustration). Keep the socket aligned with the spark plug - if it is forcibly moved to one side, the ceramic insulator may be broken off. As each plug is removed, examine it as follows.

7 Examination of the spark plugs will give a good indication of the condition of the engine. If the insulator nose of the spark plug is clean and white, with no deposits, this is indicative of a weak mixture. It could also indicate that the plug is too "hot" for the engine (a hot plug transfers heat away from the electrode slowly, a cold plug transfers heat away quickly). If this condition is apparent, either correct the mixture setting (where possible), or ensure that the correct grade of plug is fitted.

8 If the tip and insulator nose are covered with hard black-looking deposits, then this is indicative that the mixture is too rich. Should the plug be black and oily, then it is likely that the engine is fairly worn, as well as the mixture being too rich.

9 If the insulator nose is covered with light tan to greyish-brown deposits, then the mixture is correct, and it is likely that the engine is in good condition.

10 The spark plug electrode gap is of considerable importance as, if it is too large or too small, the size of the spark and its efficiency will be seriously impaired. The gap should be set to the value given in the Specifications at the beginning of this Chapter (see illustration).

11 To set it, measure the gap with a feeler blade. If necessary, bend the outer plug electrode open or closed until the correct gap is achieved (see illustration). The centre electrode should never be bent, as this may crack the insulator and cause plug failure, if nothing worse.

12 Special spark plug electrode gap adjusting tools are available from most motor accessory shops.

13 Before fitting the spark plugs, check that the threaded connector sleeves (on top of the plug) are tight, and that the plug exterior surfaces and threads are clean. Apply a smear of copper-based anti-seize compound to the plug threads (see Haynes Hint).

14 Once the plug begins to screw in correctly, remove the rubber hose (if used), and tighten the plug to the specified torque using the spark plug socket and a torque

HAYNES HiNT

It's often difficult to insert spark plugs into their holes without cross-threading them. To avoid this possibility, fit a short piece of rubber hose over the end of the spark plug. The flexible hose acts as a universal joint, to help align the plug with the plug hole. Should the plug begin to cross-thread, the hose will slip on the spark plug, preventing thread damage.

wrench. Refit the remaining spark plugs in the same manner.

15 On 1.8 and 2.0 litre models, refit the ignition coil unit to the head cover. Refit the retaining bolts, tightening them securely, then reconnect the coil unit wiring connectors.

16 On 1.6 litre models, connect the HT leads in their correct order, and refit any components removed for access.

Ignition system check

17 On 1.6 litre models, the condition cylinder of the HT leads should be checked as described in the following paragraphs. On 1.8 and 2.0 litre models, there are no HT leads, so the only relevant check is that all the primary (LT) circuit wiring connectors are clean and free of corrosion.

18 Ensure that the leads are numbered before removing them, to avoid confusion when refitting. Pull the leads from the plugs by gripping the end fitting, not the lead, otherwise the lead connection may be fractured.

19 Check inside the end fitting for signs of corrosion, which will look like a white crusty powder. Push the end fitting back onto the spark plug, ensuring that it is a tight fit on the plug. If not, remove the lead again, and use pliers to carefully crimp the metal connector inside the end fitting until it fits securely on the end of the spark plug.

20 Using a clean rag, wipe the entire length of the lead to remove any built-up dirt and grease. Once the lead is clean, check for burns, cracks and other damage. Do not bend the lead excessively, or pull the lead lengthwise - the conductor inside might break.

21 Disconnect the other end of the lead from the ignition coil. Again, pull only on the end fitting. Check for corrosion and a tight fit in the same manner as the spark plug end. Refit the lead securely on completion.

22 Check the remaining leads one at a time, in the same way.

23 If new spark plug (HT) leads are required, purchase a set for your specific car and engine.

1A

16.1 On 1.6 litre models, disconnect the inlet duct from the front of the cylinder head cover . . .

16.2a . . . then slacken the retaining screws (arrowed) . . .

16.2b . . . and release the retaining clips

16.2c Lift off the filter cover . . .

16.2d . . . and withdraw the filter element

16.5 On 1.8 and 2.0 litre models, slacken the retaining clip (arrowed) and disconnect the inlet duct from the air filter housing lid

16 Air filter element renewal

1.6 litre models

1 Slacken the retaining clip, and disconnect the inlet duct from the front of the cylinder head cover **(see illustration)**.
2 Slacken and remove the two retaining screws situated at the front of the cylinder head cover, then release the two air filter cover retaining clips. Remove the filter cover from the cylinder head cover, and withdraw the filter element **(see illustrations)**.
3 Fit the new element in position in the cylinder head cover. Refit the filter cover, securing it in position with its retaining screws and clips.
4 Reconnect the inlet duct to the cylinder head cover, and securely tighten its retaining clip.

1.8 and 2.0 litre models

5 Slacken the retaining clip and disconnect the inlet duct from the air filter housing lid **(see illustration)**.
6 Undo the screws securing the lid to the air filter housing body and lift off the lid **(see illustration)**.
7 Lift out the filter element and wipe clean the housing body and lid.
8 Place the new element in position in the

housing body. Refit the filter housing lid, securing it in position with its retaining screws.
9 Reconnect the inlet duct to the lid, and securely tighten its retaining clip.

17 Fuel filter renewal

⚠ **Warning: Before carrying out the following operation, refer to the precautions given in "Safety first!" at the beginning of this manual, and follow them implicitly. Petrol is a highly-dangerous and volatile liquid, and the precautions necessary when handling it cannot be overstressed.**

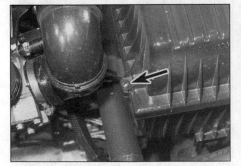

16.6 Undo the screws (arrowed) securing the lid to the housing body

1 The fuel filter is located beneath the right-hand side of the vehicle, adjacent to the fuel tank **(see illustration)**. To gain access to the filter, chock the front wheels, then jack up the rear of the car and support it on axle stands.
2 Clamp the fuel inlet hose on the tank side of the filter. Bearing in mind the information given in the relevant Part of Chapter 4 on depressurising the fuel system, disconnect the quick-release fuel hose connections and remove the fuel hoses from the filter. Be prepared for fuel spillage.
3 Pull the upper end of the filter retaining strap upward to disengage it from the slot in the retaining bracket, move the strap aside and remove the filter.
4 Dispose of the old filter safely; it will be highly-inflammable, and may explode if thrown on a fire.

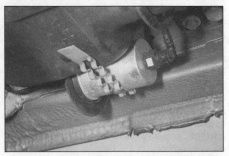

17.1 The fuel filter is situated underneath the right-hand side of the vehicle, adjacent to the fuel tank

5 Locate the new filter in position and secure it with the retaining strap. Make sure that the lug on the strap fully engages with the slot in the retaining bracket.

6 Connect the fuel hoses to the filter and remove the hose clamp.

7 Start the engine, and check the filter hose connections for leaks. Lower the vehicle to the ground on completion.

18 Auxiliary drivebelt check and renewal

Note: *Depending on model and equipment fitted, access to the auxiliary drivebelt can be extremely limited. Where necessary, greater working clearance can be gained by removing the fuel injection/ignition electronic control unit (ECU) and its mounting box (Chapter 4A).*

Note: *On models with a manually adjusted drivebelt, Peugeot specify the use of a special electronic tool (SEEM C105.5) to correctly set the drivebelt tension. If access to this equipment cannot be obtained, an approximate setting can be achieved using the method described below. If this method is used, the tension should be checked using the special electronic tool at the earliest opportunity.*

1 All models are equipped with a single poly-V type, multi-ribbed auxiliary drivebelt. The belt tension is adjusted manually on models without air conditioning, and automatically, by means of a spring-loaded tensioner, on models with air conditioning.

Checking the auxiliary drivebelt condition

2 Apply the handbrake, then jack up the front of the car and support it on axle stands. Remove the right-hand front roadwheel.

3 Release the screws and clips and remove the wheel arch liner from under the right-hand front wing for access to the crankshaft pulley bolt. Where fitted, also remove the splash guard from under the front of the engine.

4 Using a suitable socket and bar fitted to the crankshaft pulley bolt, rotate the crankshaft so that the entire length of the drivebelt can be examined. Examine the drivebelt for cracks, splitting, fraying or damage. Check also for signs of glazing (shiny patches) and for separation of the belt plies. Renew the belt if worn or damaged.

5 If the condition of the belt is satisfactory, on models without air conditioning, check the drivebelt tension as described below. On models with air conditioning, there is no need to check the drivebelt tension.

Auxiliary drivebelt (models without air conditioning) - removal, refitting and tensioning

Removal

6 If not already done, proceed as described in paragraphs 2 and 3.

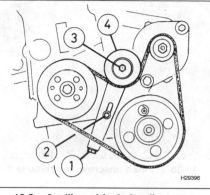

18.8a Auxiliary drivebelt adjustment details (1.6 and 1.8 litre models without air conditioning)

1 *Adjuster bolt*
2 *Tensioning pulley assembly lower securing bolt*
3 *Tensioning pulley assembly upper retaining bolt*
4 *Tensioning pulley*

7 Disconnect the battery negative lead.

8 Slacken the two bolts securing the tensioning pulley assembly to the engine **(see illustrations)**.

9 Rotate the adjuster bolt to move the tensioner pulley away from the drivebelt until there is sufficient slack for the drivebelt to be removed from the pulleys.

Refitting

10 Fit the drivebelt around the pulleys in the following order:

a) *Power steering pump.*
b) *Crankshaft.*
c) *Alternator.*
d) *Idler pulley (2.0 litre models).*
e) *Tensioner pulley.*

11 Ensure that the ribs on the belt are correctly engaged with the grooves in the pulleys, and that the drivebelt is correctly routed. Take all the slack out of the belt by turning the tensioner pulley adjuster bolt. Tension the belt as follows.

Tensioning

12 If not already done, proceed as described in paragraphs 2 and 3.

13 Correct tensioning of the drivebelt will ensure that it has a long life. A belt which is too slack will slip and perhaps squeal. Beware, however, of overtightening, as this can cause wear in the alternator bearings.

14 The belt should be tensioned so that, under firm thumb pressure, there is about 5.0 mm of free movement at the mid-point between the pulleys on the longest belt run.

15 To adjust the tension, with the two tensioner pulley assembly retaining bolts slackened, rotate the adjuster bolt until the correct tension is achieved. Once the belt is correctly tensioned, rotate the crankshaft four complete revolutions in the normal direction of rotation and recheck the tension.

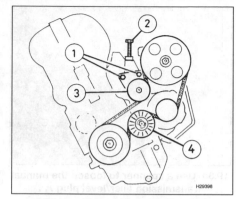

18.8b Auxiliary drivebelt adjustment details (2.0 litre models without air conditioning)

1 *Tensioning pulley assembly securing bolts*
2 *Adjuster bolt*
3 *Tensioning pulley*
4 *Idler pulley*

16 When the belt is correctly tensioned, tighten the tensioner pulley assembly retaining bolts to the specified torque, then reconnect the battery negative lead.

17 Refit the wheel arch liner and, where fitted, the engine splash guard. Refit the roadwheel, and lower the car to the ground.

Auxiliary drivebelt (models with air conditioning) - removal, refitting and tensioning

Removal

18 If not already done, proceed as described in paragraphs 2 and 3.

19 Disconnect the battery negative lead.

20 Move the tensioner pulley away from the drivebelt, using a ratchet handle or extension bar with the same size square-section end as the hole in the base of the automatic tensioner arm **(see illustration)**. Once the tensioner is

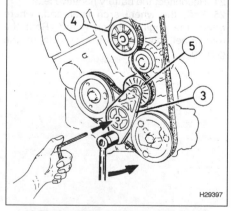

18.20 Auxiliary drivebelt adjustment details (models with air conditioning)

1 *Tensioner arm square-section end*
2 *Setting hole (for 4.0 mm Allen key)*
3 *Tensioner arm*
4 *Idler pulley*

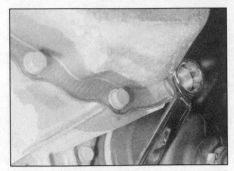

19.3a **Use a spanner to loosen the manual transmission filler/level plug . . .**

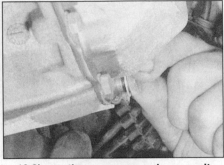

19.3b **. . . then unscrew and remove it**

19.4 **Topping-up the transmission oil level**

released, retain it in the released position by inserting a 4.0 mm Allen key in the hole provided. Disengage the drivebelt from all the pulleys, noting its correct routing. Remove the drivebelt from the engine, noting that in some cases, it may be necessary to slacken the automatic tensioner mounting bolts to disengage the belt from behind the tensioner pulley.

Refitting and tensioning
21 Fit the drivebelt around the pulleys in the following order:
   a) *Automatic tensioner pulley.*
   b) *Crankshaft.*
   c) *Air conditioning compressor.*
   d) *Power steering pump.*
   e) *Idler pulley*
   f) *Alternator.*
22 Where necessary, securely tighten the automatic tensioner mounting bolts to the specified torque.
23 Ensure that the ribs on the belt are correctly engaged with the grooves in the pulleys. Take the load off the tensioner arm and remove the Allen key. Release the tensioner arm; the tensioner is spring-loaded, removing the need to manually adjust the belt tension.
24 Reconnect the battery negative lead.
25 Refit the wheel arch liner and, where fitted, the engine splash guard. Refit the roadwheel, and lower the vehicle to the ground.

19 Manual transmission oil level check

Note: *A new sealing washer will be required for the transmission filler/level plug, when refitting.*

1 Jack up the front and rear of the car and securely support it on axle stands so that it remains level. If the car has been recently driven, wait at least 5 minutes after the engine has been switched off. If the oil level is checked immediately after driving the car, some of the oil will remain distributed around the transmission components, resulting in an inaccurate level reading.
2 Remove the left-hand front roadwheel then release the screws and clips and remove the wheel arch liner from under the wing for access to the filler/level plug.
3 Wipe clean the area around the filler/level plug, which is the largest bolt among those securing the end cover to the transmission. Unscrew the plug and clean it; discard the sealing washer **(see illustrations)**.
4 The oil level should reach the lower edge of the filler/level hole. A certain amount of oil will have gathered behind the filler/level plug, and will trickle out when it is removed; this does *not* necessarily indicate that the level is correct. To ensure that a true level is established, wait until the initial trickle has stopped, then add oil as necessary until a trickle of new oil can be seen emerging **(see illustration)**. The level will be correct when the flow ceases; use only good-quality oil of the specified type.

5 Refilling the transmission is an awkward operation; above all, allow plenty of time for the oil level to settle properly before checking it. If a large amount had to be added to the transmission, or if a large amount flowed out on checking the level, refit the filler/level plug and take the vehicle on a short journey. With the new oil distributed fully around the transmission components, recheck the level after allowing time for it to settle again.
6 If the transmission has been overfilled so that oil flows out as soon as the filler/level plug is removed, first check that the car is completely level (front-to-rear and side-to-side). Allow any surplus oil to drain off into a suitable container.
7 When the level is correct, fit a new sealing washer to the filler/level plug. Tighten the plug to the specified torque wrench setting. Wash off any spilt oil. Refit the wheel arch liner, and secure it in position with its retaining screws and clips. Refit the roadwheel.
8 Frequent need for topping-up indicates a leak, which should be found and corrected before it becomes serious.

20 Rear brake shoe check

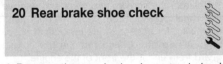

1 Remove the rear brake drums and check the brake shoes for signs of wear or contamination. At the same time, also check the wheel cylinders for signs of leakage and the brake drums for signs of wear. Refer to the relevant Sections of Chapter 9 for further information.

21 Brake fluid renewal

⚠️ **Warning: Brake hydraulic fluid can harm your eyes and damage painted surfaces, so use extreme caution when handling and pouring it. Do not use fluid that has been standing open for some time, as it absorbs moisture from the air. Excess moisture can cause a dangerous loss of braking effectiveness.**

1 The procedure is similar to that for the bleeding of the hydraulic system as described in Chapter 9, except that the brake fluid reservoir should be emptied by siphoning, using a clean poultry baster or similar before starting, and allowance should be made for the old fluid to be expelled when bleeding a section of the circuit.

2 Working as described in Chapter 9, open the first bleed screw in the sequence, and pump the brake pedal gently until nearly all the old fluid has been emptied from the master cylinder reservoir.

HAYNES HiNT *Old brake fluid is invariably much darker in colour than the new, making it easy to distinguish the two.*

3 Top-up to the "MAX" level with new fluid, and continue pumping until only the new fluid remains in the reservoir, and new fluid can be seen emerging from the bleed screw. Tighten the screw, and top the reservoir level up to the "MAX" level line.

4 Work through all the remaining bleed screws in the sequence until new fluid can be seen at all of them. Be careful to keep the master cylinder reservoir topped-up to above the "MIN" level at all times, or air may enter the system and greatly increase the length of the task.

5 When the operation is complete, check that all bleed screws are securely tightened, and that their dust caps are refitted. Wash off all traces of spilt fluid, and recheck the master cylinder reservoir fluid level.

6 Check the operation of the brakes before taking the car on the road.

Every 72 000 miles

22 Timing belt renewal

Refer to the relevant Part of Chapter 2.

Every 72 000 miles or 2 years, whichever comes first

23 Coolant renewal

Cooling system draining

⚠️ **Warning: Wait until the engine is cold before starting this procedure. Do not allow anti-freeze to come in contact with your skin, or with the painted surfaces of the vehicle. Rinse off spills immediately with plenty of water. Never leave antifreeze lying around in an open container, or in a puddle in the driveway or on the garage floor. Children and pets are attracted by its sweet smell, but antifreeze can be fatal if ingested.**

1 With the engine completely cold, remove the expansion tank filler cap. Turn the cap anti-clockwise until it reaches the first stop. Wait until any pressure remaining in the system is released, then push the cap down, turn it anti-clockwise to the second stop, and lift it off.

2 Remove the splash guard under the engine, where fitted, then position a suitable container beneath the coolant drain outlet at the lower left-hand side of the radiator.

3 Loosen the drain plug (there is no need to remove it completely) and allow the coolant to drain into the container. If desired, a length of tubing can be fitted to the drain outlet to direct the flow of coolant during draining (see illustration).

4 To assist draining, open the cooling system bleed screws. These are located in the heater matrix outlet hose union (to improve access, it may be located in an extension hose) on the engine compartment bulkhead, and on the top of the thermostat housing (see illustration). On some models, there may also be a bleed screw in the top left-hand end of the radiator.

5 When the flow of coolant stops, reposition the container below the cylinder block drain plug. On 1.6 and 1.8 litre models, the drain plug is located at the front of the cylinder block and on 2.0 litre models it is at the rear of the cylinder block.

6 Remove the drain plug, and allow the coolant to drain into the container.

7 If the coolant has been drained for a reason other than renewal, then provided it is clean and less than two years old, it can be re-used, though this is not recommended.

8 Refit the radiator and cylinder block drain plugs on completion of draining.

Cooling system flushing

9 If coolant renewal has been neglected, or if the antifreeze mixture has become diluted, then in time, the cooling system may gradually lose efficiency, as the coolant passages become restricted due to rust, scale deposits, and other sediment. The cooling system efficiency can be restored by flushing the system clean.

10 The radiator should be flushed independently of the engine, to avoid contamination.

Radiator flushing

11 To flush the radiator, first tighten the radiator drain plug, and the radiator bleed screw, where applicable.

1A

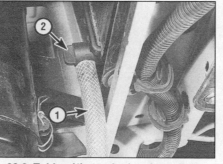

23.3 Tubing (1) attached to the radiator drain outlet and coolant drain plug (2)

23.4 Heater hose bleed screw (arrowed)

12 Disconnect the top and bottom hoses and any other relevant hoses from the radiator, with reference to Chapter 3.
13 Insert a garden hose into the radiator top inlet. Direct a flow of clean water through the radiator, and continue flushing until clean water emerges from the radiator bottom outlet.
14 If after a reasonable period, the water still does not run clear, the radiator can be flushed with a good proprietary cleaning agent. It is important that their manufacturer's instructions are followed carefully. If the contamination is particularly bad, insert the hose in the radiator bottom outlet, and reverse-flush the radiator.

Engine flushing

15 To flush the engine, first refit the cylinder block drain plug, and tighten the cooling system bleed screws.
16 Remove the thermostat (see Chapter 3), then temporarily refit the thermostat cover.
17 With the top and bottom hoses disconnected from the radiator, insert a garden hose into the radiator top hose. Direct a clean flow of water through the engine, and continue flushing until clean water emerges from the radiator bottom hose.
18 On completion of flushing, refit the thermostat and reconnect the hoses with reference to Chapter 3.

Cooling system filling

19 Before attempting to fill the cooling system, make sure that all hoses and clips are in good condition, and that the clips are tight. Note that an antifreeze mixture must be used all year round, to prevent corrosion of the engine components (see following sub-Section). Also check that the radiator and cylinder block drain plugs are in place and tight.
20 Remove the expansion tank filler cap.

Cut the bottom off an old antifreeze container to make a "header tank" for use when refilling the cooling system. The seal at the point arrowed should be as tight as possible - use an O-ring if available, or seal the joint by some other means

21 Open all the cooling system bleed screws (see paragraph 4).
22 Some of the cooling system hoses are positioned at a higher level than the top of the radiator expansion tank. It is therefore necessary to use a "header tank" when refilling the cooling system, to reduce the possibility of air being trapped in the system. Although Peugeot dealers use a special header tank, the same effect can be achieved by using a suitable bottle, with a seal between the bottle and the expansion tank (see **Haynes Hint**).
23 Fit the "header tank" to the expansion tank and slowly fill the system. Coolant will emerge from each of the bleed screws in turn, starting with the lowest screw. As soon as coolant free from air bubbles emerges from the lowest screw, tighten that screw, and watch the next bleed screw in the system. Repeat the procedure until the coolant is emerging from the highest bleed screw in the

cooling system and all bleed screws are securely tightened.
24 Ensure that the "header tank" is full (at least 0.5 litres of coolant). Start the engine, and run it at a fast idle speed (do not exceed 2000 rpm) until the cooling fan cuts in, and then cuts out. Stop the engine. **Note:** *Take great care not to scald yourself with the hot coolant during this operation.*
25 Allow the engine to cool, then remove the "header tank".
26 When the engine has cooled, check the coolant level as described in *"Weekly checks"*. Top-up the level if necessary, and refit the expansion tank cap. Where applicable, refit the splash guard under the engine.

Antifreeze mixture

27 The antifreeze should always be renewed at the specified intervals. This is necessary not only to maintain the antifreeze properties, but also to prevent corrosion which would otherwise occur as the corrosion inhibitors become progressively less effective.
28 Always use an ethylene-glycol based antifreeze which is suitable for use in mixed-metal cooling systems. The quantity of antifreeze and levels of protection are indicated in the Specifications.
29 Before adding antifreeze, the cooling system should be completely drained, preferably flushed, and all hoses checked for condition and security.
30 After filling with antifreeze, a label should be attached to the expansion tank, stating the type and concentration of antifreeze used, and the date installed. Any subsequent topping-up should be made with the same type and concentration of antifreeze.
31 Do not use engine antifreeze in the washer system, as it will cause damage to the vehicle paintwork. A screenwash additive should be added to the washer system in the quantities stated on the bottle.

Chapter 1 Part B:
Routine maintenance & servicing - diesel models

Contents

Degrees of difficulty

| **Easy,** suitable for novice with little experience | | **Fairly easy,** suitable for beginner with some experience | | **Fairly difficult,** suitable for competent DIY mechanic | | **Difficult,** suitable for experienced DIY mechanic | | **Very difficult,** suitable for expert DIY or professional | |

Lubricants and fluids

Refer to *"Weekly checks"*

Capacities

Engine oil

1.9 litre engine:
Models with air conditioning .... 4.2 litres
Models without air conditioning .... 4.5 litres
2.1 litre engine:
Models with air conditioning .... 4.3 litres
Models without air conditioning .... 4.8 litres

Cooling system

All engines (approximate) .... 8.0 litres

Transmission

1.9 litre models (approximate) .... 2.0 litres
2.1 litre models (approximate) .... 1.8 litres
Fuel tank .... 70 litres

Engine

Oil filter .... Champion F118
Auxiliary drivebelt tension (for use with Peugeot electronic tool - see text):
New belt .... 120 SEEM units
Used belt .... 90 SEEM units

Cooling system

Antifreeze mixture:
50% antifreeze .... Protection down to -37°C (5°F)
55% antifreeze .... Protection down to -45°C (-22°F)
Note: *Refer to antifreeze manufacturer for latest recommendations.*

Fuel system

Air filter element .... Champion U543
Fuel filter .... Champion L141

Brakes

Brake pad friction material minimum thickness .... 2.0 mm
Brake shoe friction material minimum thickness .... 1.5 mm

Tyre pressures

See end of *"Weekly checks"*

Torque wrench settings	Nm	lbf ft
Auxiliary drivebelt tensioner pulley assembly retaining bolts (models without air conditioning)	22	16
Auxiliary drivebelt tensioner roller retaining bolt (models with air conditioning)	50	37
Manual transmission filler/level plug	20	15
Roadwheel bolts	90	66

The maintenance intervals in this manual are provided with the assumption that you, not the dealer, will be carrying out the work. These are the minimum maintenance intervals recommended by us for vehicles driven daily. If you wish to keep your vehicle in peak condition at all times, you may wish to perform some of these procedures more often. We encourage frequent maintenance, because it enhances the efficiency, performance and resale value of your vehicle.

When the vehicle is new, it should be serviced by a factory-authorised dealer service department, in order to preserve the factory warranty.

Weekly, or every 250 miles (400 km)
☐ Refer to *"Weekly checks"*

Every 6000 miles (10 000 km) or 12 months - whichever comes sooner
In addition to all the items listed above, carry out the following:
☐ Renew the engine oil and filter (Section 3)
☐ Drain any water from the fuel filter (Section 4)
☐ Check all underbonnet components and hoses for fluid leaks (Section 5)
☐ Check the operation of the clutch (Section 6)
☐ Check the condition of the driveshaft rubber gaiters (Section 7)
☐ Check the steering and suspension components for condition and security (Section 8)
☐ Lubricate all hinges and locks (Section 9)

Every 12 000 miles (20 000 km)
In addition to all the items listed above, carry out the following:
☐ Renew the pollen filter (where fitted) (Section 10)

Every 18 000 miles (30 000 km)
In addition to all the items listed above, carry out the following:
☐ Renew the air filter (Section 11)
☐ Renew the fuel filter (Section 12)
☐ Check the condition of the front brake pads, and renew if necessary (Section 13)
☐ Check the condition of the rear brake pads and renew if necessary - rear disc brake models (Section 14)
☐ Check the operation of the handbrake (Section 15)
☐ Carry out a road test (Section 16)

Every 36 000 miles (60 000 km)
In addition to all the items listed above, carry out the following:
☐ Check the manual transmission oil level, and top-up if necessary (Section 17)
☐ Check the condition of the auxiliary drivebelt, and renew if necessary (Section 18)
☐ Check the condition of the rear brake shoes and renew if necessary - rear drum brake models (Section 19)

Every 36 000 miles (60 000 km) or 2 years, whichever comes sooner
In addition to all the items listed above, carry out the following:
☐ Renew the brake fluid (Section 20)

Every 72 000 miles (120 000 km)
In addition to all the items listed above, carry out the following:
☐ Renew the timing belt (Section 21)

Note: It is strongly recommended that the timing belt renewal interval is halved to 36 000 miles (60 000 km) on vehicles which are subjected to intensive use, ie. mainly short journeys or a lot of stop-start driving. The actual belt renewal interval is therefore very much up to the individual owner, but bear in mind that severe engine damage will result if the belt breaks.

Every 72 000 miles (120 000 km) or every 2 years, whichever comes sooner
In addition to all the items listed above, carry out the following:
☐ Renew the coolant (Section 22)

1B

Underbonnet view of a 2.1 litre model

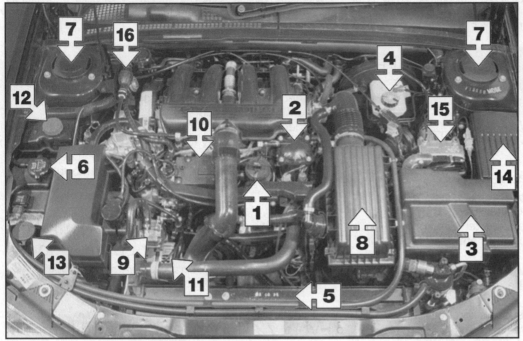

1 Engine oil filler cap/dipstick
2 Fuel filter housing
3 Battery
4 Brake fluid reservoir
5 Radiator
6 Coolant expansion tank
7 Suspension strut upper
   mounting
8 Air filter housing
9 Power steering pump
10 Injection pump
11 Alternator
12 Power steering fluid reservoir
13 Washer fluid reservoir
14 Fuse/relay box
15 Anti-lock braking system (ABS)
   hydraulic unit
16 Fuel system priming pump

Front underbody view

1 Engine oil drain plug
2 Air conditioning compressor
3 Driveshaft intermediate bearing
4 Brake caliper
5 Front suspension lower arm
6 Track rod
7 Front suspension anti-roll bar

Rear underbody view

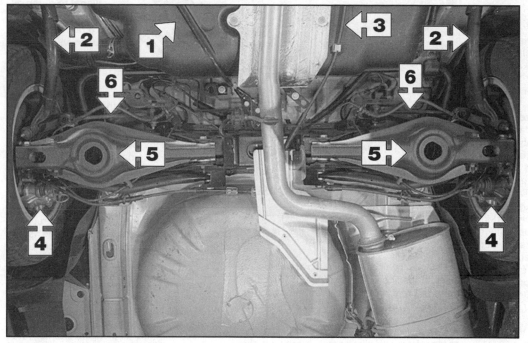

1 Fuel tank
2 Rear suspension trailing arm
3 Handbrake cable
4 Brake caliper
5 Rear suspension lower arm
6 Rear suspension track arm

Maintenance procedures

1 General information

This Chapter is designed to help the home mechanic maintain his/her vehicle for safety, economy, long life and peak performance.

The Chapter contains a master maintenance schedule, followed by Sections dealing specifically with each task in the schedule. Visual checks, adjustments, component renewal and other helpful items are included. Refer to the accompanying illustrations of the engine compartment and the underside of the vehicle for the locations of the various components.

Servicing your vehicle in accordance with the mileage/time maintenance schedule and the following Sections will provide a planned maintenance programme, which should result in a long and reliable service life. This is a comprehensive plan, so maintaining some items but not others at the specified service intervals, will not produce the same results.

As you service your vehicle, you will discover that many of the procedures can - and should - be grouped together, because of the particular procedure being performed, or because of the proximity of two otherwise-unrelated components to one another. For example, if the vehicle is raised for any reason, the exhaust can be inspected at the same time as the suspension and steering components.

The first step in this maintenance programme is to prepare yourself before the actual work begins. Read through all the Sections relevant to the work to be carried out, then make a list and gather all the parts and tools required. If a problem is encountered, seek advice from a parts specialist, or a dealer service department.

2 Intensive maintenance

1 If, from the time the vehicle is new, the routine maintenance schedule is followed closely, and frequent checks are made of fluid levels and high-wear items, as suggested throughout this manual, the engine will be kept in relatively good running condition, and the need for additional work will be minimised.
2 It is possible that there will be times when the engine is running poorly due to the lack of regular maintenance. This is even more likely if a used vehicle, which has not received regular and frequent maintenance checks, is purchased. In such cases, additional work may need to be carried out, outside of the regular maintenance intervals.
3 If engine wear is suspected, a compression test (refer to Chapter 2B) will provide valuable information regarding the overall performance of the main internal components. Such a test can be used as a basis to decide on the extent of the work to be carried out. If, for example, a compression test indicates serious internal engine wear, conventional maintenance as described in this Chapter will not greatly improve the performance of the engine, and may prove a waste of time and money, unless extensive overhaul work is carried out first.
4 The following series of operations are those most often required to improve the performance of a generally poor-running engine:

Primary operations

a) Clean, inspect and test the battery (refer to "Weekly checks").
b) Check all the engine-related fluids (refer to "Weekly checks").
c) Check the condition and tension of the auxiliary drivebelt (Section 18).
d) Check the condition of the air filter, and renew if necessary (Section 11).
e) Check the condition of all hoses, and check for fluid leaks (Section 5).
f) Renew the fuel filter (Section 12).

5 If the above operations do not prove fully effective, carry out the following secondary operations:

Secondary operations

All items listed under "Primary operations", plus the following:

a) Check the charging system (refer to Chapter 5).
b) Check the preheating system (refer to Chapter 5).
c) Check the fuel system (refer to Chapter 4).

1B

3 Engine oil and filter renewal

1 Frequent oil and filter changes are the most important preventative maintenance procedures which can be undertaken by the DIY owner. As engine oil ages, it becomes diluted and contaminated, which leads to premature engine wear.

2 Before starting this procedure, gather together all the necessary tools and materials. Also make sure that you have plenty of clean rags and newspapers handy, to mop up any spills. Ideally, the engine oil should be warm, as it will drain better, and more built-up sludge will be removed with it. Take care, however, not to touch the exhaust or any other hot parts of the engine when working under the vehicle. To avoid any possibility of scalding, and to protect yourself from possible skin irritants and other harmful contaminants in used engine oils, it is advisable to wear gloves when carrying out this work. Access to the underside of the vehicle will be greatly improved if it can be raised on a lift, driven onto ramps, or jacked up and supported on axle stands. Whichever method is chosen, make sure that the vehicle remains level, or if it is at an angle, that the drain plug is at the lowest point. Where fitted, remove the splash guard from under the engine.

3 Slacken the drain plug about half a turn, position the draining container under the drain plug, then remove the plug completely **(see illustration)**. If possible, try to keep the plug pressed into the sump while unscrewing it by hand the last couple of turns **(see Haynes Hint)**. Recover the sealing ring from the drain plug

4 Allow some time for the old oil to drain, noting that it may be necessary to reposition the container as the oil flow slows to a trickle.

5 After all the oil has drained, wipe off the drain plug with a clean rag, and fit a new sealing washer. Clean the area around the drain plug opening, and refit the plug. Tighten the plug securely.

6 If the filter is also to be renewed, move the

As the drain plug releases from the threads, move it away sharply so the stream of oil issuing from the sump runs into the container, not up your sleeve!

container into position under the oil filter, which is located on the front side of the cylinder block.

7 Using an oil filter removal tool if necessary, slacken the filter initially, then unscrew it by hand the rest of the way **(see illustration)**. Empty the oil in the old filter into the container.

8 Use a clean rag to remove all oil, dirt and sludge from the filter sealing area on the engine. Check the old filter to make sure that the rubber sealing ring hasn't stuck to the engine. If it has, carefully remove it.

9 Apply a light coating of clean engine oil to the sealing ring on the new filter, then screw it into position on the engine. Tighten the filter firmly by hand only - **do not** use any tools. Where necessary, refit the splash guard under the engine.

10 Remove the old oil and all tools from under the car, then lower the car to the ground (if applicable).

11 Remove the dipstick, then unscrew the oil filler cap from the top of the filler tube on the front side of the cylinder block. Fill the engine, using the correct grade and type of oil (see "Weekly checks"). An oil can spout or funnel may help to reduce spillage. Pour in half the specified quantity of oil first, then wait a few minutes for the oil to fall to the sump. Continue adding oil a small quantity at a time

OIL CARE
FOLLOW THE CODE
OIL BANK LINE
0800 66 33 66

Note: It is antisocial and illegal to dump oil down the drain. To find the location of your local oil recycling bank, call this number free.

until the level is up to the lower mark on the dipstick. Adding approximately 1.0 litre will bring the level up to the upper mark on the dipstick. Refit the filler cap.

12 Start the engine and run it for a few minutes; check for leaks around the oil filter seal and the sump drain plug. Note that there may be a delay of a few seconds before the oil pressure warning light goes out when the engine is first started, as the oil circulates through the engine oil galleries and the new oil filter (where fitted) before the pressure builds up.

13 Switch off the engine, and wait a few minutes for the oil to settle in the sump once more. With the new oil circulated and the filter completely full, recheck the level on the dipstick, and add more oil as necessary.

14 Dispose of the used engine oil safely, with reference to *"General Repair Procedures"*.

4 Fuel filter water draining

1 A water drain plug and tube are provided at the base of the fuel filter housing.

2 Place a suitable container beneath the drain tube, and cover the surrounding area with rags. Take care not to allow fuel to enter the transmission bellhousing which is just below.

3 Open the drain plug by turning it anti-clockwise. Allow fuel and water to drain until fuel which is free from water, emerges from the end of the tube **(see illustration)**. Close the drain plug.

4 Dispose of the drained fuel safely.

5 Start the engine. If difficulty is experienced, bleed the fuel system (Chapter 4B).

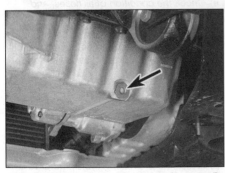

3.3 Engine oil sump drain plug (arrowed)

3.7 Using an oil filter removal tool to slacken the oil filter

4.3 Fuel filter water drain plug (arrowed) and tube, located at the base of the fuel filter housing

5 Hose and fluid leak check

 Warning: Refer to the safety information given in 'Safety First' and Chapter 3 before disturbing any of the cooling system components.

1 Carefully check the radiator and heater coolant hoses along their entire length. Renew any hose which is cracked, swollen or which shows signs of deterioration. Cracks will show up better if the hose is squeezed. Pay close attention to the clips that secure the hoses to the cooling system components. Hose clips that have been over-tightened can pinch and puncture hoses, resulting in cooling system leaks.

2 Inspect all the cooling system components (hoses, joint faces etc.) for leaks. Where any problems of this nature are found on system components, renew the component or gasket with reference to Chapter 3.

3 A leak from the cooling system will usually show up as white or rust-coloured deposits, on the area surrounding the leak **(see Haynes Hint)**.

Fuel

 Warning: Refer to the safety information given in 'Safety First' and Chapter 4 before disturbing any of the fuel system components.

4 Check all fuel lines at their connections to the injection pump, injectors and fuel filter housing.

5 Examine each fuel hose/pipe along its length for splits or cracks. Check for leakage from the union nuts and examine the unions between the metal fuel lines and the fuel filter housing. Also check the area around the fuel injectors for signs of leakage.

6 To identify fuel leaks between the fuel tank and the engine bay, the vehicle should raised and securely supported on axle stands. Inspect the fuel tank and filler neck for punctures, cracks and other damage. The connection between the filler neck and tank is especially critical. Sometimes a rubber filler neck or connecting hose will leak due to loose retaining clamps or deteriorated rubber.

7 Carefully check all rubber hoses and metal fuel lines leading away from the fuel tank. Check for loose connections, deteriorated hoses, kinked lines, and other damage. Pay particular attention to the vent pipes and hoses, which often loop up around the filler neck and can become blocked or kinked, making tank filling difficult. Follow the fuel supply and return lines to the front of the vehicle, carefully inspecting them all the way for signs of damage or corrosion. Renew damaged sections as necessary.

Engine oil

8 Inspect the area around the camshaft cover, cylinder head, oil filter and sump joint faces. Bear in mind that, over a period of time, some very slight seepage from these areas is to be expected - what you are really looking for is any indication of a serious leak caused by gasket failure. Engine oil seeping from the base of the timing belt cover or the transmission bellhousing may be an indication of crankshaft or input shaft oil seal failure. Should a leak be found, renew the failed gasket or oil seal by referring to the appropriate Chapters in this manual.

Power assisted steering (PAS) fluid

9 Examine the hose running between the fluid reservoir and the power steering pump, and the return hose running from the steering rack to the fluid reservoir. Also examine the high pressure supply hose between the pump and the steering rack.

10 Where applicable, check the hoses leading to the PAS fluid cooler at the front of the engine bay. Look for deterioration caused by corrosion and damage from grounding, or debris thrown up from the road surface.

11 Pay particular attention to crimped unions, and the area surrounding the hoses that are secured with adjustable worm drive clips. Like automatic transmission fluid, PAS fluid is a thin oil, and is usually red in colour.

Air conditioning refrigerant

 Warning: Refer to the safety information given in 'Safety First' and Chapter 3, regarding the dangers of disturbing any of the air conditioning system components.

12 The air conditioning system is filled with a liquid refrigerant, which is retained under high pressure. If the air conditioning system is opened and depressurised without the aid of specialised equipment, the refrigerant will immediately turn into gas and escape into the atmosphere. If the liquid comes into contact with your skin, it can cause severe frostbite. In addition, the refrigerant contains substances which are environmentally damaging; for this reason, it should not be allowed to escape into the atmosphere.

13 Any suspected air conditioning system leaks should be immediately referred to a Peugeot dealer or air conditioning specialist. Leakage will be shown up as a steady drop in the level of refrigerant in the system.

14 Note that water may drip from the condenser drain pipe, underneath the car, immediately after the air conditioning system has been in use. This is normal, and should not be cause for concern.

Brake (and clutch) fluid

 Warning: Refer to the safety information given in 'Safety First' and Chapter 9, regarding the dangers of handling brake fluid.

15 With reference to Chapter 9, examine the area surrounding the brake pipe unions at the master cylinder for signs of leakage. Check the area around the base of fluid reservoir, for signs of leakage caused by seal failure. Also examine the brake pipe unions at the ABS hydraulic unit.

16 If fluid loss is evident, but the leak cannot be pinpointed in the engine bay, the brake calipers and underbody brake lines and should be carefully checked with the vehicle raised and supported on axle stands. Leakage of fluid from the braking system is serious fault that must be rectified immediately.

17 On models with a hydraulically-operated clutch, refer to Chapter 6 and check for leakage around the hydraulic fluid line connections to the clutch master cylinder at the bulkhead, and to the clutch slave cylinder, bolted to the side of the transmission bellhousing.

18 Brake/clutch hydraulic fluid is a toxic substance with a watery consistency. New fluid is almost colourless, but it becomes darker with age and use.

Unidentified fluid leaks

19 If there are signs that a fluid of some description is leaking from the vehicle, but you cannot identify the type of fluid or its exact origin, park the vehicle overnight and slide a large piece of card underneath it. Providing that the card is positioned in roughly in the right location, even the smallest leak will show up on the card. Not only will this help you to pinpoint the exact location of the leak, it should be easier to identify the fluid from its colour. Bear in mind, though, that the leak may only be occurring when the engine is running!

Vacuum hoses

20 Although the braking system is hydraulically-operated, the brake servo unit amplifies the effort you apply at the brake pedal, by making use of the vacuum created by the pump (see Chapter 9). Vacuum is ported to the servo by means of a large-bore hose. Any leaks that develop in this hose will reduce the effectiveness of the braking system.

1B

A leak in the cooling system will usually show-up as white- or rust-coloured deposits on the area adjoining the leak

7.1 Checking a driveshaft gaiter for damage

8.2 Checking a steering gear gaiter for damage

8.4 Check for wear in the hub bearings by grasping the wheel and trying to rock it

21 In addition, many of the underbonnet components, particularly the emission control components, are driven by vacuum supplied from the vacuum pump via narrow-bore hoses. A leak in a vacuum hose means that air is being drawn into the hose (rather than escaping from it) and this makes leakage very difficult to detect. One method is to use an old length of vacuum hose as a kind of stethoscope - hold one end close to (but not in!) your ear and use the other end to probe the area around the suspected leak. When the end of the hose is directly over a vacuum leak, a hissing sound will be heard clearly through the hose. Care must be taken to avoid contacting hot or moving components, as the engine must be running, when testing in this manner. Renew any vacuum hoses that are found to be defective.

6 Clutch operation check

1 Diesel engine models covered by this manual are equipped with either a cable-operated, or hydraulically operated self-adjusting clutch mechanism which is virtually maintenance-free.
2 The only maintenance necessary is to check that the clutch pedal moves smoothly and easily through its full travel, and that the clutch itself functions correctly, with no trace of slip or drag. Note that the hydraulically operated clutch mechanism is a completely sealed assembly. Checking or topping-up of the hydraulic fluid level is not necessary (and is not even possible).
3 If any problems are experienced, refer to Chapter 6 for further details.

7 Driveshaft gaiter check

1 With the vehicle raised and securely supported on axle stands, turn the steering to full left or right lock, then slowly rotate the roadwheel. Inspect the outer constant velocity

(CV) joint rubber gaiters, squeezing the gaiters to open out the folds **(see illustration)**. Check for signs of cracking, splits or deterioration of the rubber, which may allow the grease to escape, or water and grit to enter. Also check the security and condition of the retaining clips. Repeat these checks on the inner CV joints. If any damage or deterioration is found, the gaiters should be renewed (see Chapter 8).
2 At the same time, check the general condition of the CV joints themselves by first holding the driveshaft and attempting to rotate the wheel. Repeat this check whilst holding the inner joint and attempting to rotate the driveshaft. Any appreciable movement indicates wear in the CV joints, wear in the driveshaft splines, or a loose driveshaft retaining nut.

8 Steering and suspension component check

Front suspension and steering check

1 Raise the front of the vehicle, and securely support it on axle stands.
2 Visually inspect the balljoint dust covers and the steering rack-and-pinion gaiters for splits, chafing or deterioration **(see illustration)**. Any wear of these components will cause loss of lubricant, together with dirt and water entry, resulting in rapid deterioration of the balljoints or steering gear.
3 Check the power steering fluid hoses for chafing or deterioration, and the pipe and hose unions for fluid leaks. Also check for signs of fluid leakage under pressure from the steering gear rubber gaiters, which would indicate failed fluid seals within the steering gear.
4 Grasp the roadwheel at the 12 o'clock and 6 o'clock positions, and try to rock it **(see illustration)**. Very slight free play may be felt, but if the movement is appreciable, further investigation is necessary to determine the source. Continue rocking the wheel while an assistant depresses the footbrake. If the

movement is now eliminated or significantly reduced, it is likely that the hub bearings are at fault. If the free play is still evident with the footbrake depressed, then there is wear in the suspension joints or mountings.
5 Now grasp the wheel at the 9 o'clock and 3 o'clock positions, and try to rock it as before. Any movement felt now may again be caused by wear in the hub bearings or the steering track-rod balljoints. If the inner or outer balljoint is worn, the visual movement will be obvious.
6 Using a large screwdriver or flat bar, check for wear in the suspension mounting bushes by levering between the relevant suspension component and its attachment point. Some movement is to be expected as the mountings are made of rubber, but excessive wear should be obvious. Also check the condition of any visible rubber bushes, looking for splits, cracks or contamination of the rubber.
7 With the car standing on its wheels, have an assistant turn the steering wheel back and forth about an eighth of a turn each way. There should be very little, if any, lost movement between the steering wheel and roadwheels. If this is not the case, closely observe the joints and mountings previously described, but in addition, check the steering column universal joints for wear, and the rack-and-pinion steering gear itself.

Suspension strut/shock absorber check

8 Check for any signs of fluid leakage around the suspension strut/shock absorber body, or from the rubber gaiter around the piston rod. Should any fluid be noticed, the suspension strut/shock absorber is defective internally, and should be renewed. **Note:** *Suspension struts/shock absorbers should always be renewed in pairs on the same axle.*
9 The efficiency of the suspension strut/shock absorber may be checked by bouncing the vehicle at each corner. Generally speaking, the body will return to its normal position and stop after being depressed. If it rises and returns on a rebound, the suspension strut/shock absorber is probably suspect. Examine also the suspension strut/shock absorber upper and lower mountings for any signs of wear.

9 Hinge and lock lubrication

1 Lubricate the hinges of the bonnet, doors and tailgate with a light general-purpose oil.

Similarly, lubricate all latches, locks and lock strikers - don't overdo it, or it will get on your clothes as you get in! At the same time, check the security and operation of all the locks, adjusting them if necessary (see Chapter 11).
2 Lightly lubricate the bonnet release mechanism and cable with a suitable grease.

Every 12 000 miles

10 Pollen filter renewal

1 Operate the windscreen wipers and switch of the ignition so the wiper arms stop at the top of their travel.
2 Unscrew the retaining nut then unclip and remove the passenger side plastic intake vent cover from the base of the windscreen (see illustration).
3 Unclip the passenger side intake vent panel and remove the panel from beneath the windscreen to gain access to the pollen filter (see illustration).
4 Ease the pollen filter out of its housing and remove it from the vehicle (see illustrations).
5 Wipe clean the housing then install the new filter, making sure it is clipped securely in position.
6 Clip the vent panel into position, making sure it is correctly engaged with the driver's side panel, then refit the vent cover and retaining nut.
7 Switch the ignition back on and return the wiper arm to the at rest position.

10.2 Undo the nut and remove the passenger side half of the intake vent cover . . .

10.3 . . . then unclip the intake vent panel from the vehicle

10.4a Carefully ease the pollen filter out from its housing . . .

10.4b . . . and remove it from the vehicle

1B

Every 18 000 miles

11 Air filter element renewal

1 Slacken the clip and disconnect the intake duct from the filter housing lid (see illustration).
2 On 2.1 litre models, release the coolant hose and the oil separator from their locations on the air filter housing lid (see illustrations). On 1.9 litre models, release the accelerator cable from the air filter housing lid.
3 Undo the screws securing the lid to the air filter housing body, lift off the lid and remove the filter element (see illustrations).
4 Wipe clean the housing body and lid.
5 Place the new element in position in the housing body. Refit the filter housing lid, securing it in position with its retaining screws.

11.1 Slacken the clip and disconnect the intake duct from the air filter housing lid

11.2a On 2.1 litre models, release the coolant hose . . .

11.2b . . . and the oil separator from the air filter housing lid

11.3a Undo the screws securing the lid to the air filter housing body . . .

11.3b . . . lift off the lid and remove the filter element

12.5 Remove the fuel filter housing cover and lift out the filter

6 Refit the coolant hose, oil separator or accelerator cable, as applicable, to their locations, then reconnect the intake duct and securely tighten its retaining clip.

12 Fuel filter renewal

1 The fuel filter is located in a plastic housing at the front of the engine.
2 Where applicable, cover the clutch bellhousing with a piece of plastic sheeting to protect the clutch from fuel spillage.
3 Position a suitable container under the end of the fuel filter drain hose. Open the drain screw on the front of the filter housing and allow the fuel to drain completely.
4 Using a suitable Allen key or hexagon bit, remove the four filter housing cover securing screws, then lift off the cover.
5 Lift the filter from the housing **(see illustration)**.
6 Place the new filter in the housing.
7 Coat the threads of the filter cover securing bolts with thread-locking compound, then refit the cover and secure with the bolts.
8 Close the fuel filter drain screw.
9 Prime the fuel system (see Chapter 4).
10 Open the drain screw until clean fuel flows from the hose, then close the drain screw and withdraw the container from under the hose.

13 Front brake pad check

1 Firmly apply the handbrake, then jack up the front of the car and support it securely on axle stands. Remove the front roadwheels.
2 For a comprehensive check, the brake pads should be removed and cleaned. The operation of the caliper can then also be checked, and the condition of the brake disc itself can be fully examined on both sides. Refer to Chapter 9 for further information **(see Haynes Hint)**.
3 If any pad's friction material is worn to the specified thickness or less, *all four pads must be renewed as a set.*

14 Rear brake pad check

1 Chock the front wheels, then jack up the rear of the vehicle and support it on axle stands. Remove the rear roadwheels.
2 For a quick check, the thickness of friction material remaining on each brake pad can be measured through the top of the caliper body. If any pad's friction material is worn to the specified thickness or less, all four pads must be renewed as a set.
3 For a comprehensive check, the brake pads should be removed and cleaned. This will permit the operation of the caliper to be checked, and the condition of the brake disc itself to be fully examined on both sides. Refer to Chapter 9 for further information.
4 If any pad's friction material is worn to the specified thickness or less, *all four pads must be renewed as a set.*

15 Handbrake check

1 Check and, if necessary, adjust the handbrake (see Chapter 9). Check that the handbrake cables are free to move easily and lubricate all exposed linkages/cable pivots.

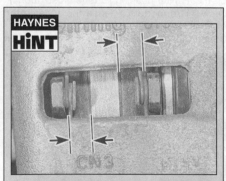

For a quick check, the thickness of the friction material on each brake pad can be measured through the aperture in the caliper body

16 Road test

Instruments and electrical equipment

1 Check the operation of all instruments and electrical equipment.
2 Make sure that all instruments read correctly, and switch on all electrical equipment in turn, to check that it functions properly.

Steering and suspension

3 Check for any abnormalities in the steering, suspension, handling or road "feel".
4 Drive the vehicle, and check that there are no unusual vibrations or noises.
5 Check that the steering feels positive, with no excessive "sloppiness", or roughness, and check for any suspension noises when cornering and driving over bumps.

Drivetrain

6 Check the performance of the engine, clutch, transmission and driveshafts.
7 Listen for any unusual noises from the engine, clutch and transmission.
8 Make sure that the engine runs smoothly when idling, and that there is no hesitation when accelerating.
9 Check that the clutch action is smooth and progressive, that the drive is taken up smoothly, and that the pedal travel is not excessive. Also listen for any noises when the clutch pedal is depressed.
10 Check that all gears can be engaged smoothly without noise, and that the gear lever action is not abnormally vague or "notchy".

Check the operation and performance of the braking system

11 Make sure that the vehicle does not pull to one side when braking, and that the wheels do not lock prematurely when braking hard.
12 Check that there is no vibration through the steering when braking.
13 Check that the handbrake operates

correctly without excessive movement of the lever, and that it holds the vehicle stationary on a slope.

14 Test the operation of the brake servo unit as follows. With the engine off, depress the footbrake four or five times to exhaust the vacuum. Hold the brake pedal depressed, then start the engine. As the engine starts, there should be a noticeable "give" in the brake pedal as vacuum builds up. Allow the engine to run for at least two minutes, and then switch it off. If the brake pedal is depressed now, it should be possible to detect a hiss from the servo as the pedal is depressed. After about four or five applications, no further hissing should be heard, and the pedal should feel considerably harder.

Every 36 000 miles

17 Manual transmission oil level check

Note: *A new sealing washer will be required for the transmission filler/level plug, when refitting.*

1 Jack up the front and rear of the car and securely support it on axle stands so that it remains level. If the car has been recently driven, wait at least 5 minutes after the engine has been switched off. If the oil level is checked immediately after driving the car, some of the oil will remain distributed around the transmission components, resulting in an inaccurate level reading.

2 On 1.9 litre models, remove the left-hand front roadwheel then release the screws and clips and remove the wheel arch liner from under the wing for access to the filler/level plug.

3 On 2.1 litre models, remove the splash guard from under the engine.

4 Wipe clean the area around the filler/level plug. On 1.9 litre models the filler/level plug is the largest bolt among those securing the end cover to the transmission; on 2.1 litre models the filler/level plug is located on the rear face of the differential housing. Unscrew the plug and clean it; discard the sealing washer **(see illustrations)**.

5 The oil level should reach the lower edge of the filler/level hole. A certain amount of oil will have gathered behind the filler/level plug, and will trickle out when it is removed; this does *not* necessarily indicate that the level is correct. To ensure that a true level is established, wait until the initial trickle has stopped, then add oil as necessary until a trickle of new oil can be seen emerging. The level will be correct when the flow ceases; use only good-quality oil of the specified type.

6 Refilling the transmission is an awkward operation; above all, allow plenty of time for the oil level to settle properly before checking it. If a large amount had to be added to the transmission, or if a large amount flowed out on checking the level, refit the filler/level plug and take the vehicle on a short journey. With the new oil distributed fully around the transmission components, recheck the level after allowing time for it to settle again.

7 If the transmission has been overfilled so that oil flows out as soon as the filler/level plug is removed, first check that the car is completely level (front-to-rear and side-to-side). Allow any surplus oil to drain off into a suitable container.

8 When the level is correct, fit a new sealing washer to the filler/level plug. Tighten the plug to the specified torque wrench setting. Wash off any spilt oil. Refit the wheel arch liner or splash guard, and secure it in position with its retaining screws and clips. Refit the roadwheel (if removed) then lower the car to the ground.

9 Frequent need for topping-up indicates a leak, which should be found and corrected before it becomes serious.

18 Auxiliary drivebelt check and renewal

Note: *Depending on model and equipment fitted, access to the auxiliary drivebelt can be extremely limited. Where necessary, greater working clearance can be gained by removing the diesel injection electronic control unit (ECU) and its mounting box as described in Chapter 4B. If working on the 2.1 litre model,* the help of an assistant will also be beneficial.

Note: *On models with a manually adjusted drivebelt, Peugeot specify the use of a special electronic tool (SEEM C105.5) to correctly set the drivebelt tension. If access to this equipment cannot be obtained, an approximate setting can be achieved using the method described below. If the method described is used, the tension should be checked using the special electronic tool at the earliest opportunity.*

1 All models are equipped with a single poly-V type, multi-ribbed auxiliary drivebelt. The belt tension is adjusted manually on models without air conditioning, and automatically (once an initial setting procedure has been carried out), by means of a spring-loaded tensioner, on models with air conditioning.

Checking the auxiliary drivebelt condition

2 Apply the handbrake, then jack up the front of the car and support it on axle stands. Remove the right-hand front roadwheel.

3 Release the screws and clips and remove the wheel arch liner from under the right-hand front wing for access to the crankshaft pulley bolt. Where fitted, also remove the splash guard from under the front of the engine.

4 Using a suitable socket and bar fitted to the crankshaft pulley bolt, rotate the crankshaft so that the entire length of the drivebelt can be examined. Examine the drivebelt for cracks, splitting, fraying or damage. Check also for signs of glazing (shiny patches) and for separation of the belt plies. Renew the belt if worn or damaged.

5 If the condition of the belt is satisfactory, on models without air conditioning, check the drivebelt tension as described below. On models with air conditioning, there is no need to check the drivebelt tension.

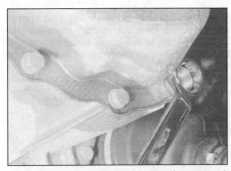

17.4a Use a spanner to loosen the manual transmission filler/level plug . . .

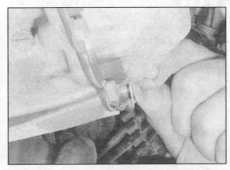

17.4b . . . then unscrew and remove it (1.9 litre models)

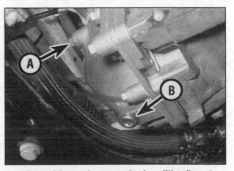

17.4c Manual transmission filler/level plug (A) and drain plug (B) (2.1 litre models)

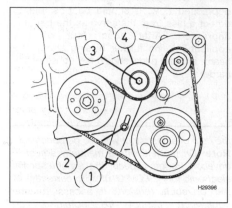

18.8 Auxiliary drivebelt adjustment details (models without air conditioning)

1 *Adjuster bolt*
2 *Tensioning pulley assembly lower securing bolt*
3 *Tensioning pulley assembly upper retaining bolt*
4 *Tensioning pulley*

Auxiliary drivebelt (models without air conditioning) - removal, refitting and tensioning

Removal

6 If not already done, proceed as described in paragraphs 2 and 3.
7 Disconnect the battery negative lead.
8 Slacken the two bolts securing the tensioning pulley assembly to the engine **(see illustration)**.
9 Rotate the adjuster bolt to move the tensioner pulley away from the drivebelt until there is sufficient slack for the drivebelt to be removed from the pulleys.

Refitting

10 Fit the drivebelt around the pulleys in the following order:
a) *Power steering pump.*
b) *Crankshaft.*
c) *Alternator.*
d) *Tensioner pulley.*
11 Ensure that the ribs on the belt are correctly engaged with the grooves in the pulleys, and that the drivebelt is correctly routed. Take all the slack out of the belt by turning the tensioner pulley adjuster bolt. Tension the belt as follows.

Tensioning

12 If not already done, proceed as described in paragraphs 2 and 3.
13 Correct tensioning of the drivebelt will ensure that it has a long life. A belt which is too slack will slip and perhaps squeal.

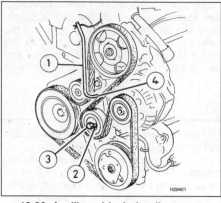

18.20 Auxiliary drivebelt adjustment details (models with air conditioning)

1 *Setting tool*
2 *Square hole on front face of the eccentric tensioner pulley*
3 *Eccentric tensioner pulley retaining bolt*
4 *8.0 mm hole in arm of automatic tensioner pulley (for insertion of setting tool)*

Beware, however, of overtightening, as this can cause wear in the alternator bearings.
14 The belt should be tensioned so that, under firm thumb pressure, there is approximately 5.0 mm of free movement at the mid-point between the pulleys on the longest belt run.
15 To adjust the tension, with the two tensioner pulley assembly retaining bolts slackened, rotate the adjuster bolt until the correct tension is achieved. Once the belt is correctly tensioned, rotate the crankshaft four complete revolutions in the normal direction of rotation and recheck the tension.
16 When the belt is correctly tensioned, tighten the tensioner pulley assembly retaining bolts to the specified torque, then reconnect the battery negative lead.
17 Refit the wheel arch liner and, where fitted, the engine splash guard. Refit the roadwheel, and lower the vehicle to the ground.

Auxiliary drivebelt (models with air conditioning) - removal, refitting and tensioning

Removal

18 If not already done, proceed as described in paragraphs 2 and 3.
19 Disconnect the battery negative lead.
20 Working under the wheel arch, slacken the retaining bolt located in the centre of the eccentric tensioner pulley **(see illustration)**.
21 Insert a cranked, 7.0 mm square section bar (a quarter inch square drive socket bar for

example) into the square hole on the front face of the eccentric tensioner pulley.
22 Using the bar, turn the eccentric tensioner pulley until the hole in the arm of the automatic tensioner pulley is aligned with the hole in the mounting bracket behind. When the holes are aligned, slide a suitable setting tool (a bolt, or cranked length of bar of approximately 8.0 mm diameter) through the hole in the arm and into the mounting bracket.
23 With the automatic tensioner locked, turn the eccentric tensioner pulley until the drivebelt tension is released sufficiently to enable the belt to be removed.

Refitting and tensioning

24 Fit the drivebelt around the pulleys in the following order:
a) *Air conditioning compressor.*
b) *Crankshaft.*
c) *Automatic tensioner pulley.*
d) *Power steering pump.*
e) *Alternator.*
f) *Eccentric tensioner pulley.*
25 Ensure that the ribs on the belt are correctly engaged with the grooves in the pulleys.
26 Turn the eccentric tensioner pulley to apply tension to the drivebelt, until the load is released from the setting bolt. Without altering the position of the eccentric tensioner pulley, tighten its retaining bolt to the specified torque.
27 Remove the setting bolt from the automatic tensioner arm, then rotate the crankshaft four complete revolutions in the normal direction of rotation.
28 Check that the holes in the automatic adjuster arm and the mounting bracket are still aligned by re-inserting the setting bolt. If the bolt will not slide in easily, repeat the tensioning procedure from paragraph 26 onward.
29 On completion, reconnect the battery negative lead, refit the wheel arch liner and, where fitted, the engine splash guard. Refit the roadwheel, and lower the vehicle to the ground.

19 Rear brake shoe check

1 Remove the rear brake drums and check the brake shoes for signs of wear or contamination. At the same time, also check the wheel cylinders for signs of leakage and the brake drums for signs of wear. Refer to the relevant Sections of Chapter 9 for further information.

20 Brake fluid renewal

⚠️ **Warning: Brake hydraulic fluid can harm your eyes and damage painted surfaces, so use extreme caution when handling and pouring it. Do not use fluid that has been standing open for some time, as it absorbs moisture from the air. Excess moisture can cause a dangerous loss of braking effectiveness.**

1 The procedure is similar to that for the bleeding of the hydraulic system as described in Chapter 9, except that the brake fluid reservoir should be emptied by siphoning, using a clean poultry baster or similar before starting, and allowance should be made for the old fluid to be expelled when bleeding a section of the circuit.

2 Working as described in Chapter 9, open the first bleed screw in the sequence, and pump the brake pedal gently until nearly all the old fluid has been emptied from the master cylinder reservoir.

3 Top-up to the "MAX" level with new fluid, and continue pumping until only the new fluid remains in the reservoir, and new fluid can be

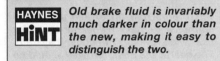
HAYNES HiNT *Old brake fluid is invariably much darker in colour than the new, making it easy to distinguish the two.*

seen emerging from the bleed screw. Tighten the screw, and top the reservoir level up to the "MAX" level line.

4 Work through all the remaining bleed screws in the sequence until new fluid can be seen at all of them. Be careful to keep the master cylinder reservoir topped-up to above the "MIN" level at all times, or air may enter the system and greatly increase the length of the task.

5 When the operation is complete, check that all bleed screws are securely tightened, and that their dust caps are refitted. Wash off all traces of spilt fluid, and recheck the master cylinder reservoir fluid level.

6 Check the operation of the brakes before taking the car on the road.

Every 72 000 miles

21 Timing belt renewal

Refer to the relevant Part of Chapter 2.

Every 72 000 miles or 2 years

22 Coolant renewal

Cooling system draining

⚠️ **Warning: Wait until the engine is cold before starting this procedure. Do not allow anti-freeze to come in contact with your skin, or with the painted surfaces of the vehicle. Rinse off spills immediately with plenty of water. Never leave antifreeze lying around in an open container, or in a puddle in the driveway or on the garage floor. Children and pets are attracted by its sweet smell, but antifreeze can be fatal if ingested.**

1 With the engine completely cold, remove the expansion tank filler cap. Turn the cap anti-clockwise until it reaches the first stop. Wait until any pressure remaining in the system is released, then push the cap down, turn it anti-clockwise to the second stop, and lift it off.

2 Position a suitable container beneath the coolant drain outlet at the lower left-hand side of the radiator.

3 Loosen the drain plug (there is no need to remove it completely) and allow the coolant to drain into the container. If desired, a length of tubing can be fitted to the drain outlet to direct the flow of coolant during draining **(see illustration).**

4 To assist draining, open the cooling system bleed screws. These are located in the heater matrix outlet hose on the engine compartment bulkhead, in the extension hose (clipped to the rear of the cylinder head) from the thermostat housing and in the coolant bypass

hose, dependant on model **(see illustrations)**. There may also be a bleed screw in the top left-hand end of the radiator.

5 When the flow of coolant stops, reposition the container below the cylinder block drain plug, located at the rear of the cylinder block.

6 Remove the drain plug, and allow the coolant to drain into the container.

7 If the coolant has been drained for a reason other than renewal, then provided it is clean and less than two years old, it can be re-used, though this is not recommended.

8 Refit the radiator and cylinder block drain plugs on completion of draining.

Cooling system flushing

9 If coolant renewal has been neglected, or if the antifreeze mixture has become diluted, then in time, the cooling system may gradually lose efficiency, as the coolant passages

1B

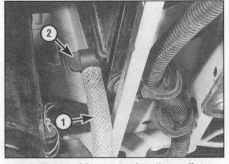
22.3 Tubing (1) attached to the radiator drain outlet and coolant drain plug (2)

22.4a Heater hose bleed screw (arrowed) in the heater matrix outlet hose . . .

22.4b . . . and in the coolant bypass hose (arrowed)

become restricted due to rust, scale deposits, and other sediment. The cooling system efficiency can be restored by flushing the system clean.

10 The radiator should be flushed independently of the engine, to avoid unnecessary contamination.

Radiator flushing

11 To flush the radiator, first tighten the radiator drain plug, and the radiator bleed screw, where applicable.

12 Disconnect the top and bottom hoses and any other relevant hoses from the radiator, with reference to Chapter 3.

13 Insert a garden hose into the radiator top inlet. Direct a flow of clean water through the radiator, and continue flushing until clean water emerges from the radiator bottom outlet.

14 If after a reasonable period, the water still does not run clear, the radiator can be flushed with a good proprietary cleaning agent. It is important that their manufacturer's instructions are followed carefully. If the contamination is particularly bad, insert the hose in the radiator bottom outlet, and reverse-flush the radiator.

Engine flushing

15 To flush the engine, first refit the cylinder block drain plug, and tighten the cooling system bleed screws.

16 Remove the thermostat as described in Chapter 3, then temporarily refit the thermostat cover.

17 With the top and bottom hoses disconnected from the radiator, insert a garden hose into the radiator top hose. Direct a clean flow of water through the engine, and continue flushing until clean water emerges from the radiator bottom hose.

18 On completion of flushing, refit the thermostat and reconnect the hoses with reference to Chapter 3.

Cooling system filling

19 Before attempting to fill the cooling system, make sure that all hoses and clips are

Cut the bottom off an old antifreeze container to make a "header tank" for use when refilling the cooling system. The seal at the point arrowed should be as tight as possible - use an O-ring if available, or seal the joint by some other means

in good condition, and that the clips are tight. Note that an antifreeze mixture must be used all year round, to prevent corrosion of the engine components (see following sub-Section). Also check that the radiator and cylinder block drain plugs are in place and tight.

20 Remove the expansion tank filler cap.

21 Open all the cooling system bleed screws (see paragraph 4).

22 Some of the cooling system hoses are positioned at a higher level than the top of the radiator expansion tank. It is therefore necessary to use a "header tank" when refilling the cooling system, to reduce the possibility of air being trapped in the system. Although Peugeot dealers use a special header tank, the same effect can be achieved by using a suitable bottle, with a seal between the bottle and the expansion tank (see **Haynes Hint**).

23 Fit the "header tank" to the expansion tank and slowly fill the system. Coolant will emerge from each of the bleed screws in turn, starting with the lowest screw. As soon as

coolant free from air bubbles emerges from the lowest screw, tighten that screw, and watch the next bleed screw in the system. Repeat the procedure until the coolant is emerging from the highest bleed screw in the cooling system and all bleed screws are securely tightened.

24 Ensure that the "header tank" is full (at least 0.5 litres of coolant). Start the engine, and run it at a fast idle speed (do not exceed 2000 rpm) until the cooling fan cuts in, and then cuts out. Stop the engine. **Note:** *Take great care not to scald yourself with the hot coolant during this operation.*

25 Allow the engine to cool, then remove the "header tank".

26 When the engine has cooled, check the coolant level as described in "Weekly checks". Top-up the level if necessary, and refit the expansion tank cap.

Antifreeze mixture

27 The antifreeze should always be renewed at the specified intervals. This is necessary not only to maintain the antifreeze properties, but also to prevent corrosion which would otherwise occur as the corrosion inhibitors become progressively less effective.

28 Always use an ethylene-glycol based antifreeze which is suitable for use in mixed-metal cooling systems. The quantity of antifreeze and levels of protection are indicated in the Specifications.

29 Before adding antifreeze, the cooling system should be completely drained, preferably flushed, and all hoses checked for condition and security.

30 After filling with antifreeze, a label should be attached to the expansion tank, stating the type and concentration of antifreeze used, and the date installed. Any subsequent topping-up should be made with the same type and concentration of antifreeze.

31 Do not use engine antifreeze in the washer system, as it will cause damage to the vehicle paintwork. A screenwash additive should be added to the washer system in the quantities stated on the bottle.

Chapter 2 Part A:
Petrol engine in-car repair procedures

Contents

Degrees of difficulty

Easy, suitable for novice with little experience	Fairly easy, suitable for beginner with some experience	Fairly difficult, suitable for competent DIY mechanic	Difficult, suitable for experienced DIY mechanic	Very difficult, suitable for expert DIY or professional

Specifications

Engine (general)

Designation:
1.6 litre (1580 cc engine)	XU5
1.8 litre (1761 cc engine)	XU7
2.0 litre (1998 cc engine)	XU10

Engine codes*:
1.6 litre engine	BFZ (XU5 JP/Z/L/L3)
1.8 litre engine	LFY (XU7 JP4/Z/L/L3)
2.0 litre engine	RFV (XU10 J4R/Z/L/L3) or R6E (XU10 J4R/K)

Bore:
1.6 litre engine	83.00 mm
1.8 litre engine	83.00 mm
2.0 litre engine	86.00 mm

Stroke:
1.6 litre engine	73.00 mm
1.8 litre engine	81.40 mm
2.0 litre engine	86.00 mm
Direction of crankshaft rotation	Clockwise (viewed from the right-hand side of vehicle)
No 1 cylinder location	At the transmission end of block

Compression ratio:
1.6 litre engine	9.25 : 1
1.8 litre engine	10.4 : 1
2.0 litre engine	10.4 : 1

*The engine code is stamped on a plate attached to the front left-hand end of the cylinder block on 1.6 litre and 1.8 litre engines and stamped directly onto the front face of the cylinder block (just to the left of the oil filter) on 2.0 litre engines. This is the code most often used by Peugeot. The code given in brackets is the factory identification number, and is not often referred to by Peugeot or this manual.

Camshaft

Drive	Toothed belt
No of bearings	5
Camshaft bearing journal diameter	Not available at time of writing
Cylinder head bearing journal diameter	Not available at time of writing

Valve clearances (1.6 litre engine only)

Inlet	0.20 mm ± 0.05 mm
Exhaust	0.40 mm ± 0.05 mm

2A

Lubrication system

Oil pump type	Gear-type, chain-driven off the crankshaft right-hand end
Minimum oil pressure at 80°C	5.3 bars (approximate) at 4000 rpm
Oil pressure warning switch operating pressure	0.5 bars

Torque wrench settings

	Nm	lbf ft
1.6 litre engines		
Alternator bracket bolts	22	16
Big-end bearing cap nuts:		
Stage 1	40	30
Fully slacken all nuts, then tighten to:		
Stage 2	20	15
Stage 3	Angle-tighten through 70°	
Camshaft bearing cap nuts	15	11
Camshaft sprocket retaining bolt	35	26
Crankshaft pulley retaining bolt	120	88
Cylinder head bolts:		
Stage 1	60	44
Fully slacken all bolts, then tighten to:		
Stage 2	20	15
Stage 3	Angle-tighten a further 300°	
Cylinder head cover nuts/bolts	10	7
Engine-to-transmission fixing bolts	45	33
Engine/transmission right-hand mounting:		
Bracket-to-engine bolts	45	33
Mounting bracket retaining nuts	45	33
Flywheel/driveplate retaining bolts	50	37
Front oil seal carrier bolts	16	12
Left-hand engine/transmission mounting:		
Mounting bracket-to-body	30	22
Rubber mounting-to-bracket bolts	30	22
Mounting stud-to-transmission	60	44
Mounting stud bracket-to-transmission	60	44
Centre nut	65	48
Lower engine movement limiter-to-driveshaft intermediate bearing housing	50	37
Lower engine movement limiter-to-subframe	85	62
Main bearing cap nuts/bolts:		
Retaining nuts/bolts	54	40
Centre bearing cap side bolts	25	18
Oil pump retaining bolts	16	12
Right-hand engine/transmission mounting:		
Mounting bracket-to-engine nuts	45	33
Mounting bracket-to-rubber mounting nut	45	33
Rubber mounting-to-body nut	40	29
Upper engine movement limiter bolts	50	37
Sump retaining bolts	19	14
Timing belt cover bolts	8	6
Timing belt tensioner pulley bolt	20	15
1.8 and 2.0 litre engines		
Big-end bearing cap nuts:		
Stage 1	20	15
Stage 2	Angle-tighten through 70°	
Camshaft bearing housings:		
Stage 1	5	4
Stage 2	10	7
Camshaft sprocket-to-hub retaining bolts	10	7
Camshaft sprocket hub-to-camshaft retaining bolts	75	55
Crankshaft pulley retaining bolt	120	88
Cylinder head cover nuts/bolts	10	7
Cylinder head bolts:		
1.8 litre engines:		
Stage 1	60	44
Fully slacken all bolts, then tighten to:		
Stage 2	20	15
Stage 3	Angle-tighten a further 300°	

Torque wrench settings (continued)

	Nm	lbf ft
1.8 and 2.0 litre engines (continued)		
Cylinder head bolts:		
2.0 litre engines:		
Stage 1	35	26
Stage 2	70	52
Stage 3	Angle-tighten through 160°	
Engine-to-transmission fixing bolts	45	33
Flywheel/driveplate retaining bolts	50	37
Front oil seal carrier bolts	16	12
Left-hand engine/transmission mounting:		
Mounting bracket-to-body	30	22
Rubber mounting-to-bracket bolts	30	22
Mounting stud-to-transmission	60	44
Mounting stud bracket-to-transmission	60	44
Centre nut	65	48
Lower engine movement limiter-to-driveshaft intermediate bearing housing	50	37
Lower engine movement limiter-to-subframe	85	62
Main bearing cap bolts:		
1.8 litre engine:		
Bearing bolts	55	40
Side securing bolts	25	18
2.0 litre engine	70	52
Oil pump retaining bolts	16	12
Piston oil jet spray tube bolt	10	7
Right-hand engine/transmission mounting:		
1.8 litre engines:		
Mounting bracket-to-engine nuts	45	33
Mounting bracket-to-engine bolts	60	44
Mounting bracket-to-rubber mounting nut	45	33
Rubber mounting-to-body nut	40	29
Upper engine movement limiter bolts	50	37
2.0 litre engines:		
Mounting bracket-to-engine nuts/bolts	80	59
Mounting bracket-to-rubber mounting nut	45	33
Rubber mounting-to-body nut	40	29
Upper engine movement limiter bolts	50	37
Sump retaining bolts	16	12
Timing belt cover bolts	8	6
Timing belt tensioner pulley bolt	20	15

1 General information

How to use this Chapter

This Part of Chapter 2 describes those repair procedures that can reasonably be carried out on the engine, while it remains in the car. If the engine has been removed from the car and is being dismantled as described in Part C, any preliminary dismantling procedures can be ignored.

Note that, while it may be possible physically to overhaul items such as the piston/connecting rod assemblies while the engine is in the car, such tasks are not usually carried out as separate operations. Usually, several additional procedures (not to mention the cleaning of components and oilways) have to be carried out. For this reason, all such tasks are classed as major overhaul procedures, and are described in Part C of this Chapter.

Part C describes the removal of the engine/transmission unit from the vehicle, and the full overhaul procedures that can then be carried out.

XU series engine description

The engine is of the in-line four-cylinder type, mounted transversely at the front of the car. The clutch and transmission are attached to its left-hand end.

The crankshaft runs in five main bearings. Thrustwashers are fitted to No 2 main bearing cap, to control crankshaft endfloat.

The connecting rods rotate on horizontally-split bearing shells at their big-ends. The pistons are attached to the connecting rods by gudgeon pins. On 2.0 litre models the gudgeon pins are a sliding fit in the connecting rods and are secured in position with circlips. On all other models they are an interference fit in the connecting rod small-end eyes. The aluminium alloy pistons are fitted with three piston rings - two compression rings and an oil control ring.

On aluminium block engines, the cylinder block is of the "wet-liner" type. The cylinder block is cast in aluminium alloy, and the bores have replaceable cast-iron liners that are located from the top of the cylinder block. Sealing O-rings are fitted at the base of each liner, to prevent the escape of coolant into the sump.

On cast iron block engines, the engine is of the conventional "dry-liner" type. The cylinder block is cast in iron, and no separate bore liners are fitted.

On all models, the camshaft is driven by a toothed timing belt, and it operates the eight valves (1.6 litre models) or sixteen valves (1.8 and 2.0 litre models) via followers located beneath each cam lobe. On 1.6 litre models, the valve clearances are adjusted by shims, positioned between the followers and the tip of the valve stem; on all other models the valve clearances are self-adjusting by means of hydraulic tappets fitted to the cam followers. The camshaft runs in bearing caps which are bolted to the top of the cylinder

2A

head. The inlet and exhaust valves are each closed by coil springs, and operate in guides pressed into the cylinder head. Both the valve seats and guides can be renewed separately if worn.

The coolant pump is driven by the timing belt and located in the right-hand end of the cylinder block.

Lubrication is by means of an oil pump which is driven (via a chain and sprocket) off the crankshaft right-hand end. It draws oil through a strainer located in the sump, and then forces it through an externally-mounted filter into galleries in the cylinder block/crankcase. From there, the oil is distributed to the crankshaft (main bearings) and camshaft. The big-end bearings are supplied with oil via internal drillings in the crankshaft; the camshaft bearings also receive a pressurised supply. The camshaft lobes and valves are lubricated by splash, as are all other engine components. An oil cooler is fitted to certain models to keep the oil temperature constant under severe operating conditions - it is mounted behind the oil filter. The oil cooler is supplied with coolant from the engine cooling system.

Throughout the manual, it is often necessary to identify the engines not only by their cubic capacity, but also by their engine code. The engine code consists of three letters (eg. BFZ). The code is stamped on a plate attached to the front, left-hand end of the cylinder block, or stamped directly onto the front face of the cylinder block, on the machined surface located just to the left of the oil filter (next to the crankcase vent hose union).

Repair operations possible with the engine in the car

The following work can be carried out with the engine in the car:

a) Compression pressure - testing.
b) Cylinder head cover - removal and refitting.
c) Crankshaft pulley - removal and refitting.
d) Timing belt covers - removal and refitting.
e) Timing belt - removal, refitting and adjustment.
f) Timing belt tensioner and sprockets - removal and refitting.
g) Camshaft oil seal(s) - renewal.
h) Camshaft(s) and followers - removal, inspection and refitting.
i) Valve clearances - checking and adjustment.
j) Cylinder head - removal and refitting.
k) Cylinder head and pistons - decarbonising.
l) Sump - removal and refitting.
m) Oil pump - removal, overhaul and refitting.
n) Crankshaft oil seals - renewal.
o) Engine/transmission mountings - inspection and renewal.
p) Flywheel/driveplate - removal, inspection and refitting.
q) Oil cooler - removal and refitting

2 Compression test - description and interpretation

1 When engine performance is down, or if misfiring occurs which cannot be attributed to the ignition or fuel systems, a compression test can provide diagnostic clues as to the engine's condition. If the test is performed regularly, it can give warning of trouble before any other symptoms become apparent.

2 The engine must be fully warmed-up to normal operating temperature, the battery must be fully charged, and all the spark plugs must be removed (Chapter 1A). The aid of an assistant will also be required.

3 Disable the fuel system by disconnecting the wiring connectors from the fuel injectors, referring to Chapter 4A for further information.

4 Fit a compression tester to the No 1 cylinder spark plug hole - the type of tester which screws into the plug thread is to be preferred.

5 Have the assistant hold the throttle wide open, and crank the engine on the starter motor; after one or two revolutions, the compression pressure should build up to a maximum figure, and then stabilise. Record the highest reading obtained.

6 Repeat the test on the remaining cylinders, recording the pressure in each.

7 All cylinders should produce very similar pressures; a difference of more than 2 bars between any two cylinders indicates a fault. Note that the compression should build up quickly in a healthy engine; low compression on the first stroke, followed by gradually-increasing pressure on successive strokes, indicates worn piston rings. A low compression reading on the first stroke, which does not build up during successive strokes, indicates leaking valves or a blown head gasket (a cracked head could also be the cause). Deposits on the undersides of the valve heads can also cause low compression.

8 Although Peugeot do not specify exact compression pressures, as a guide, any cylinder pressure of below 10 bars can be considered as less than healthy. Refer to a Peugeot dealer or other specialist if in doubt as to whether a particular pressure reading is acceptable.

9 If the pressure in any cylinder is low, carry out the following test to isolate the cause. Introduce a teaspoonful of clean oil into that cylinder through its spark plug hole, and repeat the test.

10 If the addition of oil temporarily improves the compression pressure, this indicates that bore or piston wear is responsible for the pressure loss. No improvement suggests that leaking or burnt valves, or a blown head gasket, may be to blame.

11 A low reading from two adjacent cylinders is almost certainly due to the head gasket having blown between them; the presence of coolant in the engine oil will confirm this.

12 If one cylinder is about 20 percent lower than the others and the engine has a slightly rough idle, a worn camshaft lobe could be the cause.

13 If the compression reading is unusually high, the combustion chambers are probably coated with carbon deposits. If this is the case, the cylinder head should be removed and decarbonised.

14 On completion of the test, refit the spark plugs and reconnect the ignition system.

3 Engine assembly/valve timing holes - general information and usage

Note: *Do not attempt to rotate the engine whilst the crankshaft/camshaft are locked in position. If the engine is to be left in this state for a long period of time, it is a good idea to place suitable warning notices inside the vehicle, and in the engine compartment. This will reduce the possibility of the engine being accidentally cranked on the starter motor, which is likely to cause damage with the locking pins in place.*

1 On all models, timing holes are drilled in the camshaft sprocket(s) and crankshaft pulley. The holes are used to align the crankshaft and camshaft, to prevent the possibility of the valves contacting the pistons when refitting the cylinder head, or when refitting the timing belt. When the holes are aligned with their corresponding holes in the cylinder head and cylinder block (as appropriate), suitable diameter pins can be inserted to lock both the camshaft and crankshaft in position. Proceed as follows:

2 Remove the timing belt upper cover with reference to Section 6.

3 Jack up the front of the car and support it on axle stands. Remove the right-hand front roadwheel.

4 From underneath the front of the car, unscrew the bolts and prise out the clips securing the plastic cover to the inner wing valance. Remove the cover to gain access to the crankshaft pulley bolt. The crankshaft can then be turned using a suitable socket and extension bar fitted to the pulley bolt. Note that the crankshaft must always be turned in a clockwise direction (viewed from the right-hand side of vehicle).

1.6 litre models

5 Rotate the crankshaft pulley until the timing hole in the camshaft sprocket is aligned with its corresponding hole in the cylinder head. Note that the holes are aligned when the sprocket hole is in the 8 o'clock position, when viewed from the right-hand end of the engine.

6 With the camshaft sprocket timing hole correctly positioned, insert an 8 mm diameter bolt or drill through the timing (8 mm diameter) hole in the crankshaft pulley, and locate it in the corresponding hole in the end of the

3.6 8 mm diameter drill inserted through the crankshaft pulley timing hole

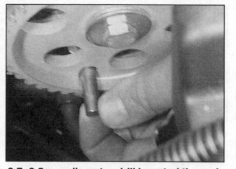

3.7 9.5 mm diameter drill inserted through the camshaft pulley timing hole

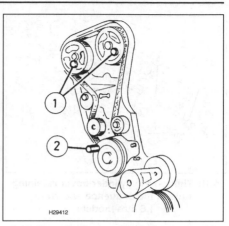

3.11 Camshaft sprocket timing holes (1) and crankshaft pulley timing hole (2) locked with suitable timing pins - 1.8 and 2.0 litre models

cylinder block (see illustration). Note that it may be necessary to rotate the crankshaft slightly, to get the holes to align.

7 Once the crankshaft pulley is locked in position, insert an 9.5 mm diameter bolt or drill through the camshaft sprocket hole and locate it in the cylinder head (see illustration).

8 The crankshaft and camshaft are now locked in position, preventing rotation.

1.8 and 2.0 litre models

9 Rotate the crankshaft pulley until the timing holes in both camshafts are aligned with their corresponding holes in the cylinder head. The holes are aligned when the inlet camshaft sprocket hole is in approximately the 5 o'clock position and the exhaust camshaft sprocket hole is in approximately the 7 o'clock position, when viewed from the right-hand end of the engine.

10 With the camshaft sprocket holes correctly positioned, insert a 6 mm diameter bolt or drill through the timing hole in the crankshaft pulley, and locate it in the corresponding hole in the end of the engine. Note that the hole size may vary according to the type of pulley fitted and auxiliary drivebelt arrangement. If the bolt or drill is not a snug fit, try a larger size until a good fit is achieved in both the pulley and cylinder block.

11 With the crankshaft locked in position, insert a suitable bolt or drill through the timing hole in each camshaft sprocket and locate it in the cylinder head (see illustration).

12 The crankshaft and camshafts are now locked in position, preventing rotation.

4 Cylinder head cover(s) - removal and refitting

Removal

1 Disconnect the battery negative terminal.

1.6 litre models

2 Slacken the retaining clips, and disconnect the breather hoses from the front right-hand end of the cover (see illustration). Where the original crimped-type Peugeot hose clips are still fitted, cut them off and discard them; use standard worm-drive hose clips on refitting.

3 Slacken the retaining clip, and disconnect the air cleaner-to-throttle housing duct from the front of the cylinder head cover. Also remove the intake duct from the left-hand side of the head cover.

4 Release the two retaining clips, then undo the two retaining screws located at the front, and remove the air cleaner element cover from the cylinder head cover. Remove the air cleaner element, and store it with the cover.

5 Evenly and progressively unscrew the ten cylinder head cover retaining nuts, lift off the cylinder head cover, and remove it along with its rubber seal (see illustrations). Examine the seal for signs of damage and deterioration, and if necessary, renew it.

1.8 and 2.0 litre models

6 Refer to Chapter 4A, Section 13 and remove the fuel rail and fuel injectors.

7 Disconnect the wiring connector at the left-hand end of the ignition coil unit, located in the centre of the cylinder head covers. Undo the six retaining bolts and lift the coil unit upwards, off the spark plugs and from its location between the cylinder head covers.

8 Slacken the retaining clips, and disconnect the breather hoses from the front left-hand side of the front cover. Where the original crimped-type Peugeot hose clips are still fitted, cut them off and discard them; use standard worm-drive hose clips on refitting.

9 Working in a spiral sequence starting from the outside and working inwards, progressively slacken, then remove the retaining bolts of each cylinder head cover, noting the correct fitted position of any brackets or clips.

10 Lift off each cover in turn and remove it along with its rubber seal.

Refitting

1.6 litre models

11 Clean the cylinder head and cover mating surfaces, and remove all traces of oil.

12 Locate the rubber seal in the cover groove, ensuring that it is correctly located along its entire length.

13 Apply a smear of sealant to each camshaft end bearing cap around the area where the cap contacts the cylinder head mating surface.

2A

4.2 Breather hoses on the right-hand end of the cylinder head cover

4.5a Cylinder head cover retaining nuts (arrowed)

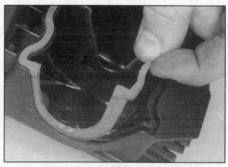

4.5b Removing the cylinder head cover seal

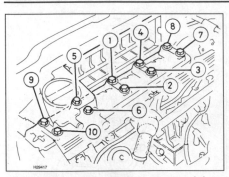

4.15 Tighten the cylinder cover retaining nuts in the sequence shown - 1.6 litre models

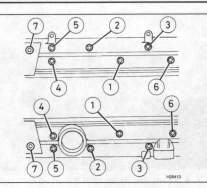

4.21 Cylinder head cover nut tightening sequence - 1.8 and 2.0 litre models

5.2 Use a fabricated tool like this one to lock the flywheel ring gear and prevent the crankshaft rotation

14 Carefully refit the cylinder head cover to the engine, taking great care not to displace the rubber seal.

15 Check that the seal is correctly located, then refit the cover retaining nuts and, working in the sequence shown, tighten them evenly and progressively to the specified torque **(see illustration).**

16 Refit the air cleaner element, and install the element cover. Securely tighten the cover retaining screws, and secure it in position with the retaining clips.

17 Reconnect the breather hoses, intake duct and throttle housing duct to the cover, tightening their retaining clips securely. Reconnect the battery.

1.8 and 2.0 litre models

18 Clean the cylinder head and cover mating surfaces, and remove all traces of oil.

19 Locate the rubber seal in the groove of each cover, ensuring that it is correctly located along its entire length.

20 Carefully refit the cylinder head covers to the engine, taking great care not to displace the rubber seals.

21 Check that the seal is correctly located, then refit the cover retaining nuts and, working in the sequence shown, tighten them evenly and progressively to the specified torque **(see illustration).**

22 Reconnect the breather hoses to the front cover and securely tighten the retaining clips.

23 Refit the ignition coil unit between the cylinder head covers. Refit the retaining bolts,

tightening them securely, then reconnect the coil unit wiring connectors.

24 Refer to Chapter 4A, Section 13 and refit the fuel rail and fuel injectors.

25 Reconnect the battery negative terminal. On completion, start the engine and check the fuel hose unions for signs of leakage.

5 Crankshaft pulley - removal and refitting

Removal

1 Remove the auxiliary drivebelt (Chapter 1A).

2 To prevent the crankshaft turning whilst the pulley retaining bolt is being slackened, select 4th gear and have an assistant apply the brakes firmly. If the engine has been removed from the vehicle, lock the flywheel ring gear using the arrangement shown **(see illustration)**. *Do not attempt to lock the pulley by inserting a bolt/drill through the timing hole.* If the locking pin is in position, temporarily remove it prior to slackening the pulley bolt, then refit it once the bolt has been slackened.

3 Unscrew the retaining bolt and washer, then slide the pulley off the end of the crankshaft **(see illustrations)**. If the pulley locating roll pin or Woodruff key (as applicable) is a loose fit, remove it and store it with the pulley for safe-keeping. If the pulley is a tight fit, it can be drawn off the crankshaft using a suitable puller.

Refitting

4 Ensure that the Woodruff key is correctly located in its crankshaft groove, or that the roll pin is in position (as applicable). Refit the pulley to the end of the crankshaft, aligning its locating groove or hole with the Woodruff key or pin.

5 Thoroughly clean the threads of the pulley retaining bolt, then apply a coat of locking compound to the bolt threads. Peugeot recommend the use of Loctite Frenetanche (available from your Peugeot dealer); in the absence of this, any good-quality locking compound may be used.

6 Refit the crankshaft pulley retaining bolt and washer. Tighten the bolt to the specified torque, preventing the crankshaft from turning using the method employed on removal.

7 Refit and tension the auxiliary drivebelt as described in Chapter 1A.

6 Timing belt covers - removal and refitting

1.6 litre models

Upper cover

1 Release the retaining clips, and free the fuel hoses from the top of the cover.

2 Undo the two cover retaining bolts (situated at the base of the cover), and remove the cover from the engine compartment.

Centre cover

3 Slacken and remove the two cover retaining bolts (located directly beneath the mounting bracket). Move the cover upwards to free it from the two locating pins situated at the base of the cover, and remove it from the engine compartment.

Lower cover

4 Remove the crankshaft pulley as described in Section 5.

5 Remove the centre cover as described in paragraph 3.

6 Undo the two cover retaining bolts, and remove the cover from the engine. Note that

5.3a Removing the crankshaft pulley retaining bolt

5.3b Removing the crankshaft pulley from the end of the crankshaft

on some models it may be necessary to unbolt the auxiliary drivebelt tensioner assembly and remove it from the engine in order to allow the cover to be removed.

1.8 and 2.0 litre models

Upper (outer) cover

7 Undo the upper and lower retaining bolts securing the outer cover to the inner cover. Slide the cover retaining clip upwards to release it from its fasteners.

8 Ease the outer cover upwards and away from the engine, freeing it from its lower locations.

Lower cover

9 Remove the crankshaft pulley as described in Section 5.

10 Remove the upper (outer) cover as described above.

11 Slacken and remove the three retaining bolts, then remove the lower timing belt cover from the engine. Note that on some models it may be necessary to unbolt the auxiliary drivebelt tensioner assembly and remove it from the engine in order to allow the cover to be removed.

Upper (inner) cover

12 Remove the timing belt as described in Section 7.

13 Remove both camshaft sprockets as described in Section 8.

14 Remove the six bolts securing the cover to the side of the cylinder head, and remove the cover from the engine.

Refitting

15 Refitting is a reversal of the relevant removal procedure, ensuring that each cover section is correctly located, and that the cover retaining nuts and/or bolts are securely tightened to the specified torque, where given.

---

7 Timing belt - general information, removal and refitting

Note: *Peugeot specify the use of a special electronic tool (SEEM C105.5) to correctly set the timing belt tension. If access to this equipment cannot be obtained, an approximate setting can be achieved using the method described below. If the method described is used, the tension must be checked using the special electronic tool at the earliest possible opportunity. Do not drive the vehicle over large distances, or use high engine speeds, until the belt tension is known to be correct. Refer to a Peugeot dealer for advice.*

General information

1 The timing belt drives the camshaft and coolant pump from a toothed sprocket on the front of the crankshaft. If the belt breaks or

slips in service, the pistons are likely to hit the valve heads, resulting in extensive (and expensive) damage.

2 The timing belt should be renewed at the specified intervals (see Chapter 1A), or earlier if it is contaminated with oil, or if it is at all noisy in operation (a 'scraping' noise due to uneven wear).

3 If the timing belt is being removed, it is a wise precaution to check the condition of the coolant pump at the same time (check for signs of coolant leakage). This may avoid the need to remove the timing belt again at a later stage, should the coolant pump fail.

Removal

1.6 litre models

4 Disconnect the battery negative terminal.

5 Jack up the front of the vehicle and support it on axle stands. Remove the right-hand front wheel.

6 Prise out the clips and unbolt the inner splash guard.

7 Remove the auxiliary drivebelt as described in Chapter 1A. Also unbolt and remove the auxiliary drivebelt tensioner.

8 Unbolt and remove the upper timing belt cover as described in Section 6.

9 Align the engine assembly/valve timing holes as described in Section 3, and lock the camshaft sprocket and crankshaft pulley in position. *Do not* attempt to rotate the engine whilst the pins are in position.

10 Remove the crankshaft pulley (Section 5).

11 Remove the centre and lower timing belt covers as described in Section 6.

12 Loosen the timing belt tensioner pulley retaining bolt. Pivot the pulley in a clockwise direction, using a suitable square-section key fitted to the hole in the pulley hub, then securely retighten the retaining bolt.

13 If the timing belt is to be re-used, use white paint or chalk to mark the direction of rotation on the belt (if markings do not already exist), then slip the belt off the sprockets. Note that the crankshaft must not be rotated whilst the belt is removed.

14 Check the timing belt carefully for any signs of uneven wear, splitting, or oil contamination. Pay particular attention to the roots of the teeth. Renew it if there is the slightest doubt about its condition. If the engine is undergoing an overhaul, and has covered more than 36 000 miles (60 000 km) with the existing belt fitted, renew the belt as a matter of course, regardless of its apparent condition. The cost of a new belt is nothing compared with the cost of repairs, should the belt break in service. If signs of oil contamination are found, trace the source of the oil leak and rectify it. Wash down the engine timing belt area and all related components, to remove all traces of oil.

1.8 and 2.0 litre models

15 Disconnect the battery negative terminal.

16 Align the engine assembly/valve timing holes as described in Section 3, and lock the

camshaft sprockets and crankshaft pulley in position. *Do not* attempt to rotate the engine whilst the pins are in position.

17 Remove the timing belt upper (outer) and lower covers as described in Section 6.

18 Move the engine wiring harness clear of the working area as necessary. This will entail the disconnection of certain connectors, and the removal of the harness from various cable clips and supports. Label any disconnected wiring and components as an aid to refitting.

19 Support the engine on a jack and remove the right-hand engine mounting components as described in Section 18.

20 Loosen the timing belt rear tensioner pulley retaining bolt and pivot the pulley in a clockwise direction, using a suitable square-section key fitted to the hole in the pulley hub, then retighten the retaining bolt.

21 Check that the camshaft sprocket locking pins are still in position, then remove and inspect the belt as described in paragraphs 13 and 14.

Refitting

1.6 litre models

22 Before refitting, thoroughly clean the timing belt sprockets. Check that the tensioner pulley rotates freely, without any sign of roughness. If necessary, renew the tensioner pulley as described in Section 8.

23 Ensure that the camshaft sprocket locking pin is still in position. Temporarily refit the crankshaft pulley, and insert the locking pin through the pulley timing hole to ensure that the crankshaft is still correctly positioned.

24 Remove the crankshaft pulley. Manoeuvre the timing belt into position, ensuring that any arrows on the belt are pointing in the direction of rotation (clockwise when viewed from the right-hand end of the engine).

25 Do not twist the timing belt sharply while refitting it. Fit the belt over the crankshaft and camshaft sprockets. Ensure that the belt "front run" is taut - ie, any slack should be on the tensioner pulley side of the belt. Fit the belt over the water pump sprocket and tensioner pulley. Ensure that the belt teeth are seated centrally in the sprockets.

26 Temporarily refit the crankshaft pulley at this stage and tighten the bolt moderately, then refit the locking pin. **Note:** *The timing belt is tensioned with the timing covers removed, then the pulley is removed to fit the covers and finally refitted.*

27 Loosen the tensioner pulley retaining bolt. Using the square-section key, pivot the pulley anti-clockwise to remove all free play from the timing belt.

28 If the special belt tension measuring equipment is available, it should be fitted to the "front run" of the timing belt. The tensioner roller should be adjusted so that the initial belt tension is 30 ± 2 units.

29 Remove the locking pins, then rotate the crankshaft through two complete rotations in a clockwise direction (viewed from the right-hand

2A

end of the engine). Realign the camshaft and crankshaft engine assembly/valve timing holes (see Section 3). *Do not* at any time rotate the crankshaft anti-clockwise. Both camshaft and crankshaft timing holes should be aligned so that the locking pins can be easily inserted. This indicates that the valve timing is correct. If all is well, remove the pins.

30 If the timing holes are not correctly positioned, repeat the fitting procedure so far.

31 If the tension is being set without using the special measuring tool, proceed as follows. Check that, under moderate pressure from the thumb and forefinger, the belt can just be twisted through 90° at the mid-point of the "front run" of the belt. Note that this method is only an initial setting, and the belt tension *must* be checked at the earliest available opportunity using the special measuring tool. Failure to do so could lead to the belt breaking (through over-tightening) or "jumping a tooth" (through slackness), resulting in serious engine damage. If necessary, readjust the tensioner pulley position as required. Tighten its retaining bolt to the specified torque on completion.

32 If the special measuring tool is being used, rotate the crankshaft two more turns without turning backwards and refit the camshaft locking pin, then check that the final belt tension on the taut "front run" of the belt is 44 ± 2 units. If not, repeat the complete fitting procedure.

33 With the belt tension correctly set remove the camshaft locking pin, then remove the crankshaft pulley and refit the timing cover(s).

34 Refit the crankshaft pulley but this time apply locking fluid to the threads of the bolt before inserting it. Tighten the bolt to the specified torque and refer to Section 5 if necessary.

35 Refit the auxiliary drivebelt tensioner then refit and tension the drivebelt with reference to Chapter 1A.

36 Refit the inner splash guard and front right-hand wheel, then lower the vehicle to the ground.

37 Reconnect the battery negative terminal.

1.8 and 2.0 litre models

38 Before refitting, thoroughly clean the timing belt sprockets. Check that the tensioner pulley rotates freely, without any sign of roughness. If necessary, renew the tensioner pulley as described in Section 8.

39 Ensure that the camshaft sprocket locking pin is still in position. Temporarily refit the crankshaft pulley, and insert the locking pin through the pulley timing hole to ensure that the crankshaft is still correctly positioned.

40 Remove the crankshaft pulley. Manoeuvre the timing belt into position on the crankshaft sprocket, ensuring that any arrows on the belt are pointing in the direction of rotation (clockwise when viewed from the right-hand end of the engine).

41 Refit the timing belt lower cover and the crankshaft pulley (Sections 6 and 5).

42 Refit the locking pin to the crankshaft pulley.

43 Without removing the locking pins, slacken the six camshaft sprocket retaining bolts (three on each sprocket). Check that both sprockets are free to turn within the limits of their elongated bolt holes.

44 Tighten the six camshaft sprocket retaining bolts finger tight, then slacken them all by one sixth of a turn.

45 Turn each sprocket clockwise to the ends of their retaining bolt slots.

46 With the timing belt engaged with the crankshaft sprocket, keep it tight on its right-hand run and engage it with the front idler pulley then up and into engagement with the inlet camshaft sprocket.

47 Keeping the belt tight and rotating the inlet camshaft sprocket anti-clockwise as necessary, feed the belt over the exhaust camshaft sprocket, taking care not to let the belt jump a tooth on the crankshaft sprocket as it is being fitted.

48 While still keeping the belt tight, feed it over the rear tensioner pulley and finally around the coolant pump.

49 If the special belt tension measuring equipment is available, proceed as described in paragraphs 50 to 58, and then to paragraph 66 onward. If the tension is being set without the use of the special measuring equipment, proceed to paragraph 60.

50 If the special belt tension measuring equipment is available, it should be fitted to the "front run" of the timing belt. The tensioner pulley should be adjusted, by turning it anti-clockwise to give a belt pre-tensioning setting of 45 units. Hold the tensioner pulley in this position and tighten the retaining bolt to the specified torque.

51 Remove one retaining bolt from each camshaft sprocket and check that the sprockets are not at the end of their retaining bolt slots. If they are, repeat the refitting operation. If all is satisfactory, refit the two removed bolts, and tighten all six sprocket retaining bolts to the specified torque.

52 Remove the locking pins, then rotate the crankshaft through two complete rotations in a clockwise direction (viewed from the right-hand end of the engine). Realign the crankshaft engine assembly/valve timing hole and refit the locking pin to the crankshaft pulley.

53 Slacken the six camshaft sprocket retaining bolts, retighten them finger tight, then slacken them all by one sixth of a turn.

54 Refit the camshaft sprocket locking pins, then slacken the tensioner pulley retaining bolt once more. Refit the belt tension measuring equipment to the front run of the belt and turn the tensioner pulley to give an initial setting of 26 units on the tensioning gauge. Hold the tensioner pulley in this position and tighten the retaining bolt to the specified torque.

55 Retighten all six sprocket retaining bolts to the specified torque.

56 Remove the locking pins, then rotate the crankshaft once again through two complete rotations in a clockwise direction. Realign the crankshaft engine assembly/valve timing hole and refit the locking pin to the crankshaft pulley.

57 Slacken the six camshaft sprocket retaining bolts, retighten them finger tight, then slacken them all by one sixth of a turn.

58 Refit the camshaft sprocket locking pins, then slacken the tensioner pulley retaining bolt once more. Refit the belt tension measuring equipment to the front run of the belt and turn the tensioner pulley to give a final setting of between 32 and 40 units on the tensioning gauge. Hold the tensioner pulley in this position and tighten the retaining bolt to the specified torque.

59 Retighten all six sprocket retaining bolts to the specified torque.

60 If the tension is being set without the use of the special measuring equipment, the tensioner pulley should be adjusted, by turning it anti-clockwise until all free play is removed from the belt. Hold the tensioner pulley in this position and tighten the retaining bolt to the specified torque.

61 Remove one retaining bolt from each camshaft sprocket and check that the sprockets are not at the end of their retaining bolt slots. If they are, repeat the refitting operation. If all is satisfactory, refit the two removed bolts, and tighten all six sprocket retaining bolts to the specified torque.

62 Remove the locking pins, then rotate the crankshaft through two complete rotations in a clockwise direction (viewed from the right-hand end of the engine). Realign the crankshaft engine assembly/valve timing hole and refit the locking pin to the crankshaft pulley.

63 Slacken the six camshaft sprocket retaining bolts, retighten them finger tight, then slacken them all by one sixth of a turn.

64 Refit the camshaft sprocket locking pins, then slacken the tensioner pulley retaining bolt once more. Turn the tensioner pulley to tension the belt until, under moderate pressure from the thumb and forefinger, the belt can just be twisted through 45° at the mid-point between the inlet camshaft sprocket and the idler pulley. Note that this method is only an initial setting and the belt tension must be checked at the earliest opportunity using the special belt tensioning equipment. Failure to do this could lead to the belt breaking (through over-tightening) or slipping (through slackness), resulting in serious engine damage. With the tension set, hold the tensioner pulley in this position and tighten the retaining bolt to the specified torque.

65 Retighten all six sprocket retaining bolts to the specified torque.

66 Once the belt tension has been correctly set, refit the right-hand engine mounting components as described in Section 18, and reconnect all the disconnected engine wiring.

67 Refit the timing belt upper (outer) and lower covers as described in Section 6, and reconnect the battery negative terminal.

8 Timing belt tensioner and sprockets - removal, inspection and refitting

Note: *This Section describes the removal and refitting of the components concerned as individual operations - if more than one is to be removed at the same time, start by removing the timing belt as described in Section 7; remove the actual component as described below, ignoring the preliminary dismantling steps.*

Removal

1 Disconnect the battery negative terminal.
2 Align the engine assembly/valve timing holes as described in Section 3, locking the camshaft sprocket(s) and the crankshaft pulley in position, and proceed as described under the relevant sub-heading. *Do not attempt to rotate the engine whilst the pins are in position.*

Camshaft sprocket - 1.6 litre models

3 Remove the upper timing belt cover as described in Section 6.
4 Loosen the timing belt tensioner pulley retaining bolt. Rotate the pulley in a clockwise direction, using a suitable square-section key fitted to the hole in the pulley hub, then retighten the retaining bolt.
5 Remove the locking pin from the camshaft sprocket. Disengage the timing belt from the sprocket and position it clear, taking care not to bend or twist the belt sharply.
6 Slacken the camshaft sprocket retaining bolt and remove it, along with its washer. To prevent the camshaft rotating as the bolt is slackened, a sprocket holding tool will be required. In the absence of the special Peugeot tool, an acceptable substitute can be fabricated at home **(see Tool Tip).** *Do not attempt to use the sprocket locking pin to prevent the sprocket from rotating whilst the bolt is slackened.*

Using a home-made tool to retain the camshaft sprocket whilst the sprocket retaining bolt is tightened

7 With the retaining bolt removed, slide the sprocket off the end of the camshaft. If the locating peg is a loose fit in the rear of the sprocket, remove it for safe-keeping. Examine the camshaft oil seal for signs of oil leakage and, if necessary, renew it as described in Section 9.

Camshaft sprockets - 1.8 and 2.0 litre models

8 Remove the timing belt upper (outer) and lower covers as described in Section 6.
9 Move the engine wiring harness clear of the working area as necessary. This will entail the disconnection of certain connectors, and the removal of the harness from various cable clips and supports. Label any disconnected wiring and components as an aid to refitting.
10 Support the engine on a jack and remove the right-hand engine mounting components as described in Section 18.
11 Loosen the timing belt rear tensioner pulley retaining bolt and pivot the pulley in a clockwise direction, using a suitable square-section key fitted to the hole in the pulley hub, then retighten the retaining bolt.
12 Check that the camshaft sprocket locking pins are still in position, then disengage the timing belt from the camshaft sprockets and position it clear, taking care not to bend or twist the belt sharply.
13 If the sprockets are to be removed without their hubs, undo the three retaining bolts and remove the relevant sprocket. Suitably mark the sprockets "inlet" and/or "exhaust" as they are removed.
14 If both the sprockets and the hubs are to be removed, remove the sprocket locking pins, then slacken the sprocket hub centre retaining bolt. To prevent the sprockets rotating as the bolt is slackened, a sprocket holding tool will be required. In the absence of the special Peugeot tool, an acceptable substitute can be fabricated at home **(see Tool Tip).** *Do not* attempt to use the sprocket locking pin to prevent the sprocket from rotating whilst the bolt is slackened.
15 Undo the three retaining bolts and remove the relevant sprocket. Remove the previously slackened hub retaining bolt and withdraw the hub from the end of the camshaft. Note that the hubs are marked for identification with a single digit on their front face. On 1.8 litre models, the inlet hub is marked "1" and the exhaust hub is marked "2". On 2.0 litre models the inlet hub is marked "3" and the exhaust hub is marked "4".

Crankshaft sprocket - 1.6 litre models

16 Remove the upper, centre and/or lower timing belt cover(s) (as applicable) as described in Section 6.
17 Loosen the timing belt tensioner pulley retaining bolt. Rotate the pulley in a clockwise direction, using a suitable square-section key fitted to the hole in the pulley hub, then retighten the retaining bolt.
18 Disengage the timing belt from the crankshaft sprocket, and slide the sprocket

off the end of the crankshaft. Remove the Woodruff key from the crankshaft, and store it with the sprocket for safe-keeping. Where necessary, also slide the spacer (where fitted) off the end of the crankshaft.
19 Examine the crankshaft oil seal for signs of oil leakage and, if necessary, renew it as described in Section 16.

Crankshaft sprocket - 1.8 and 2.0 litre models

20 Remove the timing belt upper (outer) and lower covers as described in Section 6.
21 Move the engine wiring harness clear of the working area as necessary. This will entail the disconnection of certain connectors, and the removal of the harness from various cable clips and supports. Label any disconnected wiring and components as an aid to refitting.
22 Support the engine on a jack and remove the right-hand engine mounting components as described in Section 18.
23 Loosen the timing belt rear tensioner pulley retaining bolt and pivot the pulley in a clockwise direction, using a suitable square-section key fitted to the hole in the pulley hub, then retighten the retaining bolt.
24 Check that the camshaft sprocket locking pins are still in position, then disengage the timing belt from the crankshaft sprocket and slide the sprocket off the end of the crankshaft. Remove the Woodruff key from the crankshaft, and store it with the sprocket for safe-keeping.
25 Examine the crankshaft oil seal for signs of oil leakage and, if necessary, renew it as described in Section 16.

Tensioner pulley - 1.6 litre models

26 Remove the upper and where necessary the centre timing belt covers as described in Section 6.
27 Slacken and remove the timing belt tensioner pulley retaining bolt, and slide the pulley off its mounting stud. Examine the mounting stud for signs of damage and if necessary, renew it.

Tensioner and idler pulleys - 1.8 and 2.0 litre models

28 Remove the timing belt upper (outer) and lower covers as described in Section 6.
29 Move the engine wiring harness clear of the working area as necessary. This will entail the disconnection of certain connectors, and the removal of the harness from various cable clips and supports. Label any disconnected wiring and components as an aid to refitting.
30 Support the engine on a jack and remove the right-hand engine mounting components as described in Section 18.
31 Loosen the timing belt rear tensioner pulley retaining bolt and pivot the pulley in a clockwise direction, using a suitable square-section key fitted to the hole in the pulley hub, then retighten the retaining bolt.
32 Check that the camshaft sprocket locking pins are still in position, then disengage the timing belt from the camshaft sprockets and

2A

position it clear, taking care not to bend or twist the belt sharply.

33 Undo the tensioner and idler pulley retaining bolts and remove them from the engine.

Inspection

34 Clean the camshaft/crankshaft sprockets thoroughly, and renew any that show signs of wear, damage or cracks.

35 Clean the tensioner/idler pulleys but do not use any strong solvent which may enter the pulley bearings. Check that the pulleys rotate freely, with no sign of stiffness or free play. Renew them if there is any doubt about their condition, or if there are any obvious signs of wear or damage.

Refitting

Camshaft sprocket - 1.6 litre models

36 Refit the locating peg (where removed) to the rear of the sprocket. Locate the sprocket on the end of the camshaft, ensuring that the locating peg is correctly engaged with the cut-out in the camshaft end.

37 Refit the sprocket retaining bolt and washer, and tighten it to the specified torque. Retain the sprocket with the tool used on removal.

38 Realign the hole in the camshaft sprocket with the corresponding hole in the cylinder head, and refit the locking pin. Check that the crankshaft pulley locking pin is still in position.

39 Refit the timing belt to the camshaft sprocket. Ensure that the "front run" of the belt is taut - ie, that any slack is on the tensioner pulley side of the belt. Do not twist the belt sharply while refitting it, and ensure that the belt teeth are seated centrally in the sprockets.

40 With the timing belt correctly engaged on the sprockets, tension the belt as described in Section 7.

41 Once the belt is correctly tensioned, refit the timing belt covers (see Section 6).

Camshaft sprockets - 1.8 and 2.0 litre models

42 If both the sprockets and the hubs have been removed, engage the sprocket hub with the camshaft. Ensure that the correct hub is fitted to the relevant camshaft by observing the hub identification markings described in paragraph 15.

43 Refit the sprocket retaining bolt and washer, and tighten it to the specified torque. Temporarily refit the sprockets to allow the hub to be held stationary with the tool as the bolt is tightened.

44 Turn the hub so that the locking pin can be engaged.

45 If the sprockets have been removed, leaving the hubs in place, position the sprocket on its hub and refit the three bolts finger tight only at this stage. Ensure that the correct sprocket is fitted to the relevant camshaft according to the identification made on removal.

46 Relocate and tension the timing belt as described in Section 7.

Crankshaft sprocket - 1.6 litre models

47 Slide the spacer (where fitted) into position, taking great care not to damage the crankshaft oil, and refit the Woodruff key to its slot in the crankshaft end.

48 Slide on the crankshaft sprocket, aligning its slot with the Woodruff key.

49 Ensure that the camshaft sprocket locking pin is still in position. Temporarily refit the crankshaft pulley, and insert the locking pin through the pulley timing hole, to ensure that the crankshaft is still correctly positioned.

50 Remove the crankshaft pulley. Engage the timing belt with the crankshaft sprocket. Ensure that the belt "front run" is taut - ie, that any slack is on the tensioner pulley side of the belt. Fit the belt over the water pump sprocket and tensioner pulley. Do not twist the belt sharply while refitting it, and ensure that the belt teeth are seated centrally in the sprockets.

51 Tension the timing belt as described in Section 7.

52 Remove the crankshaft pulley, then refit the timing belt cover(s) as described in Section 6.

53 Refit the crankshaft pulley as described in Section 5, and reconnect the battery negative terminal.

Crankshaft sprocket - 1.8 and 2.0 litre models

54 Refit the Woodruff key to its slot in the crankshaft end.

55 Slide on the crankshaft sprocket, aligning its slot with the Woodruff key.

56 Relocate and tension the timing belt as described in Section 7.

Tensioner pulley - 1.6 litre models

57 Refit the tensioner pulley to its mounting stud, and fit the retaining bolt.

58 Ensure that the "front run" of the belt is taut - ie, that any slack is on the pulley side of the belt. Check that the belt is centrally located on all its sprockets. Rotate the pulley anti-clockwise to remove all free play from the timing belt, and securely tighten the pulley retaining nut.

59 Tension the belt as described in Section 7.

60 Once the belt is correctly tensioned, refit the timing belt covers as described in Section 6.

Tensioner and idler pulleys - 1.8 and 2.0 litre models

61 Refit the tensioner and idler pulleys and secure with the retaining bolts.

62 Relocate and tension the timing belt as described in Section 7.

9 Camshaft oil seal(s) - renewal

Note: If the camshaft oil seal is to be renewed with the timing belt still in place, check first that the belt is free from oil contamination. (Renew the belt as a matter of course if signs of oil contamination are found; see Section 7). Cover the belt, to protect it from contamination by oil, while work is in progress. If the timing belt is removed, ensure that all traces of oil are removed from the area before the belt is refitted.

1 Remove the camshaft sprocket (s)as described in Section 8. On 1.8 and 2.0 litre models, remove the sprockets and sprocket hubs.

2 Punch or drill two small holes opposite each other in the oil seal. Screw a self-tapping screw into each, and pull on the screws with pliers to extract the seal.

3 Clean the seal housing, and polish off any burrs or raised edges, which may have caused the seal to fail in the first place.

4 Lubricate the lips of the new seal with clean engine oil, and drive it into position until it seats on its locating shoulder. Use a suitable tubular drift, such as a socket, which bears only on the hard outer edge of the seal. Take care not to damage the seal lips during fitting. Note that the seal lips should face inwards.

5 Refit the camshaft sprocket(s) as described in Section 8.

10 Camshaft(s) and followers - removal, inspection and refitting

Removal

1 Disconnect the battery negative terminal, then remove the cylinder head cover as described in Section 4. Proceed as described under the relevant sub-heading.

1.6 litre models

2 Remove the camshaft sprocket as described in Section 8.

3 Remove the ignition HT coil as described in Chapter 5B.

4 With the coil removed, slacken the upper bolt securing the thermostat housing to the left-hand end of the cylinder head. Remove the bolt, along with its sealing washer. This is necessary since the bolt screws into the left-hand (No 1) camshaft bearing cap.

5 Carefully ease the oil supply pipe out from the top of the camshaft bearing caps, and remove it. Note the O-ring seals fitted to each of the pipe unions **(see illustration)**. Also note the position of the adaptors at each end of the supply tube.

6 The camshaft bearing caps should be numbered 1 to 5, number 1 being at the transmission end of the engine. If not, make

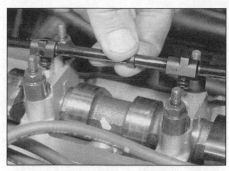

10.5 Removing the oil supply pipe from the camshaft bearing caps

10.7 Working as described in the text, unscrew the retaining nuts . . .

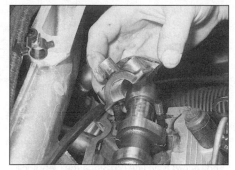

10.8 . . . and remove the camshaft bearing caps . . .

10.9 . . . then lift the camshaft away from the cylinder head

identification marks on the caps, using white paint or a suitable marker pen. Also mark each cap in some way to indicate its correct fitted orientation. This will avoid the possibility of installing the caps the wrong way around on refitting.

7 Evenly and progressively slacken the camshaft bearing cap retaining nuts by one turn at a time. This will relieve the valve spring pressure on the bearing caps gradually and evenly. Once the pressure has been relieved, the nuts can be fully unscrewed and removed **(see illustration)**.

8 Note the correct fitted orientation of the bearing caps, then remove them from the cylinder head **(see illustration)**.

9 Lift the camshaft away from the cylinder head, and slide the oil seal off the camshaft end **(see illustration)**.

10 Obtain eight small, clean plastic containers, and number them 1 to 8; alternatively, divide a larger container into eight compartments. Using a rubber sucker, withdraw each follower in turn, and place it in its respective container. Do not interchange the cam followers, or the rate of wear will be much-increased. If necessary, also remove the shim from the top of the valve stem, and store it with its respective follower. Note that the shim may stick to the inside of the follower as it is withdrawn. If this happens, take care not to allow it to drop out as the follower is removed.

1.8 and 2.0 litre models

11 Remove both cylinder head covers as described in Section 4.

12 Refer to Section 8 and remove both camshaft sprockets together with their hubs, and also remove the timing belt tensioner pulley.

13 Remove the timing belt upper (inner) cover as described in Section 6.

14 Progressively slacken, by a few turn at a time, the twelve bolts securing each camshaft bearing housing to the cylinder head. Release the bearing housings from their dowels and cylinder head locations. When each housing is free, remove the bolts and washers completely, and lift off the bearing housings.

15 As both camshafts are identical, suitably mark them inlet and exhaust, or front and rear before removal.

16 Tilt the camshafts by pressing them down at their transmission end to release the centralising bearing at the timing belt end. Carefully lift the camshafts up and out of their locations and slide the oil seal off each camshaft end.

17 Obtain sixteen small, clean plastic containers, and number them inlet 1 to 8 and exhaust 1 to 8; alternatively, divide a larger container into sixteen compartments and number each compartment accordingly. Using a rubber sucker, withdraw each hydraulic tappet in turn, and place it in its respective container. Do not interchange the tappets, or the rate of wear will be much-increased.

Inspection

18 Examine the camshaft bearing surfaces and cam lobes for signs of wear ridges and scoring. Renew the camshaft if any of these

conditions are apparent. Examine the condition of the bearing surfaces, both on the camshaft journals and in the cylinder head/bearing caps. If the head bearing surfaces are worn excessively, the cylinder head will need to be renewed. If suitable measuring equipment is available, camshaft bearing journal wear can be checked by direct measurement (where the necessary specifications have been quoted by Peugeot), noting that No 1 journal is at the transmission end of the head.

19 Examine the cam follower/hydraulic tappet bearing surfaces which contact the camshaft lobes for wear ridges and scoring. Renew any follower/tappet on which these conditions are apparent. If a follower/tappet bearing surface is badly scored, also examine the corresponding lobe on the camshaft for wear, as it is likely that both will be worn. Renew worn components as necessary.

Refitting

1.6 litre models

20 Where removed, refit each shim to the top of its original valve stem. *Do not interchange the shims, as this will upset the valve clearances (see Section 11).*

21 Liberally oil the cylinder head cam follower bores and the followers. Carefully refit the followers to the cylinder head, ensuring that each follower is refitted to its original bore. Some care will be required to enter the followers squarely into their bores.

22 Liberally oil the camshaft bearings and lobes, then refit the camshaft to the cylinder head. Temporarily refit the sprocket to the end of the shaft, and position it so that the sprocket timing hole is aligned with the corresponding cut-out in the cylinder head. Also ensure that the crankshaft is still locked in position (see Section 3).

23 Ensure that the bearing cap and head mating surfaces are completely clean, unmarked, and free from oil. Apply a smear of sealant to the thermostat housing mating surface of the left-hand (No 1) bearing cap, then refit all the caps, using the identification marks noted on removal to ensure that each is installed correctly and in its original location.

24 Evenly and progressively tighten the camshaft bearing cap nuts by one turn at a time until the caps touch the cylinder head. Then go round again and tighten all the nuts to the specified torque setting. Work only as described, to impose the pressure of the valve springs gradually and evenly on the bearing caps.

25 Examine the oil supply pipe union O-rings for signs of damage or deterioration, and renew as necessary. Apply a smear of clean engine oil to the O-rings. Ease the pipe into position in the top of the bearing caps, taking great care not to displace the O-rings.

26 Examine the sealing washer for signs of damage or deterioration, and renew it if necessary. Refit the upper retaining bolt to the

2A

thermostat housing, tightening it to the specified torque setting.

27 Refit the ignition HT coil as described in Chapter 5B.

28 Fit a new camshaft oil seal, using the information given in Section 9, then refit the camshaft sprocket as described in Section 8.

29 Check the valve clearances as described in Section 11.

30 Refit the cylinder head cover as described in Section 4, and reconnect the battery negative terminal.

1.8 and 2.0 litre models

31 Before refitting, remove all traces of oil from the bearing housing retaining bolt holes in the cylinder head, using a clean rag. Also ensure that both the cylinder head and bearing housing mating faces are clean and free from oil.

32 Liberally oil the cylinder head hydraulic tappet bores and the tappets. Carefully refit the tappets to the cylinder head, ensuring that each tappet is refitted to its original bore. Some care will be required to enter the tappets squarely into their bores. Check that each tappet rotates freely in its bore.

33 Liberally oil the camshaft bearings in the cylinder head and the camshaft lobes, then refit the camshafts to the cylinder head. Turn the camshafts so that the groove at the timing belt of each camshaft is positioned as follows:

> **1.8 litre models:** *Exhaust camshaft groove positioned at 12 o'clock, inlet camshaft groove at 11 o'clock.*
> **2.0 litre models:** *Exhaust camshaft groove positioned at 3 o'clock, inlet camshaft groove at 11 o'clock.*

34 Ensure that the four locating dowels are in position, one at each corner of the cylinder head.

35 Apply a bead of silicone based jointing compound around the perimeter of the mating faces and around the retaining bolt hole locations.

36 Liberally oil the camshaft bearings and carefully locate the bearing housings over the camshafts. Refit the retaining bolts ensuring that each has a washer under its head.

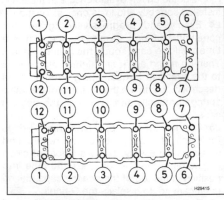

10.37 Camshaft bearing housing retaining bolt tightening sequence - 1.8 and 2.0 litre models

37 Working in the order shown, progressively tighten the bearing housing retaining bolts to the stage one torque setting then to the stage two setting **(see illustration)**.

38 Refit the timing belt upper (inner) cover as described in Section 6.

39 Refit the timing belt tensioner pulley as described in Section 8.

40 Refit the cylinder head covers as described in Section 4.

41 Fit a new camshaft oil seal(s), using the information given in Section 9, then refit the camshaft sprocket(s) and hub(s) as described in Section 8.

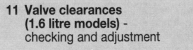

11 Valve clearances (1.6 litre models) - checking and adjustment

Checking

1 The importance of having the valve clearances correctly adjusted cannot be overstressed, as they vitally affect the performance of the engine. Checking should not be regarded as a routine operation, however. It should only be necessary when the valve gear has become noisy, after engine overhaul, or when trying to trace the cause of power loss. The clearances are checked as follows. The engine must be cold for the check to be accurate.

2 Apply the handbrake, then jack up the front of the car and support it on axle stands. Remove the right-hand front roadwheel.

3 From underneath the front of the car, prise out the retaining clips and unscrew the bolts, and remove the plastic cover from the wing valance to gain access to the crankshaft sprocket bolt. Where necessary, unclip the coolant hoses from the bracket to improve access further.

4 The engine can now be turned over using a suitable socket and extension bar fitted to the crankshaft pulley bolt.

5 Remove the cylinder head cover as described in Section 4.

6 Draw the outline of the engine on a piece of paper, numbering the cylinders 1 to 4, with No 1 cylinder at the transmission end of the engine. Show the position of each valve, together with the specified valve clearance (see paragraph 10). Above each valve, draw two lines for noting (1) the actual clearance and (2) the amount of adjustment required **(see illustration)**.

7 Turn the crankshaft until the inlet valve of No 1 cylinder (nearest the transmission end) is fully closed, with the tip of the cam facing directly away from the cam follower.

8 Using feeler blades, measure the clearance between the base of the cam and the follower **(see illustration)**. Record the clearance on line (1).

9 Repeat the measurement for the other seven valves, turning the crankshaft as necessary so that the cam lobe in question is

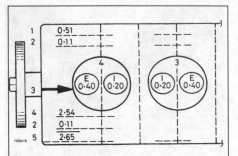

11.6 Example of valve shim thickness calculation

I Inlet
E Exhaust
1 Measured clearance
2 Difference between 1 and 3
3 Specified clearance
4 Thickness of original shim fitted
5 Thickness of new shim required

always facing directly away from the relevant follower.

10 Calculate the difference between each measured clearance and the desired value, and record it on line (2). Since the clearance is different for inlet and exhaust valves, make sure that you are aware which valve you are dealing with. The valve sequence from either end of the engine is:

Ex - In - In - Ex - Ex - In - In - Ex

11 If all the clearances are within tolerance, refit the cylinder head cover with reference to Section 4. Refit the plastic cover to the wing valance, refit the roadwheel, and lower the vehicle to the ground.

12 If any clearance measured is outside the specified tolerance, adjustment must be carried out as described in the following paragraphs.

Adjustment

13 Remove the camshaft as described in Section 10.

14 Withdraw the first follower from the cylinder head, and recover the shim from the top of the valve stem. Note that the shim may stick to the inside of the follower as it is withdrawn. If this happens, take care not to

11.8 Measuring a valve clearance using a feeler blade

11.14a Lift out the follower and remove the shim (arrowed)

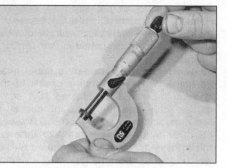

11.14b Using a micrometer to measure shim thickness

allow it to drop out as the follower is removed. Remove all traces of oil from the shim, and measure its thickness with a micrometer **(see illustrations)**. The shims usually carry thickness markings, but wear may have reduced the original thickness.

15 Refer to the clearance recorded for the valve concerned. If the clearance was more than that specified, the shim thickness must be *increased* by the difference recorded (2). If the clearance was less than that specified, the thickness of the shim must be *decreased* by the difference recorded (2).

16 Draw three more lines beneath each valve on the calculation paper, as shown in illustration 11.6. On line (4), note the measured thickness of the shim, then add or deduct the difference from line (2) to give the final shim thickness required on line (5).

17 Shims are available in thicknesses between 2.225 mm and 3.550 mm, in steps of 0.025 mm. Clean new shims before measuring or fitting them.

18 Repeat the procedure given in paragraphs 14 to 16 on the remaining valves, keeping each follower identified for position.

19 When reassembling, oil the shim, and fit it on the valve stem with the size marking face downwards. Oil the follower, and lower it onto the shim. Do not raise the follower after fitting, as the shim may become dislodged.

20 When all the followers are in position, complete with their shims, refit the camshaft as described in Section 10. Recheck the valve clearances before refitting the cylinder head cover, to make sure they are correct.

12 Cylinder head - removal and refitting

Removal

1 Disconnect the battery negative terminal.
2 Drain the cooling system as described in Chapter 1A.
3 Align the engine assembly/valve timing holes as described in Section 3, locking both the camshaft sprocket(s) and crankshaft pulley in position, and proceed as described under the relevant sub-heading. *Do not*

attempt to rotate the engine whilst the pins are in position.

1.6 litre models

4 Remove the cylinder head cover as described in Section 4.
5 Remove the air cleaner-to-throttle housing duct as described in Chapter 4A.
6 Note that the following text assumes that the cylinder head will be removed with both inlet and exhaust manifolds attached; this is easier, but makes it a bulky and heavy assembly to handle. If it is wished first to remove the manifolds, proceed as described in Chapter 4A.
7 Working as described in Chapter 4A, disconnect the exhaust system front pipe from the manifold. Where necessary, disconnect or release the lambda sensor wiring, so that it is not strained by the weight of the exhaust.
8 Carry out the following operations as described in Chapter 4A:
a) Depressurise the fuel system, and disconnect the fuel feed and return hoses. Plug all openings, to prevent loss of fuel and the entry of dirt into the system.
b) Disconnect the accelerator cable.
c) Disconnect the vacuum servo unit vacuum hose, and all the other relevant vacuum/breather hoses, from the inlet manifold and throttle housing. Release the hoses from the retaining clips on the manifold.
d) Disconnect all the electrical connector plugs from the throttle housing.
e) Disconnect the wiring connectors from the fuel injectors, and free the wiring loom from the manifold.

9 Slacken the retaining clips, and disconnect the coolant hoses from the thermostat housing (on the left-hand end of the cylinder head).
10 Depress the retaining clip(s), and disconnect the wiring connector(s) from the electrical switch(es) and/or sensor(s) which are screwed into the thermostat housing, or into the left-hand end of the cylinder head (as appropriate).
11 Slacken and remove the bolt securing the engine oil dipstick tube to the left-hand end of the cylinder head, and withdraw the tube from the cylinder block.

12 Disconnect the wiring connector from the ignition HT coil. If the cylinder head is to be dismantled for overhaul, remove the ignition HT coil as described in Chapter 5B. Note that the HT leads should be disconnected from the spark plugs instead of the coil, and the coil and leads removed as an assembly. If the cylinder numbers are not already marked on the HT leads, number each lead, to avoid the possibility of the leads being incorrectly connected on refitting.
13 Release the timing belt tensioner and disengage the timing belt from the camshaft sprocket as described in Section 8.

1.8 and 2.0 litre models

14 Remove the air cleaner assembly and intake ducting as described in Chapter 4A.
15 Remove the cylinder head cover as described in Section 4.
16 Remove the inlet manifold as described in Chapter 4A.
17 Working as described in Chapter 4A, disconnect the exhaust system front pipe from the manifold. Where necessary, disconnect or release the lambda sensor wiring, so that it is not strained by the weight of the exhaust.
18 Disconnect the radiator hose from the coolant outlet elbow.
19 Disconnect all remaining vacuum/breather hoses, and all electrical connector plugs from the cylinder head.
20 Release the timing belt tensioner and disengage the timing belt from the camshaft sprocket as described in Section 8.

All models

21 Working in the *reverse* of the sequence shown in illustration 12.38, progressively slacken the ten cylinder head bolts by half a turn at a time, until all bolts can be unscrewed by hand. Remove the bolts along with their washers, noting the correct location of the spacer fitted to the front left-hand bolt on 1.6 litre models.
22 With all the cylinder head bolts removed, the joint between the cylinder head and gasket and the cylinder block/crankcase must now be broken. On wet-liner engines, there is a risk of coolant and foreign matter leaking into the sump if the cylinder head is lifted carelessly. If care is not taken and the liners are moved, there is also a possibility of the bottom seals being disturbed, causing leakage after refitting the head.
23 To break the joint, obtain two L-shaped metal bars which fit into the cylinder head bolt holes, and gently "rock" the cylinder head free towards the front of the car. *Do not* try to swivel the head on the cylinder block/crankcase; it is located by dowels.
24 When the joint is broken, lift the cylinder head away. Seek assistance if possible, as it is a heavy assembly, especially if it is complete with the manifolds. Remove the gasket from the top of the block, noting the two locating dowels. If the locating dowels are a loose fit, remove them and store them with

2A

12.25 Cylinder liners clamped in position using suitable bolts and large flat washers

the head for safe-keeping. Do not discard the gasket; it will be needed for identification purposes.

25 On wet-liner engines, *do not* attempt to turn the crankshaft with the cylinder head removed, otherwise the liners may be displaced. Operations that require the crankshaft to be turned (eg cleaning the piston crowns), should only be carried out once the cylinder liners are firmly clamped in position. In the absence of the special Peugeot liner clamps, the liners can be clamped in position as follows. Use large flat washers positioned underneath suitable-length bolts, or temporarily refit the original head bolts, with suitable spacers fitted to their shanks **(see illustration)**.

26 If the cylinder head is to be dismantled for overhaul, remove the camshaft(s) as described in Section 10, then refer to Part C of this Chapter.

Preparation for refitting

27 The mating faces of the cylinder head and cylinder block/crankcase must be perfectly clean before refitting the head. Use a hard plastic or wooden scraper to remove all traces of gasket and carbon; also clean the piston crowns. On wet-liner engines, refer to paragraph 25 before turning the engine. Take particular care on these models, as the soft aluminium alloy is easily damaged. On all models, make sure that the carbon is not allowed to enter the oil and water passages - this is particularly important for the lubrication system, as carbon could block the oil supply to the engine's components. Using adhesive tape and paper, seal the water, oil and bolt holes in the cylinder block/crankcase. To prevent carbon entering the gap between the pistons and bores, smear a little grease in the gap. After cleaning each piston, use a small brush to remove all traces of grease and carbon from the gap, then wipe away the remainder with a clean rag. Clean all the pistons in the same way.

28 Check the mating surfaces of the cylinder block/crankcase and the cylinder head for nicks, deep scratches and other damage. If slight, they may be removed carefully with a file, but if excessive, machining may be the only alternative to renewal. If warpage of the cylinder head gasket surface is suspected,

use a straight-edge to check it for distortion. Refer to Part C of this Chapter if necessary.

29 On wet-liner engines, check the cylinder liner protrusion as described in Part C of this Chapter.

30 When purchasing a new cylinder head gasket, it is essential that a gasket of the correct thickness is obtained. On some models only one thickness of gasket is available, so this is not a problem. However on other models, there are two different thicknesses available - the standard gasket which is fitted at the factory, and a slightly thicker "repair" gasket (+ 0.2 mm), for use once the head gasket face has been machined. If the cylinder head has been machined, it should have the letter "R" stamped adjacent to the No 3 exhaust port, and the gasket should also have the letter "R" stamped adjacent to No 3 cylinder on its front upper face. The gaskets can also be identified as described in the following paragraph, using the cut-outs on the left-hand end of the gasket.

31 With the gasket fitted the correct way up on the cylinder block, there will be either a single hole, or a series of holes, punched in the tab on the left-hand end of the gasket. The standard (1.2 mm) gasket has only one hole punched in it; the slightly thicker (1.4 mm) gasket has either two or three holes punched in it, depending on its manufacturer. Identify the gasket type, and ensure that the new gasket obtained is of the correct thickness. Note that modifications to the cylinder head gasket material, type, and manufacturer are constantly taking place; seek the advice of a Peugeot dealer as to the latest recommendations.

32 Check the condition of the cylinder head bolts, and particularly their threads, whenever they are removed. Wash the bolts in a suitable solvent, and wipe them dry. Check each bolt for any sign of visible wear or damage, renewing them if necessary. Measure the length of each bolt (without the washer fitted) from the underside of its head to the end of the bolt. If all bolts are less than 176.5 mm on 1.6 litre models, less than 160 mm on 1.8 litre models, and less than 112 mm on 2.0 litre models, they may be re-used. However, if any one bolt is longer than the specified length, *all* of the bolts should be renewed as a complete set. Considering the stress which the cylinder head bolts are under, it is highly recommended that they are renewed, regardless of their apparent condition.

Refitting

33 Wipe clean the mating surfaces of the cylinder head and cylinder block/crankcase. Check that the two locating dowels are in position at each end of the cylinder block/crankcase surface. Where applicable, remove the cylinder liner clamps.

34 Position a new gasket on the cylinder block/crankcase surface, ensuring that its identification holes or the projecting tongue are at the left-hand end of the gasket.

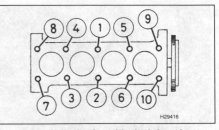

12.38 Cylinder head bolt tightening sequence

1.6 litre models

35 Check that the crankshaft pulley and camshaft sprocket are still locked in position with their respective pins. With the aid of an assistant, carefully refit the cylinder head assembly to the block, aligning it with the locating dowels.

36 Apply a smear of grease to the threads, and to the underside of the heads, of the cylinder head bolts. Peugeot recommend the use of Molykote G Rapid Plus (available from your Peugeot dealer); in the absence of the specified grease, any good-quality high-melting-point grease may be used.

37 Carefully enter each bolt and washer into its relevant hole (*do not* drop it in) and screw it in finger-tight, not forgetting to fit the spacer to the front left-hand bolt.

38 Working progressively and in the sequence shown, tighten the cylinder head bolts to their Stage 1 torque setting, using a torque wrench and a suitable socket **(see illustration)**.

39 Once all the bolts have been tightened to their Stage 1 torque, fully slacken all the head bolts, working in the reverse of the tightening sequence. Once the bolts are loose, tighten all bolts to their Stage 2 specified torque setting, again following the specified sequence.

40 With all the bolts tightened to their Stage 2 setting, working again in the specified sequence, angle-tighten the bolts through the specified Stage 3 angle, using a socket and extension bar. It is recommended that an angle-measuring gauge is used during this stage of tightening, to ensure accuracy. If a gauge is not available, use white paint to make alignment marks between the bolt head and cylinder head prior to tightening; the marks can then be used to check that the bolt has rotated sufficiently.

41 Once the cylinder head bolts are correctly tightened, reconnect the wiring connector to the ignition HT coil. Otherwise, if the head was stripped for overhaul, refit the HT coil as described in Chapter 5B.

42 Fit the timing belt over the camshaft sprocket. Refit the mounting bracket to the end of the cylinder head, and securely tighten its retaining bolts. Refit the engine right-hand mounting bracket, and tighten its retaining nuts to the specified torque. The jack can then be removed from underneath the engine.

43 Refit the timing belt to the camshaft sprocket as described in Section 8, and tension the belt as described in Section 7.

44 The remainder of the refitting procedure is a reversal of removal, noting the following points:

a) *Ensure that all wiring is correctly routed, and that all connectors are securely reconnected to the correct components.*

b) *Ensure that the coolant hoses are correctly reconnected, and that their retaining clips are securely tightened.*

c) *Ensure that all vacuum/breather hoses are correctly reconnected.*

d) *Refit the cylinder head cover as described in Section 4.*

e) *Reconnect the exhaust system to the manifold, refit the air cleaner housing and ducts, and adjust the accelerator cable, as described in Chapter 4A. If the manifolds were removed, refit these as described in Chapter 4A.*

f) *On completion, refill the cooling system as described in Chapter 1A, and reconnect the battery.*

1.8 and 2.0 litre models

45 Refit the cylinder head as described above in paragraphs 35 to 37, ignoring the remark about the spacer fitted to the front left-hand bolt.

46 Working progressively and in the sequence shown in illustration 12.38, tighten the cylinder head bolts, to their Stage 1 torque setting.

47 Once all the bolts have been tightened to their Stage 1 torque setting, fully slacken all the head bolts, working in the reverse of the tightening sequence. Once the bolts are loose, tighten all bolts to their Stage 2 specified torque setting, again following the specified sequence.

48 With all the bolts tightened to their Stage 2 setting, working again in the specified sequence, angle-tighten the bolts through the specified Stage 3 angle, using a socket and extension bar. It is recommended that an angle-measuring gauge is used during this stage of tightening, to ensure accuracy. If a gauge is not available, use white paint to make alignment marks between the bolt head and cylinder head prior to tightening; the marks can then be used to check that the bolt has rotated sufficiently.

49 Refit the timing belt to the camshaft sprocket as described in Section 8, and tension the belt as described in Section 7.

50 The remainder of the refitting procedure is a reversal of removal, noting the points made in paragraph 44.

13 Sump - removal and refitting

Removal

1 Disconnect the battery negative terminal.
2 Chock the rear wheels, jack up the front of the vehicle and support it on axle stands.

3 Drain the engine oil as described in Chapter 1A, then clean and refit the engine oil drain plug, tightening it securely. If the engine is nearing its service interval when the oil and filter are due for renewal, it is recommended that the filter is also removed, and a new one fitted. After reassembly, the engine can then be refilled with fresh oil. Refer to Chapter 1A for further information.

4 Where necessary, disconnect the wiring connector from the oil temperature sender unit, which is screwed into the sump.
5 Remove the auxiliary drivebelt as described in Chapter 1A.
6 On models with air conditioning, where the compressor is located on the side of the sump, unbolt the compressor and position it clear of the sump. Support the weight of the compressor by tying it to the vehicle, to prevent any excess strain being placed on the compressor lines. *Do not* disconnect the refrigerant lines from the compressor (refer to the warnings given in Chapter 3).
7 Progressively slacken and remove all the sump retaining bolts. Since the sump bolts vary in length, remove each bolt in turn, and store it in its correct fitted order by pushing it through a clearly-marked cardboard template. This will avoid the possibility of installing the bolts in the wrong locations on refitting.
8 Break the joint by striking the sump with the palm of your hand. Lower the sump, and withdraw it from underneath the vehicle. Remove the gasket (where fitted), and discard it; a new one must be used on refitting. While the sump is removed, take the opportunity to check the oil pump pick-up/strainer for signs of clogging or splitting. If necessary, remove the pump as described in Section 14, and clean or renew the strainer.
9 On some models, a large spacer plate is fitted between the sump and the base of the cylinder block/crankcase. If this plate is fitted, undo the two retaining screws from diagonally-opposite corners of the plate. Remove the plate from the base of the engine, noting which way round it is fitted.

Refitting

10 Clean all traces of sealant/gasket from the mating surfaces of the cylinder block/crankcase and sump, then use a clean rag to wipe out the sump and the engine's interior.
11 Where a spacer plate is fitted, remove all traces of sealant/gasket from the spacer plate, then apply a thin coating of suitable sealant (see paragraph 14) to the plate upper mating surface. Offer up the plate to the base of the cylinder block/crankcase, and securely tighten its retaining screws.
12 On models where the sump was fitted without a gasket, ensure that the sump mating surfaces are clean and dry, then apply a thin coating of suitable sealant to the sump mating surface.
13 On models where the sump was fitted with a gasket, ensure that all traces of the old

gasket have been removed, and that the sump mating surfaces are clean and dry. Position the new gasket on the top of the sump, using a dab of grease to hold it in position.
14 Offer up the sump to the cylinder block/crankcase. Refit its retaining bolts, ensuring that each is screwed into its original location. Tighten the bolts evenly and progressively to the specified torque setting.
15 On models with air conditioning, refit the compressor to the side of the sump and tighten the bolts.
16 Refit the auxiliary drivebelt (see Chapter 1A) and the pressure regulator accumulator.
17 Reconnect the wiring connector to the oil temperature sensor (where fitted).
18 Lower the vehicle to the ground, then refill the engine with oil as described in Chapter 1A and reconnect the battery negative terminal.

14 Oil pump - removal, inspection and refitting

Removal

1 Remove the sump (see Section 13).
2 Undo the two retaining screws, and slide the sprocket cover off the front of the oil pump.
3 Slacken and remove the three bolts securing the oil pump to the base of the cylinder block/crankcase. Disengage the pump sprocket from the chain, and remove the oil pump **(see illustration)**. Where necessary, also remove the spacer plate which is fitted behind the oil pump.

Inspection

4 Examine the oil pump sprocket for signs of damage and wear, such as chipped or missing teeth. If the sprocket is worn, the pump assembly must be renewed, since the sprocket is not available separately. It is also recommended that the chain and drive sprocket, fitted to the crankshaft, be renewed at the same time. To renew the chain and drive sprocket, first remove the crankshaft timing belt sprocket as described in Section 8. Unbolt the oil seal carrier from the cylinder block. The sprocket, spacer (where fitted) and chain can

14.3 Removing the oil pump

14.5a Remove the oil pump cover retaining bolts . . .

14.5b . . . then lift off the cover and remove the spring . . .

14.5c . . . and the relief valve piston, noting which way round it is fitted

then be slid off the end of the crankshaft. Refer to Part C for further information.

5 Slacken and remove the bolts (along with the baffle plate, where fitted) securing the strainer cover to the pump body. Lift off the strainer cover, and take off the relief valve piston and spring, noting which way round they are fitted **(see illustrations)**.

6 Examine the pump rotors and body for signs of wear ridges or scoring. If worn, the complete pump assembly must be renewed.

7 Examine the relief valve piston for signs of wear or damage, and renew if necessary. The condition of the relief valve spring can only be measured by comparing it with a new one; if there is any doubt about its condition, it should also be renewed. Both the piston and spring are available individually.

8 Thoroughly clean the oil pump strainer with a suitable solvent, and check it for signs of clogging or splitting. If the strainer is damaged, the strainer and cover assembly must be renewed.

9 Locate the relief valve spring and piston in the strainer cover. Refit the cover to the pump body, aligning the relief valve piston with its bore in the pump. Refit the baffle plate (where fitted) and the cover retaining bolts, and tighten them securely.

Refitting

10 Offer up the spacer plate (where fitted), then locate the pump sprocket with its drive chain. Seat the pump on the base of the cylinder block/crankcase. Refit the pump retaining bolts, and tighten them to the specified torque setting.

11 Where necessary, slide the sprocket cover into position on the pump. Refit its retaining bolts, tightening them securely.

12 Refit the sump as described in Section 13.

13 Before starting the engine, prime the oil pump as follows. Disconnect the fuel injector wiring connectors, then spin the engine on the starter until the oil pressure light goes out. Reconnect the injector wiring on completion.

15 Oil cooler - removal and refitting

Removal

1 Firmly apply the handbrake, then jack up the front of the vehicle and support it on axle stands.

2 Drain the cooling system as described in Chapter 1A. Alternatively, clamp the oil cooler coolant hoses directly above the cooler, and be prepared for some coolant loss as the hoses are disconnected.

3 Position a suitable container beneath the oil filter. Unscrew the filter using an oil filter removal tool if necessary, and drain the oil into the container. If the oil filter is damaged or distorted during removal, it must be renewed. Given the low cost of a new oil filter relative to the cost of repairing the damage which could result if a re-used filter springs a leak, it is probably a good idea to renew the filter in any case.

4 Release the hose clips, and disconnect the coolant hoses from the oil cooler.

5 Unscrew the oil cooler/oil filter mounting bolt from the cylinder block, and withdraw the cooler. Note the locating notch in the cooler flange, which fits over the lug on the cylinder block **(see illustration)**. Discard the oil cooler sealing ring; a new one must be used on refitting.

15.5 Oil cooler/oil filter mounting bolt (A) and locating notch (B)

Refitting

6 Fit a new sealing ring to the recess in the rear of the cooler, then offer the cooler to the cylinder block.

7 Ensure that the locating notch in the cooler flange is correctly engaged with the lug on the cylinder block, then refit the mounting bolt and tighten it securely.

8 Fit the oil filter, then lower the vehicle to the ground. Top-up the engine oil level as described in "Weekly Checks".

9 Refill or top-up the cooling system as described in "Weekly Checks" (as applicable). Start the engine, and check the oil cooler for signs of leakage.

16 Crankshaft oil seals - renewal

Right-hand oil seal

1 Remove the crankshaft sprocket and (where fitted) spacer, referring to Section 8. Secure the timing belt clear of the working area, so that it cannot be contaminated with oil. Make a note of the correct fitted depth of the seal in its housing.

2 Punch or drill two small holes opposite each other in the seal. Screw a self-tapping screw into each, and pull on the screws with pliers to extract the seal. Alternatively, the seal can be levered out of position. Use a flat-bladed screwdriver, and take great care not to damage the crankshaft shoulder or seal housing.

3 Clean the seal housing, and polish off any burrs or raised edges, which may have caused the seal to fail in the first place.

4 Lubricate the lips of the new seal with clean engine oil, and carefully locate the seal on the end of the crankshaft. Note that its sealing lip must be facing inwards. Take care not to damage the seal lips during fitting.

5 Fit the new seal using a suitable tubular drift, such as a socket, which bears only on the hard outer edge of the seal. Tap the seal into position, to the same depth in the housing as the original was prior to removal.

6 Wash off any traces of oil, then refit the crankshaft sprocket as described in Section 8.

Left-hand oil seal

7 Remove the flywheel/driveplate as described in Section 17. Make a note of the correct fitted depth of the seal in its housing.
8 Punch or drill two small holes opposite each other in the seal. Screw a self-tapping screw into each, and pull on the screws with pliers to extract the seal.
9 Clean the seal housing, and polish off any burrs or raised edges, which may have caused the seal to fail in the first place.
10 Lubricate the lips of the new seal with clean engine oil, and carefully locate the seal on the end of the crankshaft.
11 Fit the new seal using a suitable tubular drift, which bears only on the hard outer edge of the seal. Drive the seal into position, to the same depth in the housing as the original was prior to removal.
12 Wash off any traces of oil, then refit the flywheel/driveplate as described in Section 17.

17 Flywheel/driveplate - removal, inspection and refitting

Removal

Flywheel (models with manual transmission)

1 Remove the transmission as described in Chapter 7A, then remove the clutch assembly as described in Chapter 6.
2 Prevent the flywheel from turning by locking the ring gear teeth with a similar arrangement to that shown in illustration 5.2. Alternatively, bolt a strap between the flywheel and the cylinder block/crankcase. *Do not* attempt to lock the flywheel in position using the crankshaft pulley locking pin described in Section 3.
3 Slacken and remove the flywheel retaining bolts, and remove the flywheel from the end of the crankshaft. Be careful not to drop it; it is heavy. If the flywheel locating dowel is a loose fit in the crankshaft end, remove it and store it with the flywheel for safe-keeping. Discard the flywheel bolts; new ones must be used on refitting.

Driveplate (models with automatic transmission)

4 Remove the transmission as described in Chapter 7B. Lock the driveplate as described in paragraph 2. Mark the relationship between the torque converter plate and the driveplate, and slacken all the driveplate retaining bolts.
5 Remove the retaining bolts, along with the torque converter plate and (where fitted) the two shims (one fitted on each side of the torque converter plate). Note that the shims are of different thickness, the thicker one

17.10 If the new flywheel bolt threads are not supplied with their threads pre-coated, apply a suitable locking compound to them . . .

being on the outside of the torque converter plate. Discard the driveplate retaining bolts; new ones must be used on refitting.
6 Remove the driveplate from the end of the crankshaft. If the locating dowel is a loose fit in the crankshaft end, remove it and store it with the driveplate for safe-keeping.

Inspection

7 On models with manual transmission, examine the flywheel for scoring of the clutch face, and for wear or chipping of the ring gear teeth. If the clutch face is scored, the flywheel may be surface-ground, but renewal is preferable. Seek the advice of a Peugeot dealer or engine reconditioning specialist to see if machining is possible. If the ring gear is worn or damaged, the flywheel must be renewed, as it is not possible to renew the ring gear separately.
8 On models with automatic transmission, check the torque converter driveplate carefully for signs of distortion. Look for any hairline cracks around the bolt holes or radiating outwards from the centre, and inspect the ring gear teeth for signs of wear or chipping. If any sign of wear or damage is found, the driveplate must be renewed.

Refitting

Flywheel (models with manual transmission)

9 Clean the mating surfaces of the flywheel and crankshaft. Remove any remaining locking compound from the threads of the crankshaft holes, using the correct-size tap, if available.

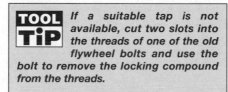

TOOL TIP *If a suitable tap is not available, cut two slots into the threads of one of the old flywheel bolts and use the bolt to remove the locking compound from the threads.*

10 If the new flywheel retaining bolts are not supplied with their threads already pre-coated, apply a suitable thread-locking compound to the threads of each bolt **(see illustration)**.

17.12 . . . then refit the flywheel, and tighten the bolts to the specified torque

11 Ensure the locating dowel is in position. Offer up the flywheel, locating it on the dowel, and fit the new retaining bolts.
12 Lock the flywheel using the method employed on dismantling, and tighten the retaining bolts to the specified torque **(see illustration)**.
13 Refit the clutch as described in Chapter 6. Remove the flywheel locking tool, and refit the transmission as described in Chapter 7A.

Driveplate (models with automatic transmission)

14 Carry out the operations described above in paragraphs 9 and 10, substituting "driveplate" for all references to the flywheel.
15 Locate the driveplate on its locating dowel.
16 Offer up the torque converter plate, with the thinner shim positioned behind the plate and the thicker shim on the outside, and align the marks made prior to removal.
17 Fit the new retaining bolts, then lock the driveplate using the method employed on dismantling. Tighten the retaining bolts to the specified torque wrench setting.
18 Remove the driveplate locking tool, and refit the transmission as described in Chapter 7B.

18 Engine/transmission mountings - inspection and renewal

Inspection

1 If improved access is required, raise the front of the car and support it securely on axle stands.
2 Check the mounting rubber to see if it is cracked, hardened or separated from the metal at any point; renew the mounting if any such damage or deterioration is evident.
3 Check that all the mounting's fasteners are securely tightened; use a torque wrench to check if possible.
4 Using a large screwdriver or a crowbar, check for wear in the mounting by carefully levering against it to check for free play. Where this is not possible, enlist the aid of an

2A

assistant to move the engine/transmission unit back and forth, or from side to side, while you watch the mounting. While some free play is to be expected even from new components, excessive wear should be obvious. If excessive free play is found, check first that the fasteners are correctly secured, then renew any worn components as described below.

Renewal

Right-hand mounting - 1.6 litre models

5 Disconnect the battery negative terminal. Release all the relevant hoses and wiring from their retaining clips, and position clear of the mounting so that they do not hinder the removal procedure.

6 Place a jack beneath the engine, with a block of wood on the jack head. Raise the jack until it is supporting the weight of the engine.

7 Slacken and remove the three nuts securing the right-hand mounting bracket to the engine unit and the single nut securing the bracket to the mounting rubber.

8 Undo the bolt securing the upper engine movement limiter to the right-hand mounting bracket, and the four bolts securing the movement limiter mounting bracket to the body. Lift away the right-hand mounting bracket and the movement limiter assembly.

9 Lift the rubber buffer plate off the mounting rubber stud, then unscrew the mounting rubber from the body and remove it from the vehicle. If necessary, the mounting bracket can be unbolted and removed from the side of the cylinder head.

10 Check all components carefully for signs of wear or damage, and renew them where necessary.

11 On reassembly, screw the mounting rubber into the vehicle body, and tighten it to the specified torque. Refit the mounting bracket to the side of the cylinder head, apply a drop of locking compound to the retaining bolts and tighten them to the specified torque.

12 Refit the engine movement limiter assembly to the engine mounting bracket and to the body and tighten the bolts to the specified torque.

13 Refit the rubber buffer plate to the mounting rubber stud, and install the mounting bracket.

14 Tighten the mounting bracket retaining nuts to the specified torque setting.

15 Remove the jack from underneath the engine, and reconnect the battery negative terminal.

Right-hand mounting - 1.8 and 2.0 litre models

16 Disconnect the battery negative terminal. Release all the relevant hoses and wiring from their retaining clips. Place the hoses/wiring clear of the mounting so that the removal procedure is not hindered.

17 Place a jack beneath the engine, with a block of wood on the jack head. Raise the jack until it is supporting the weight of the engine.

18 Slacken and remove the two nuts and two bolts securing the right-hand engine/ transmission mounting bracket to the engine. Remove the single nut securing the bracket to the mounting rubber.

19 Undo the bolt securing the upper engine movement limiter to the right-hand mounting bracket, and the four bolts securing the movement limiter mounting bracket to the body. Lift away the right-hand mounting bracket and the movement limiter assembly.

20 Lift the rubber buffer plate off the mounting rubber stud, then unscrew the mounting rubber from the body and remove it from the vehicle. If necessary, the mounting bracket can be unbolted and removed from the front of the cylinder block.

21 Check all components carefully for signs of wear or damage, and renew as necessary.

22 On reassembly, screw the mounting rubber into the vehicle body, and tighten it securely. Refit the mounting bracket to the front of the cylinder head, and securely tighten its retaining bolts.

23 Refit the engine movement limiter assembly to the engine mounting bracket and to the body and tighten the bolts to the specified torque.

24 Refit the rubber buffer plate to the mounting rubber stud, and install the mounting bracket.

25 Tighten the mounting bracket retaining nuts to the specified torque setting. Remove the jack from underneath the engine and reconnect the battery.

Left-hand mounting

26 Remove the air cleaner assembly, as described in Chapter 4A.

27 Place a jack beneath the transmission, with a block of wood on the jack head. Raise the jack until it is supporting the weight of the transmission.

28 Slacken and remove the centre nut and washer from the left-hand mounting, then undo the nuts securing the mounting in position and remove it from the engine compartment.

29 If necessary, slide the spacer (where fitted) off the mounting stud, then unscrew the stud from the top of the transmission housing, and remove it along with its washer. If the mounting stud is tight, a universal stud extractor can be used to unscrew it.

30 Check all components carefully for signs of wear or damage, and renew as necessary.

31 Clean the threads of the mounting stud, and apply a coat of thread-locking compound to its threads. Refit the stud and washer to the top of the transmission, and tighten it to the specified torque setting.

32 Slide the spacer (where fitted) onto the mounting stud, then refit the rubber mounting. Tighten both the mounting-to-body bolts and the mounting centre nut to their specified torque settings, and remove the jack from underneath the transmission.

33 Refit the air cleaner assembly, then refit the battery as described in Chapter 5A.

Lower engine movement limiter

34 If not already done, chock the rear wheels, then jack up the front of the vehicle and support it securely on axle stands.

35 Unscrew and remove the bolt securing the movement limiter link to the driveshaft intermediate bearing housing.

36 Remove the bolt securing the link to the subframe. Withdraw the link.

37 To remove the intermediate bearing housing assembly it will first be necessary to remove the right-hand driveshaft as described in Chapter 8.

38 With the driveshaft removed, undo the retaining bolts and remove the bearing housing from the rear of the cylinder block.

39 Check carefully for signs of wear or damage on all components, and renew them where necessary.

40 On reassembly, fit the bearing housing assembly to the rear of the cylinder block, and tighten its retaining bolts securely. Refit the driveshaft as described in Chapter 8.

41 Refit the movement limiter link, and tighten both its bolts to their specified torque settings.

42 Lower the vehicle to the ground.

Chapter 2 Part B:
Diesel engine in-car repair procedures

Contents

Degrees of difficulty

Easy, suitable for novice with little experience	Fairly easy, suitable for beginner with some experience	Fairly difficult, suitable for competent DIY mechanic	Difficult, suitable for experienced DIY mechanic	Very difficult, suitable for expert DIY or professional 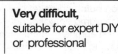

Specifications

General

Designation:
1.9 litre (1905 cc engine)	XUD9
2.1 litre (2088 cc engine)	XUD11

Engine codes*:
1.9 litre engine	DHX (XUD9BTF/Y/L3)
2.1 litre engine	P8C (XUD11BTE/Y/L/L3)

Bore:
1.9 litre engine	83.00 mm
2.1 litre engine	85.00 mm

Stroke:
1.9 litre engine	88.00 mm
2.1 litre engine	92.00 mm
Direction of crankshaft rotation	Clockwise (viewed from the right-hand side of vehicle)
No 1 cylinder location	At the transmission end of block

Compression ratio:
1.9 litre engine	21.8 : 1
2.1 litre engine	21.5 : 1

*The engine code is stamped on a plate attached to the front of the cylinder block. This is the code most often used by Peugeot. The code given in brackets is the factory identification number, and is not often referred to by Peugeot or this manual.

Compression pressures (engine hot, at cranking speed)

Normal	25 to 30 bars (363 to 435 psi)
Minimum	18 bars (261 psi)
Maximum difference between any two cylinders	5 bars (73 psi)

Camshaft

Drive	Toothed belt

No of bearings:
1.9 litre engine	3
2.1 litre engine	5

Endfloat:
1.9 litre engine	0.07 to 0.16 mm
2.1 litre engine	Not available at time of writing

2B

Valve clearances (1.9 litre engine)

Inlet	0.15 ± 0.08 mm
Exhaust	0.30 ± 0.08 mm

Lubrication system

Oil pump type	Gear-type, chain-driven off the crankshaft right-hand end
Minimum oil pressure at 90°C	4.9 bars at 4000 rpm
Oil pressure warning switch operating pressure	0.8 bars

Torque wrench settings

	Nm	lbf ft
1.9 litre engines		
Big-end bearing cap nuts:		
Stage 1	20	15
Stage 2	Tighten through a further 70°	
Camshaft bearing cap nuts	20	15
Camshaft sprocket bolt	45	33
Crankshaft pulley bolt:		
Stage 1	40	30
Stage 2	Tighten through a further 51°	
Crankshaft front oil seal housing bolts	16	12
Cylinder head bolts:		
Stage 1	20	15
Stage 2	60	44
Stage 3	Tighten through a further 220°	
Cylinder head cover bolts	10	7
Flywheel/driveplate bolts	50	37
Injection pump sprocket puller retaining screws	10	7
Injection pump sprocket nut	50	37
Left-hand engine/transmission mounting:		
Mounting bracket-to-body	30	22
Rubber mounting-to-bracket bolts	30	22
Mounting stud-to-transmission	60	44
Centre nut	65	48
Lower engine movement limiter-to-driveshaft intermediate bearing housing	50	37
Lower engine movement limiter-to-subframe	85	62
Main bearing cap bolts:		
Stage 1	15	11
Stage 2	Tighten through a further 60°	
Oil pump mounting bolts	13	10
Piston oil jet spray tube bolt	10	7
Right-hand engine/transmission mounting:		
Mounting bracket-to-engine nuts	45	33
Mounting bracket-to-rubber mounting nut	45	33
Rubber mounting-to-body nut	40	29
Upper engine movement limiter bolts	50	37
Sump bolts	16	12
Timing belt cover bolts	8	6
Timing belt tensioner adjustment bolt	20	15
Timing belt tensioner pivot nut	20	15
2.1 litre engines		
Big-end bearing cap nuts:		
Stage 1	20	15
Stage 2	Tighten through a further 70°	
Camshaft carrier bolts	25	18
Camshaft sprocket bolt	50	37
Crankshaft front oil seal housing bolts	16	12
Crankshaft pulley bolt:		
Stage 1	40	30
Stage 2	Tighten through a further 60°	
Cylinder head cover bolts	8	6
Cylinder head bolts:		
Stage 1	70	52
Stage 2	Tighten through a further 150°	
Warm up engine and allow to cool for 3.5 hours. Slacken bolts, then tighten to:		
Stage 3	70	52
Stage 4	Tighten through a further 150°	

Torque wrench settings (continued)

2.1 litre engines (continued)

	Nm	lbf ft
Flywheel/driveplate bolts	50	37
Injection pump sprocket puller retaining screws	10	7
Injection pump sprocket nut	50	37
Left-hand engine/transmission mounting:		
Mounting bracket-to-body	30	22
Rubber mounting-to-bracket bolts	30	22
Mounting stud-to-transmission	60	44
Centre nut	65	48
Lower engine movement limiter-to-driveshaft intermediate bearing housing	50	37
Lower engine movement limiter-to-subframe	85	62
Main bearing cap bolts:		
Stage 1	15	11
Stage 2	Tighten through a further 60°	
Oil pump mounting bolts	13	10
Piston oil jet spray tube bolt	10	7
Right-hand engine/transmission mounting:		
Mounting bracket-to-engine nuts	45	33
Mounting bracket-to-rubber mounting nut	45	33
Rubber mounting-to-body nut	40	29
Upper engine movement limiter bolts	50	37
Sump bolts	16	12
Timing belt idler pulley	37	27
Timing belt tensioner nut/bolt	10	7

1 General information

How to use this Chapter

This Part of Chapter 2 describes the repair procedures that can reasonably be carried out on the engine while it remains in the vehicle. If the engine has been removed from the vehicle and is being dismantled as described in Part C, any preliminary dismantling procedures can be ignored.

Note that, while it may be possible physically to overhaul items such as the piston/connecting rod assemblies while the engine is in the car, such tasks are not usually carried out as separate operations. Usually, several additional procedures are required (not to mention the cleaning of components and oilways); for this reason, all such tasks are classed as major overhaul procedures, and are described in Part C of this Chapter.

Part C describes the removal of the engine/transmission from the car, and the full overhaul procedures that can then be carried out.

XUD engine description

The engine is a turbocharged four-cylinder overhead camshaft design, mounted transversely, with the transmission mounted on the left-hand side.

An aluminium alloy cylinder head is fitted, incorporating eight valves on 1.9 litre models, and twelve valves on 2.1 litre versions. On 1.9 litre models, the valve clearances are adjusted by shims, positioned between the followers and the tip of the valve stem; on 2.1 litre models the valve clearances are self-adjusting by means of hydraulic tappets fitted to the cam followers.

The camshaft is supported by three bearings machined directly in the cylinder head on 1.9 litre models, and by five bearings within a separate carrier on 2.1 litre models. A toothed timing belt drives the camshaft, fuel injection pump and coolant pump.

The crankshaft runs in five main bearings of the usual shell type. Endfloat is controlled by thrustwashers either side of No 2 main bearing.

The pistons are selected to be of matching weight, and incorporate fully-floating gudgeon pins retained by circlips.

The oil pump is chain-driven from the front of the crankshaft. An oil cooler is fitted to all engines.

Throughout the manual, it is often necessary to identify the engines not only by their cubic capacity, but also by their engine code. The engine code consists of three letters (eg. DHX). The code is stamped on a plate attached to the front of the cylinder block.

Repair operations - precaution

Both the 1.9 and 2.1 litre engines are complex units with numerous accessories and ancillary components. The design of the 406 engine compartment is such that every conceivable space has been utilised, and access to virtually all of the engine components is extremely limited. In many cases, ancillary components will have to be removed, or moved to one side, and wiring, pipes and hoses will have to be disconnected or removed from various cable clips and support brackets.

When working on these engines, read through the entire procedure first, look at the car and engine at the same time, and establish whether you have the necessary tools, equipment, skill and patience to proceed. Allow considerable time for any operation, and be prepared for the unexpected. Any major work on these engines is not for the faint-hearted!

Because of the limited access, many of the photographs appearing in this Chapter were, by necessity, taken with the engine removed from the vehicle.

Repair operations possible with the engine in the vehicle

The following operations can be carried out without having to remove the engine from the vehicle:

1.9 litre models

a) Removal and refitting of the cylinder head.
b) Removal and refitting of the timing belt and sprockets.
c) Removal and refitting of the camshaft.
d) Removal and refitting of the sump.
e) Removal and refitting of the big-end bearings, connecting rods and pistons*.
f) Removal and refitting of the oil pump.
g) Renewal of the engine/transmission mountings.
h) Removal and refitting of the flywheel/driveplate.

*Although it is possible to remove these components with the engine in place, for reasons of access and cleanliness it is recommended that the engine is removed.

2B

2.1 litre models

a) Removal and refitting of the timing belt and sprockets.

b) Removal and refitting of the camshaft and hydraulic tappets.

c) Removal and refitting of the sump.

d) Removal and refitting of the oil pump.

e) Renewal of the engine/transmission mountings.

f) Removal and refitting of the flywheel/driveplate.

Note: On 2.1 litre models, access between the cylinder head and engine compartment bulkhead, and to the rear underside of the engine is so restricted that it is impossible to remove the cylinder head with the engine in the car. Cylinder head removal and refitting procedures are therefore contained in Part C, assuming that the engine/transmission has been removed from the vehicle.

2 Compression and leakdown tests - description and interpretation

Compression test

Note: A compression tester specifically designed for diesel engines must be used for this test.

1 When engine performance is down, or if misfiring occurs which cannot be attributed to the fuel system, a compression test can provide diagnostic clues as to the engine's condition. If the test is performed regularly, it can give warning of trouble before any other symptoms become apparent.

2 A compression tester specifically intended for diesel engines must be used, because of the higher pressures involved. The tester is connected to an adapter which screws into the glow plug or injector hole. On these models, an adapter suitable for use in the injector holes will be required, due to the limited access to the glow plug holes **(see illustration)**. It is unlikely to be worthwhile buying such a tester for occasional use, but it may be possible to borrow or hire one - if not, have the test performed by a garage.

3 Unless specific instructions to the contrary

2.2 Performing a compression test

are supplied with the tester, observe the following points:

a) The battery must be in a good state of charge, the air filter must be clean, and the engine should be at normal operating temperature.

b) All the injectors or glow plugs should be removed before starting the test. If removing the injectors, also remove the flame shield washers, otherwise they may be blown out.

c) On 1.9 litre models, the stop solenoid must be disconnected, to prevent the engine from running or fuel from being discharged. On 2.1 litre models it is normally sufficient to disconnect the fuel injection multi-function relay located in the ECU module box, but the advice of a dealer should be sought.

4 There is no need to hold the accelerator pedal down during the test, because the diesel engine air inlet is not throttled.

5 The actual compression pressures measured are not so important as the balance between cylinders. Values are given in the "Specifications".

6 The cause of poor compression is less easy to establish on a diesel engine than on a petrol one. The effect of introducing oil into the cylinders ("wet" testing) is not conclusive, because there is a risk that the oil will sit in the swirl chamber or in the recess on the piston crown instead of passing to the rings. However, the following can be used as a rough guide to diagnosis.

7 All cylinders should produce very similar pressures; any difference greater than that specified indicates the existence of a fault. Note that the compression should build up quickly in a healthy engine; low compression on the first stroke, followed by gradually-increasing pressure on successive strokes, indicates worn piston rings. A low compression reading on the first stroke, which does not build up during successive strokes, indicates leaking valves or a blown head gasket (a cracked head could also be the cause). Deposits on the undersides of the valve heads can also cause low compression.

8 A low reading from two adjacent cylinders is almost certainly due to the head gasket having blown between them; the presence of coolant in the engine oil will confirm this.

9 If the compression reading is unusually high, the cylinder head surfaces, valves and pistons are probably coated with carbon deposits. If this is the case, the cylinder head should be removed and decarbonised (see Part C).

Leakdown test

10 A leakdown test measures the rate at which compressed air fed into the cylinder is lost. It is an alternative to a compression test, and in many ways it is better, since the escaping air provides easy identification of where pressure loss is occurring (piston rings, valves or head gasket).

11 The equipment needed for leakdown testing is unlikely to be available to the home mechanic. If poor compression is suspected, have the test performed by a suitably-equipped garage.

3 Engine assembly/valve timing holes - general information and usage

Note: Do not attempt to rotate the engine whilst the crankshaft/camshaft/injection pump are locked in position. If the engine is to be left in this state for a long period of time, it is a good idea to place suitable warning notices inside the vehicle, and in the engine compartment. This will reduce the possibility of the engine being accidentally cranked on the starter motor, which is likely to cause damage with the locking pins in place.

1 On all models, timing holes are drilled in the camshaft sprocket, injection pump sprocket and flywheel. The holes are used to align the crankshaft, camshaft and injection pump and to prevent the possibility of the valves contacting the pistons when refitting the cylinder head, or when refitting the timing belt. When the holes are aligned with their corresponding holes in the cylinder head and cylinder block (as appropriate), suitable diameter bolts/pins can be inserted to lock both the camshaft, injection pump and crankshaft in position, preventing them from rotating unnecessarily. Proceed as follows. **Note:** With the timing holes aligned, No 4 cylinder is at TDC on its compression stroke.

2 Remove the upper timing belt covers as described in Section 6.

3 The crankshaft must now be turned until the bolt holes in the camshaft and injection pump sprockets (one hole in the camshaft sprocket, one or two holes in the injection pump sprocket) are aligned with the corresponding holes in the engine front plate. The crankshaft can be turned by using a spanner on the pulley bolt. To gain access to the pulley bolt, from underneath the front of the car, prise out the retaining clips and remove the screws, then withdraw the plastic wheel arch liner from the wing valance, to gain access to the crankshaft pulley bolt. Where necessary, unclip the coolant hoses from the bracket, to improve access further. The crankshaft can then be turned using a suitable socket and extension bar fitted to the pulley bolt. Note that the crankshaft must always be turned in a clockwise direction (viewed from the right-hand side of the vehicle).

4 Insert an 8 mm diameter rod or drill through the hole in the left-hand flange of the cylinder block by the starter motor; if necessary, carefully turn the crankshaft either way until the rod enters the timing hole in the flywheel/driveplate **(see illustrations)**. On 2.1 litre models, access is very restricted, and it may be easier to remove the starter motor (see Chapter 5A) to be able to locate the hole.

3.4a Suitable tools available for locking engine in position

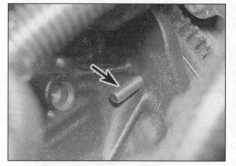

3.4b Rod (arrowed) inserted through cylinder block into timing hole in flywheel/driveplate

3.5a Bolt (arrowed) inserted through timing hole in camshaft sprocket on 1.9 litre models . . .

3.5b . . . and on 2.1 litre models

3.5c Two bolts (arrowed) inserted through timing holes in fuel injection pump sprocket on 1.9 litre models . . .

3.5d . . . and single bolt inserted through the pump sprocket on 2.1 litre models

5 Insert one 8 mm bolt through the hole in the camshaft sprocket, and two (1.9 litre models) or one (2.1 litre models) bolt(s) through the fuel injection pump sprocket, and screw them into the engine finger-tight (see illustrations).
6 The crankshaft, camshaft and injection pump are now locked in position, preventing unnecessary rotation.

4 Cylinder head cover - removal and refitting

Removal

1.9 litre models

1 Disconnect the breather hose from the front

of the cylinder head cover and remove the air cleaner inlet ducts as necessary for access.
2 Unscrew the securing bolt and remove the fuel hose bracket from the right-hand end of the cylinder head cover (see illustration).
3 Disconnect the vacuum hose from the fast idle control diaphragm unit, then undo the two bolts and move the unit to one side.
4 Note the locations of any brackets secured by the three cylinder head cover retaining bolts, then unscrew the bolts. Recover the metal and fibre washers under each bolt (see illustration).
5 Carefully move any hoses clear of the cylinder head cover.
6 Lift off the cover, and recover the rubber seal. Examine the seal for signs of damage and deterioration, and if necessary, renew it.

2.1 litre models

7 Remove the timing belt upper cover as described in Section 6.
8 Remove the inlet manifold upper part as described in Chapter 4B.
9 Disconnect the breather hose from the front of the cylinder head cover.
10 Note the locations of any brackets secured by the cylinder head cover retaining bolts, then unscrew the eleven bolts in a progressive spiral sequence.
11 Carefully move any hoses clear of the cylinder head cover.
12 Lift off the cover, and recover the rubber seal (see illustration). Examine the seal for signs of damage and deterioration, and if necessary, renew it.

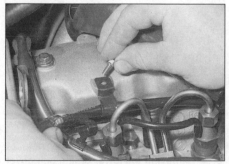

4.2 Removing the fuel hose bracket from the cylinder head cover

4.4 Remove the cylinder head cover retaining bolts and washers

4.12 Lifting off the cylinder head cover on 2.1 litre models

2B

5.1 Notched tool (arrowed) positioned on ring gear teeth to lock flywheel

Refitting

13 Refitting is a reversal of removal, bearing in mind the following points:

a) *Refit any brackets in their original positions noted before removal.*

b) *Refit the inlet manifold (2.1 litre models) and air inlet ducts described in Chapter 4B.*

5 Crankshaft pulley - removal and refitting

1 Refer to Chapter 2A, Section 5. Although not strictly necessary, due to its tightening sequence, it is recommended that the retaining bolt is renewed whenever it is disturbed. **Note:** *If the engine is in the car and it proves impossible to hold on the brakes, remove the starter motor and use the locking tool shown to retain the flywheel* **(see illustration)**.

6 Timing belt covers - removal and refitting

Removal - 1.9 litre models

Upper front cover

1 Slacken and remove the retaining screw and nut, and remove the cover from the engine.

Upper rear cover

2 Remove the front cover as described previously, then undo the retaining bolts and remove the rear cover from the engine.

Lower cover

3 Remove the crankshaft pulley as described in Section 5.

4 Remove both upper covers as described previously.

5 Slacken and remove the retaining nuts and bolts, and remove the lower cover.

Removal - 2.1 litre models

Upper cover

6 Undo the single retaining bolt, located in the centre of the cover **(see illustration)**.

7 Turn the upper fastener a quarter of a turn clockwise to release the locking peg **(see illustration)**.

8 Manipulate the cover up and off the front of the engine.

Centre cover

9 Remove the auxiliary drivebelt as described in Chapter 1B.

10 Undo the two bolts and remove the centre cover from the front of the injection pump **(see illustration)**.

Lower cover

11 Remove the crankshaft pulley as described in Section 5.

12 Remove the right-hand engine mounting assembly as described in Section 19.

13 Remove both upper covers as described previously.

14 Slacken and remove the retaining bolts, and remove the lower cover **(see illustration)**.

Refitting

15 Refitting is a reversal of the relevant removal procedure, ensuring that each cover section is correctly located, and that the cover retaining nuts and/or bolts are tightened to the specified torque.

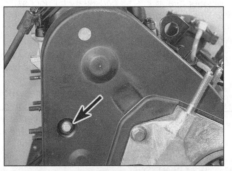

6.6 Undo the single retaining bolt (arrowed), located in the centre of the upper cover on 2.1 litre models

6.10 Removing the centre cover from the front of the injection pump on 2.1 litre models

7 Timing belt - removal, inspection, refitting and tensioning

General

1 The timing belt drives the camshaft, injection pump, and coolant pump from a toothed sprocket on the front of the crankshaft. If the belt breaks or slips in service, the pistons are likely to hit the valve heads, resulting in expensive damage.

2 The timing belt should be renewed at the specified intervals, or earlier if it is contaminated with oil, or at all noisy in operation (a "scraping" noise due to uneven wear).

3 If the timing belt is being removed, it is a wise precaution to check the condition of the coolant pump at the same time (check for signs of coolant leakage). This may avoid the need to remove the timing belt again at a later stage, should the coolant pump fail.

Removal

1.9 litre models

4 Align the engine assembly/valve timing holes as described in Section 3, and lock the camshaft sprocket, injection pump sprocket and flywheel in position. *Do not* attempt to rotate the engine whilst the pins are in position. Disconnect the battery negative terminal.

6.7 On 2.1 litre models, turn the fastener clockwise to release the cover locking peg

6.14 Removing the lower timing belt cover on 2.1 litre models

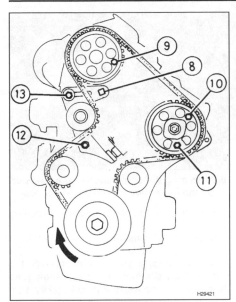

7.6 Removing the timing belt – 1.9 litre models

8 Square hole	12 Tensioner
9 Bolt	pivot nut
10 Bolt	13 Adjustment bolt
11 Bolt	

5 Remove the remaining timing belt covers as described in Section 6.

6 Remove the right-hand engine mounting and mounting bracket as described in Section 9, then loosen the timing belt tensioner pivot nut and adjustment bolt, then turn the tensioner bracket anti-clockwise to release the tension. Retighten the adjustment bolt to hold the tensioner in the released position. If available, use a 10 mm square drive extension in the hole provided, to turn the tensioner bracket against the spring tension (**see illustration**).

7 Mark the timing belt with an arrow to indicate its running direction, if it is to be re-used. Remove the belt from the sprockets.

2.1 litre models

8 Align the engine assembly/valve timing holes as described in Section 3, and lock the camshaft sprocket, injection pump sprocket

7.11 On 2.1 litre models, slacken the timing belt tensioner locking bolt using a 5 mm Allen key

and flywheel in position. *Do not* attempt to rotate the engine whilst the pins are in position. Disconnect the battery negative terminal.

9 Remove the remaining timing belt covers as described in Section 6.

10 Slacken the timing belt tensioner pulley retaining nut, situated just to the left of the engine mounting carrier bracket.

11 Using a 5 mm Allen key inserted through the hole in the engine mounting carrier bracket, slacken the timing belt tensioner locking bolt (**see illustration**).

12 Using a 10 mm socket or box spanner inserted through the same hole, retract the tensioner by turning its shaft clockwise to the extent of its travel (**see illustrations**).

13 Mark the timing belt with an arrow to indicate its running direction, if it is to be re-used. Remove the belt from the sprockets (**see illustration**).

Inspection

14 Check the timing belt carefully for any signs of uneven wear, split or oil contamination. Pay particular attention to the roots of the teeth. Renew it if there is the slightest doubt about its condition. If the engine is undergoing an overhaul, and has covered more than 36 000 miles (60 000 km) with the existing belt fitted, renew the belt as a matter of course, regardless of its apparent condition. The cost of a new belt is nothing compared with the cost of repairs, should the belt break in service. If signs of oil contamination are found, trace the source of the oil leak and rectify it. Wash down

the engine timing belt area and all related components, to remove all traces of oil. Check that the tensioner and idler pulley rotates freely, without any sign of roughness. If necessary, renew as described in Sections 9 and 10 (as applicable).

Refitting and tensioning

1.9 litre models

15 Commence refitting by ensuring that the 8 mm bolts are still fitted to the camshaft and fuel injection pump sprockets, and that the rod/drill is positioned in the timing hole in the flywheel.

16 Locate the timing belt on the crankshaft sprocket, making sure that, where applicable, the direction of rotation arrow is facing the correct way.

17 Engage the timing belt with the crankshaft sprocket, hold it in position, then feed the belt over the remaining sprockets in the following order:

a) *Idler roller.*
b) *Fuel injection pump.*
c) *Camshaft.*
d) *Tensioner roller.*
e) *Coolant pump.*

18 Be careful not to kink or twist the belt. To ensure correct engagement, locate only a half-width on the injection pump sprocket before feeding the timing belt onto the camshaft sprocket, keeping the belt taut and fully engaged with the crankshaft sprocket. Locate the timing belt fully onto the sprockets.

19 Unscrew and remove the bolts from the camshaft and fuel injection pump sprockets and remove the rod/drill from the timing hole in the flywheel.

20 With the pivot nut loose, slacken the tensioner adjustment bolt while holding the bracket against the spring tension. Slowly release the bracket until the roller presses against the timing belt. Retighten the adjustment bolt and the pivot nut.

21 Rotate the crankshaft through two complete turns in the normal running direction (clockwise). **Do not** rotate the crankshaft backwards, as the timing belt must be kept tight between the crankshaft, fuel injection pump and camshaft sprockets.

2B

7.12a Timing belt tensioner pulley retaining nut (A) and locking bolt (B) on 2.1 litre models

7.12b Timing belt tensioner arrangement on 2.1 litre models showing tensioner 10 mm shaft (arrowed)

7.13 Removing the timing belt

22 Loosen the tensioner adjustment bolt and the pivot nut to allow the tensioner spring to push the roller against the timing belt, then tighten both the adjustment bolt and pivot nut to the specified torque.

23 Check that the timing holes are all correctly positioned by reinserting the sprocket locking bolts and the rod/drill in the flywheel timing hole, as described in Section 3. If the timing holes are not correctly positioned, the timing belt has been incorrectly fitted (possibly one tooth out on one of the sprockets) - in this case, repeat the refitting procedure from the beginning.

24 The remaining refitting procedure is a reversal of removal.

2.1 litre models

25 Commence refitting by ensuring that the 8 mm bolts are still fitted to the camshaft and fuel injection pump sprockets, and that the rod/drill is positioned in the timing hole in the flywheel.

26 Ensure that the timing belt tensioner is still retracted, then tighten the tensioner pulley retaining nut. Using the 10 mm socket or box spanner, release the tensioner by turning it anti-clockwise to the extent of its travel.

27 Locate the timing belt on the crankshaft sprocket, making sure that, where applicable, the direction of rotation arrow is facing the correct way.

28 Engage the timing belt with the crankshaft sprocket, hold it in position, then feed the belt over the remaining sprockets in the following order:

   a) Idler roller.
   b) Fuel injection pump.
   c) Camshaft.
   d) Coolant pump.
   e) Tensioner roller.

29 Be careful not to kink or twist the belt. To ensure correct engagement, locate only a half-width on the injection pump sprocket before feeding the timing belt onto the camshaft sprocket, keeping the belt taut and fully engaged with the crankshaft sprocket. Locate the timing belt fully onto the sprockets.

30 Slacken the tensioner pulley retaining nut to allow the tensioner to tension the belt.

31 Unscrew and remove the bolts from the camshaft and fuel injection pump sprockets and remove the rod/drill from the timing hole in the flywheel.

32 Rotate the crankshaft through two complete turns in the normal running direction (clockwise). **Do not** rotate the crankshaft backwards, as the timing belt must be kept tight between the crankshaft, fuel injection pump and camshaft sprockets.

33 Slacken the tensioner pulley retaining nut, then rotate the crankshaft through a further two complete turns in the normal running direction, stopping at the timing setting position.

34 Slacken the tensioner pulley retaining nut one turn to allow the tensioner to finally tension the belt. Tighten tensioner pulley retaining nut and the timing belt tensioner locking bolt to the specified torque.

A sprocket holding tool can be made from two lengths of steel strip bolted together to form a forked end. Bend the ends of the strip through 90° to form the fork "prongs"

35 Check that the timing holes are all correctly positioned by reinserting the sprocket locking bolts and the rod/drill in the flywheel timing hole, as described in Section 3. If the timing holes are not correctly positioned, the timing belt has been incorrectly fitted (possibly one tooth out on one of the sprockets) - in this case, repeat the refitting procedure from the beginning.

36 The remaining refitting procedure is a reversal of removal.

8 Timing belt sprockets - removal and refitting

Camshaft sprocket

Removal

1 Remove the timing belt (see Section 7).

2 Slacken the camshaft sprocket retaining bolt and remove it, along with its washer. To prevent the camshaft rotating as the bolt is slackened, a sprocket holding tool will be required **(see Tool Tip)**. *Do not* attempt to use the sprocket locking pin to prevent the sprocket from rotating whilst the bolt is slackened. Alternatively on 1.9 litre models, remove the cylinder head cover as described in Section 4. Prevent the camshaft from turning by holding it with a suitable spanner on the lug between Nos 3 and 4 camshaft lobes **(see illustration)**.

8.5 Withdrawing the camshaft sprocket

8.2 Holding the camshaft using a spanner on the lug between Nos 3 and 4 lobes

3 Remove the camshaft sprocket retaining bolt and washer.

4 Unscrew and remove the locking bolt from the camshaft sprocket.

5 With the retaining bolt removed, slide the sprocket off the end of the camshaft **(see illustration)**. Recover the Woodruff key from the end of the camshaft if it is loose. Examine the camshaft oil seal for signs of oil leakage and, if necessary, renew it (see Section 16).

Refitting

6 Refit the Woodruff key to the end of the camshaft, then refit the camshaft sprocket. Note that the sprocket will only fit one way round (with the protruding centre boss against the camshaft), as the end of the camshaft is tapered.

7 Refit the sprocket retaining bolt and washer. Tighten the bolt to the specified torque, preventing the camshaft from turning as during removal.

8 Where applicable, refit the cylinder head cover as described in Section 4.

9 Align the holes in the camshaft sprocket and the engine front plate, and refit the 8 mm bolt to lock the camshaft in position.

10 Refit it the timing belt as described in Section 7.

11 Refit the timing belt covers as described in Section 6.

Crankshaft sprocket

Removal

12 Remove the timing belt (see Section 7).

13 Slide the sprocket off the end of the crankshaft **(see illustration)**.

8.13 Withdrawing the crankshaft sprocket

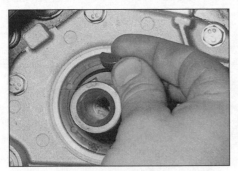

8.14 Removing the Woodruff key from the end of the crankshaft

8.21 Using a home-made tool to prevent the fuel injection pump sprocket turning

8.23 Home-made puller fitted to fuel injection pump sprocket

14 Remove the Woodruff key from the crankshaft, and store it with the sprocket for safe-keeping **(see illustration)**.
15 Examine the crankshaft oil seal for signs of oil leakage and, if necessary, renew it as described in Section 16.

Refitting

16 Refit the Woodruff key to the end of the crankshaft, then refit the crankshaft sprocket (with the flange nearest the cylinder block).
17 Refit the timing belt as described in Section 7.

Fuel injection pump sprocket

Removal

18 Remove the timing belt as described in Section 7.
19 Remove the 8 mm bolt(s) securing the fuel injection pump sprocket in the TDC position.
20 On certain models, the sprocket may be fitted with a built-in puller, which consists of a plate bolted to the sprocket. The plate contains a captive nut (the sprocket securing nut), which is screwed onto the fuel injection pump shaft. On models not fitted with the built-in puller, a suitable puller can be made up using a short length of bar, and two M7 bolts screwed into the holes provided in the sprocket.
21 The fuel injection pump shaft must be prevented from turning as the sprocket nut is unscrewed, and this can be achieved using a tool similar to that shown **(see illustration)**. Use the tool to hold the sprocket stationary by means of the holes in the sprocket.
22 On models with a built-in puller, unscrew the sprocket securing nut until the sprocket is freed from the taper on the pump shaft, then withdraw the sprocket. Recover the Woodruff key from the end of the pump shaft if it is loose. If desired, the puller assembly can be removed from the sprocket by removing the two securing screws and washers.
23 On models not fitted with a built-in puller, partially unscrew the sprocket securing nut, then fit the improvised puller, and tighten the two bolts (forcing the bar against the sprocket nut), until the sprocket is freed from the taper on the pump shaft **(see illustration)**. Withdraw the sprocket and recover the Woodruff key from the end of the pump shaft

if it is loose. Remove the puller from the sprocket.

Refitting

24 Refit the Woodruff key to the pump shaft, ensuring that it is correctly located in its groove.
25 Where applicable, if the built-in puller assembly has been removed from the sprocket, refit it, and tighten the two securing screws securely ensuring that the washers are in place.
26 Refit the sprocket, then tighten the securing nut to the specified torque, preventing the pump shaft from turning as during removal.
27 Make sure that the 8 mm bolts are fitted to the camshaft and fuel injection pump sprockets, and that the rod/drill is positioned in the flywheel timing hole.
28 Fit the timing belt around the fuel injection pump sprocket, ensuring that the marks made on the belt and sprocket before removal are aligned.
29 Tension the timing belt as described in Section 7.
30 Refit the upper timing belt covers as described in Section 6.

Coolant pump sprocket

31 The coolant pump sprocket is integral with the pump, and cannot be removed.

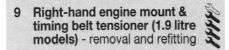

9 Right-hand engine mount & timing belt tensioner (1.9 litre models) - removal and refitting

General

1 The timing belt tensioner is operated by a spring and plunger housed in the right-hand engine mounting bracket, which is bolted to the end face of the engine. The engine mounting is attached to the mounting on the body via the engine mounting-to-body bracket.

Right-hand engine mounting-to-body bracket

Removal

2 Before removing the bracket, the engine must be supported, preferably using a

suitable hoist and lifting tackle attached to the lifting bracket at the right-hand end of the engine. Alternatively, the engine can be supported using a trolley jack and interposed block of wood beneath the sump. In which case, be prepared for the engine to tilt backwards when the bracket is removed.
3 Release the retaining clips and position all the relevant hoses and cables clear of the engine mounting assembly and suspension top mounting.
4 Unscrew the three nuts securing the bracket to the engine mounting, and the single nut securing the bracket to the body, then lift off the bracket.

Refitting

5 Refitting is a reversal of removal. Tighten the retaining nuts and bolts to the specified torque.

Timing belt tensioner and right-hand engine mounting bracket

Note: *A suitable tool will be required to retain the timing belt tensioner plunger during this operation.*

Removal

6 Remove the engine mounting-to-body bracket as described previously in this Section, and remove the auxiliary drivebelt as described in Chapter 1B.
7 If not already done, support the engine with a trolley jack and interposed block of wood beneath the sump.
8 Where applicable, disconnect the hoist and lifting tackle supporting the engine from the right-hand lifting bracket (this is necessary because the lifting bracket is attached to the engine mounting bracket, and must be removed).
9 Unscrew the two retaining bolts and remove the engine lifting bracket.
10 Align the engine assembly/valve timing holes as described in Section 3, and lock the camshaft sprocket, injection pump sprocket and flywheel in position. *Do not* attempt to rotate the engine whilst the pins are in position.
11 Loosen the timing belt tensioner pivot nut and adjustment bolt, then turn the tensioner bracket anti-clockwise until the adjustment bolt is in the middle of the slot, and retighten

2B

Fabricated tool for holding tensioner plunger in engine mounting bracket

9.15a View of timing belt end of engine
1 *Engine mounting bracket retaining bolts*
2 *Timing belt tensioner plunger*

9.15b Tool in place to hold tensioner plunger in engine mounting bracket - timing belt removed for clarity

the adjustment bolt. If available, use a 10 mm square drive extension in the hole provided, to turn the tensioner bracket against the spring tension.

12 Mark the timing belt with an arrow to indicate its running direction, if it is to be re-used. Remove the belt from the sprockets.

13 A tool must now be obtained in order to hold the tensioner plunger in the engine mounting bracket.

14 The Peugeot tool is designed to slide in the two lower bolt holes of the mounting bracket. It should be straightforward to fabricate a similar tool out of sheet metal, and using 10 mm bolts and nuts instead of metal dowel rods **(see Tool Tip)**.

15 Unscrew the two lower engine mounting bracket bolts, then fit the special tool. Grease the inner surface of the tool, to prevent any damage to the end of the tensioner plunger **(see illustrations)**. Unscrew the pivot nut and adjustment bolt, and withdraw the tensioner assembly.

16 Remove the two remaining engine mounting bracket bolts, and withdraw the bracket.

17 Compress the tensioner plunger into the engine mounting bracket, remove the special tool, then withdraw the plunger and spring.

Refitting

18 Refitting is a reversal of removal, bearing in mind the following points:
a) *Tighten all fixings to the specified torque.*
b) *Refit and tension the timing belt as described in Section 7.*
c) *Refit and tighten the auxiliary drivebelt as described in Chapter 1B.*

10 Timing belt idler roller - removal and refitting

Removal

1.9 litre models

1 Remove the auxiliary drivebelt as described in Chapter 1B.

2 Align the engine assembly/valve timing

holes as described in Section 3, and lock the camshaft sprocket, injection pump sprocket and flywheel in position. *Do not* attempt to rotate the engine whilst the pins are in position.

3 Loosen the timing belt tensioner pivot nut and adjustment bolt, then turn the tensioner bracket anti-clockwise to release the tension, and retighten the adjustment bolt to hold the tensioner in the released position. If available, use a 10 mm square drive extension in the hole provided, to turn the tensioner bracket against spring pressure.

4 Unscrew the two bolts and the stud securing the idler roller assembly to the cylinder block, noting that the upper bolt also secures the engine mounting bracket.

5 Slightly loosen the remaining four engine mounting bolts, noting that the uppermost bolt is on the inside face of the engine front plate, and also secures the engine lifting bracket. Slide out the idler roller assembly.

2.1 litre models

6 Remove the timing belt as described in Section 7.

7 Unscrew the idler roller centre bolt and remove it from the engine.

Refitting

8 Refitting is a reversal of removal, bearing in mind the following points:
a) *Tighten all fixings to the specified torque.*
b) *Refit and/or tension the timing belt as described in Section 7.*
c) *Refit and tension the auxiliary drivebelt as described in Chapter 1B.*

11 Camshaft and followers - removal, inspection and refitting

Removal

1.9 litre models

1 Remove the cylinder head cover as described in Section 4.

2 Remove the camshaft sprocket as described in Section 8.

3 Remove the braking system vacuum pump as described in Chapter 9.

4 The camshaft bearing caps should be numbered from the flywheel end of the engine **(see illustration)**. If the caps are not already numbered, identify them, numbering them from the flywheel end of the engine, and making the marks on the manifold side.

5 Progressively unscrew the nuts, then remove the bearing caps.

6 Lift the camshaft from the cylinder head. Remove the oil seal from the timing belt end of the camshaft. Discard the seal, a new one should be used on refitting.

7 Obtain eight small, clean plastic containers, and number them 1 to 8; alternatively, divide a larger container into eight compartments. Using a rubber sucker, withdraw each follower in turn, and place it in its respective container. Do not interchange the cam followers, or the rate of wear will be much-increased. If necessary, also remove the shim from the top of the valve stem, and store it with its respective follower. Note that the shim may stick to the inside of the follower as it is withdrawn. If this happens, take care not to allow it to drop out as the follower is removed.

2.1 litre models

8 Remove the cylinder head cover as described in Section 4.

9 Remove the camshaft sprocket as described in Section 8.

10 Remove the braking system vacuum pump as described in Chapter 9. Recover the

11.4 Camshaft bearing cap identification mark (arrowed)

11.10 Recover the vacuum pump oil feed tube on 2.1 litre models

11.14 On 2.1 litre models, lift the camshaft carrier, complete with camshaft, upwards off the locating dowels

11.16 Undo the two bolts securing the camshaft thrust plate (arrowed)

11.18a Lift off the rockers . . .

11.18b . . . and their guides and place them in their respective containers

11.19 Remove the oil filter tube from its cylinder head location

2B

vacuum pump oil feed tube from the end of the camshaft **(see illustration)**.

11 Refer to Chapter 4B and remove the fuel supply and leak-off pipes from the fuel injectors.

12 Disconnect the oil return hose from the front of the camshaft carrier.

13 Working in a spiral sequence, progressive slacken and remove the sixteen camshaft carrier retaining bolts.

14 Lift the camshaft carrier, complete with camshaft, upwards off the locating dowels **(see illustration)**.

15 Extract the oil seal from the end of the camshaft carrier.

16 Undo the two bolts securing the camshaft thrust plate, and carefully slide the camshaft out of the carrier **(see illustration)**.

17 Obtain twelve clean plastic containers, and number them inlet 1 to 8, and exhaust 1 to 4; alternatively, divide a larger container into twelve compartments.

18 Lift off the rockers and their guides and place them in their respective containers **(see illustrations)**. Withdraw each hydraulic tappet in turn, and place it in its respective container. Do not interchange the tappets, or the rate of wear will be much-increased.

19 Remove the oil filter tube from its location in the cylinder head **(see illustration)**.

Inspection

20 Examine the camshaft bearing surfaces and cam lobes for signs of wear ridges and scoring. Renew the camshaft if any of these conditions are apparent. Examine the condition of the bearing surfaces, both on the camshaft journals and in the cylinder head/camshaft carrier/bearing caps. If the bearing surfaces are worn excessively, the cylinder head/camshaft carrier will need to be renewed.

21 Examine the cam follower/tappet bearing surfaces which contact the camshaft lobes or rockers for wear ridges and scoring. Renew any component on which these conditions are apparent. If a follower/tappet bearing surface is badly scored, also examine the corresponding rocker or lobe on the camshaft for wear, as it is likely that both will be worn. Renew worn components as necessary.

Refitting

1.9 litre models

22 Where removed, refit each shim to the top of its original valve stem. *Do not* interchange the shims, as this will upset the valve clearances (see Section 12).

23 Liberally oil the cylinder head cam follower bores and the followers. Carefully refit the followers to the cylinder head, ensuring that each follower is refitted to its original bore. Some care will be required to enter the followers squarely into their bores.

24 Lubricate the cam lobes and bearing journals with clean engine oil of the specified grade.

25 Temporarily refit the sprocket to the end

of the camshaft and note the position of the timing hole in relation to the timing hole in the cylinder head - the lobes of No 4 cylinder should be facing upwards. Remove the sprocket, then position the camshaft in the cylinder head passing it through the engine front plate and keeping No 4 cylinder lobes facing upwards. Ensure that the crankshaft is still locked in position (see Section 3).

26 Fit the centre bearing cap the correct way round as previously noted, then screw on the nuts and tighten them two or three turns.

27 Apply sealing compound to the end bearing caps on the areas shown **(see illustration)**. Fit them in the correct positions, and tighten the nuts two or three turns.

28 Tighten all the nuts progressively to the specified torque, making sure that the camshaft remains correctly positioned.

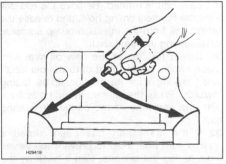

11.27 Apply sealing compound to the end camshaft bearing caps on the areas shown

11.29 **Checking the camshaft endfloat using a feeler blade**

11.37 **Lubricate each hydraulic tappet and place it in its bore**

11.38a **Position the guides . . .**

11.38b **. . . and rockers over their respective valves**

11.40a **Lubricate the lips of a new camshaft oil seal and fit the seal to the camshaft carrier . . .**

11.40b **. . . tap the seal into position using a suitable socket**

29 Check that the camshaft endfloat is as given in the Specifications, using a feeler blade. If not, the camshaft and/or the cylinder head must be renewed. To check the endfloat, push the camshaft fully towards one end of the cylinder head, and insert a feeler blade between the thrust faces of one of the camshaft lobes and a bearing cap **(see illustration)**.

30 If the original camshaft is being refitted, and it is known that the valve clearances are correct, proceed to the next paragraph. Otherwise, check and adjust the valve clearances as described in Section 12. Note that, because the timing belt is still disconnected at this stage, the crankshaft *must* be turned one quarter-turn (either way) from the TDC position, so that all the pistons are halfway down the cylinders. This will prevent the valves striking the pistons when the camshaft is rotated. Remove the rod/drill from the flywheel timing hole, and release the timing belt from the injection pump sprocket while turning the crankshaft.

31 Smear the lips of the new oil seal with clean engine oil and fit it onto the camshaft end, making sure its sealing lip is facing inwards. Press the oil seal in until it is flush with the end face of the camshaft bearing cap.

32 If the crankshaft has been turned a quarter-turn from TDC to prevent the valves from hitting the pistons, turn it back by the same amount so that pistons 1 and 4 are again at TDC. Do not turn the engine more

than a quarter-turn, otherwise pistons 2 and 3 will pass their TDC positions, and will strike the valves.

33 Refit the rod/drill to the flywheel timing hole.

34 Refit the camshaft sprocket as described in Section 8.

35 Refit the cylinder head cover as described in Section 4.

2.1 litre models

36 Liberally lubricate the camshaft and the camshaft bearing journals in the carrier and slide the camshaft into the carrier. Refit the thrust plate and secure with the two bolts.

37 Liberally lubricate each hydraulic tappet and place it in its respective bore **(see illustration)**.

38 Lubricate the guides and rockers and place all twelve over their respective valves **(see illustrations)**. Ensure that the guides are fitted with their slots facing upwards, and that the rockers engage with the guide slots.

39 Insert a new oil filter tube to its bore in the cylinder head.

40 Liberally lubricate the lips of a new camshaft oil seal and fit the seal to the camshaft carrier. Tap the seal into position using a socket of suitable diameter, or the old seal **(see illustrations)**.

41 Apply a bead of silicone sealant to the space between the groove and the outer edge of the camshaft carrier **(see illustration)**. Ensure that the sealant is applied all around the two bolt holes at the timing belt end of the carrier.

42 Locate the assembled camshaft carrier on the cylinder head, taking care not to dislodge the rockers and guides.

43 Refit the retaining bolts, then working in a spiral sequence from the centre outward, progressively tighten the camshaft carrier retaining bolts to the specified torque.

44 Reconnect the oil return hose to the front of the carrier.

45 Refit the fuel supply and leak-off pipes to the fuel injectors with reference to Chapter 4B.

46 Ensure that the oil feed tube is in place, then refit the braking system vacuum pump as described in Chapter 9.

47 Refit the camshaft sprocket as described in Section 8.

48 Refit the cylinder head cover as described in Section 4.

11.41 **Apply a bead of silicone sealant to the space between the groove and the outer edge of the camshaft carrier**

12 Valve clearances (1.9 litre models) - checking and adjustment

Checking

1 The importance of having the valve clearances correctly adjusted cannot be overstressed, as they vitally affect the performance of the engine. Checking should not be regarded as a routine operation, however. It should only be necessary when the valve gear has become noisy, after engine overhaul, or when trying to trace the cause of power loss. The clearances are checked as follows. The engine must be cold for the check to be accurate.

2 Apply the handbrake, then jack up the front of the car and support it on axle stands. Remove the right-hand front roadwheel.

3 From underneath the front of the car, remove the wheel arch liner from the wing valance to gain access to the crankshaft sprocket bolt.

4 The engine can now be turned over using a suitable socket and extension bar fitted to the crankshaft pulley bolt. **Note:** *The engine will be easier to turn if the fuel injectors or glow plugs are removed.*

5 Remove the cylinder head cover as described in Section 4.

6 On a piece of paper, draw the outline of the engine with the cylinders numbered from the flywheel end. Show the position of each valve, together with the specified valve clearance. Above each valve, draw two lines for noting (1) the actual clearance and (2) the amount of adjustment required **(see illustration)**.

7 Turn the crankshaft until the inlet valve of No 1 cylinder (nearest the transmission) is fully closed, with the tip of the cam facing directly away from the bucket tappet.

8 Using feeler blades, measure the clearance

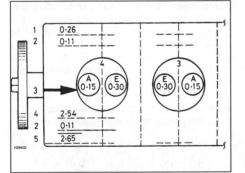

12.6 Example of valve shim thickness calculation

A *Inlet*
E *Exhaust*
1 *Measured clearance*
2 *Difference between 1 and 3*
3 *Specified clearance*
4 *Thickness of shim fitted*
5 *Thickness of shim required*

between the base of the cam and the bucket tappet. Record the clearance on line (1).

9 Repeat the measurement for the other seven valves, turning the crankshaft as necessary so that the cam lobe in question is always facing directly away from the relevant tappet.

10 Calculate the difference between each measured clearance and the desired value, and record it on line (2). Since the clearance is different for inlet and exhaust valves, make sure that you are aware which valve you are dealing with. The valve sequence from either end of the engine is:

In - Ex - Ex - In - In - Ex - Ex - In

11 If all the clearances are within tolerance, refit the cylinder head cover with reference to Section 4, and where applicable, lower the vehicle to the ground. If any clearance measured is outside the specified tolerance, adjustment must be carried out as described in the following paragraphs.

Adjustment

12 Remove the camshaft as described in Section 11.

13 Withdraw the first follower and its shim. Be careful that the shim does not fall out of the tappet. Clean the shim, and measure its thickness with a micrometer. The shims carry thickness markings, but wear may have reduced the original thickness, so be sure to check.

14 Refer to the clearance recorded for the valve concerned. If the clearance was more than that specified, the shim thickness must be increased by the difference recorded (2). If the clearance was less than that specified, the thickness of the shim must be decreased by the difference recorded (2).

15 Draw three more lines beneath each valve on the calculation paper, as shown in illustration 12.6. On line (4) note the measured thickness of the shim, then add or deduct the difference from line (2) to give the final shim thickness required on line (5).

16 Repeat the procedure given in paragraphs 13 to 15 on the remaining valves, keeping each tappet identified for position.

17 When reassembling, oil the shim and fit it into the valve retainer, with the size marking face downwards. Oil the follower and lower it onto the shim. Do not raise the follower after fitting, as the shim may become dislodged.

18 When all the followers are in position, complete with their shims, refit the camshaft as described in Section 11. Recheck the valve clearances before refitting the cylinder head cover, to make sure they are correct.

13 Cylinder head (1.9 litre models) - removal and refitting

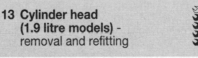

Note 1: *This is an involved procedure, and it is suggested that the Section is read thoroughly before starting work. To aid refitting, make*

notes on the locations of all relevant brackets and the routing of hoses and cables before removal.

Note 2: *Due to the limited access, it is necessary to remove the engine/transmission from the car to remove and refit the cylinder head on 2.1 litre models. Refer to Part C for the full procedure.*

Removal

1 Disconnect the battery negative terminal

2 Drain the cooling system as described in Chapter 1B.

3 Remove the inlet and exhaust manifolds as described in Chapter 4B. Alternatively, remove the inlet manifold as described in Chapter 4B, then unscrew the exhaust manifold securing nuts, remove the spacers, and remove the manifold studs from the cylinder head (using a stud extractor or two nuts locked together). The exhaust manifold can then be left in place complete with the turbocharger.

4 Ensure that the manifold and turbocharger are adequately supported, taking particular care not to strain the turbocharger oil feed pipe.

5 Disconnect and remove the fuel injector leak-off hoses.

6 Disconnect the fuel pipes from the fuel injectors and the fuel injection pump, and remove the pipes as described in Chapter 4B.

7 Unscrew the securing nut and disconnect the feed wire from the relevant glow plug. Recover the washers.

8 Disconnect the coolant hose from the rear, left-hand end of the cylinder head.

9 Disconnect the small coolant hose from the front timing belt end of the cylinder head.

10 Unclip the fuel return hose from the brackets on the cylinder head, and move it to one side.

11 Disconnect the accelerator cable from the fuel injection pump (with reference to Chapter 4B if necessary), and move the cable clear of the cylinder head.

12 Remove the fuel filter/thermostat housing as described in Chapter 3.

13 Unscrew the nut or stud securing the coolant hose bracket and the engine lifting bracket to the transmission end of the cylinder head.

14 Remove the camshaft sprocket as described in Section 8.

15 Remove the timing belt tensioner and the right-hand engine mounting bracket as described in Section 9.

16 Remove the timing belt idler roller as described in Section 10.

17 Remove the bolt securing the engine front plate to the fuel injection pump mounting bracket.

18 Remove the nut and bolt securing the engine front plate and the alternator mounting bracket to the fuel injection pump mounting bracket, then remove the engine front plate.

19 Progressively unscrew the cylinder head bolts, in the reverse order to that shown in

2B

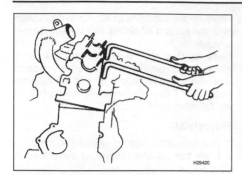

13.21 Freeing the cylinder head using angled rods

13.24 Measuring piston protrusion

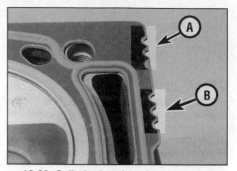

13.26 Cylinder head gasket thickness identification notches (A). Also note engine capacity and type identification notches (B)

illustration 13.34 (a T55 Torx bit will be required to loosen the bolts).

20 Lift out the bolts and recover the spacers.

21 Release the cylinder head from the cylinder block and location dowel by rocking it. The Peugeot tool for doing this consists simply of two metal rods with 90-degree angled ends **(see illustration)**. Do not prise between the mating faces of the cylinder head and block, as this may damage the gasket faces.

22 Lift the cylinder head from the block, and recover the gasket.

Gasket selection

23 Check that the timing belt is clear of the fuel injection pump sprocket, then turn the crankshaft until pistons 1 and 4 are at TDC. Position a dial test indicator (dial gauge) on the cylinder block, and zero it on the block face. Transfer the probe to the centre of No 1 piston, then slowly turn the crankshaft back and forth past TDC, noting the highest reading on the indicator. Record this reading.

24 Repeat this measurement procedure on No 4 piston, then turn the crankshaft half a turn (180°) and repeat the procedure on Nos 2 and 3 pistons **(see illustration)**.

25 If a dial test indicator is not available, piston protrusion may be measured using a straight-edge and feeler blades or vernier calipers. However, these methods are inevitably less accurate, and cannot therefore be recommended.

26 Note down the greatest piston protrusion measurement, and use this to determine the correct cylinder head gasket from the following table. Note that the notches or holes on the centre-line of the gasket identify the engine capacity and type, and have no significance for the gasket thickness **(see illustration)**.

Piston protrusion	Gasket identification
0.54 to 0.65 mm	1 notch
0.65 to 0.77 mm	2 notches
0.77 to 0.82 mm	3 notches

Cylinder head bolt examination

27 The manufacturers recommend that the cylinder head bolts are measured, to determine

whether renewal is necessary; however, some owners may wish to renew all the bolts as a matter of course. Note that, if a bolt is modified to locate the gasket (see paragraph 30), a new bolt will be required when finally refitting the cylinder head.

28 Measure the length of each bolt from the base of the head to the end of the shank. Compare the results with the values given in the following table, to determine whether the bolts and spacers should be renewed. **Note:** *Considering the stress which the cylinder head bolts are under, it is highly recommended that they are renewed, regardless of their apparent condition.*

Bolt length	Action required
145.0 to 146.5 mm	*Re-use bolts and spacers*
Above 146.5 mm	*Renew bolts and spacers*

Refitting

29 Turn the crankshaft clockwise (viewed from the timing belt end) until Nos 1 and 4 pistons pass bottom dead centre (BDC) and begin to rise, then position them halfway up their bores. Nos 2 and 3 pistons will also be at their mid-way positions, but descending their bores.

30 Fit the correct gasket the right way round on the cylinder block, with the identification notches or holes at the flywheel/driveplate end of the engine. Make sure that the locating dowel is in place at the timing belt end of the block. Note that, as there is only one locating dowel, it is possible for the gasket to move as the cylinder head is fitted, particularly when the cylinder head is fitted with the engine in the car (due to the inclination of the engine). In the worst instance, this can allow the pistons and/or the valves to hit the gasket, causing engine damage. To avoid this problem, saw the head off a cylinder head bolt, and file (or cut) a slot in the end of the bolt, to enable it to be turned with a screwdriver. Screw the bolt into one of the bolt holes at the flywheel/driveplate end of the cylinder block, then fit the gasket over the bolt and location dowel. This will ensure that the gasket is held in position as the cylinder head is fitted.

31 Lower the cylinder head onto the block.

32 Apply a smear of grease to the threads,

and to the underside of the heads, of the cylinder head bolts. Peugeot recommend the use of Molykote G Rapid Plus (available from your Peugeot dealer); in the absence of the specified grease, any good-quality high-melting-point grease may be used.

33 Carefully enter each bolt and spacer (convex sides uppermost, where applicable) into its relevant hole (*do not drop it in*) and screw it in finger-tight. Where applicable, after fitting three or four bolts to locate the cylinder head, unscrew the modified bolt fitted in paragraph 30, and fit a new bolt in its place.

34 Working progressively and in the sequence shown, tighten the cylinder head bolts to their stage 1 torque setting, using a torque wrench and suitable socket **(see illustration)**.

35 Once all the bolts have been tightened to their stage 1 torque setting, tighten all bolts to their stage 2 specified torque setting, again following the specified sequence.

36 With all the bolts tightened to their stage 2 setting, working again in the specified sequence, angle-tighten the bolts through the specified stage 3 angle using a socket and extension bar. It is recommended that an angle-measuring gauge is used during this stage of tightening, to ensure accuracy. If a gauge is not available, use white paint to make alignment marks between the bolt head and cylinder head prior to tightening; the marks can then be used to check that the bolt has rotated sufficiently.

37 The remainder of refitting is a direct reversal of the removal procedure, bearing in mind the points made in paragraph 36.

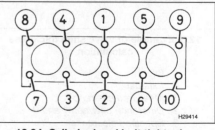

13.34 Cylinder head bolt tightening sequence

14 Sump - removal and refitting

Refer to Chapter 2A, Section 13.

15 Oil pump - removal, inspection and refitting

Refer to Chapter 2A, Section 14.

16 Oil seals - renewal

Crankshaft right-hand oil seal

1 Remove the crankshaft sprocket as described in Section 8.

2 Measure and note the fitted depth of the oil seal.

3 Pull the oil seal from the housing using a hooked instrument. Alternatively, drill a small hole in the oil seal, and use a self-tapping screw and a pair of pliers to remove it.

4 Clean the oil seal housing and the crankshaft sealing surface.

5 Dip the new oil seal in clean engine oil, and press it into the housing (open end first) to the previously-noted depth, using a suitable tube or socket. A piece of thin plastic or tape wound around the front of the crankshaft is useful to prevent damage to the oil seal as it is fitted.

6 Where applicable, remove the plastic or tape from the end of the crankshaft.

7 Refit the timing belt crankshaft sprocket as described in Section 8.

Crankshaft left-hand oil seal

8 Remove the flywheel/driveplate, as described in Section 18.

9 Proceed as described in paragraphs 2 to 6, noting that when fitted, the outer lip of the oil seal must point outwards; if it is pointing inwards, use a piece of bent wire to pull it out. Take care not to damage the oil seal.

10 Refit the flywheel/driveplate, as described in Section 18.

Camshaft right-hand oil seal

11 Remove the camshaft sprocket as described in Section 8. In principle there is no need to remove the timing belt completely, but remember that if the belt has been contaminated with oil, it must be renewed.

12 Pull the oil seal from the housing using a hooked instrument. Alternatively, drill a small hole in the oil seal and use a self-tapping screw and a pair of pliers to remove it.

13 Clean the oil seal housing and the camshaft sealing surface.

14 Smear the new oil seal with clean engine oil, then fit it over the end of the camshaft, open end first. A piece of thin plastic or tape wound around the front of the camshaft is useful to prevent damage to the oil seal as it is fitted.

15 Press the seal into the housing until it is flush with the end face of the cylinder head. Use an M10 bolt (screwed into the end of the camshaft), washers and a suitable tube or socket to press the seal into position.

16 Refit the camshaft sprocket as described in Section 8.

17 Where necessary, fit a new timing belt as described in Section 7.

Camshaft left-hand oil seal

18 No oil seal is fitted to the left-hand end of the camshaft. The sealing is provided by an O-ring fitted to the end plate flange. The O-ring can be renewed after unbolting the plate from the cylinder head.

17 Oil level, temperature and pressure sensors - general

Refer to Chapter 5A for details.

18 Flywheel/driveplate - removal, inspection and refitting

Refer to Chapter 2A, Section 17.

19 Engine/transmission mountings - inspection and renewal

Inspection

1 Refer to Chapter 2A, Section 18.

Renewal

Right-hand mounting

2 Refer to Section 9 on 1.9 litre models; refer to Chapter 2A, Section 18 on 2.1 litre models.

Left-hand mounting

3 Refer to Chapter 2A, Section 18.

Lower engine movement limiter

4 Refer to Chapter 2A, Section 18.

20 Engine oil cooler - removal and refitting

Refer to Chapter 2A, Section 15.

2B

Chapter 2 Part C:
Engine removal and overhaul procedures

Contents

Degrees of difficulty

Easy, suitable for novice with little experience	Fairly easy, suitable for beginner with some experience	Fairly difficult, suitable for competent DIY mechanic	Difficult, suitable for experienced DIY mechanic	Very difficult, suitable for expert DIY or professional

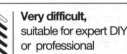

Specifications

Note: *At the time of writing, some specifications for certain engines were not available. Where the relevant specifications are not given here, refer to your Peugeot dealer for further information.*

Cylinder head

Maximum gasket face distortion:
    XU series engines . . . . 0.05 mm
    XUD series engines . . . . 0.07 mm
Swirl chamber protrusion - diesel engines only . . . . 0 to 0.03 mm

Valves

Valve head diameter:
  Inlet:
    Petrol engines:
      1.6 litre engine . . . . 41.6 mm
      1.8 litre engine . . . . Not available
      2.0 litre engine . . . . Not available
    Diesel engines:
      1.9 litre engine . . . . 38.6 mm
      2.1 litre engine . . . . 33.9 mm
  Exhaust:
    Petrol engines:
      1.6 litre engine . . . . 34.7 mm
      1.8 litre engine . . . . Not available
      2.0 litre engine . . . . Not available
    Diesel engines:
      1.9 litre engine . . . . 33.0 mm
      2.1 litre engine . . . . 33.9 mm

2C

Valves (continued)

Valve stem diameter:
  Inlet:
    Petrol engines:
      1.6 litre engine .... 7.83 to 7.98 mm
      1.8 and 2.0 litre engines .... Not available
    Diesel engines:
      1.9 litre engine .... 7.99 mm
      2.1 litre engine .... 8.005 mm
  Exhaust:
    Petrol engines:
      1.6 litre engine .... 7.83 to 7.98 mm
      1.8 and 2.0 litre engines .... Not available
    Diesel engines .... 7.97 mm
Overall length:
  Inlet:
    Petrol engines:
      1.6 litre engine .... 108.79 mm
      1.8 and 2.0 litre engines .... Not available
    Diesel engines:
      1.9 litre engine .... 112.40 mm
      2.1 litre engine .... 122.30 mm
  Exhaust:
    Petrol engines:
      1.6 litre engine .... 108.37 mm
      1.8 and 2.0 litre engines .... Not available
    Diesel engines:
      1.9 litre engine .... 111.85 mm
      2.1 litre engine .... 121.9 mm

Cylinder block

Cylinder bore diameter:
  Petrol engines:
    1.6 litre engines:
      Size group A .... 83.000 to 83.010 mm
      Size group B .... 83.010 to 83.020 mm
      Size group C .... 83.020 to 83.030 mm
    1.8 and 2.0 litre engines .... Not available
  Diesel engines:
    1.9 litre engines:
      Standard .... 83.000 to 83.018 mm
      Oversize R1 .... 83.200 to 83.218 mm
      Oversize R2 .... 83.500 to 83.518 mm
      Oversize R3 .... 83.800 to 83.818 mm
    2.1 litre engines:
      Standard .... 85.000 to 85.018 mm
      Oversize A1 .... 85.030 to 85.048 mm
      Oversize R1 .... 85.250 to 85.268 mm
      Oversize R2 .... 85.600 to 85.618 mm
Liner protrusion above block mating surface - aluminium-block engine only:
  Standard .... 0.03 to 0.10 mm
  Maximum difference between any two liners .... 0.05 mm

Pistons

Piston diameter:
  Petrol engines:
    1.6 litre engines:
      Size group A .... 82.960 ± 0.007 mm
      Size group B .... 82.970 ± 0.007 mm
      Size group C .... 82.980 ± 0.007 mm
    1.8 and 2.0 litre engines .... Not available

Pistons (continued)

Piston diameter:
  Diesel engines:
    1.9 litre engine:
      Standard . . . . 82.930 to 82.939 mm
      1st oversize . . . . 83.130 to 83.139 mm
      2nd oversize . . . . 83.430 to 83.439 mm
      3rd oversize . . . . 83.730 to 83.739 mm
    2.1 litre engine:
      Standard . . . . 84.920 to 84.929 mm
      1st oversize . . . . 84.950 to 84.959 mm
      2nd oversize . . . . 85.170 to 85.179 mm
      3rd oversize . . . . 85.520 to 85.529 mm

Crankshaft

Endfloat . . . . 0.07 to 0.32 mm
Main bearing journal diameter:
  Petrol engines:
    1.6 litre engine:
      Standard . . . . 59.981 to 60.000 mm
      Undersize . . . . 59.681 to 59.700 mm
    1.8 and 2.0 litre engines . . . . Not available
  Diesel engines:
    Standard . . . . 60.0 + 0 - 0.019 mm
    Undersize . . . . 59.7 + 0 - 0.019 mm
Big-end bearing journal diameter:
  Petrol engines:
    1.6 litre engine:
      Standard . . . . 49.984 to 50.000 mm
      Undersize . . . . 49.684 to 49.700 mm
    1.8 and 2.0 litre engines . . . . Not available
  Diesel engines:
    Standard . . . . 50.0 + 0 - 0.016 mm
    Undersize . . . . 49.7 + 0 - 0.016 mm
Maximum bearing journal out of round (all models) . . . . 0.007 mm
Main bearing running clearance:
  Petrol engines:
    1.6 litre engines . . . . 0.025 to 0.050 mm
    1.8 and 2.0 litre engines . . . . Not available
  Diesel engines** . . . . 0.025 to 0.050 mm
Big-end bearing running clearance - all models** . . . . 0.025 to 0.050 mm

*These are suggested figures, typical for this type of engine - no exact values are stated by Peugeot.

Piston rings

End gaps:
  Petrol engines:
    Top compression ring:
      1.6 litre engine* . . . . 0.4 to 0.6 mm
      1.8 and 2.0 litre engine* . . . . 0.3 to 0.5 mm
    Second compression ring:
      1.6 litre engine . . . . 0.15 to 0.35 mm
      1.8 and 2.0 litre engine* . . . . 0.3 to 0.5 mm
    Oil control ring* . . . . 0.3 to 0.5 mm
  Diesel engines:
    Top and second compression rings . . . . 0.20 to 0.40 mm
    Oil control ring . . . . 0.25 to 0.50 mm

These are suggested figures, typical for this type of engine - no exact values are stated by Peugeot.

Torque wrench settings

XU series (petrol) engine
Refer to Chapter 2A Specifications

XUD series (Diesel) engine
Refer to Chapter 2B Specifications

2C

1 General information

Included in this Part of Chapter 2 are details of removing the engine/transmission from the car and general overhaul procedures for the cylinder head, cylinder block/crankcase and all other engine internal components.

The information given ranges from advice concerning preparation for an overhaul and the purchase of replacement parts, to detailed step-by-step procedures covering removal, inspection, renovation and refitting of engine internal components.

After Section 6, all instructions are based on the assumption that the engine has been removed from the car. For information concerning in-car engine repair, as well as the removal and refitting of those external components necessary for full overhaul, refer to Part A or B of this Chapter (as applicable) and to Section 6. Ignore any preliminary dismantling operations described in Part A or B that are no longer relevant once the engine has been removed from the car.

Apart from torque wrench settings, which are given at the beginning of Part A or B (as applicable), all specifications relating to engine overhaul are at the beginning of this Part of Chapter 2.

2 Engine overhaul - general information

It is not always easy to determine when, or if, an engine should be completely overhauled, as a number of factors must be considered.

High mileage is not necessarily an indication that an overhaul is needed, while low mileage does not preclude the need for an overhaul. Frequency of servicing is probably the most important consideration. An engine which has had regular and frequent oil and filter changes, as well as other required maintenance, should give many thousands of miles of reliable service. Conversely, a neglected engine may require an overhaul very early in its life.

Excessive oil consumption is an indication that piston rings, valve seals and/or valve guides are in need of attention. Make sure that oil leaks are not responsible before deciding that the rings and/or guides are worn. Perform a compression test, as described in Part A (petrol engine) or B (diesel engine) of this Chapter, to determine the likely cause of the problem.

Check the oil pressure with a gauge fitted in place of the oil pressure switch, and compare it with that specified. If it is extremely low, the main and big-end bearings, and/or the oil pump, are probably worn out.

Loss of power, rough running, knocking or metallic engine noises, excessive valve gear noise, and high fuel consumption may also point to the need for an overhaul, especially if they are all present at the same time. If a complete service does not cure the situation, major mechanical work is the only solution.

An engine overhaul involves restoring all internal parts to the specification of a new engine. During an overhaul, the cylinder liners (where applicable), the pistons and the piston rings are renewed. New main and big-end bearings are generally fitted; if necessary, the crankshaft may be renewed to restore the journals. The valves are also serviced as well, since they are usually in less-than-perfect condition at this point. While the engine is being overhauled, other components, such as the distributor, starter and alternator, can be overhauled as well. The end result should be an as-new engine that will give many trouble-free miles.

Note: *Critical cooling system components such as the hoses, thermostat and coolant pump should be renewed when an engine is overhauled. The radiator should be checked carefully, to ensure that it is not clogged or leaking. Also, it is a good idea to renew the oil pump whenever the engine is overhauled.*

Before beginning the engine overhaul, read through the entire procedure, to familiarise yourself with the scope and requirements of the job. Overhauling an engine is not difficult if you follow carefully all of the instructions, have the necessary tools and equipment, and pay close attention to all specifications. It can, however, be time-consuming. Plan on the car being off the road for a minimum of two weeks, especially if parts must be taken to an engineering works for repair or reconditioning. Check on the availability of parts and make sure that any necessary special tools and equipment are obtained in advance. Most work can be done with typical hand tools, although a number of precision measuring tools are required for inspecting parts to determine if they must be renewed. Often the engineering works will handle the inspection of parts and offer advice concerning reconditioning and renewal.

Note: *Always wait until the engine has been completely dismantled, and until all components (especially the cylinder block/ crankcase and the crankshaft) have been inspected, before deciding what service and repair operations must be performed by an engineering works. The condition of these components will be the major factor to consider when determining whether to overhaul the original engine, or to buy a reconditioned unit. Do not, therefore, purchase parts or have overhaul work done on other components until they have been thoroughly inspected.* As a general rule, time is the primary cost of an overhaul, so it does not pay to fit worn or sub-standard parts.

As a final note, to ensure maximum life and minimum trouble from a reconditioned engine, everything must be assembled with care, in a spotlessly-clean environment.

3 Engine/transmission removal - methods and precautions

1 If you have decided that the engine must be removed for overhaul or major repair work, several preliminary steps should be taken.

2 Locating a suitable place to work is extremely important. Adequate work space, along with storage space for the car, will be needed. If a workshop or garage is not available, at the very least, a flat, level, clean work surface is required.

3 Cleaning the engine compartment and engine/transmission before beginning the removal procedure will help keep tools clean and organised.

4 An engine hoist or A-frame will also be necessary. Make sure the equipment is rated in excess of the combined weight of the engine and transmission. Safety is of primary importance, considering the potential hazards involved in lifting the engine/transmission out of the car.

5 If this is the first time you have removed an engine, an assistant should ideally be available. Advice and aid from someone more experienced would also be helpful. There are many instances when one person cannot simultaneously perform all of the operations required when lifting the engine out of the vehicle.

6 Plan the operation ahead of time. Before starting work, arrange for the hire of or obtain all of the tools and equipment you will need. Some of the equipment necessary to perform engine/transmission removal and installation safely and with relative ease (in addition to an engine hoist) is as follows: a heavy duty trolley jack, complete sets of spanners and sockets, wooden blocks, and plenty of rags and cleaning solvent for mopping up spilled oil, coolant and fuel. If the hoist must be hired, make sure that you arrange for it in advance, and perform all of the operations possible without it beforehand. This will save you money and time.

7 Plan for the car to be out of use for quite a while. An engineering works will be required to perform some of the work which the do-it-yourselfer cannot accomplish without special equipment. These places often have a busy schedule, so it would be a good idea to consult them before removing the engine, in order to accurately estimate the amount of time required to rebuild or repair components that may need work.

8 Always be extremely careful when removing and refitting the engine/transmission. Serious injury can result from careless actions. Plan ahead and take your time, and a job of this nature, although major, can be accomplished successfully.

4 Engine and manual transmission - removal, separation and refitting

Removal

Note 1: *The engine can be removed from the car only as a complete unit with the transmission; the two are then separated for overhaul.*

Note 2: *Such is the complexity of the power unit arrangement on these vehicles, and the variations that may be encountered according to model and optional equipment fitted, that the following should be regarded as a guide to the work involved, rather than a step-by-step procedure. Where differences are encountered, or additional component disconnection or removal is necessary, make notes of the work involved as an aid to refitting.*

1 Park the vehicle on firm, level ground. Chock the rear wheels, then jack up the front of the vehicle, and securely support it on axle stands. Remove both front roadwheels.

2 Set the bonnet in the upright position and secure it.

3 Disconnect the battery negative terminal.

4 Drain the cooling system as described in Chapter 1.

5 Remove both driveshafts as described in Chapter 8.

6 Remove the air cleaner assembly and intake ducting as described in Chapter 4A or 4B. Undo the bolts and remove the air cleaner support bracket.

7 On 2.1 litre diesel models, remove the fuel system ECU and module box as described in Chapter 4B.

8 Where applicable, disconnect the accelerator cable from the throttle housing or fuel injection pump.

9 On petrol models, remove the throttle housing as described in Chapter 4A.

10 As applicable, remove the wiring, cable connectors and components from the left-hand end of the cylinder head.

11 If the engine is to be dismantled, working as described in Chapter 1, first drain the oil and remove the oil filter. Clean and refit the drain plug, tightening it securely.

12 Drain the transmission oil as described in Chapter 7A. Refit the drain and filler plugs, and tighten them to their specified torque settings (see Chapter 7A).

13 Disconnect all relevant wiring from the transmission.

14 Disconnect the speedometer cable or transducer wiring from the transmission.

15 Using a flat-bladed screwdriver, carefully lever the three gearchange mechanism link rods off their respective balljoints on the transmission. Position the rods clear of the transmission unit. On 2.1 litre diesel models, carefully prise the two gearchange cable balljoints from the selector levers on the transmission.

16 Remove the cable guide, the metal bracket and the crankshaft position (RPM) sensor.

17 Release the inner cable and outer cable fittings from the clutch release lever and mounting bracket, and free the cable from the transmission housing. On 2.1 litre diesel models, release the clutch slave cylinder as described in Chapter 6.

18 Refer to Chapter 10 and remove the power steering pump without disconnecting the hydraulic hoses. Position the pump clear of the engine.

19 Remove the alternator (see Chapter 5A).

20 On models with air conditioning, unbolt the compressor, and position it clear of the engine unit. Support the weight of the compressor by tying it to the vehicle body, to prevent any excess strain being placed on the compressor lines whilst the engine is removed. *Do not* disconnect the refrigerant lines from the compressor (refer to the warnings given in Chapter 3).

21 On 2.1 litre models, unbolt the accessory bracket from the front of the cylinder block.

22 Remove the radiator as described in Chapter 3. Note that this is not strictly necessary on all models, but greatly improves clearance and removes the risk of damaging the radiator as the engine is removed.

23 On petrol models, carry out the following operations, using the information given in Chapter 4A:

a) *Depressurise the fuel system, and disconnect the fuel feed and return hoses.*

b) *Disconnect the fuel system wiring connectors.*

c) *Disconnect the purge valve from the inlet manifold (as applicable).*

d) *Remove the exhaust system front pipe.*

24 On diesel models, disconnect the fuel feed and return hoses (refer to Chapter 4B).

25 Referring to Chapter 3, release the retaining clip and disconnect the heater matrix hoses from their connection on the engine compartment bulkhead.

26 Trace the wiring harness back from the engine unit to the wiring connector(s) in the engine compartment. Unscrew the wiring connectors, then release the retaining rings and remove the connector sockets, marking them for refitting **(see illustrations)**. Unbolt the various wiring harness brackets and supports within the engine compartment as necessary for engine/transmission removal. Check that all the relevant connectors have been disconnected, and that the wiring is released from any relevant clips or ties, so that it is free to be removed with the engine/transmission.

27 Manoeuvre the engine hoist into position, and attach it to the lifting brackets bolted onto the cylinder head. Raise the hoist until it is supporting the weight of the engine.

28 Remove the left-hand and right-hand engine/transmission mountings as described in Part A or B of this Chapter.

29 From underneath the vehicle, slacken and remove the nuts and bolts securing the engine movement limiter link to the subframe and engine, and remove the link.

30 Make a final check that any components which would prevent the removal of the engine/transmission from the car have been removed or disconnected. Ensure that components such as the gearchange selector rod are secured so that they cannot be damaged on removal.

31 Lift the engine/transmission out of the car, ensuring that nothing is trapped or damaged **(see illustration)**. Enlist the help of an assistant during this procedure, as it will be necessary to tilt the assembly slightly to clear the body panels. On models equipped with anti-lock brakes, great care must be taken to ensure that the anti-lock braking system unit is not damaged during the removal procedure.

2C

4.26a Unscrew the engine wiring harness connectors (arrowed) . . .

4.26b . . . then unscrew the retaining rings and release the connector sockets from their mountings

4.31 Lifting the engine/transmission assembly out of the car

32 Once the engine is high enough, lift it out over the front of the body, and lower the unit to the ground.

Separation

33 With the engine/transmission assembly removed, support the assembly on suitable blocks of wood, on a workbench (or failing that, on a clean area of the workshop floor).
34 Undo the retaining bolts, and remove the flywheel lower cover plate (where fitted) from the transmission.
35 On models with a "pull-type" clutch release mechanism (except 2.1 litre diesel models - see Chapter 6 for further information), tap out the retaining pin or unscrew the retaining bolt (as applicable), and remove the clutch release lever from the top of the release fork shaft. This is necessary to allow the fork shaft to rotate freely, so that it disengages from the release bearing as the transmission is pulled away from the engine. Make an alignment mark across the centre of the clutch release fork shaft, using a scriber, paint or similar, and mark its relative position on the transmission housing (see Chapter 7A for further information).
36 Slacken and remove the retaining bolts, and remove the starter motor from the transmission.
37 Ensure that both engine and transmission are adequately supported, then slacken and remove the remaining bolts securing the transmission housing to the engine. Note the correct fitted positions of each bolt (and the relevant brackets) as they are removed, to use as a reference on refitting.
38 Carefully withdraw the transmission from the engine, ensuring that the weight of the transmission is not allowed to hang on the input shaft while it is engaged with the clutch friction disc.
39 If they are loose, remove the locating dowels from the engine or transmission, and keep them in a safe place.
40 On models with a "pull-type" clutch, make a second alignment mark on the transmission housing, marking the relative position of the release fork mark after removal. This should indicate the angle at which the release fork is positioned. The mark can then be used to position the release fork prior to installation, to ensure that the fork correctly engages with the clutch release bearing as the transmission is installed.

Refitting

41 If the engine and transmission have been separated, perform the operations described below in paragraphs 42 to 50. If not, proceed as described from paragraph 51 onwards.
42 Ensure that the locating dowels are correctly positioned in the engine or transmission.
43 On models with a "pull-type" clutch, before refitting, position the clutch release bearing so that its arrow mark is pointing upwards (bearing fork slots facing towards the

front of the engine unit), and align the release fork shaft mark with the second mark made on the transmission housing (release fork positioned at approximately 60° to clutch housing face). This will ensure that the release fork and bearing will engage correctly as the transmission is refitted to the engine.
44 On 2.1 litre diesel models, remove the release bearing from the clutch pressure plate, and reposition it on the transmission as described in Chapter 7A Section 9. Read through the entire procedure in Chapter 7A, Section 9, and proceed accordingly as the transmission is refitted.
45 Carefully offer the transmission to the engine, until the locating dowels are engaged. Ensure that the weight of the transmission is not allowed to hang on the input shaft as it is engaged with the clutch friction disc.
46 On models with a "pull-type" clutch, with the transmission fully engaged with the engine, check that the release fork and bearing are correctly engaged. If the release fork and bearing are correctly engaged, the mark on the release fork should be aligned with the original mark made on the transmission housing (see Chapter 7A for further information).
47 Refit the transmission housing-to-engine bolts, ensuring that all the necessary brackets are correctly positioned, and tighten them to the specified torque setting.
48 Refit the starter motor, and securely tighten its retaining bolts.
49 On models with a "pull-type" clutch release mechanism, refit the clutch release lever to the top of the release fork shaft, securing it in position with its retaining pin or bolt (as applicable).
50 Where necessary, refit the lower flywheel cover plate to the transmission, and securely tighten its retaining bolts.
51 Reconnect the hoist and lifting tackle to the engine lifting brackets. With the aid of an assistant, lift the assembly over the engine compartment.
52 The assembly should be tilted as necessary to clear the surrounding components, as during removal; lower the assembly into position in the engine compartment, manipulating the hoist and lifting tackle as necessary.
53 With the engine/transmission in position, refit the right-hand engine/transmission mounting bracket, tightening its retaining nuts and bolts (as applicable) by hand only at this stage.
54 Working on the left-hand mounting, refit the mounting bracket (where removed) to the body and tighten its retaining bolts to the specified torque. Refit the mounting rubber and refit the mounting retaining nuts and washers and the centre nut and washer, tightening them lightly only.
55 From underneath the vehicle, refit the engine movement limiter link and install both its bolts.
56 Rock the engine to settle it on its

mountings then go around and tighten all the engine/transmission mounting nuts and bolts to their specified torque settings. The hoist can then be detached from the engine and removed.
57 The remainder of the refitting procedure is a direct reversal of the removal sequence, noting the following points:
   a) *Ensure that the wiring loom is correctly routed and retained by all the relevant retaining clips; all connectors should be correctly and securely reconnected.*
   b) *Prior to refitting the driveshafts to the transmission, renew the driveshaft oil seals as described in Chapter 7A.*
   c) *Ensure that all coolant hoses are correctly reconnected, and securely retained by their clips.*
   d) *Adjust the clutch cable (where applicable) as described in Chapter 6.*
   e) *Refit the clutch slave cylinder on 2.1 litre diesel models as described in Chapter 6.*
   f) *Adjust the accelerator cable as described in the relevant Part of Chapter 4.*
   g) *Refill the engine and transmission with the correct quantity and type of lubricant, as described in Chapter 1 and 7A.*
   h) *Refill the cooling system (see "Weekly Checks").*
   i) *On diesel models, on completion bleed the fuel system as described in Chapter 4B.*

5 Engine and automatic transmission - removal, separation and refitting

Removal

Note: *The engine can be removed from the car only as a complete unit with the transmission; the two are then separated for overhaul.*

1 The procedure is essentially the same as described in Section 4, but carry out the following operations with reference to Chapter 7B.
   a) *Carefully prise the selector cable balljoint from the selector lever on the transmission multi-function switch. Extract the horseshoe shaped clip securing the cable to the mounting bracket on the transmission.*
   b) *Trace the wiring back from the multi-function switch to the wiring connector. Release the connector from the support bracket and disconnect it. Release the switch wiring from the support clip on the transmission.*
   c) *Disconnect the wiring harness at the large connector adjacent to the transmission fluid cooler. Cover the wiring connector socket on the transmission to prevent water ingress when the fluid cooler hoses are disconnected.*
   d) *Using hose clamps or similar, clamp both the fluid cooler coolant hoses to minimise coolant loss during subsequent operations.*

e) Disconnect both coolant hoses from the fluid cooler being prepared for some coolant spillage. Wash off any spilt coolant immediately with cold water, and dry the surrounding area before proceeding further.

f) Unclip the wiring connector from the support bracket located just above the fluid cooler, then remove the support bracket.

g) Disconnect the earth cable from the stud on the transmission.

h) Remove the wiring harness bracket and the hose support bracket from the transmission.

i) Disconnect the wiring from the speedometer transducer (speedometer drive) and RPM sensor, then remove the RPM sensor from the bellhousing.

j) Remove the starter motor.

k) Label and disconnect any remaining wiring connectors and support brackets connected to the transmission.

Separation

2 With the engine/transmission assembly removed, support the assembly on suitable blocks of wood, on a workbench (or failing that, on a clean area of the workshop floor).

3 Locate the access hole at the lower rear of the cylinder block, then turn the crankshaft, by means of a socket on the crankshaft pulley bolt, until one of the torque converter retaining bolts is accessible through the access hole.

4 Undo the accessible torque converter bolt then turn the crankshaft as necessary and undo the remaining two bolts.

5 Slacken and remove the bolts securing the transmission housing to the engine. Note the correct fitted positions of each bolt, and the necessary brackets, as they are removed, to use as a reference on refitting. Make a final check that all components have been disconnected, and are positioned clear of the transmission so that they will not hinder the removal procedure.

6 With the bolts removed, pull the transmission off the engine, to free it from its locating dowels. Once the transmission is free, and sufficient clearance exists, insert a bolt with a suitable washer, through the RPM sensor hole in the transmission bellhousing, to retain the torque converter on the transmission.

Preparation for reconnection

7 Prior to reconnection it is necessary to make a simple tool to align the torque converter with the driveplate as the transmission is refitted. To make the tool, obtain a bolt of the same size as the torque converter retaining bolts, but long enough to extend through the access hole in the cylinder block when the transmission is refitted.

8 Cut the head off the bolt and cut a slot (to enable it to be unscrewed) in the plain end. Check that the tool will slide easily through

the torque converter retaining bolt hole in the driveplate.

9 Turn the engine crankshaft so that one of the torque converter retaining bolt holes in the driveplate, is aligned with the access hole in the cylinder block. Screw the alignment tool (finger tight only) into one of the retaining bolt holes in the torque converter. Turn the torque converter so that the alignment tool is in approximately the correct position, relative to the cylinder block access hole. As the transmission is refitted, the alignment tool will pass through the retaining bolt hole in the driveplate and through the access hole. It can then be unscrewed with a screwdriver and the first torque converter retaining bolt fitted in its place.

10 Check that the torque converter support bush fitted to the centre of the crankshaft is in good condition, and in place.

11 Ensure that the engine/transmission locating dowels are correctly positioned prior to installation.

Reconnection

12 The transmission is reconnected by a reversal of the removal procedure, bearing in mind the following points:

a) Guide the transmission into position ensuring that the alignment tool passes through the driveplate and access hole.

b) Remove the bolt used to retain the torque converter in place, just before the transmission engages with the engine.

c) Once the transmission is bolted to the engine, remove the alignment tool and fit the first torque converter retaining bolt. Turn the crankshaft as necessary and fit the other two bolts.

Refitting

13 Refit the starter motor, and securely tighten its retaining bolts.

14 Refit the engine unit to the vehicle as described in the relevant refitting paragraphs of Section 4.

15 The remainder of the refitting procedure is a reversal of the removal sequence, noting the following points:

a) Ensure that the wiring loom is correctly routed, and retained by all the relevant retaining clips; all connectors should be correctly and securely reconnected.

b) Prior to refitting the driveshafts to the transmission, renew the driveshaft oil seals as described in Chapter 7B.

c) Ensure that all coolant hoses are correctly reconnected, and securely retained by their retaining clips.

d) Adjust the accelerator cable as described in Chapter 4.

e) Refill the engine and transmission with correct quantity and type of lubricant, as described in Chapter 1 and 7B.

f) Refill the cooling system (see "Weekly Checks").

6 Engine overhaul - dismantling sequence

1 It is much easier to dismantle and work on the engine if it is mounted on a portable engine stand. These stands can often be hired from a tool hire shop. Before the engine is mounted on a stand, the flywheel/driveplate should be removed, so that the stand bolts can be tightened into the end of the cylinder block/crankcase.

2 If a stand is not available, it is possible to dismantle the engine with it blocked up on a sturdy workbench, or on the floor. Be extra-careful not to tip or drop the engine when working without a stand.

3 If you are going to obtain a reconditioned engine, all the external components must be removed first, to be transferred to the replacement engine (just as they will if you are doing a complete engine overhaul yourself). These components include the following:

a) Alternator and/or accessory bracket.

b) Thermostat and housing, and coolant outlet chamber/elbow - petrol models (Chapter 3).

c) Fuel filter/thermostat housing - diesel models

d) Dipstick tube if not removed already.

e) Fuel system components (Chapter 4).

f) All electrical switches and sensors.

g) Inlet and exhaust manifolds (Chapter 4).

h) Oil filter (Chapter 1).

i) All engine brackets and attachments.

j) Flywheel/driveplate (Part A or B of this Chapter).

Note: When removing the external components from the engine, pay close attention to details that may be helpful or important during refitting. Note the fitted position of gaskets, seals, spacers, pins, washers, bolts, and other small items.

4 If you are obtaining a "short" engine (which consists of the engine cylinder block/crankcase, crankshaft, pistons and connecting rods all assembled), then the cylinder head, sump, oil pump, and timing belt will have to be removed also.

5 If you are planning a complete overhaul, the engine can be dismantled, and the internal components removed, in the order given below, referring to Part A or B of this Chapter unless otherwise stated.

a) Inlet and exhaust manifolds (Chapter 4).

b) Timing belt, sprockets and tensioner(s).

c) Cylinder head.

d) Flywheel/driveplate.

e) Sump.

f) Oil pump.

g) Pistons/connecting rods (Section 11).

h) Crankshaft (Section 12).

6 Before beginning the dismantling and overhaul procedures, make sure that you have all of the correct tools necessary. See "Tools and working facilities" for further information.

2C

7.4 On 2.1 litre diesel models, undo the bolts and remove the engine mounting attachment bracket

7 Cylinder head (2.1 litre diesel models) - removal and refitting

Removal

1 Remove the camshaft and followers as described in Part B, Section 11.

2 Refer to Chapter 4B and remove the inlet manifold lower part, and the exhaust manifold.

3 Remove the fuel injection pump sprocket as described in Part B of this Chapter.

4 Undo the bolts and remove the engine mounting attachment bracket from the front of the engine **(see illustration)**.

5 Disconnect the remaining wiring, hoses, support brackets and connections at the cylinder head.

6 Progressively unscrew the cylinder head bolts, in the reverse order to that shown in illustration 13.34, in Part B of this Chapter.

7 Lift out the bolts and recover the spacers.

8 Release the cylinder head from the cylinder block and location dowel by rocking it. The Peugeot tool for doing this consists simply of two metal rods with 90-degree angled ends (refer to Chapter 4B) . Do not prise between the mating faces of the cylinder head and block, as this may damage the gasket faces.

9 Lift the cylinder head from the block, and recover the gasket.

Preparation for refitting

10 The mating faces of the cylinder head and cylinder block/crankcase must be perfectly clean before refitting the head. Use a hard plastic or wooden scraper to remove all traces of gasket and carbon; also clean the piston crowns. Make sure that the carbon is not allowed to enter the oil and water passages - this is particularly important for the lubrication system, as carbon could block the oil supply to the engine's components. Using adhesive tape and paper, seal the water, oil and bolt holes in the cylinder block/crankcase. To prevent carbon entering the gap between the pistons and bores, smear a little grease in the gap. After cleaning each piston, use a small brush to remove all traces of grease and carbon from the gap, then wipe away the remainder with a clean rag. Clean all the pistons in the same way.

11 Check the mating surfaces of the cylinder block/crankcase and the cylinder head for nicks, deep scratches and other damage. If slight, they may be removed carefully with a file, but if excessive, machining may be the only alternative to renewal. If warpage of the cylinder head gasket surface is suspected, use a straight-edge to check it for distortion.

12 When purchasing a new cylinder head gasket, it is essential that a gasket of the correct thickness is obtained. Modifications to the cylinder head gasket material, type, and manufacturer are constantly taking place; seek the advice of a Peugeot dealer as to the latest recommendations.

13 It is a requirement of this engine type that the cylinder head bolts must be renewed.

Refitting

14 Wipe clean the mating surfaces of the cylinder head and cylinder block/crankcase. Check that the two locating dowels are in position at each end of the cylinder block/crankcase surface.

15 Position a new gasket on the cylinder block/crankcase surface, ensuring that its identification holes or the projecting tongue are at the left-hand end of the gasket **(see illustration)**.

16 Lower the cylinder head onto the block **(see illustration)**.

17 Apply a smear of grease to the threads, and to the underside of the heads, of the cylinder head bolts. Peugeot recommend the use of Molykote G Rapid Plus (available from your Peugeot dealer); in the absence of the specified grease, any good-quality high-melting-point grease may be used **(see illustration)**.

18 Carefully enter each bolt into its relevant hole (*do not drop it in*) and screw it in finger-tight.

19 Working progressively and in the sequence shown (see illustration 13.34 in Part B of this Chapter), tighten the cylinder head bolts to their Stage 1 torque setting, using a torque wrench and suitable socket. See Chapter 2B for the relevant torque wrench settings **(see illustration)**.

20 With all the bolts tightened to their Stage 1 setting, working again in the specified sequence, angle-tighten the bolts through the specified Stage 2 angle using a socket and extension bar. It is recommended that an angle-measuring gauge is used during this stage of tightening, to ensure accuracy **(see illustration)**. If a gauge is not available, use

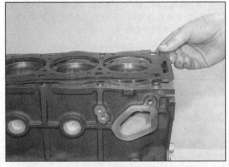

7.15 Position a new gasket on the cylinder block . . .

7.16 . . . then lower the cylinder head into position

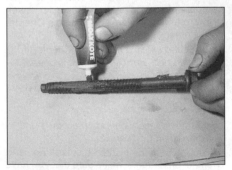

7.17 Apply suitable grease to the cylinder head bolt threads prior to refitting

7.19 Tighten the cylinder head bolts to the specified torque . . .

7.20 . . . and then through the specified angle using an angle-measuring gauge

8.4a On 2.1 litre diesel models, remove the timing belt tensioner centre stud by locking two nuts together . . .

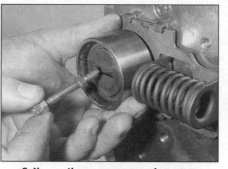

8.4b . . . then unscrew and remove the stud

8.5a Compress the valve spring using a spring compressor then extract the collets and release the compressor

8.5b Remove the spring retainer . . .

8.5c . . . followed by the valve spring . . .

8.5d . . . and the spring seat

white paint to make alignment marks between the bolt head and cylinder head prior to tightening; the marks can then be used to check that the bolt has rotated sufficiently.

21 The remainder of refitting is a direct reversal of the removal procedure.

22 Once the engine/transmission has been refitted to the car, the engine should be started and allowed to warm up until the radiator cooling fan has operated at least twice. The engine should then be stopped and allowed to cool down for three and a half hours. After that time, remove the cylinder head cover, release any residual pressure in the cooling system by removing the expansion tank cap then re-torque the cylinder head bolts as follows.

23 Working progressively and in the sequence shown (see illustration 13.34 in Part B of this Chapter), slacken each cylinder head bolt, one at a time, then tighten it to the Stage 3 torque setting, using a torque wrench, and then through the Stage 4 angle using an angle-measuring gauge.

24 On completion, refit the cylinder head cover and the cooling system expansion tank cap.

8   Cylinder head - dismantling

Note: *New and reconditioned cylinder heads are available from the manufacturer, and from engine overhaul specialists. Be aware that some specialist tools are required for the dismantling and inspection procedures, and new components may not be readily available. It may therefore be more practical and economical for the home mechanic to purchase a reconditioned head, rather than dismantle, inspect and recondition the original head.*

1 Remove the cylinder head as described in Part A or B of this Chapter, or in this Part (as applicable).

2 If not already done, remove the inlet and exhaust manifolds with reference to the relevant Part of Chapter 4. Remove any remaining brackets or housings as required.

3 Remove the camshaft, followers and shims (as applicable) as described in Part A or B of this Chapter.

4 On diesel models, remove the glow plugs as described in Chapter 5C and the injectors as described in Chapter 4B. On 2.1 litre diesel models, remove the timing belt tensioner centre retaining stud by screwing on a second nut and locking the two nuts together. Unscrew the stud by means of the locked nuts. Undo the retracting cam retaining bolt and remove the tensioner assembly **(see illustrations)**.

5 On all models, using a valve spring compressor, compress each valve spring in turn until the split collets can be removed. Release the compressor, and lift off the spring retainer, spring and spring seat. Using a pair of pliers, carefully extract the valve stem oil seal from the top of the guide **(see illustrations)**.

6 If, when the valve spring compressor is screwed down, the spring retainer refuses to free and expose the split collets, gently tap the top of the tool, directly over the retainer, with a light hammer. This will free the retainer.

7 Withdraw the valve through the combustion chamber.

8 It is essential that each valve is stored together with its collets, retainer, spring, and spring seat. The valves should also be kept in their correct sequence, unless they are so badly worn that they are to be renewed. If they are going to be kept and used again, place each valve assembly in a labelled polythene bag or similar small container **(see illustration)**. Note that No 1 valve is nearest to the transmission (flywheel/driveplate) end of the engine.

8.8 Place each valve and its associated components in a labelled polythene bag

9 Cylinder head and valves - cleaning and inspection

1 Thorough cleaning of the cylinder head and valve components, followed by a detailed inspection, will enable you to decide how much valve service work must be carried out during the engine overhaul. **Note:** *If the engine has been severely overheated, it is best to assume that the cylinder head is warped - check carefully for signs of this.*

Cleaning

2 Scrape away all traces of old gasket material from the cylinder head.
3 Scrape away the carbon from the combustion chambers and ports, then wash the cylinder head thoroughly with paraffin or a suitable solvent.
4 Scrape off any heavy carbon deposits that may have formed on the valves, then use a power-operated wire brush to remove deposits from the valve heads and stems.

Inspection

Note: *Be sure to perform all the following inspection procedures before concluding that the services of a machine shop or engine overhaul specialist are required. Make a list of all items that require attention.*

Cylinder head

5 Inspect the head very carefully for cracks, evidence of coolant leakage, and other damage. If cracks are found, a new cylinder head should be obtained.
6 Use a straight-edge and feeler blade to check that the cylinder head gasket surface is not distorted **(see illustration)**. If it is, it may be possible to have it machined, provided that the cylinder head is not reduced to less than the specified height. **Note:** *On diesel engines, it will be necessary to recut the combustion chambers and valve seats if more than 0.1 mm has been machined off the cylinder head. This is necessary in order to maintain the correct dimensions between the valve heads, valve guides and cylinder head gasket face.*
7 Examine the valve seats in each of the combustion chambers. If they are severely pitted, cracked, or burned, they will need to be renewed or re-cut by an engine overhaul specialist. If they are only slightly pitted, this can be removed by grinding-in the valve heads and seats with fine valve-grinding compound, as described below.
8 Check the valve guides for wear by inserting the relevant valve, and checking for side-to-side motion of the valve. A very small amount of movement is acceptable. If the movement seems excessive, remove the valve. Measure the valve stem diameter (see below), and renew the valve if it is worn. If the valve stem is not worn, the wear must be in the valve guide, and the guide must be renewed. The renewal of valve guides is best

carried out by a Peugeot dealer or engine overhaul specialist, who will have the necessary tools available. Where no valve stem diameter is specified, seek the advice of a Peugeot dealer on the best course of action.
9 If renewing the valve guides, the valve seats should be re-cut or re-ground only *after* the guides have been fitted.
10 On diesel models, inspect the swirl chambers for burning or damage such as cracking. Small cracks in the chambers are acceptable; renewal of the chambers will only be required if chamber tracts are badly burned and disfigured, or if they are no longer a tight fit in the cylinder head. If there is any doubt as to the swirl chamber condition, seek the advice of a Peugeot dealer or a suitable repairer who specialises in diesel engines. Swirl chamber renewal should be entrusted to a specialist. Using a dial test indicator, check that the swirl chamber protrusion is within the limits given in the Specifications **(see illustration)**. Zero the dial test indicator on the gasket surface of the cylinder head, then measure the protrusion of the swirl chamber. If the protrusion is not within the specified limits, the advice of a Peugeot dealer or suitable repairer who specialises in diesel engines should be sought.

Valves

11 Examine the head of each valve for pitting, burning, cracks, and general wear. Check the valve stem for scoring and wear ridges. Rotate the valve, and check for any obvious indication that it is bent. Look for pits or excessive wear on the tip of each valve stem. Renew any valve that shows any such signs of wear or damage.

12 If the valve appears satisfactory at this stage, measure the valve stem diameter at several points using a micrometer **(see illustration)**. Any significant difference in the readings obtained indicates wear of the valve stem. Should any of these conditions be apparent, the valve(s) must be renewed.
13 If the valves are in satisfactory condition, they should be ground (lapped) into their respective seats, to ensure a smooth, gas-tight seal. If the seat is only lightly pitted, or if it has been re-cut, fine grinding compound *only* should be used to produce the required finish. Coarse valve-grinding compound should *not* be used, unless a seat is badly burned or deeply pitted. If this is the case, the cylinder head and valves should be inspected by an expert, to decide whether seat re-cutting, or even the renewal of the valve or seat insert (where possible) is required.
14 Valve grinding is carried out as follows. Place the cylinder head upside-down on a bench.
15 Smear a trace of (the appropriate grade of) valve-grinding compound on the seat face, and press a suction grinding tool onto the valve head **(see illustration)**. With a semi-rotary action, grind the valve head to its seat, lifting the valve occasionally to redistribute the grinding compound. A light spring placed under the valve head will greatly ease this operation.
16 If coarse grinding compound is being used, work only until a dull, matt even surface is produced on both the valve seat and the valve, then wipe off the used compound, and repeat the process with fine compound. When a smooth unbroken ring of light grey matt

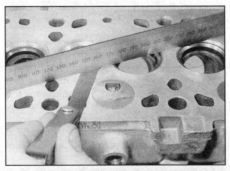

9.6 Checking the cylinder head gasket surface for distortion

9.10 Checking a swirl chamber protrusion - diesel models

9.12 Measuring a valve stem diameter

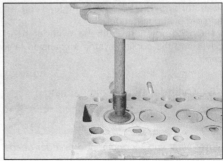

9.15 Grinding-in a valve

finish is produced on both the valve and seat, the grinding operation is complete. *Do not* grind-in the valves any further than absolutely necessary, or the seat will be prematurely sunk into the cylinder head.

17 When all the valves have been ground-in, carefully wash off *all* traces of grinding compound using paraffin or a suitable solvent, before reassembling the cylinder head.

Valve components

18 Examine the valve springs for signs of damage and discoloration. No minimum free length is specified by Peugeot, so the only way of judging valve spring wear is by comparison with a new component.

19 Stand each spring on a flat surface, and check it for squareness. If any of the springs are damaged, distorted or have lost their tension, obtain a complete new set of springs. It is normal to renew the valve springs as a matter of course if a major overhaul is being carried out.

20 Renew the valve stem oil seals regardless of their apparent condition.

10 Cylinder head - reassembly

1 Lubricate the stems of the valves, and insert the valves into their original locations **(see illustration)**. If new valves are being fitted, insert them into the locations to which they have been ground.

2 Refit the spring seat then, working on the first valve, dip the new valve stem seal in fresh engine oil. Carefully locate it over the valve and onto the guide. Take care not to damage the seal as it is passed over the valve stem. Use a suitable socket or metal tube to press the seal firmly onto the guide **(see illustration)**.

3 Locate the valve spring on top of its seat, then refit the spring retainer.

4 Compress the valve spring, and locate the split collets in the recess in the valve stem. Release the compressor, then repeat the procedure on the remaining valves.

10.1 Lubricate the valve stems prior to refitting

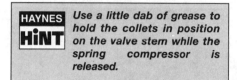

> **HAYNES HINT**
> *Use a little dab of grease to hold the collets in position on the valve stem while the spring compressor is released.*

5 With all the valves installed, support the cylinder head and, using a hammer and interposed block of wood, tap the end of each valve stem to settle the components.

6 Refit the camshaft, followers and shims (as applicable) as described in Part A or B of this Chapter.

7 Refit any remaining components using the reverse of the removal sequence and with new seals or gaskets as necessary. On 2.1 litre diesel models, refit the timing belt tensioner using thread locking compound on the centre stud. Tighten the stud using the locked nuts, then remove the second nut from the end of the stud.

8 The cylinder head can then be refitted as described in Part A or B of this Chapter, or in this Part (as applicable).

11 Piston/connecting rod assembly - removal

1 Remove the cylinder head, sump and oil pump as described in Part A or B of this Chapter, or in this Part (as applicable).

10.2 Fitting a valve stem oil seal using a socket

2 If there is a pronounced wear ridge at the top of any bore, it may be necessary to remove it with a scraper or ridge reamer, to avoid piston damage during removal. Such a ridge indicates excessive wear of the cylinder bore.

3 Using a hammer and centre-punch, paint or similar, mark each connecting rod big-end bearing cap with its respective cylinder number on the flat machined surface provided; if the engine has been dismantled before, note carefully any identifying marks made previously **(see illustration)**. Note that No 1 cylinder is at the transmission (flywheel) end of the engine.

4 Turn the crankshaft to bring pistons 1 and 4 to BDC (bottom dead centre).

5 Unscrew the nuts from No 1 piston big-end bearing cap. Take off the cap, and recover the bottom half bearing shell **(see illustration)**. If the bearing shells are to be re-used, tape the cap and the shell together.

6 To prevent the possibility of damage to the crankshaft bearing journals, tape over the connecting rod stud threads **(see illustration)**.

7 Using a hammer handle, push the piston up through the bore, and remove it from the top of the cylinder block. Recover the bearing shell, and tape it to the connecting rod for safe-keeping.

8 Loosely refit the big-end cap to the connecting rod, and secure with the nuts - this will help to keep the components in their correct order.

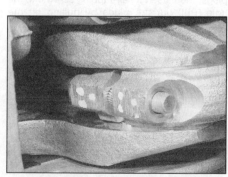

11.3 Connecting rod and big-end bearing cap marked for identification (No 3 cylinder shown)

11.5 Removing a big-end bearing cap and shell

11.6 To protect the crankshaft journals, tape over the connecting rod stud threads prior to removal

2C

12.4 Removing the oil seal carrier from the front of the cylinder block - XU and XUD engines

12.5a Remove the oil pump drive chain . . .

12.5b . . . then slide off the drive sprocket . . .

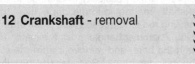

12.5c . . . and remove the Woodruff key from the crankshaft

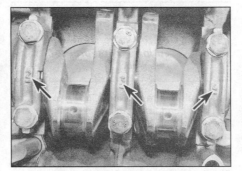

12.6 Main bearing cap identification markings (arrowed)

12.8 Removing No 2 main bearing cap. Note the thrustwasher (arrowed)

9 Remove No 4 piston assembly in the same way.
10 Turn the crankshaft through 180° to bring pistons 2 and 3 to BDC (bottom dead centre), and remove them in the same way.

12 Crankshaft - removal

1 Remove the crankshaft sprocket and the oil pump as described in Part A or B of this Chapter (as applicable).
2 Remove the pistons and connecting rods, as described in Section 10. If no work is to be done on the pistons and connecting rods, there is no need to remove the cylinder head, or to push the pistons out of the cylinder bores. The pistons should just be pushed far enough up the bores so that they are positioned clear of the crankshaft journals.
3 Check the crankshaft endfloat as described in Section 15, then proceed as follows.
4 Slacken and remove the retaining bolts, and remove the oil seal carrier from the front (timing belt) end of the cylinder block, along with its gasket (where fitted) **(see illustration)**.
5 Remove the oil pump drive chain, and slide the drive sprocket and spacer (where fitted) off the end of the crankshaft. Remove the Woodruff key, and store it with the sprocket for safe-keeping **(see illustrations)**.
6 The main bearing caps should be numbered 1 to 5, starting from the transmission (flywheel/

driveplate) end of the engine **(see illustration)**. If not, mark them accordingly using a centre-punch. Also note the correct fitted depth of the rear crankshaft oil seal in the bearing cap.
7 On 1.6 and 1.8 litre petrol engines, undo the two bolts (one at the front of the block, and one at the rear) securing the centre main bearing cap to the block. Remove the bolts, along with their sealing washers.
8 On all engines, slacken and remove the main bearing cap retaining bolts/nuts, and lift off each bearing cap. Recover the lower bearing shells, and tape them to their respective caps for safe-keeping. Also recover the lower thrustwasher halves from the side of No 2 main bearing cap **(see illustration)**. Remove the rubber sealing strips from the sides of No 1 main bearing cap, and discard them.
9 Lift out the crankshaft, and discard the rear oil seal **(see illustration)**.

12.9 Lifting out the crankshaft - XU and XUD engines

10 Recover the upper bearing shells from the cylinder block, and tape them to their respective caps for safe-keeping **(see illustration)**. Remove the upper thrustwasher halves from the side of No 2 main bearing, and store them with the lower halves.

13 Cylinder block/crankcase - cleaning and inspection

Cleaning

1 Remove all external components and electrical switches/sensors from the block. For complete cleaning, the core plugs should ideally be removed. Drill a small hole in the plugs, then insert a self-tapping screw into the hole. Pull out the plugs by pulling on the

12.10 Remove the upper main bearing shells from the cylinder block/crankcase, and store them with their lower shells

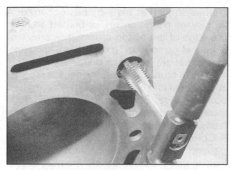

13.9 Cleaning a cylinder block threaded hole using a suitable tap

13.18a On aluminium block engines, remove each liner . . .

13.18b . . . and recover the bottom O-ring seal (arrowed)

screw with a pair of grips, or by using a slide hammer.

2 On aluminium block engines with wet liners, remove the liners, referring to paragraph 18.

3 Where applicable, undo the retaining bolt and remove the piston oil jet spray tube from inside the cylinder block.

4 Scrape all traces of gasket from the cylinder block/crankcase, and from the main bearing ladder (where fitted), taking care not to damage the gasket/sealing surfaces.

5 Remove all oil gallery plugs (where fitted). The plugs are usually very tight - they may have to be drilled out, and the holes re-tapped. Use new plugs when reassembling.

6 If any of the castings are extremely dirty, all should be steam-cleaned.

7 After the castings are returned, clean all oil holes and oil galleries one more time. Flush all internal passages with warm water until the water runs clear. Dry thoroughly, and apply a light film of oil to all mating surfaces, to prevent rusting. On cast-iron block engines, also oil the cylinder bores. If you have access to compressed air, use it to speed up the drying process, and to blow out all the oil holes and galleries.

 Warning: Wear eye protection when using compressed air!

8 If the castings are not very dirty, you can do an adequate cleaning job with hot (as hot as you can stand!), soapy water and a stiff brush. Take plenty of time, and do a thorough job. Regardless of the cleaning method used, be sure to clean all oil holes and galleries very thoroughly, and to dry all components well. On cast-iron block engines, protect the cylinder bores as described above, to prevent rusting.

9 All threaded holes must be clean, to ensure accurate torque readings during reassembly. To clean the threads, run the correct-size tap into each of the holes to remove rust, corrosion, thread sealant or sludge, and to restore damaged threads **(see illustration)**. If possible, use compressed air to clear the holes of debris produced by this operation.

 A good alternative is to inject water-dispersant lubricant into each hole, using the long spout usually supplied.

 Warning: Wear eye protection when cleaning out these holes in this way!

10 Apply suitable sealant to the new oil gallery plugs, and insert them into the holes in the block. Tighten them securely.

11 Where applicable, clean the threads of the piston oil jet retaining bolt, and apply a drop of thread-locking compound to the bolt threads. Refit the piston oil jet spray tube to the cylinder block, and tighten its retaining bolt to the specified torque setting.

12 If the engine is not going to be reassembled right away, cover it with a large plastic bag to keep it clean; protect all mating surfaces and the cylinder bores as described above, to prevent rusting.

Inspection

Cast-iron cylinder block

13 Visually check the castings for cracks and corrosion. Look for stripped threads in the threaded holes. If there has been any history of internal water leakage, it may be worthwhile having an engine overhaul specialist check the cylinder block/crankcase with special equipment. If defects are found, have them repaired if possible, or renew the assembly.

14 Check each cylinder bore for scuffing and scoring. Check for signs of a wear ridge at the top of the cylinder, indicating that the bore is excessively worn.

15 If the necessary measuring equipment is available, measure the bore diameter of each cylinder liner at the top (just under the wear ridge), centre, and bottom of the cylinder bore, parallel to the crankshaft axis.

16 Next, measure the bore diameter at the same three locations, at right-angles to the crankshaft axis. Compare the results with the figures given in the Specifications. Where no figures are stated by Peugeot, if there is any doubt about the condition of the cylinder bores seek the advice of a Peugeot dealer or suitable engine reconditioning specialist.

17 At the time of writing, it was not clear whether oversize pistons were available for all models. Consult your Peugeot dealer for the latest information on piston availability. If oversize pistons are available, then it may be possible to have the cylinder bores rebored and fit the oversize pistons. If oversize pistons

are not available, and the bores are worn, a new block seems to be the only option.

Aluminium cylinder block with wet liners

18 Remove the liner clamps (where used), then use a hard wood drift to tap out each liner from the inside of the cylinder block. When all the liners are released, tip the cylinder block/crankcase on its side and remove each liner from the top of the block. As each liner is removed, stick masking tape on its left-hand (transmission side) face, and write the cylinder number on the tape. No 1 cylinder is at the transmission (flywheel/driveplate) end of the engine. Remove the O-ring from the base of each liner, and discard it **(see illustrations)**.

19 Check each cylinder liner for scuffing and scoring. Check for a wear ridge at the top of the liner, indicating that the bore is badly worn.

20 If the necessary measuring equipment is available, measure the bore diameter of each cylinder liner at the top (just under the wear ridge), centre, and bottom of the cylinder bore, parallel to the crankshaft axis.

21 Next, measure the bore diameter at the same three locations, at right-angles to the crankshaft axis. Compare the results with the figures given in the Specifications.

22 Repeat the procedure for the remaining cylinder liners.

23 If the liner wear exceeds the permitted tolerances at any point, or if the cylinder liner walls are badly scored or scuffed, then renewal of the relevant liner assembly will be necessary. If there is any doubt about the condition of the cylinder bores, seek the advice of a Peugeot dealer or engine reconditioning specialist.

24 If renewal is necessary, new liners, complete with pistons and piston rings, can be purchased from a Peugeot dealer. Note that it is not possible to buy liners individually - they are supplied only as a matched assembly complete with piston and rings.

25 To allow for manufacturing tolerances, pistons and liners are separated into three size groups. The size group of each piston is indicated by a letter (A, B or C) stamped onto its crown, and the size group of each liner is indicated by a series of 1 to 3 notches on the upper lip of the liner; a single notch for group A,

2C

two notches for group B, and three notches for group C. Ensure that each piston and its respective liner are both of the same size group. It is permissible to have different size group piston and liner assemblies fitted to the same engine, but never fit a piston of one size group to a liner in a different group.

26 Prior to installing the liners, thoroughly clean the liner mating surfaces in the cylinder block, and use fine abrasive paper to polish away any burrs or sharp edges which might damage the liner O-rings. Clean the liners and wipe dry, then fit a new O-ring to the base of each liner. To aid installation, apply a smear of oil to each O-ring and to the base of the liner.

27 If the original liners are being refitted, use the marks made on removal to ensure that each is refitted the correct way round, and is inserted into its original bore. Insert each liner into the cylinder block, taking care not to damage the O-ring, and press it home as far as possible by hand. Using a hammer and a block of wood, tap each liner lightly but fully onto its locating shoulder. Wipe clean, then lightly oil, all exposed liner surfaces, to prevent rusting.

28 With all four liners correctly installed, use a dial gauge (or a straight-edge and feeler blade) to check that the protrusion of each liner above the upper surface of the cylinder block is within the limits given in the Specifications. The maximum difference between any two liners must not be exceeded.

29 If new liners are being fitted, it is permissible to interchange them to bring the difference in protrusion within limits. Remember to keep each piston with its respective liner.

30 If liner protrusion cannot be brought within limits, seek the advice of a Peugeot dealer or engine reconditioning specialist before proceeding with the engine rebuild.

14 Piston/connecting rod assembly - inspection

1 Before the inspection process can begin, the piston/connecting rod assemblies must be cleaned, and the original piston rings removed from the pistons.

2 Carefully expand the old rings over the top of the pistons. The use of two or three old feeler blades will be helpful in preventing the rings dropping into empty grooves **(see illustration)**. Be careful not to scratch the piston with the ends of the ring. The rings are brittle, and will snap if they are spread too far. They are also very sharp - protect your hands and fingers. Note that the third ring incorporates an expander. Always remove the rings from the top of the piston. Keep each set of rings with its piston if the old rings are to be re-used.

3 Scrape away all traces of carbon from the top of the piston. A hand-held wire brush (or a piece of fine emery cloth) can be used, once

14.2 Removing a piston ring with the aid of a feeler blade

the majority of the deposits have been scraped away.

4 Remove the carbon from the ring grooves in the piston, using an old ring. Break the ring in half to do this (be careful not to cut your fingers - piston rings are sharp). Be careful to remove only the carbon deposits - do not remove any metal, and do not nick or scratch the sides of the ring grooves.

5 Once the deposits have been removed, clean the piston/connecting rod assembly with paraffin or a suitable solvent, and dry thoroughly. Make sure that the oil return holes in the ring grooves are clear.

6 If the pistons and cylinder bores are not damaged or worn excessively, and if the cylinder block does not need to be rebored, the original pistons can be refitted. Normal piston wear shows up as even vertical wear on the piston thrust surfaces, and slight looseness of the top ring in its groove. New piston rings should always be used when the engine is reassembled.

7 Carefully inspect each piston for cracks around the skirt, around the gudgeon pin holes, and at the piston ring "lands" (between the ring grooves).

8 Look for scoring and scuffing on the piston skirt, holes in the piston crown, and burned areas at the edge of the crown. If the skirt is scored or scuffed, the engine may have been suffering from overheating, and/or abnormal combustion which caused excessively high operating temperatures. The cooling and lubrication systems should be checked thoroughly. Scorch marks on the sides of the

pistons show that blow-by has occurred. A hole in the piston crown, or burned areas at the edge of the piston crown, indicates that abnormal combustion (pre-ignition, knocking, or detonation) has been occurring. If any of the above problems exist, the causes must be investigated and corrected, or the damage will occur again. The causes may include incorrect ignition/injection pump timing, or a faulty injector (as applicable).

9 Corrosion of the piston, in the form of pitting, indicates that coolant has been leaking into the combustion chamber and/or the crankcase. Again, the cause must be corrected, or the problem may persist in the rebuilt engine.

10 On aluminium-block engines with wet liners, it is not possible to renew the pistons separately; pistons are only supplied with piston rings and a liner, as a part of a matched assembly (see Section 12). On iron-block engines, pistons can be purchased from a Peugeot dealer.

11 Examine each connecting rod carefully for signs of damage, such as cracks around the big-end and small-end bearings. Check that the rod is not bent or distorted. Damage is highly unlikely, unless the engine has been seized or badly overheated. Detailed checking of the connecting rod assembly can only be carried out by a Peugeot dealer or engine repair specialist with the necessary equipment.

12 On all engines, due to the tightening procedure for the connecting rod big-end cap retaining nuts, it is highly recommended that the big-end cap nuts and bolts are renewed as a complete set prior to refitting.

13 On all petrol engines, the gudgeon pins are an interference fit in the connecting rod small-end bearing. Therefore, piston and/or connecting rod renewal should be entrusted to a Peugeot dealer or engine repair specialist, who will have the necessary tooling to remove and install the gudgeon pins.

14 On diesel engines, the gudgeon pins are of the floating type, secured in position by two circlips. On these engines, the pistons and connecting rods can be separated as follows.

15 Using a small flat-bladed screwdriver, prise out the circlips, and push out the gudgeon pin **(see illustrations)**. Hand pressure should be sufficient to remove the

14.15a On diesel engines, prise out the circlip . . .

14.15b . . . withdraw the gudgeon pin . . .

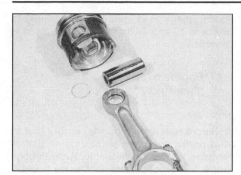

14.15c ... and separate the piston from the connecting rod

pin. Identify the piston and rod to ensure correct reassembly. Discard the circlips - new ones *must* be used on refitting.

16 Examine the gudgeon pin and connecting rod small-end bearing for signs of wear or damage. Wear can be cured by renewing both the pin and bush. Bush renewal, however, is a specialist job - press facilities are required, and the new bush must be reamed accurately.

17 The connecting rods themselves should not be in need of renewal, unless seizure or some other major mechanical failure has occurred. Check the alignment of the connecting rods visually, and if the rods are not straight, take them to an engine overhaul specialist for a more detailed check.

18 Examine all components, and obtain any new parts from your Peugeot dealer. If new pistons are purchased, they will be supplied complete with gudgeon pins and circlips. Circlips can also be purchased individually.

19 Position the piston so that the arrow on the piston crown is positioned as shown **(see illustration)**, in relation to the connecting rod big-end bearing shell cutouts. Apply a smear of clean engine oil to the gudgeon pin. Slide it into the piston and through the connecting rod small-end. Check that the piston pivots freely on the rod, then secure the gudgeon pin in position with two new circlips. Ensure that each circlip is correctly located in its groove in the piston.

15 Crankshaft - inspection

Checking crankshaft endfloat

1 If the crankshaft endfloat is to be checked, this must be done when the crankshaft is still installed in the cylinder block/crankcase, but is free to move (see Section 11).

2 Check the endfloat using a dial gauge in contact with the end of the crankshaft. Push the crankshaft fully one way, and then zero the gauge. Push the crankshaft fully the other way, and check the endfloat. The result can be compared with the specified amount, and will give an indication as to whether new thrustwashers are required **(see illustration)**.

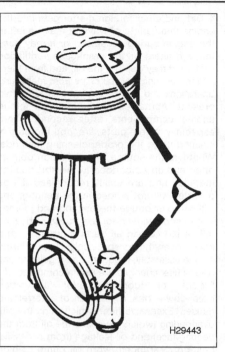

14.19 On diesel engines, ensure that the piston cutout is positioned as shown, in relation to the connecting rod bearing shell cutout

3 If a dial gauge is not available, feeler gauges can be used. First push the crankshaft fully towards the flywheel end of the engine, then use feeler gauges to measure the gap between the web of No 2 crankpin and the thrustwasher.

Inspection

4 Clean the crankshaft using paraffin or a suitable solvent, and dry it, preferably with compressed air if available.

⚠️ *Warning: Wear eye protection when using compressed air! Be sure to clean the oil holes with a pipe cleaner or similar probe, to ensure that they are not obstructed.*

5 Check the main and big-end bearing journals for uneven wear, scoring, pitting and cracking.

6 Big-end bearing wear is accompanied by distinct metallic knocking when the engine is running (particularly noticeable when the engine is pulling from low speed) and by some loss of oil pressure.

7 Main bearing wear is accompanied by severe engine vibration and rumble - getting progressively worse as engine speed increases - and again by loss of oil pressure.

8 Check the bearing journal for roughness by running a finger lightly over the bearing surface. Any roughness (which will be accompanied by obvious bearing wear) indicates that the crankshaft requires regrinding (where possible) or renewal.

9 If the crankshaft has been reground, check for burrs around the crankshaft oil holes (the holes are usually chamfered, so burrs should not be a problem unless regrinding has been

15.2 Checking crankshaft endfloat using a dial gauge

carried out carelessly). Remove any burrs with a fine file or scraper, and thoroughly clean the oil holes as described previously.

10 Using a micrometer, measure the diameter of the main and big-end bearing journals, and compare the results with the Specifications **(see illustration)**. By measuring the diameter at a number of points around each journal's circumference, you will be able to determine whether or not the journal is out-of-round. Take the measurement at each end of the journal, near the webs, to determine if the journal is tapered. Compare the results obtained with those given in the Specifications. Where no specified journal diameters are quoted, seek the advice of a Peugeot dealer.

11 Check the oil seal contact surfaces at each end of the crankshaft for wear and damage. If the seal has worn a deep groove in the surface of the crankshaft, consult an engine overhaul specialist; repair may be possible, but otherwise a new crankshaft will be required.

12 At the time of writing, it was not clear whether Peugeot produce oversize bearing shells for all of these engines. On some

2C

15.10 Measuring a crankshaft big-end journal diameter

engines, if the crankshaft journals have not already been reground, it may be possible to have the crankshaft reconditioned, and to fit oversize shells (see Section 18). If no oversize shells are available and the crankshaft has worn beyond the specified limits, it will have to be renewed. Consult your Peugeot dealer or engine specialist for further information on parts availability.

16 Main and big-end bearings - inspection

1 Even though the main and big-end bearings should be renewed during the engine overhaul, the old bearings should be retained for close examination, as they may reveal valuable information about the condition of the engine. The bearing shells are graded by thickness, the grade of each shell being indicated by the colour code marked on it.
2 Bearing failure can occur due to lack of lubrication, the presence of dirt or other foreign particles, overloading the engine, or corrosion **(see illustration)**. Regardless of the cause of bearing failure, the cause must be corrected (where applicable) before the engine is reassembled, to prevent it from happening again.
3 When examining the bearing shells, remove them from the cylinder block/crankcase, the main bearing ladder/caps (as appropriate), the connecting rods and the connecting rod big-end bearing caps. Lay them out on a clean surface in the same general position as their location in the engine. This will enable you to match any bearing problems with the corresponding crankshaft journal. *Do not* touch any shell's bearing surface with your fingers while checking it, or the delicate surface may be scratched.

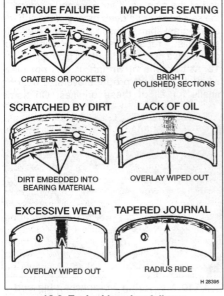

FATIGUE FAILURE   IMPROPER SEATING

CRATERS OR POCKETS   BRIGHT (POLISHED) SECTIONS

SCRATCHED BY DIRT   LACK OF OIL

DIRT EMBEDDED INTO BEARING MATERIAL   OVERLAY WIPED OUT

EXCESSIVE WEAR   TAPERED JOURNAL

OVERLAY WIPED OUT   RADIUS RIDE

H 28395

16.2 Typical bearing failures

4 Dirt and other foreign matter gets into the engine in a variety of ways. It may be left in the engine during assembly, or it may pass through filters or the crankcase ventilation system. It may get into the oil, and from there into the bearings. Metal chips from machining operations and normal engine wear are often present. Abrasives are sometimes left in engine components after reconditioning, especially when parts are not thoroughly cleaned using the proper cleaning methods. Whatever the source, these foreign objects often end up embedded in the soft bearing material, and are easily recognised. Large particles will not embed in the bearing, and will score or gouge the bearing and journal. The best prevention for this cause of bearing failure is to clean all parts thoroughly, and keep everything spotlessly-clean during engine assembly. Frequent and regular engine oil and filter changes are also recommended.
5 Lack of lubrication (or lubrication breakdown) has a number of interrelated causes. Excessive heat (which thins the oil), overloading (which squeezes the oil from the bearing face) and oil leakage (from excessive bearing clearances, worn oil pump or high engine speeds) all contribute to lubrication breakdown. Blocked oil passages, which usually are the result of misaligned oil holes in a bearing shell, will also oil-starve a bearing, and destroy it. When lack of lubrication is the cause of bearing failure, the bearing material is wiped or extruded from the steel backing of the bearing. Temperatures may increase to the point where the steel backing turns blue from overheating.
6 Driving habits can have a definite effect on bearing life. Full-throttle, low-speed operation (labouring the engine) puts very high loads on bearings, tending to squeeze out the oil film. These loads cause the bearings to flex, which produces fine cracks in the bearing face (fatigue failure). Eventually, the bearing material will loosen in pieces, and tear away from the steel backing.
7 Short-distance driving leads to corrosion of bearings, because insufficient engine heat is produced to drive off the condensed water and corrosive gases. These products collect in the engine oil, forming acid and sludge. As the oil is carried to the engine bearings, the acid attacks and corrodes the bearing material.
8 Incorrect bearing installation during engine assembly will lead to bearing failure as well. Tight-fitting bearings leave insufficient bearing running clearance, and will result in oil starvation. Dirt or foreign particles trapped behind a bearing shell result in high spots on the bearing, which lead to failure.
9 *Do not* touch any shell's bearing surface with your fingers during reassembly; there is a risk of scratching the delicate surface, or of depositing particles of dirt on it.
10 As mentioned at the beginning of this Section, the bearing shells should be renewed as a matter of course during engine overhaul;

to do otherwise is false economy. Refer to Sections 19 and 20 for details of bearing shell selection.

17 Engine overhaul - reassembly sequence

1 Before reassembly begins, ensure that all new parts have been obtained, and that all necessary tools are available. Read through the entire procedure to familiarise yourself with the work involved, and to ensure that all items necessary for reassembly of the engine are at hand. In addition to all normal tools and materials, thread-locking compound will be needed. A suitable tube of liquid sealant will also be required for the joint faces that are fitted without gaskets. It is recommended that Peugeot's own product(s) are used, which are specially formulated for this purpose; the relevant product names are quoted in the text of each Section where they are required.
2 In order to save time and avoid problems, engine reassembly can be carried out in the following order:
a) *Crankshaft (Section 19).*
b) *Piston/connecting rod assemblies (Section 20).*
c) *Oil pump (See Part A or B - as applicable).*
d) *Sump (See Part A or B - as applicable).*
e) *Flywheel (See Part A or B - as applicable).*
f) *Cylinder head (See Part A or B, or this Part - as applicable).*
g) *Timing belt tensioner and sprockets, and timing belt (See Part A or B - as applicable).*
h) *Engine external components.*
3 At this stage, all engine components should be absolutely clean and dry, with all faults repaired. The components should be laid out (or in individual containers) on a completely clean work surface.

18 Piston rings - refitting

1 Before fitting new piston rings, the ring end gaps must be checked as follows.
2 Lay out the piston/connecting rod assemblies and the new piston ring sets, so that the ring sets will be matched with the same piston and cylinder during the end gap measurement and subsequent engine reassembly.
3 Insert the top ring into the first cylinder, and push it down the bore using the top of the piston. This will ensure that the ring remains square with the cylinder walls. Position the ring near the bottom of the cylinder bore, at the lower limit of ring travel. Note that the top and second compression rings are different. The second ring is easily identified by the step on its lower surface, and by the fact that its outer face is tapered.
4 Measure the end gap using feeler gauges.

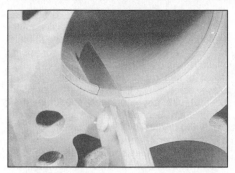

18.5 Measuring a piston ring end gap

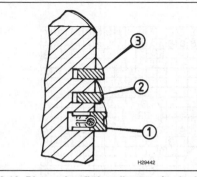

18.10 Piston ring fitting diagram (typical)

1 Oil control ring
2 Second compression ring
3 Top compression ring

19 Crankshaft - refitting and main bearing running clearance check

Selection of new bearing shells

XU series (petrol) engine

Note: *At the time of writing, no information was available on bearing shell selection on 1.8 and 2.0 litre engines. Consult a Peugeot dealer as to the latest information on these engines.*

1 On some early engines, both the upper and lower bearing shells were of the same thickness.

2 However, on later engines the main bearing running clearance was significantly reduced. To enable this to be done, four different grades of bearing shell were introduced. The grades are indicated by a colour-coding marked on the edge of each shell, which denotes the shell's thickness, as listed in the following table. The upper shell on all bearings is of the same size, and the running clearance is controlled by fitting a lower bearing shell of the required thickness.

1.6 litre engines

Bearing colour code	Thickness (mm)	
	Standard	Undersize
Upper bearing:		
Yellow	1.856	2.006
Lower bearing:		
Blue (Class A)	1.836	1.986
Black (Class B)	1.848	1.998
Green (Class C)	1.859	2.009
Red (Class D)	1.870	2.020

Note: *On all XU series engines, upper shells are easily distinguished from lower shells, by their grooved bearing surface; the lower shells have a plain surface.*

3 On most later engines, new bearing shells can be selected using the reference marks on the cylinder block/crankcase. The cylinder block marks identify the diameter of the bearing bores and the crankshaft marks, the diameter of the crankshaft journals. Where no marks are present, the bearing shells can only

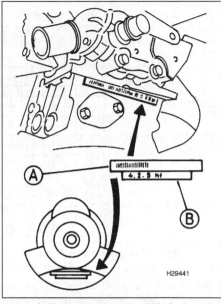

19.4 Cylinder block and crankshaft main bearing reference marking locations - XU engines

A Bar Code (for production use only)
B Reference marks

be selected by checking the running clearance (see below).

4 The cylinder block reference marks are on the left-hand (flywheel/driveplate) end of the block, and the crankshaft reference marks are on the end web of the crankshaft **(see illustration)**. These marks can be used to select bearing shells of the required thickness as follows.

5 On both the crankshaft and block there are two lines of identification: a bar code, which is used by Peugeot during production, and a row of five letters. The first letter in the sequence refers to the size of No 1 bearing (at the flywheel/driveplate end). The last letter in the sequence (which is followed by an arrow) refers to the size of No 5 main bearing. These marks can be used to select the required bearing shell grade as follows.

6 Obtain the identification number/letter of both the relevant crankshaft journal and the cylinder block bearing bore. Noting that the crankshaft references are listed across the top of the chart, and the cylinder block references down the side, trace a vertical line down from the relevant crankshaft reference, and a horizontal line across from the relevant cylinder block reference, and find the point at which both lines cross. This crossover point will indicate the grade of lower bearing shell required to give the correct main bearing running clearance. For example, the illustration shows crankshaft reference 6, and cylinder block reference H, crossing at a point within the RED area, indicating that a Red-coded (Class D) lower bearing shell is required to give the correct main bearing running clearance **(see illustration)**.

5 Repeat the procedure with the ring at the top of the cylinder bore, at the upper limit of its travel, and compare the measurements with the figures given in the Specifications **(see illustration)**. Where no figures are given, seek the advice of a Peugeot dealer or engine reconditioning specialist.

6 If the gap is too small (unlikely if genuine Peugeot parts are used), it must be enlarged, or the ring ends may contact each other during engine operation, causing serious damage. Ideally, new piston rings providing the correct end gap should be fitted. As a last resort, the end gap can be increased by filing the ring ends very carefully with a fine file. Mount the file in a vice equipped with soft jaws, slip the ring over the file with the ends contacting the file face, and slowly move the ring to remove material from the ends. Take care, as piston rings are sharp, and are easily broken.

7 With new piston rings, it is unlikely that the end gap will be too large. If the gaps are too large, check that you have the correct rings for your engine and for the particular cylinder bore size.

8 Repeat the checking procedure for each ring in the first cylinder, and then for the rings in the remaining cylinders. Remember to keep rings, pistons and cylinders matched up.

9 Once the ring end gaps have been checked and if necessary corrected, the rings can be fitted to the pistons.

10 Fit the piston rings using the same technique as for removal. Fit the bottom (oil control) ring first, and work up. When fitting the oil control ring, first insert the expander (where fitted), then fit the ring with its gap positioned 180° from the expander gap. Ensure that the second compression ring is fitted the correct way up, with its identification mark (either a dot of paint or the word "TOP" stamped on the ring surface) at the top, and the stepped surface at the bottom **(see illustration)**. Arrange the gaps of the top and second compression rings 120° either side of the oil control ring gap. **Note:** *Always follow any instructions supplied with the new piston ring sets - different manufacturers may specify different procedures. Do not mix up the top and second compression rings, as they have different cross-sections.*

2C

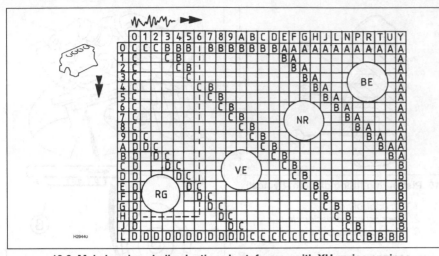

19.6 Main bearing shell selection chart, for use with XU series engines - see text for further information

7 Repeat this procedure so that the required bearing shell grade is obtained for each of the five main bearing journals.

8 Seek the advice of your Peugeot dealer on parts availability, and on the best course of action when ordering new bearing shells. **Note:** *On early models, at overhaul it is recommended that the later bearing shell arrangement is fitted. This, however, should only be done if the lubrication system components are upgraded (necessitating replacement of the oil pump relief valve piston and spring as well as the pump sprocket and drive chain) at the same time. If the new bearing arrangement is to be used without uprating the lubrication system, Blue (Class A) lower bearing shells should be fitted. Refer to your Peugeot dealer for further information.*

XUD series (diesel) engine

9 On all diesel engines both the upper and lower bearing shells are of the same thickness. Peugeot produce both a standard set of shells and an undersize set of shells.

Main bearing running clearance check

XU series (petrol) engine

10 On early engines, if the later bearing shells are to be fitted, obtain a set of new upper bearing shells, and new blue (as applicable) lower bearing shells (see paragraph 2). On later engines where the modified bearing shells are already fitted, the running clearance check can be carried out using the original bearing shells. However, it is preferable to use a new set, since the results obtained will be more conclusive.

11 Clean the backs of the bearing shells, and the bearing locations in both the cylinder block/crankcase and the main bearing caps.

12 Press the bearing shells into their locations, ensuring that the tab on each shell engages in the notch in the cylinder block/crankcase or bearing cap. Take care not to touch any shell's bearing surface with your fingers. Note that the upper bearing shells all have a grooved bearing surface, whereas the lower shells have a plain bearing surface. If the original bearing shells are being used for the check, ensure that they are refitted in their original locations.

13 The clearance can be checked in either of two ways.

14 One method (which will be difficult to achieve without a range of internal micrometers or internal/external expanding calipers) is to refit the main bearing caps to the cylinder block/crankcase, with bearing shells in place. With the cap retaining bolts tightened to the specified torque, measure the internal diameter of each assembled pair of bearing shells. If the diameter of each corresponding crankshaft journal is measured and then subtracted from the bearing internal diameter, the result will be the main bearing running clearance.

15 The second, and more accurate, method is to use Plastigage. This consists of a fine thread of perfectly-round plastic, which is compressed between the bearing shell and the journal. When the shell is removed, the plastic is deformed, and can be measured with a special card gauge supplied with the kit. The running clearance is determined from this gauge. Plastigage should be available

from your Peugeot dealer; otherwise, enquiries at one of the larger specialist motor factors should produce the name of a stockist in your area. The procedure for using Plastigage is as follows.

16 With the main bearing upper shells in place, carefully lay the crankshaft in position. Do not use any lubricant; the crankshaft journals and bearing shells must be perfectly clean and dry.

17 Cut several lengths of the appropriate-size Plastigage (they should be slightly shorter than the width of the main bearings), and place one length on each crankshaft journal axis **(see illustration)**.

18 With the main bearing lower shells in position, refit the main bearing caps and tighten them as described later in this Section. Take care not to disturb the Plastigage, and *do not* rotate the crankshaft at any time during this operation.

19 Remove the main bearing caps, again taking great care not to disturb the Plastigage or rotate the crankshaft.

20 Compare the width of the crushed Plastigage on each journal to the scale printed on the Plastigage envelope, to obtain the main bearing running clearance **(see illustration)**. Compare the clearance measured with that given in the Specifications at the start of this Chapter.

21 If the clearance is significantly different from that expected, the bearing shells may be the wrong size (or excessively worn, if the original shells are being re-used). Before deciding that different-size shells are required, make sure that no dirt or oil was trapped between the bearing shells and the caps or block when the clearance was measured. If the Plastigage was wider at one end than at the other, the crankshaft journal may be tapered.

22 If the clearance is not as specified, use the reading obtained, along with the shell thicknesses quoted above, to calculate the necessary grade of bearing shells required. When calculating the bearing clearance required, bear in mind that it is always better to have the running clearance towards the lower end of the specified range, to allow for wear in use.

23 Where necessary, obtain the required

19.17 Plastigage in place on a crankshaft main bearing journal

19.20 Measure the width of the deformed Plastigage using the scale on the card

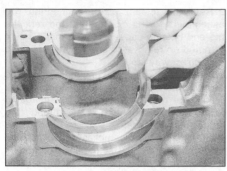

19.27 Fitting a thrustwasher to No 2 main bearing upper location

grades of bearing shell, and repeat the running clearance checking procedure as described above.

24 On completion, carefully scrape away all traces of the Plastigage material from the crankshaft and bearing shells. Use your fingernail, or a wooden or plastic scraper which is unlikely to score the bearing surfaces.

XUD series (diesel) engine

25 The running clearance check can be carried out using the original bearing shells. However, it is preferable to use a new set, since the results obtained will be more conclusive. Perform the check using the information given in the preceding paragraphs.

Final crankshaft refitting

XU and XUD series engines

26 Carefully lift the crankshaft out of the cylinder block once more.

27 Using a little grease, stick the upper thrustwashers to each side of the No 2 main bearing upper location. Ensure that the oilway grooves on each thrustwasher face outwards (away from the cylinder block) **(see illustration)**.

28 Place the bearing shells in their locations as described earlier **(see illustration)**. If new shells are being fitted, ensure that all traces of protective grease are cleaned off using paraffin. Wipe dry the shells and connecting rods with a lint-free cloth. Liberally lubricate each bearing shell in the cylinder block/crankcase and cap with clean engine oil.

29 Lower the crankshaft into position so that Nos 2 and 3 cylinder crankpins are at TDC; Nos 1 and 4 cylinder crankpins will be at BDC, ready for fitting No 1 piston. Check the crankshaft endfloat, referring to Section 15.

30 Lubricate the lower bearing shells in the main bearing caps with clean engine oil. Make sure that the locating lugs on the shells engage with the corresponding recesses in the caps.

31 Fit main bearing caps Nos 2 to 5 to their correct locations, ensuring that they are fitted the correct way round (the bearing shell tab recesses in the block and caps must be on the same side). Insert the bolts/nuts, tightening them only loosely at this stage.

32 Apply a small amount of sealant to the No 1 main bearing cap mating face on the cylinder block, around the sealing strip holes **(see illustration)**.

33 Locate the tab of each sealing strip over the pins on the base of No 1 bearing cap, and press the strips into the bearing cap grooves. It is now necessary to obtain two thin metal strips, of 0.25 mm thickness or less, in order to prevent the strips moving when the cap is being fitted. Peugeot garages use the tool shown, which acts as a clamp. Metal strips (such as old feeler blades) can be used, provided all burrs which may damage the sealing strips are first removed **(see illustrations)**.

34 Where applicable, oil both sides of the metal strips, and hold them on the sealing strips. Fit the No 1 main bearing cap, insert the bolts loosely, then carefully pull out the metal strips in a horizontal direction, using a pair of pliers **(see illustrations)**.

35 Tighten all the main bearing cap bolts/nuts evenly to the specified torque. Using a sharp knife, trim off the ends of the No 1 bearing cap sealing strips, so that they protrude above the cylinder block/crankcase mating surface by approximately 1 mm **(see illustrations)**.

36 On 1.6 and 1.8 litre petrol engines, refit the centre main bearing side retaining bolts and sealing washers (one at the front of the block, and one at the rear) and tighten them both to the specified torque.

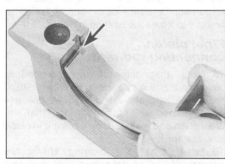

19.28 Ensure that the tab (arrowed) is correctly located in the cap when fitting the bearing shells

19.32 Applying sealant to the cylinder block No 1 main bearing cap mating face

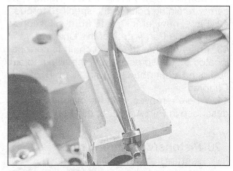

19.33a Fitting a sealing strip to No 1 main bearing cap

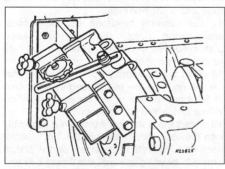

19.33b Using the Peugeot special tool to fit No 1 main bearing cap

19.34a Fitting No 1 main bearing cap, using metal strips to retain the side seals

19.34b Removing a metal strip from No 1 main bearing cap using a pair of pliers

19.35a With all bearing caps correctly installed, tighten their retaining nuts and bolts to the specified torque . . .

19.35b . . . then trim the ends of No 1 bearing cap sealing strips, so that they protrude above the cylinder block mating surface by approximately 1 mm

37 Fit a new crankshaft rear oil seal as described in Part A or B of this Chapter (as applicable).

38 Refit the piston/connecting rod assemblies to the crankshaft as described in Section 20.

39 Refit the Woodruff key, then slide on the oil pump drive sprocket and spacer (where fitted), and locate the drive chain on the sprocket.

40 Ensure that the mating surfaces of the front oil seal carrier and cylinder block are clean and dry. Note the correct fitted depth of the oil seal then, using a large flat-bladed screwdriver, lever the old seal out of the housing.

41 Apply a smear of suitable sealant to the oil seal carrier mating surface. Ensure that the locating dowels are in position, then slide the carrier over the end of the crankshaft and into position on the cylinder block. Tighten the carrier retaining bolts to the specified torque.

42 Fit a new crankshaft front oil seal as described in Part A or B of this Chapter.

43 Ensuring that the drive chain is correctly located on the sprocket, refit the oil pump and sump as described in Part A or B of this Chapter.

44 Where removed, refit the cylinder head as described in Part A or B, or this Part.

20 Pistons/connecting rods - refitting and big-end bearing running clearance check

Selection of bearing shells

1 On most engines, there are two sizes of big-end bearing shell produced by Peugeot; a standard size for use with the standard crankshaft, and an oversize for use once the crankshaft journals have been reground.

2 Consult your Peugeot dealer for the latest information on parts availability. To be safe, always quote the diameter of the crankshaft big-end crankpins when ordering bearing shells.

3 Prior to refitting the piston/connecting rod assemblies, it is recommended that the big-end bearing running clearance is checked as follows.

Big-end bearing running clearance check

4 Clean the backs of the bearing shells, and the bearing locations in both the connecting rod and bearing cap.

5 Press the bearing shells into their locations, ensuring that the tab on each shell engages in the notch in the connecting rod and cap. Take care not to touch any shell's bearing surface with your fingers **(see illustration)**. If the original bearing shells are being used for the check, ensure they are refitted in their original locations. The clearance can be checked in either of two ways.

6 One method is to refit the big-end bearing cap to the connecting rod, ensuring they are fitted the correct way around (see paragraph 20), with the bearing shells in place. With the cap retaining nuts correctly tightened, use an internal micrometer or vernier caliper to measure the internal diameter of each assembled pair of bearing shells. If the diameter of each corresponding crankshaft journal is measured and then subtracted from the bearing internal diameter, the result will be the big-end bearing running clearance.

7 The second, and more accurate method is to use Plastigage (see Section 19).

8 Ensure that the bearing shells are correctly fitted. Place a strand of Plastigage on each (cleaned) crankpin journal.

20.5 Fitting a bearing shell to a connecting rod - ensure that the tab (arrowed) engages with the recess in the connecting rod

9 Refit the (clean) piston/connecting rod assemblies to the crankshaft, and refit the big-end bearing caps, using the marks made or noted on removal to ensure they are fitted the correct way around.

10 Tighten the bearing cap nuts as described below in paragraph 21 or 22 (as applicable). Take care not to disturb the Plastigage or rotate the connecting rod during the tightening sequence.

11 Dismantle the assemblies without rotating the connecting rods. Use the scale printed on the Plastigage envelope to obtain the big-end bearing running clearance.

12 If the clearance is significantly different from that expected, the bearing shells may be the wrong size (or excessively worn, if the original shells are being re-used). Make sure that no dirt or oil was trapped between the bearing shells and the caps or block when the clearance was measured. If the Plastigage was wider at one end than at the other, the crankshaft journal may be tapered.

13 Note that Peugeot do not specify a recommended big-end bearing running clearance. The figure given in the Specifications is a guide figure, which is typical for this type of engine. Before condemning the components concerned, refer to your Peugeot dealer or engine reconditioning specialist for further information on the specified running clearance. Their advice on the best course of action to be taken can then also be obtained.

14 On completion, carefully scrape away all traces of the Plastigage material from the crankshaft and bearing shells. Use your fingernail, or some other object which is unlikely to score the bearing surfaces.

Final piston/ connecting rod refitting

15 Note that the following procedure assumes that the cylinder liners (where fitted) are in position in the cylinder block/crankcase as described in Section 12, and that the crankshaft and main bearing caps are in place (see Section 19).

16 Ensure that the bearing shells are correctly fitted as described earlier. If new shells are being fitted, ensure that all traces of the protective grease are cleaned off using paraffin. Wipe dry the shells and connecting rods with a lint-free cloth.

17 Lubricate the cylinder bores, the pistons, and piston rings, then lay out each piston/connecting rod assembly in its respective position.

18 Start with assembly No 1. Make sure that the piston rings are still spaced as described in Section 18, then clamp them in position with a piston ring compressor.

19 Insert the piston/connecting rod assembly into the top of cylinder/liner No 1. On petrol engines, ensure that the arrow on the piston crown is pointing towards the timing belt end of the engine and on diesel engines, ensure that the cloverleaf-shaped cut-out on the

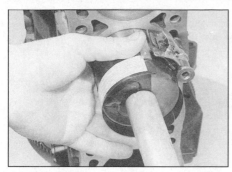

20.19 Tap the piston into the bore using a hammer handle

20.22a Tighten the big-end bearing cap nuts using a torque wrench . . .

20.22b . . . and an angle-measuring gauge

piston crown is towards the front (oil filter side) of the cylinder block. Using a block of wood or hammer handle against the piston crown, tap the assembly into the cylinder/liner until the piston crown is flush with the top of the cylinder/liner **(see illustration)**.

20 Ensure that the bearing shell is still correctly installed. Liberally lubricate the crankpin and both bearing shells. Taking care not to mark the cylinder/liner bores, pull the piston/connecting rod assembly down the bore and onto the crankpin.

21 Refit the big-end bearing cap, tightening its retaining nuts finger-tight at first. Note that the faces with the identification marks must match (which means that the bearing shell locating tabs abut each other).

22 On 1.6 litre petrol engines, tighten the bearing cap retaining nuts evenly and progressively to the stage 1 torque setting. Fully slacken both nuts, then tighten them to the stage 2 torque setting. Once both nuts have been tightened to the stage 2 setting, angle-tighten them through the specified stage 3 angle, using a socket and extension bar. It is recommended that an angle-measuring gauge is used during this stage of the tightening, to ensure accuracy **(see illustrations)**. If a gauge is not available, use a dab of white paint to make alignment marks between the nut and bearing cap prior to tightening; the marks can then be used to check that the nut has been rotated sufficiently during tightening. On all other engines, tighten the bearing cap retaining nuts evenly and progressively to the stage 1 torque setting. Once both nuts have been tightened to the stage 1 setting, angle-tighten them through the specified stage 2 angle, using a socket and extension bar.

23 On all engines, once the bearing cap retaining nuts have been correctly tightened, rotate the crankshaft. Check that it turns freely; some stiffness is to be expected if new components have been fitted, but there should be no signs of binding or tight spots.

24 Refit the remaining three piston/connecting rod assemblies in the same way.

25 Refit the cylinder head and oil pump as described in Part A or B of this Chapter, or this Part (as applicable).

21 Engine - initial start-up after overhaul

1 With the engine refitted in the vehicle, double-check the engine oil and coolant levels. Make a final check that everything has been reconnected, and that there are no tools or rags left in the engine compartment.

Petrol engine models

2 Remove the spark plugs and disable the fuel system by disconnecting the wiring connectors from the fuel injectors, referring to Chapter 4A for further information.

3 Turn the engine on the starter until the oil pressure warning light goes out. Refit the spark plugs, and reconnect the ECU.

Diesel engine models

4 To prevent the engine starting, on 1.9 litre models, disconnect the wiring from the stop solenoid on the injection pump (Chapter 4B), then turn the engine on the starter motor until the oil pressure warning light goes out. Reconnect the wire to the stop solenoid. On 2.1 litre models it is normally sufficient to disconnect the fuel injection multi-function

relay located in the ECU module box, but the advice of a dealer should be sought.

5 Prime the fuel system (refer to Chapter 4B).

6 Fully depress the accelerator pedal, turn the ignition key to position "M", and wait for the preheating warning light to go out.

All models

7 Start the engine, noting that this may take a little longer than usual, due to the fuel system components having been disturbed.

8 While the engine is idling, check for fuel, water and oil leaks. Don't be alarmed if there are some odd smells and smoke from parts getting hot and burning off oil deposits.

9 Assuming all is well, keep the engine idling until hot water is felt circulating through the top hose, then switch off the engine.

10 Check the ignition timing (petrol engines) or injection pump timing (diesel engines), and the idle speed settings (as appropriate), then switch the engine off.

11 After a few minutes, recheck the oil and coolant levels as described in "Weekly Checks", and top-up as necessary.

12 On 2.1 litre diesel engines it will be necessary to re-tighten the cylinder head after the engine has cooled (see Section 7). On all other engines, if they were tightened as described, there is no need to re-tighten the cylinder head bolts once the engine has first run after reassembly.

13 If new pistons, rings or crankshaft bearings have been fitted, the engine must be treated as new, and run-in for the first 500 miles (800 km). *Do not* operate the engine at full-throttle, or allow it to labour at low engine speeds in any gear. It is recommended that the oil and filter be changed at the end of this period.

2C

Chapter 3
Cooling, heating and ventilation systems

Contents

Degrees of difficulty

Easy, suitable for novice with little experience	Fairly easy, suitable for beginner with some experience	Fairly difficult, suitable for competent DIY mechanic	Difficult, suitable for experienced DIY mechanic	Very difficult, suitable for expert DIY or professional

Specifications

General
Maximum system pressure .... 1.4 bar

Thermostat
Opening temperature (all models)
  Petrol models:
    8-valve engines .... 89°C
    16-valve engines .... 83°C
  Diesel models .... 83°C

3

---

1 General information and precautions

General information

The cooling system is of pressurised type, comprising a coolant pump driven by the timing belt, an aluminium crossflow radiator, electric cooling fan(s), a thermostat, heater matrix, and all associated hoses and switches.

The system functions as follows. Cold coolant in the bottom of the radiator passes through the bottom hose to the coolant pump, where it is pumped around the cylinder block and head passages, and through the oil cooler(s) (where fitted). After cooling the cylinder bores, combustion surfaces and valve seats, the coolant reaches the underside of the thermostat, which is initially closed. The coolant passes through the heater, and is returned via the cylinder block to the coolant pump.

When the engine is cold, the coolant circulates only through the cylinder block, cylinder head, and heater. When the coolant

reaches a predetermined temperature, the thermostat opens, and the coolant passes through the top hose to the radiator. As the coolant circulates through the radiator, it is cooled by the inrush of air when the car is in forward motion. The airflow is supplemented by the action of the electric cooling fan(s) when necessary. Upon reaching the bottom of the radiator, the coolant has now cooled, and the cycle is repeated.

When the engine is at normal operating temperature, the coolant expands, and some of it is displaced into the expansion tank. Coolant collects in the tank, and is returned to the radiator when the system cools.

On models with automatic transmission, a proportion of the coolant is recirculated from the bottom of the radiator through the transmission fluid cooler mounted on the transmission. On models fitted with an engine oil cooler, the coolant is also passed through the oil cooler.

The electric cooling fan(s) in front of the radiator are controlled by a thermostatic switch. At a predetermined coolant temperature, the switch/sensor actuates the fan.

Precautions

Warning: Do not attempt to remove the expansion tank filler cap, or to disturb any part of the cooling system, while the engine is hot, as there is a high risk of scalding. If the expansion tank filler cap must be removed before the engine and radiator have fully cooled (even though this is not recommended), the pressure in the cooling system must first be relieved. Cover the cap with a thick layer of cloth to avoid scalding, and slowly unscrew the filler cap until a hissing sound is heard. When the hissing has stopped, indicating that the pressure has reduced, slowly unscrew the filler cap until it can be removed; if more hissing sounds are heard, wait until they have stopped before unscrewing the cap completely. At all times, keep well away from the filler cap opening, and protect your hands.

Warning: Do not allow antifreeze to come into contact with your skin, or with the painted surfaces of the vehicle. Rinse off

spills immediately, with plenty of water. Never leave antifreeze lying around in an open container, or in a puddle in the driveway or on the garage floor. Children and pets are attracted by its sweet smell, but antifreeze can be fatal if ingested.

 Warning: If the engine is hot, the electric cooling fan may start rotating even if the engine is not running. Be careful to keep your hands, hair, and any loose clothing well clear when working in the engine compartment.

 Warning: Refer to Section 10 for precautions to be observed when working on models equipped with air conditioning.

2 Cooling system hoses - disconnection and renewal

Note: *Refer to the warnings given in Section 1 of this Chapter before proceeding. Hoses should only be disconnected once the engine has cooled sufficiently to avoid scalding.*

1 If the checks described in Chapter 1 reveal a faulty hose, it must be renewed as follows.
2 First drain the cooling system (Chapter 1). If the coolant is not due for renewal, it may be re-used, providing it is collected in a clean container.
3 To disconnect a hose, proceed as follows, according to the type of hose connection.

Conventional hose connections

4 On conventional connections, the clips used to secure the hoses in position may be either standard worm-drive clips or disposable crimped types. The crimped type of clip is not designed to be re-used, and should be replaced with a worm-drive type on reassembly.
5 To disconnect a hose, use a screwdriver to slacken or release the clips, then move them along the hose, clear of the relevant inlet/outlet **(see illustration)**. Carefully work the hose free. The hoses can be removed with relative ease when new - on an older car, they may have stuck.
6 If a hose proves to be difficult to remove, try to release it by rotating its ends before attempting to free it. Gently prise the end of the hose with a blunt instrument (such as a flat-bladed screwdriver), but do not apply too much force, and take care not to damage the pipe stubs or hoses. Note in particular that the radiator inlet stub is fragile; do not use excessive force when attempting to remove the hose. If all else fails, cut the hose with a sharp knife, then slit it so that it can be peeled off in two pieces. Although this may prove expensive if the hose is otherwise undamaged, it is preferable to buying a new radiator. Check first, however, that a new hose is readily available.
7 When fitting a hose, first slide the clips onto

2.5 Disconnecting a conventional coolant hose

> **HAYNES HiNT** *If the hose is stiff, use a little soapy water as a lubricant, or soften the hose by soaking it in hot water. Do not use oil or grease, which may attack the rubber.*

the hose, then work the hose into position. If crimped-type clips were originally fitted, use standard worm-drive clips when refitting the hose.
8 Work the hose into position, checking that it is correctly routed, then slide each clip back along the hose until it passes over the flared end of the relevant inlet/outlet, before tightening the clip securely.
9 Refill the cooling system (see Chapter 1).

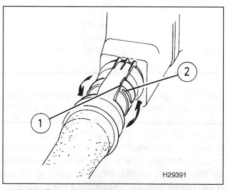
2.12 To release a bayonet-type hose, turn the locking ring (2) until it contacts the stop (1) . . .

2.17 Prior to refitting, fit a new sealing ring (arrowed) to the hose union

10 Check thoroughly for leaks as soon as possible after disturbing any part of the cooling system.

Bayonet-type connection

Note: *A new sealing ring should be used when reconnecting the hose.*
11 On certain models, some hoses may be secured in position using a plastic bayonet-type connection. To disconnect this type of connector, proceed as follows.
12 Turn the locking ring (2) anti-clockwise until it contacts the stop (1) **(see illustration)**.
13 Press the connector away from the hose, to ensure that the two retaining lugs (3) are free **(see illustration)**.
14 Pull the hose and its connector from the radiator.
15 Recover the sealing ring from the connector, and discard it; a new one must be used on refitting.
16 On refitting, wipe the connector and the stub on the radiator thoroughly with a clean, lint-free cloth.
17 Fit a new sealing ring to the male half of the connector, ensuring that it is correctly seated **(see illustration)**.
18 Turn the locking ring clockwise until it clicks.
19 Offer the hose to the union making sure the cut-out is correctly positioned to align with the locating lug **(see illustration)**.
20 Push the connector fully into position until both the retaining lugs click into position. Make sure that the sealing ring is not trapped.

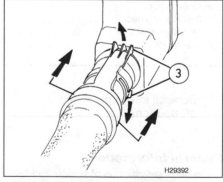
2.13 . . . then press the connector away from the hose to ensure that the retaining lugs (3) are free

2.19 When the hose is reconnected ensure its cut-out (arrowed) is correctly positioned

21 Pull the connector rearwards (away from the stub) to adjust the position of the retaining lugs if necessary.

22 Refill the cooling system (see Chapter 1).

23 Check thoroughly for leaks as soon as possible after disturbing any part of the cooling system.

Click-fit connection

Note: *A new sealing ring should be used when reconnecting the hose.*

24 On certain models, some cooling system hoses are secured in position with click-fit connectors where the hose union is retained by a large circlip.

25 To disconnect this type of hose, using a small flat-bladed screwdriver, carefully prise the circlip out of position. The hose connection can then be slid out of position and the sealing ring removed **(see illustrations)**. Once the hose is disconnected, refit the circlip to the female end of the connection.

26 On refitting, ensure that the circlip is correctly located in its groove in the female end of the connection, and fit the new sealing ring to the hose union. Push the hose connection into position, taking care not trap the sealing ring, until it clicks into position.

27 Ensure that the hose is securely retained by the circlip then refill the cooling system as described in Chapter 1.

28 Check thoroughly for leaks as soon as possible after disturbing any part of the cooling system.

3 Radiator - removal, inspection and refitting

Note: *New sealing rings must be used when reconnecting bayonet-type/click fit radiator hoses - see Section 2. If leakage is the reason for removing the radiator, bear in mind that minor leaks can often be cured using a radiator sealant with the radiator in situ.*

Removal

1 Disconnect the battery negative lead.

2 Drain the cooling system (see Chapter 1).

3 Where necessary, disconnect the wiring connector from the cooling fan switch which is screwed into the radiator.

4 Disconnect the coolant hoses from the radiator with reference to Section 2.

5 Working at the top of the radiator, release the retaining clips then tilt the radiator towards the rear **(see illustrations)**. Lift the radiator out of position, taking care not to damage the radiator fins on surrounding components; on diesel models, it will be necessary to free the intercooler from the radiator as it is removed. Take care not to lose the radiator lower mounting rubbers.

Inspection

6 If the radiator has been removed due to suspected blockage, reverse-flush it as

2.25a To disconnect a click-fit connector, lever out the circlip . . .

3.5a Lift up the retaining clips . . .

described in Chapter 1. Clean dirt and debris from the radiator fins, using an air line (in which case, wear eye protection) or a soft brush. Be careful, as the fins are sharp, and easily damaged.

7 If necessary, a radiator specialist can perform a "flow test" on the radiator, to establish whether an internal blockage exists.

8 A leaking radiator must be referred to a specialist for permanent repair. Do not attempt to weld or solder a leaking radiator, as damage to the plastic components may result.

9 In an emergency, minor leaks from the radiator can be cured by using a suitable radiator sealant, in accordance with its manufacturer's instructions, with the radiator *in situ*.

10 If the radiator is to be sent for repair or renewed, remove all hoses and the cooling fan switch (where fitted).

11 Inspect the condition of the radiator mounting rubbers, and renew them if necessary.

Refitting

12 Refitting is a reversal of removal, bearing in mind the following points:

a) *Ensure that the lower lugs on the radiator are correctly engaged with the mounting rubbers in the body panel. On diesel models, also ensure that the intercooler is correctly engaged with the radiator.*

b) *Reconnect the hoses with reference to Section 2, using new sealing rings where applicable.*

c) *On completion, refill the cooling system as described in Chapter 1.*

2.25b . . . then ease the hose union out of position and remove the sealing ring (arrowed)

3.5b . . . then tilt the radiator upwards and out of position to release its lower mounting pegs

4 Thermostat - removal, testing and refitting

Note: *A new thermostat sealing ring will be required on refitting.*

Removal

1 Disconnect the battery negative lead.

2 Drain the cooling system as described in Chapter 1. On 2.1 litre turbo diesel models, the thermostat housing is mounted onto the rear of the cylinder block on its right-hand end; to gain access, firmly apply the handbrake then jack up the front of the vehicle and support it on axle stands. On all other models, the thermostat housing is mounted on the left-hand end of the cylinder head **(see illustration)**.

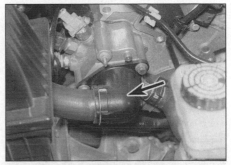

4.2 On 1.8 and 2.0 litre 16-valve models, the thermostat housing (arrowed) is on the left-hand end of the cylinder head

3

4.10a Fit a new sealing ring to the thermostat . . .

4.10b . . . then fit the thermostat to the housing, making sure its spring is correctly positioned (2.1 litre diesel shown)

3 Where necessary, release any relevant wiring and hoses from the retaining clips, and position clear of the thermostat housing to improve access.

4 Disconnect the coolant hose(s) from the thermostat housing (see Section 2).

5 Unscrew the retaining nuts/bolts (as applicable) and carefully withdraw the thermostat housing cover to expose the thermostat.

6 Lift the thermostat from the housing, and recover the sealing ring.

Testing

7 A rough test of the thermostat may be made by suspending it with a piece of string in a container full of water. Heat the water to bring it to the boil - the thermostat must open by the time the water boils. If not, renew it.

8 If a thermometer is available, the precise opening temperature of the thermostat may be determined; compare with the figures given in the Specifications. The opening temperature is also marked on the thermostat.

9 A thermostat which fails to close as the water cools must also be renewed.

Refitting

10 Refitting is a reversal of removal, bearing in mind the following points:

a) *Always fit a new sealing ring and ensure that the thermostat is fitted the correct way round, with the spring(s) facing into the housing* **(see illustrations)**.

b) *On models where the coolant hose is secured to the housing with a click-fit connector, renew the connector sealing ring (see Section 2).*

c) *On completion, refill the cooling system as described in Chapter 1.*

---

5 Electric cooling fan(s) - testing, removal and refitting

Testing

1 Current supply to the cooling fan(s) is via the ignition switch and a fuse (Chapter 12). On petrol models without air conditioning, the circuit is completed by the cooling fan thermostatic switch, which is mounted in the left-hand side of the radiator. On petrol models with air conditioning and all diesel models, the cooling fans are controlled by the "Bitron" sensor - see Section 6.

2 If a fan does not appear to work, run the engine until normal operating temperature is reached, then allow it to idle. The fan should cut in within a few minutes (before the temperature gauge needle enters the red section, or before the coolant temperature warning light comes on). If not, switch off the ignition and disconnect the wiring plug from the cooling fan switch. Bridge the two contacts in the wiring plug using a length of spare wire, and switch on the ignition. If the fan now operates, the switch is probably faulty, and should be renewed.

3 If the fan still fails to operate, check that battery voltage is available at the feed wire to the switch; if not, then there is a fault in the feed wire (possibly due to a fault in the fan motor, or a blown fuse). If there is no problem with the feed, check that there is continuity between the switch earth terminal and a good earth point on the body; if not, then the earth connection is faulty, and must be re-made.

4 If the switch and the wiring are in good condition, the fault must lie in the motor itself. The motor can be checked by disconnecting it from the wiring loom and connecting a 12-volt supply directly to it.

Removal

5 Remove the radiator (see Section 3). On diesel models it will also be necessary to remove the intercooler (see Chapter 4).

6 On models with air conditioning, slacken and remove the retaining screws, then remove the retaining clip securing the condenser assembly to the fan shroud. Carefully ease the condenser assembly backwards and position it clear of the shroud so that access can be gained to the fan motor retaining nuts.

⚠️ **Warning: Do not attempt to open the refrigerant circuit. Refer to the precautions in Section 10.**

7 Remove the fasteners (pull out the centre pins then lever out the complete fastener) securing the grille panel to the bonnet crossmember. Release the side retaining clips then, using a large flat-bladed screwdriver, depress the centre clip and slide the grille panel forwards and away from the vehicle.

8 Slacken and remove the nuts securing the fan shroud to the bonnet lock crossmember then undo the retaining bolts securing the crossmember in position. Unhook the bonnet release cable from the lock and remove the crossmember assembly.

9 Undo the retaining nuts then pull the motor assembly away from the shroud (the wiring connector will disconnect automatically) and manoeuvre it out from between the shroud and bumper **(see illustrations)**.

10 If necessary, slide off retaining clip/undo the retaining screw (as applicable) and remove the fan from the motor spindle **(see illustration)**. The motor can then be unbolted and removed from the shroud. If the motor is faulty, the complete unit must be renewed, as no spares are available.

5.9a Undo the retaining nuts (arrowed) . . .

5.9b . . . then manoeuvre the cooling fan out of position

5.10 The cooling fan is secured to the motor by a screw on most models

Refitting

11 Refitting is a reversal of removal, noting the following points.

a) Prior to refitting, inspect the fan shroud mountings, renewing them if they show signs of wear or damage.

b) Ensure that the wiring is correctly routed and secured in position with all the relevant clips and ties so that it is no danger of contacting the fan.

c) Refit the radiator as described in Section 3.

---

6 Cooling system electrical switches and sensors - testing, removal and refitting

Electric cooling fan thermostatic switch - petrol models without air conditioning

Testing

1 Testing of the switch is described in Section 5, as part of the electric cooling fan test procedure.

Removal

2 The switch is located in the left-hand side of the radiator. The engine and radiator should be cold before removing the switch.

3 Disconnect the battery negative lead.

4 Partially drain the cooling system to just below the level of the switch (as described in Chapter 1). Alternatively, have ready a suitable bung to plug the switch aperture in the radiator when the switch is removed. If this method is used, take great care not to damage the radiator, and do not use anything which will allow foreign matter to enter the radiator.

5 Disconnect the wiring plug from the switch.

6 Carefully unscrew the switch from the radiator, and recover the sealing ring (where fitted). If the system has not been drained, plug the switch aperture to prevent further coolant loss.

Refitting

7 If the switch was originally fitted using a sealing ring, use a new sealing ring on refitting. Where no sealing ring was fitted, clean the switch threads thoroughly and coat them with fresh sealing compound.

8 Refitting is a reversal of removal. Tighten the switch securely. Refill (or top-up) the cooling system as described in Chapter 1.

9 On completion, start the engine and run it until it reaches normal operating temperature. Continue to run the engine, and check that the cooling fan cuts in and out correctly.

Electric cooling fan thermostatic switch - petrol models with air conditioning, and all diesel models

10 The cooling fans are controlled by the "Bitron" sensor. This is located in the thermostat housing, which is bolted onto the left-hand end of the cylinder head - see paragraphs 19 to 21.

Coolant temperature gauge/temperature warning light sender

Testing

Note: *On petrol engine models with air conditioning and diesel engine models, the sender provides a signal to the gauge only. The coolant temperature warning light is operated by the "Bitron" temperature sensor described later in this Section.*

11 The coolant temperature gauge/warning light sender is screwed into the left-hand end of the cylinder head. The sender can be identified by its blue wiring connector **(see illustration).**

12 The temperature gauge (where fitted) is fed with a stabilised voltage from the instrument panel feed (via the ignition switch and a fuse). The gauge earth is controlled by the sender. The sender contains a thermistor - an electronic component whose electrical resistance decreases at a predetermined rate as its temperature rises. When the coolant is cold, the sender resistance is high, current flow through the gauge is reduced, and the gauge needle points towards the blue (cold) end of the scale. As the coolant temperature rises and the sender resistance falls, current flow increases, and the gauge needle moves towards the upper end of the scale. If the sender is faulty, it must be renewed.

13 On models with a temperature warning light, the light is fed with a voltage from the instrument panel. The light earth is controlled by the sender. The sender is effectively a switch, which operates at a predetermined temperature to earth the light and complete the circuit. If the light is fitted in addition to a gauge, the senders for the gauge and light are incorporated in a single unit, with two wires, one each for the light and gauge earths.

14 If the gauge develops a fault, first check the other instruments; if they do not work at all, check the instrument panel electrical feed. If the readings are erratic, there may be a fault in the voltage stabiliser, which will necessitate renewal of the stabiliser (the stabiliser is integral with the instrument panel printed

6.11 On 1.8 and 2.0 litre 16-valve models, the switches/senders are screwed into the thermostat housing (arrowed)

circuit board - see Chapter 12). If the fault lies in the temperature gauge alone, check it as follows.

15 If the gauge needle remains at the "cold" end of the scale when the engine is hot, disconnect the sender wiring plug, and earth the relevant wire to the cylinder head. If the needle then deflects when the ignition is switched on, the sender unit is proved faulty, and should be renewed. If the needle still does not move, remove the instrument panel (Chapter 12) and check the continuity of the wire between the sender unit and the gauge, and the feed to the gauge unit. If continuity is shown, and the fault still exists, then the gauge is faulty, and the gauge unit should be renewed.

16 If the gauge needle remains at the "hot" end of the scale when the engine is cold, disconnect the sender wire. If the needle then returns to the "cold" end of the scale when the ignition is switched on, the sender unit is proved faulty, and should be renewed. If the needle still does not move, check the remainder of the circuit as described previously.

17 The same basic principles apply to testing the warning light. The light should illuminate when the relevant sender wire is earthed.

Removal and refitting

18 The procedure is similar to that described previously in this Section for the electric cooling fan thermostatic switch. On some models, access to the switch is very poor, and other components may need to be removed before the sender unit can be reached.

"Bitron" temperature sensor - petrol models with air conditioning, and all diesel models

Testing

19 The sensor forms part of the air conditioning "Bitron" control system (see Section 10). Testing of the sensor should be entrusted to a Peugeot dealer.

Removal and refitting

20 The "Bitron" temperature sensor is screwed into the thermostat housing (petrol models) or fuel filter housing (diesel models), which is bolted onto the left-hand end of the cylinder head. The sensor can be identified by its brown wiring connector.

21 The procedure is similar to that described previously in this Section for the electric cooling fan thermostatic switch. On some models, access to the switch is very poor, and other components may need to be removed before the sender unit can be reached.

Coolant temperature (fuel system) sensor

Testing

22 The fuel injection system coolant temperature sensor is screwed into the thermostat housing, which is bolted onto the

3

left-hand end of the cylinder head. The sensor can be identified by its green wiring connector.

23 The sensor is a thermistor (see paragraph 13). The fuel injection/engine management electronic control unit (ECU) supplies the sensor with a set voltage and then, by measuring the current flowing in the sensor circuit, it determines the engine's temperature. This information is then used, in conjunction with other inputs, to control the injector opening time (pulse width). On some models, the idle speed and/or ignition timing settings are also temperature-dependent.

24 If the sensor circuit should fail to provide adequate information, the ECU's back-up facility will override the sensor signal. In this event, the ECU assumes a predetermined setting which will allow the fuel injection/engine management system to run, albeit at reduced efficiency. When this occurs, the warning light on the instrument panel will come on, and the advice of a Peugeot dealer should be sought. The sensor itself can only be tested using special Peugeot diagnostic equipment. *Do not* attempt to test the circuit using any other equipment, as there is a high risk of damaging the ECU.

Removal and refitting

25 The procedure is similar to that described previously in this Section for the electric cooling fan thermostatic switch. On some models, access to the switch is very poor, and certain components may need to be removed before the sensor can be reached.

7 Coolant pump - removal and refitting

Removal

1 Drain the cooling system (see Chapter 1).
2 Remove the timing belt (see Chapter 2).
3 Slacken and remove the retaining bolts and withdraw the pump assembly from the engine, along with its gasket. Discard the gasket, a new one must be used on refitting.

Refitting

4 Ensure that the pump and cylinder block/housing mating faces are clean and dry.
5 Offer up the new gasket and fit the pump assembly, tighten its retaining bolts securely.
6 Refit the timing belt as described in the relevant Part of Chapter 2.
7 Refill the cooling system (see Chapter 1).

8 Heating and ventilation system - general information

The heating/ventilation system consists of a fully adjustable blower motor (housed behind the facia), face level vents in the centre and at each end of the facia, and air ducts to the front footwells.

The control unit is located in the facia, and the controls operate flap valves to deflect and mix the air flowing through the various parts of the heating/ventilation system. The flap valves are contained in the air distribution housing, which acts as a central distribution unit, passing air to the various ducts and vents.

Cold air enters the system through the grille at the rear of the engine compartment. If required, the airflow is boosted by the blower, and then flows through the various ducts, according to the settings of the controls. Stale air is expelled through ducts at the rear of the vehicle. If warm air is required, the cold air is passed over the heater matrix, which is heated by the engine coolant.

A recirculation lever/switch enables the outside air supply to be closed off, while the air inside the vehicle is recirculated. This can be useful to prevent unpleasant odours entering from outside the vehicle, but should only be used briefly, as the recirculated air inside the vehicle will soon become stale.

9 Heater/ventilation components - removal and refitting

Heater/ventilation control unit

Removal

1 Disconnect the battery negative lead.
2 Remove the radio/cassette unit and the facia centre switch panel unit as described in Chapter 12.
3 Remove the control unit retaining screws and carefully withdraw the control unit from the facia **(see illustration)**.
4 Working at the rear of the control unit, release the securing clips, and disconnect the control cables from the unit. Note the locations of the cables to ensure correct refitting. **Note:** *This will not be necessary on models with fully automatic air conditioning system.*
5 Disconnect the wiring connector(s) from the rear of the control unit and withdraw the unit from the facia **(see illustration)**.

9.3 Undo the retaining screws (arrowed) . . .

Refitting

6 Refitting is a reversal of removal, but ensure that the control cables (where fitted) are securely reconnected to their original locations. Check the operation of the controls prior to refitting the radio/cassette and display units.

Heater/ventilation control cables

Removal

7 Disconnect the cables from the heater/ventilation control unit, as described previously in this Section during the control unit removal procedure.
8 Working through the facia aperture or under the facia (it may be necessary to remove certain facia panels for access - refer to Chapter 11 - depending on which cable is to be removed), release the clips and disconnect the relevant cable from the heater assembly. Note the routing of the cable to ensure correct refitting.

Refitting

9 Refitting is a reversal of removal, ensuring that the cables are correctly routed, and securely reconnected. Check the cable operation before refitting the trim panels.

Heater matrix

Note: *New heater matrix union sealing rings must be used on refitting. If leakage is the reason for removing the matrix, bear in mind that minor leaks can often be cured using a radiator sealant with the matrix in situ.*

Removal

10 Drain the cooling system as described in Chapter 1. Alternately, clamp the heater matrix hoses as close as possible to the engine compartment bulkhead.
11 On left-hand drive models, remove the steering column as described in Chapter 10. Undo the retaining bolts and remove the facia mounting support bracket to gain access to the heater matrix.
12 On right-hand drive models remove the glovebox as described in Chapter 11. Remove the retaining clips and lower the undercover away from the passenger side of the facia.
13 Position a container beneath the unions on the side of the heater matrix, and place

9.5 . . . then manoeuvre the control unit out of position, and disconnect its wiring connectors (fully automatic unit shown)

9.14a Undo the retaining screw (shown with the facia removed for clarity) . . .

9.14b . . . then disconnect the coolant pipes from the heater matrix and recover the sealing rings (arrowed)

9.15a Undo the retaining screws (arrowed) . . .

9.15b . . . then carefully slide the heater matrix out from its housing

9.19 Disconnect the wiring connectors, then undo the retaining screws . . .

9.20 . . . and lower the blower motor out of position (facia removed for clarity)

absorbent rags around the container as a precaution.

14 Slacken and remove the retaining bolt, and ease the coolant pipes away from the matrix, allowing the coolant to drain into the container. Remove the sealing rings from the pipe ends and discard them; new ones must be used on refitting **(see illustrations)**.

15 Slacken and remove the heater matrix screws, and slide the matrix out of position **(see illustrations)**. **Note:** *On some models, the end of the facia mounting bracket may prevent removal of the matrix. If so, trim the end of the bracket off to gain the necessary clearance. As the matrix is being removed, try to keep the pipe unions uppermost to minimise coolant spillage. Mop up any spilt coolant immediately with a damp cloth to prevent staining.*

Refitting

16 Refitting is a reversal of removal, bearing in mind the following points:

a) *Fit new sealing rings to the pipe unions.*
b) *Slide the matrix into position and engage the pipes fully with the matrix union. Refit the retaining bolts and union bolt, and tighten them securely. Remove the hose clamps (where fitted).*
c) *Refill/top-up the cooling system as described in Chapter 1.*

Heater blower motor

Removal

17 The blower motor assembly is located on the passenger side of the facia, in the base of the blower motor housing.

18 Disconnect the battery negative lead. Remove the retaining clips, and unclip the undercover from the bottom of the passenger side of the facia. If necessary, to further improve access remove the glovebox as described in Chapter 11.

19 Disconnect the wiring connector(s) from the motor and release the wiring harness from its retaining clips **(see illustration)**.

20 Slacken and remove the motor retaining screws, and lower the motor assembly away from the housing **(see illustration)**.

Refitting

21 Refitting is a reversal of removal.

Heater blower motor control module

Removal

22 Remove the blower motor as described in paragraphs earlier in this Section.

23 Release the wiring harness grommet from the base of the motor assembly. Disconnect the connector from the module/motor and remove the harness **(see illustration)**.

24 Depress the motor retaining clips and separate the motor from its mounting plate **(see illustrations)**.

3

9.23 Disconnect the wiring connector . . .

9.24a . . . then release the retaining clips (arrowed) . . .

9.24b . . . and separate the blower motor and mounting plate

9.25 Undo the screws (arrowed) and remove the blower motor control module

25 Slacken and remove the retaining screws and remove the control module from the mounting plate **(see illustration)**.

Refitting

26 Refitting is the reverse of removal, ensuring that the motor is clipped securely into position on the mounting plate. Also make sure that the wiring is correctly routed and retained by all the necessary clips.

10 Air conditioning system - general information and precautions

General information

1 An air conditioning system is available on certain models. It enables the temperature of incoming air to be lowered, and also dehumidifies the air, which makes for rapid demisting and increased comfort.

2 The cooling side of the system works in the same way as a domestic refrigerator. Refrigerant gas is drawn into a belt-driven compressor, and passes into a condenser mounted on the front of the radiator, where it loses heat and becomes liquid. The liquid passes through an expansion valve to an evaporator, where it changes from liquid under high pressure to gas under low pressure. This change is accompanied by a drop in temperature, which cools the evaporator. The refrigerant returns to the compressor, and the cycle begins again.

3 Air blown through the evaporator passes to the air distribution unit, where it is mixed with hot air blown through the heater matrix to achieve the desired temperature.

4 The heating side of the system works the same way as on models without air conditioning (see Section 8).

5 The operation of the system is controlled electronically by the "Bitron" control unit, which controls the electric cooling fan(s), the compressor and the facia-mounted warning light. Any problems with the system should be referred to a Peugeot dealer.

Precautions

6 When an air conditioning system is fitted, it is necessary to observe special precautions whenever dealing with any part of the system, or its associated components. If for any reason the system must be disconnected, entrust this task to your Peugeot dealer or a refrigeration engineer.

 Warning: The refrigeration circuit may contain a liquid refrigerant (Freon), and it is therefore dangerous to disconnect any part of the system without specialised knowledge and equipment.

7 The refrigerant is potentially dangerous, and it should therefore only be handled by qualified persons, such as your Peugeot dealer. If it is splashed onto the skin, it can cause frostbite. It is not itself poisonous, but in the presence of a naked flame (including a cigarette) it forms a poisonous gas. Uncontrolled discharging of the refrigerant is dangerous, and potentially damaging to the environment.

8 Do not operate the air conditioning system if it is known to be short of refrigerant, as this may damage the compressor.

11 Air conditioning system components - removal and refitting

 Warning: Do not attempt to open the refrigerant circuit. Refer to the precautions in Section 10.

1 The only operation which can be carried out easily without discharging the refrigerant is the renewal of the compressor drivebelt. This is described in Chapter 1. (The "Bitron" temperature sensor may be renewed using the information in Section 6). All other operations must be referred to a Peugeot dealer or an air conditioning specialist.

2 If necessary, the compressor can be unbolted and moved aside, without disconnecting its flexible hoses, after removing the drivebelt.

Chapter 4 Part A:
Fuel and exhaust system - petrol models

Contents

Degrees of difficulty

Easy, suitable for novice with little experience	**Fairly easy,** suitable for beginner with some experience	**Fairly difficult,** suitable for competent DIY mechanic	**Difficult,** suitable for experienced DIY mechanic	**Very difficult,** suitable for expert DIY or professional

4A

Specifications

System type
1.6 litre models	Magneti Marelli 8P
1.8 litre models	Bosch Motronic MP5.1.1
2.0 litre models	Bosch Motronic MP5.1.1 or MP5.2

Fuel system data
Fuel pump type	Electric, immersed in tank
Fuel pump regulated constant pressure (at specified idle speed):	
Bosch system	3.0 ± 0.2 bars
Magneti Marelli system	2.5 ± 0.2 bars
Specified idle speed	850 ± 50 rpm (not adjustable - controlled by ECU)
Idle mixture CO content	Less than 0.4 % (not adjustable- controlled by ECU)

Recommended fuel
Minimum octane rating	95 RON unleaded (UK unleaded premium). Leaded fuel must **not** be used on models equipped with a catalytic converter

Torque wrench settings
	Nm	lbf ft
Inlet manifold nuts	20	15
Exhaust manifold nuts	35	26

1 General information and precautions

The fuel supply system consists of a fuel tank (which is mounted under the rear of the car, with an electric fuel pump immersed in it), a fuel filter, fuel feed and return lines. The fuel pump supplies fuel to the fuel rail, which acts as a reservoir for the four fuel injectors which inject fuel into the inlet tracts. The fuel filter incorporated in the feed line from the pump to the fuel rail ensures that the fuel supplied to the injectors is clean.

Refer to Section 6 for further information on the operation of each fuel injection system. Throughout this Section, it is also occasionally necessary to identify vehicles by their engine codes rather than by engine capacity alone. Refer to the relevant Part of Chapter 2 for further information on engine code identification.

 Warning: Many of the procedures in this Chapter require the removal of fuel lines and connections, which may result in some fuel spillage. Before carrying out any operation on the fuel system, refer to the precautions given in 'Safety first!' at the beginning of this manual, and follow them implicitly. Petrol is a highly dangerous and volatile liquid, and the precautions necessary when handling it cannot be overstressed.

Note: *Residual pressure will remain in the fuel lines long after the vehicle was last used. When disconnecting any fuel line, first depressurise the fuel system (see Section 7).*

2 Air cleaner assembly and intake ducts - removal and refitting

Removal

1.6 litre models

1 Slacken the retaining clip(s) and disconnect the breather hose(s) from the side of the air cleaner-to-throttle housing duct. Slacken the duct retaining clips, then disconnect it from the air cleaner and throttle housing, and remove it from the vehicle. Where necessary, recover the rubber sealing ring from the throttle housing.

2 Release the two retaining clips, then slacken and remove the two retaining screws from the front of the cylinder head cover, and remove the air cleaner element cover from the head. Withdraw the air cleaner element.

3 To remove the inlet duct, undo the bolt securing the rear section of the duct to the end of the cylinder head, then slacken the retaining clip and disconnect the duct from the cylinder head cover. Undo the bolt securing the front of the duct to the crossmember and manoeuvre the duct out of the engine compartment.

2.4 Slacken the clip (arrowed) and disconnect the intake duct from the throttle housing

1.8 and 2.0 litre models

4 Slacken the retaining clips and disconnect the intake duct from the throttle housing and air cleaner housing lid **(see illustration)**.

5 Undo the screws securing the lid to the air cleaner housing body. Lift off the lid and take out the filter element.

6 Lift the housing body upward to disengage it from the lower locating lugs. On some models, as the housing is lifted up, it will be necessary to disengage a small plastic retaining tag at the front securing the housing to the cold air intake duct underneath.

7 To remove the cold air intake duct, undo the air cleaner housing mounting bracket bolts and withdraw the bracket. Release the cold air intake from the bracket as it is removed.

8 Release the other end of the cold air intake from its body attachments and manipulate the duct from the car.

Refitting

9 Refitting is a reversal of the removal procedure, ensuring that all hoses are properly reconnected, and that all ducts are correctly seated and securely held by their retaining clips.

3 Accelerator cable - removal, refitting and adjustment

Removal

1 Working in the engine compartment, free the accelerator inner cable from the cam on the throttle housing, then pull the outer cable out from its mounting bracket rubber grommet. Slide the flat washer off the end of the cable, and remove the spring clip **(see illustration)**.

2 Working back along the length of the cable, free it from any retaining clips or ties, noting its correct routing.

3 Working from inside the vehicle, open up the engine immobiliser key pad, then rotate the fastener through 90° and lower the fusebox cover. Disconnect the wiring connector from the key pad then slacken and

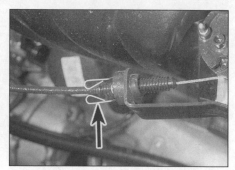

3.1 Accelerator cable spring clip (arrowed)

remove the retaining screws and remove the driver's side lower panel from the facia.

4 Release the retaining clip, and detach the inner cable from the top of the accelerator pedal.

5 Release the outer cable from its retainer on the pedal mounting bracket, then tie a length of string to the end of the cable.

6 Return to the engine compartment, release the cable grommet from the bulkhead and withdraw the cable. When the end of the cable appears, untie the string and leave it in position - it can then be used to draw the cable back into position on refitting.

Refitting

7 Tie the string to the end of the cable, then use the string to draw the cable into position through the bulkhead. Once the cable end is visible, untie the string, then clip the outer cable into its pedal bracket retainer, and clip the inner cable into position in the pedal end.

8 Check that the cable is securely retained, then refit the lower panel to the facia.

9 Within the engine compartment, ensure the outer cable is correctly seated in the bulkhead grommet, then work along the cable, securing it in position with the retaining clips and ties, and ensuring the cable is correctly routed.

10 Slide the flat washer onto the cable end, and refit the spring clip.

11 Pass the outer cable through the mounting bracket grommet on the throttle housing, and reconnect the inner cable to the throttle cam. Adjust the cable as described below.

Adjustment

12 Remove the spring clip from the accelerator outer cable. Ensuring that the throttle cam is fully against its stop, gently pull the cable out of its grommet until all free play is removed from the inner cable.

13 With the cable held in this position, refit the spring clip to the last exposed outer cable groove in front of the rubber grommet and washer. When the clip is refitted and the outer cable is released, there should be only a small amount of free play in the inner cable.

14 Have an assistant depress the accelerator pedal, and check that the throttle cam opens fully and returns smoothly to its stop.

4 Accelerator pedal - removal and refitting

Removal

1 Disconnect the accelerator cable from the pedal as described in Section 3.

2 According to type either remove the screws from the pedal pivot bush, or unscrew the nut (or remove the spring clip) from the end of the pedal pivot shaft. Where a pivot shaft and nut arrangement is used, unscrew the nut whilst retaining the pivot shaft with an open-ended spanner on the flats provided.

3 Remove the pedal, or pull the pedal and pivot shaft assembly from the support bracket according to type.

Refitting

4 Refitting is a reversal of the removal procedure, applying a little multi-purpose grease to the pedal pivot point. On completion, adjust the accelerator cable as described in Section 3.

5 Unleaded petrol - general information and usage

Note: *The information given in this Chapter is correct at the time of writing. If updated information is thought to be required, check with a Peugeot dealer. If travelling abroad, consult one of the motoring organisations (or a similar authority) for advice on the fuel available.*

1 The fuel recommended by Peugeot is given in the Specifications Section of this Chapter, followed by the equivalent petrol currently on sale in the UK.

2 All Peugeot 406 petrol models are designed to run on unleaded fuel with a minimum octane rating of 95 (RON). However not all models have a catalytic converter - 2.0 litre R6E2 engines and certain other export models not available in the UK, are not fitted with a catalytic converter. On models not fitted with a catalytic converter, it is permissible to use leaded fuel. All catalytic converter models must be run on unleaded fuel **only**. Under no circumstances should leaded fuel (UK "4-star") be used, as this may damage the converter.

3 Super unleaded petrol (98 RON) can also be used in all models if wished, though there is no advantage in doing so.

6 Fuel injection systems - general information

Note: *The fuel injection ECU is of the "self-learning" type, meaning that as it operates, it also monitors and stores the settings which* give optimum engine performance under all operating conditions. When the battery is disconnected, these settings are lost and the ECU reverts to the base settings programmed into its memory at the factory. On restarting, this may lead to the engine running/idling roughly for a short while, until the ECU has re-learned the optimum settings. This process is best accomplished by taking the vehicle on a road test (for approximately 15 minutes), covering all engine speeds and loads, concentrating mainly in the 2,500 to 3,500 rpm region.

Magneti Marelli 8P and Bosch Motronic MP5.1.1 systems

1 The Magneti Marelli 8P system is fitted to 1.6 litre (BFZ) engines, and the Bosch Motronic MP5.1.1 system is fitted to 1.8 litre (LFY) engines and 2.0 litre (RFV) engines. Both systems are full engine management (fuel injection/ignition) systems incorporating both a closed-loop catalytic converter and evaporative emission control to comply with the very latest emission standards. Refer to Chapter 5 for information on the ignition side of the system; the fuel side of both systems is very similar and operates as follows.

2 The fuel pump (which is immersed in the fuel tank) supplies fuel from the tank to the fuel rail, via a filter mounted underneath the rear of the vehicle. Fuel supply pressure is controlled by the pressure regulator in the fuel rail. When the optimum operating pressure of the fuel system is exceeded, the regulator allows excess fuel to return to the tank.

3 The electrical control system consists of the ECU, along with the following sensors:

  a) *Throttle potentiometer - informs the ECU of the throttle position, and the rate of throttle opening/closing.*

  b) *Coolant temperature sensor - informs the ECU of engine temperature.*

  c) *Inlet air temperature sensor - informs the ECU of the temperature of the air passing through the throttle housing.*

  d) *Lambda (oxygen) sensor - informs the ECU of the oxygen content of the exhaust gases (explained in greater detail in Part C of this Chapter).*

  e) *Crankshaft (RPM) sensor - informs the ECU of the crankshaft position and speed of rotation.*

  f) *Manifold Absolute Pressure (MAP) sensor - informs the ECU of the load on the engine (expressed in terms of inlet manifold vacuum).*

  g) *Vehicle speed sensor - informs the ECU of the vehicle speed.*

  h) *Knock sensor - informs the ECU of pre-ignition (detonation) within the cylinders. Fitted to Motronic systems only.*

4 All the above signals are analysed by the ECU which selects the fuelling response appropriate to those values. The ECU controls the fuel injectors (varying the pulse width - the length of time the injectors are held open - to provide a richer or weaker mixture, as appropriate). The mixture is constantly varied by the ECU, to provide the best setting for cranking, starting (with either a hot or cold engine), warm-up, idle, cruising and acceleration.

5 The ECU also has full control over the engine idle speed via a stepper motor fitted to the throttle housing. The motor has a pushrod controlling the opening of an air passage which bypasses the throttle valve. When the throttle valve is closed, the ECU controls the movement of the motor pushrod, which regulates the amount of air which flows through the throttle housing passage, so controlling the idle speed. The bypass passage is also used as an additional air supply during cold starting.

6 The ECU also controls the exhaust and evaporative emission control systems, which are described in detail in Part C of this Chapter.

7 An electric heating element is fitted to the throttle housing; the heater is supplied with current by the ECU, and warms the throttle housing on cold starts to prevent possible icing of the throttle valve.

8 If there is an abnormality in any of the readings obtained from either the coolant temperature sensor, the inlet air temperature sensor or the lambda sensor, the ECU enters its back-up mode. In this event, it ignores the abnormal sensor signal and assumes a pre-programmed value which will allow the engine to continue running (albeit at reduced efficiency). If the ECU enters this back-up mode, the warning light on the instrument panel will come on, and the relevant fault code will be stored in the ECU memory.

9 If the warning light comes on, the vehicle should be taken to a Peugeot dealer at the earliest opportunity. A complete test of the engine management system can then be carried out, using a special electronic diagnostic test unit which is simply plugged into the system's diagnostic connector located near the fusebox on the facia.

Bosch Motronic MP5.2 system

10 The Bosch Motronic MP5.2 engine management (fuel injection/ignition) system is fitted to 2.0 litre models without a catalytic converter (R6E engine). Refer to Chapter 5B for information on the ignition side of the system.

11 The system is similar in operation to the MP5.1.1 system described above, however on this system there is no lambda (oxygen) sensor and no evaporative emission control system.

12 At the time of writing there was very little information available on the MP5.2 system, but the component layout within the engine compartment is similar, and the majority of the procedures described for the other two systems will be applicable.

4A

7 Fuel injection system - depressurisation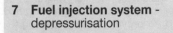

Note: *Refer to the warning note in Section 1 before proceeding.*

> ⚠️ **Warning: The following procedure will merely relieve the pressure in the fuel system - remember that fuel will still be present in the system components and take precautions accordingly before disconnecting any of them.**

1 The fuel system referred to in this Section is defined as the tank-mounted fuel pump, the fuel filter, the fuel injectors, the fuel rail and the pressure regulator, and the metal pipes and flexible hoses of the fuel lines between these components. All these contain fuel which will be under pressure while the engine is running, and/or while the ignition is switched on. The pressure will remain for some time after the ignition has been switched off, and must be relieved in a controlled fashion when any of these components are disturbed for servicing work.
2 Disconnect the battery negative terminal.
3 Place a container beneath the connection/ union to be disconnected, and have a large rag ready to soak up any escaping fuel not being caught by the container.
4 Slowly loosen the connection or union nut to avoid a sudden release of pressure, and position the rag around the connection, to catch any fuel spray which may be expelled. Once the pressure is released, disconnect the fuel line. Plug the pipe ends, to minimise fuel loss and prevent the entry of dirt into the fuel system.

8 Fuel pump - removal and refitting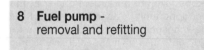

Note: *Refer to the warning note in Section 1 before proceeding.*

Removal

1 Disconnect the battery negative terminal.
2 For access to the fuel pump, remove the rear seat as described in Chapter 11.
3 Using a screwdriver, carefully prise the plastic access cover from the floor to expose the fuel pump.
4 Disconnect the wiring connector from the top of the fuel pump **(see illustration)**.

 Tape the connector to the vehicle body in order to prevent it from disappearing behind the tank.

5 Mark the hoses for identification purposes, then slacken the feed and return hose retaining clips. Where the crimped-type Peugeot hose clips are fitted, cut the clips and

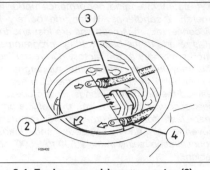

8.4 Fuel pump wiring connector (2), fuel feed hose (3) and return hose (4)

discard them; use standard worm-drive hose clips on refitting. Disconnect both hoses from the top of the pump, and plug the hose ends.
6 Noting the relationship of the notch and alignment pin on the tank and pump, and the arrow on the pump cover, unscrew the locking ring and remove it from the tank. Although Peugeot recommend the use of tool 1336 to unscrew the locking ring, this can be accomplished by using a screwdriver on the raised studs of the locking ring. Carefully tap the screwdriver to turn the ring anti- clockwise and release it. Once the locking ring is released, it will be necessary to position it to one side and lay it on the top of the fuel tank; the diameter of the ring is larger than that of the opening in the floor.
7 Lift the fuel pump assembly out of the fuel tank, taking great care not to damage the float arm, or to spill fuel inside the car.
8 Note that the fuel pump is only available as a complete assembly - no components are available separately.

Refitting

9 Carefully manoeuvre the pump assembly into the fuel tank, ensuring that the arrow on the pump cover and the notch and pin are in alignment as noted during removal. Refit the locking ring and securely tighten it using the same method as for removal..
10 Reconnect the feed and return hoses to the top of the fuel pump, using the marks made on removal to ensure that they are correctly reconnected, and securely tighten their retaining clips.

10.6 Fuel filler pipe (A), breather pipe (B) and vapour collection pipe (C) attachments at the fuel tank

11 Reconnect the pump wiring connector.
12 Reconnect the battery negative terminal and start the engine. Check the fuel pump feed and return hoses unions for signs of leakage.
13 If all is well, refit the plastic access cover. Refit the rear seat as described in Chapter 11.

9 Fuel gauge sender unit - removal and refitting

The fuel gauge sender unit is incorporated in the fuel pump - refer to Section 8.

10 Fuel tank - removal and refitting

Note: *Refer to the warning note in Section 1 before proceeding.*

Removal

1 Before removing the fuel tank, all fuel must be drained from the tank. Since a fuel tank drain plug is not provided, it is therefore preferable to carry out the removal operation when the tank is nearly empty. Before proceeding, disconnect the battery negative terminal and syphon or hand-pump the remaining fuel from the tank.
2 Disconnect the fuel pump wiring connector and the fuel feed and return hoses at the pump outlets as described in Section 8.
3 Jack up the rear of the car and support on axle stands.
4 Remove the exhaust system from the catalytic converter rearward (see Section 17).
5 Unbolt and remove the exhaust heat shield from the underbody.
6 Disconnect the fuel filler pipe, breather pipe and vapour collection pipe at their tank attachments **(see illustration)**. Where the crimped-type Peugeot hose clips are fitted, cut the clips and discard them; use standard worm-drive hose clips on refitting.
7 Disconnect the fuel supply and return pipes at their fuel tank connections **(see illustration)**.
8 Unclip the handbrake cable and move it aside as far as possible.

10.7 Fuel supply and return pipe connections at the fuel tank

10.10 Fuel tank cradle mounting bolt (arrowed)

9 Place a trolley jack with an interposed block of wood beneath the tank, then raise the jack until it is supporting the weight of the tank. Position the jack so as to allow room to remove the fuel tank cradle.
10 Unscrew the fuel tank cradle mounting bolts and remove the cradle **(see illustration)**.
11 Lower the fuel tank and remove it from under the car.
12 If the tank is contaminated with sediment or water, remove the fuel pump and swill the tank out with clean fuel. The tank is injection-moulded from a synthetic material - if seriously damaged, it should be renewed. However, in certain cases, it may be possible to have small leaks or minor damage repaired. Seek the advice of a specialist before attempting to repair the fuel tank.

Refitting

13 Refitting is the reverse of the removal procedure, noting the following points:
a) *When lifting the tank back into position, take care to ensure none of the hoses get trapped between the tank and body.*
b) *Ensure that all pipes and hoses are correctly routed, and securely held in position with their retaining clips.*
c) *On completion, refill the tank with a small amount of fuel, and check for signs of leakage prior to taking the vehicle out on the road.*

11 Fuel injection system - testing

Testing

1 If a fault appears in the fuel injection system (including the ignition system and engine management system as a whole), first ensure that all the system wiring connectors are securely connected and free of corrosion. Ensure that the fault is not due to poor maintenance; ie, check that the air cleaner filter element is clean, the spark plugs are in good condition and correctly gapped, the cylinder compression pressures are correct, and that the engine breather hoses are clear and undamaged, referring to the relevant Parts of Chapters 1, 2 and 5 for further information.
2 If these checks fail to reveal the cause of the problem, it is possible that a fault exists and a fault code may be stored in the system ECU. A diagnostic socket is incorporated in the engine management circuit, into which a fault code reader can be plugged. The socket is located next to the fusebox under the facia; to gain access, open up the engine immobiliser key pad, then rotate the fastener through 90° and lower the fusebox cover. If a fault code reader is available, follow the instructions supplied with the reader for connection and operation of the unit.
3 Although a fault code reader will identify the likely component or area in which a fault may lie, and can often provide the answer to a peculiar fault quickly, bear in mind that certain faults may not generate a fault code, and may not be detectable by the reader. In this instance (and even in cases where a fault code has been recorded) further testing to actually pinpoint the precise problem may be necessary, and additional test equipment will usually be required to do this. Tests of this nature are complex and outside the scope of this manual. For more detailed information about fuel injection system testing, Haynes Publishing produce a book in the Techbook series called "*Automotive Engine Management And Fuel Injection Systems Manual*". This incorporates information on all aspects of fuel injection and engine management diagnostics and testing.

Fault code read-out

4 Having accessed any stored fault codes by means of the fault code reader, it is now necessary to interpret the meaning of the codes. Given in the accompanying tables are the possible fuel/ignition fault codes for the Bosch Motronic 5.1.1 and Magneti Marelli 8P systems and the component or area in the system where the fault is likely to be found. Note that at the time of writing, no specific fault codes were available for the Motronic 5.2 system but they are likely to be similar to those for the 5.1.1 system.

4A

Motronic 5.1.1 system

Fault code	Interpretation
11	End of diagnosis - no faults detected
12	Initiation of diagnosis
13	Inlet air temperature sensor
14	Coolant temperature sensor
15	Fuel pump relay
21	Throttle potentiometer sensor - idle contact
31	Idle switch
32	Mixture regulation - manifold leakage or low/high fuel pressure
33	Carbon canister solenoid valve - circuit fault
34	Carbon canister solenoid valve
35	Throttle position sensor - full load contact
41	Crankshaft position (RPM) sensor
42	Injectors
43	Knock regulation - knock sensor/engine temperature/spark plugs/etc.
44	Knock regulation - other
51	Lambda (oxygen) sensor - circuit fault
52	Mixture control - supply voltage/air/exhaust leak
53	Battery voltage
54	ECU - ECU supply/injection relay
56	Immobiliser system
71	No 1 injector control
72	No 2 injector control
73	No 3 injector control
74	No 4 injector control

Magneti Marelli 8P system

Fault code	Interpretation
11	End of diagnosis - no faults detected
12	Initiation of diagnosis
13	Inlet air temperature sensor
14	Coolant temperature sensor
15	Fuel pump control
21	Throttle position sensor
22	Idle speed stepper motor
27	Vehicle speed sensor
31	Lambda (oxygen) sensor - circuit fault
33	Manifold absolute pressure sensor
34	Carbon canister solenoid valve - circuit fault
41	Crankshaft position (RPM) sensor
42	Injector control
44	Knock sensor
45	Ignition coil control (coil one)
52	Lambda (oxygen) sensor - circuit fault
53	Battery voltage
54	ECU
57	Ignition coil control (coil one)

13.2 Fuel pressure regulator vacuum pipe (arrowed)

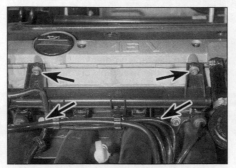

13.6 Fuel rail retaining bolts (arrowed)

13.13 Throttle potentiometer wiring connector (arrowed)

12 Throttle housing - removal and refitting

Removal

1 Disconnect the battery negative terminal.
2 Remove the air cleaner-to-throttle housing duct as described in Section 2.
3 Disconnect the accelerator inner cable from the throttle cam then withdraw the outer cable from the mounting bracket along with its flat washer and spring clip.
4 Depress the retaining clips, and disconnect the wiring connectors from the throttle potentiometer, the electric heating element, the inlet air temperature sensor and idle speed control stepper motor (as applicable).
5 Release the retaining clips (where fitted), and disconnect all the relevant vacuum and breather hoses from the throttle housing. Make identification marks on the hoses, to ensure that they are connected correctly on refitting.
6 Where necessary, undo the bolts or screws and release the accelerator cable bracket and housing support bracket.
7 Slacken and remove the retaining screws, and remove the throttle housing from the inlet manifold. Remove the O-ring from the manifold, and discard it - a new one must be used on refitting.

Refitting

8 Refitting is a reversal of the removal procedure, noting the following points:
  a) *Fit a new O-ring to the manifold, then refit the throttle housing and securely tighten its retaining nuts or screws (as applicable).*
  b) *Ensure that all hoses are correctly reconnected and, where necessary, are securely held in position by the retaining clips.*
  c) *Ensure that all wiring is correctly routed, and that the connectors are securely reconnected.*
  d) *On completion, adjust the accelerator cable as described in Section 3.*

13 Bosch Motronic MP5.1.1 system components - removal and refitting

Fuel rail and injectors

Note: *Refer to the warning note in Section 1 before proceeding.*
Note: *If a faulty injector is suspected, before condemning the injector, it is worth trying the effect of one of the proprietary injector-cleaning treatments.*
1 Disconnect the battery negative terminal.
2 Disconnect the vacuum pipe from the fuel pressure regulator **(see illustration)**.
3 Bearing in mind the information given in Section 7, slacken the retaining clips and disconnect the fuel feed and return hoses from the fuel rail. Where the original crimped-type Peugeot hose clips are still fitted, cut them and discard; replace them with standard worm-type hose clips on refitting.
4 Open the retaining clips and release the wiring and hoses running along the front of the fuel rail.
5 Depress the retaining tangs and disconnect the wiring connectors from the four injectors.
6 Slacken and remove the fuel rail retaining bolts then carefully ease the fuel rail and injector assembly out from the inlet manifold and remove it from the vehicle **(see illustration)**. Remove the O-rings from the end of each injector and discard them; they must be renewed whenever they are disturbed.
7 Slide out the retaining clip(s) and remove the relevant injector(s) from the fuel rail. Remove the upper O-ring from each disturbed injector and discard; all disturbed O-rings must be renewed.
8 Refitting is a reversal of the removal procedure, noting the following points.
  a) *Fit new O-rings to all disturbed injector unions.*
  b) *Apply a smear of engine oil to the O-rings to aid installation then ease the injectors and fuel rail into position ensuring that none of the O-rings are displaced.*
  c) *On completion start the engine and check for fuel leaks.*

Fuel pressure regulator

Note: *Refer to the warning note in Section 1 before proceeding.*
9 Disconnect the battery negative terminal.
10 Disconnect the vacuum pipe from the regulator.
11 Place a wad of rag over the regulator, to catch any fuel spray which may be released, then remove the retaining clip and ease the regulator out from the fuel rail.
12 Refitting is a reversal of the removal procedure. Examine the regulator seal for signs of damage or deterioration and renew if necessary.

Throttle potentiometer

13 Depress the retaining clip and disconnect the wiring connector from the throttle potentiometer located beneath the throttle housing **(see illustration)**.
14 Slacken and remove the two retaining screws then disengage the potentiometer from the throttle valve spindle and remove it from the vehicle.
15 Refitting is a reverse of the removal procedure ensuring that the potentiometer is correctly engaged with the throttle valve spindle.

Electronic Control Unit (ECU)

16 The ECU is located in a plastic box which is mounted on the right-hand front wheel arch.
17 Ensure that the ignition is switched off then lift off the ECU module box lid. On automatic transmission models there will be two ECU's in the box; the fuel injection/ignition ECU is the unit nearest to the engine.
18 Release the wiring connector by lifting the locking lever on top of the connector upwards. Lift the connector at the rear, disengage the tag at the front and carefully withdraw the connector from the ECU pins.
19 Lift the ECU upwards and remove it from its location.
20 Refitting is a reversal of removal. Note that if a new ECU has been fitted, the vehicle should be taken on an extensive road test. Initially, engine performance may be less than acceptable, but should improve as the ECU control circuitry adapts to the engine parameters.

Idle speed control stepper motor

21 The idle speed control stepper motor is located on the side of the throttle housing assembly.

22 Release the retaining clip, and disconnect the wiring connector from the motor.

23 Slacken and remove the two retaining screws, and withdraw the motor from the throttle housing.

24 Refitting is a reversal of the removal procedure.

Manifold absolute pressure (MAP) sensor

25 The MAP sensor is situated on the inlet manifold.

26 Disconnect the wiring connector and vacuum hose and remove the MAP sensor from the manifold.

27 Refitting is the reverse of the removal procedure.

Coolant temperature sensor

28 Refer to Chapter 3.

Inlet air temperature sensor

29 The inlet air temperature sensor is screwed into the underside of the inlet manifold.

30 Disconnect the wiring connector then unscrew the sensor and remove it from the vehicle.

31 Refitting is the reverse of removal.

Crankshaft (RPM) sensor

35 The crankshaft sensor is situated on the front face of the transmission clutch housing.

36 Trace the wiring back from the sensor to the wiring connector and disconnect it from the main harness.

37 Prise out the rubber grommet then undo the retaining bolt and withdraw the sensor from the transmission.

38 Refitting is the reverse of the removal procedure ensuring that the sensor retaining bolt is securely tightened and the grommet is correctly seated in the transmission housing.

Vehicle speed sensor

39 The vehicle speed sensor is an integral part of the transmission speedometer drive assembly. Refer to the relevant Part of Chapter 7 for removal and refitting details.

Knock sensor

40 The knock sensor is screwed into the front face of the cylinder block.

41 To gain access to the sensor, apply the handbrake then jack up the front of the car and support it on axle stands. Remove the splash guard from under the engine.

42 Trace the wiring back from the sensor to its wiring connector, and disconnect it from the main loom.

43 Undo the bolt securing the sensor to the cylinder block, and remove it from under the vehicle.

44 Refitting is a reversal of the removal procedure.

Fuel injection system relay unit

45 The relay unit is located in the ECU module box which is mounted on the right-hand front wheel arch.

46 Ensure that the ignition is switched off then lift off the ECU module box lid.

47 Disconnect the wiring connector and remove the relay unit from the mounting plate.

48 Refitting is the reverse of removal.

---

14 Magneti Marelli 8P system components - removal and refitting

Fuel injectors

Note: *Refer to the warning note in Section 1 before proceeding. If a faulty injector is suspected, before condemning the injector, it is worth trying the effect of one of the proprietary injector-cleaning treatments.*

1 Disconnect the battery negative terminal.

2 Remove the air cleaner-to-throttle housing duct as described in Section 2.

3 Undo the two bolts securing the wiring tray to the top of the manifold, and position the tray clear of the injectors.

4 Depress the retaining clip(s), and disconnect the wiring connector(s) from the injector(s).

5 Slacken the retaining screw, and remove the injector retaining plate; Nos 1 and 2 injectors are retained by one plate, Nos 3 and 4 by another.

6 Place a wad of clean rag over the injector, to catch any fuel spray which may be released, then carefully ease the relevant injector(s) out of the manifold. Remove the O-rings from the end of each disturbed injector, and discard them - these must be renewed whenever they are disturbed.

7 On refitting the injectors, fit a new O-rings to the end of each injector. Apply a smear of engine oil to the O-ring, to aid installation, then ease the injector(s) back into position in the manifold.

8 Ensure each injector connector is correctly positioned, then refit the retaining plate and securely tighten its retaining screw. Reconnect the wiring connector(s) to the injector(s).

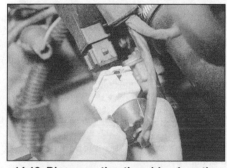

14.13 Disconnecting the wiring from the throttle potentiometer

9 Refit the wiring tray to the top of the manifold, and securely tighten its bolts.

10 Refit the air cleaner-to-throttle body duct, and reconnect the battery. Start the engine, and check the injectors for signs of leakage.

Fuel pressure regulator

11 Refer to Section 13.

Throttle potentiometer

12 The throttle potentiometer is fitted to the right-hand side of the throttle housing.

13 Depress the retaining clip, and disconnect the potentiometer wiring connector **(see illustration)**.

14 Slacken and remove the two retaining screws, and remove the potentiometer from the throttle housing.

15 Refitting is the reverse of removal, ensuring that the potentiometer is correctly engaged with the throttle valve spindle.

Electronic Control Unit (ECU)

16 Refer to Section 13.

Idle speed control stepper motor

17 The idle speed control stepper motor is located on the front of the throttle housing assembly.

18 Release the retaining clip, and disconnect the wiring connector from the motor **(see illustration)**.

19 Slacken and remove the two retaining screws, and withdraw the motor from the throttle housing.

20 Refitting is a reversal of the removal procedure.

Manifold absolute pressure (MAP) sensor

21 The MAP sensor is located at the front of the ECU module box which is mounted on the right-hand front wheel arch.

22 Ensure that the ignition is switched off then lift off the ECU module box lid.

23 Undo the retaining nut(s) or clips and free the MAP sensor from the module box.

24 Disconnect the wiring connector and vacuum hose and remove the MAP sensor from the engine compartment.

25 Refitting is the reverse of the removal procedure.

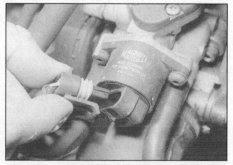

14.18 Disconnecting the idle speed control stepper motor wiring

4A

Coolant temperature sensor

26 Refer to Chapter 3.

Inlet air temperature sensor

27 The inlet air temperature sensor is located in the throttle housing.

28 To remove the sensor, first remove the throttle potentiometer as described in paragraphs 12 to 14.

29 Depress the retaining clip, and disconnect the wiring connector from the air temperature sensor.

30 Remove the screw securing the sensor connector to the top of the throttle housing, then carefully ease the sensor out of position and remove it from the throttle housing. Examine the sensor O-ring for signs of damage or deterioration, and renew if necessary.

31 Refitting is a reversal of the removal procedure, using a new O-ring where necessary, and ensuring that the throttle potentiometer is correctly engaged with the throttle valve spindle.

Crankshaft (RPM) sensor

32 Refer to Section 13.

Fuel injection system relay unit

33 Refer to Section 13.

Vehicle speed sensor

34 Refer to Section 13.

---

15 Inlet manifold - removal and refitting

Removal

1 Disconnect the battery negative terminal and proceed as described under the relevant sub-heading.

1.6 litre models

2 Remove the air cleaner-to-throttle housing duct as described in Section 2.

3 Disconnect the accelerator inner cable from the throttle cam then withdraw the outer cable from the mounting bracket along with its flat washer and spring clip.

4 Undo the two bolts securing the wiring tray to the top of the manifold, and position the tray, and its associated wiring and hoses, clear of the manifold so that it does not hinder removal.

5 Depress the retaining clips, and disconnect the wiring connectors from the four fuel injectors.

6 Bearing in mind the information given in Section 7, slacken the retaining clips, and disconnect the fuel feed and return hoses from either side of the manifold. Where the original crimped-type Peugeot hose clips are still fitted, cut them off and discard them; use standard worm-drive hose clips on refitting.

7 Slacken the retaining clip(s), and disconnect

the braking system vacuum servo unit hose, and all the relevant vacuum/ breather hoses, from the top of the manifold. Where necessary, make identification marks on the hoses, to ensure that they are correctly reconnected on refitting.

8 Undo the manifold retaining nuts, and withdraw the manifold from the engine compartment. Recover the two manifold seals, and discard them - new ones must be used on refitting.

1.8 and 2.0 litre models

9 Remove the throttle housing as described in Section 12 and the fuel rail and injectors as described in Section 13.

10 Slacken the retaining clip(s), and disconnect the braking system vacuum servo unit hose, and all the relevant vacuum/ breather hoses, from the manifold. Where necessary, make identification marks on the hoses, to ensure that they are correctly reconnected on refitting.

11 Where applicable, slacken and remove the bolt securing the dipstick tube to the side of the manifold.

12 Undo the nuts and bolts securing the manifold to the cylinder head, and remove the manifold from the engine compartment. Recover the manifold gasket/seals, and discard them - new ones must be used on refitting.

Refitting

13 Refitting is a reverse of the relevant removal procedure, noting the following points:

a) Ensure that the manifold and cylinder head mating surfaces are clean and dry, then locate the new gasket/seals on the manifold. Refit the manifold and tighten its retaining nuts and bolts to the specified torque setting.

b) Ensure that all relevant hoses are reconnected to their original positions and are securely held (where necessary) by the retaining clips.

c) Adjust the accelerator cable as described in Section 3.

---

16 Exhaust manifold - removal and refitting

Removal

1 Disconnect the hot-air inlet hose from the manifold shroud and remove it from the vehicle.

2 Slacken and remove the three retaining screws, and remove the shroud from the top of the exhaust manifold.

3 Chock the rear wheels, then jack up the front of the vehicle and support it on axle stands.

4 Where necessary, disconnect the wiring from the lambda (oxygen) sensor. Alternatively,

support the exhaust front pipe, to avoid any strain being placed on the sensor wiring.

5 Undo the nuts securing the exhaust front pipe to the manifold and recover the springs. Where applicable, remove the bolt securing the front pipe to its mounting bracket. Disconnect the front pipe from the manifold, and recover the gasket.

6 Undo the retaining nuts securing the manifold to the cylinder head. Manoeuvre the manifold out of the engine compartment, and discard the manifold gaskets.

Refitting

7 Refitting is the reverse of the removal procedure, noting the following points:

a) Examine all the exhaust manifold studs for signs of damage and corrosion; remove all traces of corrosion, and repair or renew any damaged studs.

b) Ensure that the manifold and cylinder head sealing faces are clean and flat, and fit the new manifold gasket(s). Tighten the manifold retaining nuts to the specified torque setting.

c) Reconnect the front pipe to the manifold, using the information given in Section 17.

---

17 Exhaust system - general information, removal and refitting

General information

1 A multi-section exhaust system is fitted. All exhaust sections are joined by a flanged joint. The downpipe to manifold joint is secured by nuts and bolts with a centre sealing ring. The joint is of the spring-loaded ball type, to allow for movement in the exhaust system. Other joints in the system are secured by a clamping ring.

2 Where fitted the catalytic converter is located on the front section of the exhaust.

3 The system is suspended throughout its entire length by rubber mountings.

Removal

4 Each exhaust section can be removed individually, or the system can be removed complete, then separated after removal.

5 To remove part of the system, first jack up the front or rear of the car and support it on axle stands. Alternatively, position the car over an inspection pit or on car ramps.

Front pipe

6 Undo the nuts and bolts securing the front pipe flange joint to the manifold, and recover the springs **(see illustration)**. Separate the joint and recover the sealing ring.

7 Loosen the clamp bolt securing the front pipe flange joint to the intermediate pipe/rear pipe and separate the joint. Withdraw the front pipe from underneath the vehicle, and recover the sealing ring.

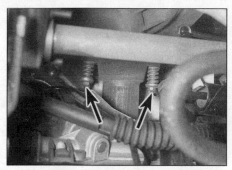

17.6 Exhaust front pipe-to-manifold retaining nuts and springs (arrowed)

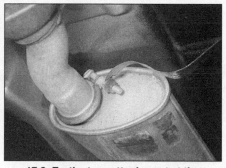

17.8 Earth strap attachment at the exhaust intermediate pipe clamp

Intermediate pipe and silencer

8 Slacken the clamping ring bolts and disengage the clamps from the front and rear flange joints. Note that there may be an earth strap attached to one of the clamp bolts **(see illustration)**.

9 Unhook the intermediate pipe and silencer from its mounting rubber and remove it from underneath the vehicle.

Tailpipe and silencer

10 Slacken the clamping ring bolt and disengage the clamp from the flange joint.

11 Unhook the tailpipe and silencer from its mounting rubbers and remove it from the car.

Heat shield(s)

12 The heat shields are secured to the underbody by various nuts and bolts. Each shield can be removed once the relevant exhaust section has been removed. If a shield is being removed to gain access to a component located behind it, it may prove sufficient in some cases to remove the retaining nuts and/or bolts, and simply lower the shield, without disturbing the exhaust system.

Refitting

13 Each section is refitted by reversing the removal sequence, noting the following:

a) *Ensure that all traces of corrosion have been removed from the flanges.*

b) *Inspect the rubber mountings for damage or deterioration, and renew as necessary.*

c) *Prior to assembling the spring-loaded joint, a smear of high-temperature grease should be applied to the joint mating surfaces.*

d) *Prior to tightening the exhaust system fasteners, ensure that all rubber mountings are correctly located, and that there is adequate clearance between the exhaust system and vehicle underbody.*

4A

Chapter 4 Part B:
Fuel and exhaust system - diesel models

Contents

Degrees of difficulty

Easy, suitable for novice with little experience	Fairly easy, suitable for beginner with some experience	Fairly difficult, suitable for competent DIY mechanic	Difficult, suitable for experienced DIY mechanic	Very difficult, suitable for expert DIY or professional

Specifications

General

System type . . . .   Rear-mounted fuel tank, distributor fuel injection pump with integral transfer pump, indirect injection. Turbocharger and intercooler

Application:
  1.9 litre (DHX engine) models . . . .   Bosch AS3 VP20
  2.1 litre (P8C engine) models . . . .   Lucas/PSA EPIC
Firing order . . . .   1-3-4-2 (No 1 at flywheel/driveplate end)
Maximum speed . . . .   5100 ± 80 rpm

Injection pump

Direction of rotation . . . .   Clockwise, viewed from sprocket end
Static timing (Bosch fuel injection pump):
  Engine position . . . .   No 4 piston at TDC
  Pump timing measurement . . . .   0.57 mm

Injectors

Type . . . .   Pintle
Opening pressure:
  Models with Bosch fuel injection pump . . . .   175 bars
  Models with Lucas fuel injection pump . . . .   163 ± 3.5 bars

Turbocharger

Type . . . .   Garrett T2
Boost pressure (approximate) . . . .   1 bar at 3000 rpm

4B

Torque wrench settings

	Nm	lbf ft
Stop solenoid	20	15
Fuel pipe union nuts	20	15
Injection pump timing hole blanking plug:		
Lucas pump	6	4
Bosch pump	15	11
Injection pump mounting nuts/bolts	20	15
Injection pump sprocket nut	50	37
Injection pump sprocket puller bolts	10	7
Injectors to cylinder head	90	66
Turbocharger mounting bolts	60	44
Turbocharger oil pipe unions	20	15

1 General information and precautions

General information

Two types of diesel fuel injection systems are fitted to models covered by this manual. 1.9 litre models are equipped with the Bosch AS3 semi-electronic system, and 2.1 litre models are fitted with the Lucas EPIC (Electronic Programmed Injection Control) full engine management system.

The Bosch system provides electronic control of the fuel injection pump fast idle operation and injection timing and also controls the operation of the exhaust gas recirculation (EGR) function and the preheater glow plugs.

The system is controlled by an electronic control unit (ECU) which receives inputs from sensors which monitor engine load, engine speed, injector operation and engine coolant temperature. From the sensor inputs, the ECU controls the fast idle operation via a vacuum operated diaphragm and cable arrangement, injection pump timing and operation of the EGR solenoid valve. Further information on the various sensors will be found in Section 16.

The Lucas EPIC system provides programmed electronic control of the fuel injection pump, and electronic control of the exhaust gas recirculation system, via the EPIC electronic control module (ECU).

For the ECU to assess fuel system requirements under all operating conditions, sensors are provided to monitor accelerator pedal position, manifold absolute pressure, crankshaft position/speed, engine coolant temperature and intake air temperature. Operation of the EGR valve is also controlled by the ECU in conjunction with a solenoid valve.

A unique feature of this system is the "drive-by-wire" throttle control. Instead of the accelerator cable being connected to the fuel injection pump, as it is in the normal mechanical system, the cable is connected to a pedal position sensor. This sensor sends pedal position signals to the ECU, which in turn controls the fuel injection pump electronically.

The fuel system itself consists of a rear-mounted fuel tank, a fuel filter with integral water separator, an electronically regulated fuel injection pump, injectors and associated components. Before passing through the filter, the fuel is heated by coolant flowing through the base of the fuel filter housing. A turbocharger and intercooler are fitted to all models.

Fuel is drawn from the fuel tank to the fuel injection pump by a vane-type transfer pump incorporated in the fuel injection pump. Before reaching the pump, the fuel passes through a fuel filter, where foreign matter and water are removed. Excess fuel lubricates the moving components of the pump, and is then returned to the tank.

The fuel injection pump is driven at half-crankshaft speed by the timing belt. The high pressure required to inject the fuel into the compressed air in the swirl chambers is achieved by a cam and piston arrangement in the pump. The fuel passes through a central rotor with a single outlet drilling which aligns with ports leading to the injector pipes.

Fuel metering is controlled by a centrifugal governor, which reacts to accelerator pedal position and engine speed. The governor is linked to a metering valve, which increases or decreases the amount of fuel delivered at each pumping stroke. A separate device also increases fuel delivery with increasing boost pressure.

Basic injection timing is determined when the pump is fitted. When the engine is running, it is varied automatically by an internal mechanism within the pump, acting under the control of the system ECU.

The four fuel injectors produce a homogeneous spray of fuel into the swirl chambers located in the cylinder head. The injectors are calibrated to open and close at critical pressures to provide efficient and even combustion. Each injector needle is lubricated by fuel, which accumulates in the spring chamber and is channelled to the injection pump return hose by leak-off pipes.

Cold starting is assisted by preheater or "glow" plugs fitted to each swirl chamber. On the Bosch system, when the engine is cold, the idling speed is increased by means of a vacuum operated cable and diaphragm arrangement acting on a fast idle lever on the side of the injection pump. On the Lucas

system, the fast idle is automatically regulated by the injection pump. On both systems, the fast idle function is regulated by the system ECU.

A stop solenoid cuts the fuel supply to the injection pump rotor when the ignition is switched off and on the Bosch fuel injection pump there is also a hand-operated stop lever for use in an emergency

Provided that the specified maintenance is carried out, the fuel injection equipment will give long and trouble-free service. The injection pump itself may well outlast the engine. The main potential cause of damage to the injection pump and injectors is dirt or water in the fuel.

Servicing of the injection pump and injectors is very limited for the home mechanic, and any dismantling or adjustment other than that described in this Chapter must be entrusted to a Peugeot dealer or fuel injection specialist.

Precautions

 Warning: It is necessary to take certain precautions when working on the fuel system components, particularly the fuel injectors. Before carrying out any operations on the fuel system, refer to the precautions given in 'Safety first!' at the beginning of this manual, and to any additional warning notes at the start of the relevant Sections.

When working on the Lucas EPIC system, the following additional precautions should be observed.

a) *Always disconnect the battery negative lead before removing any of the electronic control system's electrical connectors.*

b) *When installing a battery, be particularly careful to avoid reversing the positive and negative battery leads.*

c) *Do not subject any components of the system (especially the ECU) to severe impact during removal or installation.*

d) *Never attempt to work on the ECU, to test it (with any kind of test equipment), or to open its cover.*

e) *If you are inspecting electronic control system components during rainy weather, make sure that water does not enter any part. When washing the engine compartment, do not spray these parts or their electrical connectors with water.*

2.2 Hand-operated fuel system priming pump

2 Fuel system - priming and bleeding

1 After disconnecting part of the fuel supply system it is necessary to prime the system and bleed off any air which may have entered the system components. In the case of running out of fuel it is not necessary to carry out the full priming and bleeding procedure - add fuel to the fuel tank, then operate the starter motor with the accelerator pedal fully depressed until the engine starts. On starting the engine, increase the idling speed slightly to complete the bleeding of the fuel system.

2 All models are fitted with a hand-operated priming pump, consisting of a rubber bulb, which is located on the right-hand side of the engine compartment (see illustration).

3 To prime the system, loosen the bleed screw located in the injection pump inlet pipe union bolt.

4 Pump the priming pump until fuel free from air bubbles emerges from the bleed screw. Retighten the bleed screw.

5 Switch on the ignition (to activate the stop solenoid) and continue pumping the priming plunger until firm resistance is felt, then pump a few more times.

6 If a large amount of air has entered the pump, place a wad of rag around the fuel return union on the pump (to absorb spilt fuel), then slacken the union. Operate the priming plunger (with the ignition switched on to

activate the stop solenoid), or crank the engine on the starter motor in 10 second bursts, until fuel free from air bubbles emerges from the fuel union. Tighten the union and mop up split fuel.

 Warning: Be prepared to stop the engine if it should fire, to avoid excessive fuel spray and spillage.

7 If air has entered the injector pipes, place wads of rag around the injector pipe unions at the injectors (to absorb spilt fuel), then slacken the unions. Crank the engine on the starter motor until fuel emerges from the unions, then stop cranking the engine and retighten the unions. Mop up spilt fuel. *Refer to the warning given in the previous paragraph.*

8 Start the engine with the accelerator pedal fully depressed. Additional cranking may be necessary to finally bleed the system before the engine starts.

3 Air cleaner assembly and intake ducts - removal and refitting

Removal

Air cleaner

1 Slacken the retaining clips and disconnect the intake duct from the air cleaner housing lid.

2 On 1.9 litre models, release the accelerator cable from the air filter housing lid. On 2.1 litre models, release the coolant hose and the oil separator from their locations on the air filter housing lid.

3 Undo the screws securing the lid to the air cleaner housing body. Lift off the lid and take out the filter element.

4 Lift the housing body upward to disengage it from the lower locating lugs. On some models, as the housing is lifted up, it will be necessary to disengage a small plastic retaining tag at the front securing the housing to the cold air intake duct underneath (see illustration).

5 To remove the cold air intake duct, undo the air cleaner housing mounting bracket

3.4 Lift up the air cleaner housing and disengage the retaining tag at the front (arrowed)

bolts and withdraw the bracket. Release the cold air intake from the bracket as it is removed.

6 Release the other end of the cold air intake from its body attachments and manipulate the duct from the car.

Intake ducts

7 On both engine types the intake ducting is complex arrangement consisting of flexible hoses and rigid ducts connecting the air cleaner assembly, intercooler and turbocharger. The intake ducts pass over the top and rear of the engine and, on 2.1 litre models, also along the underside of the engine between the transmission bellhousing and the sump. To remove the underside ducts it will be necessary to jack up the front of the car and support it on axle stands, then remove the engine splash guard.

8 To remove a section of intake ducting, slacken the retaining clips at each end and undo the bolts securing the relevant duct to its mounting bracket or support. On 2.1 litre models, when removing the front duct over the engine, it will be necessary to disconnect the inlet air temperature sensor wiring connector (see illustrations).

9 Release the ends of the duct then work it from its location (see illustration).

Refitting

10 Refitting is the reverse of the relevant removal procedure.

4B

3.8a Upper and centre intake duct retaining bolt locations (arrowed) on 1.9 litre models

3.8b On 2.1 litre models, when removing the front duct, disconnect the inlet air temperature sensor wiring connector

3.9 Manipulating a front intake duct from its location

4.1 On 1.9 litre models, operate the pump control lever, and release the inner cable (arrowed) from the lever

4 Accelerator cable - removal, refitting and adjustment

Removal

1 On 1.9 litre models, operate the pump control lever on the fuel injection pump, and release the inner cable from the lever **(see illustration)**. Pull the outer cable from the grommet in the fuel injection pump bracket.

2 On 2.1 litre models, release the inner cable from the lever on the accelerator pedal position sensor located on the left-hand side of the engine compartment. Pull the outer cable from the grommet in the pedal position sensor bracket.

3 On all models, release the cable from the remaining clips and brackets in the engine compartment, noting its routing.

4 Working from inside the vehicle, open up the engine immobiliser key pad, then rotate the fastener through 90° and lower the fusebox cover. Disconnect the wiring connector from the key pad then slacken and remove the retaining screws and remove the driver's side lower panel from the facia.

5 Release the clip, and detach the inner cable from the top of the accelerator pedal.

6 Release the outer cable from its retainer on the pedal mounting bracket, then tie a length of string to the end of the cable.

7 Return to the engine compartment, release the cable grommet from the bulkhead and withdraw the cable. When the end of the cable appears, untie the string and leave it in position - it can then be used to draw the cable back into position on refitting.

Refitting

8 Tie the string to the end of the cable, then use the string to draw the cable into position through the bulkhead. Once the cable end is visible, untie the string, then clip the outer cable into its pedal bracket retainer, and clip the inner cable into position in the pedal end.

9 Check that the cable is securely retained, then refit the lower panel to the facia.

10 Within the engine compartment, ensure the outer cable is correctly seated in the bulkhead grommet, then work along the cable, securing it in position with the retaining clips and ties,

and ensuring that the cable is correctly routed.

11 Slide the flat washer onto the cable end, and refit the spring clip.

12 Pass the outer cable through the grommet on the injection pump bracket or pedal position sensor bracket and reconnect the inner cable to the lever. Adjust the cable as described below.

Adjustment

13 Remove the spring clip from the accelerator outer cable. Ensuring the control lever or pedal position sensor lever is against its stop, gently pull the cable out of its grommet until all free play is removed from the inner cable.

14 With the cable held in this position, refit the spring clip to the last exposed outer cable groove in front of the rubber grommet and washer. When the clip is refitted and the outer cable is released, there should be only a small amount of free play in the inner cable.

15 Have an assistant depress the accelerator pedal, and check that the control lever or sensor lever opens fully and returns smoothly to its stop.

5 Accelerator pedal - removal and refitting

Refer to Chapter 4A, Section 4.

6 Fuel gauge sender and pick-up unit - removal and refitting

The fuel gauge sender and pick-up unit is in the same position as the fuel pump on petrol models, and removal/refitting is similar. Refer to Chapter 4A, Section 8.

7 Fuel tank - removal and refitting

Refer to Chapter 4A, Section 10.

8 Fuel injection pump - adjustments

Note: *The following procedure only applies to the Bosch fuel injection pump. Idle, fast idle and anti-stall speed settings on the Lucas pump are controlled by the system ECU.*

1 The usual type of tachometer (rev counter), which works from ignition system pulses, cannot be used on diesel engines. A diagnostic socket is provided for the use of Peugeot test equipment, but this will not normally be available to the home mechanic. If it is not felt that adjusting the idle speed "by ear" is satisfactory, it will be necessary to purchase or hire an appropriate tachometer,

8.2 Maximum speed adjustment screw (arrowed) on the Bosch fuel injection pump

or else leave the task to a Peugeot dealer or other suitably equipped specialist.

2 Before making adjustments, warm up the engine to normal operating temperature, ensuring that the radiator cooling fan has operated at least twice. Check the accelerator cable adjustment as follows, before making any adjustments to the fuel injection pump:

a) *Have an assistant depress the accelerator pedal to the floor and hold it there.*

b) *Check that the control lever on the injection pump is in contact with the maximum speed adjustment screw (see illustration). If this is not the case, remove the spring clip from the accelerator outer cable and reposition the cable as necessary. Refit the spring clip to the last exposed outer cable groove.*

c) *Release the accelerator cable and check that the control lever is in contact with the anti-stall adjustment screw.*

Idle speed adjustment

3 Loosen the locknut, and unscrew the anti-stall adjustment screw until it is clear of the pump control lever.

4 Loosen the locknut and turn the idle speed adjustment screw as required, then retighten the locknut **(see illustration)**.

8.4 Adjustment points at the fast idle lever

B Idle speed adjustment screw
C Fast idle adjustment screw
Note: *Adjustment screws viewed from the engine compartment bulkhead side*

8.9 Slacken the locknut (A) and turn the knurled nut (B) to alter the fast idle setting

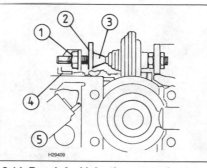

8.14 Bosch fuel injection pump damper adjustment details

1	Locknut	4	Adjustment screw
2	Shim	5	Pump control lever
3	Damper rod		

9.4 Removing the stop solenoid wiring cover

Anti-stall speed adjustment

5 Insert a 1.0 mm shim or feeler blade between the pump control lever and the anti-stall adjustment screw.

6 Start the engine and allow it to idle. The engine speed should be as specified for the anti-stall speed.

7 If adjustment is necessary, loosen the locknut and turn the anti-stall adjustment screw as required. Retighten the locknut.

8 Remove the shim or feeler blade and allow the engine to idle.

Fast idle speed adjustment

9 With the engine stopped, check that the fast idle lever is in contact with the fast idle adjustment screw. If necessary, slacken the locknut and turn the fast idle cable knurled adjustment nut, located on the fast idle control diaphragm bracket (see illustration). Tighten the locknut after adjustment.

10 Disconnect the vacuum hose at the fast idle control diaphragm and start the engine. Hold the fast idle lever against the fast idle adjustment screw and check that the engine is idling at the specified fast idle speed. If necessary, loosen the locknut and turn the fast idle adjustment screw as required, then retighten the locknut. Switch off the engine and reconnect the vacuum hose to the diaphragm.

11 Where applicable, disconnect the tachometer on completion.

12 If any adjustment was made to the fast idle speed, adjust the damper as described below.

Damper adjustment

13 Carry out all the previously described adjustments.

14 Slacken the locknut and unscrew the control lever damper adjustment screw, located on the rear of the lever, and insert a 1.0 mm shim or feeler blade between the damper rod and adjustment screw (see illustration). Make sure the pump control lever is in the idle position then position the adjustment screw so that the feeler blade/shim is a light, sliding fit between the screw and damper rod. Hold the screw in this position and securely tighten its locknut.

9 Stop solenoid - description, removal and refitting

Caution: Be careful not to allow dirt into the injection pump during this procedure.
Note: The following procedure is only applicable to the Bosch fuel injection pump.

Description

1 The stop solenoid is located on the end of the fuel injection pump. Its purpose is to cut the fuel supply when the ignition is switched off. If an open-circuit occurs in the solenoid or supply wiring, it will be impossible to start the engine, as the fuel will not reach the injectors. The same applies if the solenoid plunger jams in the "stop" position. If the solenoid jams in the "run" position, the engine will not stop when the ignition is switched off.

2 If the solenoid has failed and the engine will not run, a temporary repair may be made by removing the solenoid as described in the following paragraphs. Refit the solenoid body without the plunger and spring. Tape up the wire so that it cannot touch earth. The engine can now be started as usual, but it will be necessary to use the manual stop lever (see Section 1, paragraph 14) on the fuel injection pump (or to stall the engine in gear) to stop it.

Removal

3 Disconnect the battery negative terminal.

4 Withdraw the rubber boot (if fitted), then unscrew the terminal nut and detach the wire from the top of the solenoid (see illustration).

5 Carefully clean around the solenoid, then unscrew and withdraw the solenoid, and recover the sealing washer or O-ring (as applicable). Recover the solenoid plunger and spring if they remain in the pump. Operate the hand-priming pump as the solenoid is removed, to flush away any dirt.

Refitting

6 Refitting is a reversal of removal, using a new sealing washer or O-ring and tightening the solenoid to the specified torque setting.

10 Bosch fuel injection pump - removal and refitting

Caution: Be careful not to allow dirt into the injection pump or injector pipes during this procedure. New sealing rings should be used on the fuel pipe banjo unions when refitting.

Removal

1 Disconnect the battery negative terminal.

2 Remove the air intake ducts as described in Section 3, as necessary for access to the pump.

3 Remove the auxiliary drivebelt (Chapter 1) then, on models with air conditioning, refer to Chapter 10 and unbolt the power steering pump and move it to one side without disconnecting the hydraulic fluid pipes.

4 Remove the upper timing belt cover with reference to Chapter 2B.

5 Where necessary, disconnect the hoses from the vacuum converter on the end of the fuel injection pump.

6 Disconnect the accelerator cable from the fuel injection pump, with reference to Section 4.

7 Mark the position of the fast idle cable in relation to the fast idle lever then disconnect the cable from the fuel injection pump.

8 Loosen the clip, or undo the banjo union, and disconnect the fuel supply hose. Recover the sealing washers from the banjo union, where applicable. Cover the open end of the hose, and refit and cover the banjo bolt to keep dirt out (see illustrations).

9 Disconnect the main fuel return pipe and the injector leak-off return pipe banjo union. Recover the sealing washers from the banjo union. Again, cover the open end of the hose and the banjo bolt to keep dirt out. Take care not to get the inlet and outlet banjo unions mixed up.

10 Disconnect all relevant wiring from the pump. This can be achieved by simply disconnecting the wiring connectors at the brackets on the pump (see illustration).

11 Unscrew the union nuts securing the injector pipes to the fuel injection pump and

4B

10.8a Disconnecting the fuel pump fuel supply banjo union. Note sealing washers (arrowed)

10.8b Refitting the fuel supply banjo bolt with a small section of fuel hose (arrowed) to prevent dirt ingress

10.10 Fuel injection pump wiring plug (arrowed)

injectors. Counterhold the unions on the pump, while unscrewing the pipe-to-pump union nuts. Remove the pipes as a set. Cover open unions to keep dirt out (see Haynes Hint).

12 Using a socket on the crankshaft pulley, turn the crankshaft in the normal direction of rotation until the two bolt holes in the fuel injection pump sprocket are aligned with the corresponding holes in the engine front plate. It will be easier to turn the engine if the glow plugs are removed (see Chapter 5C).

13 Insert two M8 bolts through the holes, and hand-tighten them. Note that the bolts must retain the sprocket while the fuel injection pump is removed, thereby making it unnecessary to remove the timing belt (see illustration).

14 Mark the fuel injection pump in relation to the mounting bracket, using a scriber or felt tip pen (see illustration). This will ensure that the correct pump timing is retained when refitting.

15 Unscrew the three front mounting nuts, and recover the washers. Unscrew and remove the rear mounting nut and bolt, noting the locations of the washers, and support the injection pump on a block of wood.

16 Release the injection pump sprocket from the pump shaft, as described in Chapter 2B, Section 8. Note that the sprocket can be left

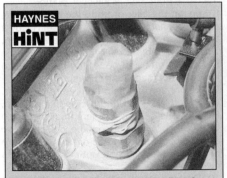

An ideal way to prevent dirt from entering open fuel lines and unions is to cut off the fingers from surgical rubber gloves and secure them in place with elastic bands.

10.13 Bolts inserted through timing holes in injection pump sprocket

engaged with the timing belt as the pump is withdrawn from its mounting bracket. Refit the M8 bolts to retain the sprocket in position while the pump is removed.

17 Carefully withdraw the pump. Recover the Woodruff key from the end of the pump shaft if it is loose, and similarly recover the bush from the rear of the mounting bracket.

Refitting

18 Commence refitting the injection pump by fitting the Woodruff key to the shaft groove (if removed).

19 Offer the pump to the mounting bracket, and support on a block of wood, as during removal.

20 Engage the pump shaft with the sprocket, and refit the sprocket as described in Chapter 2B, Section 8. Ensure that the Woodruff key does not fall out of the shaft as the sprocket is engaged.

21 Align the marks made on the pump and mounting bracket before removal. If a new pump is being fitted, transfer the mark from the old pump to give an approximate setting.

22 Refit and lightly tighten the pump mounting nuts and bolt.

23 Set up the injection timing, as described in Sections 12 and 13.

24 Refit and reconnect the injector fuel pipes.

25 Reconnect all relevant wiring to the pump.

26 Reconnect the fuel supply and return hoses, and tighten the unions, as applicable. Use new sealing washers on the banjo unions.

27 Reconnect the fast idle cable, setting it in the position noted during removal.

10.14 Mark the injection pump in relation to the mounting bracket (arrowed)

28 Reconnect and adjust the accelerator cable with reference to Section 4.

29 Where necessary, reconnect the hoses to the vacuum converter.

30 Refit the upper timing belt cover.

31 Refit the auxiliary drivebelt (Chapter 1) and, if removed, the power steering pump (Chapter 10).

32 Refit the air intake ducting removed for access.

33 Reconnect the battery negative terminal.

34 Bleed the fuel system as described in Section 2.

35 Start the engine, and check the fuel injection pump adjustments as described in Section 8.

11 Lucas fuel injection pump - removal and refitting

Caution: Be careful not to allow dirt into the injection pump or injector pipes during this procedure. New sealing rings should be used on the fuel pipe banjo unions when refitting.

Removal

1 Disconnect the battery negative terminal.

2 Remove the fuel injection system electronic control unit (ECU) and the ECU module box as described in Section 17.

3 Remove the intake ducting as described in Section 3 and the inlet manifold upper part as described in Section 18.

4 Remove the auxiliary drivebelt (Chapter 1), then refer to Chapter 10 and unbolt the power steering pump and move it to one side without disconnecting the hydraulic fluid pipes.

5 Remove the alternator as described in Chapter 5A.

6 Undo the bolts and remove the accessory bracket (power steering pump and alternator mounting bracket) from the side of the cylinder block.

7 Undo the bolts securing the wiring harness carrier to the engine and move the carrier clear of the injection pump. According to equipment fitted, it may be necessary to disconnect specific wiring connectors to enable the harness carrier to be moved sufficiently. Label all disconnected wiring to aid refitting.

8 Remove the timing belt cover over the injection pump sprocket with reference to Chapter 2B.

9 Undo the banjo unions, and disconnect the fuel supply and return hoses from the pump. Recover the sealing washers from the banjo unions. Cover the open end of the hoses, and refit and cover the banjo bolt to keep dirt out.

10 Disconnect all remaining wiring and hose clips and brackets from the pump.

11 Unscrew the union nuts securing the injector pipes to the fuel injection pump and injectors (see illustrations). Counterhold the unions on the pump, while unscrewing the pipe-to-pump union nuts. Remove the pipes as a set. Cover open unions to keep dirt out (see Haynes Hint - Section 10).

12 Using a socket on the crankshaft pulley, turn the crankshaft in the normal direction of rotation until the two bolt holes in the fuel injection pump sprocket are aligned with the corresponding holes in the engine front plate. It will be easier to turn the engine if the glow plugs are removed (see Chapter 5C).

13 Insert two M8 bolts through the holes, and hand-tighten them (see illustration 10.13). Note that the bolts must retain the sprocket while the fuel injection pump is removed, thereby making it unnecessary to remove the timing belt.

14 Mark the fuel injection pump in relation to the mounting bracket, using a scriber or felt tip pen (see illustration 10.14). This will ensure that the correct pump timing is retained when refitting.

15 Unscrew the three front mounting nuts, and recover the washers. Unscrew and remove the rear mounting nut and bolt, noting the locations of the washers, and support the injection pump on a block of wood (see illustrations).

16 Release the injection pump sprocket from the pump shaft, as described in Chapter 2B, Section 8. Note that the sprocket can be left engaged with the timing belt as the pump is withdrawn from its mounting bracket. Refit the M8 bolts to retain the sprocket in position while the pump is removed.

17 Carefully withdraw the pump. Recover the Woodruff key from the end of the pump shaft if it is loose, and similarly recover the bush from the rear of the mounting bracket (where fitted).

Refitting

18 Commence refitting the injection pump by fitting the Woodruff key to the shaft groove (if removed).

19 Offer the pump to the mounting bracket, and support on a block of wood, as during removal.

20 Engage the pump shaft with the sprocket, and refit the sprocket as described in Chapter 2B, Section 8. Ensure that the Woodruff key does not fall out of the shaft as the sprocket is engaged.

21 Align the marks made on the pump and mounting bracket before removal. If a new pump is being fitted, transfer the mark from the old pump to give an approximate setting.

22 Refit and lightly tighten the pump mounting nuts and bolt.

23 Set up the injection timing, as described in Sections 12 and 14.

24 Refit and reconnect the injector fuel pipes.

25 Reconnect all relevant wiring to the pump.

26 Reconnect the fuel supply and return hoses, and tighten the unions, as applicable. Use new sealing washers on the banjo unions.

27 Refit the timing belt cover.

28 Refit the wiring harness carrier to the engine and reconnect any disconnected wiring.

29 Refit the accessory bracket to the cylinder block.

30 Refit the alternator (Chapter 5A), the power steering pump (Chapter 10) and the auxiliary drivebelt (Chapter 1).

31 Refit the inlet manifold upper part as described in Section 18.

32 Refit the ECU module box and the ECU as described in Section 17.

33 Reconnect the battery negative terminal.

34 Bleed the fuel system as described in Section 2.

12 Injection timing - checking methods and adjustment

1 Checking the injection timing is not a routine operation. It is only necessary after the injection pump has been disturbed.

2 Dynamic timing equipment does exist, but it is unlikely to be available to the home mechanic. The equipment works by converting pressure pulses in an injector pipe into electrical signals. If such equipment is available, use it in accordance with its maker's instructions.

3 Static timing as described in this Chapter gives good results if carried out carefully. If working on the Bosch fuel injection pump, a dial test indicator will be needed, with suitable probes and adapters (see illustration). If working on the Lucas pump, a Peugeot special tool will be needed although a home-made alternative can be used. Read through the procedures before starting work, to find out what is involved.

4B

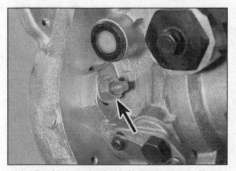

11.11a Unscrew the union nuts securing the injector pipes to the fuel injection pump . . .

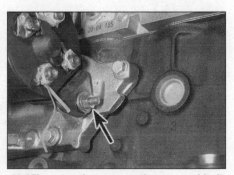

11.11b . . . and to the fuel injectors

11.15a Unscrew the injection pump front mounting nuts (arrowed) . . .

11.15b . . . and rear mounting nut and bolt (arrowed)

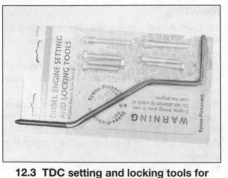

12.3 TDC setting and locking tools for injection pump timing

13 Injection timing (Bosch fuel injection pump) - checking and adjustment

Caution: Some of the injection pump settings and access plugs may be sealed by the manufacturers at the factory, using paint or locking wire and lead seals. Do not disturb the seals if the vehicle is still within the warranty period, otherwise the warranty will be invalidated. Also do not attempt the timing procedure unless accurate instrumentation is available.

Note: *A dial test indicator and an adaptor (Peugeot tool No. 0117AK) will be required for this procedure. If the Peugeot adaptor cannot be obtained, suitable alternatives to fit a range of Bosch fuel injection pumps can be purchased from most motor factors or diesel injection specialists.*

1 If the injection timing is being checked with the pump in position on the engine, rather than as part of the pump refitting procedure, disconnect the battery negative terminal and cover the alternator with a clean cloth or plastic bag to prevent the possibility of fuel being spilt onto it.

2 Remove the injector pipes as described in paragraph 11 of Section 10.

3 Referring to Chapter 2B, align the engine assembly/valve timing holes to lock the crankshaft in position. Remove the crankshaft locking tool, then turn the crankshaft **backwards** (anti-clockwise) approximately a quarter of a turn.

4 Unscrew the access screw, situated in the centre of the four injector pipe unions, from the rear of the injection pump. As the screw is removed, position a suitable container beneath the pump to catch any escaping fuel. Mop up any spilt fuel with a clean cloth.

5 Screw the adapter into the rear of the pump and mount the dial gauge in the adapter **(see illustration)**. Position the dial gauge so that its plunger is at the mid-point of its travel and securely tighten the adapter locknut.

6 Slowly rotate the crankshaft back and forth whilst observing the dial gauge, to determine when the injection pump piston is at the bottom of its travel (BDC). When the piston is correctly positioned, zero the dial gauge.

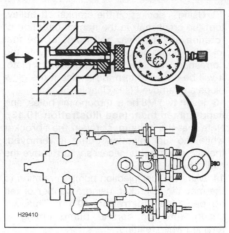

13.5 Dial test indicator and timing probe for use with Bosch pump

7 Rotate the crankshaft slowly in the correct direction until the crankshaft locking tool can be re-inserted.

8 The reading obtained on the dial gauge should be equal to the specified pump timing measurement given in the Specifications at the start of this Chapter. If adjustment is necessary, slacken the front and rear pump mounting nuts and bolts and slowly rotate the pump body until the point is found where the specified reading is obtained. When the pump is correctly positioned, tighten both its front and rear mounting nuts and bolts securely.

9 Rotate the crankshaft through one and three quarter rotations in the normal direction of rotation. Find the injection pump piston BDC as described in paragraph 6 and zero the dial gauge.

10 Rotate the crankshaft slowly in the correct direction of rotation until the crankshaft locking tool can be re-inserted (bringing the engine back to TDC). Recheck the timing measurement.

11 If adjustment is necessary, slacken the pump mounting nuts and bolts and repeat the operations in paragraphs 8 to 10.

12 When the pump timing is correctly set, unscrew the adapter and remove the dial gauge.

13 Refit the screw and sealing washer to the pump and tighten it securely.

14.3 Unscrew the cap over the timing hole on the Lucas pump

14 If the procedure is being carried out as part of the pump refitting sequence, proceed as described in Section 10.

15 If the procedure is being carried out with the pump fitted to the engine, refit the injector pipes tightening their union nuts to the specified torque setting. Reconnect the battery then bleed the fuel system as described in Section 2. Start the engine and carry out the adjustments in Section 8.

14 Injection timing (Lucas fuel injection pump) - checking and adjustment

Caution: Some of the injection pump settings and access plugs may be sealed by the manufacturers at the factory, using paint or locking wire and lead seals. Do not disturb the seals if the vehicle is still within the warranty period, otherwise the warranty will be invalidated. Also do not attempt the timing procedure unless accurate instrumentation is available.

Note: *A pump timing setting rod (available as a Peugeot special tool) will be required for the following procedure. Alternatively, a short length of approximately 1.5 mm diameter rod (ie welding rod) shaped as described in the text, can be used.*

1 Carry out the operations described in Section 11, paragraphs 1 to 9.

2 Referring to Chapter 2B, align the engine assembly/valve timing holes to lock the crankshaft in position. Remove the crankshaft locking tool, then turn the crankshaft **backwards** (anti-clockwise) approximately a quarter of a turn.

3 Unscrew the cap over the timing hole on the side of the injection pump **(see illustration)**. As the cap is removed, position a suitable container beneath the pump to catch any escaping fuel. Mop up any spilt fuel with a clean cloth.

4 If the Peugeot setting rod is not available, obtain a short length of approximately 1.5 mm diameter rod (welding rod will do) and taper one end to form a point.

5 Insert the Peugeot setting rod or the home-made alternative into the timing hole on the side of the pump **(see illustration)**. While

14.5 Using the home-made setting rod to time the Lucas pump

keeping pressure on the tool, slowly turn the crankshaft in the correct direction of rotation until the setting rod moves in further slightly to engage with a slot in the internal mechanism of the pump. This is very much a trial-and-error operation (especially if the home-made tool is being used) and it is not always immediately obvious if the setting rod has engaged internally or not. If difficulty is experienced, set the crankshaft back at the TDC position and turn it very slowly one way, then the other, until the setting rod engages in the pump. Once you have a "feel" of how the rod engages, the procedure will be easier.

6 Remove the tools, return the crankshaft to TDC to align the engine assembly/valve timing holes once more, then again turn the crankshaft **backwards** (anti-clockwise) approximately a quarter of a turn.

7 Repeat paragraph 5 until the setting rod engages internally with the pump. With the setting rod engaged, the crankshaft should be at TDC and it should be possible to insert the locking tool into the engine assembly/valve timing hole in the crankshaft.

8 If adjustment is necessary, remove the pump setting rod and turn the crankshaft to the TDC position. Insert the locking tool into the engine assembly/valve timing hole in the crankshaft.

9 Slacken the front and rear pump mounting nuts and bolts and rotate the pump away from the engine. Insert the setting rod into the timing hole on the side of the pump. While keeping pressure on the tool as before, slowly rotate the pump toward the engine until the setting rod engages internally. Tighten the front pump mounting bolts followed by the rear mounting bolt, to the specified torque.

10 Remove the setting rod and refit the cap over the timing hole.

11 Remove the locking tool from the crankshaft.

12 Refit all the components removed for access as described in Section 11, paragraphs 26 to 34.

15 Fuel injectors - testing, removal and refitting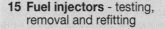

⚠️ **Warning: Exercise extreme caution when working on the fuel injectors. Never expose the hands or any part of the body to injector spray, as the high working pressure can cause the fuel to penetrate the skin, with possibly fatal results. You are strongly advised to have any work which involves testing the injectors under pressure carried out by a dealer or fuel injection specialist.**

Testing

1 Injectors do deteriorate with prolonged use, and it is reasonable to expect them to need reconditioning or renewal after 60 000 miles (100 000 km) or so. Accurate testing, overhaul and calibration of the injectors must be left to a specialist. A defective injector which is causing knocking or smoking can be located without dismantling as follows.

2 Run the engine at a fast idle. Slacken each injector union in turn, placing rag around the union to catch spilt fuel, and being careful not to expose the skin to any spray. When the union on the defective injector is slackened, the knocking or smoking will stop.

Removal

Note: *To remove the injector fitted with the needle lift sensor, a suitable slotted socket will be required to allow clearance for the sensor*

wire. These sockets are available from Peugeot dealers (as a special tool) or from diesel injection specialists.

3 On 1.9 litre models (Bosch fuel injection pump) remove the air intake ducting as described in Section 3, as necessary for access to the pump. On 2.1 litre models (Lucas fuel injection pump) remove the air intake ducting as described in Section 3 and the inlet manifold upper part (see Section 18).

4 Carefully clean around the injectors and injector pipe union nuts.

5 Unscrew the union nuts and disconnect the pipes from the injectors **(see illustration)**. If necessary, the injector pipes may be completely removed. Note carefully the locations of the pipe clamps, for use when refitting. Cover the ends of the injectors, to prevent dirt ingress.

6 Pull the leak-off pipes from the injectors.

7 Unscrew the union nuts securing the injector pipes to the fuel injection pump. Counterhold the unions on the pump when unscrewing the nuts. Cover open unions to keep dirt out, using small plastic bags, or fingers cut from discarded (but clean!) rubber gloves.

8 Bearing in mind the information given in the Note at the start of this Section, unscrew the injectors using a deep socket or box spanner (27 mm across-flats), and remove them from the cylinder head **(see illustration)**.

9 Recover the copper washers and fire seal washers from the cylinder head. Also recover the sleeves if they are loose **(see illustrations)**.

15.5 Disconnecting the fuel pipes from the fuel injectors

15.8 Unscrew the injectors and remove them from the cylinder head

15.9a Removing a fuel injector copper washer . . .

15.9b . . . fire seal washer . . .

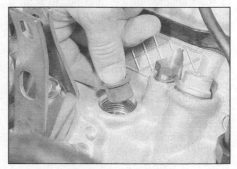

15.9c . . . and sleeve

4B

Refitting

10 Obtain new copper washers and fire seal washers. Also renew the sleeves, if they are damaged.

11 Take care not to drop the injectors, or allow the needles at their tips to become damaged. The injectors are precision-made to fine limits, and must not be handled roughly. In particular, never mount them in a bench vice.

12 Commence refitting by inserting the sleeves (if removed) into the cylinder head, followed by the fire seal washers (convex face uppermost), and copper washers.

13 Insert the injectors and tighten them to the specified torque.

14 Refit the injector pipes and tighten the union nuts. Make sure the pipe clamps are in their previously-noted positions. If the clamps are wrongly positioned or missing, problems may be experienced with pipes breaking or splitting.

15 Reconnect the leak-off pipes.

16 Refit the air intake ducting (Section 3) and, where applicable, the inlet manifold upper part (Section 18).

17 Start the engine. If difficulty is experienced, bleed the fuel system as described in Section 2.

16 Information sensors and actuators (Bosch AS3) - testing, removal and refitting

General information

Electronic Control Unit (ECU)

1 This component is the heart of the system, controlling the injection timing, fast idle speed, preheater glow plugs and exhaust gas recirculation. The ECU receives signals from sensors, which monitor engine coolant temperature, engine speed, fuel injector operation and engine load. These signals are used by the ECU to control the previously mentioned system functions.

Crankshaft (RPM) sensor

2 This is an inductive pulse generator bolted to the transmission bellhousing, to scan a reference ridge on the flywheel. As the ridge passes the sensor tip, a signal is generated, which is used by the ECU to determine engine speed.

Coolant temperature sensor

3 This component is an NTC (Negative Temperature Coefficient) thermistor - that is, a semi-conductor whose electrical resistance decreases as its temperature increases. It provides the ECU with a constantly-varying (analogue) voltage signal, corresponding to the temperature of the engine coolant. This is used to refine the calculations made by the ECU, when determining fuel metering.

Atmospheric pressure sensor

4 An atmospheric pressure sensor is located inside the ECU. The sensor is used by the ECU to regulate fuel injection timing according to altitude.

Load lever sensor

5 The load lever sensor is located on the top of the injection pump and attached to the pump control lever. The unit consists of a potentiometer whose resistance varies according to accelerator position. From this information the ECU can regulate the fuel injection timing according to driver input and engine load.

Injector needle lift sensor

6 The needle lift sensor is an integral part of one of the fuel injectors and sends a signal to the ECU whenever the injector opens.

Preheating system control unit

7 This unit is a relay, controlled by the ECU, to operate the preheating system glow plugs during cold starting conditions.

Fast idle control diaphragm

8 The fast idle control diaphragm controls the operation of the fast idle lever on the injection pump by means of a cable. When the engine is stopped, the injection pump lever remains in the fast idle position. When the engine is started, vacuum from the engine vacuum pump is supplied to the control diaphragm via an ECU controlled solenoid valve. When the ECU signals the solenoid valve to open, vacuum is supplied to the control diaphragm which returns the fast idle lever (via the cable) to the normal idle position.

EGR valve

9 Introduction of part of the exhaust gas back into the inlet manifold is controlled by the ECU in conjunction with an EGR solenoid valve and EGR valve. Vacuum from the engine vacuum pump is directed to the EGR valve, via the solenoid valve according to engine speed, load and altitude.

Testing

10 If a fault appears in the system, first ensure all the system wiring connectors are securely connected and free of corrosion. Ensure the fault is not due to poor maintenance; ie, check that the air cleaner filter element is clean, the cylinder compression pressures are correct, and that the engine breather hoses are clear and undamaged, referring to Chapters 1 and 2 for further information.

11 If these checks fail to reveal the cause of the problem, the vehicle should be taken to a suitably-equipped Peugeot dealer for testing. A wiring block connector is incorporated in the engine management circuit, into which a special electronic diagnostic tester can be plugged. The tester will locate the fault quickly and simply, alleviating the need to test all the system components individually, which is a time-consuming operation that also carries a risk of damaging the ECU.

16.14 Lift off the ECU module box lid for access to the ECU wiring connector (arrowed)

Removal and refitting

General

12 Before disconnecting any of these components, always disconnect the battery negative lead first.

ECU

Note: *The ECU is fragile. Take care not to drop it or subject it to any other kind of impact, and do not subject it to extremes of temperature, or allow it to get wet.*

13 The ECU is located in a plastic box which is mounted on the right-hand front wheel arch.

14 Lift off the ECU module box lid **(see illustration)**.

15 Release the wiring connector by lifting the locking lever on top of the connector upwards. Lift the connector at the rear, disengage the tag at the front and carefully withdraw the connector from the ECU pins.

16 Lift the ECU upwards and remove it from its location.

17 If necessary, the ECU module box can now be removed by undoing the internal and external retaining bolts.

18 Refitting is a reversal of removal.

Crankshaft (RPM) sensor

19 The crankshaft sensor is situated on the front face of the transmission clutch housing.

20 Trace the wiring back from the sensor to the wiring connector and disconnect it from the main harness.

21 Prise out the rubber grommet then undo the retaining bolt and withdraw the sensor from the transmission.

22 Refitting is reversal of removal ensuring that the sensor retaining bolt is securely tightened and the grommet is correctly seated in the transmission housing.

Coolant temperature sensor

23 Refer to Chapter 3.

Absolute pressure sensor

24 This component is an integral part of the ECU and cannot be separately removed.

16.25 Load lever sensor (arrowed) on the Bosch fuel injection pump

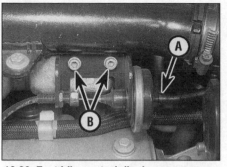

16.30 Fast idle control diaphragm vacuum hose (A) and mounting bracket bolts (B)

Load lever sensor

25 The load lever sensor is fitted to the top of the fuel injection pump (see illustration). Although it can be individually removed, Peugeot test equipment is required to adjust the sensor position when refitting. Any removal and refitting of this component should therefore be entrusted to a Peugeot dealer.

Injector needle lift sensor

26 The needle lift sensor is an integral part of the fuel injectors. Fuel injector removal and refitting procedures are contained in Section 15.

Preheating system control unit

27 Refer to Chapter 5C.

Fast idle control diaphragm

28 For improved access remove the air intake ducting over the front of the engine with reference to Section 3.
29 Mark the position of the fast idle cable in relation to the fast idle lever then disconnect the cable from the fuel injection pump.
30 Disconnect the vacuum hose from the diaphragm unit (see illustration).
31 Release the cable from the securing clips and ties, then undo the two mounting bracket bolts and remove the unit from the inlet manifold.
32 Refitting is reversal of removal, but adjust the fast idle speed as described in Section 8 on completion.

EGR valve

33 Refer to Part C of this Chapter.

---

17 Information sensors and actuators (Lucas EPIC) - testing, removal and refitting

General information

ECU (Electronic Control Unit)

1 This component is the heart of the entire engine management system, controlling the fuel injection, and emission control systems. The ECU receives signals from various sensors, which monitor changing engine

operating conditions such as inlet air temperature, coolant temperature, engine speed, accelerator pedal position, etc. These signals are used by the ECU to determine the correct fuel metering by the injection pump.

Crankshaft (RPM) sensor

2 This is an inductive pulse generator bolted to the transmission bellhousing, to scan the ridges between holes machined in the inboard face of the flywheel. As each ridge passes the sensor tip, a signal is generated, which is used by the ECU to determine engine speed.
3 The ridge between one of the holes is missing - this step in the incoming signals is used by the ECU to determine crankshaft (ie, piston) position.

Coolant temperature sensor

4 This component is an NTC (Negative Temperature Coefficient) thermistor - that is, a semi-conductor whose electrical resistance decreases as its temperature increases. It provides the ECU with a constantly-varying (analogue) voltage signal, corresponding to the temperature of the engine coolant. This is used to refine the calculations made by the ECU, when determining fuel metering.

Inlet air temperature sensor

5 This component is also an NTC thermistor - see the previous paragraph - providing the ECU with a signal corresponding to the temperature of air passing into the engine. This is also used to refine fuel metering calculations.

Accelerator pedal position sensor

6 The "drive-by-wire" throttle control information is provided by this sensor. The accelerator cable is connected to the pedal position sensor which converts accelerator pedal movement into an electrical signal. After processing this signal (and refining it using information received from the other sensors) the ECU controls the fuel injection pump electronically so that the correct fuel metering is achieved to obtain the desired road speed.

Manifold absolute pressure sensor

7 The manifold absolute pressure sensor measures inlet manifold vacuum and supplies this information to the ECU for calculation of engine load at any given throttle position.

Injector needle lift sensor

8 The needle lift sensor is an integral part of one of the fuel injectors and sends a signal to the ECU whenever the injector opens.

Preheating system control unit

9 This unit is a relay, controlled by the ECU, to operate the preheating system glow plugs during cold starting conditions.

Vehicle speed sensor

10 The vehicle speed sensor consists of a transducer incorporated into the speedometer drive unit. The ECU uses inputs from the sensor to modify fuel metering in accordance with vehicle speed.

EGR valve

11 Introduction of part of the exhaust gas back into the inlet manifold is controlled by the ECU in conjunction with an EGR solenoid valve and EGR valve. Vacuum from the engine vacuum pump is directed to the EGR valve, via the solenoid valve according to engine speed, load and altitude.

Testing

12 If a fault appears in the system, first ensure that all the system wiring connectors are securely connected and free of corrosion. Ensure that the fault is not due to poor maintenance; ie, check that the air cleaner filter element is clean, the cylinder compression pressures are correct, and that the engine breather hoses are clear and undamaged, referring to Chapters 1 and 2 for further information.
13 If these checks fail to reveal the cause of the problem, the vehicle should be taken to a suitably-equipped Peugeot dealer for testing. A wiring block connector is incorporated in the engine management circuit, into which a special electronic diagnostic tester can be plugged. The tester will locate the fault quickly and simply, alleviating the need to test all the system components individually, which is a time-consuming operation that also carries a risk of damaging the ECU.

Removal and refitting

General

14 Before disconnecting any of these components, always disconnect the battery negative lead first.

ECU

Note: The ECU is fragile. Take care not to drop it or subject it to any other kind of impact, and do not subject it to extremes of temperature, or allow it to get wet.
15 The ECU is located in a plastic box which is mounted on the right-hand front wheel arch.
16 Lift off the ECU module box lid.
17 Release the wiring connector by lifting the locking lever on top of the connector

4B

17.17a On the Lucas EPIC system ECU, lift the locking lever upwards . . .

17.17b . . . and disconnect the wiring connector

17.18 Lift the ECU upwards and remove it from the module box

17.19a Turn the injection pump wiring connector clockwise, disengage the retaining lug using a screwdriver . . .

17.19b . . . then turn the connector anti-clockwise and lift off

17.20 Undo the two base retaining screws and lift off the connector base

upwards. Lift the connector at the rear, disengage the tag at the front and carefully withdraw the connector from the ECU pins **(see illustrations)**.

18 Lift the ECU upwards and remove it from its location **(see illustration)**.

19 To remove the ECU module box, turn the injection pump wiring connector on the top of the box clockwise, disengage the retaining lug using a screwdriver, then turn the connector anti-clockwise and lift off **(see illustrations)**.

20 Undo the two screws securing the wiring connector base to the module box and lift off the connector base **(see illustration)**.

21 Undo the internal and external retaining bolts and remove the module box **(see illustrations)**.

22 Refitting is a reversal of removal.

Crankshaft (RPM) sensor

23 The crankshaft sensor is situated on the top face of the transmission clutch housing.

24 Trace the wiring back from the sensor to the wiring connector and disconnect it from the main harness.

25 Prise out the rubber grommet then undo the retaining bolt and withdraw the sensor from the transmission.

26 Refitting is reversal of removal ensuring that the sensor retaining bolt is securely tightened and the grommet is correctly seated in the transmission housing.

Coolant temperature sensor

27 Refer to Chapter 3.

Inlet air temperature sensor

28 Disconnect the wiring connector then unscrew the sensor from the intake ducting over the front of the engine **(see illustration)**.

29 Refitting is a reversal of removal.

17.21a Undo the internal and external retaining bolts . . .

17.28 Disconnect the inlet air temperature sensor wiring connector

Accelerator pedal position sensor

30 Release the accelerator inner cable from the lever on the pedal position sensor located on the left-hand side of the engine compartment **(see illustration)**. Pull the outer

17.21b . . . and remove the module box

17.30 Accelerator pedal position sensor

cable from the grommet in the pedal position sensor bracket.

31 Disconnect the wiring connector, undo the mountings and withdraw the sensor complete with mounting bracket. If it is necessary to remove the sensor from the mounting bracket, mark the position of the sensor in relation to the bracket, then undo the two screws and remove the unit. When refitting, align the marks made on removal. If a new unit is to be fitted, align it centrally within the mounting holes initially, then have the sensor adjusted by a Peugeot dealer.

32 The remainder of refitting is a reversal of removal.

Manifold absolute pressure sensor

33 The sensor may be located beneath the air cleaner assembly or in various locations at the front left-hand side of the engine compartment.

34 Disconnect the vacuum hose and wiring multiplug then undo the two sensor mounting bolts.

35 Withdraw the sensor from its location.

36 Refitting is a reversal of removal.

Injector needle lift sensor

37 The needle lift sensor is an integral part of the fuel injectors. Fuel injector removal and refitting procedures are contained in Section 15.

Preheating system control unit

38 Refer to Chapter 5C.

EGR valve

39 Refer to Part C of this Chapter.

---

18 Inlet manifold - removal and refitting

1.9 litre models

Note: *The inlet and exhaust manifolds share the same gasket. Therefore, it is recommended that both manifolds are removed, whenever one is removed, in order that the gasket can be renewed. It is possible to remove the manifolds individually, in which case the original gasket would be re-used, but this is not recommended.*

Removal

1 Disconnect the battery negative terminal.

2 Remove the air intake ducting over the top of the engine and attached to the inlet manifold, with reference to Section 3.

3 Disconnect the vacuum hose, then undo the two bolts securing the fast idle control diaphragm assembly to the manifold. Move the diaphragm assembly to one side.

4 Jack up the front of the car and support it on axle stands. Remove the splash guard from under the engine.

5 If not already removed with the intake ducting, disconnect the inlet and outlet ducts from the turbocharger. Cover the turbocharger openings with clean rag.

6 Undo the two bolts securing the EGR valve to the top of the exhaust manifold.

7 Using a suitable hexagon bit or Allen key, remove the bolts securing the inlet manifold. Loosen, but do not remove, the central hexagon manifold securing bolt - the manifold is slotted.

8 Withdraw the manifold from the cylinder head.

Refitting

9 Refitting is a reversal of removal, bearing in mind the following points.
a) *Renew the gasket(s) upon refitting.*
b) *Tighten all fixings to the specified torques, where applicable.*
c) *Renew the gasket when refitting the EGR valve.*
d) *Ensure that all relevant hoses and pipes are correctly reconnected and routed.*

2.1 litre models

Removal - upper part

Note: *There is insufficient clearance between the inlet manifold and the engine compartment bulkhead to gain access to the inlet manifold lower part attachments. The upper part can be removed with the engine in the car, however, if the lower part is to be removed it will be necessary to remove the engine/transmission assembly first.*

10 Slacken the retaining clip and disconnect the air intake duct from the manifold upper part **(see illustration)**.

11 Remove the clip securing the flexible portion of the EGR pipe to the manifold. If the original crimped clip is still in place, cut it off; new clips are supplied by Peugeot parts stockists with a screw clamp fixing **(see illustration)**. If a screw clamp type clip is fitted, undo the screw and manipulate the clip off the pipe.

12 Undo the four retaining bolts and lift off the manifold upper part. Recover the four rubber connecting tubes from the lower part **(see illustrations)**.

Refitting - upper part

13 Refitting is a reversal of removal, bearing in mind the following points.
a) *Renew the four rubber connecting tubes as a set if any one shows signs of deterioration.*
b) *Tighten all fixings to the specified torques, where applicable.*

18.10 Slacken the retaining clip and disconnect the air intake duct from the inlet manifold upper part

18.11 Remove the clip securing the flexible portion of the EGR pipe to the manifold

4B

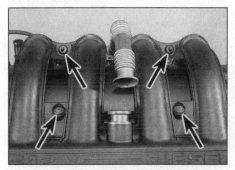

18.12a Undo the four retaining bolts (arrowed) . . .

18.12b . . . lift off the manifold upper part . . .

18.12c . . . and recover the four rubber connecting tubes

18.13 Secure the EGR pipe with a screw clamp type clip (arrowed) when refitting

18.16 Note the location of the support bracket (arrowed) when removing the inlet manifold lower part

18.17 Withdrawing the manifold from the cylinder head

c) *Secure the EGR pipe with a new screw clamp type clip, if a crimped type was initially fitted (see illustration).*

Removal - lower part

14 Remove the engine/transmission as described in Chapter 2C.

15 Remove the manifold upper part as described previously.

16 Undo the manifold retaining bolts, noting the location of the pipe support bracket at the right-hand end of the manifold **(see illustration)**.

17 Withdraw the manifold from the cylinder head, ease the EGR pipe aside, and manipulate the manifold out from between the EGR pipe and head **(see illustration)**.

18 Remove the manifold gasket.

Refitting - lower part

19 Refitting is a reversal of removal, bearing in mind the following points.

a) *Renew the gasket when refitting the manifold.*

b) *Tighten all fixings to the specified torques, where applicable.*

c) *Refit the manifold upper part as described previously.*

d) *Refit the engine/transmission as described in Chapter 2C.*

19 Exhaust manifold - removal and refitting

Removal

1.9 litre models

1 Remove the inlet manifold as described in Section 18.

2 Remove the turbocharger (see Section 21).

3 On certain models, it may be necessary to unbolt the resonator chamber from the manifold, to allow sufficient clearance for the manifold to be removed.

4 Unscrew the six exhaust manifold securing nuts, and recover the spacers from the studs.

5 Lift the exhaust manifold from the cylinder head, and recover the gasket(s) (where fitted).

6 It is possible that some of the manifold studs may be unscrewed from the cylinder

head when the manifold securing nuts are unscrewed. In this event, the studs should be screwed back into the cylinder head once the manifolds have been removed, using two manifold nuts locked together.

2.1 litre models

Note: *There is insufficient working clearance from above or below to allow removal of the exhaust manifold with the engine in the car. The only alternative, therefore, is to remove the engine/transmission assembly first.*

7 Remove the engine/transmission as described in Chapter 2C.

8 Remove the clip securing the flexible portion of the EGR pipe to the manifold. If the original crimped clip is still in place, cut it off; new clips are supplied by Peugeot parts stockists with a screw clamp fixing **(see illustration 18.11)**. If a screw clamp type clip is fitted, undo the screw and manipulate the clip off the pipe.

9 Unscrew the union nut and disconnect the oil feed pipe from the top of the turbocharger.

10 Undo the two bolts and separate the oil return pipe flange from the base of the turbocharger **(see illustration)**. Recover the gasket.

11 Undo the turbocharger steady bracket bolt.

12 Undo the nuts securing the manifold to the cylinder head studs, noting the position of the various support brackets.

13 Withdraw the manifold, complete with turbocharger, from the cylinder head and recover the gasket.

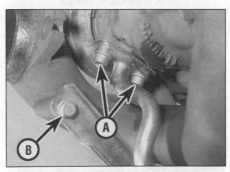

19.10 Turbocharger oil return pipe flange bolts (A) and steady bracket bolt (B) on 2.1 litre models

Refitting

14 Refitting is a reversal of removal, bearing in mind the following points.

a) *Renew all gaskets when refitting.*

b) *On 1.9 litre models refit the turbocharger (Section 21) and the inlet manifold (Section 18).*

c) *Tighten all fixings to the specified torque, where applicable.*

d) *On 2.1 litre models, secure the EGR pipe with a new screw clamp type clip, if a crimped type was initially fitted.*

e) *On 2.1 litre models refit the engine/transmission as described in Chapter 2C.*

20 Turbocharger - description and precautions

Description

A turbocharger is fitted to all diesel engines covered by this manual. It increases engine efficiency by raising the pressure in the inlet manifold above atmospheric pressure. Instead of the air simply being sucked into the cylinders, it is forced in. Additional fuel is supplied by the injection pump in proportion to the increased air inlet.

Energy for the operation of the turbocharger comes from the exhaust gas. The gas flows through a specially-shaped housing (the turbine housing) and in so doing, spins the turbine wheel. The turbine wheel is attached to a shaft, at the end of which is another vaned wheel known as the compressor wheel. The compressor wheel spins in its own housing, and compresses the inlet air on the way to the inlet manifold.

Between the turbocharger and the inlet manifold, the compressed air passes through an intercooler. This is an air-to-air heat exchanger, mounted in front of the radiator and supplied with cooling air from the front grille and electric cooling fans. The purpose of the intercooler is to remove from the inlet air some of the heat gained in being compressed. Because cooler air is denser, removal of this heat further increases engine efficiency.

Boost pressure (the pressure in the inlet manifold) is limited by a wastegate, which diverts the exhaust gas away from the turbine wheel in response to a pressure-sensitive actuator.

The turbo shaft is pressure-lubricated by an oil feed pipe from the main oil gallery. The shaft "floats" on a cushion of oil. A drain pipe returns the oil to the sump.

Precautions

The turbocharger operates at extremely high speeds and temperatures. Certain precautions must be observed, to avoid premature failure of the turbo, or injury to the operator.

Do not operate the turbo with any of its parts exposed, or with any of its hoses removed. Foreign objects falling onto the rotating vanes could cause excessive damage, and (if ejected) personal injury.

Do not race the engine immediately after start-up, especially if it is cold. Give the oil a few seconds to circulate.

Always allow the engine to return to idle speed before switching it off - do not blip the throttle and switch off, as this will leave the turbo spinning without lubrication.

Allow the engine to idle for several minutes before switching off after a high-speed run.

Observe the recommended intervals for oil and filter changing, and use a reputable oil of the specified quality. Neglect of oil changing, or use of inferior oil, can cause carbon formation on the turbo shaft, leading to subsequent failure.

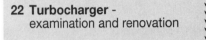

21 Turbocharger -
removal and refitting

Note: *On 1.9 litre models the turbocharger can be removed with the engine in the car; on 2.1 litre models, access is so restricted that the only alternative is to remove the engine/transmission first.*

Removal

1.9 litre models

1 Apply the handbrake, then jack up the front of the vehicle and support securely on axle stands (see *"Jacking and Vehicle Support"*).
2 Disconnect the exhaust frontpipe from the turbocharger, with reference to Chapter 4A, Section 17.
3 Unscrew the union nut, and disconnect the oil feed pipe from the top of the turbocharger.
4 Undo the two bolts and separate the oil return pipe flange from the base of the turbocharger. Recover the gasket.
5 Disconnect the inlet and outlet ducts from the turbocharger. Cover the turbocharger openings with clean rag.
6 Slacken and remove the nuts securing the anti-roll bar connecting links to the suspension struts.

7 Slacken and remove the lower engine movement limiter bracket through-bolt and nut, then undo the nut and bolt securing the bracket to the subframe and remove the bracket.
8 Make alignment marks between the intermediate shaft joint and the steering gear pinion then slacken and remove the clamp bolt and nut.
9 Place a jack and a suitable block of wood under the subframe to support the subframe as it is lowered.
10 Slacken and remove the four subframe mounting bolts then carefully lower the subframe assembly to the limit of the steering gear flexible hoses (approximately 300 mm).
11 Unscrew and remove the two lower turbocharger securing bolts.
12 Support the turbocharger, then remove the upper turbocharger securing bolt, and recover the spacer.
13 Carefully lower the turbocharger and remove it from under the car. If it is to be refitted, store the turbocharger carefully, and plug its openings to prevent dirt ingress.

2.1 litre models

14 Remove the engine/transmission assembly as described in Chapter 2C.
15 Unscrew the union nut and disconnect the oil feed pipe from the top of the turbocharger.
16 Undo the two bolts and separate the oil return pipe flange from the base of the turbocharger. Recover the gasket.
17 Undo the turbocharger steady bracket bolt.
18 Undo the three bolts securing the turbocharger to the underside of the exhaust manifold **(see illustration)**.
19 Withdraw the turbocharger from the manifold.

Refitting

20 Refitting is a reversal of removal, bearing in mind the following points:
   a) *If a new turbo is being fitted, change the engine oil and filter. Also renew the filter (where fitted) in the oil feed pipe.*
   b) *On 1.9 litre models, do not fully tighten the oil feed pipe unions until both ends of the pipe are in place. When tightening the oil return pipe union, position it so that the return hose is not strained.*

21.18 Turbocharger-to-manifold retaining bolts (arrowed) on 2.1 litre models

   c) *On 1.9 litre models, refer to Chapter 10 for torque wrench settings applicable to the front subframe.*
   d) *On 2.1 litre models refit the engine/transmission as described in Chapter 2C.*
   e) *Before starting the engine, prime the turbo lubrication circuit by disconnecting the stop solenoid lead at the fuel pump, and cranking the engine on the starter for three ten-second bursts.*

22 Turbocharger -
examination and renovation

1 With the turbocharger removed, inspect the housing for cracks or other visible damage.
2 Spin the turbine or the compressor wheel, to verify that the shaft is intact and to feel for excessive shake or roughness. Some play is normal, since in use, the shaft is "floating" on a film of oil. Check that the wheel vanes are undamaged.
3 The Garrett turbocharger wastegate actuator is a separate unit. Consult a Peugeot dealer or other specialist if it is thought that testing or renewal is necessary.
4 If the exhaust or induction passages are oil-contaminated, the turbo shaft oil seals have probably failed. (On the induction side, this will also have contaminated the intercooler, which should if necessary be flushed with a suitable solvent.)
5 No DIY repair of the turbo is possible. A new unit may be available on an exchange basis.

23 Intercooler -
removal and refitting

4B

Removal

1 The intercooler is located in front of the radiator. To remove it first remove the radiator as described in Chapter 3.
2 Disconnect the air hoses from each end of the intercooler then remove the unit from the front cross panel **(see illustration)**.

23.2 Removing the intercooler

Refitting

3 Refitting is a reversal of removal with reference to Chapter 3 when refitting the radiator.

24 Exhaust system - general information, removal and refitting

Refer to Part A, Section 17.

Chapter 4 Part C:
Emission control systems

Contents

Degrees of difficulty

Easy, suitable for novice with little experience   **Fairly easy,** suitable for beginner with some experience   **Fairly difficult,** suitable for competent DIY mechanic   **Difficult,** suitable for experienced DIY mechanic   **Very difficult,** suitable for expert DIY or professional

1 General information

All petrol engine models have the ability to use unleaded petrol and also have various other features built into the fuel system to help minimise harmful emissions. On top of this, all models are equipped with the crankcase emission-control system described below. Most petrol models are also equipped with a catalytic converter and an evaporative emission control system (See Chapter 4A or 4B for further information).

All diesel engine models are also designed to meet strict emission requirements and are also equipped with a crankcase emission control system and a catalytic converter. To further reduce emissions, all diesel models are fitted with an exhaust gas recirculation (EGR) system.

The emission control systems function as follows.

Petrol models

Crankcase emission control

To reduce the emission of unburned hydrocarbons from the crankcase into the atmosphere, the engine is sealed and the blow-by gases and oil vapour are drawn from inside the crankcase, through a wire mesh oil separator, into the inlet tract to be burned by the engine during normal combustion.

Under conditions of high manifold depression (idling, deceleration) the gases will be sucked positively out of the crankcase. Under conditions of low manifold depression (acceleration, full-throttle running) the gases are forced out of the crankcase by the (relatively) higher crankcase pressure; if the engine is worn, the raised crankcase pressure (due to increased blow-by) will cause some of the flow to return under all manifold conditions.

Exhaust emission control

To minimise the amount of pollutants which escape into the atmosphere, a catalytic converter is fitted in the exhaust system. On all models where a catalytic converter is fitted, the system is of the closed-loop type, in which a lambda (oxygen) sensor in the exhaust system provides the fuel-injection/ignition system ECU with constant feedback, enabling the ECU to adjust the mixture to provide the best possible conditions for the converter to operate.

The lambda sensor has a heating element built-in that is controlled by the ECU through the lambda sensor relay to quickly bring the sensor's tip to an efficient operating temperature. The sensor's tip is sensitive to oxygen and sends the ECU a varying voltage depending on the amount of oxygen in the exhaust gases; if the inlet air/fuel mixture is too rich, the exhaust gases are low in oxygen so the sensor sends a low-voltage signal, the voltage rising as the mixture weakens and the amount of oxygen rises in the exhaust gases. Peak conversion efficiency of all major pollutants occurs if the inlet air/fuel mixture is maintained at the chemically-correct ratio for the complete combustion of petrol of 14.7 parts (by weight) of air to 1 part of fuel (the 'stoichiometric' ratio). The sensor output voltage alters in a large step at this point, the ECU using the signal change as a reference point and correcting the inlet air/fuel mixture accordingly by altering the fuel injector pulse width.

Evaporative emission control

To minimise the escape into the atmosphere of unburned hydrocarbons, an evaporative emission control system is fitted to models equipped with a catalytic converter. The fuel tank filler cap is sealed and a charcoal canister is mounted behind the radiator on the left-hand side of the engine compartment to collect the petrol vapours generated in the tank when the car is parked. It stores them until they can be cleared from the canister (under the control of the fuel-injection/ignition system ECU) via the purge valve into the inlet tract to be burned by the engine during normal combustion.

To ensure that the engine runs correctly when it is cold and/or idling and to protect the catalytic converter from the effects of an over-rich mixture, the purge control valve is not opened by the ECU until the engine has warmed up, and the engine is under load; the valve solenoid is then modulated on and off to allow the stored vapour to pass into the inlet tract.

Diesel models

Crankcase emission control

Refer to paragraphs 4 and 5.

Exhaust emission control

To minimise the level of exhaust pollutants released into the atmosphere, a catalytic converter is fitted in the exhaust system of all models.

The catalytic converter consists of a canister containing a fine mesh impregnated with a catalyst material, over which the hot exhaust gases pass. The catalyst speeds up the oxidation of harmful carbon monoxide, unburnt hydrocarbons and soot, effectively reducing the quantity of harmful products released into the atmosphere via the exhaust gases.

Exhaust gas recirculation system

This system is designed to recirculate small quantities of exhaust gas into the inlet tract, and therefore into the combustion process. This process reduces the level of oxides of nitrogen present in the final exhaust gas which is released into the atmosphere.

The volume of exhaust gas recirculated is controlled by the system electronic control unit.

A vacuum-operated valve is fitted to the exhaust manifold, to regulate the quantity of exhaust gas recirculated. The valve is operated by the vacuum supplied by the solenoid valve.

Exhaust system

The exhaust system is fully described in Part A of this Chapter.

4C

2 Emission control systems - testing and component renewal

Petrol models

Crankcase emission control

1 The components of this system require no attention other than to check that the hose(s) are clear and undamaged at regular intervals.

Evaporative emission control system

Testing

2 If the system is thought to be faulty, disconnect the hoses from the charcoal canister and purge control valve and check that they are clear by blowing through them. If the purge control valve or charcoal canister are thought to be faulty, they must be renewed.

Charcoal canister - renewal

3 The charcoal canister is located under the wheel arch on the right-hand side. To gain access, jack up the front of the car and support it on axle stands. Remove the roadwheel and the wheel arch liner (where necessary).

4 Identify the location of the two hoses then disconnect them from the top of the canister. Where the crimped-type hose clips are fitted, cut the clips and discard them, replace them with standard worm-drive hose clips on refitting. Where the hoses are equipped with quick-release fittings depress the centre collar of the fitting with a small flat-bladed screwdriver then detach the hose from the canister.

5 Unscrew the mounting nuts and remove the canister from its mounting bracket. If necessary unbolt and remove the mounting bracket.

6 Refitting is a reverse of the removal procedure ensuring that the hoses are correctly reconnected.

Purge valve - renewal

7 The purge valve is located in the right-hand side of the engine compartment near the front suspension strut tower.

8 To renew the purge valve, disconnect the battery negative terminal then depress the retaining clip and disconnect the wiring connector from the valve.

9 Disconnect the hoses from either end of the valve then release the valve from its retaining clip and remove it from the engine compartment, noting which way around it is fitted.

10 Refitting is a reversal of the removal procedure ensuring that the valve is fitted the correct way around and the hoses are securely connected.

Exhaust emission control

Testing

11 The performance of the catalytic converter can be checked only by measuring the exhaust gases using a good-quality, carefully-calibrated exhaust gas analyser as described in Chapter 1.

12 If the CO level at the tailpipe is too high, the vehicle should be taken to a Peugeot dealer so that the complete fuel-injection and ignition systems, including the lambda sensor, can be thoroughly checked using the special diagnostic equipment. Once these have been checked and are known to be free from faults, the fault must be in the catalytic converter, which must be renewed as described in Part A of this Chapter.

Catalytic converter - renewal

13 Refer to Part A of this Chapter.

Lambda sensor - renewal

Note: *The lambda sensor is delicate and will not work if it is dropped or knocked, if its power supply is disrupted, or if any cleaning materials are used on it.*

14 Trace the wiring back from the lambda sensor, which is screwed into the top of the exhaust front pipe, to the top of the transmission. Disconnect both wiring connectors and free the wiring from any relevant retaining clips or ties.

15 Unscrew the sensor from the exhaust system front pipe and remove it along with its sealing washer **(see illustration)**.

16 Refitting is a reverse of the removal procedure using a new sealing washer. Prior to installing the sensor apply a smear of high temperature grease to the sensor threads. Ensure that the sensor is securely tightened and that the wiring is correctly routed and in no danger of contacting either the exhaust system or engine.

Diesel models

Crankcase emission control

17 The components of this system require no attention other than to check that the hose(s) are clear and undamaged at regular intervals.

Exhaust emission control

Testing

18 The performance of the catalytic converter can be checked only by measuring the exhaust gases using a good-quality, carefully-calibrated exhaust gas analyser.

19 If the catalytic converter is thought to be faulty, before assuming the catalytic converter is faulty, it is worth checking the problem is not due to a faulty injector(s). Refer to your Peugeot dealer for further information.

Catalytic converter - renewal

20 Refer to Part A of this Chapter.

Exhaust gas recirculation system

Testing

21 Testing of the system should be entrusted to a Peugeot dealer.

Component renewal

22 At the time of writing, no specific information was available regarding removal and refitting of the system components.

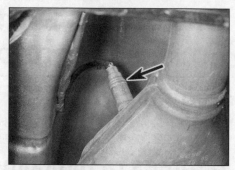

2.15 Lambda sensor location (arrowed) in the top of the exhaust front pipe

3 Catalytic converter - general information and precautions

1 The catalytic converter is a reliable and simple device which needs no maintenance in itself, but there are some facts of which an owner should be aware if the converter is to function properly for its full service life.

Petrol models

a) DO NOT use leaded petrol in a car equipped with a catalytic converter - the lead will coat the precious metals, and will eventually destroy the converter.

b) Always keep the ignition and fuel systems well-maintained to the service schedule.

c) If the engine develops a misfire, do not drive the car at all (or at least as little as possible) until the fault is cured.

d) DO NOT push- or tow-start the car - this will soak the catalytic converter in unburned fuel, causing it to overheat when the engine does start.

e) DO NOT switch off the ignition at high engine speeds.

f) DO NOT use fuel or engine oil additives - these may contain substances harmful to the catalytic converter.

g) DO NOT continue to use the car if the engine burns oil to the extent of leaving a visible trail of blue smoke.

h) Remember that the catalytic converter operates at very high temperatures. DO NOT, therefore, park the car in dry undergrowth, over long grass or piles of dead leaves after a long run.

i) Remember that the catalytic converter is FRAGILE - do not strike it with tools.

j) In some cases a sulphurous smell (like that of rotten eggs) may be noticed from the exhaust. This is common to many catalytic converter-equipped cars and once the car has covered a few thousand miles the problem should disappear.

k) If the converter is no longer effective it must be renewed.

Diesel models

2 Refer to parts f, g, h and i of the *"petrol models"* information given above.

Chapter 5 Part A:
Starting and charging systems

Contents

Degrees of difficulty

Easy, suitable for novice with little experience	Fairly easy, suitable for beginner with some experience	Fairly difficult, suitable for competent DIY mechanic	Difficult, suitable for experienced DIY mechanic	Very difficult, suitable for expert DIY or professional

Specifications

System type .... 12-volt, negative earth

Battery
Type .... Low maintenance or "maintenance-free" sealed for life
Charge condition:
  Poor .... 12.5 volts
  Normal .... 12.6 volts
  Good .... 12.7 volts

Alternator
Type .... Valeo or Mitsubishi (depending on model)

Starter motor
Type .... Valeo or Bosch (depending on model)

1 General information and precautions

General information

The engine electrical system consists mainly of the charging and starting systems. Because of their engine-related functions, these components are covered separately from the body electrical devices such as the lights, instruments, etc (which are covered in Chapter 12). On petrol engine models refer to Part B for information on the ignition system, and on diesel models refer to Part C for information on the preheating system.

The electrical system is of the 12-volt negative earth type.

The battery is of the low maintenance or "maintenance-free" (sealed for life) type and is charged by the alternator, which is belt-driven from the crankshaft pulley.

The starter motor is of the pre-engaged type incorporating an integral solenoid. On starting, the solenoid moves the drive pinion into engagement with the flywheel ring gear before the starter motor is energised. Once the engine has started, a one-way clutch prevents the motor armature being driven by the engine until the pinion disengages from the flywheel.

Precautions

Further details of the various systems are given in the relevant Sections of this Chapter. While some repair procedures are given, the usual course of action is to renew the component concerned. The owner whose interest extends beyond mere component renewal should obtain a copy of the "Automobile Electrical & Electronic Systems Manual", available from the publishers of this manual.

It is necessary to take extra care when working on the electrical system to avoid damage to semi-conductor devices (diodes and transistors), and to avoid the risk of personal injury. In addition to the precautions given in "Safety first!" at the beginning of this manual, observe the following when working on the system:

 Always remove rings, watches, etc before working on the electrical system. Even with the battery disconnected, capacitive discharge could occur if a component's live terminal is earthed through a metal object. This could cause a shock or nasty burn.

Do not reverse the battery connections. Components such as the alternator, electronic control units, or any other components having semi-conductor circuitry could be irreparably damaged.

If the engine is being started using jump leads and a slave battery, connect the batteries positive-to-positive and negative-to-negative (see "Booster battery (jump) starting"). This also applies when connecting a battery charger.

Never disconnect the battery terminals, the alternator, any electrical wiring or any test instruments when the engine is running.

Do not allow the engine to turn the alternator when the alternator is not connected.

Never "test" for alternator output by "flashing" the output lead to earth.

Never use an ohmmeter of the type incorporating a hand-cranked generator for circuit or continuity testing.

Always ensure that the battery negative lead is disconnected when working on the electrical system.

Before using electric-arc welding equipment on the car, disconnect the battery, alternator and components such as the fuel injection/ignition electronic control unit to protect them from the risk of damage.

The radio/cassette unit fitted as standard equipment by Peugeot is equipped with a built-in security code to deter thieves. If the power source to the unit is cut, the anti-theft system will activate. Even if the power source is immediately reconnected, the radio/ cassette unit will not function until the correct security code has been entered. Therefore, if you do not know the correct security code for the radio/cassette unit do not disconnect the battery negative terminal of the battery or remove the radio/cassette unit from the vehicle. Refer to the "Radio/cassette unit anti-theft system precaution" Section for further information.

2 Electrical fault finding - general information

Refer to Chapter 12.

3 Battery - testing and charging

Standard and low maintenance battery - testing

1 If the vehicle covers a small annual mileage, it is worthwhile checking the specific gravity of the electrolyte every three months to determine the state of charge of the battery. Use a hydrometer to make the check and compare the results with the following table. Note that the specific gravity readings assume an electrolyte temperature of 15°C (60°F); for every 10°C (18°F) below 15°C (60°F) subtract 0.007. For every 10°C (18°F) above 15°C (60°F) add 0.007.

	Above 25°C	Below 25°C
Fully-charged	1.210 to 1.230	1.270 to 1.290
70% charged	1.170 to 1.190	1.230 to 1.250
Discharged	1.050 to 1.070	1.110 to 1.130

2 If the battery condition is suspect, first check the specific gravity of electrolyte in each cell. A variation of 0.040 or more

between any cells indicates loss of electrolyte or deterioration of the internal plates.

3 If the specific gravity variation is 0.040 or more, the battery should be renewed. If the cell variation is satisfactory but the battery is discharged, it should be charged as described later in this Section.

Maintenance-free battery - testing

4 In cases where a "sealed for life" maintenance-free battery is fitted, topping-up and testing of the electrolyte in each cell is not possible. The condition of the battery can therefore only be tested using a battery condition indicator or a voltmeter.

5 Certain models may be fitted with a "Delco" type maintenance-free battery, with a built-in charge condition indicator. The indicator is located in the top of the battery casing, and indicates the condition of the battery from its colour. If the indicator shows green, then the battery is in a good state of charge. If the indicator shows black, then the battery requires charging, as described later in this Section. If the indicator shows blue, then the electrolyte level in the battery is too low to allow further use, and the battery should be renewed. **Do not** attempt to charge, load or jump start a battery when the indicator shows blue.

6 If testing the battery using a voltmeter, connect the voltmeter across the battery and compare the result with those given in the Specifications under "charge condition". The test is only accurate if the battery has not been subjected to any kind of charge for the previous six hours. If this is not the case, switch on the headlights for 30 seconds, then wait four to five minutes before testing the battery after switching off the headlights. All other electrical circuits must be switched off, so check that the doors, boot and/or tailgate are fully shut when making the test.

7 If the voltage reading is less than 12.2 volts, then the battery is discharged, whilst a reading of 12.2 to 12.4 volts indicates a partially discharged condition.

8 If the battery is to be charged, remove it from the vehicle (Section 4) and charge it as described later in this Section.

Standard and low maintenance battery - charging

Note: The following is intended as a guide only. Always refer to the manufacturer's recommendations (often printed on a label attached to the battery) before charging a battery.

9 Charge the battery at a rate of 3.5 to 4 amps and continue to charge the battery at this rate until no further rise in specific gravity is noted over a four hour period.

10 Alternatively, a trickle charger charging at the rate of 1.5 amps can safely be used overnight.

11 Specially rapid "boost" charges which are claimed to restore the power of the battery in 1 to 2 hours are not recommended, as they

can cause serious damage to the battery plates through overheating.

12 While charging the battery, note that the temperature of the electrolyte should never exceed 37.8°C (100°F).

Maintenance-free battery - charging

Note: The following is intended as a guide only. Always refer to the manufacturer's recommendations (often printed on a label attached to the battery) before charging a battery.

13 This battery type takes considerably longer to fully recharge than the standard type, the time taken being dependent on the extent of discharge.

14 A constant voltage type charger is required, to be set, when connected, to 13.9 to 14.9 volts with a charger current of 5.0 amps maximum. Using this method, the battery should be charged within twenty four hours.

4 Battery - removal and refitting

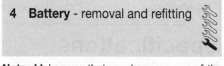

Note: Make sure that you have a copy of the radio/cassette unit security code number before disconnecting the battery.

Removal

1 The battery is located on the front left-hand side of the engine compartment.

2 Lift off the battery cover then slacken the battery negative (earth) terminal connector (coloured green). Lift the terminal connector off the battery post.

3 Disconnect the positive terminal connector (coloured red) in the same way.

4 Unscrew the two bolts and remove the battery retaining clamp.

5 Lift the battery out of the engine compartment.

6 To remove the battery box, remove the air cleaner assembly as described in the relevant Part of Chapter 4.

7 On models equipped with air conditioning, undo the screw securing the dehydrator retaining strap to the front of the battery box (see illustration).

4.7 Undo the screw (arrowed) securing the air conditioning dehydrator retaining strap to the front of the battery box

4.8a Undo the internal bolts (arrowed) securing the battery box and metal base to the mounting bracket . . .

4.8b . . . and the single outer bolt securing the box to the air cleaner mounting bracket

4.9 Lift the battery box out of the engine compartment

8 Undo the internal bolts securing the battery box and metal base to the mounting bracket, and the single outer bolt securing the box to the air cleaner mounting bracket (see illustrations).

9 Carefully move aside all cables and hoses, then lift the battery box out of the engine compartment (see illustration).

Refitting

10 Refitting is a reversal of removal, but smear petroleum jelly on the terminals when reconnecting the leads, and always reconnect the positive lead first, and the negative lead last.

11 With the battery reconnected, switch on the ignition and wait ten seconds before starting the engine. This will allow the vehicle electronic systems and control units to stabilise.

12 Enter the radio/cassette unit security codes with reference to the audio system documentation supplied with the vehicle.

5 Charging system - testing

Note: *Refer to the warnings given in "Safety first!" and in Section 1 of this Chapter before starting work.*

1 If the ignition warning light fails to illuminate when the ignition is switched on, first check the alternator wiring connections for security. If satisfactory, check that the warning light bulb has not blown, and that the bulbholder is secure in its location in the instrument panel. If the light still fails to illuminate, check the continuity of the warning light feed wire from the alternator to the bulbholder. If all is satisfactory, the alternator is at fault and should be renewed or taken to an auto-electrician for testing and repair.

2 If the ignition warning light illuminates when the engine is running, stop the engine and check that the drivebelt is correctly tensioned (see Chapter 1) and that the alternator connections are secure. If all is so far

satisfactory, have the alternator checked by an auto-electrician for testing and repair.

3 If the alternator output is suspect even though the warning light functions correctly, the regulated voltage may be checked as follows.

4 Connect a voltmeter across the battery terminals and start the engine.

5 Increase the engine speed until the voltmeter reading remains steady; the reading should be approximately 12 to 13 volts, and no more than 14 volts.

6 Switch on as many electrical accessories (eg, the headlights, heated rear window and heater blower) as possible, and check that the alternator maintains the regulated voltage at around 13 to 14 volts.

7 If the regulated voltage is not as stated, the fault may be due to worn brushes, weak brush springs, a faulty voltage regulator, a faulty diode, a severed phase winding or worn or damaged slip rings. The alternator should be renewed or taken to an auto-electrician for testing and repair.

6 Alternator drivebelt - removal, refitting and tensioning

Refer to the procedure given for the auxiliary drivebelt in Chapter 1.

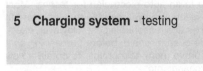

7.3 Alternator wiring connections

7 Alternator - removal and refitting

Removal

1 Disconnect the battery negative lead.

2 Slacken the auxiliary drivebelt as described in Chapter 1 and disengage it from the alternator pulley.

3 Remove the rubber covers (where fitted) from the alternator terminals, then unscrew the retaining nuts and disconnect the wiring from the rear of the alternator (see illustration).

4 On 2.1 litre diesel models, unbolt the power steering pump and move it to one side without disconnecting any hydraulic pipes or hoses (see Chapter 10).

5 Unscrew the nut/bolt securing the alternator to the upper mounting bracket (see illustration). Unscrew the lower mounting bolt. Note that, where a long through-bolt is used to secure the alternator in position, the bolt does not need to be fully removed; the alternator can be disengaged from the bolt once it has been slackened sufficiently. On some models, it may be necessary to remove the drivebelt idler/tensioner pulley to gain access to the alternator mounting nuts and bolts (depending on specification).

6 Manoeuvre the alternator away from its mounting brackets and out from the engine compartment.

5A

7.5 Alternator upper mounting bracket (2.0 litre petrol engine)

Refitting

7 Refitting is a reversal of removal, tensioning the auxiliary drivebelt as described in Chapter 1 on models with a manually adjusted tensioner, and ensuring that the alternator mountings are securely tightened.

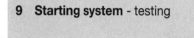

8 Alternator - testing and overhaul

If the alternator is thought to be suspect, it should be removed from the vehicle and taken to an auto-electrician for testing. Most auto-electricians will be able to supply and fit brushes at a reasonable cost. However, check on the cost of repairs before proceeding as it may prove more economical to obtain a new or exchange alternator.

9 Starting system - testing

Note: *Refer to the precautions given in "Safety first!" and in Section 1 of this Chapter before starting work.*

1 If the starter motor fails to operate when the ignition key is turned to the appropriate position, the following possible causes may be to blame.

a) The coded anti-start system is engaged.
b) The battery is faulty.
c) The electrical connections between the switch, solenoid, battery and starter motor are somewhere failing to pass the necessary current from the battery through the starter to earth.
d) The solenoid is faulty.
e) The starter motor is mechanically or electrically defective.

2 To check the battery, switch on the headlights. If they dim after a few seconds, this indicates that the battery is discharged - recharge (see Section 3) or renew the battery. If the headlights glow brightly, operate the ignition switch and observe the lights. If they dim, then this indicates that current is reaching the starter motor, therefore the fault must lie in the starter motor. If the lights continue to glow brightly (and no clicking sound can be heard from the starter motor solenoid), this indicates that there is a fault in the circuit or solenoid - see following paragraphs. If the starter motor turns slowly when operated, but the battery is in good condition, then this indicates that either the starter motor is faulty, or there is considerable resistance somewhere in the circuit.

3 If a fault in the circuit is suspected, disconnect the battery leads (including the earth connection to the body), the starter/solenoid wiring and the engine/ transmission earth strap. Thoroughly clean the connections, and reconnect the leads and wiring, then use a

10.3 Remove the two retaining nuts (arrowed) and disconnect the wiring from the starter motor solenoid

voltmeter or test lamp to check that full battery voltage is available at the battery positive lead connection to the solenoid, and that the earth is sound. Smear petroleum jelly around the battery terminals to prevent corrosion - corroded connections are amongst the most frequent causes of electrical system faults.

4 If the battery and all connections are in good condition, check the circuit by disconnecting the wire from the solenoid blade terminal. Connect a voltmeter or test lamp between the wire end and a good earth (such as the battery negative terminal), and check that the wire is live when the ignition switch is turned to the `start' position. If it is, then the circuit is sound - if not the circuit wiring can be checked as described in Chapter 12.

5 The solenoid contacts can be checked by connecting a voltmeter or test lamp between the battery positive feed connection on the starter side of the solenoid, and earth. When the ignition switch is turned to the "start" position, there should be a reading or lighted bulb, as applicable. If there is no reading or lighted bulb, the solenoid is faulty and should be renewed.

6 If the circuit and solenoid are proved sound, the fault must lie in the starter motor. In this event, it may be possible to have the starter motor overhauled by a specialist, but check on the cost of spares before proceeding, as it may prove more economical to obtain a new or exchange motor.

10 Starter motor - removal and refitting

Removal

1 Disconnect the battery negative lead.
2 So that access to the motor can be gained both from above and below, chock the rear wheels then jack up the front of the vehicle and support it on axle stands. Where applicable, to improve access to the motor remove the air cleaner and ducting as necessary as described in the relevant Part of Chapter 4.
3 Slacken and remove the two retaining nuts and disconnect the wiring from the starter

10.4 Note the main engine earth strap connection on one of the starter motor mounting bolts (2.1 litre diesel engine)

motor solenoid. Recover the washers under the nuts **(see illustration)**.
4 Undo the three mounting bolts, supporting the motor as the bolts are withdrawn. Recover the washers from under the bolt heads and note the locations of any wiring or hose brackets secured by the bolts **(see illustration)**.
5 Manoeuvre the starter motor out from underneath the engine and recover the locating dowel(s) from the motor/transmission (as applicable).

Refitting

6 Refitting is a reversal of removal, ensuring that the locating dowel(s) are correctly positioned. Also make sure that any wiring or hose brackets are in place under the bolt heads as noted prior to removal.

11 Starter motor - testing and overhaul

If the starter motor is thought to be suspect, it should be removed from the vehicle and taken to an auto-electrician for testing. Most auto-electricians will be able to supply and fit brushes at a reasonable cost. However, check on the cost of repairs before proceeding as it may prove more economical to obtain a new or exchange motor.

12 Ignition switch - removal and refitting

The ignition switch is integral with the steering column lock, and can be removed as described in Chapter 10.

13 Oil pressure warning light switch - removal and refitting

Removal

1 The switch is located at the front of the cylinder block, above the oil filter mounting. Note that on some models access to the switch may be improved if the vehicle is jacked up and supported on axle stands so that the switch can be reached from underneath.

2 Disconnect the battery negative lead.

3 Remove the protective sleeve from the wiring plug (where applicable), then disconnect the wiring from the switch.

4 Unscrew the switch from the cylinder block, and recover the sealing washer. Be prepared for oil spillage, and if the switch is to be left removed from the engine for any length of time, plug the hole in the cylinder block.

Refitting

5 Examine the sealing washer for signs of damage or deterioration and if necessary renew.

6 Refit the switch, complete with washer, and tighten it securely. Reconnect the wiring connector.

7 Lower the vehicle to the ground then check and, if necessary, top-up the engine oil as described in Chapter 1.

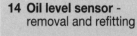

14 Oil level sensor - removal and refitting

1 The sensor is located on the rear facing side of the cylinder block at the flywheel end.

2 The removal and refitting procedure is as described for the oil pressure switch in Section 13. Access is most easily obtained from underneath the vehicle **(see illustration)**.

14.2 Removing the oil level sensor from the cylinder block

5A

Chapter 5 Part B:
Ignition system (petrol models)

Contents

Degrees of difficulty

Easy, suitable for novice with little experience	Fairly easy, suitable for beginner with some experience	Fairly difficult, suitable for competent DIY mechanic	Difficult, suitable for experienced DIY mechanic	Very difficult, suitable for expert DIY or professional

Specifications

System type . . . . Static (distributorless) ignition system controlled by engine management ECU
Firing order . . . . 1-3-4-2 (number 1 cylinder at flywheel end of engine)
Ignition timing . . . . Controlled by engine management ECU - see text

---

1 Ignition system - general information

On all models, the ignition system is integrated with the fuel injection system to form a combined engine management system under the control of one ECU (See the relevant Part of Chapter 4 for further information).

On 1.6 litre models, the ignition side of the system is of the static (distributorless) type, consisting only of a four output ignition coil. The ignition coil actually consists of two separate HT coils which supply two cylinders each (one coil supplies cylinders 1 and 4, and the other cylinders 2 and 3). Under the control of the ECU, the ignition coil operates on the "wasted spark" principle, ie. each spark plug sparks twice for every cycle of the engine, once on the compression stroke and once on the exhaust stroke. The ECU uses its inputs from the various sensors to calculate the required ignition advance setting and coil charging time.

On 1.8 and 2.0 litre models, the ignition side of the system is also of the static (distributorless) type and consists primarily of four ignition coils located in an ignition coil unit fitted to the centre of the cylinder head cover. The coils are integral with the spark plug caps and are pushed directly onto the spark plugs, one for each plug. This removes the need for any HT leads connecting the coils to the plugs. The ECU uses the inputs from the various sensors to calculate the required ignition advance setting and calculate the coil charging time.

2 Ignition system - testing

⚠ Warning: Voltages produced by an electronic ignition system are considerably higher than those produced by conventional ignition systems. Extreme care must be taken when working on the system with the ignition switched on. Persons with surgically-implanted cardiac pacemaker devices should keep well clear of the ignition circuits, components and test equipment.

1 If a fault appears in the engine management (fuel injection/ignition) system first ensure that the fault is not due to a poor electrical connection or poor maintenance; ie, check that the air cleaner filter element is clean, the spark plugs are in good condition and correctly gapped, that the engine breather hoses are clear and undamaged, referring to Chapter 1 for further information. Also check that the accelerator cable is correctly adjusted as described in the relevant part of Chapter 4. If the engine is running very roughly, check the compression pressures and the valve clearances as described in Chapter 2A.

2 If these checks fail to reveal the cause of the problem, the car should be taken to a Peugeot dealer for testing. A wiring block connector is incorporated in the engine management circuit into which a special electronic diagnostic tester can be plugged. The tester will locate the fault quickly and simply, alleviating the need to test all the system components individually, an operation that carries a high risk of damaging the ECU.

3 The only ignition system checks which can be carried out by the home mechanic are those described in Chapter 1, relating to the spark plugs. If necessary, the system wiring and wiring connectors can be checked as described in Chapter 12 ensuring that the ECU wiring connector(s) have first been disconnected.

3 Ignition HT coil(s) - removal and refitting

Removal

1.6 litre models

1 Disconnect the battery negative terminal. The ignition HT coil is mounted on the left-hand end of the cylinder head.
2 Depress the retaining clip and disconnect the wiring connector from the HT coil **(see illustration)**.

5B

3.2 Disconnect the wiring connector from the ignition coil

3 Make a note of the correct fitted positions of the HT leads then disconnect them from the coil terminals.

4 Undo the four retaining screws securing the coil to its mounting bracket and remove it from the engine compartment.

1.8 and 2.0 litre models

5 Disconnect the battery negative terminal. There are four separate ignition HT coils, one on the top of each spark plug.

6 To gain access to the coils, disconnect the wiring connectors at the left-hand end of the coil unit, then undo the six retaining bolts and lift the coil unit upwards, off the spark plugs and from its location in the cylinder head cover. The individual coils can now be removed as required.

Refitting

7 Refitting is a reversal of the relevant removal procedure ensuring that the wiring connectors are securely reconnected and, where necessary, the HT leads are correctly connected.

4 Ignition timing - checking and adjustment

1 On all models, there are no timing marks on the flywheel or crankshaft pulley. The timing is constantly being monitored and adjusted by the engine management ECU, and nominal values cannot be given. Therefore, it is not possible for the home mechanic to check the ignition timing.

2 The only way in which the ignition timing can be checked is using special electronic test equipment, connected to the engine management system diagnostic connector (refer to the relevant Part of Chapter 4 for further information).

Chapter 5 Part C:
Preheating system (diesel models)

Contents

Degrees of difficulty

Easy, suitable for novice with little experience		**Fairly easy,** suitable for beginner with some experience		**Fairly difficult,** suitable for competent DIY mechanic		**Difficult,** suitable for experienced DIY mechanic		**Very difficult,** suitable for expert DIY or professional	

Specifications

Torque wrench setting	Nm	lbf ft
Glow plugs	22	16

---

1 Preheating system - description and testing

Description

1 Each swirl chamber has a heater plug (commonly called a glow plug) screwed into it. The plugs are electrically-operated before and during start-up when the engine is cold. Electrical feed to the glow plugs is controlled by a relay/timer unit, in conjunction with the diesel injection system electronic control unit (ECU).

2 On certain models, the glow plugs provide a "post-heating" function, whereby the glow plugs remain switched on for a period after the engine has started. Once the starter has been switched off, the glow plugs begin a timed 3-minute "post-heating" cycle. The operation of the plugs cannot be cancelled for the first 15 seconds, but after the first 15 seconds, the supply to the plugs will be interrupted by:

a) *Operation of the accelerator pedal beyond a travel of 11 mm for a duration of more than 2.5 seconds.*
b) *A coolant temperature of more than 60°C.*

3 A warning light in the instrument panel tells the driver that preheating is taking place. When the light goes out, the engine is ready to be started. The voltage supply to the glow plugs continues for several seconds after the light goes out. If no attempt is made to start, the timer then cuts off the supply, in order to avoid draining the battery and overheating the glow plugs.

Testing

4 If the system malfunctions, testing is ultimately by substitution of known good units, but some preliminary checks may be made as follows.

5 Connect a voltmeter or 12-volt test lamp between the glow plug supply cable and earth (engine or vehicle metal). Make sure that the live connection is kept clear of the engine and bodywork.

6 Have an assistant switch on the ignition, and check that voltage is applied to the glow plugs. Note the time for which the warning light is lit, and the total time for which voltage is applied before the system cuts out. Switch off the ignition.

7 At an under-bonnet temperature of 20°C, typical times noted should be 5 or 6 seconds for warning light operation, followed by a further 10 seconds supply after the light goes out. Warning light time will increase with lower temperatures and decrease with higher temperatures.

8 If there is no supply at all, the relay or associated wiring is at fault.

9 To locate a defective glow plug, remove the air intake ducting (Chapter 4B) and, where necessary, disconnect the breather hose from the engine oil filler tube. Disconnect the main supply cable and the interconnecting wire or strap from the top of the glow plugs. Be careful not to drop the nuts and washers.

10 Use a continuity tester, or a 12-volt test lamp connected to the battery positive terminal, to check for continuity between each glow plug terminal and earth. The resistance of a glow plug in good condition is very low (less than 1 ohm), so if the test lamp does not light or the continuity tester shows a high resistance, the glow plug is certainly defective.

11 As a final check, the glow plugs can be removed and inspected as described in the following Section.

---

2 Glow plugs - removal, inspection and refitting

Removal

Caution: *If the preheating system has just been energised, or if the engine has been running, the glow plugs will be very hot.*

1 Disconnect the battery negative lead. To improve access, remove the air intake ducting (Chapter 4B) and, where necessary, disconnect the breather hose from the engine oil filler tube.

2 Unscrew the nut from the relevant glow plug terminal(s), and recover the washer(s). Note the main supply cable connection (usually to Number 2 cylinder glow plug) and the interconnecting wire fitted between the four plugs **(see illustration)**.

3 Where applicable, carefully move any obstructing pipes or wires to one side to enable access to the relevant glow plug(s).

4 Unscrew the glow plug(s) and remove from the cylinder head **(see illustration)**.

2.2 Unscrew the nut (arrowed) and disconnect the glow plug connecting wire

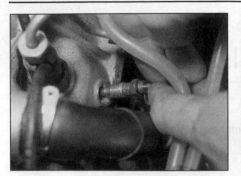

2.4 Unscrew the glow plug and remove it from the cylinder head

3.1 Preheating system control unit location on 1.9 litre models

3.4 Disconnect the wiring connector from the preheating system control unit then unscrew the two retaining nuts and free the main feed and supply wires (2.1 litre model shown)

Inspection

5 Inspect each glow plug for physical damage. Burnt or eroded glow plug tips can be caused by a bad injector spray pattern. Have the injectors checked if this sort of damage is found.

6 If the glow plugs are in good physical condition, check them electrically using a 12 volt test lamp or continuity tester as described in the previous Section.

7 The glow plugs can be energised by applying 12 volts to them to verify that they heat up evenly and in the required time. Observe the following precautions.

a) *Support the glow plug by clamping it carefully in a vice or self-locking pliers. Remember it will become red-hot.*

b) *Make sure that the power supply or test lead incorporates a fuse or overload trip to protect against damage from a short-circuit.*

c) *After testing, allow the glow plug to cool for several minutes before attempting to handle it.*

8 A glow plug in good condition will start to glow red at the tip after drawing current for 5 seconds or so. Any plug which takes much longer to start glowing, or which starts glowing in the middle instead of at the tip, is defective.

Refitting

9 Refit by reversing the removal operations. Apply a smear of copper-based anti-seize compound to the plug threads and tighten the glow plugs to the specified torque. Do not overtighten, as this can damage the glow plug element.

---

3 Preheating system control unit - removal and refitting

Removal

1 The unit is located on the left-hand side of the engine compartment, on the side of the

fusebox on 1.9 litre models, and on a bracket beneath the accelerator pedal position sensor on 2.1 litre models **(see illustration)**.

2 Disconnect the battery negative lead.

3 On 2.1 litre models, remove the air cleaner assembly and intake ducting as described in Chapter 4B.

4 Disconnect the wiring connector from the base of the unit then unscrew the two retaining nuts and free the main feed and supply wires from the unit **(see illustration)**.

5 Unscrew the retaining nut(s) and remove the unit from the engine compartment.

Refitting

6 Refitting is a reversal of removal, ensuring that the wiring connectors are correctly connected.

Chapter 6
Clutch

Contents

Degrees of difficulty

Easy, suitable for novice with little experience	Fairly easy, suitable for beginner with some experience	Fairly difficult, suitable for competent DIY mechanic	Difficult, suitable for experienced DIY mechanic	Very difficult, suitable for expert DIY or professional

Specifications

Type . . . . Single dry plate with diaphragm spring, cable or hydraulic operation

Friction plate diameter
Petrol models:
   1.6 and 1.8 litre models . . . . 200 mm
   2.0 litre models . . . . 215 mm
Diesel models . . . . 215 mm

Torque wrench setting	Nm	lbf ft
Pressure plate retaining bolts	20	15

1 General information

The clutch consists of a friction plate, a pressure plate assembly, a release bearing and the release mechanism; all of these components are contained in the large cast-aluminium alloy bellhousing, sandwiched between the engine and the transmission. The release mechanism is mechanical, and is operated by a self-adjusting cable on all models except the 2.1 litre diesel versions. On 2.1 litre diesel models the release mechanism is operated hydraulically by means of a master and slave cylinder and interconnecting hydraulic pipework.

The friction plate is fitted between the engine flywheel and the clutch pressure plate, and is allowed to slide on the transmission input shaft splines.

The pressure plate assembly is bolted to the engine flywheel. When the engine is running, drive is transmitted from the crankshaft, via the flywheel, to the friction plate (these components being clamped securely together by the pressure plate assembly) and from the friction plate to the transmission input shaft.

To interrupt the drive, the spring pressure must be relaxed. On the models covered in this manual, two different types of clutch release mechanism are used. The first is a conventional "push-type" mechanism, where an independent clutch release bearing, fitted concentrically around the transmission input shaft, is pushed onto the pressure plate assembly; this type is fitted to 1.6 and 1.8 litre petrol models. The second is a "pull-type" mechanism, where the clutch release bearing is an integral part of the pressure plate assembly, and is lifted away from the friction plate; this type is fitted to 2.0 litre petrol models and all diesel models.

On models with the conventional "push-type" mechanism, at the transmission end of the clutch cable, the outer cable is retained by a fixed mounting bracket, and the inner cable is attached to the release fork lever. Depressing the clutch pedal pulls the control cable inner wire, and this rotates the release fork by acting on the lever at the fork's upper end. The release fork then presses the release bearing against the pressure plate spring fingers. This causes the springs to deform and releases the clamping force on the pressure plate.

On 2.0 litre petrol and 1.9 litre diesel models with the "pull-type" mechanism, at the transmission end of the clutch cable the inner cable is attached to a fixed mounting bracket, and the outer cable acts against the release fork lever. Depressing the clutch pedal rotates the release fork. The release fork then lifts the release bearing, which is attached to the pressure plate springs, away from the friction plate, and releases the clamping force exerted at the pressure plate periphery.

On 2.1 litre diesel models with the "pull-type" mechanism, the clutch pedal is connected to the clutch master cylinder by a pushrod. The master cylinder is mounted on the engine compartment bulkhead with the slave cylinder mounted on the side of the transmission. A hydraulic fluid reservoir is also remotely mounted on the bulkhead and connected to the master cylinder by means of a fluid hose (see illustration). Depressing the

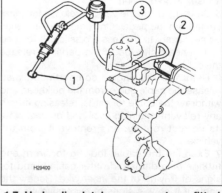

1.7 Hydraulic clutch components as fitted to 2.1 litre diesel models

1 Master cylinder   3 Fluid reservoir
2 Slave cylinder

6

clutch pedal moves the piston in the master cylinder forwards, so forcing hydraulic fluid through the clutch hydraulic pipe to the slave cylinder. The piston in the slave cylinder moves forward under hydraulic pressure and actuates the release fork by means of a short pushrod. The release fork then lifts the release bearing, which is attached to the pressure plate springs, away from the friction plate, and releases the clamping force exerted at the pressure plate periphery.

The clutch master cylinder, fluid reservoir, slave cylinder, and interconnecting fluid pipework are all part of a maintenance-free, sealed assembly. The fluid reservoir cannot be opened and the fluid level does not require topping-up. In the event of fluid leakage or any malfunction of the hydraulic system, all the components must be renewed as a complete assembly.

On all models, adjustment of the clutch to compensate for wear of the friction plate linings is automatically taken up by the hydraulic clutch components, or by the self-adjusting mechanism incorporated in the cable.

2 Clutch cable - removal and refitting

Removal

1 Disconnect the battery negative terminal.
2 Open up the engine immobiliser key pad, then rotate the fastener through 90° and lower the fusebox cover. Disconnect the wiring connector from the key pad then slacken and remove the retaining screws and remove the driver's side lower panel from the facia.
3 Remove the air cleaner housing and intake duct components as described in the relevant Part of Chapter 4.
4 Working in the engine compartment, release the inner cable and outer cable fittings from the clutch release lever and mounting bracket and free the cable from the transmission housing.
5 Working inside the vehicle, release the inner cable from the pedal. On some models it may be necessary to depress a plastic clip located just beneath the top of the pedal to release the cable.
6 Return to the engine compartment, then release the cable guide from the bulkhead and withdraw the cable forwards, releasing it from any relevant retaining clips and guides. Note its correct routing, and remove it from the vehicle.
7 Examine the cable, looking for worn end fittings or a damaged outer casing, and for signs of fraying of the inner wire. Renew the cable if it shows signs of excessive wear or any damage.

Refitting

8 Apply a thin smear of multi-purpose grease

to the cable end fittings, then pass the cable through the engine compartment bulkhead.
9 Hold the clutch pedal in its raised position by wedging a suitable tool beneath it.
10 Guide the end of the cable into the pedal end (or plastic clip) making sure that it is fully engaged.
11 In the engine compartment refit the cable to the transmission housing and release lever. Re-secure the cable with any relevant retaining clips and guides.
12 Depress and release the clutch pedal several times to operate the self-adjusting mechanism and check that the clutch pedal operates correctly.
13 Refit the lower panel to the facia then refit the air cleaner components and reconnect the battery.

3 Clutch pedal - removal and refitting

Removal

1 Disconnect the battery negative terminal.
2 Open up the engine immobiliser key pad, then rotate the fastener through 90° and lower the fusebox cover. Disconnect the wiring connector from the key pad then slacken and remove the retaining screws and remove the driver's side lower panel from the facia.
3 On models with a cable-operated clutch, release the inner cable from the pedal. On some models it may be necessary to depress a plastic clip located just beneath the top of the pedal to release the cable. Carefully release the pedal-assist spring assembly from the pedal.
4 On models with a hydraulically-operated clutch, release the master cylinder pushrod balljoint from the pedal and allow the pedal to rise until it reaches its stop.
5 Slacken and remove the pivot bolt and nut, and remove the clutch pedal from the vehicle. Slide the spacer out from the pedal pivot. Examine all components for signs of wear or damage, renewing them as necessary.

Refitting

6 Apply a smear of multi-purpose grease to the spacer, and insert it into the pedal pivot bore.
7 Manoeuvre the pedal into position, and insert the pivot bolt. Refit the nut to the pivot bolt and tighten it securely.
8 Reconnect the clutch cable or master cylinder pushrod to the pedal. On cable-operated versions, refit the pedal assist spring assembly.
9 Depress and release the clutch pedal several times and check for correct operation.
10 Refit the lower panel to the facia and reconnect the battery.

4 Clutch hydraulic system components - removal and refitting

Note 1: *The hydraulic system components (master cylinder, slave cylinder, reservoir and pipework) are a sealed assembly and cannot be separated or dismantled.*
Note 2: *Access to the master cylinder is extremely limited and Peugeot recommend the use of a special slotted socket (tool 0216J) for this purpose. A suitable alternative can be fabricated from a box spanner with a slot cut in the side to accommodate the hydraulic hose.*

Removal

1 Disconnect the battery negative terminal.
2 Remove the air cleaner housing and intake duct components as described in the relevant Part of Chapter 4.
3 Open up the engine immobiliser key pad, then rotate the fastener through 90° and lower the fusebox cover. Disconnect the wiring connector from the key pad then slacken and remove the retaining screws and remove the driver's side lower panel from the facia.
4 Release the master cylinder pushrod balljoint from the pedal and allow the pedal to rise until it reaches its stop.
5 Working in the engine compartment, unclip the master cylinder fluid reservoir from the bulkhead.
6 Engage the Peugeot special tool, or the home-made alternative over the master cylinder and turn the cylinder 90° clockwise to release it from the bulkhead attachment.
7 Release the slave cylinder from the transmission by pushing it in by hand and at the same time turning it 90° anti-clockwise **(see illustration)**.
8 Release the hydraulic pipework from the retaining clips and attachments in the engine compartment and remove the complete assembly from the vehicle.

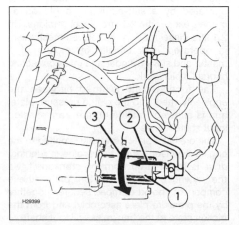

4.7 Release the slave cylinder (1) from the transmission by pushing it in (2) and turning it 90° anti-clockwise (3)

Refitting

Note: *On a new assembly, the slave cylinder pushrod is retained in the cylinder by a plastic collar which will automatically break off when the clutch pedal is depressed for the first time. Do not attempt to release this collar manually prior to fitting or the pushrod may be ejected.*

9 Push the clutch pedal to the floor by hand and retain it in this position.

10 Locate the master cylinder in position, aligning the white mark on the cylinder with the corresponding white mark on the bulkhead. Using the tool, push and turn the cylinder 90° anti-clockwise to secure.

11 Clip the master cylinder fluid reservoir into place on the bulkhead. Ensure that the fluid hoses are correctly routed and not chafing.

12 Lubricate the end of the slave cylinder pushrod with molybdenum disulphide grease then locate the slave cylinder in the transmission. Push it in by hand and at the same time turn it 90° clockwise to secure.

13 Reconnect the hydraulic pipework to the retaining clips and attachments in the engine compartment

14 Lubricate the master cylinder pushrod balljoint, then lift the clutch pedal and connect the pushrod.

15 With the assembly installed, slowly depress the clutch pedal to the floor, then slowly lift it again by hand. Wait for ten seconds and repeat this procedure. Depress the pedal again, release it and check that it rises correctly after being released.

16 Refit the lower panel to the facia then refit the air cleaner components and reconnect the battery.

---

 5 Clutch assembly - removal, inspection and refitting

⚠ **Warning: Dust created by clutch wear and deposited on the clutch components may contain asbestos, which is a health hazard. DO NOT blow it out with compressed air, or inhale any of it. DO NOT use petrol or petroleum-based solvents to clean off the dust. Brake system cleaner or methylated spirit should be used to flush the dust into a suitable receptacle. After the clutch components are wiped clean with rags, dispose of the contaminated rags and cleaner in a sealed, marked container.**

Note: *Although some friction materials may no longer contain asbestos, it is safest to assume that they do, and to take precautions accordingly.*

Removal

1 Unless the complete engine/transmission is to be removed from the car and separated for major overhaul (see Chapter 2C), the clutch can be reached by removing the transmission as described in Chapter 7A.

2 Before disturbing the clutch, mark the relationship of the pressure plate assembly to the flywheel, using a marker pen or similar.

3 Working in a diagonal sequence, slacken the pressure plate bolts by half a turn at a time, until spring pressure is released and the bolts can be unscrewed by hand.

4 Prise the pressure plate assembly off its locating dowels, and collect the friction plate, noting which way round the friction plate is fitted.

Inspection

Note: *Due to the amount of work necessary to remove and refit clutch components, it is usually considered good practice to renew the clutch friction plate, pressure plate assembly and release bearing as a matched set, even if only one of these is actually worn enough to require renewal. It is also worth considering the renewal of the clutch components on a preventative basis if the engine and/or transmission have been removed for some other reason.*

5 Separate the pressure plate and friction plate and place them on the bench.

6 When cleaning clutch components, read first the warning at the beginning of this Section; remove dust using a clean, dry cloth, and working in a well-ventilated atmosphere.

7 Check the friction plate facings for signs of wear, damage or oil contamination. If the friction material is cracked, burnt, scored or damaged, or if it is contaminated with oil or grease (shown by shiny black patches), the friction plate must be renewed.

8 If the friction material is still serviceable, check that the centre boss splines are unworn, that the torsion springs are in good condition and securely fastened, and that all the rivets are tight. If any wear or damage is found, the friction plate must be renewed.

9 If the friction material is fouled with oil, this must be due to an oil leak from the crankshaft left-hand oil seal, from the sump-to-cylinder block joint, or from the transmission input shaft. Renew the seal or repair the joint, as appropriate, as described in Chapter 2 or 7, before installing the new friction plate.

10 Check the pressure plate assembly for obvious signs of wear or damage; shake it to check for loose rivets or worn or damaged fulcrum rings, and check that the drive straps securing the pressure plate to the cover do

not show signs (such as a deep yellow or blue discoloration) of overheating. If the diaphragm spring is worn or damaged, or if its pressure is in any way suspect, the pressure plate assembly should be renewed.

11 Examine the machined bearing surfaces of the pressure plate and of the flywheel; they should be clean, completely flat, and free from scratches or scoring. If either is discoloured from excessive heat, or shows signs of cracks, it should be renewed - although minor damage of this nature can sometimes be polished away using emery paper.

12 Check that the release bearing contact surface rotates smoothly and easily, with no sign of noise or roughness. Also check that the surface itself is smooth and unworn, with no signs of cracks, pitting or scoring. If there is any doubt about its condition, the bearing must be renewed. On clutches with a "pull-type" release mechanism, this means that the complete pressure plate assembly must also be renewed.

Refitting

13 On reassembly, ensure that the bearing surfaces of the flywheel and pressure plate are completely clean, smooth, and free from oil or grease. Use solvent to remove any protective grease from new components.

14 Fit the friction plate so its spring hub faces away from the flywheel; there may also be a marking to show which way round the plate is to be refitted **(see illustration)**.

15 Refit the pressure plate assembly, aligning the marks made on dismantling (if the original pressure plate is re-used), and locating the pressure plate on its locating dowels. Fit the pressure plate bolts, but tighten them only finger-tight, so that the friction plate can still be moved.

16 The friction plate must now be centralised, so that when the transmission is refitted, its input shaft will pass through the splines at the centre of the friction plate.

17 Centralisation can be achieved by passing a screwdriver or other long bar through the friction plate and into the hole in the crankshaft; the friction plate can then be moved around until it is centred on the crankshaft hole. Alternatively, a clutch-aligning tool can be used to eliminate the guesswork; these can be obtained from most accessory shops **(see illustration)**. A home-made aligning tool can

6

5.14 Ensure the friction plate is fitted the correct way round then install the pressure plate

5.17 Using a clutch-aligning tool to centralise the friction plate

be fabricated from a length of metal rod or wooden dowel which fits closely inside the crankshaft hole, and has insulating tape wound around it to match the diameter of the friction plate splined hole.

18 When the friction plate is centralised, tighten the pressure plate bolts evenly and in a diagonal sequence to the specified torque setting.

19 Refit the transmission as described in Chapter 7A.

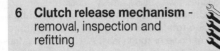

6 Clutch release mechanism - removal, inspection and refitting

Note: *Refer to the warning concerning the dangers of asbestos dust at the beginning of Section 5.*

Removal

1 Unless the complete engine/transmission is to be removed from the car and separated for major overhaul (see Chapter 2C), the clutch release mechanism can be reached by removing the transmission only, as described in Chapter 7A.

2 On models with a conventional "push-type" release mechanism, unhook the release bearing from the fork, and slide it off the input shaft **(see illustration)**. Drive out the roll pin, and remove the release lever from the top of the release fork shaft. Discard the roll pin - a new one must be used on refitting.

3 On both types of clutch, depress the retaining tabs, then slide the upper bush off the end of the release fork shaft. Disengage the shaft from its lower bush, and manoeuvre it out from the transmission. Depress the retaining tabs, and remove the lower pivot bush from the transmission housing **(see illustrations)**.

Inspection

4 Check the release mechanism, renewing any component which is worn or damaged.

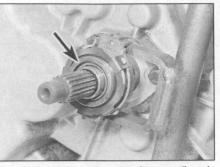

6.2 Clutch release bearing (arrowed) and release fork and shaft

6.3b . . . release fork shaft . . .

Carefully check all bearing surfaces and points of contact.

5 When checking the release bearing itself, note that it is often considered worthwhile to renew it as a matter of course. Check that the contact surface rotates smoothly and easily, with no sign of noise or roughness, and that the surface itself is smooth and unworn, with no signs of cracks, pitting or scoring. If there is any doubt about its condition, the bearing must be renewed. On models with a "pull-type" release mechanism, this means that the complete pressure plate assembly must be renewed, as described in Section 5.

Refitting

6 Apply a smear of molybdenum disulphide

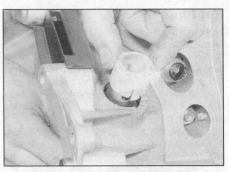

6.3a Removing the upper bush . . .

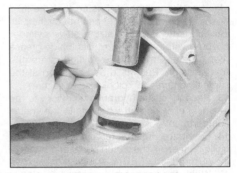

6.3c . . . and lower bush

grease to the shaft pivot bushes and the contact surfaces of the release fork.

7 Locate the lower pivot bush in the transmission, ensuring that it is securely retained by its locating tangs, and refit the release fork. Slide the upper bush down the shaft, and clip it into position in the transmission housing.

8 On models with a conventional "push-type" release mechanism, refit the release lever to the shaft. Align the lever with the shaft hole, and secure it in position by tapping a new roll pin fully into position. Slide the release bearing onto the input shaft, and engage it with the release fork.

9 Refit the transmission as described in Chapter 7A.

Chapter 7 Part A:
Manual transmission

Contents

Degrees of difficulty

Easy, suitable for novice with little experience	**Fairly easy,** suitable for beginner with some experience	**Fairly difficult,** suitable for competent DIY mechanic	**Difficult,** suitable for experienced DIY mechanic	**Very difficult,** suitable for expert DIY or professional

Specifications

General
Type .... Manual, five forward speeds and reverse. Synchromesh on all forward speeds

Designation:
All models except 2.1 litre diesel BE3
2.1 litre diesel models ML5T

Lubrication
Recommended oil .... See *"Lubricants, fluids and tyre pressures"*
Capacity .... 1.9 litres (1.8 litres after draining)

Torque wrench settings

	Nm	lbf ft
BE3 transmission:		
Gearchange selector rod to lever pivot bolt	15	11
Gearchange linkage bellcrank pivot bolt	28	21
Oil filler/level plug	20	15
Oil drain plug	30	22
Clutch release bearing guide sleeve bolts	12	9
Reversing light switch	25	18
Right-hand driveshaft intermediate bearing retaining bolt nuts	10	7
Engine movement limiter-to- driveshaft intermediate bearing housing	50	37
Engine movement limiter-to- subframe	85	62
Left-hand engine/transmission mounting:		
Rubber mounting-to- bracket bolts	30	22
Mounting stud to transmission	60	44
Mounting stud bracket-to-transmission	60	44
Centre nut	65	48
Engine-to-transmission fixing bolts	45	33
Clutch cable bracket retaining bolts ("pull-type" clutch only)	18	13
Roadwheel bolts	90	66

7A

Torque wrench settings (continued)

	Nm	lbf ft
ML5T transmission:		
Oil filler/level plug	20	15
Oil drain plug	30	22
Gearchange lever housing bolts	7	5
Clutch release bearing guide sleeve bolts	12	9
Reversing light switch	25	18
Right-hand driveshaft intermediate bearing retaining bolt nuts	10	7
Engine movement limiter-to-driveshaft intermediate bearing housing	50	37
Engine movement limiter-to-subframe	85	62
Left-hand engine/transmission mounting:		
Mounting to bracket	30	22
Mounting bracket-to-transmission	30	22
Centre nut	65	48
Engine-to-transmission fixing bolts	60	44
Roadwheel bolts	90	66

1 General information

The transmission is contained in a cast-aluminium alloy casing bolted to the engine's left-hand end, and consists of the gearbox and final drive differential. Two transmission types are fitted; all models except the 2.1 litre diesel utilise the BE3 transmission, whereas the 2.1 litre diesel is fitted with the ML5T unit. Both transmission types are similar and operate as follows.

Drive is transmitted from the crankshaft via the clutch to the input shaft, which has a splined extension to accept the clutch friction plate, and rotates in sealed ball-bearings. From the input shaft, drive is transmitted to the output shaft, which rotates in a roller bearing at its right-hand end, and a sealed ball-bearing at its left-hand end. From the output shaft, the drive is transmitted to the differential crownwheel, which rotates with the differential case and planetary gears, thus driving the sun gears and driveshafts. The rotation of the planetary gears on their shaft allows the inner roadwheel to rotate at a slower speed than the outer roadwheel when the car is cornering.

The input and output shafts are arranged side by side, parallel to the crankshaft and driveshafts, so that their gear pinion teeth are in constant mesh. In the neutral position, the relevant input shaft and output shaft gear pinions rotate freely, so that drive cannot be transmitted to the output shaft and crownwheel.

Gear selection is via a floor-mounted lever actuating a selector rod mechanism on BE3 transmissions, or a selector cable mechanism on the ML5T units. The selector rod/cables cause the appropriate selector fork to move its respective synchro-sleeve along the shaft, to lock the gear pinion to the synchro-hub. Since the synchro-hubs are splined to the input and output shafts, this locks the pinion to the shaft, so that drive can be transmitted.

To ensure that gear-changing can be made quickly and quietly, a synchro-mesh system is fitted to all forward gears, consisting of baulk rings and spring-loaded fingers, as well as the gear pinions and synchro-hubs. The synchro-mesh cones are formed on the mating faces of the baulk rings and gear pinions.

2 Manual transmission - draining and refilling

Note: *A suitable square section wrench may be required to undo the transmission filler/level and drain plugs on some models. These wrenches can be obtained from most motor factors or your Peugeot dealer.*

1 This operation is much quicker and more efficient if the car is first taken on a journey of sufficient length to warm the engine/transmission up to operating temperature.

2 Park the car on level ground, switch off the ignition and apply the handbrake firmly. To ensure that the car remains level when refilling, jack up the front and rear of the car and support it securely on axle stands.

3 On models equipped with the BE3 transmission, remove the left-hand front roadwheel then release the screws and clips and remove the wheel arch liner from under the wing for access to the filler/level plug. On all models, remove the splash guard from under the engine.

4 Wipe clean the area around the filler/level plug. On the BE3 transmission, the filler/level plug is the largest bolt among those securing the end cover to the transmission; on the ML5T transmission, the filler/level plug is located on the rear face of the differential housing. Unscrew the filler/level plug from the transmission and recover the sealing washer.

5 Position a suitable container under the drain plug (situated on the final drive casing at the rear of the transmission) and unscrew the plug **(see illustration)**.

6 Allow the oil to drain completely into the container. If the oil is hot, take precautions against scalding. Clean both the filler/level and the drain plugs, being especially careful to wipe any metallic particles off the magnetic inserts. Discard the original sealing washers; they should be renewed whenever they are disturbed.

7 When the oil has finished draining, clean the drain plug threads and those of the transmission casing, fit a new sealing washer and refit the drain plug, tightening it to the specified torque wrench setting.

8 Refilling the transmission is an extremely awkward operation. Above all, allow plenty of time for the oil level to settle properly before checking it. Note that the car must be level when checking the oil level.

9 Refill the transmission with the exact amount of the specified type of oil then check the oil level as described in the relevant Part of Chapter 1; if the correct amount was poured into the transmission and a large amount flows out on checking the level, refit the filler/level plug and take the car on a short journey so that the new oil is distributed fully around the transmission components, then check the level again on your return.

10 When the level is correct, fit a new sealing washer to the filler/level plug. Tighten the plug to the specified torque wrench setting. Wash off any spilt oil. Refit the wheel arch liner and splash guard, and secure with the retaining screws and clips. Refit the roadwheel (if removed) then lower the car to the ground.

2.5 Unscrewing the drain plug situated on the final drive casing

3 Gearchange linkage (BE3 transmission) - removal and refitting

Removal

1 Remove the centre console (Chapter 11).
2 Chock the rear wheels, then jack up the front of the vehicle and support it on axle stands.
3 Refer to the relevant Part of Chapter 4 and remove the exhaust system and heat shields, as necessary for access to the gearchange linkage.
4 Slacken and remove the nut, and withdraw the pivot bolt securing the selector rod to the base of the gearchange lever.
5 Using a flat-bladed screwdriver, carefully lever the three link rods off their balljoints on the transmission (see illustration). Disengage the selector rod from the bellcrank pivot, and remove it from underneath the vehicle.
6 Carefully prise the plastic cap off the bolt securing the gearchange linkage bellcrank to the subframe.
7 Slacken and remove the bellcrank pivot bolt and washer, then manoeuvre the bellcrank and link rod out from under the vehicle, and recover the spacer and pivot bushes from the centre of the bellcrank.
8 Inspect all the linkage components for signs of wear or damage, paying particular attention to the pivot bushes and link rod balljoints, and renew worn components as necessary. If necessary, the gearchange lever can be removed and inspected as follows.
9 Slacken and remove the selector lever retaining nuts and lift off the retaining plate then lower the lever out from underneath the vehicle.
10 Peel back the lower gaiter from the base of the gearchange lever, then disengage the lever mounting plate, and slide the upper gaiter up the lever to gain access to the gearchange lever pivot ball. Examine the lever components for signs of wear or damage, paying particular attention to the rubber gaiters, and renew components as necessary. The lever can be separated from its baseplate after the retaining ring has been unclipped.

3.5 Disconnect the three gearchange linkage link rods (arrowed) from their transmission balljoints

Refitting

11 Refitting is a reversal of the removal procedure, noting the following points:

a) Apply a smear of molybdenum disulphide grease to the gearchange lever pivot ball, the link rod balljoints and the bellcrank ball and pivot bushes.
b) Ensure that the gearchange lever rubber gaiters are correctly seated before refitting the lever assembly to the vehicle.
c) Ensure that the link rods are securely pressed onto their balljoints.
d) Refit the heat shields and exhaust components (Chapter 4) and the centre console (Chapter 11).

4 Gearchange cables (ML5T transmission) - removal and refitting

Removal

1 Remove the air cleaner assembly as described in Chapter 4B.
2 Remove the centre console as described in Chapter 11.
3 Working in the engine compartment, carefully prise the two gearchange cable balljoints from the selector levers on the transmission (see illustration).
4 Extract the two horseshoe shaped clips securing the cables to the mounting bracket on the transmission.
5 Chock the rear wheels, then jack up the front of the vehicle and support it on axle stands.
6 Refer to Chapter 4B and remove the exhaust system and heat shields, as necessary for access to the cables and gearchange lever housing.
7 From inside the car, remove the sound-proofing shim then unscrew the bolts securing the lever housing to the floor. Release any clips or ties securing the gearchange cables, then remove the lever housing and gearchange cables as an assembly from under the car.

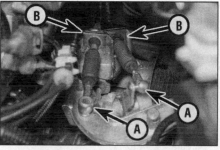

4.3 Gearchange cable balljoint attachments (A) and horseshoe shaped clips (B) securing the cables to the mounting bracket

Refitting

8 Refitting is a reversal of the removal procedure, noting the following points:

a) Ensure that the sound-proofing shim is correctly positioned when refitting the lever housing.
b) Ensure that the cables are fitted to the correct selector levers on the transmission - the 13.0 mm diameter balljoint connects to the upper lever and the 10.0 mm diameter balljoint connects to the side lever.
c) Refit the heat shields, exhaust components and air cleaner assembly (Chapter 4B) and the centre console (Chapter 11).

5 Oil seals - renewal

Driveshaft oil seals

Note: A new suspension lower balljoint nut will be required on refitting.
1 Chock the rear wheels, then jack up the front of the car and support it on axle stands. Remove the appropriate front roadwheel, and remove the splash guard from under the engine.
2 Drain the transmission oil as described in Section 2.
3 On models equipped with ABS, remove the wheel sensor as described in Chapter 9.
4 Slacken and remove the nut securing the front suspension lower balljoint to the swivel hub, and free the balljoint from the lower arm (see Chapter 10). Discard the nut and remove the protector plate (if loose).

Right-hand seal

5 Loosen the two intermediate bearing retaining bolt nuts, then rotate the bolts through 90° so that their offset heads are clear of the bearing outer race.
6 Carefully pull the swivel hub assembly outwards, and pull on the inner end of the driveshaft to free the intermediate bearing from its mounting bracket.
7 Once the driveshaft end is free from the transmission, slide the dust seal off the inner end of the shaft, noting which way around it is fitted, and support the inner end of the driveshaft to avoid damaging the constant velocity joints or gaiters.
8 Carefully prise the oil seal out of the transmission, using a large flat-bladed screwdriver (see illustration).
9 Remove all traces of dirt from the area around the oil seal aperture, then fill the space between the lips of the new oil seal with grease. Fit the new seal into its aperture, and drive it squarely into position using a suitable tubular drift (such as a socket) which bears only on the hard outer edge of the seal, until it abuts its locating shoulder. If the seal was supplied with a plastic protector sleeve, leave

7A

5.8 Use a large flat-bladed screwdriver to prise the driveshaft oil seals out of position

5.9a Fit the new seal to the transmission, noting the plastic seal protector . . .

5.9b . . . and tap it into position using a tubular drift

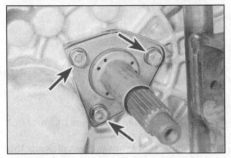

5.23a Clutch release bearing guide sleeve retaining bolts (arrowed) on the BE3 transmission . . .

5.23b . . . and on the ML5T transmission (arrowed)

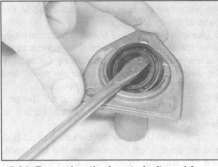

5.24 Removing the input shaft seal from the guide sleeve

this in position until the driveshaft has been refitted **(see illustrations)**.

10 Thoroughly clean the driveshaft splines, then apply a thin film of grease to the oil seal lips and to the driveshaft inner end splines.

11 Slide the dust seal into position on the end of the shaft, ensuring that its flat surface is facing the transmission.

12 Carefully locate the inner driveshaft splines with those of the differential sun gear, taking care not to damage the oil seal, then align the intermediate bearing with its mounting bracket, and push the driveshaft fully into position. If necessary, use a soft-faced mallet to tap the outer race of the bearing into position in the mounting bracket.

13 Ensure that the intermediate bearing is correctly seated, then rotate its retaining bolts back through 90° so that their offset heads are resting against the bearing outer race, and tighten the retaining nuts to the specified torque. Remove the plastic seal protector (where supplied), and slide the dust seal tight up against the oil seal.

14 Refit the protector plate (where removed) to the lower balljoint, then align the balljoint with the lower arm. Fit the new balljoint nut and tighten it to the specified torque setting (see Chapter 10).

15 Where necessary, refit the ABS wheel sensor as described in Chapter 9.

16 Refit the roadwheel and the engine splash guard, then lower the vehicle to the ground and tighten the roadwheel bolts to the specified torque.

17 Refill the transmission with the specified type and amount of fluid/oil, and check the level using the information given in Chapter 1.

Left-hand seal

18 Pull the swivel hub assembly outwards and withdraw the driveshaft inner constant velocity joint from the transmission, taking care not to damage the driveshaft oil seal. Support the driveshaft, to avoid damaging the constant velocity joints or gaiters.

19 On the BE3 transmission, renew the oil seal as described in paragraphs 8 to 10. On ML5T transmissions, unbolt the differential bearing stop plate, and prise or drift the oil seal out of the stop plate. Also remove the sealing O-ring. Thoroughly clean the stop plate, then fill the space between the lips of the new oil seal with grease. Fit the new seal into its aperture, and drive it squarely into position using a suitable tubular drift (such as a socket) which bears only on the hard outer edge of the seal, until it is fully seated. Locate a new O-ring in position then refit the stop plate to the transmission.

20 Carefully locate the inner constant velocity joint splines with those of the differential sun gear, taking care not to damage the oil seal, and push the driveshaft fully into position. Where fitted, remove the plastic protector from the oil seal.

21 Carry out the operations described above in paragraphs 14 to 17.

Input shaft oil seal

22 Remove the transmission as described in Section 8 or 9 as applicable.

23 Undo the three bolts (BE3 transmission) or two bolts (ML5T transmission) securing the clutch release bearing guide sleeve in position, and slide the guide off the input shaft, along with its O-ring or gasket **(see illustrations)**. Recover any shims or thrustwashers which have stuck to the rear of the guide sleeve, and refit them to the input shaft.

24 Carefully lever the oil seal out of the guide using a suitable flat-bladed screwdriver **(see illustration)**.

25 Before fitting a new seal, check the input shaft's seal rubbing surface for signs of burrs, scratches or other damage, which may have caused the seal to fail in the first place. It may be possible to polish away minor faults of this sort using fine abrasive paper; however, more serious defects will require the renewal of the input shaft. Ensure the input shaft is clean and greased, to protect the seal lips on refitting.

26 Dip the new seal in clean oil, and fit it to the guide sleeve.

27 Fit a new O-ring or gasket (as applicable) to the rear of the guide sleeve, then carefully slide the sleeve into position over the input shaft **(see illustration)**. Refit the retaining bolts and tighten them to the specified torque.

28 Take the opportunity to inspect the clutch components if not already done (Chapter 6). Finally, refit the transmission (Section 8 or 9).

Selector shaft oil seal (BE3 transmission)

29 Park the car on level ground, chock the rear wheels, then jack up the front of the

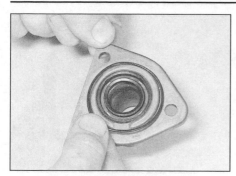

5.27 Fit a new O-ring/gasket (as applicable) to the guide sleeve

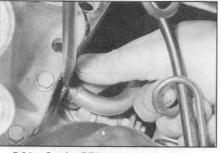

5.31a On the BE3 transmission, use a screwdriver to prise the selector shaft seal out of position . . .

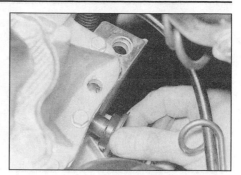

5.31b . . . then slide the seal off the shaft

vehicle and support it on axle stands . Remove the left-hand front roadwheel, then release the screws and clips and remove the wheel arch liner from under the wing.

30 Using a large flat-bladed screwdriver, lever the link rod balljoint off the transmission selector shaft, and disconnect the link rod.

31 Carefully prise the selector shaft seal out of the housing, and slide it off the end of the shaft **(see illustrations)**.

32 Before fitting a new seal, check the selector shaft's seal rubbing surface for signs of burrs, scratches or other damage, which may have caused the seal to fail in the first place. It may be possible to polish away minor faults of this sort using fine abrasive paper; however, more serious defects will require the renewal of the selector shaft.

33 Apply a smear of grease to the new seal's outer edge and sealing lip, then carefully slide the seal along the selector rod. Press the seal fully into position in the transmission housing.

34 Reconnect the link rod to the selector shaft, ensuring that its balljoint is pressed firmly onto the shaft.

35 Refit the wheel arch liner and secure it in position with its retaining screws and clips. Refit the roadwheel then lower the car to the ground.

6 Reversing light switch - testing, removal and refitting

Testing

1 The reversing light circuit is controlled by a plunger-type switch that is screwed into the top of the transmission casing. If a fault develops in the circuit, first ensure that the circuit fuse has not blown.

2 To test the switch, remove the air cleaner components as required for access (Chapter 4) then disconnect the wiring connector, and use a multimeter (set to the resistance function) or a battery-and-bulb test circuit to check that there is continuity between the switch terminals only when reverse gear is selected. If this is not the case, and there are no obvious breaks or other damage to the wires, the switch is faulty, and must be renewed.

Removal

3 Remove the air cleaner components as described in the relevant Part of Chapter 4.

4 Disconnect the wiring connector, then unscrew it from the transmission casing along with its sealing washer **(see illustration)**.

Refitting

5 Fit a new sealing washer to the switch, then screw it back into position in the top of the transmission housing and tighten it to the specified torque setting. Reconnect the wiring connector, and test the operation of the circuit. Refit any components removed for access.

7 Speedometer drive - removal and refitting

Removal

1 Chock the rear wheels, then jack up the front of the car and support it on axle stands. Remove the splash guard from under the engine. The speedometer drive is situated on the rear of the transmission housing, next to the inner end of the right-hand driveshaft. According to model either a standard cable drive unit or transducer unit is fitted **(see illustration)**.

2 On the cable type, pull out the speedometer cable retaining pin and disconnect the cable from the speedometer drive. Also disconnect

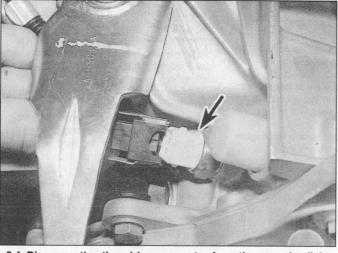

6.4 Disconnecting the wiring connector from the reversing light switch (arrowed)

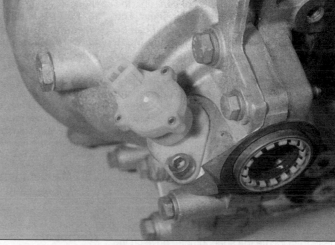

7.1 Speedometer transducer unit as fitted to the ML5T transmission

7A

7.3a Slacken and remove the retaining bolt . . .

7.3b . . . then withdraw the speedometer drive from the transmission (transmission removed for clarity)

7.6a Undo the three retaining bolts . . .

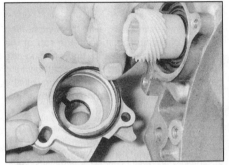

7.6b . . . and remove the housing, O-ring and drive pinion from the transmission (transmission removed for clarity)

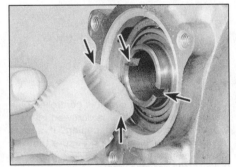

7.7 Ensure the drive pinion dogs are correctly engaged with the gear slots (arrowed)

8.5 Engine movement limiter attachments to the intermediate bearing housing and subframe

the wiring connector (where applicable). On the transducer type, disconnect the wiring.

3 Slacken and remove the retaining bolt, along with the heat shield (where fitted), and withdraw the speedometer drive and driven pinion assembly from the transmission housing, along with its O-ring **(see illustrations)**.

4 If necessary, the pinion can be slid out of the housing, and the oil seal can be removed from the top of the housing. Examine the pinion for signs of damage, and renew if necessary. Renew the housing O-ring as a matter of course.

5 If the driven pinion is worn or damaged, also examine the drive pinion in the transmission housing for similar signs. The drive pinion on the BE3 transmission can be renewed as described below; on the ML5T transmission, major dismantling is necessary which must be entrusted to a dealer.

6 To remove the drive pinion on the BE3 transmission, first disengage the right-hand driveshaft from the transmission, as described in paragraphs 1 to 7 of Section 5. Undo the three retaining bolts, and remove the speedometer drive housing from the transmission, along with its O-ring. Remove the drive pinion from the differential gear, and recover any adjustment shims from the gear **(see illustrations)**.

Refitting

7 Refit the adjustment shims to the differential gear, then locate the speedometer drive on the gear, ensuring it is correctly engaged in the gear slots **(see illustration)**. Fit a new O-ring

to the rear of the speedometer drive housing, then refit the housing to the transmission and securely tighten its retaining bolts. Inspect the driveshaft oil seal for signs of wear, and renew if necessary. Refit the driveshaft to the transmission, using the information given in Section 5.

8 Apply a smear of grease to the lips of the seal and to the driven pinion shaft, and slide the pinion into position in the speedometer drive.

9 Fit a new O-ring to the speedometer drive and refit it to the transmission, ensuring that the drive and driven pinions are correctly engaged.

10 Refit the retaining bolt and the heat shield (where fitted), and tighten the bolt.

11 On the transducer type, reconnect the wiring. On the cable type, reconnect the wiring connector to the speedometer drive where applicable, then apply a smear of oil to the speedometer cable O-rings, reconnect the cable to the drive, and secure it in position with the rubber retaining pin.

12 Refit the splash guard under the engine then lower the vehicle to the ground.

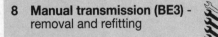

8 Manual transmission (BE3) - removal and refitting

Removal

1 Disconnect the battery negative terminal.
2 Chock the rear wheels, then jack up the

front of the vehicle, and securely support it on axle stands. Remove both front roadwheels, then release the screws and clips and remove the wheel arch liner from under the left-hand wing. Remove the splash guard from under the engine.

3 Drain the transmission oil as described in Section 2, then refit the drain and filler plugs, and tighten them to their specified torque settings.

4 Remove both driveshafts as described in Chapter 8.

5 From under the car, undo the bolts securing the engine movement limiter to the right-hand driveshaft intermediate bearing housing, and subframe **(see illustration)**. Manipulate the movement limiter from its location.

6 Remove the air cleaner assembly and intake ducting (see Chapter 4A or 4B, as applicable).

7 Disconnect the accelerator cable from the throttle housing or fuel injection pump.

8 Disconnect the wiring from the transmission including the reversing light switch, speedometer transducer and earth wiring.

9 Release the cable-ties or clips and move aside the brake pad wear warning light harness and/or the ABS wiring harness.

10 Using a flat-bladed screwdriver, carefully lever the three gearchange mechanism link rods off their respective balljoints on the transmission. Position the rods clear of the transmission.

11 Remove the cable guide, bracket and the RPM/TDC sensor.

12 Move aside the air conditioning pipes (where applicable) from the front crossmember, and the power steering high pressure pipe from the transmission.

13 Release the inner cable and outer cable fittings from the clutch release lever and mounting bracket, and free the cable from the transmission housing.

14 Undo the starter motor mounting bolts and move the starter clear without disconnecting the wiring.

15 Unbolt and remove the clutch cable bracket.

16 On the cable type speedometer cable, pull out the cable retaining pin and disconnect the cable from the speedometer drive. Also disconnect the wiring connector (where applicable). Slacken and remove the retaining bolt, along with the heat shield (where fitted), and withdraw the speedometer drive and driven pinion assembly from the transmission housing, along with its O-ring. Undo the three retaining bolts, and remove the speedometer drive housing from the transmission, along with its O-ring. Remove the drive pinion from the differential gear, and recover any adjustment shims from the gear.

17 Attach a hoist or support bar to the engine left-hand lifting eye and just take the engine weight.

18 Place a jack and block of wood beneath the transmission, and raise the jack to take the weight of the transmission. Move the transmission slightly towards the radiator.

19 Slacken and remove the centre nut and washer from the left-hand engine/transmission mounting. Undo the two bolts and remove the rubber mounting from the mounting bracket and transmission mounting stud **(see illustration)**. If the mounting stud is screwed into a separate bracket bolted to the transmission, undo the bolts and remove the transmission bracket. If the mounting stud is screwed directly into the transmission, slide off the spacer and unscrew the stud. If it is tight, use a universal stud extractor to unscrew it.

20 On models with a "pull-type" clutch release mechanism (see Chapter 6), pull out the retaining pin or unscrew the retaining bolt (as applicable) and remove the clutch release lever from the top of the release fork shaft. This is necessary to allow the fork shaft to rotate freely, to disengage from the release bearing as the transmission is pulled away from the engine. Make an alignment mark across the centre of the clutch release fork shaft using a scriber, paint or similar, and mark its position relative to the transmission housing **(see illustrations)**.

21 Unscrew the retaining bolts and remove the flywheel lower cover plate (where fitted) from the transmission.

22 Unscrew and remove the transmission mounting bolt located on the rear of the cylinder block.

23 With the jack positioned beneath the transmission taking the weight, slacken and remove the remaining bolts securing the

8.19 Engine/transmission left-hand mounting details

8.20b . . . then remove the clutch release lever . . .

transmission housing to the engine. Note the correct fitted positions of each bolt, and the necessary brackets, as they are removed, to use as a reference on refitting. Make a final check that all components have been disconnected, and are positioned clear of the transmission so that they will not hinder the removal procedure.

24 With the bolts removed, lower the engine and move the trolley jack and transmission to the left, to free it from its locating dowels. Once the transmission is free, lower the jack and manoeuvre the unit out from under the car. Remove the locating dowels from the transmission or engine if they are loose, and keep them in a safe place.

25 On models with a "pull-type" clutch, make a second alignment mark on the transmission housing, marking the relative position of the release fork mark after removal, noting the angle at which the release fork is positioned **(see illustration 8.26)**. This mark can then be used to position the release fork before refitting, to ensure that the fork correctly engages with the clutch release bearing as the transmission is installed.

Refitting

26 The transmission is refitted by a reversal of the removal procedure, bearing in mind the following points:

a) *Renew the driveshaft oil seals, as described in Section 5, prior to refitting the transmission.*

b) *Ensure that the locating dowels are correctly positioned prior to installation.*

8.20a On models with a "pull-type" clutch, withdraw the retaining pin . . .

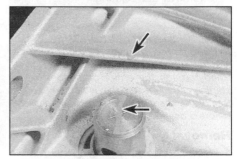
8.20c . . . and make an alignment mark between the release fork shaft and transmission housing (arrowed)

c) *On models with a "pull-type" clutch, before refitting, position the clutch release bearing so that its arrow mark is pointing upwards (bearing fork slots facing towards the front of the engine), and align the release fork shaft mark with the second mark made on the transmission housing (release fork positioned at approximately 60° to clutch housing face)* **(see illustration)**. *This will ensure that the release fork and bearing will engage correctly as the transmission is refitted to the engine. If the bearing and fork are correctly engaged, the mark on the shaft should be aligned with the original mark made on the transmission housing.* **Ensure that the release fork and bearing are correctly engaged before bolting the transmission onto the engine.**

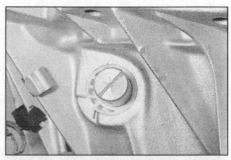
8.26 On models with a "pull-type" clutch, prior to refitting the transmission, align the release fork mark with the second mark made on removal

7A

d) Apply thread-locking fluid to the left-hand engine/transmission mounting stud and mounting bolt threads, prior to refitting. Tighten the stud/bolts to the specified torque.

e) Tighten all nuts and bolts to the specified torque (where given).

f) Refit the driveshafts as described in Chapter 8.

g) On completion, refill the transmission with the specified type and quantity of lubricant, as described in Chapter 1.

9 Manual transmission (ML5T) - removal and refitting

Note: *Peugeot special tool 0216E will be required for this operation, although details of a suitable home-made alternative are given. Read through the entire procedure before starting and make sure that either the Peugeot tool or the alternative described, are available before proceeding.*

Removal

1 Disconnect the battery negative terminal.

2 Chock the rear wheels, then jack up the front of the vehicle, and securely support it on axle stands. Remove both front roadwheels, then release the screws and clips and remove the wheel arch liner from under the left-hand wing. Remove the splash guard from under the engine.

3 Drain the transmission oil as described in Section 2, then refit the drain and filler plugs, and tighten them to their specified torque settings.

4 Remove both driveshafts as described in Chapter 8.

5 From under the car, undo the bolts securing the engine movement limiter to the right-hand driveshaft intermediate bearing housing, and subframe **(see illustration 8.5)**. Manipulate the movement limiter from its location.

6 Remove the air cleaner assembly and intake ducting as described in Chapter 4B.

7 Release the clutch slave cylinder from the transmission by pushing it in by hand and at the same time turning it 90° anti-clockwise. Withdraw the slave cylinder, together with its pushrod from the transmission. With the slave cylinder removed, retain the pushrod in place using a cable tie and suitable slotted tube or a similar arrangement **(see illustrations)**. **Do not** depress the clutch pedal with the slave cylinder removed or the push rod will be ejected. It is advisable to place a block of wood under the clutch pedal to prevent it being accidentally depressed. Release the hydraulic fluid pipe from the support clip and position the slave cylinder to one side.

8 Carefully prise the two gearchange cable balljoints from the selector levers on the transmission. Extract the two horseshoe shaped clips securing the cables to the mounting bracket on the transmission.

9 Disconnect the wiring from the transmission

including the reversing light switch, speedometer transducer and earth wiring **(see illustration)**. Unbolt and remove the TDC sensor from the top of the transmission bellhousing.

10 Undo the starter motor mounting bolts and move the starter clear without disconnecting the wiring.

11 Remove the turbocharger air intake pipe from its location between the engine sump and transmission bellhousing.

12 Unscrew the retaining bolts and remove the flywheel lower cover plate from the transmission.

13 Undo the bolts securing the power steering pipes to the transmission **(see illustrations)**.

14 Remove the front suspension subframe as described in Chapter 10.

15 Attach a hoist or support bar to the engine left-hand lifting eye and just take the engine weight.

16 Place a jack and block of wood beneath the transmission, and raise the jack to take the weight of the transmission. Move the transmission slightly towards the radiator.

17 Slacken and remove the centre nut and washer from the left-hand engine/transmission mounting **(see illustration)**. Undo the bolts and remove the rubber mounting from the mounting bracket and transmission mounting stud. Undo the bolts and remove the transmission bracket.

18 With the jack positioned beneath the

9.7a Withdraw the clutch slave cylinder from the transmission . . .

9.7b . . . and retain the pushrod using a cable tie and suitable slotted tube arrangement as shown

9.9 Engine earth cable attachment (arrowed) at the transmission

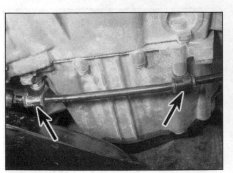

9.13a Unbolt the power steering pipe bracket bolts under the transmission (arrowed) . . .

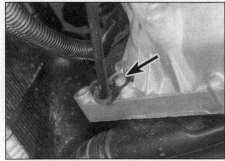

9.13b . . . and on the side of the bellhousing (arrowed)

9.17 Undo the left-hand mounting centre nut (arrowed) then undo the bolts and remove the mounting

transmission taking the weight, slacken and remove the bolts securing the transmission housing to the engine. Note the correct fitted positions of each bolt, and the necessary brackets, as they are removed, to use as a reference on refitting. Make a final check that all components have been disconnected, and are positioned clear of the transmission so that they will not hinder the removal procedure.

19 With the bolts removed, lower the engine and move the trolley jack and transmission to the left, to free it from its locating dowels. Once the transmission is free, lower the jack and manoeuvre the unit out from under the car. Remove the locating dowels from the transmission or engine if they are loose, and keep them in a safe place.

Preparation for refitting

20 The design of the clutch release bearing and clutch release fork is unusual on this type of transmission in that it is necessary to remove the "pull-type" release bearing from the clutch pressure plate, and reposition it on the transmission, before the transmission is re-attached to the engine. With the transmission refitted, the release bearing is then secured back on the pressure plate by means of a special tool. If the following procedure is not followed exactly, it will be impossible to operate the clutch on completion.

21 The Peugeot special tool (0216E) for securing the release bearing in place, consists of a T-shaped rod with a rectangular end **(see illustration)**. The rod is inserted through the slave cylinder aperture in the transmission bellhousing so that the rectangular end engages through the slot in the clutch release fork. When the tool is turned through 90° the rectangular end locks in the release fork slot. Pulling the tool sharply rearwards pivots the release fork and forces the release bearing hard against the pressure plate, causing a snap-ring on the bearing to lock into the pressure plate.

22 Before proceeding, either obtain the Peugeot special tool, or fabricate an alternative on the same pattern that will operate as described above.

23 Begin by removing the clutch assembly as described in Chapter 6.

24 Using a screwdriver, carefully remove the release bearing retaining snap-ring from the inside of the pressure plate diaphragm spring **(see illustration)**. Take care not to deform the snap-ring as it is removed.

25 Remove the release bearing from the pressure plate, then refit the snap-ring back into the groove in the release bearing boss **(see illustration)**.

26 Refit the clutch assembly (see Chapter 6).

27 Slide the release bearing onto the guide tube on the transmission input shaft, while at the same time engaging the release fork between the contact lugs on the release bearing. Check that the release fork and bearing operate smoothly and that the fork ends are correctly engaged between the bearing lugs.

28 Using the Peugeot tool or the home-made alternative, check that the tool will enter the release fork slot, and lock when turned through 90° enabling the fork to be pulled away from the bellhousing end of the transmission by means of the tool. If all is satisfactory, remove the tool.

29 Renew the drive shaft oil seals as described in Section 5 before refitting the transmission.

30 The transmission can now be refitted as follows.

Refitting

31 The transmission is refitted by a reversal of the removal procedure, bearing in mind the following points:

a) *Ensure the release bearing is in position on the transmission as previously described.*

b) *Ensure that the locating dowels are correctly positioned prior to installation.*

c) *Once the transmission is bolted to the engine, engage the Peugeot tool, or the home-made alternative as described previously, and pull on the tool so that the release bearing snap-ring engages with the clutch pressure plate. Check for correct engagement by attempting to push the release fork back towards the engine with a screwdriver; there should be slight play but no appreciable travel.*

d) *Refit the front suspension subframe as described in Chapter 10.*

e) *Tighten all nuts and bolts to the specified torque (where given).*

f) *When refitting the clutch slave cylinder, remove the tie used to retain the pushrod, and lubricate the pushrod end with molybdenum disulphide grease. Locate the slave cylinder in the transmission, push it in by hand, and at the same time turn it 90° clockwise to secure. With the cylinder installed, slowly depress the clutch pedal to the floor, then slowly lift it again by hand. Wait for ten seconds and repeat this procedure. Depress the pedal again, release it and check that it rises correctly after being released.*

g) *Ensure that the gearchange cables are fitted to the correct selector levers on the transmission - the 13.0 mm diameter balljoint connects to the upper lever and the 10.0 mm diameter balljoint connects to the side lever.*

h) *On completion, refill the transmission with the specified type and quantity of lubricant, as described in Chapter 1.*

10 Manual transmission overhaul - general information

Overhauling a manual transmission is a difficult and involved job for the DIY home mechanic. In addition to dismantling and reassembling many small parts, clearances must be precisely measured and, if necessary, changed by selecting shims and spacers. Internal transmission components are also often difficult to obtain, and in many instances, extremely expensive. Because of this, if the transmission develops a fault or becomes noisy, the best course of action is to have the unit overhauled by a specialist repairer, or to obtain an exchange reconditioned unit.

Nevertheless, it is not impossible for the more experienced mechanic to overhaul the transmission, provided the special tools are available, and the job is done in a deliberate step-by-step manner, so nothing is overlooked.

The tools necessary for an overhaul include internal and external circlip pliers, bearing pullers, a slide hammer, a set of pin punches, a dial test indicator, and possibly a hydraulic press. In addition, a large, sturdy workbench and a vice will be required.

7A

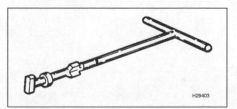

9.21 Peugeot tool for securing the release bearing to the clutch pressure plate

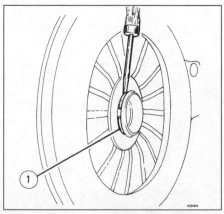

9.24 Remove the release bearing retaining snap-ring (1) from the inside of the pressure plate diaphragm spring . . .

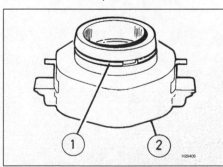

9.25 . . . then refit the snap-ring (1) back into the release bearing (2)

During dismantling of the transmission, make careful notes of how each component is fitted, to make reassembly easier and more accurate.

Before dismantling the transmission, it will help if you have some idea what area is malfunctioning. Certain problems can be closely related to specific areas in the

transmission, which can make component examination and replacement easier. Refer to the Fault finding Section at the rear of this manual for more information.

Chapter 7 Part B:
Automatic transmission

Contents

Degrees of difficulty

Easy, suitable for novice with little experience	Fairly easy, suitable for beginner with some experience	Fairly difficult, suitable for competent DIY mechanic	Difficult, suitable for experienced DIY mechanic	Very difficult, suitable for expert DIY or professional

Specifications

General

Type . . . . Automatic, four forward speeds and reverse
Designation . . . . 4 HP 20

Lubrication

Recommended fluid . . . . See "Lubricants, fluids and tyre pressures"
Capacity (approximate):
   Drain and refill . . . . 3.0 litres
   Total capacity (including torque converter) . . . . 8.3 litres

Torque wrench settings

	Nm	lbf ft
Fluid cooler mounting bolts	40	30
Multi-function switch retaining bolts	10	7
Selector lever-to-multi-function switch shaft	21	15
Left-hand engine/transmission mounting:		
Mounting stud	50	37
Centre nut	65	48
Engine-to-transmission securing bolts	60	45
Engine movement limiter-to-driveshaft intermediate bearing housing	50	37
Engine movement limiter-to-subframe	85	62
Torque converter-to-driveplate bolts	30	22
Roadwheel bolts	90	66

7B

1 General information

2.0 litre petrol models may be fitted with an optional computer controlled four-speed fully-automatic transmission, consisting of a torque converter, an epicyclic geartrain, and hydraulically-operated clutches and brakes.

The unit is controlled by an electronic control unit (ECU) which receives signal inputs from various sensors relating to transmission operating conditions. Information on engine parameters are also sent to the ECU from the engine management system. From this data, the ECU can establish the optimum gear shifting speeds according to the driving mode selected.

Drive is taken from the engine to the transmission by a torque converter. The torque converter provides a fluid coupling between the engine and transmission, and acts as an automatic clutch, also providing a degree of torque multiplication when accelerating.

The epicyclic geartrain provides either of the four forward or one reverse gear ratios, according to which of its component parts are held stationary or allowed to turn. The components of the geartrain are held or released by brakes and clutches which are activated by a hydraulic control unit. A fluid pump within the transmission provides the necessary hydraulic pressure to operate the brakes and clutches.

Driver control of the transmission is by a seven-position selector lever. The transmission has a "drive" position, and a "hold" facility on the first three gear ratios. The "drive" position "D" provides automatic changing throughout the range of all four gear ratios, and is the one to select for normal driving. An automatic kickdown facility shifts the transmission down a gear if the accelerator pedal is fully depressed. This is useful when extra acceleration is required. Kickdown, like the other transmission functions, is controlled by the ECU. The "hold" facility is very similar, but limits the number of gear ratios available - ie when the selector lever is in the "3" position, only the first three ratios can be selected; in the "2" position, only the first two can be selected, and so on. The lower ratio "hold" is useful for providing engine braking when travelling down steep gradients, or for preventing unwanted selection of top gear on twisty roads. Additionally, three driving programs, controlled by a switch to the left of the selector lever, provides additional driver control of transmission according to road conditions. In "Normal" mode the transmission adopts conventional automatic operation. In "Sport" mode, priority is given to engine performance and gear changes occur at higher engine rpm. In "Snow" mode, the vehicle starts in the second gear ratio when "D" is selected. In positions 1, 2 and 3, the gears are selected manually and the kickdown facility is inhibited.

Due to the complexity of the automatic transmission, any repair or overhaul work must be left to a Peugeot dealer with the necessary special equipment for fault diagnosis and repair. The contents of the following Sections are therefore confined to supplying general information, and any service information and instructions that can be used by the owner.

2 Automatic transmission fluid - draining and refilling

Note: *Transmission fluid renewal is not a service requirement and the following operations will normally only be necessary to allow transmission repair work to be carried out.*

1 Take the vehicle on a short run, to warm the transmission up to normal operating temperature.

2 Park the vehicle on level ground, switch off the ignition and apply the handbrake firmly. For improved access, jack up the front of the vehicle and support it securely on axle stands. Note that the vehicle must be lowered to the ground and be level, to ensure accuracy when refilling and checking the fluid level.

3 Remove the dipstick, then position a suitable container under the transmission drain plug. The drain plug is located in the centre of the transmission casing.

4 Unscrew the drain plug and allow the fluid to drain completely into the container. Note that only approximately 3.0 litres will drain out as it is not possible to completely drain the torque converter. If the fluid is hot, take precautions against scalding. Clean the drain plug, being especially careful to wipe any metallic particles off the magnetic insert. Discard the original sealing washer which should be renewed whenever it is disturbed.

5 When the fluid has finished draining, clean the drain plug threads and those of the transmission casing, fit a new sealing washer to the drain plug and refit it to the transmission, tightening securely. If the vehicle was raised for the draining operation, lower it to the ground.

6 Refilling the transmission is an extremely awkward operation, adding the specified type of fluid to the transmission a little at a time via the dipstick tube. Use a funnel with a fine mesh gauze, to avoid spillage and to ensure that no foreign matter enters the transmission. Allow plenty of time for the fluid level to settle properly before checking. Note that the vehicle must be parked on flat level ground when checking the fluid level.

7 Add approximately 3.0 litres and check the level on the dipstick continuously as the last litre is added. Once the level is up to the MAX mark on the dipstick, refit the dipstick then start the engine and allow it to idle for a few minutes. Switch the engine off and recheck the level, topping-up if necessary. Take the

vehicle on a short run to fully distribute the new fluid around the transmission, then recheck the fluid level.

3 Selector cable - removal and refitting

Removal

1 Remove the air cleaner assembly as described in Chapter 4A.

2 Move the gear selector lever to the "P" position.

3 Working in the engine compartment, carefully prise the selector cable balljoint from the selector lever on the transmission multi-function switch.

4 Extract the horseshoe shaped clip securing the cable to the mounting bracket on the transmission.

5 Remove the centre console (Chapter 11).

6 Chock the rear wheels, then jack up the front of the car and support it on axle stands.

7 Refer to Chapter 4A and remove the exhaust system and heat shields, as necessary for access to the cable and gear selector lever housing.

8 Work back along the selector cable, releasing it from any relevant retaining clips, and noting its correct routing.

9 From inside the car, remove the selector lever control grid illumination bulbholder, the control grid and the sound proofing gaiter. Unscrew the nuts securing the selector lever housing to the floor. Release any remaining clips or ties, then remove the selector lever housing and cable as an assembly from under the car.

Refitting

10 Refitting is the reverse of removal, ensuring that the selector lever is in the "P" position and the cable is correctly routed and retained with any relevant clips and ties. If a new cable is being fitted, remove the automatic adjuster locking key from the cable end fitting by turning it anti-clockwise and lifting off **(see illustration)**.

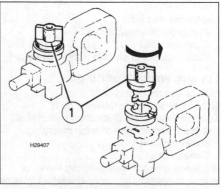

3.10 To remove the automatic adjuster locking key (1) from the selector cable end fitting, turn it anti-clockwise and lift it off

4 Oil seals - renewal

Only the driveshaft oil seals can be renewed without extensive dismantling. The procedure is as described for manual transmission models in Chapter 7A, and specifically for the BE3 transmission where two transmission types are described.

5 Speedometer drive - removal and refitting

Removal

1 Chock the rear wheels, then jack up the front of the car and support it on axle stands. Remove the splash guard from under the engine. The speedometer drive is situated on the rear of the transmission housing, next to the inner end of the right-hand driveshaft.
2 Disconnect the wiring connector from the speedometer drive housing.
3 Slacken and remove the retaining bolt, along with the heat shield, and withdraw the speedometer drive and driven pinion assembly from the transmission housing, along with its O-ring. As the drive is withdrawn, hold the pinion assembly in place as there is a possibility that it can be dislodged and fall into the transmission casing.
4 If necessary, the pinion can be slid out of the housing, and the oil seal can be removed from the top of the housing. Renew the housing O-ring as a matter of course.

Refitting

5 Fit a new O-ring to the speedometer drive and refit it to the transmission, ensuring the drive and driven pinions are correctly engaged.
6 Refit the retaining bolt and the heat shield and tighten the bolt. Reconnect the wiring.
7 Refit the splash guard under the engine then lower the vehicle to the ground.

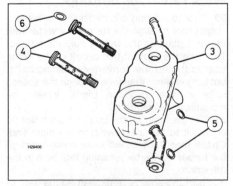

6.5 Transmission fluid cooler details

3 *Fluid cooler*
4 *Mounting bolts*
5 *Fluid cooler lower seals*
6 *Mounting bolt seals*

6 Fluid cooler - removal and refitting

Removal

1 The fluid cooler is mounted on the top of the transmission housing. To gain access to the fluid cooler, remove the air cleaner assembly and intake ducts as described in Chapter 4A.
2 Unclip the wiring connector from the support bracket located just above the fluid cooler, then remove the support bracket.
3 Using hose clamps or similar, clamp both the fluid cooler coolant hoses to minimise coolant loss during subsequent operations.
4 Disconnect both coolant hoses from the fluid cooler being prepared for some coolant spillage. Wash off any spilt coolant immediately with cold water, and dry the surrounding area before proceeding further.
5 Slacken and remove the two fluid cooler mounting bolts, and remove the cooler from the transmission. Remove the seals from the mounting bolts, and the two seals fitted to the base of the cooler, and discard them; new ones must be used on refitting **(see illustration)**.

Refitting

6 Lubricate the new seals with clean automatic transmission fluid, then fit the two new seals to the base of the fluid cooler, and a new seal to each mounting bolt.
7 Locate the fluid cooler on the top of transmission housing, with its pointed end (and the smaller of the two circular indentations on the top of the cooler) towards the front of the car. Refit the mounting bolts, and tighten to the specified torque setting.
8 Reconnect the coolant hoses to the fluid cooler and remove the hose clamps.
9 Refit the support bracket and wiring connector, then refit disturbed intake duct/air cleaner components (see Chapter 4A).
10 On completion, top-up the cooling system and check the automatic transmission fluid level as described in Chapter 1.

7 Multi-function switch - removal and refitting

Removal

1 To improve access to the switch, remove the air cleaner assembly and intake ducts as necessary, as described in Chapter 4A.
2 Place the gear selector in the "N" position.
3 If the original switch is to be refitted, mark the position of the selector lever in relation to the switch body. Ensure that the lever is in this position ("N") when refitting the switch. If a new switch is to be fitted, it will be supplied already in the "N" position.

4 Carefully prise the gear selector cable balljoint from the selector lever on the multi-function switch.
5 Trace the wiring back from the switch to the wiring connector. Release the connector from the support bracket and disconnect it.
6 Release the switch wiring from the support clip on the transmission.
7 Hold the selector lever on the switch and unscrew the lever retaining nut. Remove the selector lever from the switch shaft.
8 Unscrew the switch, and remove it from transmission housing.

Refitting

9 Refit the switch to the transmission ensuring that it is seated correctly and secure it with the retaining bolts tightened to the specified torque.
10 Ensure that the switch is in the "N" position then locate the selector lever on the switch shaft. Hold the lever to prevent internal damage to the switch, and fit and tighten the retaining nut to the specified torque.
11 Ensure that the gear selector lever is still in the "N" position then reconnect the selector cable balljoint to the selector lever.
12 Reconnect the switch wiring, locate the connector in the support bracket and secure the harness with the retaining clip.
13 Reconnect the switch wiring, then refit the support tray and securely tighten its retaining bolts.
14 Refit the air cleaner and intake ducts as described in Chapter 4A.

8 Electronic control unit (ECU) - removal and refitting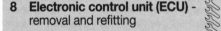

Note: *The automatic transmission ECU, together with the engine management ECU is located in the ECU module box, situated at the front right-hand side of the engine compartment, adjacent to the cooling system expansion tank.*

Removal

1 Ensure that the ignition is switched off then lift off the ECU module box lid. The automatic transmission ECU is the unit nearest to the side of the car.
2 Release the wiring connector by lifting the locking lever on top of the connector upwards. Lift the connector at the rear, disengage the tag at the front and carefully withdraw the connector from the ECU pins.
3 Lift the ECU upwards and remove it from its location.

Refitting

4 Refitting is a reversal of removal. Note that if a new ECU has been fitted, the vehicle should be taken on an extensive road test, on a route which will allow numerous gearchanges and full use of the transmission mode settings. Initially, transmission response

7B

9.18 Engine movement limiter attachments to the intermediate bearing housing and subframe

9.25 Engine/transmission left-hand mounting details

and gearchange quality may be less than acceptable, but should improve as the ECU control circuitry adapts to the transmission parameters.

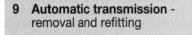

9 Automatic transmission - removal and refitting

Removal

1 Remove the battery and battery box as described in Chapter 5A.
2 Remove the air cleaner assembly and intake ducting as described in Chapter 4A.
3 Chock the rear wheels, then jack up the front of the vehicle, and securely support it on axle stands. Remove both front roadwheels, then release the screws and clips and remove the wheel arch liner from under the left-hand wing. Remove the splash guard from under the engine..
4 Drain the transmission fluid as described in Section 2, then refit the drain plug, and tighten securely.
5 Release the cable ties or clips and move aside the brake pad wear warning light harness and/or the ABS wiring harness.
6 Carefully prise the selector cable balljoint from the selector lever on the transmission multi-function switch. Extract the horseshoe shaped clip securing the cable to the mounting bracket on the transmission.
7 Trace the wiring back from the multi-function switch to the wiring connector. Release the connector from the support bracket and disconnect it. Release the switch wiring from the support clip on the transmission.
8 Disconnect the wiring harness at the large connector adjacent to the transmission fluid cooler. Cover the wiring connector socket on the transmission to prevent water ingress when the fluid cooler hoses are disconnected.
9 Using hose clamps or similar, clamp both the fluid cooler coolant hoses to minimise coolant loss during subsequent operations.
10 Disconnect both coolant hoses from the fluid cooler being prepared for some coolant spillage. Wash off any spilt coolant immediately

with cold water, and dry the surrounding area before proceeding further.
11 Unclip the wiring connector from the support bracket located just above the fluid cooler, then remove the support bracket.
12 Disconnect the earth cable from the stud on the transmission.
13 Remove the wiring harness bracket and the hose support bracket from the transmission.
14 Disconnect the wiring from the speedometer transducer (speedometer drive) and RPM sensor, then remove the RPM sensor from the bellhousing.
15 Undo the starter motor mounting bolts and move the starter clear without disconnecting the wiring.
16 Label and disconnect any remaining wiring connectors and support brackets connected to the transmission.
17 Remove both driveshafts as described in Chapter 8.
18 From under the car, undo the bolts securing the engine movement limiter to the right-hand driveshaft intermediate bearing housing, and subframe. Manipulate the movement limiter from its location **(see illustration)**.
19 Undo the bolts securing the power steering pipes to the transmission.
20 Remove the front suspension subframe as described in Chapter 10.
21 Attach a hoist or support bar to the engine left-hand lifting eye and just take the engine weight.
22 Attach a second hoist to the transmission lifting eye located next to the fluid cooler.

 Warning The transmission is a bulky unit and weighs in excess of 90 kg. Ensure that it is securely supported by means of a suitable hoist.

23 Locate the access hole at the lower rear of the cylinder block, then turn the crankshaft, by means of a socket on the crankshaft pulley bolt, until one of the torque converter retaining bolts is accessible through the access hole.
24 Undo the accessible torque converter bolt then turn the crankshaft as necessary and undo the remaining two bolts.
25 With the transmission securely supported

on the hoist, slacken and remove the centre nut and washer from the left-hand engine/transmission mounting stud, then unscrew the stud from the transmission **(see illustration)**.
26 Slacken and remove the bolts securing the transmission housing to the engine. Note the correct fitted positions of each bolt, and the necessary brackets, as they are removed, to use as a reference on refitting. Make a final check that all components have been disconnected, and are positioned clear of the transmission so that they will not hinder the removal procedure.
27 With the bolts removed, pull the transmission to the left, to free it from its locating dowels. Once the transmission is free, and sufficient clearance exists, insert a bolt with a suitable washer, through the RPM sensor hole in the transmission bellhousing, to retain the torque converter on the transmission.
28 Lower the engine and transmission hoists and manoeuvre the transmission out from under the car. Remove the locating dowels from the transmission or engine if they are loose, and keep them in a safe place.
29 With the transmission removed make sure that the bolt used initially is capable of retaining the torque converter in place.

Preparation for refitting

30 Prior to refitting it is necessary to make a simple tool to align the torque converter with the driveplate as the transmission is refitted. To make the tool, obtain a bolt of the same size as the torque converter retaining bolts, but long enough to extend through the access hole in the cylinder block when the transmission is refitted.
31 Cut the head off the bolt and cut a slot (to enable it to be unscrewed) in the plain end. Check that the tool will slide easily through the torque converter retaining bolt hole in the driveplate.
32 Turn the engine crankshaft so that one of the torque converter retaining bolt holes in the driveplate, is aligned with the access hole in the cylinder block. Screw the alignment tool (finger tight only) into one of the retaining bolt holes in the torque converter. Turn the torque

converter so that the alignment tool is in approximately the correct position, relative to the cylinder block access hole. As the transmission is refitted, the alignment tool will pass through the retaining bolt hole in the driveplate and through the access hole **(see illustration)**. It can then be unscrewed with a screwdriver and the first torque converter retaining bolt fitted in its place.

33 Check that the torque converter support bush fitted to the centre of the crankshaft is in good condition, and in place.

34 Ensure that the engine/transmission locating dowels are correctly positioned prior to installation.

Refitting

35 The transmission is refitted by a reversal of the removal procedure, bearing in mind the following points:

a) *Guide the transmission into position ensuring that the alignment tool passes through the driveplate and access hole.*

b) *Remove the bolt used to retain the torque converter in place, just before the transmission engages with the engine.*

c) *Once the transmission is bolted to the engine, remove the alignment tool and fit*

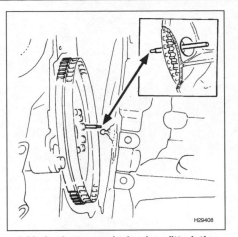

9.32 As the transmission is refitted, the alignment tool will pass through the retaining bolt hole in the driveplate and through the access hole (inset)

the first torque converter retaining bolt. Turn the crankshaft as necessary and fit the other two bolts.

d) *Refit the front suspension subframe as described in Chapter 10.*

e) *Refit the driveshafts as described in Chapter 8.*

f) *Tighten all nuts and bolts to the specified torque (where given).*

g) *On completion, refill the transmission with the specified type and quantity of lubricant, as described in Section 2 of this Chapter and in Chapter 1.*

h) *Top-up the cooling system as described in Chapter 1.*

10 Automatic transmission overhaul - general information

In the event of a fault occurring with the transmission, it is first necessary to determine whether it is of an electrical, mechanical or hydraulic nature, and to do this, special test equipment is required. It is therefore essential to have the work carried out by a Peugeot dealer if a transmission fault is suspected.

Do not remove the transmission from the car for possible repair before professional fault diagnosis has been carried out, since most tests require the transmission to be in the vehicle.

7B

Notes

Chapter 8
Driveshafts

Contents

Degrees of difficulty

Easy, suitable for novice with little experience	Fairly easy, suitable for beginner with some experience	Fairly difficult, suitable for competent DIY mechanic	Difficult, suitable for experienced DIY mechanic	Very difficult, suitable for expert DIY or professional

Specifications

Lubrication (overhaul only - see text)

Lubricant type/specification . . . . Use only special grease supplied in sachets with gaiter kits - joints are otherwise pre-packed with grease and sealed

Torque wrench settings	Nm	lbf ft
Driveshaft retaining nut	325	238
Lower suspension arm balljoint retaining nuts	45	33
Right-hand driveshaft intermediate bearing retaining bolt nuts	10	7
Roadwheel bolts	90	66

1 General information

Drive is transmitted from the differential to the front wheels by means of two solid-steel driveshafts of unequal length.

Both driveshafts are splined at their outer ends, to accept the wheel hubs, and are threaded so that each hub can be fastened by a large nut. The inner end of each driveshaft is splined, to accept the differential sun gear.

Constant velocity (CV) joints are fitted to each end of the driveshafts, to ensure that the smooth and efficient transmission of power at all suspension and steering angles. The outer constant velocity joints are of the ball-and-cage type, and the inner constant velocity joints are of the tripod type.

On the right-hand side, due to the length of the driveshaft, the inner constant velocity joint is situated approximately halfway along the shaft's length, and an intermediate support bearing is mounted in the engine/transmission rear mounting bracket. The inner end of the driveshaft passes through the bearing (which prevents any lateral movement of the driveshaft inner end) and the inner constant velocity joint outer member.

2 Driveshafts - removal and refitting

Removal

Note: *A new suspension lower balljoint nut will be required on refitting.*

1 Remove the wheel trim/hub cap (as applicable) then withdraw the R-clip and remove the locking cap from the driveshaft retaining nut. Slacken the driveshaft nut with the vehicle resting on its wheels. Also slacken the wheel bolts.

2 Chock the rear wheels of the car, firmly apply the handbrake, then jack up the front of the car and support it on axle stands. Remove the appropriate front roadwheel.

3 On manual transmission models drain the transmission oil as described in Chapter 7A, and on automatic transmission models drain the fluid as described in Chapter 7B.

4 On models equipped with ABS, remove the wheel sensor as described in Chapter 9.

5 Slacken and remove the driveshaft retaining nut. If the nut was not slackened with the wheels on the ground (see paragraph 1), withdraw the R-clip and remove the locking cap. Refit at least two roadwheel bolts to the front hub, tightening them securely, then have an assistant firmly depress the brake pedal to prevent the front hub from rotating, whilst you slacken and remove the driveshaft retaining nut. Alternatively, a tool can be fabricated from two lengths of steel strip (one long, one short) and a nut and bolt; the nut and bolt forming the pivot of a forked tool **(see Tool tip)**.

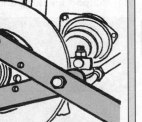

Using a fabricated tool to hold the front hub stationary whilst the driveshaft retaining nut is slackened

8

2.9a On the right-hand driveshaft, slacken the two intermediate bearing retaining bolt nuts . . .

6 Slacken and remove the nut securing the front suspension lower balljoint to the swivel hub, and free the balljoint from the lower arm (see Chapter 10). Discard the nut and remove the protector plate (if loose).

Left-hand driveshaft

7 Carefully pull the swivel hub assembly outwards, and withdraw the driveshaft outer constant velocity joint from the hub assembly. If necessary, the shaft can be tapped out of the hub using a soft-faced mallet.

8 Support the driveshaft, then withdraw the inner constant velocity joint from the transmission, taking care not to damage the driveshaft oil seal. Remove the driveshaft from the vehicle.

Note: *Do not allow the vehicle to rest on its wheels with one or both driveshafts removed, as damage to the wheel bearing(s) may result. If moving the vehicle is unavoidable, temporarily insert the outer end of the driveshaft(s) in the hub(s) and tighten the driveshaft nut(s). Support the inner end(s) of the driveshaft(s) to avoid damage.*

Right-hand driveshaft

9 Loosen the two intermediate bearing retaining bolt nuts, then rotate the bolts through 90°, so that their offset heads are clear of the bearing outer race **(see illustrations)**.

10 Carefully pull the swivel hub assembly outwards, and withdraw the driveshaft outer constant velocity joint from the hub assembly. If necessary, the shaft can be tapped out of the hub using a soft-faced mallet.

11 Support the outer end of the driveshaft,

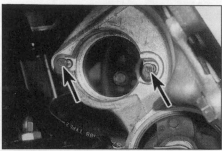

2.9b . . . then turn the bolts through 90° to disengage their offset heads (arrowed) from the bearing (driveshaft removed for clarity)

then pull on the inner end of the shaft to free the intermediate bearing from its mounting bracket.

12 Once the driveshaft end is free from the transmission, slide the dust seal (where fitted) off the inner end of the shaft, noting which way around it is fitted, and remove the driveshaft from the vehicle.

Note: *Do not allow the vehicle to rest on its wheels with one or both driveshafts removed, as damage to the wheel bearing(s) may result. If moving the vehicle is unavoidable, temporarily insert the outer end of the driveshaft(s) in the hub(s) and tighten the driveshaft nut(s). Support the inner end(s) of the driveshaft(s) to avoid damage.*

Refitting

13 Before installing the driveshaft, examine the driveshaft oil seal in the transmission for signs of damage or deterioration and, if necessary, renew it as described in Chapter 7. It is highly recommended that the seal is renewed, regardless of its apparent condition.

14 Thoroughly clean the driveshaft splines, and the apertures in the transmission and hub assembly. Apply a thin film of grease to the oil seal lips, and to the driveshaft splines and shoulders. Check that all gaiter clips are securely fastened.

Left-hand driveshaft

15 Offer up the driveshaft, and locate the joint splines with those of the differential sun gear, taking great care not to damage the oil seal. Push the joint fully into position.

16 Locate the outer constant velocity joint splines with those of the swivel hub, and slide the joint back into position in the hub.

17 Refit the protector plate (where removed) to the lower balljoint, then align the balljoint with the lower arm. Fit the new balljoint nut and tighten it to the specified torque setting (see Chapter 10).

18 Lubricate the inner face and threads of the driveshaft nut with clean engine oil, and refit it to the end of the driveshaft. Use the method employed on removal to prevent the hub from rotating (see paragraph 5), and tighten the driveshaft retaining nut to the specified torque. Check that the hub rotates freely then engage the locking cap with the driveshaft nut, so that one of its cut-outs is aligned with the driveshaft hole, and secure the cap in position with the R-clip **(see illustrations)**. Alternatively, lightly tighten the nut at this stage, and tighten it to the specified torque once the car is resting on its wheels.

19 Where necessary, refit the ABS wheel sensor as described in Chapter 9.

20 Refit the roadwheel, then lower the vehicle to the ground and tighten the roadwheel bolts to the specified torque. If not already done, tighten the driveshaft retaining nut to the specified torque then refit the locking cap, aligning its cut-outs with the drive shaft hole, and secure it in position with the R-clip.

21 Refill the transmission with the specified type and amount of fluid/oil, and check the level using the information given in Chapter 1.

Right-hand driveshaft

22 Check that the intermediate bearing rotates smoothly, without any sign of roughness or undue free play between its inner and outer races. If necessary, renew the bearing as described in Section 5. Examine the dust seal for signs of damage or deterioration, and renew if necessary.

23 Apply a smear of grease to the outer race of the intermediate bearing, and to the inner lip of the dust seal (where fitted).

24 Pass the inner end of the shaft through the bearing mounting bracket then, where necessary, carefully slide the dust seal into position on the driveshaft, ensuring that its flat surface is facing the transmission **(see illustration)**.

2.18a Tighten the driveshaft nut to the specified torque, then refit the locking cap . . .

2.18b . . . and secure it in position with the R-clip

2.24 Locate the dust seal (where fitted) on the inner end of the right-hand driveshaft, ensuring it is fitted the right way around

2.26 Pull out the swivel hub assembly and locate the outer constant velocity joint splines with those of the swivel hub

2.27 Secure the intermediate bearing in position then (where necessary) slide the dust seal up tight against the driveshaft oil seal

25 Carefully locate the inner driveshaft splines with those of the differential sun gear, taking care not to damage the oil seal. Align the intermediate bearing with its mounting bracket, and push the driveshaft fully into position. If necessary, use a soft-faced mallet to tap the outer race of the bearing into position in the mounting bracket.

26 Locate the outer constant velocity joint splines with those of the swivel hub, and slide the joint back into position in the hub (see illustration).

27 Ensure that the intermediate bearing is correctly seated, then rotate its retaining bolts back through 90°, so that their offset heads are resting against the bearing outer race. Tighten the retaining nuts to the specified torque. Where necessary, ensure that the dust seal is tight against the driveshaft oil seal (see illustration).

28 Carry out the operations described above in paragraphs 17 to 21.

3 Driveshaft rubber gaiters - renewal

Outer joint

1 Remove the driveshaft from the vehicle as described in Section 2.

2 Secure the driveshaft in a vice equipped with soft jaws, and release the two outer gaiter retaining clips. If necessary, the gaiter retaining clips can be cut to release them.

3 Slide the rubber gaiter down the shaft, to expose the outer constant velocity joint. Scoop out the excess grease.

4 Using a hammer and suitable soft metal drift, sharply strike the inner member of the outer joint to drive it off the end of the shaft. The joint is retained on the driveshaft by a circlip, and striking the joint in this manner forces the circlip into its groove, so allowing the joint to slide off.

5 Once the joint assembly has been removed, remove the circlip from the groove in the driveshaft splines, and discard it. A new circlip must be fitted on reassembly.

6 Withdraw the rubber gaiter from the driveshaft. Where necessary, slide off the gaiter inner end plastic bush.

7 With the constant velocity joint removed from the driveshaft, thoroughly clean the joint using paraffin, or a suitable solvent, and dry it thoroughly. Carry out a visual inspection of the joint.

8 Move the inner splined driving member from side to side, to expose each ball in turn at the top of its track. Examine the balls for cracks, flat spots, or signs of surface pitting.

9 Inspect the ball tracks on the inner and outer members. If the tracks have widened, the balls will no longer be a tight fit. At the same time, check the ball cage windows for wear or cracking between the windows.

10 If on inspection, any of the constant velocity joint components are found to be worn or damaged, it will be necessary to renew the complete joint assembly (where available), or even the complete driveshaft (where no joint components are available separately). Refer to your Peugeot dealer for further information on parts availability. If the joint is in satisfactory condition, obtain a repair kit consisting of a new gaiter, circlip, retaining clips, and the correct type and quantity of grease.

11 To install the new gaiter, refer to the accompanying illustrations, and perform the operations shown (see illustrations 3.11a to 3.11k). Be sure to stay in order, and follow the

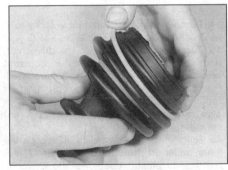

3.11a Fit the hard plastic rings to the outer CV joint gaiter . . .

3.11b . . . then slide on the new plastic bush (arrowed - where fitted), and seat it in its recess in the shaft. Slide the gaiter onto the shaft . . .

3.11c . . . and seat the gaiter inner end on top of the plastic bush/shaft (as applicable)

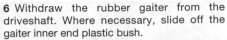

3.11d Fit the new circlip to its groove in the driveshaft splines . . .

3.11e . . . then locate the joint outer member on the splines, and slide it into position over the circlip. Ensure that the joint is securely retained by the circlip

8

3.11f Pack the joint with the grease supplied, working it into the ball tracks while twisting the joint, then locate the gaiter outer lip in its groove on the outer member

3.11g Fit the outer gaiter retaining clip and, using a hook fabricated out of welding rod and a pair of pliers, pull the clip tightly to remove all slack

3.11h Bend the clip end back over the buckle, then cut off the excess clip

3.11i Fold the clip end underneath the buckle . . .

3.11j . . . then fold the buckle firmly down onto the clip to secure the clip in position

3.11k Carefully lift the gaiter inner end to equalise air pressure in the gaiter, then secure the inner gaiter retaining clip in position using the same method

captions carefully. Note that the hard plastic rings are not fitted to all gaiters, and the gaiter retaining clips supplied with the repair kit may be different to those shown in the sequence. To secure this other type of clip in position, lock the ends of the clip together, then remove any slack in the clip by carefully compressing the raised section of the clip using a pair of side cutters.

12 Check that the constant velocity joint moves freely in all directions, then refit the driveshaft to the vehicle as described in Section 2.

Inner joint

13 Remove the driveshaft from the vehicle as described in Section 2.

14 Remove the outer constant velocity joint as described above in paragraphs 1 to 5.

15 Tape over the splines on the driveshaft, and carefully remove the outer constant velocity joint rubber gaiter, and (where fitted) the gaiter inner end plastic bush. It is recommended that the outer joint gaiter is also renewed, regardless of its apparent condition.

16 Release the retaining clips, then slide the inner gaiter off the shaft and (where fitted) remove its plastic bush. As the gaiter is released, the joint outer member will also be freed from the end of the shaft **(see illustrations)**.

17 Thoroughly clean the joint using paraffin, or a suitable solvent, and dry it thoroughly. Check

the tripod joint bearings and joint outer member for signs of wear, pitting or scuffing on their bearing surfaces. Check that the bearing rollers rotate smoothly and easily around the tripod joint, with no traces of roughness.

18 If on inspection, the tripod joint or outer member reveal signs of wear or damage, it will be necessary to renew the complete driveshaft assembly, since the joint is not available separately. If the joint is in satisfactory condition, obtain a repair kit consisting of a new gaiter, retaining clips, and the correct type and quantity of grease. Although not strictly necessary, it is also recommended that the outer constant velocity joint gaiter is renewed, regardless of its apparent condition.

3.16a Release the inner gaiter retaining clips, and remove the joint outer member

3.16b Slide the gaiter off the end of the driveshaft . . .

3.16c . . . and remove the plastic bush

19 On reassembly, pack the inner joint with the grease supplied in the gaiter kit. Work the grease well into the bearing tracks and rollers, while twisting the joint.

20 Clean the shaft, using emery cloth to remove any rust or sharp edges which may damage the gaiter, then slide the plastic bush (where fitted) and inner joint gaiter along the driveshaft. Locate the plastic bush in its recess on the shaft, and seat the inner end of the gaiter on top of the bush; where no bush is fitted, seat the inner end of the driveshaft in the recess on the shaft.

21 Fit the outer member over the end of the shaft, and locate the gaiter in the groove on the joint outer member. Push the outer member onto the joint, so that its spring-loaded plunger is compressed, then lift the outer edge of the gaiter to equalise air pressure in the gaiter. Fit both the inner and outer retaining clips, securing them in position using the information given in paragraph 11. Ensure that the gaiter retaining clips are securely tightened, then check that the joint moves freely in all directions.

22 Refit the outer constant velocity joint components using the information given in paragraph 11.

4 Driveshaft overhaul - general information

1 If any of the checks described in Chapter 1 reveal wear in any driveshaft joint, first remove the roadwheel trim or centre cap (as appropriate).

2 If the R-clip is still in position, the driveshaft nut should be correctly tightened; if in doubt, remove the R-clip and locking cap, and use a torque wrench to check that the nut is securely fastened. Once tightened, refit the locking cap and R-clip, then refit the centre cap or trim. Repeat this check on the remaining driveshaft nut.

3 Road test the vehicle, and listen for a metallic clicking from the front as the vehicle is driven slowly in a circle on full-lock. If a clicking noise is heard, this indicates wear in the outer constant velocity joint. This means that the joint must be renewed; reconditioning is not possible.

4 If vibration, consistent with road speed, is felt through the car when accelerating, there is a possibility of wear in the inner constant velocity joints.

5 To check the joints for wear, remove the driveshafts, then dismantle them as described in Section 3; if any wear or free play is found, the affected joint must be renewed. In the case of the inner joints (and on some models, the outer joints), this means that the complete driveshaft assembly must be renewed, as the joints are not available separately. Refer to your Peugeot dealer for latest information on the availability of driveshaft components.

5 Right-hand driveshaft intermediate bearing - renewal

Note: *A suitable bearing puller will be required, to draw the bearing and collar off the driveshaft end.*

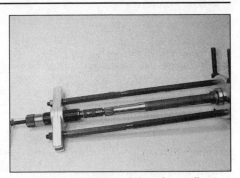

5.3 Using a long-reach bearing puller to remove the intermediate bearing from the right-hand driveshaft

1 Remove the right-hand driveshaft as described in Section 2 of this Chapter.

2 Check that the bearing outer race rotates smoothly and easily, without any signs of roughness or undue free play between the inner and outer races. If necessary, renew the bearing as follows.

3 Using a long-reach universal bearing puller, carefully draw the collar and intermediate bearing off the driveshaft inner end **(see illustration)**. Apply a smear of grease to the inner race of the new bearing, then fit the bearing over the end of the driveshaft. Using a hammer and suitable piece of tubing which bears only on the bearing inner race, tap the new bearing into position on the driveshaft, until it abuts the constant velocity joint outer member. Once the bearing is correctly positioned, tap the bearing collar onto the shaft until it contacts the bearing inner race.

4 Check that the bearing rotates freely, then refit the driveshaft as described in Section 2.

Chapter 9
Braking system

Contents

Degrees of difficulty

Easy, suitable for novice with little experience	Fairly easy, suitable for beginner with some experience	Fairly difficult, suitable for competent DIY mechanic	Difficult, suitable for experienced DIY mechanic	Very difficult, suitable for expert DIY or professional

Specifications

Front brakes
Type . . . . Disc, with single-piston sliding caliper
Disc diameter:
  1.6 and 1.8 litre petrol models . . . . 260 mm
  All other models . . . . 283 mm
Disc thickness:
  1.6 and 1.8 litre petrol models:
    New . . . . 24.0 mm
    Minimum . . . . 22.0 mm
  All other models:
    New . . . . 26.0 mm
    Minimum . . . . 24.0 mm
Maximum disc run-out . . . . 0.05 mm
Brake pad friction material thickness:
  New . . . . 13.0 mm
  Minimum . . . . 2.0 mm

Rear drum brakes
Drum internal diameter
  New . . . . 228.6 mm
  Maximum diameter after machining . . . . 230.0 mm
Brake shoe friction material thickness:
  New . . . . 4.8 mm
  Minimum . . . . 1.5 mm
Maximum drum run-out . . . . 0.07 mm

Rear disc brakes

Disc diameter	290 mm
Disc thickness:	
New	10.0 mm
Minimum thickness	8.0 mm
Maximum disc run-out	0.05 mm
Brake pad friction material thickness:	
New	11.0 mm
Minimum	2.0 mm

Torque wrench settings

	Nm	lbf ft
ABS system components:		
Electronic control unit (ECU) bolts	5	4
Regulator unit nuts	20	15
Wheel sensor retaining bolts*	10	7
Brake pedal pivot shaft nut	40	29
Crossover linkage housing nuts and bolts - right-hand drive models	25	18
Disc retaining screws	10	7
Front brake caliper:		
Guide pin bolts*	30	22
Mounting bracket bolts*	120	88
Handbrake lever nuts	20	15
Hydraulic hose/pipe union nuts	15	11
Load-sensitive pressure regulating valve bolts*	20	15
Master cylinder retaining nuts	15	11
Rear brake caliper:		
Mounting bolt*	50	37
Guide pin bolt*	30	22
Rear wheel cylinder bolts	10	7
Roadwheel bolts	90	66
Vacuum servo unit mounting nuts	20	15

*Use thread-locking compound.

1 General information

The braking system is of the servo-assisted, dual-circuit hydraulic type. The arrangement of the hydraulic system is such that each circuit operates one front and one rear brake from a tandem master cylinder. Under normal circumstances, both circuits operate in unison. However, in the event of hydraulic failure in one circuit, full braking force will still be available at two wheels.

Some large-capacity engine models have disc brakes all round as standard; all other models are fitted with front disc brakes and rear drum brakes. ABS is fitted as standard to certain models, and is offered as an option on most other models (refer to Section 23 for further information on ABS operation).

The front disc brakes are actuated by single-piston sliding type calipers, which ensure that equal pressure is applied to each disc pad.

On models with rear drum brakes, the rear brakes incorporate leading and trailing shoes, which are actuated by twin-piston wheel cylinders. A self-adjust mechanism is incorporated, to automatically compensate for brake shoe wear. As the brake shoe linings wear, the footbrake operation automatically operates the adjuster mechanism, which effectively lengthens the shoe strut and repositions the brake shoes, to remove the lining-to-drum clearance.

On models with rear disc brakes, the brakes are actuated by single-piston sliding calipers.

A pressure-regulating valve arrangement is situated in the hydraulic circuit to each rear brake; on most models, a separate valve arrangement is fitted, but on some models with rear drum brakes, the valves are incorporated into the rear wheel cylinders. The valves control the hydraulic pressure applied to the rear brakes to help to prevent rear wheel lock-up during emergency braking (see Section 21).

On all models, the handbrake provides an independent mechanical means of rear brake application. On models with rear disc brakes, the handbrake is in the form of a separate drum brake arrangement fitted in the centre of the brake disc; on models with drum brakes, the handbrake applies the rear brake shoes.

On diesel engines, there is insufficient vacuum in the inlet manifold to operate the braking system servo effectively at all times. To overcome this problem, a vacuum pump is fitted to the engine, to provide sufficient vacuum to operate the servo unit. The vacuum pump is mounted on the end of the cylinder head, and is driven directly off the end of the camshaft.

Note: *When servicing any of the system, work carefully and methodically; also observe scrupulous cleanliness when overhauling any of the hydraulic system. Always renew components (in axle sets, where applicable) if in doubt about their condition, and use only genuine Peugeot replacement parts, or at least those of known good quality. Note the warnings given in "Safety first" and at relevant points in this Chapter concerning the dangers of asbestos dust and hydraulic fluid.*

2 Hydraulic system - bleeding

⚠️ *Warning: Hydraulic fluid is poisonous; wash off immediately and thoroughly in the case of skin contact, and seek immediate medical advice if any fluid is swallowed or gets into the eyes. Certain types of hydraulic fluid are inflammable, and may ignite when allowed into contact with hot components; when servicing any hydraulic system, it is safest to assume that the fluid is inflammable, and to take precautions against the risk of fire as though it is petrol that is being handled. Hydraulic fluid is also an effective paint stripper, and will attack plastics; if any is spilt, it should be washed off immediately, using copious quantities of fresh water. Finally, it is hygroscopic (it absorbs moisture from the air) - old fluid may be contaminated and unfit for further use. When topping-up or renewing the fluid,*

always use the recommended type, and ensure that it comes from a freshly-opened sealed container.

General

1 The correct operation of any hydraulic system is only possible after removing all air from the components and circuit; this is achieved by bleeding the system.

2 During the bleeding procedure, add only clean, unused hydraulic fluid of the recommended type; never re-use fluid that has already been bled from the system. Ensure that sufficient fluid is available before starting work.

3 If there is any possibility of incorrect fluid being already in the system, the brake components and circuit must be flushed completely with uncontaminated, correct fluid, and new seals should be fitted to the various components.

4 If hydraulic fluid has been lost from the system, or air has entered because of a leak, ensure that the fault is cured before proceeding further.

5 Park the vehicle on level ground, switch off the engine and select first or reverse gear, then chock the wheels and release the handbrake.

6 Check that all pipes and hoses are secure, unions tight and bleed screws closed. Clean any dirt from around the bleed screws.

7 Unscrew the master cylinder reservoir cap, and top the master cylinder reservoir up to the "MAX" level line; refit the cap loosely, and remember to maintain the fluid level at least above the "MIN" level line throughout the procedure, or there is a risk of further air entering the system.

8 There are a number of one-man, do-it-yourself brake bleeding kits currently available from motor accessory shops. It is recommended that one of these kits is used whenever possible, as they greatly simplify the bleeding operation, and also reduce the risk of expelled air and fluid being drawn back into the system. If such a kit is not available, the basic (two-man) method must be used, which is described in detail below.

9 If a kit is to be used, prepare the vehicle as described previously, and follow the kit manufacturer's instructions, as the procedure may vary slightly according to the type being used; generally, they are as outlined below in the relevant sub-section.

10 Whichever method is used, the same sequence must be followed (paragraphs 11 and 12) to ensure that the removal of all air from the system.

Bleeding sequence

11 If the system has been only partially disconnected, and suitable precautions were taken to minimise fluid loss, it should be necessary only to bleed thatof the system (ie the primary or secondary circuit).

12 If the complete system is to be bled, then it should be done working in the following sequence:

a) *Right-hand front brake.*
b) *Left-hand front brake.*
c) *Right-hand rear brake.*
d) *Left-hand rear brake.*

Bleeding - basic (two-man) method

13 Collect a clean glass jar, a suitable length of plastic or rubber tubing which is a tight fit over the bleed screw, and a ring spanner to fit the screw. The help of an assistant will also be required.

14 Remove the dust cap from the first screw in the sequence. Fit the spanner and tube to the screw, place the other end of the tube in the jar, and pour in sufficient fluid to cover the end of the tube.

15 Ensure that the master cylinder reservoir fluid level is maintained at least above the "MIN" level line throughout the procedure.

16 Have the assistant fully depress the brake pedal several times to build up pressure, then maintain it on the final downstroke.

17 While pedal pressure is maintained, unscrew the bleed screw (approximately one turn) and allow the compressed fluid and air to flow into the jar. The assistant should maintain pedal pressure, following it down to the floor if necessary, and should not release it until instructed to do so. When the flow stops, tighten the bleed screw again, have the assistant release the pedal slowly, and recheck the reservoir fluid level.

18 Repeat the steps given in paragraphs 16 and 17 until the fluid emerging from the bleed screw is free from air bubbles. If the master cylinder has been drained and refilled, and air is being bled from the first screw in the sequence, allow approximately five seconds between cycles for the master cylinder passages to refill.

19 When no more air bubbles appear, tighten the bleed screw securely, remove the tube and spanner, and refit the dust cap. Do not overtighten the bleed screw.

20 Repeat the procedure on the remaining screws in the sequence, until all air is removed from the system and the brake pedal feels firm again.

Bleeding - using a one-way valve kit

21 As their name implies, these kits consist of a length of tubing with a one-way valve fitted, to prevent expelled air and fluid being drawn back into the system; some kits include a translucent container, which can be positioned so that the air bubbles can be more easily seen flowing from the end of the tube.

22 The kit is connected to the bleed screw, which is then opened **(see illustration)**. The user returns to the driver's seat, depresses the brake pedal with a smooth, steady stroke, and slowly releases it; this is repeated until the expelled fluid is clear of air bubbles.

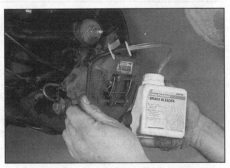

2.22 Bleeding a rear brake caliper

23 Note that these kits simplify work so much that it is easy to forget the master cylinder reservoir fluid level; ensure that this is maintained at least above the "MIN" level line at all times.

Bleeding - using a pressure-bleeding kit

24 These kits are usually operated by the reservoir of pressurised air contained in the spare tyre. However, note that it will probably be necessary to reduce the pressure to a lower level than normal; refer to the instructions supplied with the kit.

25 By connecting a pressurised, fluid-filled container to the master cylinder reservoir, bleeding can be carried out simply by opening each screw in turn (in the specified sequence), and allowing the fluid to flow out until no more air bubbles can be seen in the expelled fluid.

26 This method has the advantage that the large reservoir of fluid provides an additional safeguard against air being drawn into the system during bleeding.

27 Pressure-bleeding is particularly effective when bleeding "difficult" systems, or when bleeding the complete system at the time of routine fluid renewal.

All methods

28 When bleeding is complete, and firm pedal feel is restored, wash off any spilt fluid, tighten the bleed screws securely, and refit their dust caps.

29 Check the hydraulic fluid level in the master cylinder reservoir, and top-up if necessary (see "Weekly checks").

30 Discard any hydraulic fluid that has been bled from the system; it will not be fit for re-use.

31 Check the feel of the brake pedal. If it feels at all spongy, air must still be present in the system, and further bleeding is required. Failure to bleed satisfactorily after a reasonable repetition of the bleeding procedure may be due to worn master cylinder seals.

Note: *If difficulty is experienced in bleeding the braking circuit on models with ABS, this maybe due to air being trapped in the ABS regulator unit. If this is the case then the vehicle should be taken to a Peugeot dealer so that the system can be bled using special electronic test equipment.*

9

3 Hydraulic pipes and hoses - renewal

Caution: On models equipped with ABS, disconnect the battery before disconnecting any braking system hydraulic union and do not reconnect the battery until after the hydraulic system has been bled. Failure to do this could lead to air entering the regulator unit requiring the unit to be bled using special Peugeot test equipment (see Section 2).

Note: *Before starting work, refer to the note at the beginning of Section 2 concerning the dangers of hydraulic fluid.*

1 If any pipe or hose is to be renewed, minimise fluid loss by first removing the master cylinder reservoir cap, then tightening it down onto a piece of polythene to obtain an airtight seal. Alternatively, flexible hoses can be sealed, if required, using a proprietary brake hose clamp; metal brake pipe unions can be plugged (if care is taken not to allow dirt into the system) or capped immediately they are disconnected. Place a wad of rag under any union that is to be disconnected, to catch any spilt fluid.

2 If a flexible hose is to be disconnected, unscrew the brake pipe union nut before removing the spring clip which secures the hose to its mounting bracket.

3 To unscrew the union nuts, it is preferable to obtain a brake pipe spanner of the correct size; these are available from most large motor accessory shops **(see illustration)**. Failing this, a close-fitting open-ended spanner will be required, though if the nuts are tight or corroded, their flats may be rounded-off if the spanner slips. In such a case, a self-locking wrench is often the only way to unscrew a stubborn union, but it follows that the pipe and the damaged nuts must be renewed on reassembly. Always clean a union and surrounding area before disconnecting it. If disconnecting a component with more than one union, make a careful note of the connections before disturbing any of them.

4 If a brake pipe is to be renewed, it can be obtained, cut to length and with the union nuts and end flares in place, from Peugeot dealers. All that is then necessary is to bend it to shape, following the line of the original, before fitting it to the car. Alternatively, most motor accessory shops can make up brake pipes from kits, but this requires very careful measurement of the original, to ensure that the replacement is of the correct length. The safest answer is usually to take the original to the shop as a pattern.

5 On refitting, do not overtighten the union nuts. It is not necessary to exercise brute force to obtain a sound joint.

6 Ensure that the pipes and hoses are correctly routed, with no kinks, and that they are secured in the clips or brackets provided. After fitting, remove the polythene from the

3.3 Using a brake pipe spanner to slacken a union nut

reservoir, and bleed the hydraulic system as described in Section 2. Wash off any spilt fluid, and check carefully for fluid leaks.

4 Front brake pads - renewal

> ⚠ *Warning: Renew both sets of front brake pads at the same time - never renew the pads on only one wheel, as uneven braking may result. Note that the dust created by wear of the pads may contain asbestos, which is a health hazard. Never blow it out with compressed air, and don't inhale any of it. An approved filtering mask should be worn when working on the brakes. DO NOT use petrol or petroleum-based solvents to clean brake parts; use brake cleaner or methylated spirit only.*

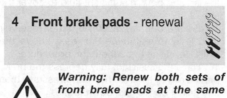
4.2 Disconnect the pad wear sensor wiring connectors and release the wiring from its retaining clips

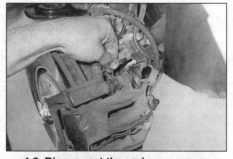
4.5 . . . then pivot the caliper upwards and away from the brake pads and tie it to the suspension strut . . .

Note: *New guide pin bolts must be used on refitting.*

1 Apply the handbrake, then jack up the front of the vehicle and support it on axle stands. Remove the front roadwheels.

2 Trace the brake pad wear sensor wiring back from the pads, and disconnect it from the wiring connector. Note the routing of the wiring, and free it from any relevant retaining clips **(see illustration)**.

3 Push the piston into its bore by pulling the caliper outwards.

4 Slacken and remove the caliper lower guide pin bolt, using a slim open-ended spanner to prevent the guide pin itself from rotating **(see illustration)**. Discard the guide pin bolt - a new one must be used on refitting.

5 With the lower guide pin bolt removed, pivot the caliper away from the brake pads and mounting bracket, and tie it to the suspension strut using a suitable piece of wire **(see illustration)**.

6 Withdraw the two brake pads from the caliper mounting bracket; the shims (where fitted) should be bonded to the pad, but may have come unstuck in use **(see illustration)**.

7 First measure the thickness of each brake pad's friction material **(see illustration)**. If either pad is worn at any point to the specified minimum thickness or less, all four pads must be renewed. Also, the pads should be renewed if any are fouled with oil or grease; there is no satisfactory way of degreasing friction material, once contaminated. If any of the brake pads are worn unevenly, or are fouled with oil or grease, trace and rectify the cause before reassembly.

4.4 Slacken and remove the caliper lower guide pin bolt . . .

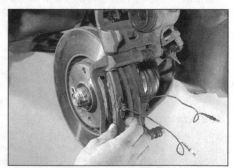
4.6 . . . the brake pads can then be removed from the mounting bracket

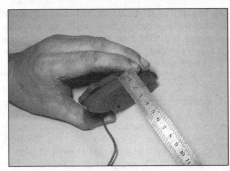

4.7 Measuring brake pad friction material thickness

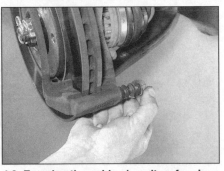

4.9 Examine the guide pin gaiters for signs of damage and renew if necessary

14 Depress the brake pedal repeatedly, until the pads are pressed into firm contact with the brake disc, and normal (non-assisted) pedal pressure is restored.
15 Repeat the above procedure on the remaining front brake caliper.
16 Refit the roadwheels, then lower the vehicle to the ground and tighten the roadwheel bolts to the specified torque.
17 Check the hydraulic fluid level as described in "Weekly checks".

> **HAYNES HiNT** *New pads will not give full braking efficiency until they have bedded in. Be prepared for this, and avoid hard braking as far as possible for the first hundred miles or so after pad renewal.*

4.12a Pivot the caliper back into position, passing the pad wear sensor wiring through the aperture . . .

4.12b . . . then fit the new guide pin bolt and tighten it to the specified torque

5 Rear brake pads - renewal

> ⚠️ *Warning: Renew both sets of rear brake pads at the same time - never renew the pads on only one wheel, as uneven braking may result. Note that the dust created by wear of the pads may contain asbestos, which is a health hazard. Never blow it out with compressed air, and don't inhale any of it. An approved filtering mask should be worn when working on the brakes. DO NOT use petrol or petroleum-based solvents to clean brake parts; use brake cleaner or methylated spirit only.*

8 If the brake pads are still serviceable, carefully clean them using a clean, fine wire brush or similar, paying particular attention to the sides and back of the metal backing. Clean out the grooves in the friction material, and pick out any large embedded particles of dirt or debris. Carefully clean the pad locations in the caliper mounting bracket.
9 Prior to fitting the pads, check that the guide pins are free to slide easily in the caliper mounting bracket, and check that the rubber guide pin gaiters are undamaged **(see illustration)**. Brush the dust and dirt from the caliper and piston, but **do not** inhale it, as it is a health hazard. Inspect the dust seal around the piston for damage, and the piston for evidence of fluid leaks, corrosion or damage. If attention to any of these components is necessary, refer to Section 10.
10 If new brake pads are to be fitted, the caliper piston must be pushed back into the cylinder to make room for them. Either use a G-clamp or similar tool, or use suitable pieces of wood as levers. Provided that the master cylinder reservoir has not been overfilled with hydraulic fluid, there should be no spillage, but keep a careful watch on the fluid level while retracting the piston. If the fluid level rises above the "MAX" level line at any time, the surplus should be siphoned off or ejected via a plastic tube connected to the bleed screw (see Section 2). **Note:** *Do not syphon the fluid by mouth, as it is poisonous; use a syringe or an old poultry baster.*
11 Ensuring that the friction material of each pad is against the brake disc, fit the pads to

the caliper mounting bracket. If the shims (where fitted) have become detached, ensure that they are correctly positioned on each pads backing plate.
12 Pivot the caliper down into position over the pads, passing the pad warning sensor wiring through the caliper aperture. If the threads of the new guide pin bolt are not already pre-coated with locking compound, apply a suitable thread-locking compound to them (Peugeot recommend Loctite Frenetanch - available from your Peugeot dealer). Press the caliper into position, then install the guide pin bolt, tightening it to the specified torque setting while retaining the guide pin with an open-ended spanner **(see illustrations)**.
13 Reconnect the brake pad wear sensor wiring connectors, ensuring that the wiring is correctly routed through the loop of the caliper bleed screw cap.

5.2a Remove the spring clips (arrowed) . . .

1 Chock the front wheels, then jack up the rear of the vehicle and support it on axle stands. Remove the rear wheels.
2 Extract the small spring clip from the each pad retaining pin then slide the retaining pins out from the caliper, noting the correct fitted location of the pad anti-rattle spring **(see illustrations)**. Remove the anti-rattle spring noting which way around it is fitted.
3 Using pliers if necessary, withdraw both the inner and outer pads from the caliper; the shims (where fitted) should be bonded to the pad, but may have come unstuck during use **(see illustration)**.

5.2b . . . then withdraw the retaining pins and recover the anti-rattle spring, noting which way around it is fitted

9

5.3 Removing the rear brake pads from the caliper

5.9 On refitting ensure the upper retaining pin passes through the centre of the anti-rattle spring and ensure the spring ends are located behind the lower pin

4 First measure the thickness of the friction material of each brake pad. If either pad is worn at any point to the specified minimum thickness or less, all four pads must be renewed. Also, the pads should be renewed if any are fouled with oil or grease; there is no satisfactory way of degreasing friction material, once contaminated. If any of the brake pads are worn unevenly, or fouled with oil or grease, trace and rectify the cause before reassembly. Examine the retaining pins for signs of wear and renew if necessary. New brake pads and retaining pin kits are available from Peugeot dealers.

5 If the brake pads are still serviceable, carefully clean them using a clean, fine wire brush or similar, paying particular attention to the sides and back of the metal backing. Clean out the grooves in the friction material, and pick out any large embedded particles of dirt or debris. Carefully clean the pad locations in the caliper body/mounting bracket.

6 Prior to fitting the pads, check that the guide sleeves are free to slide easily in the caliper body, and check that the rubber guide sleeve gaiters are undamaged. Brush the dust and dirt from the caliper and piston, but **do not** inhale it, as it is a health hazard. Inspect the dust seal around the piston for damage, and the piston for evidence of fluid leaks, corrosion or damage. If attention to any of these components is necessary, refer to Section 11.

7 If new brake pads are to be fitted, the caliper piston must be pushed back into the cylinder to make room for them. Either use a G-clamp or similar tool, or use suitable pieces of wood as levers. Provided that the master cylinder reservoir has not been overfilled with hydraulic fluid, there should be no spillage, but keep a careful watch on the fluid level while retracting the piston. If the fluid level rises above the "MAX" level line at any time, the surplus should be siphoned off or ejected via a plastic tube connected to the bleed screw (see Section 2). **Note:** *Do not syphon the fluid by mouth, as it is poisonous; use a syringe or an old poultry baster.*

8 Slide the brake pads into position in the caliper, ensuring each pad's friction material is facing the brake disc. If the shims (where fitted) have become detached, ensure that they are correctly positioned on each pad's backing plate

9 Fit the anti-rattle spring to the top of the pads, making sure it is fitted the correct way up. Slide the first pad retaining pin into position, ensuring it passes through the holes in both pad backing plates and the centre of the anti-rattle spring. Slide the second pad retaining pin into position, ensuring that the anti-rattle spring ends are correctly located behind the pin **(see illustration)**. Ensure that the anti-rattle spring and pads are correctly engaged with the retaining pins, then secure the pins in position with the spring clips.

10 Depress the brake pedal repeatedly until the pads are pressed into firm contact with the brake disc, and normal (non-assisted) pedal pressure is restored. Check that the inner pad lug is correctly engaged with one of the caliper piston slots.

11 Repeat the above procedure on the remaining rear brake caliper.

12 Refit the roadwheels, then lower the vehicle to the ground and tighten the roadwheel bolts to the specified torque setting.

13 Check the hydraulic fluid level as described in *"Weekly checks"*.

> **HAYNES HINT** *New pads will not give full braking efficiency until they have bedded in. Be prepared for this, and avoid hard braking as far as possible for the first hundred miles or so after pad renewal.*

6 Rear brake shoes - renewal

⚠️ *Warning: Brake shoes must be renewed on both rear wheels at the same time - never renew the shoes on only one wheel, as uneven braking may result. Also, the dust created by wear of the shoes may contain asbestos, which is a health hazard. Never blow it out with compressed air, and don't inhale any of it. An approved filtering mask should be worn when working on the brakes. DO NOT use petrol or petroleum-based solvents to clean brake parts; use brake cleaner or methylated spirit only.*

1 Remove the brake drum as described in Section 9.

2 Working carefully, and taking the necessary precautions, remove all traces of brake dust from the brake drum, backplate and shoes.

3 Measure the thickness of the friction material of each brake shoe at several points; if either shoe is worn at any point to the specified minimum thickness or less, all four shoes must be renewed as a set. The shoes should also be renewed if any are fouled with oil or grease; there is no satisfactory way of degreasing friction material, once contaminated.

4 If any of the brake shoes are worn unevenly, or fouled with oil or grease, trace and rectify the cause before reassembly.

5 To renew the brake shoes, proceed as follows. If all the components are in good condition, refit the brake drum as described in Section 9.

6 Note the correct fitted location of all components then, using a pair of pliers, remove the shoe retainer spring cups by depressing and turning them through 90°. With the cups removed, lift off the springs and withdraw the retainer pins **(see illustration)**.

7 Ease the shoes out one at a time from the lower pivot point, to release the tension of the return spring, then disconnect the lower return spring from both shoes.

8 Ease the upper end of both shoes out from their wheel cylinder locations, taking care not to damage the wheel cylinder seals, and disconnect the handbrake cable from the trailing shoe. The brake shoe and adjuster strut assembly can then be manoeuvred out of position and away from the backplate. Do not depress the brake pedal until the brakes are reassembled; wrap a strong elastic band around the wheel cylinder pistons to retain them.

9 With the shoe and adjuster strut assembly on a bench, make a note of the correct fitted positions of the springs and adjuster strut, to use as a guide on reassembly **(see illustration)**. Release the handbrake lever stop-peg (if not already done), then carefully

6.6 Removing a shoe retainer spring cup

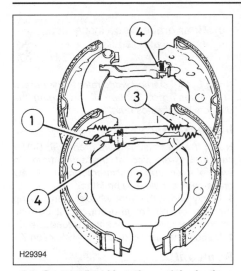

6.9 Correct fitted locations of the brake shoe adjuster strut and associated components

4 Adjuster strut bolt retaining spring
5 Adjuster strut spring
6 Upper return spring
7 Adjuster strut assembly

detach the adjuster strut bolt retaining spring from the leading shoe. Disconnect the upper return spring, then detach the leading shoe and return spring from the trailing shoe and strut assembly. Unhook the spring securing the adjuster strut to the trailing shoe, and separate the two.

10 Depending on the type of brake shoes being installed, it may be necessary to remove the handbrake lever from the original trailing shoe, and install it on the new shoe. Secure the lever in position with a new retaining clip. All return springs should be renewed, regardless of their apparent condition; spring kits are available from Peugeot dealers.

11 Withdraw the adjuster bolt from the strut, and carefully examine the assembly for signs of wear or damage. Pay particular attention to the threads of the adjuster bolt and the knurled adjuster wheel, and renew if necessary. Note that left-hand and right-hand struts are not interchangeable - they are marked "G" (gauche/left) and "D" (droit/right) respectively. Also note that the strut adjuster bolts are not interchangeable; the left-hand strut bolt has a left-handed thread (unscrews **clockwise**), and the right-hand bolt a right-handed thread.

12 Ensure that the components on the end of the strut are correctly positioned, then apply a little high-melting-point grease to the threads of the adjuster bolt. Screw the adjuster wheel onto the bolt until only a small gap exists between the wheel and the head of the bolt, then install the bolt in the strut.

13 Fit the adjuster strut retaining spring to the trailing shoe, ensuring that the shorter hook of the spring is engaged with the shoe. Attach the adjuster strut to the spring end, then ease the strut into position in its slot in the trailing shoe.

6.16 Apply a little high-melting point grease to the shoe contact points on the backplate

14 Engage the upper return spring with the trailing shoe, then hook the leading shoe onto the other end of the spring, and lever the leading shoe down until the adjuster bolt head is correctly located in its groove. Once the bolt is correctly located, hook its retaining spring into the slot on the leading shoe.

15 Peel back the rubber protective caps, and check the wheel cylinder for fluid leaks or other damage; check that both cylinder pistons are free to move easily. Refer to Section 12, if necessary, for information on wheel cylinder renewal.

16 Prior to installation, clean the backplate, and apply a thin smear of high-temperature brake grease or anti-seize compound (eg Duckhams Copper 10) to all those surfaces of the backplate which bear on the shoes, particularly the wheel cylinder pistons and lower pivot point **(see illustration)**. Do not allow the lubricant to foul the friction material.

17 Ensure that the handbrake lever stop-peg is correctly located against the edge of the trailing shoe, and remove the elastic band fitted to the wheel cylinder.

18 Manoeuvre the shoe and strut assembly into position on the vehicle, and locate the upper end of both shoes with the wheel cylinder pistons. Attach the handbrake cable to the trailing shoe lever. Fit the lower return spring to both shoes, and ease the shoes into position on the lower pivot point.

19 Tap the shoes to centralise them with the backplate, then refit the shoe retainer pins and springs, and secure them in position with the spring cups.

20 Using a screwdriver, turn the strut adjuster wheel to expand the shoes until the brake drum just slides over the shoes.

21 Refit the brake drum as described in Section 9.

22 Repeat the above procedure on the remaining rear brake.

23 Once both sets of rear shoes have been renewed, adjust the lining-to-drum clearance by repeatedly depressing the brake pedal. Whilst depressing the pedal, have an assistant listen to the rear drums, to check that the adjuster strut is functioning correctly; if so, a clicking sound will be emitted by the strut as the pedal is depressed.

24 Check and, if necessary, adjust the handbrake as described in Section 17.

25 On completion, check the hydraulic fluid level as described in "Weekly checks".

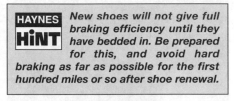

HAYNES HiNT *New shoes will not give full braking efficiency until they have bedded in. Be prepared for this, and avoid hard braking as far as possible for the first hundred miles or so after shoe renewal.*

7 Front brake disc - inspection, removal and refitting

Note: *Before starting work, refer to the note at the beginning of Section 4 concerning the dangers of asbestos dust.*

Inspection

Note: *If either disc requires renewal, BOTH should be renewed at the same time, to ensure even and consistent braking. New brake pads should also be fitted.*

1 Apply the handbrake, then jack up the front of the car and support it on axle stands. Remove the appropriate front roadwheel.

2 Slowly rotate the brake disc so that the full area of both sides can be checked; remove the brake pads if better access is required to the inboard surface. Light scoring is normal in the area swept by the brake pads, but if heavy scoring or cracks are found, the disc must be renewed.

3 It is normal to find a lip of rust and brake dust around the disc's perimeter; this can be scraped off if required. If, however, a lip has formed due to excessive wear of the brake pad swept area, then the disc's thickness must be measured using a micrometer. Take measurements at several places around the disc, at the inside and outside of the pad swept area; if the disc has worn at any point to the specified minimum thickness or less, the disc must be renewed **(see illustration)**.

4 If the disc is thought to be warped, it can be checked for run-out. Either use a dial gauge mounted on any convenient fixed point, while the disc is slowly rotated, or use feeler blades

7.3 Measuring brake disc thickness using a micrometer

9

7.4 Using a dial gauge to check brake disc runout

to measure (at several points all around the disc) the clearance between the disc and a fixed point, such as the caliper mounting bracket **(see illustration)**. If the measurements obtained are at the specified maximum or beyond, the disc is excessively warped, and must be renewed; however, it is worth checking first that the hub bearing is in good condition (Chapters 1 and/or 10). Also try the effect of removing the disc and turning it through 180°, to reposition it on the hub; if the run-out is still excessive, the disc must be renewed.

5 Check the disc for cracks, especially around the wheel bolt holes, and any other wear or damage, and renew if necessary.

Removal

6 Slacken and remove the two bolts securing the brake caliper mounting bracket to the swivel hub. Slide the caliper assembly off the disc and tie the assembly to the front coil spring, using a piece of wire or string, to avoid placing any strain on the hydraulic brake hose.

7 Use chalk or paint to mark the relationship of the disc to the hub, then remove the screws securing the brake disc to the hub, and remove the disc. If it is tight, lightly tap its rear face with a hide or plastic mallet.

Refitting

8 Refitting is the reverse of the removal procedure, noting the following points:

a) Ensure that the mating surfaces of the disc and hub are clean and flat.

b) Align (if applicable) the marks made on removal, and tighten the disc retaining screws to the specified torque setting.

c) If a new disc has been fitted, use a suitable solvent to wipe any preservative coating from the disc, before refitting the caliper.

d) Prior to installation, clean the threads of the caliper bracket mounting bolts and coat them with thread-locking compound (Peugeot recommend Loctite Frenetanch - available from your Peugeot dealer). Slide the caliper into position, making sure the pads pass either side of the disc, and tighten the caliper bracket bolts to the specified torque setting.

e) Refit the roadwheel then lower the vehicle to the ground and tighten the wheel bolts to the specified torque. Apply the footbrake several times to force the pads back into contact with the disc before driving the vehicle.

8 Rear brake disc - inspection, removal and refitting

Note: *Before starting work, refer to the note at the beginning of Section 5 concerning the dangers of asbestos dust.*

Inspection

Note: *If either disc requires renewal, BOTH should be renewed at the same time, to ensure even and consistent braking. New brake pads should also be fitted.*

1 Firmly chock the front wheels, then jack up the rear of the car and support it on axle stands. Remove the relevant rear roadwheel.

2 Inspect the disc as described in Section 7.

Removal

3 Slide out the retaining clip and release the brake pipe from its clip on the front of the hub assembly **(see illustration)**.

4 Slacken and remove the caliper mounting bolt then remove the protective cap from the guide bush and slacken and remove the guide pin bolt. Slide the caliper assembly off the disc and tie the assembly to the coil spring, using a piece of wire or string, to avoid placing any strain on the hydraulic brake pipe **(see illustrations)**.

5 Use chalk or paint to mark the relationship of the disc to the hub, then remove the screws securing the brake disc to the hub. Ensure that the handbrake is fully released then remove the disc from the vehicle, if necessary

8.3 Slide out the retaining clip and free the brake pipe from the hub assembly

8.4a Slacken and remove the mounting bolt . . .

8.4b . . . then remove the cap from the guide bush . . .

8.4c . . . and unscrew the guide pin bolt

8.4d Slide the caliper assembly off the disc and tie it to the rear suspension to avoid straining the brake pipe

8.5a Undo the retaining screws (arrowed) . . .

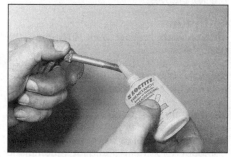

8.6a Apply locking compound to the threads of the caliper mounting and guide pin bolts . . .

8.5b . . . and remove the rear brake disc from the vehicle

8.6b . . . and tighten them to the specified torque settings

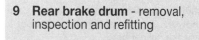

gently tap the disc to free it from the hub. If the disc is still tight on the handbrake shoes even with the brake fully released, back off the adjuster as described in Section 17 **(see illustrations)**.

Refitting

6 Refitting is the reverse of the removal procedure, noting the following points:

a) *Ensure that the mating surfaces of the disc and hub are clean and flat.*
b) *Align (if applicable) the marks made on removal, and tighten the disc retaining screws to the specified torque.*
c) *If a new disc has been fitted, use a suitable solvent to wipe any preservative coating from the disc, before refitting the caliper.*
d) *Clean the threads of the caliper mounting and guide pin bolts and coat them with thread-locking compound. Slide the caliper into position, making sure the pads pass either side of the disc, then refit the bolts tightening them to the specified torque settings* **(see illustrations)**. *Refit the cap to the guide bush.*
e) *Prior to refitting the roadwheel, adjust the handbrake shoes (refer to Section 17).*
f) *Refit the roadwheel, then lower the vehicle to the ground and tighten the roadwheel bolts to the specified torque. Depress the brake pedal several times to force the pads back into contact with the disc.*

9 Rear brake drum - removal, inspection and refitting

Note: *Before starting work, refer to the note at the beginning of Section 6 concerning the dangers of asbestos dust.*

Removal

1 Chock the front wheels, then jack up the rear of the vehicle and support it on axle stands. Remove the appropriate rear wheel.
2 Slacken and remove the screws securing the brake drum to the hub.
3 Ensure that the handbrake is fully released and remove the brake drum from the vehicle. It may be difficult to remove the drum due to the drum being corroded onto the hub, or the brake shoes binding on the inner circumference of the drum. If the drum is tight, tap the periphery of the drum using a hide or plastic mallet. If the brake shoes are binding, first check that the handbrake is fully released, then proceed as follows.
4 Referring to Section 17, fully slacken the handbrake cable adjuster to obtain maximum freeplay in the cable. Remove the access plug from the rear of the brake backplate (the plug is usually coloured blue) then, using a screwdriver or punch, push the handbrake lever outwards until the stop-peg slips behind the brake shoe web **(see illustration)**. This will retract the brake shoes fully and so allow the brake drum to be withdrawn easily. Once the drum is removed, refit the access plug to the backplate.

Inspection

Note: *If either drum requires renewal, BOTH should be renewed at the same time, to ensure even and consistent braking. New brake shoes should also be fitted.*

5 Working carefully, remove all traces of brake dust from the drum, but *avoid inhaling the dust, as it is a health hazard.*
6 Clean the outside of the drum, and check it for obvious signs of wear or damage, such as cracks around the roadwheel bolt holes; renew the drum if necessary.
7 Examine carefully the inside of the drum. Light scoring of the friction surface is normal, but if heavy scoring is found, the drum must be renewed. It is usual to find a lip on the drum's inboard edge which consists of a mixture of rust and brake dust; this should be scraped away, to leave a smooth surface which can be polished with fine (120- to 150-grade) emery paper. If, however, the lip is due to the friction surface being recessed by excessive wear, then the drum must be renewed.
8 If the drum is thought to be excessively worn, or oval, its internal diameter must be measured at several points using an internal micrometer. Take measurements in pairs, the second at right-angles to the first, and compare the two, to check for signs of ovality. Provided that it does not enlarge the drum to beyond the specified maximum diameter, it may be possible to have the drum refinished by skimming or grinding; if this is not possible, the drums on both sides must be renewed. Note that if the drum is to be skimmed, BOTH drums must be refinished, to maintain a consistent internal diameter on both sides.

Refitting

9 If a new brake drum is to be installed, use a suitable solvent to remove any preservative coating that may have been applied to its interior. Note that it may also be necessary to shorten the adjuster strut length, by rotating the strut wheel, to allow the drum to pass over the brake shoes.

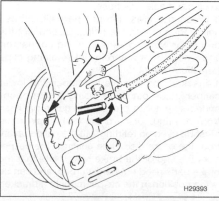

9.4 To fully release the handbrake lever, remove the access plug and use a screwdriver or punch (A) to push the lever outwards

9

10 Ensure that the handbrake lever stop-peg is correctly repositioned against the edge of the brake shoe web and that the mating surfaces of the drum and hub are clean and dry.

11 Manoeuvre the drum into position and tighten its retaining screws to the specified torque setting.

12 Depress the footbrake several times to operate the self-adjusting mechanism.

13 Repeat the above procedure on the remaining rear brake assembly (where necessary), then check and, if necessary, adjust the handbrake cable (see Section 17).

14 On completion, refit the roadwheel(s), then lower the car to the ground and tighten the wheel bolts to the specified torque.

10 Front brake caliper - removal, overhaul and refitting

Caution: On models equipped with ABS, disconnect the battery before disconnecting any braking system hydraulic union and do not reconnect the battery until after the hydraulic system has been bled. Failure to do this could lead to air entering the regulator unit requiring the unit to be bled using special Peugeot test equipment (see Section 2).

Note: *Before starting work, refer to the note at the beginning of Section 2 concerning the dangers of hydraulic fluid, and to the warning at the beginning of Section 4 concerning the dangers of asbestos dust.*

Removal

Note: *New guide pin bolts will be required on refitting.*

1 Apply the handbrake, then jack up the front of the vehicle and support it on axle stands. Remove the appropriate roadwheel.

2 Minimise fluid loss by first removing the master cylinder reservoir cap, and then tightening it down onto a piece of polythene, to obtain an airtight seal. Alternatively, use a brake hose clamp, a G-clamp or a similar tool to clamp the flexible hose.

3 Clean the area around the caliper hose union, then loosen the union. Disconnect the pad wear warning sensor wiring connector, and free it from any relevant retaining clips **(see illustration)**.

4 Slacken and remove the upper and lower caliper guide pin bolts, using a slim open-ended spanner to prevent the guide pin itself from rotating. Discard the bolts, new ones must be used on refitting. Lift the caliper away from the brake disc, then unscrew the caliper from the end of the brake hose. Note that the brake pads need not be disturbed, and can be left in position in the caliper mounting bracket.

Overhaul

5 With the caliper on the bench, wipe away all traces of dust and dirt, but *avoid inhaling the dust, as it is a health hazard.*

10.3 Disconnect the pad wear sensor wiring and free it from its retaining clips (arrowed)

6 Withdraw the partially ejected piston from the caliper body, and remove the dust seal.

> **HAYNES HiNT** *If the piston cannot be withdrawn by hand, it can be pushed out by applying compressed air to the brake hose union hole. Only low pressure should be required, such as is generated by a foot pump. As the piston is expelled, take great care not to trap your fingers between the piston and caliper.*

7 Using a small screwdriver, extract the piston hydraulic seal, taking great care not to damage the caliper bore.

8 Thoroughly clean all components, using only methylated spirit, isopropyl alcohol or clean hydraulic fluid as a cleaning medium. Never use mineral-based solvents such as petrol or paraffin, as they will attack the hydraulic system's rubber components. Dry the components immediately, using compressed air or a clean, lint-free cloth. Use compressed air to blow clear the fluid passages.

9 Check all components, and renew any that are worn or damaged. Check particularly the cylinder bore and piston; these should be renewed (note that this means the renewal of the complete body assembly) if they are scratched, worn or corroded in any way. Similarly check the condition of the guide pins and their gaiters; both pins should be undamaged and (when cleaned) a reasonably tight sliding fit in the caliper bracket. If there is any doubt about the condition of any component, renew it.

10 If the assembly is fit for further use, obtain the appropriate repair kit; the components are available from Peugeot dealers in various combinations. All rubber seals should be renewed as a matter of course; these should never be re-used.

11 On reassembly, ensure that all components are clean and dry.

12 Soak the piston and the new piston (fluid) seal in clean hydraulic fluid. Smear clean fluid on the cylinder bore surface.

13 Fit the new piston (fluid) seal, using only your fingers (no tools) to manipulate it into the cylinder bore groove.

14 Fit the new dust seal to the rear of the piston and seat the outer lip of the seal in the caliper body groove. Carefully ease the piston squarely into the cylinder bore using a twisting motion. Press the piston fully into position, and seat the inner lip of the dust seal in the piston groove.

15 If the guide pins are being renewed, lubricate the pin shafts with the special grease supplied in the repair kit, and fit the gaiters to the pin grooves. Insert the pins into the caliper bracket and seat the gaiters correctly in the bracket grooves.

Refitting

16 Screw the caliper body fully onto the flexible hose union.

17 Ensure that the brake pads are still correctly fitted in the caliper mounting bracket and refit the caliper, passing the pad warning sensor wiring through the caliper aperture.

18 If the threads of the new guide pin bolts are not already pre-coated with locking compound, apply a suitable locking compound to them (Peugeot recommend Loctite Frenetanch - available from your Peugeot dealer). Fit the new lower guide pin bolt, then press the caliper into position and fit the new upper guide pin bolt. Tighten both guide pin bolts to the specified torque while retaining the guide pin with an open-ended spanner.

19 Reconnect the brake pad wear sensor wiring connectors, ensuring that the wiring is correctly routed through the loop of the caliper bleed screw cap.

20 Tighten the brake hose union nut to the specified torque, then remove the brake hose clamp or polythene (where fitted).

21 Bleed the hydraulic system as described in Section 2. Note that, providing the precautions described were taken to minimise brake fluid loss, it should only be necessary to bleed the relevant front brake.

22 Refit the roadwheel, then lower the vehicle to the ground and tighten the roadwheel bolts to the specified torque.

11 Rear brake caliper - removal, overhaul and refitting

Caution: On models equipped with ABS, disconnect the battery before disconnecting any braking system hydraulic union and do not reconnect the battery until after the hydraulic system has been bled. Failure to do this could lead to air entering the regulator unit requiring the unit to be bled using special Peugeot test equipment (see Section 2).

Note: *Before starting work, refer to the note at the beginning of Section 2 concerning the dangers of hydraulic fluid, and to the warning*

11.8a Apply locking compound to the guide pin and mounting bolt threads . . .

11.8b . . . and tighten them to the specified torque

at the beginning of Section 5 concerning the dangers of asbestos dust.

Removal

1 Chock the front wheels, then jack up the rear of the vehicle and support on axle stands. Remove the relevant rear wheel.

2 Remove the brake pads as described in Section 5.

3 Minimise fluid loss by first removing the master cylinder reservoir cap, and then tightening it down onto a piece of polythene, to obtain an airtight seal. Alternatively, use a brake hose clamp, a G-clamp or a similar tool to clamp the flexible hose at the nearest convenient point to the brake caliper.

4 Wipe away all traces of dirt around the brake hose union on the caliper. Unscrew the union nut and disconnect the brake pipe from the caliper. Plug the pipe and caliper unions to minimise fluid loss and prevent dirt entry.

5 Slacken and remove the caliper mounting bolt then remove the protective cap from the guide bush and slacken and remove the guide pin bolt. Remove the caliper from the vehicle.

Overhaul

6 The caliper can be overhauled as described in Section 10. The only notable difference between the front and rear caliper is in the guide pin/bush arrangement. If either the guide bush or spacer show signs of wear or damage they must be renewed; both components are available in repair kits from Peugeot dealers.

Refitting

7 Clean the threads of the caliper mounting and guide pin bolts and coat them with thread-locking compound (Peugeot recommend Loctite Frenetanch - available from your Peugeot dealer).

8 Refit the caliper and insert the mounting and guide pin bolts, tightening them to the specified torque settings **(see illustrations)**. Refit the protective cap to the guide bush.

9 Reconnect the brake pipe to the caliper, and tighten the brake hose union nut to the specified torque. Remove the brake hose clamp or polythene (where fitted).

10 Refit the brake pads as described in Section 5.

11 Bleed the hydraulic system as described in Section 2. Note that, providing the precautions described were taken to minimise brake fluid loss, it should only be necessary to bleed the relevant front brake.

12 Refit the roadwheel, then lower the vehicle to the ground and tighten the roadwheel bolts to the specified torque.

12 Rear wheel cylinder - removal and refitting

Caution: On models equipped with ABS, disconnect the battery before disconnecting any braking system hydraulic union and do not reconnect the battery until after the hydraulic system has been bled. Failure to do this could lead to air entering the regulator unit requiring the unit to be bled using special Peugeot test equipment (see Section 2).

Note: Before starting work, refer to the note at the beginning of Section 2 concerning the dangers of hydraulic fluid, and to the warning at the beginning of Section 6 concerning the dangers of asbestos dust.

Removal

1 Remove the brake drum as described in Section 9.

2 Minimise fluid loss by first removing the master cylinder reservoir cap, and then tightening it down onto a piece of polythene, to obtain an airtight seal. Alternatively, use a

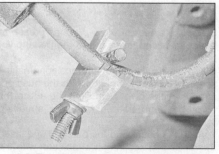

12.2 To minimise fluid loss, clamp the brake hose at the nearest convenient point to the wheel cylinder

brake hose clamp, a G-clamp or a similar tool to clamp the flexible hose at the nearest convenient point to the wheel cylinder **(see illustration)**.

3 Using pliers, carefully unhook the upper brake shoe return spring, and remove it from both brake shoes. Pull the upper ends of the shoes away from the wheel cylinder to disengage them from the pistons.

4 Wipe away all traces of dirt around the brake pipe union at the rear of the wheel cylinder, and unscrew the union nut **(see illustration)**. Carefully ease the pipe out of the wheel cylinder, and plug or tape over its end to prevent dirt entry. Wipe off any spilt fluid immediately.

5 Unscrew the two wheel cylinder retaining bolts from the rear of the backplate, and remove the cylinder, taking great care not to allow surplus hydraulic fluid to contaminate the brake shoe linings.

6 Note that it is not possible to overhaul the cylinder, since no components are available separately. If faulty, the complete wheel cylinder assembly must be renewed.

Refitting

7 Ensure that the backplate and wheel cylinder mating surfaces are clean, then spread the brake shoes and manoeuvre the wheel cylinder into position.

8 Engage the brake pipe, and screw in the union nut two or three turns to ensure that the thread has started.

9 Insert the two wheel cylinder retaining bolts, tightening them to the specified torque, then tighten the brake pipe union nut to the specified torque.

10 Remove the clamp from the flexible brake hose, or the polythene from the master cylinder reservoir (as applicable).

11 Ensure that the brake shoes are correctly located in the cylinder pistons, then carefully refit the brake shoe upper return spring, using a screwdriver to stretch the spring into position.

12 Refit the brake drum as described in Section 9.

13 Bleed the brake hydraulic system as described in Section 2. Providing suitable precautions were taken to minimise loss of fluid, it should only be necessary to bleed the relevant rear brake.

12.4 Using a brake pipe spanner to unscrew the wheel cylinder union nut

9

13 Master cylinder - removal, overhaul and refitting

Caution: On models equipped with ABS, disconnect the battery before disconnecting any braking system hydraulic union and do not reconnect the battery until after the hydraulic system has been bled. Failure to do this could lead to air entering the regulator unit requiring the unit to be bled using special Peugeot test equipment (see Section 2).

Note: *Before starting work, refer to the warning at the beginning of Section 2 concerning the dangers of hydraulic fluid.*

Removal

1 To provide improved access on some models it will be necessary to remove the air cleaner housing duct (see Chapter 4).

2 Remove the master cylinder reservoir cap and filter, and syphon the hydraulic fluid from the reservoir. **Note:** *Do not syphon the fluid by mouth, as it is poisonous; use a syringe or an old poultry baster.* Alternatively, open any convenient bleed screw in the system, and gently pump the brake pedal to expel the fluid through a plastic tube connected to the screw (see Section 2). Disconnect the wiring connector from the brake fluid level sender unit.

3 Remove the retaining clip then slide out the fluid reservoir retaining pin. Lift the reservoir upwards and away from the master cylinder body, and recover the mounting seals from the cylinder ports. If the mounting seals show signs of wear or deterioration, they must be renewed.

4 Wipe clean the area around the brake pipe unions on the side of the master cylinder, and place absorbent rags beneath the pipe unions to catch any surplus fluid. Make a note of the correct fitted positions of the unions, then unscrew the union nuts and carefully withdraw the pipes. Plug or tape over the pipe ends and master cylinder orifices, to minimise the loss of brake fluid, and to prevent the entry of dirt into the system. Wash off any spilt fluid immediately with cold water.

5 Slacken and remove the two nuts securing the master cylinder to the vacuum servo unit, then withdraw the unit from the engine compartment. If the sealing ring fitted to the rear of the master cylinder shows signs of damage or deterioration, it must be renewed.

Overhaul

6 The master cylinder can be overhauled after obtaining the relevant repair kit from a Peugeot dealer. Ensure that the correct repair kit is obtained for the master cylinder being worked on. Note the locations of all components to ensure correct refitting, and lubricate the new seals using clean brake fluid. Follow the assembly instructions supplied with the repair kit.

Refitting

7 Prior to refitting, measure the distance from the end of the vacuum servo unit pushrod to the servo master cylinder mating surface. This should be 22.3 ± 0.1 mm; if not seek the advice of a Peugeot dealer before refitting the master cylinder.

8 Remove all traces of dirt from the master cylinder and servo unit mating surfaces and ensure that the sealing ring is correctly fitted to the rear of the master cylinder.

9 Fit the master cylinder to the servo unit, ensuring that the servo unit pushrod enters the master cylinder bore centrally. Refit the master cylinder mounting nuts, and tighten them to the specified torque.

10 Wipe clean the brake pipe unions and refit them to the master cylinder ports, tightening them to the specified torque.

11 Press the mounting seals fully into the master cylinder ports then carefully ease the fluid reservoir into position. Slide the reservoir retaining pin into position and secure it in position, making sure the retaining clip is correctly located in the pin groove.

12 Refit any components removed to improve access then refill the master cylinder reservoir with new fluid. Bleed the complete hydraulic system as described in Section 2.

14 Brake pedal - removal and refitting

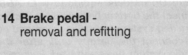

Removal

1 Disconnect the battery negative terminal.

2 Open up the engine immobiliser key pad, then rotate the fastener through 90° and lower the fusebox cover. Disconnect the wiring connector from the key pad then slacken and remove the retaining screws and remove the driver's side lower panel from the facia.

3 Slide off the retaining clip(s) and withdraw the clevis pin securing the pedal crossover linkage/servo unit pushrod to the pedal.

4 Slacken and remove the pivot bolt and nut, and remove the brake pedal from the vehicle. Slide the spacer out from the pedal pivot. Examine all components for signs of wear or damage, renewing them as necessary.

Refitting

5 Apply a smear of multi-purpose grease to the spacer, and insert it into the pedal pivot bore.

6 Manoeuvre the pedal into position, making sure it is correctly engaged with the pushrod, and insert the pivot bolt. Refit the nut to the pivot bolt and tighten it to the specified torque.

7 Align the pedal with the pushrod and insert the clevis pin, securing it in position with the retaining clip(s).

8 Refit the lower panel to the facia and reconnect the battery.

15 Vacuum servo unit - testing, removal and refitting

Testing

1 To test the operation of the servo unit, depress the footbrake several times to exhaust the vacuum, then start the engine whilst keeping the pedal firmly depressed. As the engine starts, there should be a noticeable "give" in the brake pedal as the vacuum builds up. Allow the engine to run for at least two minutes, then switch it off. If the brake pedal is now depressed it should feel normal, but further applications should result in the pedal feeling firmer, with the pedal stroke decreasing with each application.

2 If the servo does not operate as described, first inspect the servo unit check valve as described in Section 16. On diesel engine models, also check the operation of the vacuum pump as described in Section 26.

3 If the servo unit still fails to operate satisfactorily, the fault lies within the unit itself. Repairs to the unit are not possible - if faulty, the servo unit must be renewed.

Removal

4 Remove the master cylinder as described in Section 13.

5 Slacken the retaining clip (where fitted) and disconnect the vacuum hose from the servo unit check valve. Proceed as described under the relevant sub-heading.

Right-hand drive models

Note: *Access to the servo unit and crossover linkage is exceptionally poor (especially on diesel models) but can only be improved by removing the cylinder head (where possible) or the engine!.*

6 Undo the retaining screws and remove the cover from the right-hand end of the pedal crossover linkage housing.

7 Slacken and remove the pivot bolt and nut securing the crossover linkage rod to the pedal end pivot, then unscrew the two bolts securing the linkage housing to the pedal end bracket.

8 Unclip the cover from the servo end of the crossover linkage housing then slacken and remove the four nuts securing the housing to the bulkhead.

9 Ease the housing away from the bulkhead, then slacken and remove the servo unit retaining nuts. Remove the retaining clip, then slide out the clevis pin securing the servo unit to the linkage pivot.

10 Manoeuvre the servo unit out of position, along with its gasket which is fitted between the servo and housing. Renew the gasket if it shows signs of damage.

Left-hand drive models

11 Disconnect the servo unit pushrod from the brake pedal as described in paragraphs 2 and 3 of Section 14.

12 Slacken and remove the nuts securing the servo unit to the bulkhead, and manoeuvre the unit out of position. Recover the seal which is fitted between the servo and bulkhead.

Refitting

Right-hand drive models

13 Refitting is the reverse of removal, noting the following points.

a) Prior to refitting, measure the distance from the end of the vacuum servo unit pushrod to the servo master cylinder mating surface. This should be 22.3 ± 0.1 mm; if not seek the advice of a Peugeot dealer before refitting the master cylinder.

b) Lubricate all crossover linkage pivot points with multi-purpose grease.

c) Tighten the servo unit and mounting bracket nuts and bolts to their specified torque settings.

d) Refit the master cylinder as described in Section 13 and bleed the complete hydraulic system as described in Section 2.

Left-hand drive models

14 Prior to refitting, measure the distance from the end of the vacuum servo unit pushrod to the servo master cylinder mating surface. This should be 22.3 ± 0.1 mm; if not seek the advice of a Peugeot dealer before refitting the master cylinder.

15 Ensure that the gasket is correctly fitted to the rear of the servo unit, then manoeuvre the unit into position.

16 Make sure the pushrod is correctly engaged with the pedal, then refit the servo unit mounting nuts and tighten them to the specified torque.

17 Align the pedal with the pushrod and insert the clevis pin, securing it in position with the retaining clip(s). Refit the lower panel to the facia.

18 Connect the vacuum hose to the check valve and securely tighten its retaining clip.

19 Refit the master cylinder as described in Section 13, and bleed the complete hydraulic system as described in Section 2.

16 Vacuum servo unit check valve - removal, testing and refitting

Removal

1 Slacken the retaining clip (where fitted), and disconnect the vacuum hose from the servo unit check valve.

2 Withdraw the valve from its rubber sealing grommet, using a pulling and twisting motion. Remove the grommet from the servo.

Testing

3 Examine the check valve for signs of damage, and renew if necessary. The valve may be tested by blowing through it in both directions. Air should flow through the valve in one direction only - when blown through from the servo unit end of the valve. Renew the valve if this is not the case.

4 Examine the rubber sealing grommet and flexible vacuum hose for signs of damage or deterioration, and renew as necessary.

Refitting

5 Fit the sealing grommet into position in the servo unit.

6 Carefully ease the check valve into position, taking great care not to displace or damage the grommet. Reconnect the vacuum hose to the valve and, where necessary, securely tighten its retaining clip.

7 On completion, start the engine and check for air leaks from the check valve-to-servo unit connection.

17 Handbrake - adjustment

Rear drum brake models

1 To check the handbrake adjustment, fully release the handbrake then apply the footbrake firmly several times to establish correct shoe-to-drum clearance, then apply and release the handbrake several times to ensure that the self-adjust mechanism is fully

adjusted. Applying normal moderate pressure, pull the handbrake lever to the fully-applied position, counting the number of clicks emitted from the handbrake ratchet mechanism. If adjustment is correct, there should be between 10 and 11 clicks before the handbrake is fully applied. If this is not the case, adjust as follows.

2 Chock the front wheels, then jack up the rear of the vehicle and support it on axle stands.

3 To gain access to the handbrake adjuster, unscrew the retaining nuts/bolts and remove the exhaust system rear heatshield.

4 With the handbrake lever fully released, slacken the locknut and rotate the adjuster on the left-hand side of the relay mechanism. Screw the adjuster in or out (as applicable) until there is approximately 0.5 to 1.0 mm of freeplay between the front cable and the right-hand rear cable **(see illustrations)**. Once the adjuster is correctly positioned, securely tighten the locknut.

5 Check the handbrake adjustment by applying the handbrake fully, counting the clicks emitted from the handbrake ratchet and, if necessary, re-adjust.

6 Refit the heatshield then lower the vehicle to the ground.

Rear disc brake models

7 To check the handbrake adjustment, applying normal moderate pressure, pull the handbrake lever to the fully-applied position, counting the number of clicks emitted from the handbrake ratchet mechanism. If adjustment is correct, there should be between 6 and 7 clicks before the handbrake is fully applied. If this is not the case, adjust as follows noting that it should only be necessary to adjust the cable if the handbrake shoes have not been disturbed.

Adjusting the handbrake shoes

8 Chock the front wheels, then jack up the rear of the vehicle and support it on axle stands. Remove both rear roadwheels.

9 Working on the first disc, using a pair of pointed nose pliers, remove the adjuster access plug from the front of the brake disc **(see illustration)**.

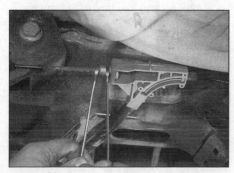

17.4a Slacken the lock nut and rotate the adjuster nut . . .

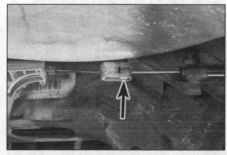

17.4b . . . to obtain the correct amount of freeplay between the right-hand cable and front cable end fittings

17.9 On models with rear disc brakes, remove the access plug from brake disc

9

17.11a Using a flat-bladed screwdriver inserted through the access hole . . .

17.11b . . . rotate the adjuster knurled ring (shown with disc removed) as described in text to correctly set the handbrake shoe-to-drum clearance

10 Rotate the disc and position the access hole directly opposite the brake caliper so that access can be gained to the handbrake shoe adjuster knurled ring.

11 Make sure the handbrake is fully released, then insert a screwdriver in through the access hole and fully expand the handbrake shoes by rotating the adjuster knurled ring **(see illustrations)**. When the disc can no longer be turned, back the knurled ring off by 5 or 6 teeth (catches) so that the wheel is free to rotate easily.

12 Refit the access plug to the brake disc. Ensure that the plug is positioned correctly so that its slot is at right-angles to the centre line from the hub to the plug hole.

13 Repeat paragraphs 9 to 12 on the opposite disc.

14 Refit the roadwheels then adjust the cable as follows. On completion lower the vehicle to the ground and tighten the wheelbolts to the specified torque setting.

Adjusting the handbrake cable

15 The handbrake cable is adjusted as described in paragraphs 2 to 6.

18 Handbrake lever - removal and refitting

Removal

1 Chock the front wheels then jack up the rear of the vehicle and support it on axle stands.

2 Referring to Section 17, release the handbrake lever and back off the adjuster to obtain maximum freeplay in the cable.

3 Remove the centre console as described in Chapter 11.

4 Peel back the gaiter (where necessary) and disconnect the wiring connector from the handbrake warning light switch.

5 Detach the handbrake cable from the lever then slacken and remove the lever retaining nuts, and remove the lever from the vehicle.

Refitting

6 Refitting is a reversal of removal. Tighten the lever retaining nuts to the specified torque, and adjust the handbrake (see Section 17).

19 Handbrake cables - removal and refitting

Removal

1 The handbrake cable consists of three sections, a front section which incorporates the adjuster mechanism and right- and left-hand rear sections which connect the rear brakes to the adjuster mechanism on the front cable. Each section can be removed individually.

2 Firmly chock the front wheels, then jack up the rear of the vehicle and support it on axle stands.

3 Referring to Section 17, remove the heatshield and slacken the adjuster to obtain maximum freeplay in the cable. Proceed as described under the relevant sub-heading.

19.12a Tap the handbrake outer cable out from the backplate . . .

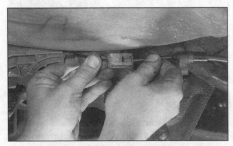

19.12c The right-hand cable end fitting simply unhooks from the front cable . . .

Front cable

4 Remove the centre console (Chapter 11).

5 Fully release the handbrake then detach the cable from the handbrake lever, and release the cable from its retaining clips and ties.

6 From underneath the vehicle, detach the right-hand rear cable from the front cable adjuster, then unscrew the adjuster and detach the left-hand rear cable.

7 Free the front cable from its retaining clips and ties, and withdraw the cable from underneath the vehicle.

Rear cable - drum brake models

8 Remove the relevant rear brake drum as described in Section 9.

9 Detach the end of the inner cable from the brake shoe lever, and tap the outer cable out of the rear of the backplate.

10 Work back along the length of the cable, freeing it from any relevant retaining clips and ties. Free the cable from the adjuster mechanism (the right-hand cable is clipped in position and the left-hand cable screwed in) and remove it from underneath the vehicle.

Rear cable - disc brake models

11 Remove the relevant set of handbrake shoes as described in Section 20, and detach the expander mechanism from the end of the cable.

12 Tap the outer cable out of the backplate then work back along the length of the cable, freeing it from any relevant retaining clips and ties. Free the cable from the adjuster mechanism (the right-hand cable is clipped in position and the left-hand cable screwed in) and remove it from underneath the vehicle **(see illustrations)**.

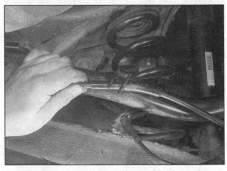

19.12b . . . and free the cable from its retaining clips

19.12d . . . whereas the left-hand cable needs to be unscrewed

20.2 Rotate the handbrake upper shoe retaining spring through 90° and remove it from the vehicle

20.3a Unhook the upper return spring . . .

20.3b . . . and remove the adjuster from between the handbrake shoes

20.4 Disengage the upper shoe from the expander then remove the shoe and lower return spring

20.5a Remove the retaining spring and lower shoe . . .

20.5b . . . and detach the expander mechanism from the end of the cable, noting its fitted arrangement and taking care not to lose the pivot pin (arrowed)

Refitting

13 Refitting is a reversal of the removal procedure, adjusting the handbrake as described in Section 17.

---

20 Handbrake shoes (rear disc brake models) - removal and refitting

Removal

1 Remove the brake disc as described in Section 8, and make a note of the correct fitted position of all components.
2 Using an Allen key, compress the upper shoe retaining spring, then rotate it through 90° and remove it from the backplate **(see illustration)**.
3 Carefully unhook and remove the handbrake shoe upper return spring then free the adjuster, noting which way around it is fitted, and remove it from between the shoes **(see illustrations)**.
4 Free the upper shoe from the expander mechanism, then carefully unhook the lower return spring and remove both components **(see illustration)**.
5 Remove the lower shoe retaining spring (see paragraph 2) and remove the handbrake shoe, taking great care not to drop the expander. Note the correct fitted orientation of the expander assembly, then detach it from the end of the handbrake cable **(see illustrations)**.
6 Inspect the handbrake shoes for signs of

wear or contamination, and renew if necessary. It is recommended that the return springs are renewed as a matter of course. Peugeot do not state any wear limit for the shoe friction material thickness, but anything less than 1 mm is not ideal.
7 Whilst the shoes are removed, clean and inspect the condition of the shoe adjuster and expander mechanisms, renew them if they show signs of wear or damage **(see illustration)**. If all is well, apply a fresh coat of high-temperature grease to the threads of the adjuster and sliding surfaces of the expander mechanism. Do allow the grease to contact the shoe friction material.

Refitting

8 Prior to installation, clean the backplate, and apply a thin smear of high-temperature brake grease or anti-seize compound to all

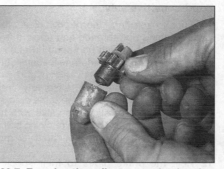

20.7 Examine the adjuster mechanism for signs of wear or damage

those surfaces of the backplate which bear on the shoes. Do not allow the lubricant to foul the friction material.
9 Ensure that the expander mechanism is correctly assembled, then engage it with the end of the handbrake cable **(see illustration)**.
10 Ensure that the expander legs are correctly positioned against the back plate stops, then fit the lower handbrake shoe. Ensure that the shoe is correctly engaged with the expander and secure it in position retaining spring **(see illustration)**.
11 Offer up the upper shoe and lower return spring. Hook the spring into position on both shoes, then manoeuvre the upper shoe into position on the backplate. Ensure that the upper shoe is correctly engaged with the expander, then secure it in position with the retaining spring.
12 Fully retract the adjuster assembly and

20.9 Ensure the expander mechanism is correctly engaged with the cable . . .

9

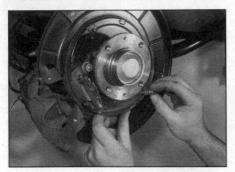

20.10 . . . then fit the lower handbrake shoe and secure it in position with the retaining spring

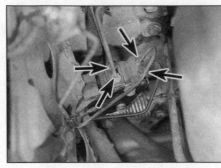

21.6 Load-sensitive pressure regulating valve pipe unions (arrowed)

21.8 Undo the retaining bolts (1) then detach the spring (2) and remove the valve from underneath the vehicle

manoeuvre it into position between the shoes. Using pliers, hook the upper return spring onto the lower shoe, then stretch it into position in the upper shoe.

13 Check all components are correctly fitted, and centralise the handbrake shoes.

14 Refit the brake disc (see Section 8). Prior to refitting the roadwheel, adjust the handbrake shoes and cable (see Section 17).

21 Rear brake pressure-regulating valve - testing, removal and refitting

Caution: On models equipped with ABS, disconnect the battery before disconnecting any braking system hydraulic union, and do not reconnect the battery until after the hydraulic system has been bled. Failure to do this could lead to air entering the regulator unit, requiring the unit to be bled using special Peugeot test equipment (see Section 2).

Testing

1 On most models, a load-sensitive pressure regulating valve is fitted into the hydraulic circuit to each rear brake. The valve is mounted onto the underside of the rear of the vehicle, and is attached to the rear suspension anti-roll bar by a spring. The valve measures the load on the rear axle, via the movement of the anti-roll bar, and regulates the hydraulic pressure being applied to the rear brakes to help prevent rear wheels locking up under hard braking.

2 On some smaller-capacity models with rear drum brakes, the valves are incorporated into the wheel cylinders; on these models, the valves are pressure-sensitive only, and are not affected by the load being carried.

3 Specialist equipment is required to check the performance of the valve(s), so if the valve is thought to be faulty, the car should be taken to a suitably-equipped Peugeot dealer for testing. Repairs are not possible and, if faulty, the valve must be renewed; on models with a load-sensitive valve, adjustment is possible, but again specialist equipment is needed to carry out this procedure.

Removal

Note: *Before starting work, refer to the warning at the beginning of Section 2 concerning the dangers of hydraulic fluid.*

Load-sensitive valve

4 Firmly chock the front wheels, then jack up the rear of the vehicle and support it on axle stands.

5 Minimise fluid loss by first removing the master cylinder reservoir cap, and then tightening it down onto a piece of polythene, to obtain an airtight seal.

6 Wipe clean the area around the brake pipe unions on the valve, and place absorbent rags beneath the pipe unions to catch any surplus fluid **(see illustration)**. To avoid confusion on refitting, make alignment marks between the pipes and valve assembly.

7 Slacken the union nuts and disconnect the brake pipes from the valve. Plug or tape over the pipe ends and valve orifices, to minimise the loss of brake fluid, and to prevent the entry of dirt into the system. Wash off any spilt fluid immediately with cold water.

8 Slacken and remove the valve retaining bolts, then unhook the valve spring from its bracket and remove the valve assembly from underneath the vehicle **(see illustration)**.

Pressure-sensitive valve

9 The valve is an integral part of the rear wheel cylinder. Refer to Section 12 for removal and refitting details.

Refitting

Load-sensitive valve

10 Prior to refitting, thoroughly clean the valve retaining bolt threads and apply a few drops of thread-locking compound (Peugeot recommend Loctite Frenetanch - available from your Peugeot dealer) to each one.

11 Manoeuvre the valve assembly into position, and hook the spring into the bracket on the anti-roll bar. Align the valve with its mounting bracket, and refit the retaining bolts, tightening them to the specified torque setting.

12 Refit the brake pipes to their specific unions on the valve, and tighten the union nuts to the specified torque setting.

13 Remove the polythene from the master cylinder reservoir, and bleed the complete hydraulic system as described in Section 2. If a new valve assembly has been fitted, it is recommended that the vehicle is taken to a Peugeot dealer so that the valve operation can be checked and, if necessary, adjusted using their special test equipment.

Pressure-sensitive valve

14 Refit the wheel cylinder (see Section 12).

22 Stop-light switch - removal, refitting and adjustment

Note: *On some models it will be necessary to remove the steering column to gain access to the switch.*

Removal

1 The stop-light switch is located on the pedal bracket behind the facia. On models with automatic transmission there are two switches fitted to the bracket - the stop-light switch is the left-hand of the two.

2 Open up the engine immobiliser key pad, then rotate the fastener through 90° and lower the fusebox cover. Disconnect the wiring connector from the key pad, then slacken and remove the retaining screws and remove the driver's side lower panel from the facia. Access to the switch is very poor, and can only be improved by removing the steering column (see Chapter 10) **(see illustration)**.

22.2 Stop-light switch (arrowed) viewed with the steering column removed

3 Disconnect the wiring, then unscrew the switch and remove it from the bracket.

Refitting and adjustment

4 Screw the switch back into position in the mounting bracket, until the gap between the end of the main body of the switch and the lug on the brake pedal is around 2 to 3 mm.
5 Once the stop-light switch is correctly positioned, reconnect the wiring connector, and check the operation of the stop-lights. The stop-lights should illuminate after the brake pedal has travelled about 5 mm. Adjust the switch as necessary, then refit the steering column (where removed) lower facia panel.

23 Anti-lock braking system (ABS) - general information

ABS is fitted to some larger-capacity models as standard and was available as an option on all others. The system comprises a hydraulic regulator unit and the four roadwheel sensors. The regulator unit contains the electronic control unit (ECU), the eight hydraulic solenoid valves (two for each brake - one inlet and one outlet) and the electrically-driven return pump. The purpose of the system is to prevent the wheel(s) locking during heavy braking. This is achieved by automatic release of the brake on the relevant wheel, followed by re-application of the brake. In the case of the rear wheels both brakes are applied at the same time.

The solenoid valves are controlled by the ECU, which itself receives signals from the four wheel sensors (front sensors are fitted to the hubs, and the rear sensors are fitted to the caliper mounting brackets), which monitor the speed of rotation of each wheel. By comparing these signals, the ECU can determine the speed at which the vehicle is travelling. It can then use this speed to determine when a wheel is decelerating at an abnormal rate, compared to the speed of the vehicle, and therefore predicts when a wheel is about to lock. During normal operation, the system functions in the same way as a non-ABS braking system.

If the ECU senses that a wheel is about to lock, it closes the relevant outlet solenoid valves in the hydraulic unit, which then isolates the relevant brake(s) on the wheel(s) which is/are about to lock from the master cylinder, effectively sealing-in the hydraulic pressure.

If the speed of rotation of the wheel continues to decrease at an abnormal rate, the ECU opens the inlet solenoid valves on the relevant brake(s), and operates the electrically-driven return pump which pumps the hydraulic fluid back into the master cylinder, releasing the brake. Once the speed of rotation of the wheel returns to an acceptable rate, the pump stops; the solenoid valves switch again, allowing the hydraulic master cylinder pressure to return to the caliper, which then re-applies the brake. This cycle can be carried out many times a second.

The action of the solenoid valves and return pump creates pulses in the hydraulic circuit. When the ABS system is functioning, these pulses can be felt through the brake pedal.

The operation of the ABS system is entirely dependent on electrical signals. To prevent the system responding to any inaccurate signals, a built-in safety circuit monitors all signals received by the ECU. If an inaccurate signal or low battery voltage is detected, the ABS system is automatically shut down, and the warning light on the instrument panel is illuminated, to inform the driver that the ABS system is not operational. Normal braking should still be available, however.

If a fault does develop in the ABS system, the vehicle must be taken to a Peugeot dealer for fault diagnosis and repair.

24 Anti-lock braking system (ABS) components - removal and refitting

Regulator assembly

Caution: Disconnect the battery before disconnecting the regulator hydraulic unions, and do not reconnect the battery until after the hydraulic system has been bled. Also ensure that the unit is stored upright (in the same position as it is fitted to the vehicle) and is not tipped onto its side or upside down. Failure to do this could lead to air entering the regulator unit, requiring the unit to be bled using special Peugeot test equipment on refitting (see Section 2).
Note: *Before starting work, refer to the warning at the beginning of Section 2 concerning the dangers of hydraulic fluid.*

Removal

1 Disconnect the battery negative lead.
2 Release the retaining clip and disconnect the main wiring connector from the regulator assembly. Unscrew the retaining nut and disconnect the earth lead from the regulator.
3 Mark the locations of the hydraulic fluid pipes to ensure correct refitting, then unscrew the union nuts, and disconnect the pipes from the regulator assembly. Be prepared for fluid spillage, and plug the open ends of the pipes and the regulator, to prevent dirt ingress and further fluid loss.

24.16a Slacken and remove the retaining bolt and nut (arrowed) . . .

4 Slacken and remove the regulator mounting nuts and remove the assembly from the engine compartment. If necessary, the mounting bracket can then be unbolted and removed from the vehicle. Renew the regulator mountings if they show signs of wear or damage.

Refitting

5 Manoeuvre the regulator into position and locate it in the mounting bracket. Refit the mounting nuts and tighten them to the specified torque setting.
6 Reconnect the hydraulic pipes to the correct unions on the regulator and tighten the union nuts to the specified torque.
7 Reconnect the wiring connector to the regulator and connect the earth lead, tightening its retaining nut securely.
8 Bleed the complete hydraulic system as described in Section 2. Once the system is correctly bled, reconnect the battery.

Electronic control unit (ECU)

Removal

9 The ECU can be removed with the regulator unit in position on the vehicle. To gain access to the ECU, remove the battery and battery tray (see Chapter 5).
10 Release the retaining clip and disconnect the wiring connector from the ECU.
11 Slacken and remove the retaining bolts, and carefully ease the ECU squarely away from the regulator.

Refitting

12 Align the ECU with the regulator connectors, and ease the unit into position. Refit the retaining bolts and tighten them to the specified torque setting.
13 Reconnect the wiring connector and refit the battery.

Front wheel sensor

Removal

14 Disconnect the battery negative lead.
15 Apply the handbrake, then jack up the front of the vehicle and support securely on axle stands. To improve access, remove the roadwheel.
16 Slacken and remove the retaining nut and screw, and remove the protective shield from the sensor **(see illustrations)**.

24.16b . . . and remove the protective shield

9

24.18a Slacken and remove the retaining bolt . . .

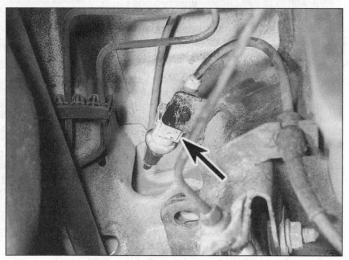

24.18b . . . and withdraw the front wheel sensor from the hub

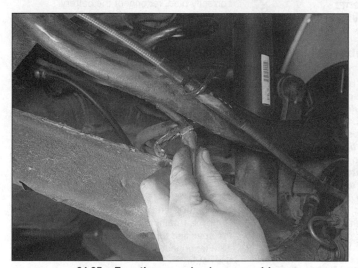

24.25a Free the rear wheel sensor wiring
from its retaining clips . . .

24.25b . . . and disconnect the sensor
wiring connector (arrowed) . . .

17 Trace the wiring back from the sensor, releasing it from all the relevant clips and ties whilst noting its correct routing, and disconnect the wiring connector.
18 Slacken and remove the retaining bolt and withdraw the sensor from the swivel hub **(see illustrations)**.

Refitting

19 Ensure that the mating faces of the sensor and the swivel hub are clean, and apply a little grease to the swivel hub bore before refitting.
20 Make sure the sensor tip is clean and ease it into position in the swivel hub.
21 Clean the threads of the sensor bolt and apply a few drops of thread-locking compound (Peugeot recommend Loctite Frenetanch - available from your Peugeot dealer). Refit the retaining bolt and tighten it to the specified torque.
22 Work along the sensor wiring, making sure it is correctly routed, securing it in

position with all the relevant clips and ties. Reconnect the wiring connector.
23 Refit the protective shield to the sensor and securely tighten its retaining nut and screw. Lower the vehicle and (where necessary) tighten the wheel bolts to the specified torque.

Rear wheel sensor

Removal

24 Chock the front wheels, then jack up the rear of the vehicle and support it on axle stands. To improve access, remove the appropriate roadwheel.
25 Trace the wiring back from the sensor, releasing it from all the relevant clips and ties whilst noting its correct routing, and disconnect the wiring connector **(see illustrations)**.
26 Slacken and remove the retaining bolt and withdraw the sensor **(see illustration)**.

Refitting

27 Ensure that the mating faces of the sensor and the hub are clean, and apply a little grease to the hub bore before refitting.
28 Make sure the sensor tip is clean and ease it into position in the swivel hub.

24.26 . . . then remove the retaining bolt (arrowed) and remove sensor

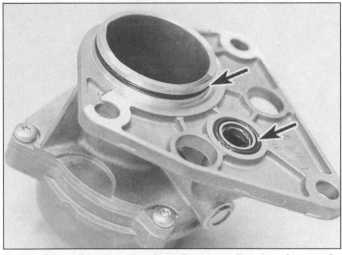

25.4a On 1.9 litre diesel engines, fit new sealing rings (arrowed) to the pump recesses . . .

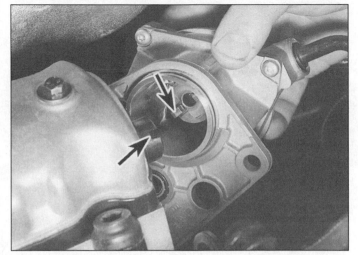

25.4b . . . then refit the pump, ensuring the drive dog is correctly aligned with the camshaft slot (arrowed)

29 Clean the threads of the sensor bolt and apply a few drops of thread-locking compound (Peugeot recommend Loctite Frenetanch - available from your Peugeot dealer). Refit the retaining bolt and tighten it to the specified torque.

30 Work along the sensor wiring, making sure it is correctly routed, securing it in position with all the relevant clips and ties. Reconnect the wiring connector, then lower the vehicle and (where necessary) tighten the wheel bolts to the specified torque.

25 Vacuum pump (diesel engine models) - removal and refitting

Removal

1 If necessary, to improve access to the vacuum pump, remove the air cleaner duct (see Chapter 4).

2 Release the retaining clip and disconnect the vacuum hose from the pump.

3 Slacken and remove the retaining bolts/nut (as applicable) securing the pump to the left-hand end of the cylinder head, then remove the pump. On 1.9 litre engines, the pump has two sealing rings (one large and one small); on 2.1 litre engines, there is only one. Discard the sealing rings - new ones must be used on refitting.

Refitting

4 Fit new sealing ring(s) to the pump recess(es), then align the drive dog with the slot in the end of the camshaft, and refit the pump to the cylinder head, ensuring that the sealing ring(s) remain correctly seated (see illustrations).

5 Refit the pump mounting bolts/nut (as applicable) and tighten them securely.

6 Reconnect the vacuum hose to the pump, tightening its retaining clip securely, and (where necessary) refit the air cleaner duct.

26 Vacuum pump (diesel engine models) - testing

1 The operation of the braking system vacuum pump can be checked using a vacuum gauge.

2 Disconnect the vacuum pipe from the pump, and connect the gauge to the pump union using a suitable length of hose.

3 Start the engine and allow it to idle, then measure the vacuum created by the pump. As a guide, after one minute, a minimum of approximately 500 mm Hg should be recorded. If the vacuum registered is significantly less than this, it is likely that the pump is faulty. However, seek the advice of a Peugeot dealer before condemning the pump.

4 Overhaul of the vacuum pump is not possible, since no components are available separately for it. If faulty, the complete pump assembly must be renewed.

Notes

Chapter 10
Suspension and steering

Contents

Degrees of difficulty

Easy, suitable for novice with little experience	Fairly easy, suitable for beginner with some experience	Fairly difficult, suitable for competent DIY mechanic	Difficult, suitable for experienced DIY mechanic	Very difficult, suitable for expert DIY or professional

Specifications

Wheel alignment and steering angles
Front wheel:
Toe setting .... 0 ± 0.5 mm toe-in
Camber .... 0° ± 30'
Castor .... 3° 30' ± 30'
King pin inclination .... 11° 30' ± 30'
Rear wheel:
Toe setting .... 1.5 ± 0.5 mm toe-in
Camber .... 1° 50' ± 30'

Roadwheels
Type .... Pressed-steel or aluminium alloy (depending on model)
Size .... 5J x 14, 6J x 15 or 6.5J x 15 (depending on model)
Tyre pressures .... See "Weekly checks"

10

Torque wrench settings

	Nm	lbf ft
Front suspension		
Anti-roll bar:		
Mounting clamp bolts	65	48
Connecting link nuts	65	48
Driveshaft retaining nut	325	238
Lower arm:		
Front pivot bolt	130	95
Rear mounting bracket bolts	60	44
Lower balljoint:		
Retaining nut	45	33
Balljoint-to-swivel hub	250	183
Subframe mounting bolts	120	88
Suspension strut:		
Upper mounting bolts	40	29
Upper mounting plate nut	65	48
Swivel hub clamp bolt	55	40
Rear suspension		
Anti-roll bar:		
Mounting clamp bolts	40	29
Connecting link nuts	40	29
Hub nut	275	202
Leading arm:		
Mounting bracket to body bolts	100	73
Front pivot bolt	95	70
Rear pivot bolt	75	55
Lower arm:		
Inner pivot bolt	75	55
Outer pivot bolt	95	70
Shock absorber:		
Upper mounting nut	35	26
Lower mounting bolt	75	55
Subframe mounting bolts	65	48
Track arm:		
Balljoint nut	65	48
Inner pivot bolt nut	40	29
Upper arm:		
Inner pivot bolt	95	70
Outer pivot bolt	75	55
Steering		
Column-to-intermediate shaft clamp bolt	22	16
Intermediate shaft-to-steering gear clamp bolt	25	18
Steering column mounting bolts	20	15
Steering gear mounting bolts	80	59
Steering wheel bolt	35	26
Track rod:		
Balljoint-to-swivel hub nut	35	26
Balljoint locknut	60	44
Inner balljoint-to-steering rack	50	37
Roadwheels		
Wheel bolts	90	66

1 General information

The independent front suspension is of the MacPherson strut type, incorporating coil springs and integral telescopic shock absorbers. The MacPherson struts are located by transverse lower suspension arms, which utilise rubber inner mounting bushes, and incorporate a balljoint at the outer ends.

The front swivel hubs, which carry the wheel bearings, brake calipers and the hub/disc assemblies, are bolted to the MacPherson struts, and connected to the lower arms via the balljoints. A front anti-roll bar is fitted to all models. The anti-roll bar is rubber-mounted onto the subframe, and is connected directly to the front suspension struts.

The independent rear suspension is of multi-link type. The stub axles are linked to the subframe by upper and lower arms and a track arm, and are attached to the vehicle underbody by leading arms. The anti-roll bar is mounted onto the subframe and is attached to the swivel hubs by connecting links.

The steering column has a universal joint fitted to its lower end, which is connected to an intermediate shaft having a second universal joint at its lower end. The lower universal joint is clamped to the steering gear pinion by means of a clamp bolt.

The steering gear is mounted onto the front subframe, and is connected by two track rods, with balljoints at their outer ends, to the steering arms projecting rearwards from the swivel hubs. The track rod ends are threaded, to facilitate adjustment. The hydraulic steering system is powered by a belt-driven pump, which is driven off the crankshaft pulley.

There are two different types of power steering fitted to the models covered in this manual; the steering can be either variable or invariable (depending on model). The hydraulic pump on the variable system alters the hydraulic pressure supplied to the steering gear to suit all conditions, ie. supplies high pressure when the vehicle is being driven slowly/parked and lower pressure when the vehicle is being driven at speed. On the invariable system the pump supplies the fluid at constant pressure, regardless of the vehicle speed.

2 Front swivel hub assembly - removal and refitting

Note: *A new track rod balljoint nut, lower balljoint nut, and swivel hub clamp bolt and nut will be required on refitting.*

Removal

1 Remove the wheel trim/hub cap (as applicable) then withdraw the R-clip and remove the locking cap from the driveshaft retaining nut. Slacken the driveshaft nut with the vehicle resting on its wheels **(see illustrations)**. Also slacken the wheel bolts.
2 Chock the rear wheels of the car, firmly apply the handbrake, then jack up the front of the car and support it on axle stands. Remove the appropriate front roadwheel.
3 On models equipped with ABS, unbolt the wheel sensor and position it clear of the hub assembly (see Chapter 9). Note that there is no need to disconnect the wiring.
4 Slacken and remove the driveshaft retaining nut. If the nut was not slackened with the wheels on the ground (see paragraph 1), withdraw the R-clip and remove the locking cap. Refit at least two roadwheel bolts to the front hub, tightening them securely, then have an assistant firmly depress the brake pedal to

prevent the front hub from rotating, whilst you slacken and remove the driveshaft retaining nut. Alternatively, a tool can be fabricated to hold the hub stationary (see Chapter 8, Section 2).
5 Slacken and remove the nut securing the steering gear track rod to the swivel hub then free the balljoint from the hub and recover the protector plate. If the balljoint is tight, use a universal balljoint separator to free it. Discard the nut, a new one should be used on refitting.
6 If the hub bearings are to be disturbed, remove the brake disc as described in Chapter 9. If not, unscrew the two bolts securing the brake caliper/mounting bracket assembly to the swivel hub, and slide the caliper assembly off the disc. Using a piece of wire or string, tie the caliper to the front suspension coil spring, to avoid placing any strain on the hydraulic brake hose.
7 Where necessary, slacken and remove the bolts securing the bracket to the top of the swivel hub **(see illustration)**.
8 Slacken and remove the lower balljoint nut and free the balljoint shank from the lower arm, if necessary, using a universal balljoint separator. Discard the nut and lift off the protector plate (if loose).
9 Undo the nut and withdraw the swivel hub-to-suspension strut clamp bolt, noting that the bolt fits from the rear of the vehicle. Discard the nut and clamp bolt, they should be renewed whenever they are disturbed.
10 Free the swivel hub assembly from the end of the strut, then release it from the outer constant velocity joint splines, and remove it from the vehicle. If the swivel hub is a tight fit on the strut, use a large flat-bladed screwdriver to carefully open up the clamp a little.

Refitting

11 Ensure that the driveshaft outer constant velocity joint and hub splines are clean, then slide the hub fully onto the driveshaft splines.
12 Slide the hub assembly fully onto the suspension strut, aligning the split in the hub clamp with the lug on the back of the strut. Also ensure that the raised rim on the strut is in contact with the top surface of the swivel

hub. Insert the new clamp bolt from the rear side of the strut then fit the new nut and tighten it to the specified torque.
13 Refit the protector plate (where removed) to the lower balljoint. Align the balljoint with the lower arm and fit the new retaining nut, tightening it to the specified torque.
14 Refit the protector plate and engage the track rod balljoint in the swivel hub, then fit the new retaining nut and tighten it to the specified torque.
15 Where necessary, refit the brake disc to the hub, referring to Chapter 9 for further information. Thoroughly clean the threads of the caliper bracket mounting bolts and coat them with thread locking compound (Peugeot recommend Loctite Frenetanch - available from your Peugeot dealer). Slide the caliper into position, making sure the pads pass either side of the disc, and tighten the caliper bracket bolts to the specified torque setting (see Chapter 9).
16 On models with ABS, refit the wheel sensor as described in Chapter 9.
17 Where applicable, refit the wiring retaining bracket to the top of the swivel hub, and tighten its retaining bolt securely.
18 Lubricate the inner face and threads of the driveshaft retaining nut with clean engine oil, and refit it to the end of the driveshaft. Use the method employed on removal to prevent the hub from rotating (see paragraph 4), and tighten the driveshaft retaining nut to the specified torque. Check that the hub rotates freely then engage the locking cap with the driveshaft nut, so that one of its cut-outs is aligned with the driveshaft hole, and secure the cap in position with the R-clip. Alternatively, lightly tighten the nut at this stage and tighten it to the specified torque once the vehicle is resting on its wheels again.
19 Refit the roadwheel, then lower the vehicle to the ground and tighten the roadwheel bolts to the specified torque. If not already having done so, tighten the driveshaft retaining nut to the specified torque then refit the locking cap, aligning its cut-outs with the drive shaft hole, and secure it in position with the R-clip.

2.1a Withdraw the R-clip . . .

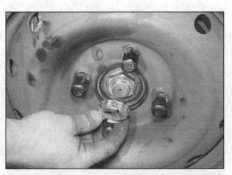
2.1b . . . then remove the locking cap and slacken the driveshaft nut

2.7 Undo the bolts (arrowed) and free the mounting bracket from the swivel hub

10

3 Front hub bearings - renewal

Note: *The bearing is a sealed, pre-adjusted and pre-lubricated, double-row roller type, and is intended to last the car's entire service life without maintenance or attention. Never overtighten the driveshaft nut beyond the specified torque wrench setting in an attempt to "adjust" the bearing.*

Note: *A press will be required to dismantle and rebuild the assembly; if such a tool is not available, a large bench vice and spacers (such as large sockets) will serve as an adequate substitute. The bearing's inner races are an interference fit on the hub; if the inner race remains on the hub when it is pressed out of the hub carrier, a knife-edged bearing puller will be required to remove it. A new bearing retaining circlip must be used on refitting.*

1 Remove the swivel hub assembly as described in Section 2.

2 Support the swivel hub securely on blocks or in a vice. Using a tubular spacer which bears only on the inner end of the hub flange, press the hub flange out of the bearing. If the bearing's outboard inner race remains on the hub, remove it using a bearing puller (see note above).

3 Extract the bearing retaining circlip from the inner end of the swivel hub assembly **(see illustration)**.

4 Where necessary, refit the inner race back in position over the ball cage, and securely support the inner face of the swivel hub. Using a tubular spacer which bears only on the inner race, press the complete bearing assembly out of the swivel hub.

5 Thoroughly clean the hub and swivel hub, removing all traces of dirt and grease, and polish away any burrs or raised edges which might hinder reassembly. Check both for cracks or any other signs of wear or damage, and renew them if necessary. Renew the circlip, regardless of its apparent condition.

6 On reassembly, apply a light film of oil (Peugeot recommend Molykote 321R - available from your Peugeot dealer) to the bearing outer race and hub flange shaft, to aid installation of the bearing.

7 Securely support the swivel hub, and locate the bearing in the hub. Press the bearing fully into position, ensuring that it enters the hub squarely, using a tubular spacer which bears only on the bearing outer race.

8 Once the bearing is correctly seated, secure the bearing in position with the new circlip, ensuring that it is correctly located in the groove in the swivel hub.

9 Securely support the outer face of the hub flange, and locate the swivel hub bearing inner race over the end of the hub flange. Press the bearing onto the hub, using a tubular spacer which bears only on the inner race of the hub bearing, until it seats against the hub shoulder. Check that the hub flange

3.3 Front wheel bearing retaining clip

4.2b . . . then undo the retaining bolts and free the mounting bracket from the hub

rotates freely, and wipe off any excess oil or grease.

10 Refit the swivel hub assembly as described in Section 2.

4 Front suspension strut - removal and refitting

Note: *At the time of writing, no information on the active suspension system was available. If your car has active suspension, consult your Peugeot dealer for details of any relevant changes to the following procedure before attempting to remove/refit the strut assembly.*

Note: *A new swivel hub clamp bolt and nut, a lower balljoint nut and a anti-roll bar connecting link nut will be required on refitting.*

Removal

1 Chock the rear wheels, apply the handbrake, then jack up the front of the car

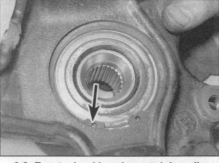
4.5a Slacken and remove the nut . . .

4.2a Unclip the wiring . . .

4.4 Undo the retaining nut and free the anti-roll bar connecting link from the strut

and support on axle stands. Remove the appropriate roadwheel.

2 Unclip the wiring and/or hoses from the strut/body then undo the retaining bolts and free the mounting bracket from the swivel hub **(see illustrations)**.

3 Slacken and remove the lower balljoint nut and free the balljoint shank from the lower arm, if necessary, using a universal balljoint separator. Discard the nut and lift off the protector plate (if loose).

4 Unscrew the nut securing the anti-roll bar connecting link to the strut, and position the link clear of the strut; if necessary, retain the balljoint shank with an Allen key to prevent rotation whilst the nut is slackened **(see illustration)**. Discard the nut, a new one should be used on refitting.

5 Undo the nut and withdraw the swivel hub-to-suspension strut clamp bolt, noting that the bolt fits from the rear of the strut; discard the nut and bolt, new ones will be needed on refitting **(see illustrations)**. To prevent the

4.5b . . . then withdraw the clamp bolt securing the swivel hub to the strut

4.7a Remove the plastic cover . . .

4.7b . . . then undo the upper mounting bolts (arrowed) . . .

4.7c . . . and remove the front suspension strut from underneath the wheelarch

swivel hub assembly dropping whilst the strut is removed support the lower arm or alternately tie the hub to the subframe with a piece of wire.
6 Release the strut from the swivel hub. If the swivel hub is a tight fit on the strut, carefully open up the clamp a little using a large flat-bladed screwdriver or similar tool. Take care not to strain the brake hose and the wiring attached to the brake caliper and the swivel hub.
7 Working in the engine compartment, remove the plastic cover then slacken and remove the suspension strut upper mounting bolts and withdraw the strut from under the wheel arch (see illustrations). Temporarily locate the hub assembly balljoint in the lower arm to help support it whilst the strut is removed.

Refitting

8 Manoeuvre the strut assembly into position, ensuring that the top mounting plate locating pin is correctly located in the corresponding hole in the body. Engage the lower end of the strut with the hub assembly aligning the split in the hub clamp with the lug on the back of the strut.
9 Refit the strut upper mounting bolts and tighten them to the specified torque setting.
10 Ensure that the raised rim on the strut is in contact with the top surface of the swivel hub then insert the new clamp bolt from the rear side of the strut. Fit the new nut to the clamp bolt and tighten it to the specified torque.
11 Refit the protector plate (where removed) to the lower balljoint. Align the balljoint with the lower arm and fit the new retaining nut, tightening it to the specified torque.
12 Reconnect the anti-roll bar connecting link to the strut. Fit a new nut to the connecting link, and tighten it to the specified torque.
13 Where applicable, clip any wiring/hoses into position on the strut.
14 Refit the roadwheel, then lower the vehicle to the ground and tighten the roadwheel bolts to the specified torque.

5 Front suspension strut - overhaul

Note: At the time of writing, no information on the active suspension system was available. If your car has active suspension, consult your Peugeot dealer for details of any relevant changes to the following procedure before attempting to overhaul the strut assembly.

⚠ Warning: Before attempting to dismantle the front suspension strut, a suitable tool to hold the coil spring in compression must be obtained. Adjustable coil spring compressors are readily-available, and are recommended for this operation. Any attempt to dismantle the strut without such a tool is likely to result in damage or personal injury.

5.1 Using spring compressors, compress the spring sufficiently to relieve pressure from the spring seats

5.3a . . . then lift off the upper mounting plate . . .

Note: A new mounting plate nut will be required.
1 With the strut removed from the car, clean away all external dirt, then mount it upright in a vice. Fit the spring compressor and compress the coil spring until tension is relieved from the spring seats (see illustration).
2 Slacken and remove the upper mounting plate nut whilst retaining the shock absorber piston with a suitable Allen key (see illustration).
3 Remove the nut and washer then lift off the mounting plate followed by the spacer and upper spring seat (see illustrations).
4 Lift off the coil spring and remove the washer, dust gaiter and rubber bump stop from the shock absorber piston (see illustrations). Slide off the lower spring seat.
5 Examine the shock absorber for signs of fluid leakage. Check the piston for signs of pitting along its entire length, and check the

5.2 Slacken and remove the upper mounting plate nut . . .

5.3b . . . the spacer and the upper spring seat (arrowed)

10

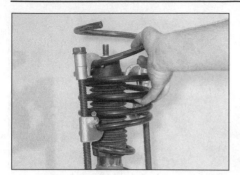

5.4a Lift off the coil spring . . .

5.4b . . . then slide off the washer, dust gaiter . . .

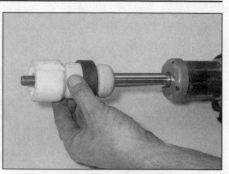

5.4c . . . rubber bump stop . . .

5.4d . . . and lower spring seat

5.7 On refitting ensure the dust gaiter is correctly located on the strut body

5.8 Ensure the upper spring seat stop (arrowed) is correctly located against the spring end

shock body for signs of damage. While holding it in an upright position, test the operation of the shock absorber by moving the piston through a full stroke, and then through short strokes of 50 to 100 mm. In both cases, the resistance felt should be smooth and continuous. If the resistance is jerky, or uneven, or if there is any visible sign of wear or damage to the shock absorber, renewal is necessary.

6 Inspect all other components for signs of damage or deterioration, and renew any that are suspect.

7 Fit the lower spring seat to the shock absorber then slide the rubber bump stop onto the piston. Fit the dust gaiter and washer making sure the lower end of gaiter is correctly positioned over the shock absorber end **(see illustration)**.

8 Refit the coil spring, making sure its lower end is correctly seated against the spring seat stop. Fit the upper spring seat, aligning its

stop with the spring end, then fit the spacer and mounting plate **(see illustration)**.

9 Refit the washer and screw on the new nut. Retain the shock absorber piston and tighten the mounting plate nut to the specified torque.

6 Front suspension lower arm - removal, overhaul and refitting

Note: A new lower balljoint nut will be required on refitting.

Removal

1 Chock the rear wheels, firmly apply the handbrake, then jack up the front of the vehicle and support on axle stands. Remove the appropriate front roadwheel.

2 Slacken and remove the nut, then free the lower balljoint shank from the lower arm, if

necessary, using a universal balljoint separator. Discard the nut and lift off the protector plate (if loose).

3 Slacken and remove the lower arm front pivot bolt and nut **(see illustration)**.

4 Unscrew the two bolts securing the lower arm rear mounting bush to the subframe **(see illustration)**.

5 Manoeuvre the lower arm assembly out from underneath the vehicle.

Overhaul

6 Thoroughly clean the lower arm and the area around the arm mountings, removing all traces of dirt and underseal if necessary, then check carefully for cracks, distortion or any other signs of wear or damage, paying particular attention to the pivot bushes, and renew components as necessary.

7 Renewal of the front pivot bush and rear mounting bracket will required the use of a hydraulic press, a bearing puller and several spacers and should therefore be entrusted to a Peugeot dealer with access to the necessary equipment.

Refitting

8 Manoeuvre the lower arm assembly into position, and refit the front pivot bolt and nut, tightening it finger-tight only.

9 Refit the rear pivot bush retaining bolts and tighten them to the specified torque.

10 Refit the protector plate (where removed) to the lower balljoint, then locate the balljoint shank in the lower arm. Fit the new retaining nut and tighten it to the specified torque.

6.3 Front suspension lower arm front pivot bolt (arrowed)

6.4 Front suspension lower arm rear mounting bush bolts (arrowed)

7.2 Tapping off the lower balljoint protector plate

11 Refit the roadwheel, then lower the vehicle and tighten the roadwheel bolts to the specified torque. Rock the car to settle the disturbed components in position, then tighten the lower arm front pivot bolt to the specified torque.

12 Check and, if necessary, adjust the front wheel alignment as described in Section 32.

7 Front suspension lower balljoint - removal and refitting

Note: *A special peg socket (Peugeot number 0615J) is required to remove and refit the balljoint. If access to this tool is not available, then balljoint renewal should be entrusted to a Peugeot dealer.*

Removal

1 Remove the swivel hub assembly as described in Section 2.

2 Remove the protector plate from the balljoint and mount the assembly securely in a vice **(see illustration)**.

3 Using a hammer and pointed-nose chisel, tap up the staking securing the balljoint in position.

4 Fit the special tool to the balljoint, engaging the tool with the cut-outs in the balljoint, and secure it in position by screwing on the old balljoint nut **(see illustration)**. Unscrew the balljoint and remove it from the swivel hub.

Refitting

5 Screw the balljoint into the swivel hub assembly. Fit the special tool, taking care not

7.4 Engage the special tool with the cut-outs (arrowed) in the balljoint

to damage the balljoint gaiter, and tighten the balljoint to the specified torque. Secure the balljoint in position by firmly staking it into one of the swivel hub notches using a hammer and punch.

6 Fit the new protector plate to the balljoint and secure it in position by staking it into the one of the balljoint notches.

7 Refit the swivel hub (see Section 2).

8 Front suspension anti-roll bar - removal and refitting

Note: *New connecting link nuts will be required on refitting.*

Removal

1 Chock the rear wheels, firmly apply the handbrake, then jack up the front of the vehicle and support on axle stands. Remove both front roadwheels.

2 Slacken and remove the nuts securing the left- and right-hand connecting links to the anti-roll bar, and position the links clear of the bar; if necessary, retain the balljoint shank with an Allen key to prevent rotation whilst the nut is slackened **(see illustration)**. Discard the nuts new ones should be used on refitting.

3 Slacken the two anti-roll bar mounting clamp retaining bolts and nuts, and remove both clamps from the top of the subframe **(see illustration)**.

4 Manoeuvre the anti-roll bar out from underneath the vehicle, and remove the mounting bushes from the bar.

5 Carefully examine the anti-roll bar components for signs of wear, damage or deterioration, paying particular attention to the mounting bushes. Renew worn components as necessary.

Refitting

6 Fit the rubber mounting bushes to the anti-roll bar. Position each bush so that its flat surface is at the bottom and its internal flats are correctly engaged with the flats on the anti-roll bar; the bush split should be facing towards the rear.

7 Offer up the anti-roll bar, and manoeuvre it into position on the subframe. Refit the mounting clamps, ensuring that their ends are correctly located in the hooks on the subframe, and refit the retaining bolts and nuts. Engage the connecting links with the ends of the bar then tighten the mounting clamp retaining bolts to the specified torque.

8 Fit the new retaining nuts to the connecting links and tighten them to the specified torque setting.

9 Refit the roadwheels then lower the vehicle to the ground and tighten the wheel bolts to the specified torque.

9 Front suspension anti-roll bar connecting link - removal and refitting

Note: *New connecting link nuts will be required on refitting.*

Removal

1 Chock the rear wheels, firmly apply the handbrake, then jack up the front of the vehicle and support on axle stands. Remove the relevant roadwheel.

2 Slacken and remove the nuts securing the connecting link to the anti-roll bar and suspension strut and remove the link from the vehicle; if necessary, retain the balljoint shanks with an Allen key to prevent rotation whilst each nut is slackened **(see illustration)**. Discard the nuts, new ones should be used on refitting.

3 Inspect the link for signs of wear or damage and renew if necessary.

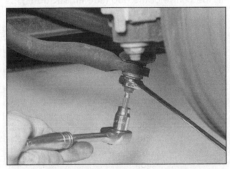

8.2 Unscrew the nut and detach the connecting rods from the anti-roll bar ends

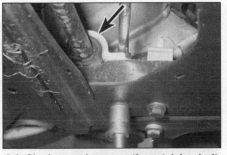

8.3 Slacken and remove the retaining bolt and nut, and remove the anti-roll bar mounting clamp (arrowed)

9.2 Unscrew the balljoint nuts and remove the anti-roll bar connecting link

10

11.2 Tap the cap out from the centre of the hub and discard it

11.3 Using a hammer and punch, tap out the hub nut staking

11.5 Using a puller to remove the rear hub assembly from the stub axle

Refitting

4 Refitting is the reverse of removal, using new nuts and tightening them to the specified torque setting.

10 Front suspension subframe - removal and refitting

Note: *New connecting link nuts and lower balljoint nuts will be required on refitting.*

Removal

1 Chock the rear wheels, firmly apply the handbrake, then jack up the front of the vehicle and support it on axle stands. Remove both front roadwheels.
2 Remove the anti-roll bar connecting links as described in Section 9.
3 Slacken and remove the rear engine/transmission through-bolt and nut, then undo the nut and bolt securing the mounting bracket to the subframe and remove the bracket.
4 Slacken and remove the left-hand lower balljoint nut and free the balljoint shank from the lower arm, if necessary, using a universal balljoint separator. Discard the nut and lift off the protector plate (if loose). Repeat the procedure on the right-hand side.
5 Slacken and remove the steering gear mounting bolts and washers then recover the washers from the top of the steering gear and the spacers which are fitted between steering gear and subframe. Free the power steering pipes/hoses from their brackets on the subframe so the subframe can be removed, leaving the steering gear in position.
6 Referring to Chapter 7, on all models except 2.1 litre Diesel engine models, slacken and remove the bolt securing the gearchange linkage bellcrank to the subframe. Withdraw the spacer from the bellcrank and store it with the pivot bolt for safe-keeping.
7 Make a final check that all control cables/hoses that are attached to the subframe have been released and positioned clear so that they will not hinder the removal procedure.
8 Place a jack and a suitable block of wood under the subframe to support the subframe as it is lowered.

9 Slacken and remove the four subframe mounting bolts then carefully lower the subframe assembly out of position and remove it from underneath the vehicle, taking great care to ensure that the subframe assembly does not catch the power steering pipes as it is lowered out of position.

Refitting

10 Refitting is a reversal of the removal procedure, noting the following points:
- a) *Use new connecting link and lower balljoint nuts.*
- b) *Tighten all nuts and bolts to the specified torque settings (where given).*
- c) *On completion check and, if necessary, adjust the front wheel alignment as described in Section 32.*

11 Rear hub assembly - removal and refitting

Removal

Note: *Do not remove the hub assembly unless it is absolutely necessary. A puller will be required to draw the hub assembly off the stub axle, and the hub bearing will almost certainly be damaged by the removal procedure, necessitating renewal of the hub assembly. A new hub nut and centre cap must be used on refitting.*
1 Remove the rear brake drum/disc (as applicable) as described in Chapter 9.
2 Prise out the cap from the centre of the hub

11.10a Fit the new hub nut . . .

and discard; a new cap should be used on refitting **(see illustration)**.
3 Using a hammer and punch, tap up the staking securing the hub retaining nut to the groove in the stub axle **(see illustration)**.
4 Using a socket and long bar, unscrew the rear hub nut and discard it; a new hub nut should be used on refitting.
5 Using a puller, draw the hub assembly off the stub axle, along with the outer bearing race **(see illustration)**. If necessary, with the hub removed, use the puller to draw the inner bearing race off the stub axle.
6 Check the hub bearing for signs of roughness. It is recommended that the hub bearings should be renewed as a matter of course, as it is likely to have been damaged during removal. This means that the complete hub assembly must be renewed, since it is not possible to obtain the bearing separately.
7 With the hub removed, examine the stub axle shaft for signs of wear or damage, and if necessary renew it (see Section 15).

Refitting

8 Ensure that the bearing is packed with grease and lubricate the stub axle shaft with clean engine oil.
9 Fit the new bearing assembly, tapping it fully onto the stub axle using a hammer and a tubular drift which bears only on the flat inside edge of the bearing inner race.
10 Fit the new hub nut and tighten it to the specified torque. Stake the nut firmly into the groove on the stub axle to secure it in position, then tap the new hub cap into place in the centre of the hub **(see illustrations)**.

11.10b . . . and tighten it to the specified torque

11.10c Stake the hub nut firmly into the stub axle groove

11.10d . . . and securely fit a new cap to the centre of the hub assembly

11 Refit the rear brake disc/drum as described in Chapter 9.

12 Rear hub bearings - renewal

1 The hub bearing is an integral part of the hub assembly and is not available separately. If the bearing is worn, renew the complete hub assembly as described in Section 11.

13 Rear suspension shock absorber - removal, testing and refitting

Note: *At the time of writing, no information on the active suspension system was available. If your car has active suspension, consult your Peugeot dealer for details of any relevant changes to the following procedure before attempting to remove/refit the shock absorber.*
Note: *A new shock absorber upper mounting nut and lower mounting bolt nut will be required on refitting.*

Removal

1 On Saloon models, from inside the vehicle luggage compartment, slacken and remove the retaining screws and remove the rear trim panel. Release the retaining clips (pull out the centre pins then prise out the complete clip) and peel back the trim panel to gain access to

the strut upper mounting, it may also prove necessary to undo the retaining screw and remove the tie-down hook **(see illustration)**. On some models, if work is being carried out on the left-hand side it will also be necessary to unscrew the fastener and remove the storage compartment to gain the necessary clearance required.
2 On Estate models, open up the tailgate and peel the sealing strip away from the base and relevant side of the body. Undo the retaining screws and remove the rear trim plate then unclip and remove the side storage compartment cover. Remove the retaining clips (pull out the centre pins then remove the complete clip) securing the side of the carpet to the floor then release the retaining clips and remove the plastic storage compartment. Peel back the side trim panel to reveal the strut upper mounting **(see illustration)**.
3 Chock the front wheels, then jack up the rear of the vehicle and support it on axle stands. Remove the relevant rear roadwheel.
4 Using a trolley jack, raise the lower arm until the rear suspension coil spring is slightly compressed.
5 From inside the luggage compartment, slacken and remove the upper mounting nut; discard the nut, a new one should be used on refitting, and lift off the upper mounting rubber, noting which way around it is fitted.
6 From underneath the vehicle, slacken and remove the lower mounting bolt and nut then manoeuvre the shock absorber out of position complete with its mounting rubber and bump

stop/dust cover **(see illustration)**. Slide off the mounting, noting which way around it is fitted, and lift off the bump stop/dust cover.

Testing

7 Examine the shock absorber for signs of fluid leakage or damage. Test the operation of the shock absorber, while holding it in an upright position, by moving the piston through a full stroke and then through short strokes of 50 to 100 mm. In both cases, the resistance felt should be smooth and continuous. If the resistance is jerky, or uneven, or if there is any visible sign of wear or damage, renewal is necessary. Also check the rubber mountings for damage and deterioration. Renew worn components as necessary. Inspect the shank of the mounting bolt for signs of wear or damage, and renew as necessary. The self-locking nuts should be renewed as a matter of course.

Refitting

8 Prior to refitting the shock absorber, mount it upright in the vice, and operate it fully through several strokes in order to prime it. Apply a smear of multi-purpose grease to the lower mounting bolt and contact face of the new nut (Peugeot recommend Molykote G Rapide Plus - available from your Peugeot dealer).
9 Fit the bump stop/dust cover to the shock absorber piston followed by the mounting rubber.
10 Fully extend the piston and manoeuvre the assembly into position. Have an assistant refit the upper mounting cup and rubber to the inside of the vehicle and screw the new upper mounting nut on a few turns.
11 Align the shock absorber lower mounting with the lower arm and refit the mounting bolt. Fit the new nut, tightening it lightly only at this stage.
12 Tighten the upper mounting nut to the specified torque and refit the trim panel(s) in the luggage compartment.
13 Refit the rear roadwheel then lower the vehicle to the ground and tighten the wheel bolts to the specified torque. Rock the vehicle to settle the shock absorber in position then tighten the shock absorber lower mounting to the specified torque setting.

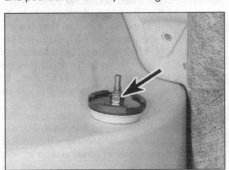

13.1 On Saloon models, peel back the luggage compartment side trim panel to gain access to the shock absorber upper mounting (arrowed)

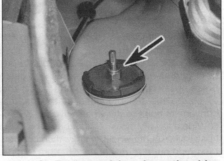

13.2 On Estate models, release the side trim panel as described in text to gain access to the shock absorber upper mounting (arrowed)

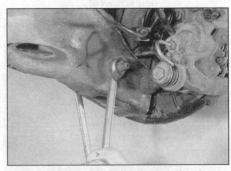

13.6 Slackening the shock absorber lower mounting bolt

10

14 Rear suspension coil spring - removal and refitting

Note: *A new shock absorber lower mounting bolt nut and lower arm pivot bolt nuts will be required on refitting.*

Removal

1 Chock the front wheels, then jack up the rear of the vehicle and support it on axle stands. Remove the relevant rear roadwheel.

2 Position a trolley jack underneath the outer end of the lower arm and raise the arm until the rear suspension coil spring is slightly compressed.

3 Slacken and remove the lower arm outer pivot bolt and nut then unscrew the nut from the inner pivot bolt **(see illustrations)**.

4 Unscrew the shock absorber lower mounting bolt nut and withdraw the bolt. Discard the nut; a new should be used on refitting.

5 Unclip the brake hose and wiring (as applicable) from any relevant clips on the lower arm, so that the arm is free to be lowered.

6 Slowly lower the jack until all spring pressure is released, then remove the coil spring along with its upper and lower spring seats.

7 Inspect the coil spring and its seats for signs of wear or damage and renew if necessary.

Refitting

8 Fit the lower spring seat in position on the lower arm, and seat the upper seat on top of

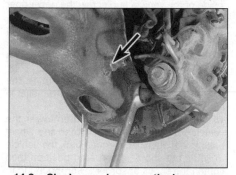

14.3a Slacken and remove the lower arm outer pivot bolt and nut (shock absorber bolt arrowed) . . .

14.3b . . . and loosen the inner pivot bolt

the coil spring. Lubricate the shanks of the shock absorber and lower arm bolts and the contact faces of the new nuts with multi-purpose grease (Peugeot recommend Molykote G Rapide Plus - available from your Peugeot dealer).

9 Manoeuvre the spring into position and carefully raise the lower arm with the jack, ensuring that the coil spring ends are correctly aligned with both seats.

10 Align the lower arm with the swivel hub and insert the outer pivot bolt. Fit the new nuts to the inner and outer pivot bolts tightening them by hand only at this stage.

11 Align the shock absorber with the lower arm and refit its mounting bolt. Fit the new nut to bolt, tightening it lightly only at this stage.

12 Remove the jack from underneath the lower arm and secure the brake hose and wiring (as applicable) in position with all the relevant clips and ties.

13 Refit the rear roadwheel then lower the vehicle to the ground and tighten the wheel bolts to the specified torque. Rock the vehicle to settle the lower arm in position then tighten the shock absorber lower mounting and the lower arm pivot bolts to their specified torque settings.

15 Rear suspension stub axle - removal, overhaul and refitting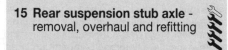

Note: *On refitting new leading arm, lower arm and upper arm pivot bolt nuts will be required on refitting as will a track arm balljoint nut and an anti-roll bar connecting link nut. It is almost certain that a new hub assembly will also be required on refitting.*

Removal

1 Chock the front wheels then jack up the rear of the vehicle and support it on axle stands. Remove the relevant roadwheel.

2 On models equipped with ABS, unbolt the wheel sensor and position it clear of the stub axle (see Chapter 9). Note that there is no need to disconnect the wiring.

3 Remove the hub assembly as described in Section 11. Proceed as described under the relevant sub-heading.

Models with rear drum brakes

4 Minimise fluid loss by first removing the master cylinder reservoir cap, and then tightening it down onto a piece of polythene, to obtain an airtight seal. Alternatively, use a brake hose clamp, a G-clamp or a similar tool to clamp the flexible hose at the nearest convenient point to the wheel cylinder.

5 Wipe away all traces of dirt around the brake hose union on the wheel cylinder then unscrew the union nut and disconnect the brake pipe. Plug the pipe and wheel cylinder unions to minimise fluid loss and prevent dirt entry.

6 Unclip the handbrake cable then slacken and remove the four bolts securing the brake

backplate assembly in position then carefully ease the assembly off the stub axle. Position the plate clear of the stub axle so that it does not hinder removal.

7 Position a hydraulic jack underneath the outer end of the lower arm and raise the jack until the coil spring is slightly compressed.

8 Unscrew the retaining nut and free the anti-roll bar connecting link from the stub axle.

9 Unscrew the retaining nut and free the track arm balljoint from the stub axle.

10 Slacken and remove the upper and lower arm outer pivot bolts and nuts.

11 Unscrew the nut and withdraw the bolt securing the leading arm to the stub axle and remove the stub axle from the vehicle.

12 Inspect the stub axle for signs of wear or damage paying particular attention to the pivot bush. If the stub axle shaft is worn or damage then the assembly must be renewed. The pivot bush is available separately, however renewal is best entrusted to a Peugeot dealer since a hydraulic press and spacers will be required.

Models with rear disc brakes

13 Remove the stub axle as described in paragraphs 6 to 12.

Refitting

14 Obtain all the new nuts required (see Note) and lubricate the shanks of the pivot bolts and contact faces of the new nuts with multi-purpose grease (Peugeot recommend Molykote G Rapide Plus - available from your Peugeot dealer).

15 Offer up the stub axle and insert the upper and lower arm pivot bolts and the leading arm bolt. Fit the new nuts to the bolts, tightening them lightly only at this stage.

16 Locate the anti-roll bar connecting link and track arm balljoints correctly in position then fit the new nuts and tighten them to their specified torque settings.

17 Locate the backplate assembly on the stub axle and tighten its retaining bolts to the specified torque.

18 Fit the new hub assembly as described in Section 11.

19 On models with rear drum brakes, working as described in Chapter 9, reconnect the pipe to the wheel cylinder and tighten its union nut to the specified torque. Remove the clamp/polythene (as applicable) and bleed the hydraulic system noting that if the precautions described have been taken it should only be necessary to bleed the relevant rear brake.

20 On models with ABS, refit the wheel sensor to the stub axle (see Chapter 9).

21 Refit the rear roadwheel then lower the vehicle to the ground and tighten the wheel bolts to the specified torque. Rock the vehicle to settle the stub axle in position then tighten the upper and lower arm pivot bolts and the leading arm pivot bolt to their specified torque settings.

22 Check and, if necessary, adjust the rear wheel alignment as described in Section 32.

16 Rear suspension lower arm - removal, overhaul and refitting

Note: *A new shock absorber lower mounting bolt nut and lower arm pivot bolt nuts will be required on refitting.*

Removal

1 Remove the coil spring as described in Section 14.
2 Withdraw the inner pivot bolt and remove the lower arm from the vehicle.

Overhaul

3 Thoroughly clean the lower arm and the area around the arm mountings, removing all traces of dirt and underseal if necessary, then check carefully for cracks, distortion or any other signs of wear or damage, paying particular attention to the pivot bushes (the outer bush is pressed into the stub axle), and renew components as necessary.
4 Renewal of the inner pivot bush will required the use of a hydraulic press and several spacers and should therefore be entrusted to a Peugeot dealer with access to the necessary equipment. If renewal of outer pivot bush is necessary, it will be necessary to remove the stub axle (see Section 15).

Refitting

5 Lubricate the shanks of the pivot bolts and the contact faces of the new nuts with multi-purpose grease (Peugeot recommend Molykote G Rapide Plus - available from your Peugeot dealer).
6 Offer up the lower arm and insert the inner pivot bolt.
7 Refit the coil spring with reference to Section 14. On completion check and, if necessary, adjust the rear wheel alignment as described in Section 32.

17 Rear suspension upper arm - removal and refitting

Right-hand arm

1 To gain the necessary clearance required to withdraw the inner pivot bolt, it is necessary to drop the complete rear suspension and subframe assembly out of position **(see illustration)**. This task should be entrusted to a Peugeot dealer. On refitting they will fit the bolt the opposite way around so that it can be removed in future, should the need arise.
2 A way around this is to cut the head off the original pivot bolt so that it can be withdrawn in the opposite direction. This avoids the need to remove the rear suspension and subframe assembly, so saving a lot of time and effort. Using this method, the arm can be removed and refitted as described below.

Left-hand arm

Note: *New pivot bolt nuts will be required on refitting.*

Removal

3 Chock the front wheels then jack up the rear of the vehicle and support it on axle stands. Remove the relevant roadwheel.
4 Position a hydraulic jack underneath the outer end of the lower arm and raise the jack until the coil spring is slightly compressed.
5 Slacken and remove the nuts then withdraw the inner and outer pivot bolts and remove the arm from underneath the vehicle, freeing it from the handbrake cable **(see illustrations)**.
6 Thoroughly clean the arm and the area around the arm mountings, removing all traces of dirt and underseal if necessary, then check carefully for cracks, distortion or any other signs of wear or damage, paying particular attention to the pivot bushes. If there is any sign of wear or damage the arm must be renewed.

Refitting

7 Lubricate the shanks of the pivot bolts and the contact faces of the nuts with multi-purpose grease (Peugeot recommend Molykote G Rapide Plus - available from your Peugeot dealer).
8 Offer up the arm and insert the pivot bolts. Fit the new nuts to the bolts tighten them lightly only at this stage.
9 Refit the rear roadwheel then lower the vehicle to the ground and tighten the wheel bolts to the specified torque. Rock the vehicle to settle the stub axle in position then tighten the upper arm pivot bolts to the specified torque setting.
10 On completion check and, if necessary, adjust the rear wheel alignment as described in Section 32.

18 Rear suspension leading arm - removal, overhaul and refitting

Note: *New leading arm pivot bolt nuts will be required on refitting.*

Removal

1 Chock the front wheels then jack up the rear of the vehicle and support it on axle stands. Remove the relevant roadwheel.
2 Position a hydraulic jack underneath the outer end of the lower arm and raise the jack until the coil spring is slightly compressed.
3 Unscrew the nut and remove the washer then withdraw the pivot bolt and washer securing the leading arm to the stub axle **(see illustration)**.
4 Unscrew the three bolts securing the leading arm mounting bracket to the vehicle body and remove the arm assembly **(see illustration)**. **Note:** *Do not slacken the leading arm pivot bush bolt unless renewal of the bush/mounting bracket is necessary.*

Overhaul

5 Slacken and remove the nut and pivot bolt and separate the front mounting bracket and trailing arm.

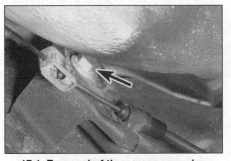

17.1 Removal of the rear suspension right-hand upper arm may require removal of the subframe - see text

17.5a Slacken and remove the inner pivot bolt and nut . . .

17.5b . . . and the outer pivot bolt and nut, and remove the upper arm from the rear suspension

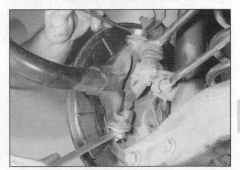

18.3 Slacken and remove the pivot bolt and nut securing the leading arm to the stub axle . . .

10

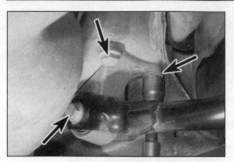

18.4 . . . then undo the three mounting bracket-to-body bolts (arrowed), and remove the leading arm assembly

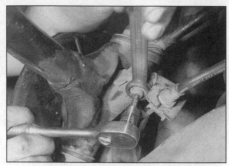

19.4 Unscrew the nut and free the track arm balljoint from the stub axle . . .

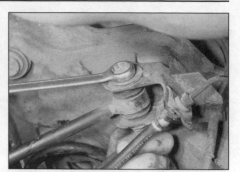

19.5 . . . then remove the inner pivot bolt arrangement and remove the arm

6 Thoroughly clean the leading arm and the area around the arm mountings, removing all traces of dirt and underseal if necessary, then check carefully for cracks, distortion or any other signs of wear or damage paying particular attention to the mounting bushes. If either bush requires renewal, it is recommended that the task is entrusted to a Peugeot dealer or suitably equipped garage with access to a hydraulic press and spacers which will be needed to press the bushes out of position and install the new ones. If the front bush requires renewal, it may prove easier/more cost effective to renew the complete mounting bracket assembly. Inspect the pivot bolts for signs of wear or damage and renew as necessary.

Refitting

7 Lubricate the shanks of the bolts and the contact faces of the new nuts with multi-purpose grease (Peugeot recommend Molykote G Rapide Plus - available from your Peugeot dealer).

8 If the trailing arm and bracket were separated, refit the pivot bolt and screw on the new nut, tightening it by hand only at this stage.

9 Manoeuvre the arm assembly into position and refit the mounting bracket retaining bolts.

10 Insert the pivot bolt and washer securing the arm to the stub axle then fit the washer and new nut, tightening it lightly only at this stage.

11 Tighten the mounting bracket to body bolts to the specified torque then refit the roadwheel and lower the vehicle to the ground. Tighten the wheel bolts to the specified torque then rock the vehicle to settle the stub axle in position. Tighten the leading arm front and (where slackened) rear pivot bolt to their specified torque settings.

12 On completion check and, if necessary, adjust the rear wheel alignment (Section 32).

19 Rear suspension track arm - removal and refitting

Note: *A new track arm pivot bolt nut and balljoint nut will be required on refitting.*

Removal

1 Chock the front wheels then jack up the

rear of the vehicle and support it on axle stands. Remove the relevant roadwheel.

2 Position a hydraulic jack underneath the outer end of the lower arm and raise the jack until the coil spring is slightly compressed.

3 Prior to disturbing the track arm, make alignment marks between the inner pivot bolt special washer and subframe. These marks can then be used on refitting to set the rear wheel alignment.

4 Slacken and remove the nut securing the track arm balljoint to the stub axle and free the balljoint shank; if necessary, prevent the balljoint shank from rotating by retaining it with an Allen key whilst the nut is slackened (see illustration).

5 Unscrew the nut from the inner pivot bolt and remove the special washer (see illustration). Withdraw the pivot bolt and remove the track arm from the vehicle.

6 Thoroughly clean the arm and the area around the arm mountings, removing all traces of dirt and underseal if necessary, then check carefully for cracks, distortion or any other signs of wear or damage, paying particular attention to the balljoint. If there is any sign of wear or damage the complete arm must be renewed.

Refitting

7 Clean the threads of the pivot bolt and balljoint and lubricate the contact faces of the new nuts with multi-purpose grease (Peugeot recommend Molykote G Rapide Plus - available from your Peugeot dealer).

8 Manoeuvre the track arm into position and insert the pivot bolt. Slide the special washer

onto the rear of the bolt, making sure it is correctly engaged with the bolts and is positioned against the lug on the subframe, and fit the new nut tightening it lightly only. Align the marks made prior to removal and tighten the bolt to the specified torque setting.

9 Locate the balljoint shank in the stub axle and fit the new nut, tightening it to the specified torque setting.

10 Refit the rear roadwheel then lower the vehicle to the ground and tighten the wheel bolts to the specified torque.

11 On completion check and, if necessary, adjust the rear wheel alignment as described in Section 32.

20 Rear suspension anti-roll bar - removal and refitting

Note: *New connecting link nuts will be required on refitting.*

Removal

1 Chock the front wheels then jack up the rear of the vehicle and support it on axle stands. Remove both rear roadwheels.

2 Unscrew the retaining nuts and free the connecting links from either end of the anti-roll bar (see illustration).

3 Prior to removal make alignment marks between the mounting bushes and the anti-roll.

4 Slacken and remove the retaining nuts/bolt (as applicable) and remove the anti-roll bar mounting clamps (see illustration).

20.2 Unscrew the nuts, and free the connecting links from the anti-roll bar ends

20.4 Unscrew the nuts/bolt (arrowed) and remove the anti-roll bar mounting clamps

22.4 On refitting, tighten the steering wheel retaining bolt to the specified torque

22.7 Unscrew the retaining bolt and make alignment marks between the steering wheel and column . . .

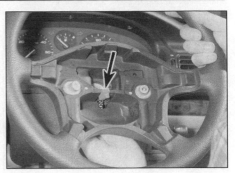

22.8 . . . then remove the wheel, taking great care not to damage the airbag unit wiring (arrowed)

5 Manoeuvre the anti-roll bar out from underneath the vehicle, and remove the mounting bushes from the bar.

6 Carefully examine the anti-roll bar components for signs of wear, damage or deterioration, paying particular attention to the mounting bushes. Renew worn components as necessary.

Refitting

7 Fit the rubber mounting bushes to the anti-roll bar. Align the bushes with the marks made prior to removal and position them so that their flat surfaces are at the top and the bush splits are facing towards the front.

8 Offer up the anti-roll bar, and manoeuvre it into position. Refit the mounting clamps and refit the retaining bolt and nuts. Engage the connecting links with the ends of the bar then tighten the mounting clamp retaining bolts to the specified torque.

9 Fit the new retaining nuts to the connecting links and tighten them to the specified torque setting.

10 Refit the roadwheels then lower the vehicle to the ground and tighten the wheel bolts to the specified torque.

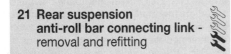

21 Rear suspension anti-roll bar connecting link - removal and refitting

Note: *New connecting link nuts will be required on refitting.*

Removal

1 Chock the front wheels then jack up the rear of the vehicle and support on axle stands. Remove the relevant roadwheel.

2 Slacken and remove the nuts securing the connecting link to the anti-roll bar and stub axle and remove the link from the vehicle; if necessary, retaining the balljoint shank with an Allen key to prevent rotation as the nut is slackened. Discard the nuts, new ones should be used on refitting.

3 Inspect the link for signs of wear or damage and renew if necessary.

Refitting

4 Refitting is the reverse of removal, using new nuts and tightening them to the specified torque setting.

22 Steering wheel - removal and refitting

Note: *Models equipped with a driver's side airbag have the word AIRBAG stamped on the steering wheel pad.*

Models without air bag

Removal

1 Set the front wheels in the straight-ahead position, and engage the steering lock.

2 Carefully ease off the steering wheel centre pad/trim plate, then slacken and remove the steering wheel retaining bolt.

3 Mark the steering wheel and steering column shaft in relation to each other, then lift the steering wheel off the column splines.

> **HAYNES HiNT**
> *If the wheel is tight, tap it up near the centre, using the palm of your hand, or twist it from side to side, whilst pulling upwards to release it from the shaft splines.*

Refitting

4 Refitting is a reversal of removal, noting the following points:

a) *Prior to refitting, ensure that the indicator switch stem is in its central position. Failure to do this could lead to the steering wheel lug breaking the switch tab as the steering wheel is refitted.*

b) *On refitting, align the marks made on removal, and tighten the retaining bolt to the specified torque* **(see illustration)**.

Models with an air bag

 Warning: Refer to the precautions given in Chapter 12 before proceeding.

Removal

5 Remove the air bag unit as described in Chapter 12.

6 Position the front wheels in the straight-ahead position and engage the steering lock.

7 Slacken and remove the steering wheel retaining bolt then mark the steering wheel and steering column shaft in relation to each other **(see illustration)**.

8 Release the airbag unit wiring connector from its retaining clips and lift the steering wheel off the column splines, taking care not to damage the wiring **(see illustration)**.

> **HAYNES HiNT**
> *If the wheel is tight, tap it up near the centre, using the palm of your hand, or twist it from side to side, whilst pulling upwards to release it from the shaft splines.*

Refitting

9 Refitting is a reversal of removal, noting the points listed in paragraph 4. Prior to refitting the steering wheel, ensure that the front wheels are still in the straight-ahead position and check that the airbag contact unit is correctly centralised (see Chapter 12, Section 26). On completion, refit the airbag unit as described in Chapter 12

23 Steering column - removal, inspection and refitting

Note: *On models equipped with a driver's side airbag, refer to the precautions given in Chapter 12 before proceeding.*

Note: *A special socket (Peugeot no 0718) will be required to remove/refit the column mounting bolts. A new clamp bolt nut will also be needed on refitting.*

Removal

1 Disconnect the battery negative terminal.

2 Remove the steering wheel as described in Section 22.

10

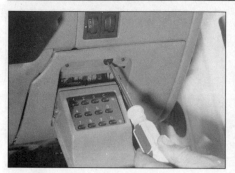

23.6a Lower the fuse box cover . . .

23.6b . . . then disconnect the wiring from the key pad. Undo the screws and remove the driver's side lower facia panel

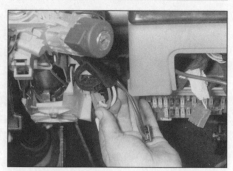

23.7 Disconnect the ignition switch wiring connectors, and free the wiring from its retaining clips

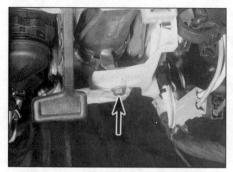

23.8 Undo the retaining bolt (arrowed) and free the wiring bracket from the steering column

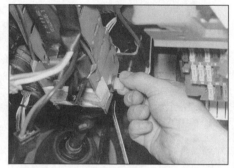

23.9 Lock the column in position by pressing in the locking button on the column base

23.10 Make alignment marks between the column joint and intermediate shaft, then remove the clamp bolt (arrowed)

3 On models with an airbag, remove the contact unit from the top of the steering column as described in Chapter 12.

4 On all models, remove the combination switches from the top of the steering column as described in Chapter 12.

5 Open up the engine immobiliser key pad.

6 Rotate the fastener through 90° and lower the fusebox cover. Disconnect the wiring connector from the key pad, then slacken and remove the retaining screws, and remove the driver's side lower panel from the facia **(see illustrations)**.

7 Trace the wiring back from the ignition switch and disconnect it at the wiring connectors **(see illustration)**.

8 Undo the retaining bolt and free the wiring retaining bracket from the column **(see illustration)**. Release the wiring from its

retaining clips and position it clear so that it does hinder column removal.

9 Lock the steering column in position by pressing in the locking button on the base of the column shaft **(see illustration)**.

10 Using paint or a suitable marker pen, make alignment marks between the column universal joint and the intermediate shaft then slacken and remove the clamp bolt **(see illustration)**.

11 Slacken and remove the mounting bolts from the top of the column. Slide the column assembly upwards, to release its rear retaining clip and free it from the intermediate shaft, and remove it from the vehicle **(see illustrations)**.

Inspection

12 Before refitting the steering column, examine the column and mountings for signs of damage and deformation, and renew as

necessary. Check the steering shaft for signs of free play in the column bushes, and check the universal joints for signs of damage or roughness in the joint bearings. If any damage or wear is found on the steering column universal joint or shaft bushes, the column must be renewed as an assembly.

Refitting

13 Prior to refitting release the clamp bolt nut retainer tang and remove the old nut **(see illustration)**. Fit the new nut into the retainer, making sure it is fitted the correct way around, and securely refit the retainer to the column.

14 Align the marks made prior to removal and engage the column universal joint with the intermediate shaft.

15 Slide the column assembly into position making sure its mounting bracket is correctly

23.11a Slacken and remove the mounting bolts (arrowed) . . .

23.11b . . . then free the column from the intermediate shaft and remove it

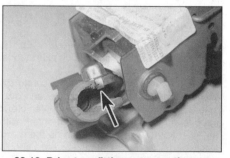

23.13 Prior to refitting, remove the nut retainer (arrowed) and renew the clamp bolt nut

25.4 Turn the ignition key to the first position, and slide out the lock cylinder retaining clip (shown with steering column removed for clarity)

25.5a Remove the key then disengage the wiring clip . . .

25.5b . . . and manoeuvre the ignition switch wiring block away from steering column

engaged with the bracket. Refit the column mounting bolts and tighten them to the specified torque setting.

16 Refit the universal joint clamp bolt and tighten it to the specified torque setting. Unlock the column by pulling out the locking button.

17 The remainder of refitting is a direct reversal of the removal procedure, noting the following.

a) Ensure that all wiring is correctly routed and retained by all the necessary clips and ties.

b) Refit the steering wheel as described in Section 22.

24 Steering column intermediate shaft - removal, inspection and refitting

Note: New clamp bolt nuts will be required on refitting.

Removal

1 Remove the steering column as described in Section 23.

2 Firmly apply the handbrake then jack up the front of the vehicle and support it on axle stands.

3 Make alignment marks between the intermediate shaft joint and the steering gear pinion then slacken and remove the clamp bolt and nut. Discard the nut, a new one should be used on refitting.

4 Slacken and remove the three nuts securing the intermediate shaft gaiter to the bulkhead.

5 From inside the car, slide the gaiter off the intermediate shaft then detach the shaft from the steering gear and remove it from the car.

Inspection

6 Inspect the intermediate shaft assembly for signs of wear or damage, paying particular attention to the universal joint. If the shaft or joint show any sign of wear then the complete shaft assembly must be renewed. Renew the rubber gaiter if it shows signs of damage or deterioration.

Refitting

7 Align the marks made prior to removal and engage the intermediate shaft with the steering gear pinion splines.

8 Slide the rubber gaiter along the intermediate shaft and into position in the bulkhead.

9 From underneath the vehicle, fit the intermediate shaft clamp bolt and the new retaining nut and tighten it to the specified torque setting.

10 Refit the gaiter retaining nuts and tighten them securely.

11 Refit the steering column as described in Section 23.

25 Ignition switch/ steering column lock - removal and refitting

Ignition switch wiring block

Removal

1 Disconnect the battery negative terminal.

2 Open up the engine immobiliser key pad and disconnect the wiring connector. Rotate the fastener through 90° and lower the fusebox cover then slacken and remove the retaining screws and remove the driver's side lower panel from the facia.

3 Undo the retaining screws securing the steering column lower shroud in position then unclip both the upper and lower shrouds from the column, disconnecting the cruise control and/or radio control switch wiring connector(s) (as applicable). Remove lower shroud and position the upper shroud clear of the ignition switch.

4 Insert the key into the lock and turn it to the first (A) position. Slide out the retaining clip then return the key to the off position and remove it from the lock cylinder **(see illustration)**.

5 Manoeuvre the ignition switch block wiring clip out of position and remove the wiring block from the rear of the lock housing **(see illustrations)**.

6 Trace the wiring back from the ignition switch, and disconnect its wiring connectors from the main wiring harness.

Refitting

7 Prior to refitting, it will be necessary to align the wiring block centre pin correctly with the lock cylinder. The two are located together by means of a Y-shaped dog on the lock cylinder centre pin; the dog is not symmetrical and the cylinder and wiring block will only engage correctly in one position.

8 Slide the ignition switch wiring block into position and refit the wiring clip, making sure it is correctly engaged with the lock housing.

9 Fit the key and turn the lock cylinder to position (A) so that the lock cylinder fully engages with the housing. Slide the retaining clip into position then check the operation of the ignition switch/steering column lock.

10 Reconnect the wiring to the main harness ensuring it is correctly routed and retained by all the necessary clips.

11 The remainder of refitting is the reverse of removal.

Lock cylinder

Removal

12 Remove the wiring block as described in paragraphs 1 to 5.

13 Slide the lock cylinder assembly out of position, noting the correct fitted position of the steering lock wedge, and separate it from its cover. Note the correct fitted position of the locating pins in the housing and, if necessary, remove them for safe-keeping **(see illustrations)**.

Refitting

14 Engage the steering lock wedge with the lock cylinder arm then refit the trim cover to the lock cylinder assembly. Ensure that the locating pins are in position and insert the assembly into the housing, aligning the steering lock wedge with the housing slot.

15 Refit the ignition switch wiring block as described earlier.

10

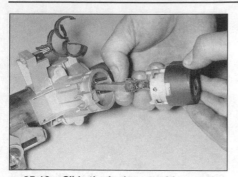
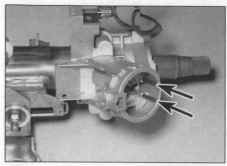
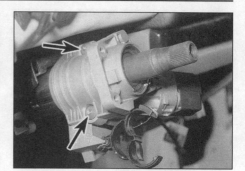

25.13a Slide the lock assembly out of position, noting the correct fitted position of the wedge . . .

25.13b . . . and the locating pins (arrowed)

25.18 Steering lock assembly shear-bolts (arrowed)

Lock assembly

Note: *New shear-bolts will be required on refitting.*

Removal

16 Carry out the operations described in paragraphs 1 to 3.
17 Trace the wiring back from the ignition switch, and disconnect its wiring connectors from the main wiring harness.
18 Using a hammer and suitable punch, tap the lock assembly retaining bolts around until they can be unscrewed by hand **(see illustration)**. Remove the bolts and lift the lock assembly away from the steering column.

Refitting

19 Offer up the lock assembly, making sure it is correctly engaged with the column, and fit the new shear-bolts.
20 Evenly and progressively tighten the shear-bolts until both are lightly tightened. Check the operation of the lock assembly then tighten each bolt until its head shears off.
21 Reconnect the wiring to the main harness ensuring it is correctly routed and retained by all the necessary clips then refit all the disturbed trim panels.

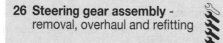

26 Steering gear assembly - removal, overhaul and refitting

Note: *New track rod balljoint nuts and an intermediate shaft clamp bolt nut will be required on refitting.*

Removal

1 Firmly apply the handbrake then jack up the front of the vehicle and support it on axle stands. Remove both front roadwheels.
2 Release the cable-ties and unclip the heatshield from the top of the steering gear. Where necessary, depress the retaining clip and disconnect the wiring connector from the steering gear pinion housing.
3 Slacken and remove the nuts securing the steering gear track rod balljoints to the swivel hubs. Release the balljoint tapered shanks using a universal balljoint separator and

recover the protector plates. Discard the nuts, new ones will be needed on refitting.
4 Using paint or a suitable marker pen, make alignment marks between the intermediate shaft joint and the steering gear pinion, then slacken and remove the clamp bolt and nut. Discard the nut, a new one should be used on refitting **(see illustration)**.
5 Using brake hose clamps, clamp both the supply and return hoses near the power steering fluid reservoir. This will minimise fluid loss during subsequent operations.
6 Mark the unions to ensure that they are correctly positioned on reassembly, then unscrew the feed and return pipe union nuts/bolts (as applicable) from the steering gear assembly; be prepared for fluid spillage, and position a suitable container beneath the pipes whilst unscrewing the union nuts. Disconnect both pipes, and plug the pipe ends and steering gear orifices, to prevent fluid leakage and to keep dirt out of the hydraulic system.
7 Free the power steering pipes from any retaining clips, and position them clear of the steering gear.
8 Slacken the steering gear mounting bolts, and recover the nuts and washers from the top of the steering gear **(see illustration)**. Withdraw the mounting bolts, and recover the spacers which are fitted between the steering gear and the subframe.
9 Free the steering gear pinion from the intermediate shaft joint and manoeuvre it out towards the driver's side of the vehicle.

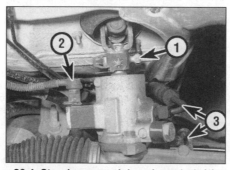

26.4 Steering gear pinion clamp bolt (1), wiring connector (2) and fluid pipes (3)

Overhaul

10 Examine the steering gear assembly for signs of wear or damage, and check that the rack moves freely throughout the full length of its travel, with no signs of roughness or excessive free play between the steering gear pinion and rack. Inspect all the steering gear fluid unions for signs of leakage, and check that all union nuts are securely tightened. On models with invariable power steering, also examine the steering gear hydraulic ram for signs of fluid leakage or damage, and if necessary renew it.
11 It is possible to overhaul the steering gear assembly housing components, but this task should be entrusted to a Peugeot dealer. The only components which can be renewed easily by the home mechanic are the steering gear gaiters, the track rod balljoints and the track rods. Track rod balljoint, steering gear gaiter and track rod renewal procedures are covered elsewhere in this Chapter.

Refitting

12 Manoeuvre the steering gear into position and engage it with the intermediate shaft, aligning the marks made prior to removal.
13 Slide the spacers into position between the subframe and steering gear and fit the washers and nuts to the top of the steering gear. Insert the mounting bolts and tighten them to the specified torque.
14 Reconnect the fluid pipes to the steering gear and securely tighten their union

26.8 Slacken and remove the steering gear-to-subframe bolts (arrowed)

nuts/bolts. Secure the pipes in position with all the necessary clips and ties and remove the clamps from the hoses.

15 Fit the intermediate shaft clamp bolt and the new nut, tightening it to the specified torque.

16 Ensure that the protector plates are in position then locate the track rod balljoints in the swivel hubs. Fit the new retaining nuts and tighten them to the specified torque.

17 Reconnect the wiring connector (where fitted) then refit the heatshield to the steering gear and secure it in position with new cable-ties. Refit the roadwheels then lower the vehicle to the ground and tighten the roadwheel bolts to the specified torque.

18 Top-up the fluid reservoir and bleed the hydraulic system as described in Section 28.

19 On completion check and, if necessary, adjust the front wheel alignment as described in Section 32.

27 Steering gear rubber gaiters - renewal

Models with variable steering

1 Remove the track rod balljoint as described in Section 30.

2 Mark the correct fitted position of the gaiter on the track rod, then release the retaining clips (where fitted) and slide the gaiter off the steering gear housing and track rod end.

3 Thoroughly clean the track rod and the steering gear housing, using fine abrasive paper to polish off any corrosion, burrs or sharp edges, which might damage the new gaiter's sealing lips on installation. Scrape off all the grease from the old gaiter, and apply it to the track rod inner balljoint. (This assumes that grease has not been lost or contaminated as a result of damage to the old gaiter. Use fresh grease if in doubt.)

4 Carefully slide the new gaiter onto the track rod end, and locate it on the steering gear housing. Align the outer edge of the gaiter with the mark made on the track rod prior to removal, then secure it in position with new retaining clips (where fitted).

5 Refit the track rod balljoint as described in Section 30.

Models with invariable steering

6 On these models, it is only possible to renew the gaiter nearest the drive pinion, ie the right-hand gaiter on right-hand-drive models, and the left-hand gaiter on left-hand-drive models. This can be renewed as described above in paragraphs 1 to 5.

7 The task of renewing the opposite gaiter should be entrusted to a Peugeot dealer. This is necessary since it is not possible to pass the gaiter over the steering rack stud to which the hydraulic ram is fixed. Therefore, the steering gear must be dismantled and the

rack removed from the housing to allow the gaiter to be renewed.

8 The only task on this end of the assembly which can be carried out by the home mechanic is the renewal of the track rod inner balljoint dust cover. The dust cover can be renewed once the track rod balljoint has been removed as described in Section 30. On refitting, ensure that the dust cover is correctly located on the track rod and steering rack, then refit the balljoint.

28 Power steering system - bleeding

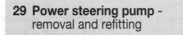

1 This procedure will only be necessary when anyof the hydraulic system has been disconnected.

2 Referring to "Weekly checks", remove the fluid reservoir filler cap, and top-up with the specified fluid to the upper level mark.

3 With the engine stopped, slowly move the steering from lock-to-lock several times to purge out the trapped air, then top-up the level in the fluid reservoir. Repeat this procedure until the fluid level in the reservoir does not drop any further.

4 Start the engine, then slowly move the steering from lock-to-lock several times to purge out any remaining air in the system. Repeat this procedure until bubbles cease to appear in the fluid reservoir.

5 If, when turning the steering, an abnormal noise is heard from the fluid lines, it indicates that there is still air in the system. Check this by turning the wheels to the straight-ahead position and switching off the engine. If the fluid level in the reservoir rises, then air is present in the system, and further bleeding is necessary.

6 Once all traces of air have been removed from the power steering hydraulic system, turn the engine off and allow the system to cool. Once cool, check that fluid level is up to the upper mark on the power steering fluid reservoir, topping-up if necessary.

29 Power steering pump - removal and refitting

Removal

1 Release the drivebelt tension as described in Chapter 1, and unhook the drivebelt from the pump pulley. The power steering pump is mounted directly above, or directly below the alternator, depending on engine type and specification level. If the pump is mounted below the alternator, access is most easily obtained from underneath the car.

2 Using brake hose clamps, clamp both the supply and return hoses near the power steering fluid reservoir. This will minimise fluid loss during subsequent operations.

3 Undo the retaining nut, and free the fluid hose retaining clip from the rear of the pump (where fitted).

4 Slacken the retaining clip, and disconnect the fluid supply hose from the pump then slacken the union nut, and disconnect the feed pipe. Be prepared for some fluid spillage as the pipe and hose are disconnected, and plug the hose/pipe end and pump unions, to minimise fluid loss and prevent the entry of dirt into the system.

5 Slacken and remove the pump mounting bolts and withdraw the pump from its bracket.

6 If the power steering pump is faulty it must be renewed. The pump is a sealed unit and cannot be overhauled.

Refitting

7 Manoeuvre the pump into position, then refit its mounting bolts and tighten them securely.

8 Reconnect the feed pipe to the pump and securely tighten the union nut. Refit the supply pipe to the pump, and securely tighten its retaining clip. Remove the brake hose clamps used to minimise fluid loss.

9 Where applicable, refit the fluid hose retaining clip to the rear of the pump, and securely tighten its retaining nut.

10 Refit the drivebelt to the pump pulley, and tension it as described in Chapter 1.

11 On completion, bleed the hydraulic system as described in Section 28.

30 Track rod balljoint - removal and refitting

Note: A new balljoint retaining nut will be required on refitting.

Removal

1 Apply the handbrake, then jack up the front of the vehicle and support it on axle stands. Remove the appropriate front roadwheel.

2 If the balljoint is to be re-used, use a straight-edge and a scriber, or similar, to mark its relationship to the track rod.

3 Hold the track rod, and unscrew the balljoint locknut by a quarter of a turn. Do not move the locknut from this position, as it will serve as a handy reference mark on refitting.

4 Slacken and remove the nut securing the track rod balljoint to the swivel hub; discard the nut a new one will be needed on refitting. Release the balljoint tapered shank using a universal balljoint separator and recover the protector plate (if loose) **(see illustrations)**.

5 Counting the **exact** number of turns necessary to do so, unscrew the balljoint from the track rod end.

6 Count the number of exposed threads between the end of the balljoint and the locknut, and record this figure. If a new balljoint is to be fitted, unscrew the locknut from the old balljoint.

10

30.4a Slacken and remove the track rod balljoint retaining nut . . .

30.4b . . . then release the balljoint shank using a universal balljoint separator

7 Carefully clean the balljoint and the threads. Renew the balljoint if its movement is sloppy or too stiff, if excessively worn, or if damaged in any way; carefully check the stud taper and threads. If the balljoint gaiter is damaged, the complete balljoint assembly must be renewed; it is not possible to obtain the gaiter separately.

Refitting

8 If a new balljoint is to be fitted, screw the locknut onto its threads, and position it so that the same number of exposed threads are visible, as was noted prior to removal.
9 Screw the balljoint into the track rod by the number of turns noted on removal. This should bring the balljoint locknut to within a quarter of a turn from the track rod, with the alignment marks that were made on removal (if applicable) lined up.
10 Ensure that the protector plate is in position then locate the balljoint shank in the swivel hub. Fit a new retaining nut and tighten it to the specified torque.
11 Refit the roadwheel, then lower the vehicle to the ground and tighten the roadwheel bolts to the specified torque.
12 Check and, if necessary, adjust the front wheel alignment as described in Section 32, then securely tighten the balljoint locknut.

31 Track rod - removal and refitting

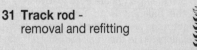

Note: A special wrench (Peugeot number 0707) will be required to remove/refit the track rod inner balljoint from the end of the steering rack. The special wrench engages with the balljoint housing allowing the track rod to be easily slackened/tightened without the risk of damage. Note that without access to the special tool, track rod removal will be difficult, especially without causing damage.
Note: A new balljoint retaining nut will be required on refitting.

Removal

1 Remove the track rod balljoint as described in Section 30.
2 Either release the retaining clips and slide the steering gear gaiter off the end of the track

rod, or release the track rod balljoint dust cover from rack, and slide it off the track rod (as applicable). Refer to Section 27 for further information.
3 Using the special wrench (see note at the start of the Section), unscrew the track rod inner balljoint from the steering rack end. Take great care not to place excess strain on the rack as the joint is unscrewed, if necessary, prevent the steering rack from turning by holding it carefully with a pair of grips. Take great care not to mark the surfaces of the rack and balljoint.
4 Remove the track rod assembly. Examine the track rod inner balljoint for signs of slackness or tight spots, and check that the track rod itself is straight and free from damage. If necessary, renew the track rod; it is also recommended that the steering gear gaiter/dust cover is renewed.

Refitting

5 Screw the balljoint into the steering rack, and tighten it to the specified torque. If necessary, retain the steering rack with a pair of grips, again taking great care not to damage or mark the track rod balljoint or steering rack.
6 Where a gaiter was removed, carefully slide on the new gaiter, and locate it on the steering gear housing. Turn the steering fully from lock-to-lock, to check that the gaiter is correctly positioned on the track rod, then secure it in position with new retaining clips (where fitted).
7 Where a dust cover was removed, carefully slide on the new cover, and locate it in its grooves on the steering rack collar and track rod.
8 Refit the track rod balljoint as described in Section 30.

32 Wheel alignment and steering angles - information, checking and adjustment

Definitions

1 A car's steering and suspension geometry is defined in four basic settings - all angles are expressed in degrees (toe settings are also expressed as a measurement); the steering

axis is defined as an imaginary line drawn through the axis of the suspension strut, extended where necessary to contact the ground.
2 **Camber** is the angle between each roadwheel and a vertical line drawn through its centre and tyre contact patch, when viewed from the front or rear of the car. Positive camber is when the roadwheels are tilted outwards from the vertical at the top; negative camber is when they are tilted inwards. The camber angle is not adjustable
3 **Castor** is the angle between the steering axis and a vertical line drawn through each roadwheel's centre and tyre contact patch, when viewed from the side of the car. Positive castor is when the steering axis is tilted so that it contacts the ground ahead of the vertical; negative castor is when it contacts the ground behind the vertical. The castor angle is not adjustable.
4 **Toe** is the difference, viewed from above, between lines drawn through the roadwheel centres and the car's centre-line. "Toe-in" is when the roadwheels point inwards, towards each other at the front, while "toe-out" is when they splay outwards from each other at the front.
5 The front wheel toe setting is adjusted by screwing the track rod in or out of its balljoints, to alter the effective length of the track rod assembly.
6 Rear wheel toe setting is also adjustable. The toe setting is adjusted by slackening and rotating the track arm inner pivot bolt.

Checking and adjustment

7 Due to the special measuring equipment necessary to check the wheel alignment and steering angles, and the skill required to use it properly, the checking and adjustment of these settings is best left to a Peugeot dealer or similar expert. Note that most tyre-fitting shops now possess sophisticated checking equipment. The following is provided as a guide, should the owner decide to carry out a DIY check.

Front wheel toe setting

8 The front wheel toe setting is checked by measuring the distance between the front and rear inside edges of the roadwheel rims. Proprietary toe measurement gauges are available from motor accessory shops. Adjustment is made by screwing the balljoints in or out of their track rods, to alter the effective length of the track rod assemblies.
9 For **accurate** checking, the vehicle **must** be at the kerb weight, ie unladen and with a full tank of fuel.
10 Before starting work, check first that the tyre sizes and types are as specified, then check the tyre pressures and tread wear, the roadwheel run-out, the condition of the hub bearings, the steering wheel free play, and the condition of the front suspension components (see "Weekly checks" and Chapter 1). Correct any faults found.

11 Park the vehicle on level ground, check that the front roadwheels are in the straight-ahead position, then rock the rear and front ends to settle the suspension. Release the handbrake, and roll the vehicle backwards 1 metre, then forwards again, to relieve any stresses in the steering and suspension components.

12 Measure the distance between the front edges of the wheel rims and the rear edges of the rims. Subtract the rear measurement from the front measurement, and check that the result is within the specified range.

13 If adjustment is necessary, apply the handbrake, then jack up the front of the vehicle and support it securely on axle stands. Turn the steering wheel onto full-left lock, and record the number of exposed threads on the right-hand track rod end. Now turn the steering onto full-right lock, and record the number of threads on the left-hand side. If there are the same number of threads visible on both sides, then subsequent adjustment should be made equally on both sides. If there are more threads visible on one side than the other, it will be necessary to compensate for this during adjustment. **Note:** *It is most important that after adjustment, the same number of threads are visible on each track rod end.*

14 First clean the track rod threads; if they are corroded, apply penetrating fluid before starting adjustment. Release the rubber gaiter outboard clips (where necessary), and peel back the gaiters; apply a smear of grease to

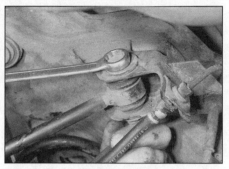

32.20 Rear wheel toe setting is adjusted by slackening and rotating the track arm inner pivot bolt

the inside of the gaiters, so that both are free, and will not be twisted or strained as their respective track rods are rotated.

15 Use a straight-edge and a scriber or similar to mark the relationship of each track rod to its balljoint then, holding each track rod in turn, unscrew its locknut fully.

16 Alter the length of the track rods, bearing in mind the note made in paragraph 13. **Note:** *One complete rotation of the track rod equals approximately 2 mm of adjustment.* Screw them onto or off the balljoints, rotating the track rod using an open-ended spanner fitted to the flats provided on the track rod. Shortening the track rods (screwing them into their balljoints) will reduce toe-in/increase toe-out.

17 When the setting is correct, hold the track rods and tighten the balljoint locknuts to the specified torque setting. Check that the balljoints are seated correctly in their sockets, and count the exposed threads to check the length of both track rods. If they are not the same, then the adjustment has not been made equally, and problems will be encountered with tyre scrubbing in turns; also, the steering wheel spokes will no longer be horizontal when the wheels are in the straight-ahead position.

18 If the track rod lengths are the same, lower the vehicle to the ground and re-check the toe setting; re-adjust if necessary. When the setting is correct, tighten the track rod balljoint locknuts to the specified torque. Ensure that the rubber gaiters are seated correctly, and are not twisted or strained, and secure them in position with new retaining clips (where necessary).

Rear wheel toe setting

19 The procedure for checking the rear toe setting is same as described for the front in paragraphs 8 to 12.

20 To adjust the setting, chock the front wheels then jack up the rear of the vehicle and support it on axle stands. Slacken the track arm inner pivot bolt nut and rotate the pivot bolt until the toe setting is correctly set **(see illustration)**. Hold the pivot bolt stationary and tighten the pivot bolt nut to the specified torque.

21 Check that the toe setting has been correctly adjusted by lowering the vehicle to the ground and re-checking the toe setting; re-adjust if necessary.

Chapter 11
Bodywork and fittings

Contents

Degrees of difficulty

Easy, suitable for novice with little experience	**Fairly easy,** suitable for beginner with some experience	**Fairly difficult,** suitable for competent DIY mechanic
Difficult, suitable for experienced DIY mechanic	**Very difficult,** suitable for expert DIY or professional	

1 General information

The bodyshell is made of pressed-steel sections. Most components are welded together, but some use is made of structural adhesives.

The bonnet, door, and some other vulnerable panels are made of zinc-coated metal, and are further protected by being coated with an anti-chip primer before being sprayed.

Extensive use is made of plastic materials, mainly in the interior, but also in exterior components. The front and rear bumpers and front grille are injection-moulded from a synthetic material that is very strong and yet light. Plastic components such as wheel arch liners are fitted to the underside of the vehicle, to improve the body's resistance to corrosion.

2 Maintenance - bodywork and underframe

1 The general condition of a vehicle's bodywork is the one thing that significantly affects its value. Maintenance is easy, but needs to be regular. Neglect, particularly after minor damage, can lead quickly to further deterioration and costly repair bills. It is important also to keep watch on those parts of the vehicle not immediately visible, for instance the underside, inside all the wheel arches, and the lower of the engine compartment.

2 The basic maintenance routine for the bodywork is washing - preferably with a lot of water, from a hose. This will remove all the loose solids which may have stuck to the vehicle. It is important to flush these off in such a way as to prevent grit from scratching the finish. The wheel arches and underframe need washing in the same way, to remove any accumulated mud which will retain moisture and tend to encourage rust. Paradoxically enough, the best time to clean the underframe and wheel arches is in wet weather, when the mud is thoroughly wet and soft. In very wet weather, the underframe is usually cleaned of large accumulations automatically, and this is a good time for inspection.

3 Periodically, except on vehicles with a wax-based underbody protective coating, it is a good idea to have the whole of the underframe of the vehicle steam-cleaned, engine compartment included, so that a thorough inspection can be carried out to see what minor repairs and renovations are necessary. Steam cleaning is available at many garages, and is necessary for the removal of the accumulation of oily grime, which sometimes is allowed to become thick in certain areas. If steam-cleaning facilities are not available, there are some excellent grease solvents available which can be brush-applied; the dirt can then be simply hosed off. Note that these methods should not be used on vehicles with wax-based underbody protective coating, or the coating will be removed. Such vehicles should be inspected annually, preferably just before Winter, when the underbody should be washed down, and repair any damage to the wax coating. Ideally, a completely fresh coat should be applied. It would also be worth considering the use of such wax-based protection for injection into door panels, sills, box sections, etc, as an additional safeguard against rust damage, where such protection is not provided by the vehicle manufacturer.

4 After washing paintwork, wipe off with a chamois leather to give an unspotted clear finish. A coat of clear protective wax polish will give added protection against chemical pollutants in the air. If the paintwork sheen has dulled or oxidised, use a cleaner/polisher combination to restore the brilliance of the shine. This requires a little effort, but such dulling is usually caused because regular washing has been neglected. Care needs to be taken with metallic paintwork, as special non-abrasive cleaner/polisher is required to avoid damage to the finish. Always check that the door and ventilator opening drain holes and pipes are completely clear, so that water can be drained out. Brightwork should be treated in the same way as paintwork. Windscreens and windows can be kept clear of the smeary film which often appears, by proprietary glass cleaner. Never use any form of wax or other body or chromium polish on glass.

11

3 Maintenance - upholstery and carpets

1 Mats and carpets should be brushed or vacuum-cleaned regularly, to keep them free of grit. If they are badly stained, remove them from the vehicle for scrubbing or sponging, and make quite sure they are dry before refitting. Seats and interior trim panels can be kept clean by wiping with a damp cloth. If they do become stained (which can be more apparent on light-coloured upholstery), use a little liquid detergent and a soft nail brush to scour the grime out of the grain of the material. Do not forget to keep the headlining clean in the same way as the upholstery. When using liquid cleaners inside the vehicle, do not over-wet the surfaces being cleaned. Excessive damp could get into the seams and padded interior, causing stains, offensive odours or even rot. If the inside of the vehicle gets wet accidentally, it is worthwhile taking some trouble to dry it out properly, particularly where carpets are involved. *Do not leave oil or electric heaters inside the vehicle for this purpose.*

4 Minor body damage - repair

Repairs of minor scratches in bodywork

1 If the scratch is very superficial, and does not penetrate to the metal of the bodywork, repair is very simple. Lightly rub the area of the scratch with a paintwork renovator or a very fine cutting paste to remove loose paint from the scratch, and to clear the surrounding bodywork of wax polish. Rinse the area with clean water.

2 Apply touch-up paint to the scratch using a fine paint brush; continue to apply fine layers of paint until the surface of the paint in the scratch is level with the surrounding paintwork. Allow the new paint at least two weeks to harden, then blend it into the surrounding paintwork by rubbing the scratch area with a paintwork renovator or a very fine cutting paste. Finally, apply wax polish.

3 Where the scratch has penetrated right through to the metal of the bodywork, causing the metal to rust, a different repair technique is required. Remove any loose rust from the bottom of the scratch with a penknife, then apply rust-inhibiting paint to prevent the formation of rust in the future. Using a rubber or nylon applicator, fill the scratch with bodystopper paste. If required, this paste can be mixed with cellulose thinners to provide a very thin paste which is ideal for filling narrow scratches. Before the stopper-paste in the scratch hardens, wrap a piece of smooth cotton rag around the top of a finger. Dip the finger in cellulose thinners, and quickly sweep it across the surface of the stopper-paste in the scratch; this will ensure that the surface of the stopper-paste is slightly hollowed. The scratch can now be painted over as described earlier in this Section.

Repairs of dents in bodywork

4 When deep denting of the vehicle's bodywork has taken place, the first task is to pull the dent out, until the affected bodywork almost attains its original shape. There is little point in trying to restore the original shape completely, as the metal in the damaged area will have stretched on impact, and cannot be reshaped fully to its original contour. It is better to bring the level of the dent up to a point which is about 3 mm below the level of the surrounding bodywork. In cases where the dent is very shallow anyway, it is not worth trying to pull it out at all. If the underside of the dent is accessible, it can be hammered out gently from behind, using a mallet with a wooden or plastic head. Whilst doing this, hold a suitable block of wood firmly against the outside of the panel, to absorb the impact from the hammer blows and thus prevent a large area of the bodywork from being "belled-out".

5 Should the dent be in a section of the bodywork which has a double skin, or some other factor making it inaccessible from behind, a different technique is called for. Drill several small holes through the metal inside the area - particularly in the deeper section. Then screw long self-tapping screws into the holes, just sufficiently for them to gain a good purchase in the metal. Now the dent can be pulled out by pulling on the protruding heads of the screws with a pair of pliers.

6 The next stage of the repair is the removal of the paint from the damaged area, and from an inch or so of the surrounding "sound" bodywork. This is accomplished most easily by using a wire brush or abrasive pad on a power drill, although it can be done just as effectively by hand, using sheets of abrasive paper. To complete the preparation for filling, score the surface of the bare metal with a screwdriver or the tang of a file, or alternatively, drill small holes in the affected area. This will provide a good "key" for the filler paste.

7 To complete the repair, see the Section on filling and respraying.

Repairs of rust holes or gashes in bodywork

8 Remove all paint from the affected area, and from an inch or so of the surrounding "sound" bodywork, using an abrasive pad or a wire brush on a power drill. If these are not available, a few sheets of abrasive paper will do the job most effectively. With the paint removed, you will be able to judge the severity of the corrosion, and therefore decide whether to renew the whole panel (if this is possible) or to repair the affected area. New body panels are not as expensive as most people think, and it is often quicker and more satisfactory to fit a new panel than to attempt to repair large areas of corrosion.

9 Remove all fittings from the affected area, except those which will act as a guide to the original shape of the damaged bodywork (eg headlight shells etc). Then, using tin snips or a hacksaw blade, remove all loose metal and any other metal badly affected by corrosion. Hammer the edges of the hole inwards, to create a slight depression for the filler paste.

10 Wire-brush the affected area to remove the powdery rust from the surface of the remaining metal. Paint the affected area with rust-inhibiting paint; if the back of the rusted area is accessible, treat this also.

11 Before filling can take place, it will be necessary to block the hole in some way. This can be achieved with aluminium or plastic mesh, or aluminium tape.

12 Aluminium or plastic mesh, or glass-fibre matting, is probably the best material to use for a large hole. Cut a piece to the approximate size and shape of the hole to be filled, then position it in the hole so that its edges are below the level of the surrounding bodywork. It can be retained in position by several blobs of filler paste around its periphery.

13 Aluminium tape should be used for small or very narrow holes. Pull a piece off the roll, trim it to the approximate size and shape required, then pull off the backing paper (if used) and stick the tape over the hole; it can be overlapped if the thickness of one piece is insufficient. Burnish down the edges of the tape with the handle of a screwdriver or similar, to ensure that the tape is securely attached to the metal underneath.

Bodywork repairs - filling and respraying

14 Before using this Section, see the Sections on dent, deep scratch, rust holes and gash repairs.

15 Many types of bodyfiller are available, but generally speaking, those proprietary kits which contain a tin of filler paste and a tube of resin hardener are best for this type of repair which can be used directly from the tube. A wide, flexible plastic or nylon applicator will be found invaluable for imparting a smooth and well-contoured finish to the surface of the filler.

16 Mix up a little filler on a clean piece of card or board - measure the hardener carefully (follow the maker's instructions on the pack), otherwise the filler will set too rapidly or too slowly. Using the applicator, apply the filler paste to the prepared area; draw the applicator across the surface of the filler to achieve the correct contour and to level the surface. When a contour that approximates to the correct one is achieved, stop working the paste - if you carry on too long, the paste will become sticky and begin to "pick-up" on the applicator. Continue to add thin layers of filler paste at 20-minute intervals, until the level of the filler is just proud of the surrounding bodywork.

17 Once the filler has hardened, the excess can be removed using a metal plane or file. From then on, progressively-finer grades of abrasive paper should be used, starting with a 40-grade production paper, and finishing with a 400-grade wet-and-dry paper. Always wrap the abrasive paper around a flat rubber, cork, or wooden block - otherwise the surface of the filler will not be completely flat. During the smoothing of the filler surface, the wet-and-dry paper should be periodically rinsed in water. This will ensure that a very smooth finish is imparted to the filler at the final stage.

18 At this stage, the "dent" should be surrounded by a ring of bare metal, which in turn should be encircled by the finely "feathered" edge of the good paintwork. Rinse the repair area with clean water, until all the dust produced by the rubbing-down operation has gone.

19 Spray the whole area with a light coat of primer - this will show up any imperfections in the surface of the filler. Repair these imperfections with fresh filler paste or bodystopper, and again smooth the surface with abrasive paper. If bodystopper is used, it can be mixed with cellulose thinners, to form a thin paste which is ideal for filling small holes. Repeat this spray-and-repair procedure until you are satisfied that the surface of the filler, and the feathered edge of the paintwork, are perfect. Clean the repair area with clean water, and allow to dry fully.

20 The repair area is now ready for final spraying. Paint spraying must be carried out in a warm, dry, windless and dust-free atmosphere. This condition can be created artificially if you have access to a large indoor working area, but if you are forced to work in the open, you will have to pick your day very carefully. If you are working indoors, dousing the floor in the work area with water will help to settle the dust which would otherwise be in the atmosphere. If the repair area is confined to one body panel, mask off the surrounding panels; this will help to minimise the effects of a slight mis-match in paint colours. Bodywork fittings (eg chrome strips, door handles etc) will also need to be masked off. Use genuine masking tape, and several thickness of newspaper, for the masking operations.

21 Before starting to spray, agitate the aerosol can thoroughly, then spray a test area (an old tin, or similar) until the technique is mastered. Cover the repair area with a thick coat of primer; the thickness should be built up using several thin layers of paint, rather than one thick one. Using 400 grade wet-and-dry paper, rub down the surface of the primer until it is smooth. While doing this, the work area should be thoroughly doused with water, and the wet-and-dry paper periodically rinsed in water. Allow to dry before spraying on more paint.

22 Spray on the top coat, again building up the thickness by using several thin layers of paint. Start spraying in the centre of the repair area, and then, using a circular motion, work outwards until the whole repair area and about 2 inches of the surrounding original paintwork is covered. Remove all masking material 10 to 15 minutes after spraying on the final coat of paint.

23 Allow the new paint at least two weeks to harden, then, using a paintwork renovator or a very fine cutting paste, blend the edges of the paint into the existing paintwork. Finally, apply wax polish.

Plastic components

24 With the use of more and more plastic body components by the vehicle manufacturers (eg bumpers. spoilers, and in some cases major body panels), rectification of more serious damage to such items has become a matter of either entrusting repair work to a specialist in this field, or renewing complete components. Repair of such damage by the DIY owner is not feasible, owing to the cost of the equipment and materials required for effecting such repairs. The basic technique involves making a groove along the line of the crack in the plastic, using a rotary burr in a power drill. The damaged is then welded back together, using a hot air gun to heat up and fuse a plastic filler rod into the groove. Any excess plastic is then removed, and the area rubbed down to a smooth finish. It is important that a filler rod of the correct plastic is used, as body components can be made of a variety of different types (eg polycarbonate, ABS, polypropylene).

25 Damage of a less serious nature (abrasions, minor cracks etc) can be repaired by the DIY owner using a two-part epoxy filler repair material which can be used directly from the tube. Once mixed in equal proportions, this is used in similar fashion to the bodywork filler used on metal panels. The filler is usually cured in twenty to thirty minutes, ready for sanding and painting.

26 If the owner is renewing a complete component himself, or if he has repaired it with epoxy filler, he will be left with the problem of finding a suitable paint for finishing which is compatible with the type of plastic used. At one time, the use of a universal paint was not possible, owing to the complex range of plastics met with in body component applications. Standard paints, generally speaking, will not bond to plastic or rubber satisfactorily, but professional matched paints, to match any plastic or rubber finish, can be obtained from some dealers. However, it is now possible to obtain a plastic body parts finishing kit which consists of a pre-primer treatment, a primer and coloured top coat. Full instructions are normally supplied with a kit, but basically the method of use is to first apply the pre-primer to the component concerned, and allow it to dry for up to

30 minutes. Then the primer is applied, and left to dry for about an hour before finally applying the special-coloured top coat. The result is a correctly coloured component, where the paint will flex with the plastic or rubber, a property that standard paint does not normally posses.

5 Major body damage - repair

Where serious damage has occurred, or large areas need renewal due to neglect, it means that complete new panels will need welding-in, and this is best left to professionals. If the damage is due to impact, it will also be necessary to check completely the alignment of the bodyshell, and this can only be carried out accurately by a Peugeot dealer using special jigs. If the body is left misaligned, it is primarily dangerous, as the car will not handle properly, and secondly, uneven stresses will be imposed on the steering, suspension and possibly transmission, causing abnormal wear, or complete failure, particularly to such items as the tyres.

6 Front bumper - removal and refitting

Removal

1 Remove the headlights as described in Chapter 12.

2 Firmly apply the handbrake then jack up the front of the vehicle and support it on axle stands.

3 Undo the retaining screws securing the left- and right-hand front wheelarch liners to the bumper **(see illustration)**. Release each liner from the from the bumper then slacken and remove the retaining bolt securing the left- and right-hand ends of the bumper to the body.

4 On models with front foglights, depress the retaining clips and disconnect the wiring connectors from the foglights.

6.3 Release the wheelarch liners and remove the bumper end retaining bolts

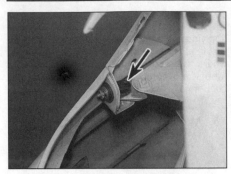

6.6a Rotate the bumper fasteners (arrowed) through 90° . . .

6.6b . . . and remove the front bumper from the vehicle

5 Undo the bumper two upper mounting bolts and the three lower mounting bolts.

6 Release the left- and right-hand retaining clips (situated by the headlight apertures) by rotating them through 90° then, with the aid of an assistant, manoeuvre the bumper assembly forwards and away from the vehicle **(see illustrations)**.

7 Inspect the bumper mountings for signs of damage and renew if necessary.

Refitting

8 Refitting is a reverse of the removal procedure, ensuring that the bumper mounting bolts are securely tightened.

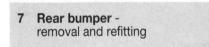

7 Rear bumper -
removal and refitting

Removal

1 On Saloon models, from inside the vehicle luggage compartment, slacken and remove the retaining screws and remove the rear trim panel. Undo the retaining screws and remove the tie-down hooks from the left- and right-hand corners of the luggage compartment. Release the retaining clips (pull out the centre pins then prise out the complete clip) and peel back the side trim panels to gain access to the bumper mountings. On some models, it will also be necessary to unscrew the fastener and remove the storage compartment to allow the trim panel to be freed **(see illustrations)**.

2 On Estate models, open up the tailgate and peel the sealing strip away from the base and sides of the body. Remove the storage compartment covers, undo the retaining screws and remove the rear trim plate, then

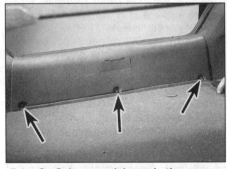

7.1a On Saloon models, undo the screws (arrowed - viewed from inside the car) . . .

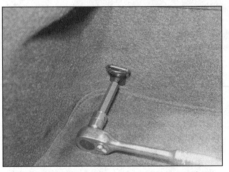

7.1c Undo the screw and remove the tie-down hook . . .

7.3 Undo the retaining nuts and remove the vent assembly from the right-hand side

unclip and remove the left- and right-hand lower rear side trim panels. Remove the retaining clips (pull out the centre pins then remove the complete clip) securing the sides of the carpet to the floor, then release the retaining clips and remove the plastic storage compartments. Peel back each side trim panel to reveal the bumper mountings (see Section 27 for illustrations).

3 On all models, undo the retaining nuts and remove the vent assembly from the right-hand rear corner of the luggage compartment **(see illustration)**.

4 From outside the vehicle, slacken and remove the retaining screws securing the rear of each wheelarch liner to the bumper. Free the liners from the bumper then slacken and remove the retaining nuts and rubbers securing the left- and right-hand ends of the bumper to the body **(see illustrations)**.

7.1b . . . and remove the rear trim panel from the luggage compartment

7.1d . . . then prise out the fasteners and peel back the side trim panel to gain access to the bumper retaining nuts

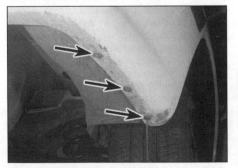

7.4a Undo the retaining screws (arrowed) and free the wheelarch liner . . .

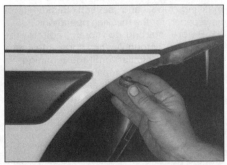

7.4b . . . then slacken and remove the bumper retaining nut and mounting rubber

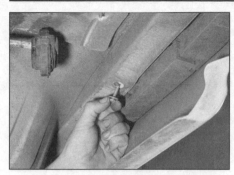

7.5 Slacken and remove the lower retaining bolts . . .

7.6 . . . then undo the upper retaining nuts and rubbers

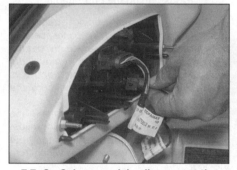

7.7 On Saloon models, disconnect the number plate light wiring connector from the left-hand rear light cluster, and free the wiring from all clips

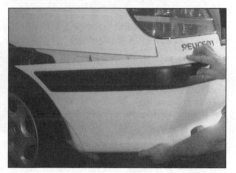

7.8 Lower the bumper to release it from the body and remove it from the vehicle

5 Slacken and remove the bolts securing the rear of the bumper to the vehicle underbody **(see illustration)**.

6 Returning to the luggage compartment, slacken and remove the remaining bumper upper retaining nuts and mounting rubbers (there are six in total) **(see illustration)**.

7 On Saloon models, trace the number plate light wiring back to the left-hand rear light cluster assembly and disconnect the wiring connector **(see illustration)**.

8 With the aid of an assistant, carefully release the bumper ends and remove the bumper from the vehicle, freeing the number plate light wiring grommet (Saloon models) from the body **(see illustration)**.

Refitting

9 Refitting is a reverse of the removal procedure. If any of the upper retaining nut studs were unscrewed from the mounting plates on removal, prior to refitting, remove the nuts and rubbers from the stud, then refit the studs and plates to the bumper and tighten securely.

8 Bonnet - removal, refitting and adjustment

Removal

1 Open the bonnet to the vertical position and place a wad of rag underneath each corner of

the bonnet to protect against possible damage should the bonnet slip.

2 Disconnect the washer hose from the right-hand side of the bonnet.

3 Using a pencil or felt tip pen, mark the outline of each retaining nut relative to the bonnet, to use as a guide on refitting.

4 With the aid of an assistant, support the bonnet then (where necessary) carefully lift the retaining clips and detach the support struts from the bonnet **(see illustration)**.

5 Slacken and remove the left- and right-hand hinge to bonnet nuts and carefully remove the bonnet from the vehicle.

6 Inspect the bonnet hinges for signs of wear and free play at the pivots, and if necessary renew; the hinges are bolted to the body.

8.4 Lift the retaining clip and detach the support struts (where fitted) from the bonnet

Refitting and adjustment

7 With the aid of an assistant, engage the bonnet with the hinges. Refit the retaining nuts and tighten them by hand only. Align the nuts with the marks made on removal, then tighten them securely. Where necessary, clip the support struts securely onto the bonnet.

8 Close the bonnet, and check for alignment with the adjacent panels. If necessary, slacken the hinge bolts and re-align the bonnet to suit; the height of the bonnet is altered by moving the rubber stops on the bonnet crossmember. If necessary, further adjustment can be gained by slackening the hinge retaining bolts and repositioning the hinge slightly. Once the bonnet is correctly aligned, securely tighten the hinge nuts/bolts (as applicable). Once the bonnet is correctly aligned, check that the bonnet fastens and releases satisfactorily.

9 Bonnet release cable - removal and refitting

Removal

1 The bonnet release cable is in two sections; the main section, linking the release lever to the driver's side lock, and the joining section, linking the locks. Proceed as described under the relevant sub-heading.

Main cable

2 Remove the driver's side headlight as described in Chapter 12.

3 Undo the retaining screw and release the cable retaining clamp from the headlight aperture **(see illustration)**.

4 Tie a piece of string to the end of the release cable and free the cable from all the necessary retaining clips and ties.

5 From inside the vehicle, undo the retaining bolt and withdraw the bonnet release handle from underneath the facia, withdrawing the cable into the passenger engine compartment. When the end of the string appears from the bulkhead, untie it and leave it in position; the string can then be used on refitting to draw the cable back into position.

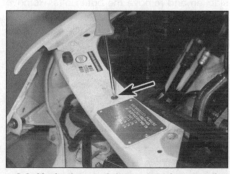

9.3 Undo the retaining screw (arrowed) and detach the bonnet release cable from its clamp

10.1 Remove the fasteners then release the retaining clips and remove the grille panel from the vehicle

10.2 Undo the retaining bolts, then detach the lock from the release cable(s)

10.5 Adjust the release cable by slackening the clamp screw and repositioning the outer cable

Joining cable

6 Remove the grille panel as described in Section 10.
7 Detach the cable from each lock assembly and remove it from the vehicle.

Refitting

8 Refitting is the reverse of removal, ensuring that the cable is correctly routed, and secured to all the relevant retaining clips. Prior to closing the bonnet, operate the release handle and have an assistant check that the lock hook moves easily and smoothly to its stop. The cable is adjusted by slacken the main cable retaining clamp screw and repositioning the outer cable as necessary.

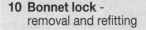

10 Bonnet lock -
removal and refitting

Removal

1 Open up the bonnet and remove the fasteners (pull out the centre pins then lever out the complete fastener) securing the grille panel to the bonnet crossmember. Release the side retaining clips then, using a large flat-bladed screwdriver, depress the centre clip and slide the grille panel forwards and away from the vehicle **(see illustration)**.
2 Using a suitable marker pen, draw around the outline of each lock retaining bolt then slacken and remove the both bolts. Remove

the lock from the vehicle, freeing it from the release cable(s) **(see illustration)**.

Refitting

3 Connect the release cable(s) to the lock, and seat the lock on the crossmember.
4 Refit the retaining bolts, aligning them with the marks made prior to removal, and tighten them securely.
5 Check the lock operation then lubricate the lock with multi-purpose grease. If adjustment is necessary, slacken the release cable clamp retaining screw and reposition the cable (see Section 9) **(see illustration)**.
6 Once the lock is operating correctly, clip the grille panel back into position and secure it with the fasteners.

11 Door - removal, refitting and adjustment

Removal

1 Disconnect the battery negative terminal and proceed as described under the relevant sub-heading.

Front door

2 If the door contains any electrical components, remove the door inner trim panel as described in Section 12. To gain access to the wiring clips, it is necessary to peel/cut the foam insulation panel carefully away from the door. **Note:** *This is likely to*

result in the panel being damaged, necessitating its renewal. If the panel needs to be renewed, it will be necessary to drill out the rivets (see Section 13) and remove the armrest/trim panel brackets; new pop rivets will be required on refitting to secure the brackets in position.
3 Disconnect the wiring connectors and free the wiring from any relevant retaining clips. Ease the rubber grommet out from the front edge of the door and withdraw the wiring from the door.
4 Using a pencil or felt tip pen, mark the outline of each hinge relative to the door, to use as a guide on refitting.
5 Undo the retaining bolts securing the check link to the pillar and remove the rubber cover **(see illustrations)**.
6 With the aid of an assistant, support the door then unscrew the hinge retaining bolts and remove the door from the vehicle.
7 Examine the hinges for signs of wear or damage. If renewal is necessary, mark the position of the hinge(s) then undo the retaining bolts and remove them from the door. Fit the new hinge(s), align with the marks made before removal, and securely tighten the retaining bolts.

Rear door

8 Open up the front door to gain access to the rear door wiring connector. Rotate the connector locking ring anti-clockwise until it is possible to disconnect the wiring connector **(see illustration)**.

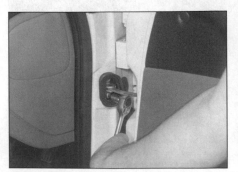

11.5a Undo the retaining screws securing the check link to the door pillar . . .

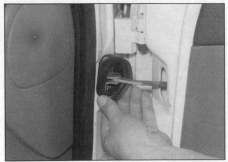

11.5b . . . and remove the rubber cover

11.8 Unscrew the locking ring to detach the rear door wiring connector from the pillar

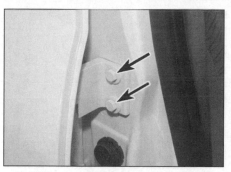

11.9 Unscrew the hinge retaining bolts (arrowed) and remove the rear door

9 Remove the door as described in paragraphs 4 to 7 **(see illustration)**.

Refitting

Front door

10 Manoeuvre the door into position and refit the hinge retaining bolts. Align the hinges with the marks made prior to removal, then tighten them to the securely.
11 Refit the rubber cover onto the check link, then align the link with the pillar and securely tighten its retaining bolts.
12 Where necessary, feed the wiring back into the door, and seat the rubber grommet in position. Ensure that the wiring is correctly routed and securely reconnected, then secure it in position with the necessary clips and ties. Seat the insulation panel back in position, and refit the trim panel as described in Section 12.
13 Check the door alignment and, if necessary, adjust. If the paintwork around the hinges has been damaged, paint the affected area with a suitable touch-in brush to prevent corrosion.

Rear door

14 Carry out the operations described in paragraphs 10, 11 and 13. Reconnect the wiring connector and secure it in position by rotating the locking ring until the index marks align **(see illustration)**.

Adjustment

15 Close the door and check the door alignment with surrounding body panels. If

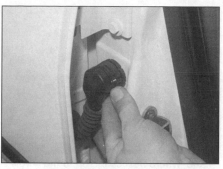

11.14 On refitting, secure the wiring connector by rotating the locking ring until the index marks are aligned

necessary, slight adjustment of the door position can be made by slackening the hinge retaining bolts and repositioning the hinge/door as necessary. Once the door is correctly positioned, tighten the hinge bolts to the specified torque. If the paintwork around the hinges has been damaged, paint the affected area with a suitable touch-in brush to prevent corrosion.

12 Door inner trim panel - removal and refitting

Removal

Note: *Door trim panel design varies according to the equipment level of the vehicle, and*

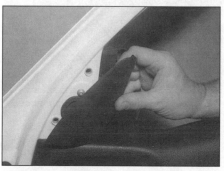

12.2 Removing the mirror inner trim panel from the door

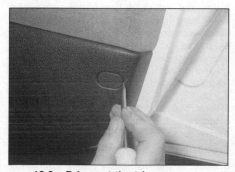

12.6a Prise out the trim cover . . .

12.6b . . . then slacken and remove the trim panel retaining screw

therefore some trim panel fastener locations on your vehicle might be different to those shown in the accompanying illustrations.
1 Disconnect the battery negative terminal and proceed as described under the relevant sub-heading.

Front door

2 Carefully unclip the exterior mirror inner trim panel from the front of the door **(see illustration)**. On models with manually-adjusted mirrors, remove the rubber gaiter from the adjustment handle prior to unclipping the trim panel.
3 On models with manually-operated windows, pull the window regulator handle off its spindle and remove the spacer.
4 Working as described in Chapter 12, remove the switch(es) from the door armrest and also remove the loudspeaker from the door.
5 Lift the door lock inner handle and carefully prise out the handle surround **(see illustration)**.
6 Prise out the trim cover from the lower rear corner of the trim panel, and slacken and remove the retaining screw **(see illustrations)**.
7 Remove the trim cover(s) and slacken and remove the screw(s) securing the underside of the armrest to the door.
8 Where necessary, remove the trim cover from the base of the armrest pocket, then slacken and remove the retaining screw and lift the pocket out of position. Also slacken and remove the screw (where fitted) securing the switch panel section of the trim panel in position **(see illustrations)**.

12.5 Removing the inner handle surround

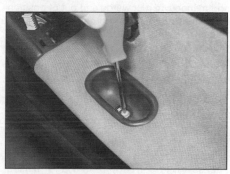

12.8a Remove the trim cover then undo the retaining screw . . .

11

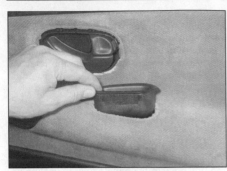

12.8b . . . and remove the armrest pocket from the trim panel

12.8c Where necessary, undo the screw securing the switch panel section of the trim panel in position

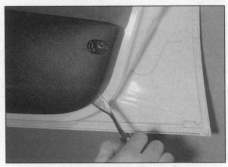

12.9a Unclip the trim panel . . .

12.9b . . . and move it upwards and away from the door

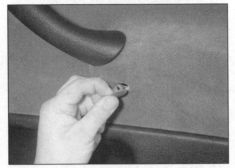

12.10a On the rear door, remove the trim covers . . .

12.10b . . . and undo the retaining screws (arrowed)

13.2a Carefully peel the insulation panel away from the door . . .

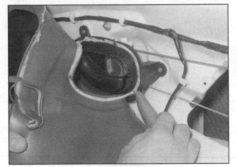

13.2b . . . and inner handle to gain access to the lock components

13.2c If the insulation panel is to be removed completely it will be necessary to drill out the rivets and remove the trim panel mounting brackets

9 Make a final check that all the retaining screws have been removed, then carefully unclip the base of the trim panel from the door and manoeuvre it upwards and out of position **(see illustrations)**. As the panel is removed, free the wiring harness noting its correct routing.

Rear door

10 Remove the trim panel as described in paragraphs 3 to 9 **(see illustrations)**.

Refitting

11 Refitting of the trim panel is the reverse of removal. Prior to clipping the panel in position, ensuring all the wiring (where necessary) is correctly routed and passed through the relevant apertures. On completion check the operation of all switches.

13 Door handle and lock components - removal and refitting

Removal

1 Remove the inner trim panel as described in Section 12.
2 To gain access to the handle and lock components, it is necessary to peel/cut the foam insulation panel away from the door. **Note:** *This is likely to result in the panel being damaged, necessitating its renewal. If the panel needs to be renewed, it will be necessary to drill out the rivets (see paragraph 4) and remove the armrest/trim panel brackets; new pop rivets will be required on refitting to secure the brackets in position* **(see illustrations)**.

Door lock inner handle

Note: *A pop rivet gun and suitable rivets will be required on refitting.*
3 Peel/cut the insulation panel sufficiently away from the door to gain access to the handle (see paragraph 2).
4 Carefully drill the heads off the rivets securing the handle to the door, whilst taking great care not to damage the handle itself. Recover the remains of the rivets from inside the door.
5 Free the handle from the door, then disconnect the link rods and remove the handle assembly **(see illustration)**.

Front door lock cylinder

6 Peel/cut the insulation panel sufficiently away from the door to gain access to the lock assembly (see paragraph 2).

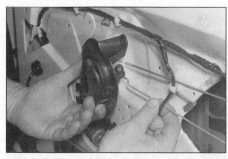

13.5 Drill out the rivets then detach the inner handle from the link rods and remove it from the door

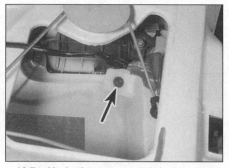

13.7a Undo the upper retaining screws (arrowed) . . .

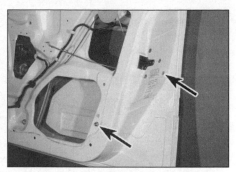

13.7b . . . and lower nut (arrowed) . . .

13.7c . . . and manoeuvre the lock protective cover from the front door

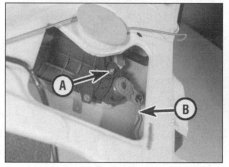

13.9a Undo the retaining nut (A) then detach the link rod (B) . . .

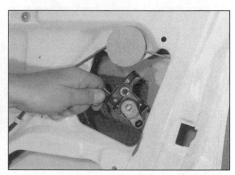

13.9b . . . and remove the lock cylinder mounting plate from the door

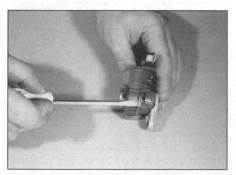

13.10a Slide out the retaining clip . . .

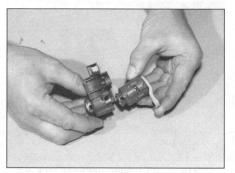

13.10b . . . then separate the lock cylinder housing and mounting plate

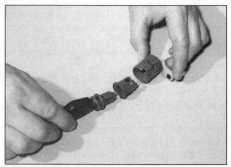

13.10c Insert the key and withdraw the lock cylinder from its housing

7 Slacken and remove the lower retaining nut and the upper retaining screws, and manoeuvre the lock protective cover out from inside the door assembly **(see illustrations)**.

8 To improve access to the lock cylinder, release the retaining clip and disconnect the wiring connector from the lock assembly.

9 Slacken and remove the rear retaining nut from the exterior handle, then manoeuvre the lock cylinder mounting plate assembly out of position, disconnecting it from the link rod **(see illustrations)**.

10 To remove the lock cylinder, prise out the retaining clip then separate the lock cylinder, housing and mounting plate. Insert the key into the lock cylinder and withdraw it from the housing **(see illustrations)**.

Front door exterior handle

11 Remove the lock cylinder assembly as described in paragraphs 6 to 9.

12 Undo the front retaining nut then detach the link rod from the handle and manoeuvre the handle out from the door, along with its rubber seal **(see illustrations)**.

Front door lock assembly

13 Peel/cut the insulation panel sufficiently away from the door to gain access to the lock and handle components (see paragraph 2).

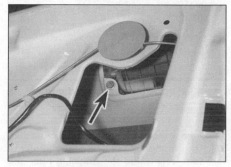

13.12a Undo the retaining nut (arrowed) . . .

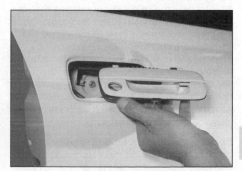

13.12b . . . and remove the handle and seal from the door

11

13.16 Lift the clip and disconnect the wiring connector from the lock assembly

13.17a Undo the retaining screws (arrowed) . . .

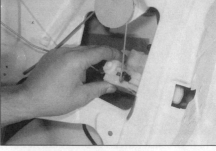

13.17b . . . and manoeuvre the lock assembly out of position

13.20a Detach the link rod (arrowed) . . .

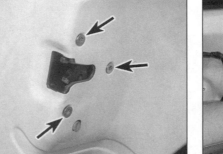

13.20b . . . then undo the lock retaining screws (arrowed)

13.21a Detach the link rods from the lock . . .

14 Slacken and remove the lower retaining nut and the upper retaining screws, and manoeuvre the lock protective cover out from inside the door assembly (see paragraph 7).

15 Remove the inner handle as described in paragraphs 4 and 5.

16 Release the retaining clip and disconnect the wiring connector from the lock assembly **(see illustration)**.

17 Slacken and remove the retaining screws, then unhook the link rods from the lock assembly and manoeuvre it out from the door **(see illustrations)**. Do not attempt to dismantle the lock assembly, if it is faulty the complete unit must be renewed.

Rear door lock assembly

18 Peel/cut the insulation panel sufficiently away from the door to gain access to the lock and handle components (see paragraph 2).

19 Remove the inner handle as described in paragraphs 4 and 5.

20 Unhook the link rod connecting the lock to the handle, then slacken and remove the lock retaining screws **(see illustrations)**.

21 Manoeuvre the lock assembly out of position and remove it from the door. Note that it may be necessary to unhook the inner handle link rods from the lock assembly, noting there correct fitted locations, in order to gain the clearance required **(see illustrations)**.

Rear door exterior handle

22 Peel/cut the insulation panel sufficiently away from the door to gain access to the lock and handle components (see paragraph 2).

23 Release the retaining clip and disconnect the wiring connector from the lock.

13.21b . . . and manoeuvre the lock out from the door

13.25b . . . then unscrew the front retaining nut . . .

24 Unhook the link rod from the door handle.

25 Remove the access plug from the rear of the door, then undo the retaining nuts and remove the handle and seal from the outside of the door **(see illustrations)**.

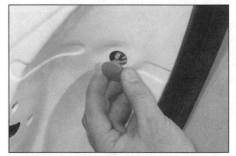

13.25a Remove the access plug from the rear of the door, then slacken and remove the handle rear retaining nut . . .

13.25c . . . and remove the handle and seal from the rear door

Refitting

26 Refitting is the reverse of removal, ensuring that all link rods are clipped securely in position. Prior to sticking the insulation

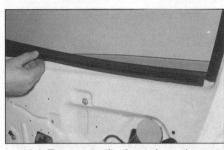

14.4 To remove the front door glass, remove the inner sealing strip from the top of the door . . .

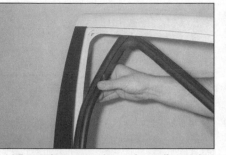

14.5 . . . then ease the main sealing strip out from the door frame

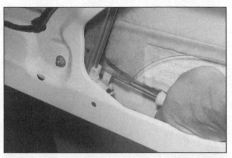

14.6 Release the regulator guide clip . . .

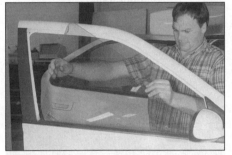

14.7 . . . and carefully work the window glass out through the top of the door

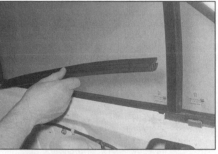

14.8 To remove the rear door glass, remove the inner sealing strip . . .

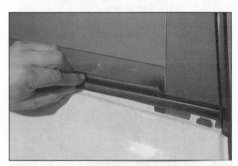

14.9 . . . then free the outer sealing strip . . .

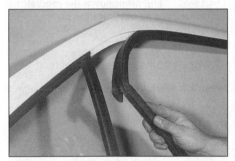

14.10 . . . and the main sealing strip from the door

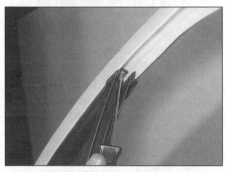

14.11a Undo the upper . . .

14.11b . . . and lower retaining screws . . .

panel to the door, reconnect the battery and check the operation of the lock and handles. If all is well, stick the insulation securely in position then refit the trim panel (Section 12).

14 Door window glass and regulator - removal and refitting

Note: *A pop rivet gun and suitable rivets will be required on refitting. The door foam insulation panel is almost certainly going to be damaged on removal, necessitating its renewal.*

Removal

1 Fully lower the window glass then remove the inner trim panel (see Section 12).
2 Noting each brackets correct fitted location, carefully drill off the head of the pop rivets and remove the armrest/trim panel mounting brackets from the door. New pop rivets will be required on refitting.

3 Carefully peel/cut the foam insulation panel away from the door to gain access to the window/regulator. If the panel is damaged on removal it should be renewed. Proceed as described under the relevant sub-heading.

Front door window

4 Remove the inner sealing strip away from the door, noting which way around it is fitted **(see illustration)**.
5 Carefully peel the main sealing strip out from the door frame and remove it from the vehicle **(see illustration)**.
6 Using a long, flat-bladed screwdriver, depress and release the retaining clip, and free the window glass from the regulator guide clip **(see illustration)**.
7 Carefully manoeuvre the glass upwards and out from the top of the door **(see illustration)**.

Rear door window

8 Carefully ease the window inner seal out of position, noting which way around it is fitted, and remove it from the door frame **(see illustration)**.

9 Free the window section of the outer sealing strip from the door, and position it clear of the glass **(see illustration)**.
10 Carefully peel the main sealing strip out from the door frame and remove it from the vehicle **(see illustration)**.
11 Slacken and remove the two retaining screws, then manoeuvre the window rear guide rail out of position and remove it from the door **(see illustrations)**.

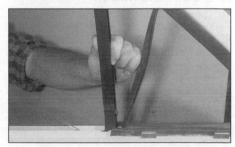

14.11c . . . and manoeuvre the window guide rail out of position

11

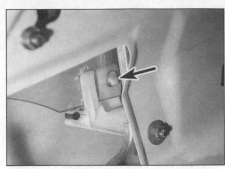

14.12a Release the regulator guide clip (arrowed) . . .

14.12b . . . and manoeuvre the glass out of the top of the door

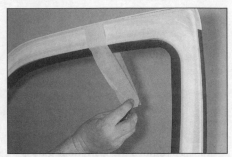

14.13 Release the glass from the regulator then slide up and tape it securely to the door frame

14.14 On models with electric windows, lift the retaining clip and detach the wiring connector from the window motor

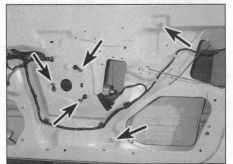

14.15a Undo the retaining nuts (arrowed) . . .

14.15b . . . and manoeuvre the regulator assembly out from the door

12 Depress the retaining clip and free the window glass from the regulator guide. The window glass can then be removed from the top of the door **(see illustrations)**.

Window regulator

13 Depress the retaining clip (on the front door it will be necessary to use a screwdriver to reach the clip) and free the window glass from the regulator guide. Slide the window glass fully up and hold it in position by taping it to the door frame **(see illustration)**.

14 On models with electric windows, lift the retaining clip and disconnect the wiring connector from the regulator motor **(see illustration)**.

15 On all models, undo the five retaining nuts securing the regulator assembly to the door, then carefully manoeuvre the assembly out through the door lower aperture **(see illustrations)**.

Rear door fixed window

16 Carry out the operations described in paragraphs 8 to 11, noting that it is not necessary to remove the main sealing strip completely, it only needs to be freed from window guide.

17 The fixed window can then be eased out position complete with the outer sealing strip.

Refitting

18 Refitting is the reverse of the relevant removal procedure, noting the following:
a) *Ensure that all sealing strips are correctly located in the door frame.*

b) *On refitting the window glass, take care to ensure it engages correctly with its guides and the regulator slide, and is clipped securely in position.*
c) *Check the operation of the window prior to sticking the insulation panel in position. On models with electric windows, the windows will not function correctly until they have been reprogrammed (see Section 20).*
d) *Fit the insulation panel securely to the door, and secure the armrest/trim panel brackets in position with new pop rivets. Refit the inner trim panel as described in Section 12.*

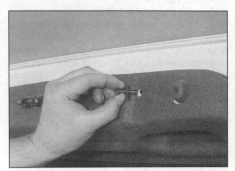

15.2a Remove the retaining fasteners . . .

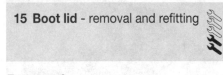

15 Boot lid - removal and refitting

Removal

Boot lid

1 Open up the boot lid and disconnect the battery negative terminal.

2 Remove the fasteners securing the inner trim panel to the boot lid, then unclip the panel and remove it from the vehicle; the fasteners are removed by pulling out their centre pins before prising out the complete clip **(see illustrations)**.

3 Prise out the retaining clip and release the wiring cover from the left-hand boot lid hinge to gain access to the wiring harness **(see illustration)**.

15.2b . . . and lift the inner trim panel away from the boot lid

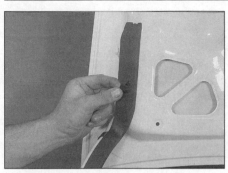

15.3a Remove the retaining clip . . .

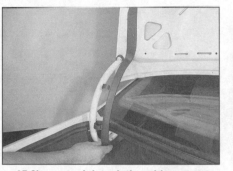

15.3b . . . and detach the wiring cover from the boot lid hinge

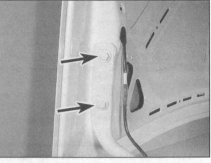

15.5 Undo the hinge bolts (arrowed) and remove the boot lid

15.6 With the parcel shelf removed, the hinge pivot bolt (arrowed) can be removed

15.7 Access to the support strut front mounting is best obtained from the front

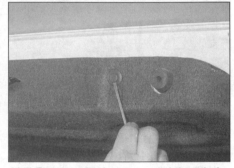

16.2 Remove the fasteners and detach the inner trim panel from the boot lid

4 Disconnect the wiring connectors from the boot lid electrical components, noting their correct fitted locations, and tie a piece of string to the end of the wiring. Noting the correct routing of the wiring harness, withdraw the wiring. When the end of the wiring appears, untie the string and leave it in position in the boot lid; it can then be used on refitting to draw the wiring into position.
5 Draw around the outline of each hinge with a suitable marker pen, then slacken and remove the hinge retaining bolts and remove the boot lid from the vehicle **(see illustration)**.
6 To remove the boot lid hinge, it will first be necessary to remove the parcel shelf (see rear seat belt removal - Section 27). The hinge pivot bolt can then be unscrewed and the hinge removed **(see illustration)**.

Support strut

7 To remove a support strut, using a small flat-bladed screwdriver, carefully lift the retaining clips and unhook the strut from its balljoints. **Note:** *Access to the strut front mounting can be improved by removing the rear seat back side cushion (models with a folding rear seat) or the complete seat back (models with a fixed rear seat - Section 25). The mounting can then be reached from the front* **(see illustration)**.

Refitting

Boot lid

8 Refitting is the reverse of removal, aligning

the hinges with the marks made before removal.
9 On completion, close the boot lid and check its alignment with the surrounding panels. If necessary, slight adjustment can be made by slackening the retaining bolts and repositioning the boot lid on its hinges. If the paintwork around the hinges has been damaged, paint the affected area with a suitable touch-in brush to prevent corrosion.

Support strut

10 Refitting is the reverse of removal, ensuring that the strut is securely clipped in position.

16 Boot lid lock components - removal and refitting

Removal

1 Open up the boot lid then disconnect the battery negative terminal.
2 Remove the retaining clips (pull out the centre pins then prise out the complete clip) and remove the inner trim panel from the boot lid **(see illustration)**. Proceed as described under the relevant sub-heading.

Lock mechanism

3 Slacken and remove the retaining bolts, then unhook the link rod and remove the lock from the boot lid **(see illustrations)**.

11

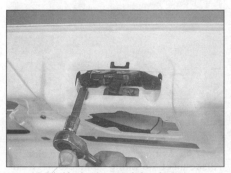

16.3a Undo the retaining bolts . . .

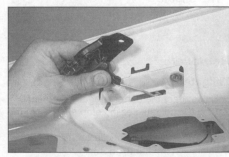

16.3b . . . then unhook the link rod and remove the lock from the boot lid

16.4 Undo the lock cylinder housing screws and remove the trim cover and seal from the boot lid

16.5 Detach the link rods and remove the lock cylinder housing

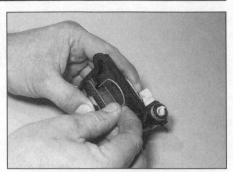

16.6a Slide out the retaining clip . . .

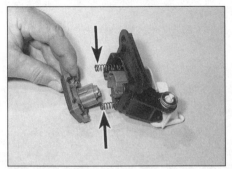

16.6b . . . then remove the lock button (spring locations arrowed) . . .

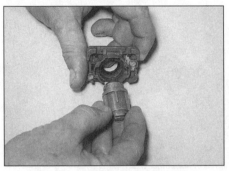

16.6c . . . and separate the button and lock cylinder

17.2 Peel away the tailgate sealing strip then unclip the upper trim panels to gain access to the tailgate wiring

Lock cylinder housing

4 Slacken and remove the retaining screws securing the lock cylinder housing in position, and remove the trim cover and seal from the outside of the boot lid **(see illustration)**.
5 Detach the link rods and remove the lock cylinder housing from the boot lid **(see illustration)**.
6 To remove the lock cylinder, slide out the retaining clip then separate the lock button and main housing, noting the correct fitted locations of the springs. The lock cylinder can then be withdrawn **(see illustrations)**.

Refitting

7 Refitting is the reverse of removal. Prior to refitting the trim panel, check the operation of the lock assembly and (where necessary) the central locking actuator.

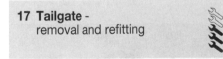

17 Tailgate -
removal and refitting

Removal

Tailgate

1 Disconnect the battery negative terminal.
2 Peel the tailgate sealing strip away from the left- and right-hand rear pillar upper trim panels, then carefully unclip both panels from the vehicle **(see illustration)**.
3 Disconnect the tailgate wiring connectors, which are clipped to the left-hand rear

pillar, then release the grommet and withdraw the wiring harness from the body **(see illustrations)**.
4 Disconnect the wiring connector and undo the bolt securing the earth lead to the right-

17.3a Working on the left-hand side, disconnect the wiring connectors (arrowed) . . .

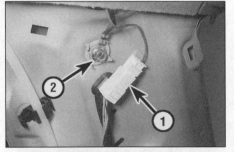

17.4a Working on the left-hand side, disconnect the wiring connector (1) then undo the earth lead bolt (2) . . .

hand rear pillar. Work back along the washer hose and disconnect it, then free the grommet and withdraw the wiring and hose from the body **(see illustrations)**.
5 Using a pencil or felt tip pen, mark the

17.3b . . . then free the grommet and withdraw the harness from the rear

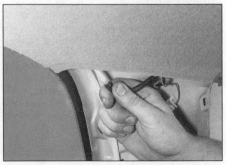

17.4b . . . and disconnect the tailgate washer jet hose from its union

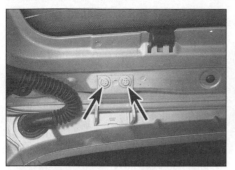

17.7 Undo the hinge bolts (arrowed) and remove the tailgate from the vehicle

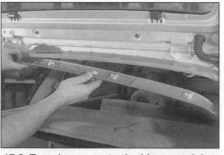

17.8 To gain access to the hinge retaining nuts, unclip the upper trim panel and peel back the headlining

17.9 To remove a support strut, carefully lift the retaining clips using a small, flat-bladed screwdriver

outline of each hinge on the tailgate, to use as a guide on refitting.

6 Have an assistant support the tailgate, then carefully lift the retaining clips and detach the support struts.

7 Slacken and remove the bolts securing the hinges to the tailgate and remove the tailgate from the vehicle **(see illustration)**.

8 Inspect the hinges for signs of wear or damage. If renewal is necessary, draw around the outline of the hinge then unclip the upper trim panel from the roof **(see illustration)**. Carefully peel back the headlining then undo the retaining nuts and remove the hinges from the vehicle. Fit the new hinges, aligning them with the marks made prior to removal and securely tighten the retaining nuts. Clip the headlining back in position and refit the upper trim panel.

Support strut

9 Have an assistant support the tailgate then,

using a small flat-bladed screwdriver, carefully lift the retaining clips and unhook the strut from its balljoints **(see illustration)**.

Refitting

Tailgate

10 Refitting is the reverse of removal, aligning the hinges with the marks made before removal. Prior to refitting the trim panels and sealing strip, connect the battery and check the operation of all the tailgate electrical components. On completion, ensure that the tailgate is correctly aligned with all its surrounding body components; adjustments can be made by slacken the hinge bolts and repositioning the tailgate.

Support strut

11 Refitting is the reverse of removal, making sure the strut is clipped securely in position.

18 Tailgate lock components - removal and refitting

Removal

1 Disconnect the battery negative terminal.

2 Open up the tailgate then undo the retaining screws and remove the inner handle. Unclip the surround from the lock inner button, then prise out the trim clips and remove the trim panel from the tailgate **(see illustrations)**. Proceed as described under the relevant sub-heading.

Lock assembly

3 Undo the retaining screws then free the lock from the link rod and remove it from the tailgate **(see illustrations)**.

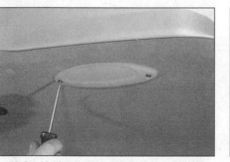

18.2a Undo the screws (arrowed) and remove the inner handle from the tailgate

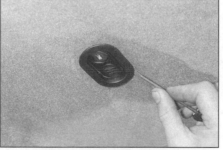

18.2b Prise out the surround from the lock inner button . . .

18.2c . . . then remove the retaining clips . . .

18.2d . . . and remove the inner trim panel from the tailgate

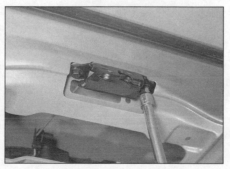

18.3a Undo the retaining bolts . . .

18.3b . . . then detach the link rod and remove the tailgate lock

11

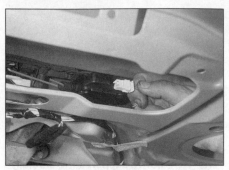

18.5a Disconnect the wiring connector from the central locking motor . . .

18.5b . . . then undo the retaining bolts and remove the lock cylinder housing

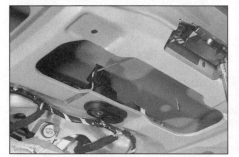

18.6 Note how the link rod engages with the inner button then unclip it from the lock and cylinder, and remove it

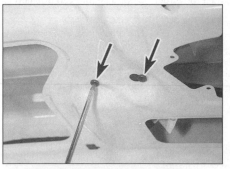

18.7 Slide out the retaining clip and remove the button from the tailgate

Lock cylinder housing

4 Release the clip and detach the link rod from the assembly.

5 Disconnect the wiring connector from the central locking motor then undo the retaining bolts and remove the assembly from the tailgate **(see illustrations)**. In order to gain the necessary clearance required, it will probably be necessary to unclip the number plate lights.

Lock inner button

6 Remove the lock assembly (refer to paragraph 3). Note how the link rod is engaged with the button, then detach the rod from the lock cylinder housing and remove it from the tailgate **(see illustration)**.

7 Slide out the retaining clip and remove the button assembly from the tailgate **(see illustration)**.

Refitting

8 Refitting is the reverse of removal. Check the operation of the lock assembly components prior to refitting the trim panel to the tailgate.

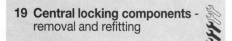

19 Central locking components - removal and refitting

Removal

Door lock motor

1 Each door lock motor is integral with the

lock assembly, and cannot be renewed separately. If the motor is faulty, the complete lock assembly must be renewed (refer to Section 13).

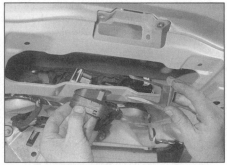

19.3a On Saloon models, undo the retaining screws (arrowed) . . .

19.5a Undo the retaining screws (arrowed) . . .

Boot lid lock motor - Saloon models

2 Open up the boot lid. Remove the retaining clips (pull out the centre pins then prise out the complete clip) and remove the inner trim panel from the boot lid.

3 Disconnect the wiring connector, then undo the retaining screws and remove the motor from the boot lid, unhooking it from the link rod **(see illustrations)**.

Tailgate lock motor - Estate models

4 Remove the lock cylinder housing as described in Section 18.

5 Slacken and remove the retaining screws, then detach the motor from its link rod and remove it from the assembly **(see illustrations)**.

Electronic control units (ECU)

6 Due to the complexity of the central locking system there are three control units; the remote receiver unit, the central lock control unit and the deadlocking control unit. All units are located behind the passenger side of the facia.

7 To gain access to the units, open up the glovebox then slide out the hinge pins and remove the glovebox. Undo the retaining screw(s) and remove the access cover from the facia, then prise out the retaining clips and remove the undercover from the facia **(see illustrations)**.

8 The remote receiver unit is the upper left-hand control unit, the central locking unit is the upper right-hand control unit, and the deadlocking unit is located directly below the pair.

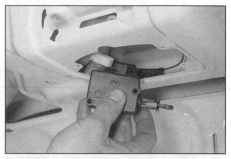

19.3b . . . then disconnect the wiring connector and link rod and remove the central locking motor from the boot lid

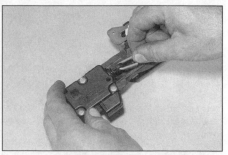

19.5b . . . then unhook the link rod and remove the central locking motor from the bracket

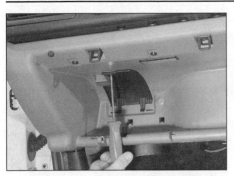

19.7a Undo the retaining screw . . .

19.7b . . . and remove the cover from the facia to gain (limited) access to the ECUs

19.9 Removing the remote receiver unit (shown with facia removed for clarity)

19.10 Removing the deadlocking unit (shown with facia removed for clarity)

9 To remove the remote receiver or central locking unit, disconnect the wiring then release the retaining clip and slide the unit out from its mounting bracket **(see illustration)**.

10 To remove the deadlocking unit, disconnect the wiring connectors then unbolt the mounting bracket from bulkhead. Slacken and remove the retaining screws, and slide the control unit out of position **(see illustration)**.

Refitting

11 Refitting is the reverse of removal. Prior to refitting any trim panels removed for access, thoroughly check the operation of the central locking system.

20 Electric window components - removal and refitting

Note: *If the battery is disconnected with a window open, the window will need to be reprogrammed once the battery is reconnected. To do this, turn on the ignition switch and fully lower the window to its stop. Hold the switch until the relay clicks then, within two seconds, fully raise the window (it will rise in short steps). Once the window is fully closed, keep the switch depressed for a few seconds; this will initialise the ECU so that it learns the fully closed position. Release the switch and check that the window operates normally. Repeat the procedure as necessary.*

Window switches

1 Refer to Chapter 12.

Window winder motors

2 At the time of writing, it was unclear whether the window winder motors were available separately or whether the complete

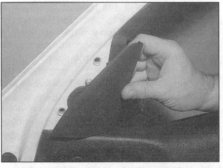

21.4 Unclip the inner trim panel . . .

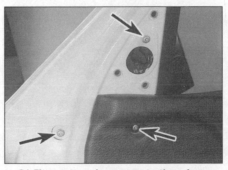

21.5b . . . to gain access to the mirror retaining screws (arrowed)

regulator assembly would have to be renewed. Refer to your Peugeot dealer for the latest information. Regulator removal and refitting is described in Section 14.

21 Exterior mirrors and associated components - removal and refitting

Manually-adjusted mirror

1 Remove the rubber gaiter from the mirror adjustment handle, then carefully unclip the mirror inner trim panel from the door.

2 Prise out the trim covers to reveal the mirror lower retaining screws, then undo the retaining screws and remove the mirror from the door. Recover the rubber seal which is fitted between the door and mirror; if the seal is damaged, it must be renewed.

3 Refitting is the reverse of removal.

Electrically-operated mirror

4 Carefully unclip the mirror inner trim panel from the door **(see illustration)**.

5 Prise out the trim covers to reveal the mirror lower retaining screws, then undo the retaining screws and remove the mirror from the door, disconnect the wiring connector as it becomes accessible **(see illustrations)**. Recover the rubber seal which is fitted between the door and mirror; if the seal is damaged it must be renewed.

6 Refitting is the reverse of removal.

21.5a . . . then remove the trim covers (arrowed) . . .

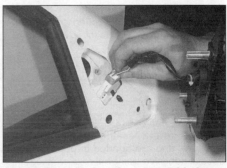

21.5c Remove the mirror assembly from the door and disconnect the wiring

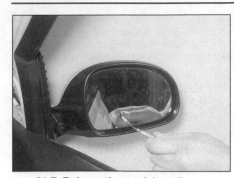

21.7 Release the retaining clip . . .

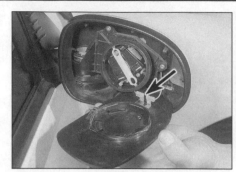

21.8 . . . then carefully unclip the glass from the mirror and (where necessary disconnect its wiring connectors

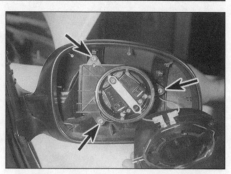

21.12 Mirror motor is retained by three screws (arrowed)

Mirror glass

Note: *The mirror glass is clipped into position. Removal of the glass is likely to result in breakage if carried out carelessly. It is advisable to wear gloves when carrying out this procedure.*

7 Tilt the mirror glass fully upwards, and insert a wide plastic or wooden wedge between the mirror glass and mirror housing. Release the lower retaining clip and carefully prise the glass from the motor/adjuster **(see illustration)**. Take great care when removing the glass; do not use excessive force as the glass is easily broken.

8 Remove the glass from the mirror, where necessary, disconnect the wiring connectors from the mirror heating element **(see illustration)**.

9 On refitting, reconnect the wiring to the glass and clip the glass onto the motor/adjuster, taking great care not to break it. Ensure that the glass is clipped securely into position and adjust as necessary.

Mirror switch

10 Refer to Chapter 12.

Mirror motor

11 Remove the mirror glass as described above.

12 Undo the retaining screws and remove the motor, disconnecting its wiring connector as it becomes accessible **(see illustration)**.

13 On refitting reconnect the wiring connector and securely tighten the motor screws. Check the operation of the motor then refit the glass as described above.

22 Windscreen and rear screen glass - general information

These areas of glass are secured by the tight fit of the weatherstrip in the body aperture, and are bonded in position with a special adhesive. Renewal of such fixed glass is a difficult, messy and time-consuming task, which is beyond the scope of the home mechanic. It is difficult, unless one has plenty of practice, to obtain a secure, waterproof fit. Furthermore, the task carries a high risk of breakage; this applies especially to the laminated glass windscreen. In view of this, owners are strongly advised to have this sort of work carried out by one of the many specialist windscreen fitters.

23 Sunroof - general information

1 Due to the complexity of the sunroof mechanism, considerable expertise is needed to repair, replace or adjust the sunroof components successfully. Removal of the roof first requires the headlining to be removed, which is a complex and tedious operation in itself, and not a task to be undertaken lightly. Therefore, any problems with the sunroof should be referred to a Peugeot dealer.

2 On models with an electric sunroof, if the sunroof motor fails to operate, first check the relevant fuse. If the fault cannot be traced and rectified, the sunroof can be opened and closed manually using an Allen key to turn the motor spindle. To gain access to the motor, remove the overhead console from the roof (see Chapter 12). Using the Allen key, rotate the motor spindle and move the sunroof to the required position **(see illustration)**.

23.2 Using an Allen key to manually move the electric sunroof

24 Body exterior fittings - removal and refitting

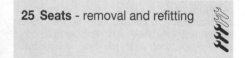

Wheel arch liners and body under-panels

1 The various plastic covers fitted to the underside of the vehicle are secured in position by a mixture of screws, nuts and retaining clips, and removal will be fairly obvious on inspection. Work methodically around the panel, removing its retaining screws and releasing its retaining clips until the panel is free and can be removed from the underside of the vehicle. Most clips used on the vehicle are simply prised out of position. Other clips can be released by unscrewing/prising out the centre pins and then removing the clip.

2 On refitting, renew any retaining clips that may have been broken on removal, and ensure that the panel is securely retained by all the relevant clips and screws.

Body trim strips and badges

3 The various body trim strips and badges are held in position with a special adhesive tape. Removal requires the trim/badge to be heated, to soften the adhesive, and then cut away from the surface. Due to the high risk of damage to the vehicle's paintwork during this operation, it is recommended that this task should be entrusted to a Peugeot dealer.

25 Seats - removal and refitting

Removal

Front seat

⚠️ *Warning: On models equipped with front seat belt tensioners, refer to Section 26 before proceeding.*

1 Slacken and remove the screw from the rear of the seat outer trim panel, then unclip

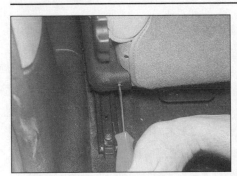

25.1a Undo the retaining screw . . .

25.1b . . . and unclip the outer trim panel from the front seat

25.2 Undo the lower mounting bolt and detach the seat belt from the seat

25.3 Slide the seat fully forwards and undo the rear mounting bolts . . .

25.4 . . . then slide it fully backwards and undo the front mounting bolts

the trim panel in an upwards direction (see illustrations).

2 Slacken and remove the mounting bolt, and free the seat belt from the seat base (see illustration).

3 Slide the seat fully forwards, then slacken and remove the bolts and washers securing the rear of the seat rails in position (see illustration).

4 Slide the seat fully backwards, then slacken and remove the seat rail front mounting bolts (see illustration).

5 Carefully manoeuvre the seat out of position, disconnecting the wiring connectors from the seat belt tensioner and (where applicable) seat motors as they become accessible (see illustration).

Rear seat
(models with folding rear seat)

6 Remove the rubber covers from the seat cushion mounting studs then unscrew the seat retaining nuts (see illustration). Slide the seat cushion forwards slightly and lift it to release it from the rear retaining pegs. Remove the cushion from the vehicle, freeing it from the seat belt buckles.

7 To remove the seat side cushions, slacken and remove the retaining bolt from the base of the cushion, then slide the cushion upwards and out of the vehicle (see illustrations).

8 To remove the rear seat back assembly on

25.5 Carefully lift the seat and disconnect the various wiring connectors before removing the seat from the vehicle

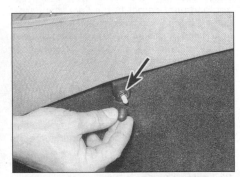

25.6 Remove the rubber cover then undo the seat cushion retaining nut (arrowed)

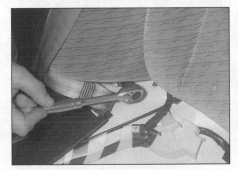

25.7a Undo the retaining bolt . . .

25.7b . . . then unclip the rear seat side section from the vehicle

11

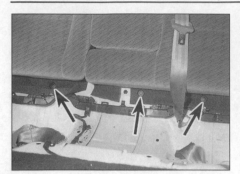

25.8a On models with a split rear seat, remove the fasteners (arrowed) . . .

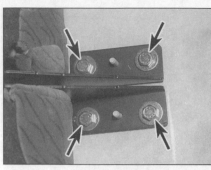

25.8b . . . and peel back the carpet to gain access to the centre bolts (arrowed)

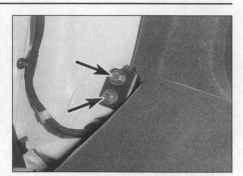

25.9a Rear seat back side mounting bolts - Saloon model

25.9b On Estate models, unclip the access cover to reveal the seat side bolts

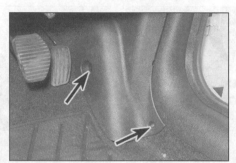

27.5 Undo the retaining screws and fasteners (arrowed) and remove the side panel from the footwell

models with a split rear seat, it is first necessary to remove the retaining clips (prise out the centre pins then remove the complete clips) securing the front of the luggage compartment carpet to the floor; the carpet can then be folded back to gain access to the seat centre mounting bolts (see illustrations). On Estate models, it will be necessary to unbolt the centre set belt lower mounting from the body.

9 Slacken and remove all the mounting bolts and remove the seat assembly from the vehicle; on Estate models, it will be necessary to unclip the access covers from the side trim panels to gain access to the mounting bolts (see illustrations).

Rear seat
(models with fixed rear seat)

10 Remove the seat cushion as described in paragraph 6.
11 Slacken and remove the seat back retaining bolts then lift the back upwards and out of position.

Refitting

12 Refitting is the reverse of removal, ensuring all bolts are securely tightened.

26 Front seat belt tensioning mechanism - general information

Most models covered in this manual are fitted with a front seat belt tensioner system.

The system is designed to instantaneously take up any slack in the seat belt in the case of a sudden frontal impact, therefore reducing the possibility of injury to the front seat occupants. Each front seat is fitted with the system, the tensioner being attached directly to the seat belt stalk.

The seat belt tensioner is operated by the airbag control unit (see Chapter 12). The tensioner is electrically triggered by a frontal impact above a pre-determined force. Lesser impacts, including impacts from behind, will not trigger the system.

When the system is triggered, the fuel inside the tensioner cylinder ignites. This forces the tensioner piston forwards which then removes all slack from the seat belt by retracting the seat belt stalk. The strength of the explosion in the tensioner cylinder is calibrated to retract the seat belt sufficiently to securely retain the occupant of the seat without forcing them into the seat. Once the tensioner has been triggered, the seat belt will be permanently locked and the assembly must be renewed.

To prevent the risk of injury if the system is triggered inadvertently when working on the vehicle, if any work is to be carried out on the seat, disconnect the battery and disable the tensioner. To do this, remove the centre console, and disconnect the wiring connector from the seat belt tensioning/airbag control unit (see Chapter 12).

Also note the following warnings carefully before contemplating any work on the front seat belts.

 Warning: Before carrying out any operations on the seatbelt tensioning system, disconnect the battery negative terminal and wait at least two minutes. Remove the centre console (see Section 29) then release the retaining clip and disconnect the main wiring connector from the seat belt tensioning control unit (Chapter 12). When operations are complete, reconnect the control unit and refit the centre console.

 Warning: If the tensioner mechanism is dropped, it must be renewed, even it has suffered no apparent damage.
Warning: Do not allow any solvents to come into contact with the tensioner mechanism.
Warning: Do not subject the seat to any form of shock, as this could accidentally trigger to the seat belt tensioner.
Warning: Do not subject the tensioner assembly to temp-eratures above 100° C.

27 Seat belt components - removal and refitting

Removal

Front seat belt

1 Disconnect the battery negative terminal.
2 Remove the relevant front seat as described in Section 25.
3 Prise out the retaining clips and remove the undercover from beneath the facia.
4 If the work is being carried out on the driver's side, slacken the retaining bolt(s) and free the bonnet release lever from the side of the footwell.
5 Remove the footwell side panel retaining screws/nut and clips (as applicable), and carefully unclip the panel from the vehicle (see illustration).
6 Slacken and remove the retaining screw, then peel away the sealing strip and unclip the

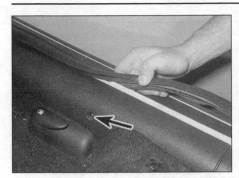

27.6a Peel back the sealing strip and undo the retaining screw (arrowed) . . .

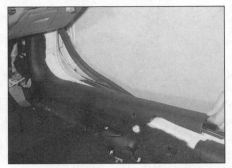

27.6b . . . then unclip the trim panel from the sill

27.7 Peel the front and rear sealing strips away from the pillar . . .

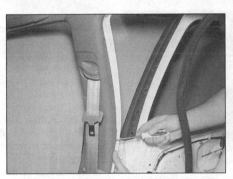

27.8 . . . then unclip the trim panel and remove it from the vehicle

27.9 Undo the retaining screws (arrowed), and unclip the front of the rear door sill trim panel to gain access to the inertia reel

front door sill trim panel and remove it from the vehicle **(see illustrations)**.

7 Peel away the front and rear sealing strips from the door centre pillar **(see illustration)**.

8 Unclip the centre pillar trim panel (starting at the top and working down) and free it from the seat belt **(see illustration)**.

9 Undo the front retaining screws, then carefully unclip the front of the rear door sill trim panel sufficiently to reveal the seat belt inertia reel **(see illustration)**. It is not necessary to remove the trim panel completely (this would require the rear seat to be removed).

10 Slacken and remove the two retaining screws, and remove the seat belt guide from the door pillar **(see illustration)**.

11 Unscrew the upper mounting nut and detach the seat belt from its height adjuster **(see illustration)**.

12 Slacken and remove the inertia reel mounting bolt and remove the seat belt assembly from the vehicle **(see illustration)**.

13 If necessary, the height adjustment mechanism can be removed once its retaining bolt has been undone.

Rear seat belt - Saloon models

14 Remove the rear seat cushion and side cushions (models with a folding rear seat) or the complete seat back (models with a fixed rear seat) as described in Section 25.

15 Slacken and remove the lower mounting bolt securing the seat belt to the floor.

16 Pull out the centre pins and remove the retaining clips securing the front of the parcel shelf to the body **(see illustration)**.

17 Carefully unclip the seat belt trim covers from the front of the parcel shelf, then disengage them from the seat belts **(see illustrations)**.

18 Remove the rear loudspeakers as described in Chapter 12.

19 Where necessary, open up the storage compartment in the centre of the shelf and

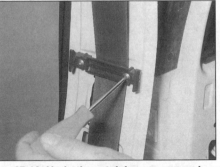

27.10 Undo the retaining screws and remove the seat belt guide from the pillar

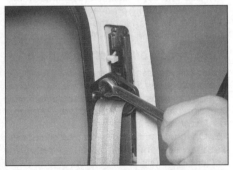

27.11 Undo the upper mounting nut . . .

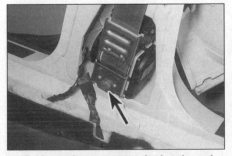

27.12 . . . then unscrew the inertia reel mounting bolt (arrowed) and remove the front seat belt assembly from the vehicle

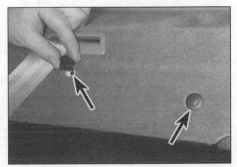

27.16 Remove the retaining clips securing the front of the parcel shelf in position

11

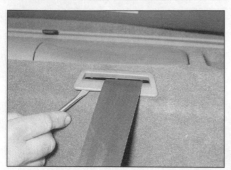

27.17a Carefully prise out the seat belt trim covers . . .

27.17b . . . and detach them from the seat belts

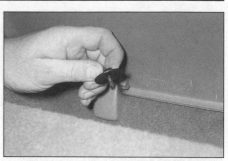

27.19 On models with a storage compartment, remove the parcel shelf bolt from the centre of the compartment

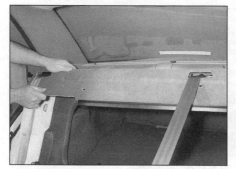

27.20 Unclip the front of the parcel shelf and remove it from the vehicle

27.21 Rear seat belt inertia reel retaining bolt (arrowed)

then unclip the lower side trim panel (see illustrations). Release the retaining clips and remove the storage compartment.
24 Unclip the trim cover then slacken and remove the seat belt lower mounting bolt.
25 Remove the trim cover from the seat belt upper mounting point. Slacken and remove the mounting bolt and free the seat belts from the pillar, noting the correct fitted locations and arrangements of the spacers and belt holder (see illustrations).
26 Peel the rear door sealing strip away from the front edge of the upper trim panel, then carefully unclip the upper trim panel and remove it from the vehicle (see illustrations).
27 Using a flat-bladed screwdriver, prise out the ventilation grille from the rear window lower trim panel. Slacken and remove the retaining screws, then unclip the trim panel and free it from the seat belts (see illustrations).

slacken and remove the shelf retaining bolt (see illustration).
20 Release the front edge of the parcel shelf from the body, and slide the assembly forwards and out of position (see illustration).
21 Slacken and remove the inertia reel retaining bolt, and remove the seat belt assembly from the vehicle (see illustration).

Rear seat belt - Estate models

Note: *The rear seat centre belt is built into the seat back. At the time of writing, it was unclear whether it is possible to separate the belt from the seat assembly. Refer to your Peugeot dealer for further information.*
22 Open up the tailgate and peel the sealing strip away from the relevant side of the vehicle. Carefully unclip the upper trim panel from the rear pillar, and remove the luggage compartment side storage compartment

cover. Release the luggage compartment cover assembly and remove it from the car.
23 Undo the retaining screws and remove the rear trim panel from the luggage compartment,

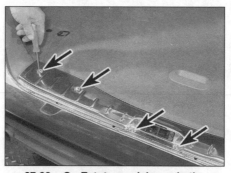

27.23a On Estate models, undo the retaining screws (arrowed) . . .

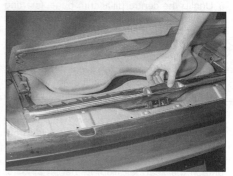

27.23b . . . and remove the rear trim panel . . .

27.23c . . . then unclip the lower side trim panel from the luggage compartment

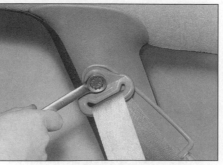

27.25a Remove the trim cover, then slacken and remove the upper bolt . . .

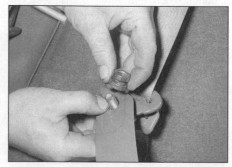

27.25b . . . noting the correct fitted order of the plain spacers, belt holder . . .

27.25c . . . and the stepped spacer

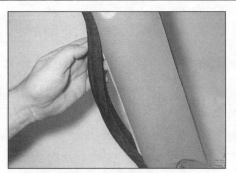

27.26a Peel away the rear door sealing strip . . .

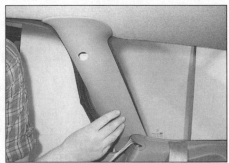

27.26b . . . then unclip the upper trim panel from the pillar

27.27a Unclip the ventilation grille . . .

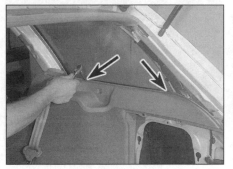
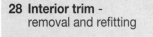

27.27b . . . then undo the retaining screws (arrowed) . . .

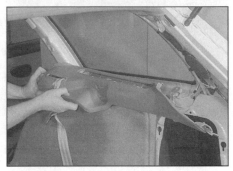

27.27c . . . and remove the lower trim panel from the rear window

28 Peel back the luggage compartment side trim panel to gain access to the seat belt inertia reels. Slacken and remove the retaining bolt and remove the relevant belt from the vehicle (see illustration).

Refitting

29 Refitting is the reverse of removal, making sure the inertia reel is correctly engaged with the body, and that all mounting bolts are securely tightened. Also ensure that all trim panels removed are correctly clipped into position and retained by all the relevant clips and screws.

28 Interior trim - removal and refitting

Interior trim panels

1 The interior trim panels are secured using either screws or various types of trim fasteners, usually studs or clips.
2 Check that there are no other panels overlapping the one to be removed; usually there is a sequence that has to be followed that will become obvious on close inspection.
3 Remove all obvious fasteners, such as screws. If the panel will not come free, it is held by hidden clips or fasteners. These are usually situated around the edge of the panel, and can be prised up to release them; note, however that they can break quite easily, so replacements should be available. The best

way of releasing such clips without the correct type of tool, is to use a large flat-bladed screwdriver. Note in many cases that the adjacent sealing strip must be prised back to release a panel.
4 When removing a panel, never use excessive force or the panel may be damaged; always check carefully that all fasteners have been removed or released before attempting to withdraw a panel.
5 Refitting is the reverse of the removal procedure; secure the fasteners by pressing them firmly into place and ensure that all disturbed components are correctly secured to prevent rattles.

Glovebox

6 Open up the glovebox, then slide out the hinge pins and remove the glovebox (see illustrations).
7 Refitting is the reverse of removal.

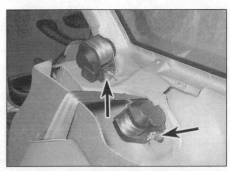

27.28 Rear seat belt inertia reel retaining bolts (arrowed) - Estate models

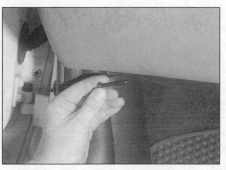

28.6a Slide out the hinge pins . . .

28.6b . . . and remove the glovebox lid from the facia

11

29.1 Slide the seat forwards and remove the rear bolts from the centre console

29.3a Remove the ashtray insert . . .

29.3b . . . then unclip the surround and remove it from the console . . .

29.3c . . . disconnecting its wiring as it is removed

29.4a Undo the retaining screws in the ashtray aperture . . .

29.4b . . . and unclip the side panels from the front of the console

Carpets

8 The passenger compartment floor carpet is in one piece, and is secured at its edges by screws or clips, usually the same fasteners used to secure the various adjoining trim panels.

9 Carpet removal and refitting is reasonably straightforward but very time-consuming, because all adjoining trim panels must be removed first, as must components such as the seats, the centre console and seat belt lower anchorages.

Headlining

10 The headlining is clipped to the roof, and can be withdrawn only once all fittings such as the grab handles, sun visors, sunroof (if fitted), windscreen and rear quarterwindows and related trim panels have been removed and the door, tailgate and sunroof aperture sealing strips have been prised clear.

11 Note that headlining removal requires considerable skill and experience if it is to be carried out without damage, and is therefore best entrusted to an expert.

29 Centre console - removal and refitting

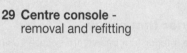

Removal

1 Slide the front seats fully forwards, then slacken and remove the rear retaining screws from the left- and right-hand sides of the centre console (see illustration).

2 Slide the front seats fully backwards and disconnect the battery negative terminal.

3 Open up the ashtray then push the lid forwards to release the ashtray insert. Carefully unclip the ashtray surround and remove it from centre console, disconnecting

its wiring connectors as they become accessible (see illustrations).

4 Working inside the ashtray aperture, slacken and remove the retaining screws securing the left- and right-hand side panels to the centre console. Unclip the front of each panel and remove both panels from the console (see illustrations).

5 On manual transmission models, unclip the gearchange lever gaiter from the console (see illustration).

6 On automatic transmission models, pull the knob off the top of the gear selector lever.

7 On all models, carefully unclip the handbrake lever trim cover from the top of the console (see illustration).

8 Where necessary, unclip the front seat armrest(s) to gain the necessary clearance required to remove the console.

9 Slacken and remove the two mounting nuts securing the front of the console to the floor (see illustration).

29.5 On manual transmission models, unclip the gearchange lever gaiter

29.7 Carefully prise the handbrake lever trim cover out from the console

29.9 Undo the front mounting nuts (arrowed) . . .

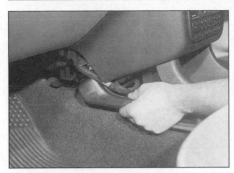

29.10 . . . and unclip the heater ducts from the housing

29.11a Lift the rear of the console and disconnect the cigarette lighter wiring . . .

29.11b . . . then manoeuvre the console out of position

10 Free the heater ducts (situated at the front of the console) from the base of the housing, then lift up the rear of the console **(see illustration)**. Reach in and push the console switch panel (where fitted) out of position, disconnect the wiring connectors and remove the panel from the vehicle.

11 Disconnect the wiring connectors from the cigarette lighter, then lift up the console and remove it from the vehicle **(see illustrations)**.

Refitting

12 Refitting is the reverse of removal, making sure the heater ducts are correctly engaged with the housing. Ensure that all wiring is correctly routed and all fasteners are securely tightened. On completion, check the operation of all switches.

---

30 Facia panel assembly -
removal and refitting

Removal

HAYNES HiNT

Attach an identification label to each wiring connector as it is disconnected. The labels can then be used on refitting to help ensure that all wiring is correctly routed through the relevant facia apertures.

1 Remove the centre console as described in Section 29.

2 Working as described in Chapter 12, remove the following components.

  a) *Instrument panel. The instrument panel wiring can be clipped into the holder on the bulkhead to hold it in position whilst the facia is removed.*
  b) *Driver's side and centre facia switch panels. On the driver's side, disconnect the wiring connector from the lights-on warning buzzer and free the wiring harness from its retaining clips so that it does not hinder facia removal.*
  c) *Radio/cassette unit.*
  d) *Clock.*
  e) *Facia loudspeakers.*
  f) *Driver's side airbag and contact unit. Also, where necessary, disconnect the*

passenger airbag wiring connectors from the control unit so the airbag is free to be removed with the facia.
  g) *Windscreen wiper motor.*

3 Remove the steering column (Chapter 10).
4 Referring to Chapter 3, undo the heater control panel retaining screws and free the panel from the facia. On models equipped with a fully-automatic air conditioning system, disconnect the wiring connectors and remove the panel from the vehicle. On all other models the panel can be left connected.
5 Undo the retaining nuts and free the facia wiring connector mounting plate from its bracket **(see illustrations)**.
6 Slacken and remove the upper and lower mounting bolts and remove the facia mounting bracket support strut from the side of the driver's footwell **(see illustrations)**.

30.5a Undo the retaining nuts . . .

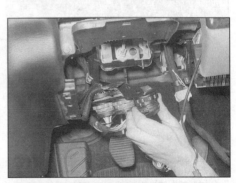

30.5b . . . and free the wiring connector mounting plate from the facia

30.6a Slacken and remove the upper (arrowed) . . .

30.6b . . . and lower mounting bolts (arrowed) . . .

30.6c . . . and remove the facia support strut

11

30.7 Undo the retaining screws securing the facia to the heater housing

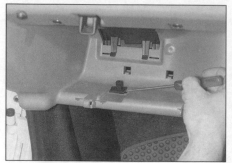

30.8a Prise out the glovebox light switch . . .

30.8b . . . and the illumination light and remove them from the facia

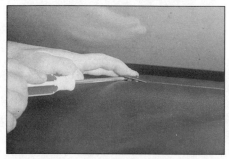

30.9a On models with automatic air conditioning, carefully prise the sunshine sensor out from the top of the facia . . .

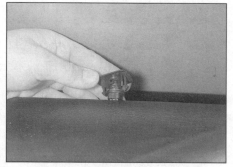

30.9b . . . and unclip the sensor mounting plate

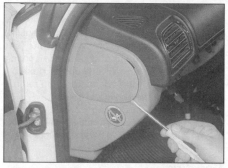

30.10 Removing the side cover from the passenger end of the facia

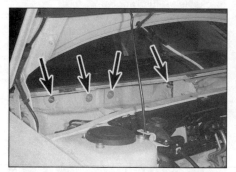

30.11 Facia retaining nuts and bolts (arrowed)

30.12a Slacken and remove the end bolts then release the retaining clips . . .

30.12b . . . and remove the facia from the vehicle

7 Slacken and remove the two heater housing-to-facia screws (see illustration).
8 Slide out the hinge pins and remove the glovebox lid. Carefully prise the illumination light and switch out from the facia, and disconnect them from the wiring connectors (see illustrations). Prise out the retaining clips and remove the undercover from the passenger side of the facia.
9 On models with a fully-automatic air conditioning system, carefully prise the sunshine sensor out from the centre of the top of the facia. Free the sensor from its mounting plate so that it is free to pass through the facia aperture (see illustrations).

10 Carefully prise out the side cover from the passenger end of the facia (see illustration).
11 From within the engine compartment, slacken and remove the three nuts and two bolts securing the facia mounting bracket to the bulkhead (see illustration).
12 From inside the vehicle, slacken and remove the facia mounting bolts from the left- and right-hand end of the mounting bracket. With the aid of an assistant, release the end clips then carefully manoeuvre the facia assembly away from the bulkhead and out from the vehicle, detaching the heater vents from the heater housing (see illustrations).

Refitting

13 Refitting is a reversal of the removal procedure, ensuring that the heater vents engage correctly with the housing. Prior to refitting the facia mounting nuts and bolts, ensure that all the necessary wiring connectors are fed through the relevant facia apertures. Ensure that the facia bracket is clipped securely in position, then refit the mounting nuts and bolts; tighten them all by hand at first before going around and tightening them securely. On completion, reconnect the battery and check that all the electrical components and switches function correctly.

Chapter 12
Body electrical system

Contents

Degrees of difficulty

Easy, suitable for novice with little experience	**Fairly easy,** suitable for beginner with some experience	**Fairly difficult,** suitable for competent DIY mechanic	**Difficult,** suitable for experienced DIY mechanic	**Very difficult,** suitable for expert DIY or professional

Specifications

System type	12-volt negative earth

Bulbs

Wattage

Exterior lights

Headlight	55 (H7 type)
Front foglight	55 (H1 type)
Front sidelight	5
Direction indicator	21
Direction indicator side repeater	5
Stop/tail	21/5
Reversing light	21
Rear foglight	21
Number plate light	5

Interior light

Front courtesy lights	5
Rear courtesy lights	5
Luggage compartment light	5

Torque wrench setting	Nm	lbf ft
Airbag control unit nuts	8	6

1 General information and precautions

⚠ *Warning: Before carrying out any work on the electrical system, read through the precautions given in Safety First! at the beginning of this manual and Chapter 5.*

The electrical system is of the 12 volt negative earth type. Power for the lights and all electrical accessories is supplied by a lead/acid type battery which is charged by the alternator.

This Chapter covers repair and service procedures for the various electrical components not associated with engine. Information on the battery, alternator and starter motor can be found in Chapter 5.

It should be noted that prior to working on any component in the electrical system, the battery negative terminal should first be disconnected, to prevent the possibility of electrical short circuits and/or fires.

2 Electrical fault finding - general information

Note: *Refer to the precautions given in 'Safety first!' and in Section 1 of this Chapter before starting work. The following tests relate to testing of the main electrical circuits, and should not be used to test delicate electronic circuits (such as anti-lock braking systems), particularly where an electronic control module (ECU) is used.*

General

1 A typical electrical circuit consists of an electrical component, any switches, relays, motors, fuses, fusible links or circuit breakers related to that component, and the wiring and connectors which link the component to both the battery and the chassis. To help to pinpoint a problem in an electrical circuit, wiring diagrams are included at the end of this Manual.

2 Before attempting to diagnose an electrical fault, first study the appropriate wiring diagram to obtain a complete understanding of the components included in the particular circuit concerned. The possible sources of a fault can be narrowed down by noting if other components related to the circuit are operating properly. If several components or circuits fail at one time, the problem is likely to be related to a shared fuse or earth connection.

3 Electrical problems usually stem from simple causes, such as loose or corroded connections, a faulty earth connection, a blown fuse, a melted fusible link, or a faulty relay (refer to Section 3 for details of testing relays). Visually inspect the condition of all fuses, wires and connections in a problem circuit before testing the components. Use the wiring diagrams to determine which terminal connections will need to be checked in order to pinpoint the trouble spot.

4 The basic tools required for electrical fault-finding include a circuit tester or voltmeter (a 12-volt bulb with a set of test leads can also be used for certain tests); a self-powered test light (sometimes known as a continuity tester); an ohmmeter (to measure resistance); a battery and set of test leads; and a jumper wire, preferably with a circuit breaker or fuse incorporated, which can be used to bypass suspect wires or electrical components. Before attempting to locate a problem with test instruments, use the wiring diagram to determine where to make the connections.

5 To find the source of an intermittent wiring fault (usually due to a poor or dirty connection, or damaged wiring insulation), a 'wiggle' test can be performed on the wiring. This involves wiggling the wiring by hand to see if the fault occurs as the wiring is moved. It should be possible to narrow down the source of the fault to a particular section of wiring. This method of testing can be used in conjunction with any of the tests described in the following sub-Sections.

6 Apart from problems due to poor connections, two basic types of fault can occur in an electrical circuit - open circuit, or short circuit.

7 Open circuit faults are caused by a break somewhere in the circuit, which prevents current from flowing. An open circuit fault will prevent a component from working, but will not cause the relevant circuit fuse to blow.

8 Short circuit faults are caused by a 'short' somewhere in the circuit, which allows the current flowing in the circuit to 'escape' along an alternative route, usually to earth. Short circuit faults are normally caused by a breakdown in wiring insulation, which allows a feed wire to touch either another wire, or an earthed component such as the bodyshell. A short circuit fault will normally cause the relevant circuit fuse to blow.

Finding an open circuit

9 To check for an open circuit, connect one lead of a circuit tester or voltmeter to either the negative battery terminal or a known good earth.

10 Connect the other lead to a connector in the circuit being tested, preferably nearest to the battery or fuse.

11 Switch on the circuit, bearing in mind that some circuits are live only when the ignition switch is moved to a particular position.

12 If voltage is present (indicated either by the tester bulb lighting or a voltmeter reading, as applicable), this means that the section of the circuit between the relevant connector and the battery is problem-free.

13 Continue to check the remainder of the circuit in the same fashion.

14 When a point is reached at which no voltage is present, the problem must lie between that point and the previous test point with voltage. Most problems can be traced to a broken, corroded or loose connection.

Finding a short circuit

15 To check for a short circuit, first disconnect the load(s) from the circuit (loads are the components which draw current from a circuit, such as bulbs, motors, heating elements, etc).

16 Remove the relevant fuse from the circuit, and connect a circuit tester or voltmeter to the fuse connections.

17 Switch on the circuit, bearing in mind that some circuits are live only when the ignition switch is moved to a particular position.

18 If voltage is present (indicated either by the tester bulb lighting or a voltmeter reading, as applicable), this means that there is a short circuit.

19 If no voltage is present, but the fuse still blows with the load(s) connected, this indicates an internal fault in the load(s).

Finding an earth fault

20 The battery negative terminal is connected to 'earth'- the metal of the engine/transmission and the car body - and most systems are wired so that they only receive a positive feed, the current returning through the metal of the car body. This means that the component mounting and the body form of that circuit. Loose or corroded mountings can therefore cause a range of electrical faults, ranging from total failure of a circuit, to a puzzling partial fault. In particular, lights may shine dimly (especially when another circuit sharing the same earth point is in operation), motors (eg. wiper motors or the radiator cooling fan motor) may run slowly, and the operation of one circuit may have an apparently unrelated effect on another. Note that on many vehicles, earth straps are used between certain components, such as the engine/transmission and the body, usually where there is no metal-to-metal contact between components due to flexible rubber mountings, etc.

21 To check whether a component is properly earthed, disconnect the battery and connect one lead of an ohmmeter to a known good earth point. Connect the other lead to the wire or earth connection being tested. The resistance reading should be zero; if not, check the connection as follows.

22 If an earth connection is thought to be faulty, dismantle the connection and clean back to bare metal both the bodyshell and the wire terminal or the component earth connection mating surface. Be careful to remove all traces of dirt and corrosion, then use a knife to trim away any paint, so that a clean metal-to-metal joint is made. On reassembly, tighten the joint fasteners securely; if a wire terminal is being refitted, use serrated washers between the terminal and the bodyshell to ensure a clean and secure connection. When the connection is

3.2a Open up the immobiliser keypad then rotate the fastener 90° and lower the fusebox cover . . .

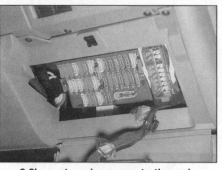

3.2b . . . to gain access to the main fusebox

3.2c Unclip the lid to gain access to the engine compartment fuses

remade, prevent the onset of corrosion in the future by applying a coat of petroleum jelly or silicone-based grease or by spraying on (at regular intervals) a proprietary ignition sealer or a water-dispersant lubricant.

3 Fuses and relays - general information

Fuses

1 The majority of fuses are located in the fusebox situated behind the driver's side lower facia panel. Additional fuses (including the larger, higher-rated fuses) are located in the fuse/relay box on the left-hand side of the engine compartment.

2 To gain access to the main fusebox, fold down the engine immobiliser keypad then rotate the fastener through 90° and lower the fusebox cover. To gain access to the fuses in the engine compartment, simply unclip the cover from the fuse/relay box; some of the higher-rated fuses are located in a separate box mounted in front of the main box **(see illustrations)**.

3 A list of the circuits each fuse protects is given on the fusebox cover.

4 To remove a fuse, first switch off the circuit concerned (or the ignition), then pull the fuse out of its terminals. The wire within the fuse should be visible; if the fuse is blown it will be broken or melted.

5 Always renew a fuse with one of an identical rating; never use a fuse with a different rating from the original, nor substitute anything else. Never renew a fuse more than once without tracing the source of the trouble. The fuse rating is stamped on top of the fuse; note that the fuses are also colour-coded for easy recognition.

6 If a new fuse blows immediately, find the cause before renewing it again; a short to earth as a result of faulty insulation is most likely. Where a fuse protects more than one circuit, try to isolate the defect by switching on each circuit in turn (if possible) until the fuse blows again. Always carry a supply of

spare fuses of each relevant rating on the vehicle, a spare of each rating should be clipped into the base of the fusebox.

Relays

7 The majority of relays are either located in the fuse/relay box in the engine compartment or behind the driver's side lower facia panel; the exceptions are as follows.

  a) The sunroof relay - located behind the overhead console.
  b) Rear screen/tailgate wiper relay - fitted to the wiper motor bracket.
  c) Cooling fan relay(s) - located in the fan shroud or at the side of the radiator.

8 If a circuit or system controlled by a relay develops a fault and the relay is suspect, operate the system; if the relay is functioning it should be possible to hear it click as it is energised. If this is the case, the fault lies with the components or wiring of the system. If the relay is not being energised, then either the relay is not receiving a main supply or a switching voltage or the relay itself is faulty. Testing is by the substitution of a known good unit, but be careful; while some relays are identical in appearance and in operation, others look similar but perform different functions.

9 To renew a relay, first ensure that the ignition switch is off. The relay can then simply be pulled out from the socket and the new relay pressed in.

4.3a Slacken the retaining screws (arrowed) . . .

4 Switches - removal and refitting

Note: *Disconnect the battery negative lead before removing any switch, and reconnect the lead after refitting the switch.*

Ignition switch/ steering column lock

1 Refer to Chapter 10.

Steering column combination switches

2 Undo the retaining screws securing the steering column lower shroud in position then unclip both the upper and lower shrouds from the column, disconnecting the cruise control and/or radio control switch wiring connector(s) (as applicable). Remove the lower shroud and position the upper shroud clear of the switches.

3 To remove an individual switch assembly, disconnect the wiring, then remove the retaining screws and slide the switch out of its mounting bracket **(see illustrations)**.

4 To remove the complete switch and mounting bracket assembly it will first be necessary to remove the steering wheel (see Chapter 10); on models with a driver's airbag, also remove the contact unit as described in Section 26. On all models, disconnect the wiring connectors from the switches, then

4.3b . . . then slide the combination switch out of position and disconnect its wiring (shown with steering wheel removed)

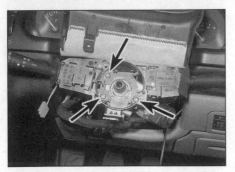

4.4 To remove the complete combination switch assembly, disconnect the wiring connectors then undo the screws (arrowed)

4.7 Undo the retaining screws (arrowed) and remove the radio switch from the steering column lower shroud

4.10 Undo the retaining screws (arrowed) . . .

4.11a . . . and remove the driver's side switch panel from the facia. Disconnect the wiring connector . . .

4.11b . . . and remove the relevant switch from the panel

4.14 Prise out the blanking plug to reveal the centre switch panel retaining screws

undo the retaining screws and remove the assembly from the top of the steering column **(see illustration)**.

5 Refitting is the reverse of removal, ensuring all wiring connectors are securely reconnected.

Radio control/ cruise control switches

6 Undo the retaining screws securing the steering column lower shroud in position and remove the shroud, disconnecting the switch wiring connector(s).

7 Undo the retaining screws and remove the relevant switch assembly from the lower shroud **(see illustration)**.

8 Refitting is the reverse of removal, ensuring that the switch wiring is correctly routed.

Driver's side facia switches

9 Open up the engine immobiliser keypad then rotate the fastener 90° and lower the fusebox cover.

10 Slacken and remove the screws from the base of the switch panel **(see illustration)**.

11 Withdraw the switch panel from the facia and disconnect its wiring connectors. Each individual switch can then be unclipped and removed from the mounting panel **(see illustrations)**.

12 Refitting is the reverse of removal noting that the correct fitted location of each switch is indicated by symbols on the switch panel.

Centre facia switches

13 Remove the multi-function display as described in Section 11. On models with no multi-function display unit, carefully prise out the storage compartment from the right-hand side of the switches.

14 Carefully prise out the blanking plug from the end of the switch panel to reveal the panel retaining screws; on some models, the alarm LED is fitted to the blanking plug **(see illustration)**.

15 Slacken and remove the retaining screws then remove the switch panel from the facia, disconnecting the wiring connectors as they become accessible. Each individual switch

can then be unclipped and remove from the mounting panel **(see illustrations)**.

16 Refitting is the reverse of removal.

Centre console switches

17 The switch panel can be pushed out of position once the centre console assembly has been unbolted from the floor. See Chapter 11 for centre console removal and refitting details. Each individual switch can then be unclipped and removed from the panel.

Door mounted switches

18 Carefully prise the switch panel cover out from the armrest **(see illustration)**.

4.15a Undo the retaining screws (arrowed) and remove the switch panel assembly from the vehicle . . .

4.15b . . . each switch can then be pushed out of position

4.18 Carefully prise out the switch panel cover . . .

4.19a . . . then ease the relevant switch out of position . . .

4.19b . . . and disconnect it from the wiring

4.21 Unclip the cover from the overhead console . . .

4.22a . . . and undo the retaining screws (arrowed) . . .

4.22b . . . then lower the console out and disconnect the wiring connectors

19 Each individual switch can then be carefully prised out of position and its wiring disconnected **(see illustrations)**.

20 Refitting is the reverse of removal.

Overhead console switches

21 Unclip the cover from the rear of the overhead console **(see illustration)**.

22 Undo the two retaining screws and free the console from the roof lining. Disconnect the wiring connectors and remove the console from the vehicle **(see illustrations)**.

23 To remove the sunroof switch, slacken and remove the retaining screws and lift off

the printed circuit board; the switch can then be slid out of position **(see illustrations)**. All the other switches are integral with the console and can only be renewed by replacing the complete console assembly.

24 Refitting is the reverse of removal ensuring that the wiring is correctly routed. Do not overtighten the circuit board screws, as the board is easily broken.

Seat switches

25 Carefully prise the switch out from the side of the seat, and disconnect it from the wiring connector(s).

26 Reconnect the wiring connector, and clip the switch back into position.

Stop-light switch

27 Refer to Chapter 9.

Handbrake warning light switch

28 Remove the centre console as described in Chapter 11.

29 Disconnect the wiring connector from the warning light switch, then unclip the switch and remove it from the handbrake lever.

30 Refitting in the reverse of removal.

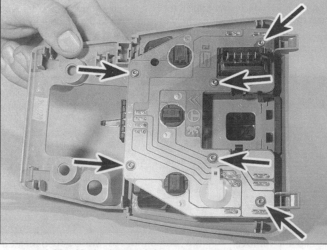

4.23a Undo the retaining screws and remove the printed circuit board . . .

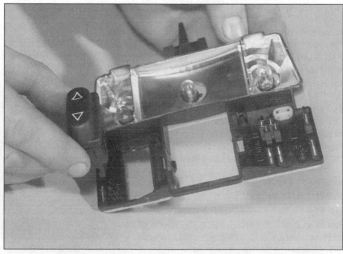

4.23b . . . the sunroof switch can then be slid out of position

12

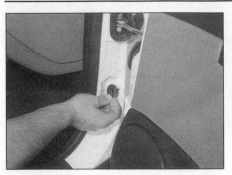

4.31a Remove the rubber cover . . .

4.31b . . . then release the retaining clips . . .

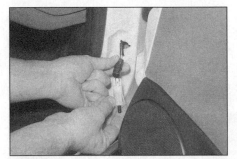

4.31c . . . and remove the courtesy light switch from the door pillar, disconnecting it from the wiring

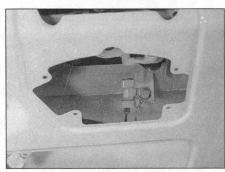

4.35 Luggage compartment light switch - Saloon models

Courtesy light switch

31 Open the door and remove the rubber cover from the switch. Release the retaining clips and carefully ease the switch out from the pillar, disconnecting its wiring connector as it becomes accessible (see illustrations). Tie a piece of string to the wiring to prevent it falling back into the door pillar.

32 Refitting is a reverse of the removal procedure. Refit the rubber cover to the switch prior to clipping it into the door pillar.

Luggage compartment light switch

33 On Saloon models, open up the boot lid then remove the retaining clips and lift off the inner trim panel to gain access to the switch.

34 On Estate models, open up the tailgate then undo the retaining screws and remove the inner handle. Unclip the surround from the lock inner button then prise out the trim clips and remove the inner trim panel from the tailgate.

35 Undo the retaining bolt and remove the switch, disconnecting it from the wiring connector (see illustration).

36 Refitting is the reverse of removal.

Windscreen wiper rain sensor switch

37 Carefully unclip the rear view mirror housing from its mounting on the inside of the windscreen by pulling it gently downwards.

38 Disconnect the wiring connector then carefully release the side retaining clips and remove the rain sensor from the windscreen.

Caution: Do not touch the rain sensor lens or the windscreen glass in the area of the sensor. These areas must be kept spotlessly clean if the sensor is to function correctly.

39 Refitting is the reverse of removal, ensuring that the sensor and mirror are clipped securely in position.

---

5 Bulbs (exterior lights) - renewal

General

1 Whenever a bulb is renewed, note the following points.

a) *Disconnect the battery negative lead before starting work.*

5.2 Depress the retaining clip and remove the access cover from the rear of the headlight unit

b) *Remember that if the light has just been in use, the bulb may be extremely hot.*

c) *Always check the bulb contacts and holder, ensuring that there is clean metal-to-metal contact between the bulb and its live(s) and earth. Clean off any corrosion or dirt before fitting a new bulb.*

d) *Wherever bayonet-type bulbs are fitted (see Specifications) ensure that the live contact(s) bear firmly against the bulb contact.*

e) *Always ensure that the new bulb is of the correct rating and that it is completely clean before fitting it; this applies particularly to headlight/foglight bulbs (see below).*

Headlight

2 Release the retaining clips and remove the access cover from the rear of the headlight unit (see illustration).

3 Disconnect the wiring connector from the rear of the bulb (see illustration).

4 Unhook and release the ends of the bulb retaining clip and release it from the rear of the light unit. Withdraw the bulb.

5 When handling the new bulb, use a tissue or clean cloth to avoid touching the glass with the fingers; moisture and grease from the skin can cause blackening and rapid failure of this type of bulb. If the glass is accidentally touched, wipe it clean using methylated spirit.

6 Install the new bulb, ensuring that its locating tabs are correctly located in the light cut-outs, and secure it in position with the retaining clip.

7 Reconnect the wiring connector and refit the access cover, making sure it is securely refitted.

Front sidelight

8 Depress the retaining clip and remove the access cover from the rear of the headlight unit.

9 Rotate the sidelight bulbholder and release it from the headlight unit. The bulb is of the capless (push-fit) type, and can be removed by simply pulling it out of the bulbholder.

10 Refitting is the reverse of the removal procedure, making sure the access cover is securely refitted.

5.3 Disconnect the wiring connector then release the retaining clip and remove the bulb

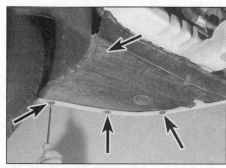

5.12 Undo the screws (arrowed) and remove the cover from beneath the foglight

5.13a Disconnect the wiring connector . . .

5.13b . . . then release the clip and remove the reflector assembly from the foglight

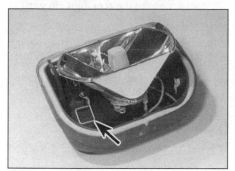

5.14 Unhook the spring clip (arrowed) and pivot the reflector away from the cover

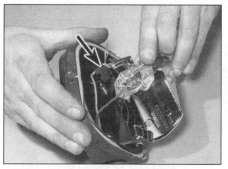

5.15a Disconnect the wiring connector (arrowed) then release the retaining clip . . .

5.15b . . . and remove the foglight bulb

Front foglight

11 If necessary, to improve access, firmly apply the handbrake then jack up the front of the vehicle and support it on axle stands.
12 Undo the retaining screws and remove the plastic cover from beneath the foglight (see illustration).
13 Disconnect the wiring connector then release the retaining clip and remove the rear cover assembly from the foglight (see illustrations).
14 Disengage the spring clip and tilt the reflector assembly away from the cover (see illustration).
15 Disconnect the wiring connector then unhook the bulb retaining clip and remove the bulb (see illustrations).
16 When handling the new bulb, use a tissue or clean cloth to avoid touching the glass with the fingers; moisture and grease from the skin

can cause blackening and rapid failure of this type of bulb. If the glass is accidentally touched, wipe it clean using methylated spirit.
17 Install the new bulb, ensuring that its locating tabs are correctly located in the reflector cut-outs, and secure it in position with the retaining clip.
18 Reconnect the wiring connector and clip the reflector back into position on the cover.
19 Refit the cover assembly and secure it in position with the retaining clip.
20 Reconnect the wiring connector then refit the plastic cover, tightening its retaining screws securely. Where necessary, lower the vehicle to the ground.

Front direction indicator

21 To improve access on the left-hand side, remove the protective cover from the battery.
22 Rotate the bulbholder anti-clockwise and remove it from the rear of the light unit. The

bulb is a bayonet fit in the holder, and can be removed by pressing it and twisting in an anti-clockwise direction (see illustration).
23 Refitting is a reverse of the removal procedure.

Front direction indicator side repeater

24 Carefully unclip the light unit and withdraw it from the wing (see illustration).
25 Twist the bulbholder anti-clockwise and remove it from the light. The bulb is of the capless (push-fit) type, and can be removed by simply pulling it out of the bulbholder (see illustration).
26 Refitting is a reversal of removal.

Rear light cluster - Saloon models

27 From inside the luggage compartment, slacken and remove the retaining screws and

5.22 Removing the front direction indicator bulb

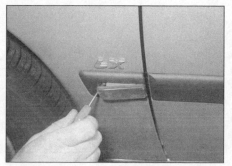

5.24 Carefully prise the side repeater light out from the wing . . .

5.25 . . . then free the bulbholder and pull out the bulb

5.27a On Saloon models, undo the retaining screws and remove the rear trim panel from the luggage compartment

5.27b Remove the storage compartment (fastener location arrowed) . . .

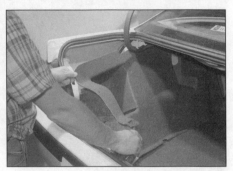

5.27c . . . then release the rear retaining clips and peel back the side trim panel to gain access to the rear light cluster

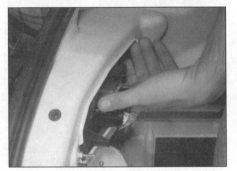

5.28 Depress the retaining clips and remove the bulbholder from the rear cluster . . .

5.29 . . . the relevant bulb can then be removed by pressing it in and turning anti-clockwise

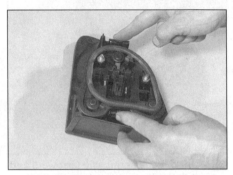

5.32 On Estate models, release the retaining clips and remove the bulbholder from the rear light unit . . .

remove the rear trim panel. Release the retaining clips (pull out the centre pins then prise out the complete clip) and peel back the trim panel to gain access to the rear of the light assembly, it may also prove necessary to undo the retaining screw and remove the tie-down hook. On some models, if work is being carried out on the left-hand side it will also be necessary to unscrew the fastener and remove the storage compartment to gain the necessary clearance required (see illustrations).
28 Release the retaining clips and remove the bulbholder assembly from the rear of the light cluster (see illustration).
29 All bulbs have bayonet fittings. The relevant bulb can be removed by pressing in and rotating anti-clockwise (see illustration).

Note that the stop/taillight bulb has offset pins to ensure it is fitted the correct way around.
30 Refitting is the reverse of the removal sequence.

Rear light - Estate models

31 Remove the light unit (see Section 7).
32 Release the retaining clips and remove the bulbholder from the rear of the light unit (see illustration).
33 All bulbs have bayonet fittings. The relevant bulb can be removed by pressing in and rotating anti-clockwise (see illustration). Note that the stop/taillight bulb has offset pins to ensure it is fitted the correct way around.
34 Refitting is the reverse of the removal sequence.

Number plate light - Saloon models

35 Release the retaining clips and remove the lens from the light unit. The bulb is of the capless (push-fit) type, and can be removed by simply pulling it out of the light unit (see illustrations).
36 Refitting is the reverse of removal, ensuring that the lens is clipped securely in position.

Number plate light - Estate models

37 Undo the retaining screw and remove the lens from the light unit. The bulb is of the capless (push-fit) type, and can be removed

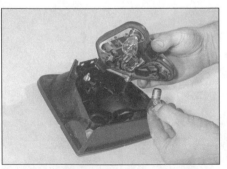

5.33 . . . remove the relevant bulb by pressing it in and turning anti-clockwise

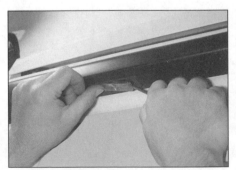

5.35a On Saloon models carefully prise out the number plate light lens . . .

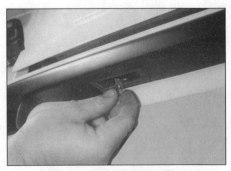

5.35b . . . and pull the bulb out from its holder

5.37a On Estate models, undo the retaining screw and remove the lens from the number plate light . . .

by simply pulling it out of the light unit **(see illustrations).**

38 Refitting is the reverse of removal. Do not overtighten the screw, as the lens is easily cracked.

6 Bulbs (interior lights) - renewal

General

1 Refer to Section 5, paragraph 1.

Front seat courtesy light and reading light

Models with an overhead console

2 Using a flat-bladed screwdriver, carefully unclip the lens from the overhead console **(see illustration).**

5.37b . . . then pull out the bulb from the light unit

3 Each individual bulb can then be removed by simply pulling it out of its holder **(see illustration).**

4 Refitting is the reverse of removal.

Models without an overhead console

5 Using a small, flat-bladed screwdriver, carefully prise light unit assembly out of position **(see illustration).**

6 Twist the bulbholder anti-clockwise and remove it from the light. The bulb is of the capless (push-fit) type, and can be removed by simply pulling it out of the bulbholder **(see illustrations).**

7 Refitting is the reverse of removal.

Rear courtesy light

8 Refer to the information given above in paragraphs 5 to 7.

Luggage compartment light

9 Refer to the information given above in paragraphs 5 to 7.

Instrument panel illumination/warning lights

10 Remove the instrument panel as described in Section 9.
11 Twist the relevant bulbholder anti-clockwise and withdraw it from the rear of the panel **(see illustration).**
12 All bulbs are integral with their holders. Be very careful to ensure the new bulbs are of the correct rating, the same as those removed; this is especially important in the case of the ignition/battery charging warning light.
13 Refit the bulbholder to the rear of the instrument panel then refit the instrument panel as described in Section 9.

Glovebox illumination light bulb

14 Open up the glovebox and renew the bulb as described in paragraphs 6 to 8.

Heater control panel illumination bulb

15 Remove the heater control panel from the facia as described in Chapter 3, noting that it is not necessary to detach the control cables (where fitted).
16 Twist the relevant bulbholder anti-clockwise and remove it from the control unit.
17 The bulb is of the capless (push-fit) type, and can be removed by simply pulling it out of the bulbholder.
18 Refitting is the reverse of removal.

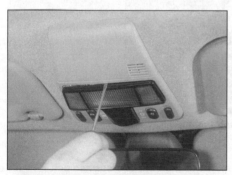

6.2 Carefully prise out the lens from the overhead console . . .

6.3 . . . then pull the relevant bulb out of position

6.5 Carefully prise the courtesy light unit out from the headlining . . .

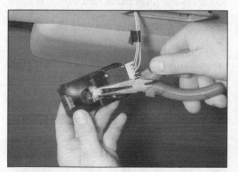

6.6a . . . then remove the bulbholder from the rear of the light . . .

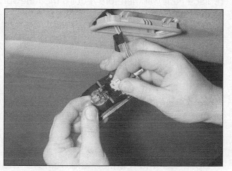

6.6b . . . and pull out the bulb

6.11 Removing an instrument panel bulbholder

6.20 Removing the clock illumination bulb

6.23 Removing a multi-function display illumination bulb

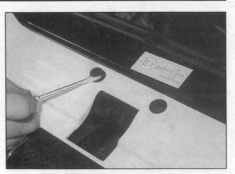

7.1a Remove the fasteners . . .

7.1b . . . then release the retaining clips and remove the grille panel from the car

7.2a Undo the retaining nut and bolts . . .

7.2b . . . then detach the bonnet release cable and remove crossmember assembly from the vehicle

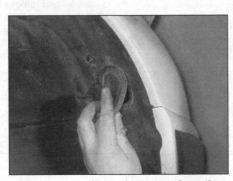

7.3a Remove the access cover from the wheelarch liner . . .

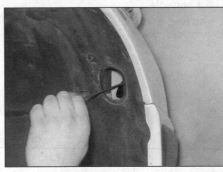

7.3b . . . and unhook the headlight retaining spring

Clock illumination bulb

19 Remove the clock (see Section 13).
20 Using a pair of pliers, twist the bulbholder through 90° and remove it from the side of the clock **(see illustration)**.
21 Refitting is the reverse of removal.

Multi-function display bulb

22 Remove the multi-function display as described in Section 11.
23 Twist the relevant bulbholder through 90° and remove it from the display **(see illustration)**.
24 Refitting is the reverse of removal.

Switch illumination bulbs

25 All of the switches are fitted with illuminating bulbs; some are also fitted with a bulb to show when the circuit concerned is

operating. On most switches, these bulbs are an integral part of the switch assembly, and cannot be obtained separately. Bulb replacement will therefore require the renewal of the complete switch assembly.

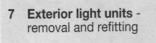

7 Exterior light units - removal and refitting

Note: *Disconnect the battery negative lead before removing any light unit, and reconnect the lead after refitting the light.*

Headlight

1 Open up the bonnet and remove the fasteners (pull out the centre pins then lever out the complete fastener) securing the grille

panel to the bonnet crossmember. Release the side retaining clips then, using a large flat-bladed screwdriver, depress the centre clip and slide the grille panel forwards and away from the vehicle **(see illustrations)**.
2 Slacken and remove the nuts securing the fan shroud to the bonnet lock crossmember, then undo the retaining bolts securing the crossmember in position. Unhook the bonnet release cable from the lock and remove the crossmember assembly **(see illustrations)**.
3 From underneath the wheelarch, prise out the small access cover from the liner to gain access to the headlight retaining spring. Using a pair of pointed-nose pliers or a piece of welding rod with a hooked end, unhook the spring from the body **(see illustrations)**. On some models it may be possible to access the spring from inside the engine compartment.

7.4a Undo the headlight retaining bolts . . .

7.4b . . . then manoeuvre the headlight unit out of position . . .

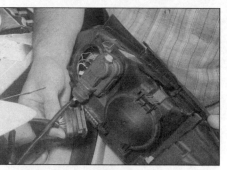
7.4c . . . and disconnect the wiring connectors

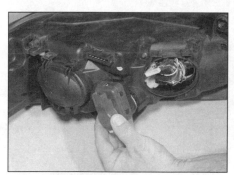
7.5a Twist the headlight levelling motor anti-clockwise to free it from the light . . .

7.5b . . . then unclip the motor balljoint from the reflector assembly

7.7 Undo the retaining screws and remove the plastic cover from beneath the foglight

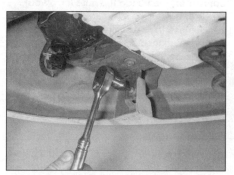
7.8a Unhook the upper retaining spring then undo the lower retaining screw . . .

7.8b . . . and remove the foglight from underneath the bumper

7.9 The foglight can be adjusted via the cover access hole using an Allen key

4 Slacken and remove the headlight retaining bolts (there are three in total) then disconnect the wiring and manoeuvre the headlight unit out of position (see illustrations).

5 On models equipped with a headlight levelling system, if necessary, remove the motor from the rear of the light unit by rotating it anti-clockwise and carefully unclipping its balljoint from the rear of the reflector assembly (see illustrations).

6 Refitting is a direct reversal of the removal procedure. Lightly tighten the retaining screws and check the alignment of the headlight with the bumper and bonnet. Once the light unit is correctly positioned, securely tighten the retaining screws and check the headlight beam alignment using the information given in Section 8.

Front foglight

7 To improve access, firmly apply the handbrake then jack up the front of the vehicle and support it on axle stands. Undo the retaining screws and remove the plastic cover from beneath the foglight (see illustration).

8 Disconnect the wiring connector then undo the lower retaining screw. Unhook the light unit upper retaining spring then manoeuvre the foglight out from underneath the front bumper (see illustrations).

9 Refitting is the reverse of removal, ensuring that the upper retaining spring is correctly engaged with the light unit lug. If necessary, adjust the foglight aim using the adjuster on the rear of the light unit; the adjuster can be rotated using an Allen key once the access plug has been removed from the cover,

alternatively remove the cover completely and rotate the adjuster by hand (see illustration).

Front direction indicator side repeater

10 Unclip the rear of the light unit and withdraw it from the wing. Free the bulbholder by rotating it anti-clockwise, and remove the light unit from the vehicle

11 Refitting is a reverse of the removal procedure.

Rear light cluster - Saloon models

12 From inside the luggage compartment, slacken and remove the retaining screws and remove the rear trim panel. Release the retaining clips (pull out the centre pins then

12

7.13 On Saloon models, disconnect the wiring connector(s) . . .

7.14a . . . then undo the retaining nuts . . .

7.14b . . . and remove the rear light unit

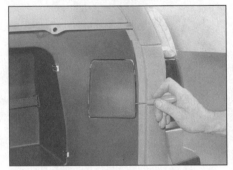

7.16 On Estate models, unclip the access cover . . .

7.17 . . . then disconnect the wiring connector. Unscrew the nut (arrowed) and remove the rear wing light unit

7.20a On Estate models, open up the access cover and disconnect the wiring connector, then undo the nuts (arrowed) . . .

prise out the complete clip) and peel back the trim panel to gain access to the rear of the light assembly, it may also prove necessary to undo the retaining screw and remove the tie-down hook. On some models, if work is being carried out on the left-hand side it will also be necessary to unscrew the fastener and remove the storage compartment to gain the necessary clearance required (see Section 5 for illustrations).

13 Depress the retaining clip(s) and disconnect the wiring connector(s) from the rear of the light cluster **(see illustration)**.

14 Slacken and remove the retaining nuts and remove the light unit from the vehicle **(see illustrations)**.

15 Refitting is the reverse of removal, ensuring that the retaining nuts are securely tightened.

Rear wing light - Estate models

16 Remove the storage compartment cover from the luggage compartment, and open up the access cover in the compartment to reveal the light unit **(see illustration)**.

17 Depress the retaining clip and disconnect the wiring connector, then undo the retaining nut and remove the light unit from the wing **(see illustration)**.

18 Refitting is the reverse of removal, tightening the retaining nut securely.

Tailgate light unit - Estate models

19 Open up the tailgate then release the retaining clips and open up the light unit access cover in the tailgate trim panel.

20 Depress the retaining clip and disconnect the wiring connector. Undo the retaining nuts then release the retaining clips and remove the light unit from the tailgate **(see illustrations)**.

21 Refitting is the reverse of removal, tightening the retaining nut securely.

High-level stop-light

Saloon models

22 Using hooked pieces of welding rod, insert the rods into the cut-outs on each end of the light unit and release the retaining clips by pulling them downwards **(see illustration)**.

23 Slide the light unit backwards to free it from its guides and remove it from the vehicle, disconnecting the wiring connector as it becomes accessible **(see illustration)**.

24 Refitting is the reverse of removal.

7.20b . . . and remove the rear light unit from the tailgate

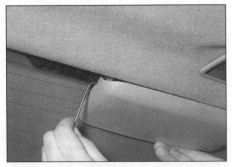

7.22 On Saloon models, using a hooked piece of welding rod, release the clips . . .

7.23 . . . then free the high-level stop-light from its guides and disconnect the wiring

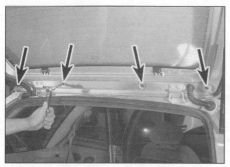

7.25 On Estate models undo the tailgate spoiler retaining screws (arrowed) . . .

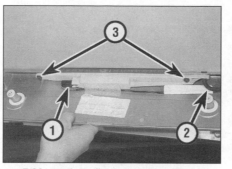

7.26 . . . then disconnect the wiring connector (1) and washer hose (2). Undo the retaining screws (3) and separate the high-level stop-light and spoiler

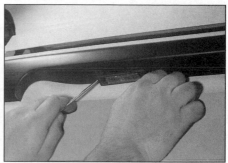

7.28a On Saloon models carefully prise out the number plate light from the bumper . . .

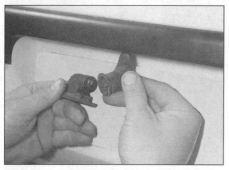

7.28b . . . and disconnect it from the wiring

7.30 On Estate models, remove the tailgate inner trim panel . . .

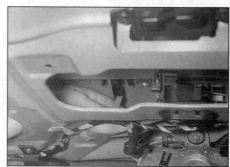

7.31a . . . then disconnect the wiring connector . . .

7.31b . . . and push the number plate light unit out of position

Estate models

25 Open up the tailgate then slacken and remove the spoiler retaining screws from the top edge of the tailgate **(see illustration)**.
26 Release the spoiler then disconnect the wiring connector and washer hose and remove it from the tailgate. Undo the retaining screws and separate the stop-light and spoiler **(see illustration)**.
27 Refitting is the reverse of removal.

Number plate light

Saloon models

28 Carefully prise the light unit out from the bumper/tailgate, disconnecting its wiring connector as it becomes accessible **(see illustrations)**.

29 On refitting, reconnect the wiring connector and clip the light unit securely in position.

Estate models

30 Open up the tailgate then undo the retaining screws and remove the inner handle. Unclip the surround from the lock inner button, then prise out the trim clips and remove the trim panel from the tailgate **(see illustration)**.
31 Disconnect the wiring connector from the rear of the light unit and push the light out of position **(see illustrations)**.
32 Refitting is the reverse of removal.

---

8 Headlight beam alignment - general information

Accurate adjustment of the headlight beam is only possible using optical beam setting equipment, and this work should therefore be carried out by a Peugeot dealer or suitably-equipped workshop.

For reference, the headlights can be adjusted by rotating the adjuster Allen screws on the rear of the headlight unit. The upper screw adjusts the headlight beam vertical aim, and the lower screw the headlight beam horizontal aim.

On models equipped with headlight levelling, ensure that the headlight beam

adjuster switch is set to position "0" before the headlights are adjusted. On models not equipped with headlight levelling, ensure that the manual adjuster on the rear of each light unit is set to position "0" before adjustment.

---

9 Instrument panel - removal and refitting

Removal

1 Disconnect the battery negative terminal.
2 Fully lower the steering column to improve access to the instrument panel.
3 Carefully prise out the access cover from the driver's end of the facia **(see illustration)**.

9.3 Prise out the access cover from the driver's end of the facia

9.4a Undo the retaining screws (arrowed) . . .

9.4b . . . then unclip the base of the shroud from the facia . . .

9.4c . . . and remove it from the vehicle (steering wheel removed for clarity)

9.5a Undo the retaining screws (arrowed) . . .

9.5b . . . then release the clip and withdraw the instrument panel from the facia

9.6 Release the clips and disconnect the instrument panel wiring connectors

4 Slacken and remove the three retaining screws from the top of the instrument panel. Carefully unclip the shroud and remove it from the vehicle; the shroud can be pushed out from behind, via the facia aperture **(see illustrations)**.

5 Unscrew the four instrument panel retaining screws. Insert a screwdriver between the top of the panel and the facia, and carefully lever the instrument panel out of position **(see illustrations)**.

6 Withdraw the panel until the wiring connectors are accessible, then release the retaining clips and disconnect both connectors **(see illustration)**. The instrument panel can then be removed from the vehicle.

Refitting

7 Reconnect the wiring connectors, securing them in position with the retaining clips, and clip the instrument panel back into position in the facia. Refit the panel retaining screws and tighten securely.

8 Clip the shroud back into position and securely tighten its retaining screws. Refit the cover to the end of the facia.

9 Reconnect the battery and check the operation of the panel warning lights to ensure that they are functioning correctly.

10 Instrument panel components - removal and refitting

At the time of writing, it was unclear if any of the instrument panel components were

available separately. Refer to your Peugeot dealer for the latest parts information; they will be able to advise you on the best course of action should the instrument(s) develop a fault.

11 Multi-function display - removal and refitting

Removal

1 Taking great care not to damage either the unit or facia, carefully prise the multi-function display from the facia **(see illustration)**. If preferred, to avoid damage, remove the instrument panel shroud as described in paragraphs 1 to 4 of Section 10, then reach in behind the multi-function display and push it out of position.

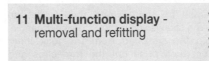

11.1 Carefully prise the multi-function display out of position . . .

2 Disconnect the wiring connector and remove the unit from the facia **(see illustration)**.

Refitting

3 Refitting is the reverse of removal.

12 Cigarette lighter - removal and refitting

Removal

1 Disconnect the battery negative terminal.

Manual transmission models

2 Unclip the gearchange lever gaiter from the centre console.

3 Reach in behind the cigarette lighter, then disconnect the wiring connector(s) and push the cigarette lighter out of position.

11.2 . . . and disconnect the wiring

Automatic transmission models

4 Remove the centre console as described in Chapter 11. The cigarette lighter can then easily be pushed out of position.

Refitting

5 Refitting is a reversal of the removal procedure, ensuring all the wiring connectors are securely reconnected.

13 Clock - removal and refitting

Removal

1 Disconnect the battery negative terminal.
2 Taking great care not to damage the clock or facia, gently prise the clock out of position and disconnect it from the wiring connector (see illustrations).

Refitting

3 Refitting is the reverse of removal.

14 Horn(s) - removal and refitting

Removal

Models fitted with an air horn

1 The air horn assembly (both the horn and compressor) are located behind the left-hand front wing.
2 To gain access to the assembly, firmly apply the handbrake then jack up the front of the vehicle and support it on axle stands.
3 Disconnect the wiring connector(s) then slacken and remove the horn and compressor mounting nuts and remove the assembly from the vehicle. The horn and compressor can then be separated.

Models fitted with conventional horns

4 Models not fitted with an air horn are fitted with twin conventional horns. The horns are located behind the front bumper, one is fitted on the right-hand side and the other on the left-hand side.
5 To gain access to the assembly, firmly apply the handbrake then jack up the front of the vehicle and support it on axle stands. Undo the retaining screws, and free the wheelarch liner/cover from the underside of the bumper and wheelarch (as applicable).
6 Disconnect the wiring connector(s) then slacken and remove the mounting nut(s) and remove the horn(s) from the vehicle.

Refitting

7 Refitting is the reverse of removal.

13.2a Carefully prise out the clock from the facia panel . . .

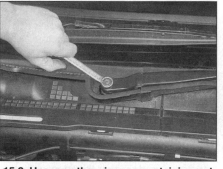
15.2 Unscrew the wiper arm retaining nut and remove the arm

15 Wiper arm - removal and refitting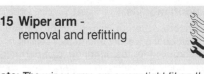

Note: *The wiper arms are a very tight fit on the spindles, and it is likely that a puller will be needed to remove them safely, without damage.*

Removal

1 Operate the wiper motor then switch it off so that the wiper arm returns to the at-rest position.
2 Prise off the wiper arm retaining nut cover (where fitted) then slacken and remove the nut (see illustration).
3 Lift the blade off the glass and pull the wiper arm off the motor. Carefully lever the arm off the spindle using a large, flat-bladed screwdriver. If the arm is very tight, free it from the spindle using a suitable puller (see illustration).

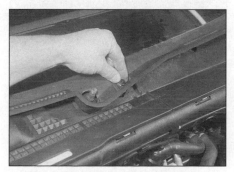
16.3a Unscrew the retaining nut . . .

13.2b . . . and disconnect its wiring connector

15.3 If the arm is a tight-fit, a puller will be required to free it from the spindle

Refitting

4 Ensure that the wiper and spindle are clean and dry, then refit the arm. Ensure that the arm is correctly positioned, then securely tighten the retaining nut. Where necessary, refit the spindle nut cover.

16 Windscreen wiper motor and linkage - removal and refitting

Removal

1 Disconnect the battery negative terminal.
2 Remove the wiper arms as described in the previous Section.
3 Unscrew the retaining nut, then unclip and remove the left- and right-hand plastic inlet vent covers from the base of the windscreen (see illustrations).

16.3b . . . then unclip and remove the left- and right-hand inlet vent covers . . .

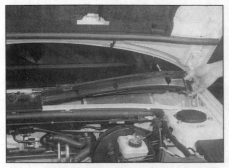

16.4 . . . and vent panels to gain access to the wiper motor

16.5 Depress the clip and disconnect the wiper motor wiring connector

16.6a Slacken and remove the mounting nuts and bolt (arrowed) . . .

16.6b . . . then manoeuvre the wiper motor out of position . . .

16.6c . . . and recover the spacers from the motor mounting rubbers

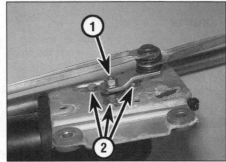

16.7 Wiper motor spindle nut (1) and mounting bolts (2)

4 Unclip the left- and right-hand inlet vent panels, and remove them from beneath the windscreen to gain access to the wiper motor **(see illustration)**.
5 Trace the wiring back from the wiper motor and disconnect it at the wiring connector **(see illustration)**.
6 Slacken and remove the wiper motor mounting nuts and bolt, and manoeuvre the wiper motor assembly out of position. Recover the spacers from the motor mounting rubbers **(see illustrations)**.
7 If necessary, mark the relative positions of the motor shaft and crank, then unscrew the retaining nut and washer and free the wiper linkage from the motor spindle. Unscrew the motor retaining bolts, and separate the motor and linkage **(see illustration)**.

Refitting

8 Refitting is the reverse of removal, ensuring all fasteners are securely tightened. Also ensure that the inlet vent panels are correctly clipped in position prior to refitting the wiper arms.

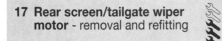

17 Rear screen/tailgate wiper motor - removal and refitting

Removal

1 Disconnect the battery negative terminal.
2 Remove the wiper arm as described in Section 15 and proceed as described under the relevant sub-heading.

Saloon models

3 Unscrew the nut from the motor spindle, and lift off the washer and rubber sealing ring.
4 From inside the luggage compartment, disconnect the wiring connector, then slacken and remove the nuts/bolts and manoeuvre the wiper motor assembly out of position.
5 Recover the inner seal from the wiper spindle and the spacers from the motor mounting rubbers.

Estate models

6 Open up the tailgate then prise out the retaining clips and remove the inner trim panel.
7 Slacken and remove the wiper motor retaining nuts and carefully manoeuvre the motor out of position, disconnecting its wiring connector as it becomes accessible. **Note:** *It may be necessary to slide the spacer off the motor spindle to gain the necessary clearance required to withdraw the motor.* Recover the

spacers from the motor mounting rubbers and remove the rubber sealing grommet from the tailgate glass **(see illustrations)**.

Refitting

8 Refitting is the reverse of removal. Prior to refitting, check the mounting rubbers, washers and sealing grommet (as applicable) for damage and renew if necessary.

18 Washer system components - removal and refitting

1 The washer reservoir is located behind the right-hand front wing. On Estate models, the reservoir also supplies the tailgate washer. On models equipped with headlight washers, the reservoir also supplies the headlight washer jets via an additional pump.

17.7a On Estate models, slacken and remove the retaining nuts (arrowed) . . .

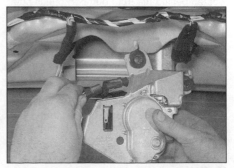

17.7b . . . then manoeuvre the motor out of position and disconnect the wiring . . .

17.7c ... noting that it may first be necessary to slide off the spacer

Washer system reservoir

2 Working in the engine compartment, remove the filler cap and unscrew the washer reservoir filler neck **(see illustration)**.
3 Firmly apply the handbrake then jack up the front of the vehicle and support it on axle stands. Remove the right-hand front roadwheel. Remove the retaining screws and fasteners, and peel back the wheelarch liner to reveal the reservoir.
4 If necessary, drain the reservoir by remove the rubber plug from the union on the reservoir base. Once all the fluid has drained, securely refit the plug.
5 Release the retaining clip(s) and disconnect the hose(s) from the washer pump union(s) (as applicable). Where there is more than one hose connection, make alignment marks to ensure that the hoses are correctly reconnected on refitting **(see illustration)**.
6 Disconnect the wiring connectors from the washer pump(s) and the fluid level sender unit.
7 Slacken and remove the retaining bolt from the top of the reservoir and remove it from the vehicle. **Note:** *Access to the bolt is very poor, and the bolt can only be easily reached if the headlight is removed* **(see illustration)**.
8 Refitting is the reverse of removal, ensuring that the hose(s) are securely reconnected. Refill the reservoir and check for leakage.

Washer pump

9 Disconnect the wiring connector and washer hose(s) from the pump. Drain the fluid reservoir (see paragraphs 3 to 5).
10 Carefully ease the pump out from the reservoir, and recover its sealing grommet. Wash off any spilt fluid with cold water.
11 Refitting is the reverse of removal, using a new sealing grommet if the original one shows signs of damage or deterioration. Refill the reservoir, and check the pump grommet for leaks.

Washer reservoir level switch

12 Firmly apply the handbrake then jack up the front of the vehicle and support it on axle stands. Remove the right-hand front roadwheel. Remove the retaining screws and fasteners, and peel back the wheelarch liner to reveal the reservoir.

17.7d **Remove the sealing grommet from the tailgate and examine it for signs of damage or deterioration**

13 Disconnect the wiring connector from the level switch, and carefully ease the switch out from the reservoir. Recover the sealing grommet and wash off any spilt fluid with cold water.
14 Refitting is the reverse of removal, using a new sealing grommet if the original one shows signs of damage or deterioration.

Windscreen washer jets

15 Open up the bonnet to gain access to the windscreen washer jets. Disconnect the washer hoses from the relevant jet, then depress the retaining clips and carefully ease the jet away from the bonnet.
16 On refitting, securely connect the jet to the hose, and clip it into position in the bonnet. Check the operation of the jet. If necessary adjust the nozzles using a pin, aiming one nozzle to a point slightly above the centre of the swept area, and the other to

18.2 **Unscrew the large nut (arrowed) and remove the filler neck from the washer reservoir**

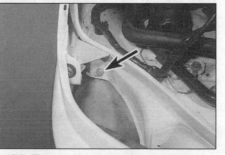

18.7 **The washer reservoir retaining bolt (arrowed) is only easily accessible once the headlight is removed**

slightly below the centre point to ensure complete coverage.

Tailgate washer jet

17 Open up the tailgate then undo the retaining screws and free the spoiler from the upper edge of the tailgate.
18 Disconnect the washer hose then unclip the jet and remove it from the spoiler.
19 Refitting is the reverse of removal. If necessary adjust the nozzle using a pin.

Headlight washer jets

20 Remove the front bumper (Chapter 11).
21 Disconnect the washer hose then undo the retaining screws and remove the jet assembly from the bumper.
22 Refitting is the reverse of removal.

19 Radio/cassette player - removal and refitting

Note: *The following removal and refitting procedure is for the range of equipment fitted by Peugeot. Note that it is likely the special removal tools will be required to withdraw the audio unit from the facia - refer to your Peugeot dealer for further information.*

Removal

1 Insert the tools into the holes in each side of the unit to release the retaining clips **(see illustration)**. **Note:** *If the special tools are not available, it may be possible to release the clips using two lengths of welding rod.*

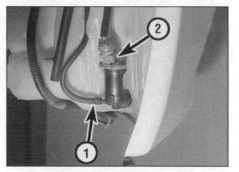

18.5 **Washer pump hose (1) and wiring connector (2)**

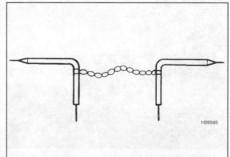

19.1 **Special Peugeot tools for removing the radio/cassette player**

12

19.2 Slide out the radio/cassette unit and disconnect the wiring and aerial lead

2 Carefully slide the audio unit out of position whilst ensuring that the wiring does not become trapped or caught. Disconnect the wiring connectors and aerial lead and remove the unit from the vehicle (see illustration). Note: If there is insufficient wiring to allow the unit to be withdrawn, remove the ashtray insert then carefully unclip the ashtray surround and remove it from centre console. Working inside the ashtray aperture, slacken and remove the retaining screws and remove centre console side panels (see Chapter 11) to allow access to the wiring from behind.

Refitting

3 Refitting is the reverse of removal.

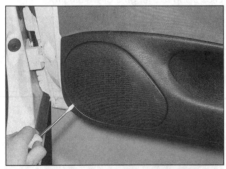

20.4 Carefully prise out the speaker grille from the door trim panel . . .

20.7 On Saloon models, unscrew the retaining ring from within the luggage compartment . . .

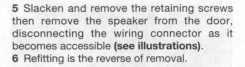

20 Loudspeakers - removal and refitting

Facia loudspeaker

1 Carefully prise the speaker out of position, taking great care not to damage the facia panel or speaker grille (see illustration).
2 Disconnect the wiring connector and remove the speaker from the vehicle (see illustration).
3 Refitting is the reverse of removal, ensuring the speaker is clipped securely in position.

Front door speaker

4 Carefully prise the speaker out of position, taking great care not to damage the door panel or speaker grille (see illustration).

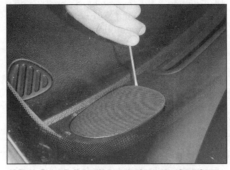

20.1 Carefully prise out the speaker from the top of the facia . . .

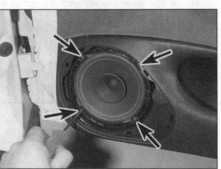

20.5a . . . then undo the retaining screws (arrowed) . . .

20.8 . . . then lift the rear speaker out of position and disconnect its wiring

5 Slacken and remove the retaining screws then remove the speaker from the door, disconnecting the wiring connector as it becomes accessible (see illustrations).
6 Refitting is the reverse of removal.

Rear speaker - Saloon models

7 From within the luggage compartment, unscrew the retaining ring from the base of the speaker (see illustration).
8 From inside the vehicle, lift the speaker out of position, disconnecting its wiring as it becomes accessible (see illustration).
9 Refitting is the reverse of removal.

Rear speaker - Estate models

10 Open up the tailgate. Peel the tailgate sealing strip away from the relevant rear pillar upper trim panel, then unclip the trim panel and remove it from the car (see illustration).

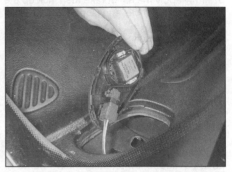

20.2 . . . and disconnect its wiring connector (viewed through windscreen)

20.5b . . . and remove the speaker, disconnecting it from the wiring

20.10 On Estate models, unclip the trim panel from the rear pillar to gain access to the rear speaker

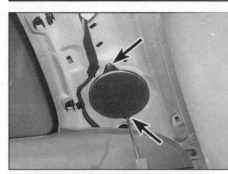

20.11a Undo the retaining screws (arrowed) . . .

20.11b . . . then remove the speaker and disconnect it from the wiring

21.2a Remove the insulating cap . . .

21.2b . . . to gain access to the aerial retaining nut (arrowed)

11 Undo the retaining screws and remove the speaker, disconnecting its wiring connector as it becomes accessible (see illustrations).
12 Refitting is the reverse of removal.

21 Radio aerial - removal and refitting

Removal

1 The aerial mast can is a screw-fit in its base, and is easily removed.
2 To remove the complete aerial, remove the overhead console or courtesy light (as applicable - see Section 6) to gain access to the mounting nut. Remove the insulating cap then slacken and remove the aerial lead nut (see illustrations). Detach the aerial lead and lift the aerial off from the roof, noting its rubber seal.

Refitting

3 Refitting is the reverse of removal.

22 Cruise control system components - removal and refitting

1 The cruise control system is vacuum-operated. The main components of the system are the electronic control unit (ECU), the vacuum pump, the solenoid valve, the

actuator and the cable. The system is controlled by the switch on the steering column, and there are also switches on the brake and (where necessary) clutch pedals.

Removal

Electronic control unit (ECU)

2 The cruise control ECU is located behind the glovebox. Prior to removal, disconnect the battery negative terminal.
3 Slide out the hinge pins and remove the glovebox from the facia. Undo the retaining screw(s) and remove the access cover from the facia to reveal the ECU.
4 Remove the retaining clips (pull out the centre pins then prise them out) and remove the undercover from beneath the passenger side of the facia.
5 Disconnect the wiring connector(s) then undo the retaining screws and remove the ECU from underneath the facia.

Vacuum pump

6 The vacuum pump is situated in the engine compartment. Prior to removal, disconnect the battery negative terminal.
7 Disconnect the wiring connector and vacuum hose from the pump, then undo the retaining screws and remove the pump from its mounting bracket.

Solenoid valve

8 The solenoid valve is mounted onto the same bracket as the vacuum pump.
9 Disconnect the battery negative terminal, then disconnect the solenoid wiring connector and vacuum hose.

10 Undo the screws and remove the solenoid valve from the engine compartment.

Throttle actuator and cable

11 Unclip the cable from the throttle cam balljoint, then carefully prise off the retaining clip and free the outer cable from its mounting bracket.
12 Disconnect the vacuum hose from the actuator unit, then undo the retaining nut and remove the actuator and cable assembly from the engine compartment.
13 If necessary, remove the outer cable retaining clip and detach the cable and bracket from the actuator.

System operating switch

14 Refer to Section 4.

Brake and clutch pedal switches

15 Refer to Chapter 9.

Refitting

16 Refitting is the reverse of removal. On completion check the operation of the cruise control system.

23 Anti-theft alarm and engine immobiliser system - general information

Note: *This information is applicable only to the anti-theft alarm system fitted by Peugeot as standard equipment.*

General

Most models in the range are fitted with an anti-theft alarm system as standard equipment. The alarm is automatically armed and disarmed using the remote central locking transmitter (where applicable). When the system is activated, the alarm indicator light, located on the centre console, will flash continuously. In addition to the alarm function, the system also incorporates an engine immobiliser.

Additionally, most models are also fitted with a coded engine immobiliser device, operated by a key pad mounted in the driver's side facia lower panel. The immobiliser indicator light is located in the facia centre switch panel.

Anti-theft alarm system

Note that if the doors are operated using the key, the alarm will not be armed or disarmed (as applicable). If for some reason the remote central locking transmitter fails whilst the alarm is armed, the alarm can be disarmed using the key. To do this, open the door with the key, then enter the vehicle, noting that the alarm will sound as the door is opened, and switch on the ignition switch whilst depressing the small alarm button, located on the centre console. Note that the ignition switch must be turned on and the button depressed within 10 seconds of opening the door.

The alarm system has switches on the bonnet, tailgate and each of the doors. It also has ultrasonic sensing, which detects movement inside the vehicle, via sensors mounted on either side of the vehicle interior. If required, the ultrasonic sensing facility can be switched off, whilst retaining the switched side of the system. To switch off the ultrasonic sensing, with the ignition switch off, depress the alarm switch (located on the centre console) until the alarm indicator light is continuously lit. Now, when the doors are locked using the remote central locking transmitter, and the alarm is armed, only the switched side of the alarm system is operational (and the alarm indicator light will revert to its flashing mode). This facility is useful, as it allows you to leave the windows/sunroof open, and still arm the alarm. If the windows/sunroof are left open with the ultrasonic sensing not switched off, the alarm may be falsely triggered by a gust of wind.

To deactivate the complete alarm system, switch on the ignition switch and then depress the alarm switch on the centre console and hold for approximately two seconds. The alarm indicator light should then flash rapidly for three seconds, indicating the alarm is disarmed. To reactivate the system, simply lock then unlock the vehicle using the remote transmitter; the alarm will be functional again the next time the vehicle is locked with the remote control.

Should the alarm system become faulty, the vehicle should be taken to a Peugeot dealer for examination.

Coded engine immobiliser

> ⚠ **Warning: Do not forget the immobiliser code - if the correct code cannot be entered, the engine management electronic control unit may have to be renewed.**

This device prevents the engine from being started unless a confidential code is keyed into the pad located in the driver's side facia lower panel. The immobiliser has two modes of operation - manual, where the owner must enter the code every time in order to enable the vehicle to be started, or automatic, where the system is automatically disarmed (for 1 minute only) using the remote central locking unit. The mode of operation can be chosen by the owner, and full details are given in the vehicle handbook. The owner can also change the code, if wished.

When the ignition is turned on, if the green light on the key pad is illuminated, the system is disabled and the engine can be started normally. If the red light is illuminated, the system is working (the engine cannot be started, and the alarm will sound if starting is attempted).

Should the immobiliser system become faulty, the vehicle should be taken to a Peugeot dealer for examination.

Disconnecting the battery

Prior to disconnecting the battery, the alarm system must be deactivated as described in paragraph 5. Failure to deactivate the alarm will lead to the siren sounding when the battery is disconnected. Once the battery is reconnected, reactivate the alarm using the remote central locking unit.

24 Electric front seat components - removal and refitting

Renewal of the front seat heater pads and/or electric motors should be entrusted to a Peugeot dealer. Renewal involves dismantling of the complex seat assembly. Heater pad renewal is especially difficult to achieve successfully. In practice, it will be very difficult for the home mechanic to carry out the job without ruining the upholstery. The only items which are easily removed or refitted are the operating switches (see Section 4).

25 Airbag system - general information and precautions

Both a driver's and passenger airbag are fitted as standard to some models in the range; on other models they were available as an optional extra. Models fitted with a driver's side airbag have the word AIRBAG stamped on the airbag unit, which is fitted to the centre of the steering wheel. Models also equipped with a passenger side airbag also have the word AIRBAG stamped on the passenger airbag unit which is fitted to the top of the facia. The airbag system comprises of the airbag unit(s) (complete with gas generators), the control unit (with an integral impact sensor) and a warning light in the instrument panel.

The airbag system is triggered in the event of a heavy frontal impact above a predetermined force, depending on the point of impact. The airbag is inflated within milliseconds, and forms a safety cushion between the driver and steering wheel and (where fitted) the passenger and facia. This prevents contact between the upper body and wheel/facia, and therefore greatly reduces the risk of injury. The airbag then deflates almost immediately. The control unit also operates the front seat belt tensioner mechanisms at the same time as the airbag(s) (see Chapter 11).

Every time the ignition is switched on, the airbag control unit performs a self-test. The self-test takes approximately 6 seconds and during this time the airbag warning light in the instrument panel is illuminated. After the self-test has been completed, the warning light should go out. If the warning light fails to come on, remains illuminated after the initial period, or comes on at any time when the vehicle is being driven, there is a fault in the airbag system. The vehicle should be taken to a Peugeot dealer for examination at the earliest possible opportunity.

25.4 To disable the airbag system, disconnect the battery then disconnect the airbag control unit wiring (see text)

> ⚠ **Warning: Before carrying out any operations on the airbag system, disconnect the battery negative terminal and wait at least two minutes. Remove the centre console (see Chapter 11) then release the retaining clip and disconnect the main wiring connector from the airbag control unit (see illustration). When operations are complete, reconnect the control unit and refit the centre console. Make sure no one is inside the vehicle when the battery is reconnected then, with the driver's door open, switch the ignition on from outside the vehicle.**

> ⚠ **Warning: Note that the airbag(s) must not be subjected to temperatures in excess of 100°C. When the airbag is removed, ensure that it is stored the correct way up to prevent possible inflation.**
> **Warning: Do not allow any solvents or cleaning agents to contact the airbag assemblies. They must be cleaned using only a damp cloth.**
> **Warning: The airbags and control unit are both sensitive to impact. If either is dropped or damaged they should be renewed.**
> **Warning: Disconnect the airbag control unit wiring plug prior to using arc-welding equipment on the vehicle.**

26 Airbag system components - removal and refitting

Note: *Refer to the warnings in Section 25 before carrying out the following operations.*
1 Disconnect the battery negative terminal, wait at least two minutes, then remove the centre console as described in Chapter 11. Release the retaining clip and disconnect the main wiring connector from the airbag control unit. This will disable the airbag system.

26.3 Remove the driver's airbag unit from the steering wheel and disconnect its wiring connector

26.4 Tighten the driver's airbag unit screws to the specified torque, making sure the left-hand screw is tightened first

26.8 Passenger airbag unit retaining nuts (arrowed)

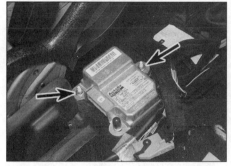

26.11 Airbag control unit retaining nuts (arrowed)

26.16a Undo the screws and remove the steering column lower shroud . . .

26.16b . . . disconnect the switch wiring connector(s)

Driver's side airbag

Removal

2 Slacken and remove the two airbag retaining screws from the rear of the steering wheel, rotating the wheel as necessary to gain access to the screws.

3 Return the steering wheel to the straight-ahead position, then carefully lift the airbag assembly away from the steering wheel and disconnect the wiring connector from the rear of the unit **(see illustration)**. Note that the airbag must not be knocked or dropped, and should be stored the correct way up with its padded surface uppermost.

Refitting

4 Ensure that the wiring connector is securely reconnected, and seat the airbag unit centrally in the steering wheel, making sure the wire does not become trapped. Fit the retaining screws and tighten them to the specified torque, noting the left-hand retaining screw should be tightened first **(see illustration)**.

5 Reconnect the airbag control unit wiring connector then refit the centre console as described in Chapter 11.

6 Ensure no one is inside the vehicle and reconnect the battery. With the driver's door open, turn on the ignition switch and check the operation of the airbag warning light.

Passenger side airbag

Removal

7 Remove the facia (see Chapter 11).

8 Slacken and remove the retaining nuts then release the airbag unit from its mountings and remove it from the facia **(see illustration)**.

Refitting

9 Manoeuvre the airbag into position, making sure it is correctly engaged with its mounting tangs, then refit the mounting nuts and tighten them securely.

10 Refit the facia as described in Chapter 11 and reconnect the battery (see paragraph 6).

Airbag control unit

Removal

11 Unscrew the retaining nuts and remove the control unit from the vehicle **(see illustration)**.

Refitting

12 Refit the control unit, making sure the arrow on the top of the unit is pointing towards the front of the vehicle. Refit the mounting nuts and tighten them to the specified torque setting.

13 Reconnect the wiring connector and refit the centre console (see Chapter 11).

14 Ensure no one is inside the vehicle, then reconnect the battery. With the driver's door open, turn on the ignition switch and check the operation of the airbag warning light.

Airbag wiring contact unit

Removal

15 Remove the driver's side airbag unit then remove the steering wheel as described in

Chapter 10. Ensure that the front wheels are pointing in the straight-ahead position.

16 Undo the retaining screws securing the steering column lower shroud in position, then unclip and remove both the upper and lower shrouds from the column, disconnecting the cruise control and/or radio control switch wiring connector(s) (as applicable) **(see illustrations)**.

17 Trace the wiring back from the contact unit and disconnect it at the connector **(see illustration)**.

18 Slacken and remove the retaining screws and remove the contact unit from the top of the steering column **(see illustrations)**.

Refitting

19 Prior to refitting it is necessary to ensure that the contact unit is correctly centralised, with the arrow markings on the top of the unit

26.17 Disconnect the contact unit wiring connector . . .

12

26.18a . . . then undo the retaining screws (arrowed) . . .

26.18b . . . and remove the unit from the top of the steering column

26.19 Prior to refitting the steering wheel, centralise the contact unit as described in text so that the index marks (arrowed) are aligned

correctly aligned, and that the front wheels are pointing in the straight-ahead position. If there is any doubt about the unit position, rotate the contact unit insert in a clockwise direction until resistance is felt. From this point, rotate the insert back through two to two and a half rotations until the arrows on the top surface of the unit are correctly aligned; the wiring harness will be at the bottom **(see illustration)**. Do not rotate the unit from now on.

20 Slide the contact unit into position, making sure its wiring is correctly routed, and engage it with the switch housing column. Ensure that the contact ring is correctly seated and securely tighten its retaining screws.

21 Reconnect the contact unit wiring connector, making sure it is correctly routed.

22 Reconnect the wiring connector(s) and refit the steering column shrouds. Ensure that the wiring is not trapped by the shrouds, then refit the retaining screws and tighten them securely.

23 Refit the steering wheel as described in Chapter 10, then refit the airbag unit as described in paragraphs 4 to 6.

Key to symbols

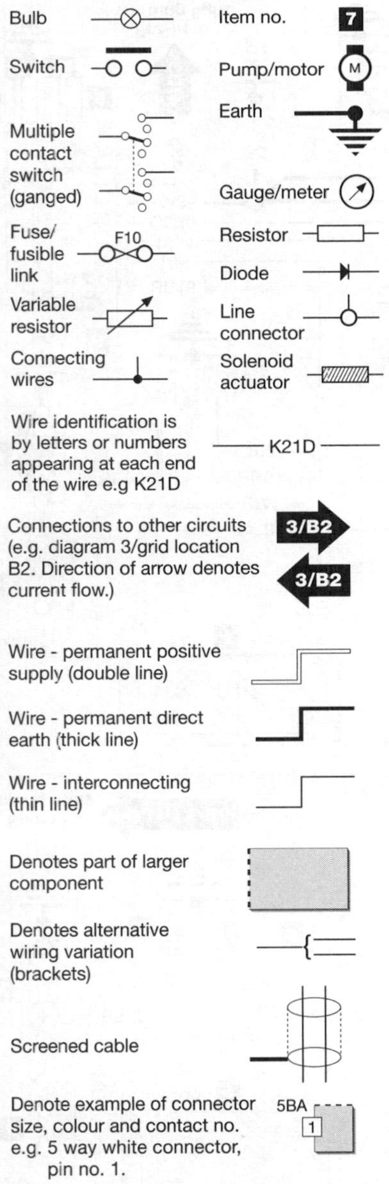
Bulb
Item no.
7
Switch
Pump/motor
M
Multiple contact switch (ganged)
Earth
Gauge/meter
Fuse/ fusible link
F10
Resistor
Diode
Variable resistor
Line connector
Connecting wires
Solenoid actuator
Wire identification is by letters or numbers appearing at each end of the wire e.g K21D
K21D
Connections to other circuits (e.g. diagram 3/grid location B2. Direction of arrow denotes current flow.)
3/B2
3/B2
Wire - permanent positive supply (double line)
Wire - permanent direct earth (thick line)
Wire - interconnecting (thin line)
Denotes part of larger component
Denotes alternative wiring variation (brackets)
Screened cable
Denote example of connector size, colour and contact no. e.g. 5 way white connector, pin no. 1.
5BA
1

Battery fusebox 1

Fuse	*Rating*	*Circuit protected*
F1	50A	Anti-theft system
F2	50A	Post ignition anti-theft system
F3	50A	Main battery supply
F4	50A	Lighting control, anti-start

Battery fusebox 2

Fuse	*Rating*	*Circuit protected*
F5	50A	ABS
F6	20/40A	Fan 1
F7	20/40A	Fan 2
F8	40A	Heated rear screen

Engine fusebox

Fuse	*Rating*	*Circuit protected*
F1	-	Spare
F2	-	Free
F3	25A	ABS
F4	20A	Engine running
F5	15A	Double relay
F6	-	Free
F7	15A	Headlight washer
F8	-	Free
F9	10A	Oxygen sensor
F10	10A	Fuel pump
F11	-	Free
F12	10A	LH front foglight
F13	10A	RH front foglight
F14	10A	LH main beam
F15	10A	RH main beam

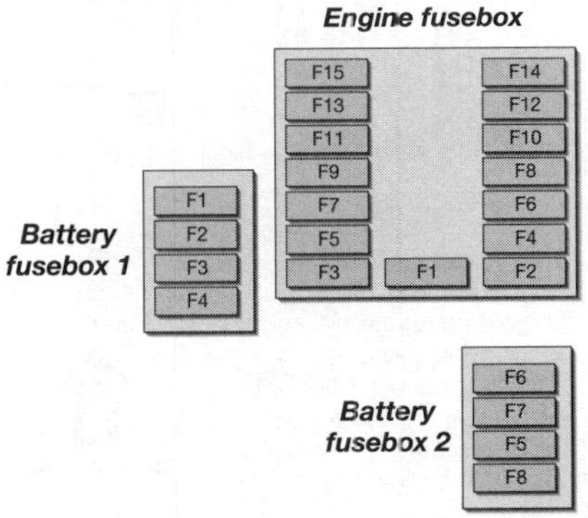
Engine fusebox
F15
F14
F13
F12
F11
F10
F9
F8
F7
F6
F5
F4
F3
F1
F2
Battery fusebox 1
F1
F2
F3
F4
Battery fusebox 2
F6
F7
F5
F8

Passenger fusebox

Fuse	*Rating*	*Circuit protected*
F1	10A	Cigar lighter
F1A		
F2	5A	Radiator water level, water in fuel warning light (diesel), instrument panel, power steering, gears interface housing
F3	10A	Electronic suspension
F4	5A	LH front, RH rear side lights, lighting rheostat
F5	10A	Headlight adjustment, headlight washer, RH dipped beam and warning light
F6	15A	Automatic gearbox ECU and position switch
F7	20A	Caravan
F8	-	Shunt
F9	5A	Front RH, LH rear side lights
F10	30A	Memory seats and mirrors
F11	30A	Front left seat
F12	15A	Reversing lights, air conditioning, alarm ECU and siren, stop lights
F13	30A	Front right seat
F14	30A	Rear window mechanism
F15	20A	Central locking, alarm
F16	10A	Radio
F16A	10A	Radio
F17	20A	Central locking
F18	5A	Rear fog light
F19	5A	Interior illumination
F20	10A	LH headlight dipped beam
F21	10A	Air conditioning/heating and ventilation
F22	20A	Rear wiper
F23	-	Shunt
F24	30A	Windscreen wiper, heated rear window, cruise control
F25	10A	Radio, clock, instrument panel, trip computer front/rear courtesy light
F26	15A	Hazard warning lights
F27	30A	One touch electric window
F28	10A	Trip computer, electric mirrors, one touch electric windows, memory seats and mirrors, central locking receiver, front electric windows, sunroof, stop lights and clock
F29	30A	Front electric windows and sunroof
F30	15A	Front/rear interior light, vanity mirror, glove box light, lights on buzzer

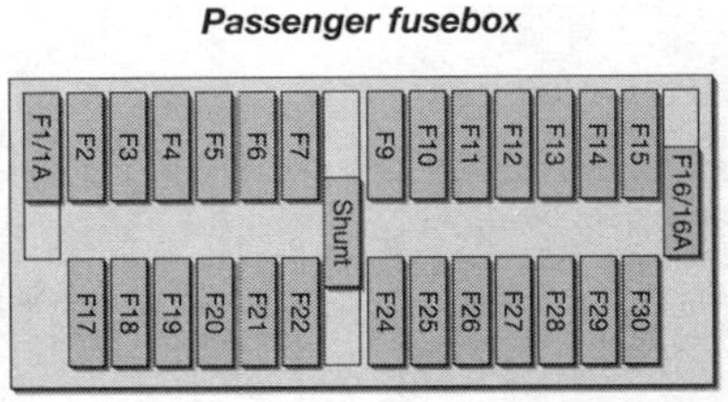
Passenger fusebox
F1/1A
F2
F3
F4
F5
F6
F7
Shunt
F9
F10
F11
F12
F13
F14
F15
F16/16A
F17
F18
F19
F20
F21
F22
F24
F25
F26
F27
F28
F29
F30
H29460

Diagram 1 : Information for wiring diagrams

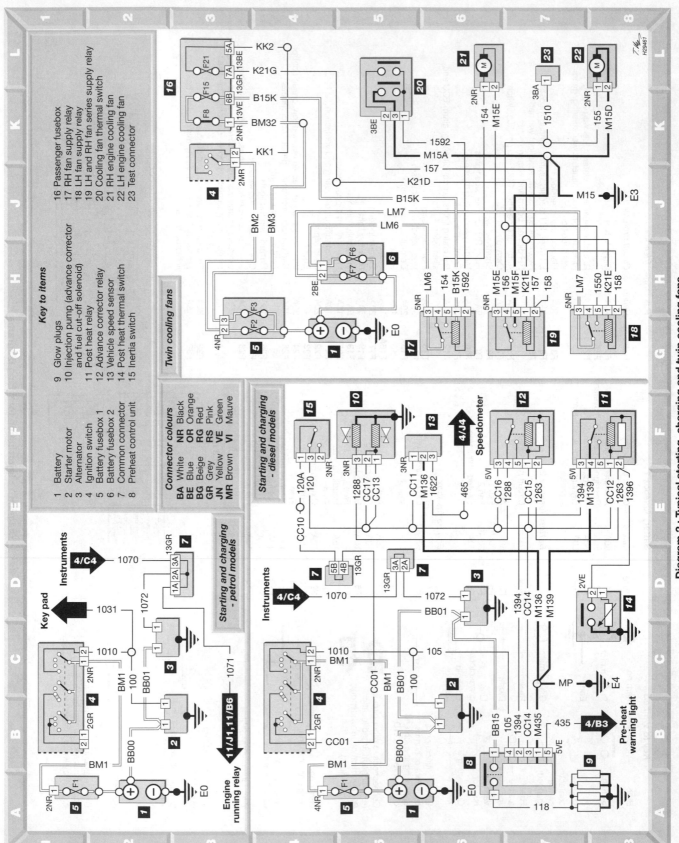

Key to items

1 Battery
2 Starter motor
3 Alternator
4 Ignition switch
5 Battery fusebox 1
6 Battery fusebox 2
7 Common connector
8 Preheat control unit

9 Glow plugs
10 Injection pump (advance corrector and fuel cut-off solenoid)
11 Post heat relay
12 Advance corrector relay
13 Vehicle speed sensor
14 Post heat thermal switch
15 Inertia switch

16 Passenger fusebox
17 RH fan supply relay
18 LH fan supply relay
19 LH and RH fan series supply relay
20 Cooling fan thermal switch
21 RH engine cooling fan
22 LH engine cooling fan
23 Test connector

Connector colours

BA White   NR Black
BE Blue   OR Orange
BG Beige   RG Red
GR Grey   RS Pink
JN Yellow   VE Green
MR Brown   VI Mauve

Twin cooling fans

Starting and charging - diesel models

Starting and charging - petrol models

Speedometer

Instruments

Key pad

Engine running relay

Pre-heat warning light

Diagram 2 : Typical starting, charging and twin cooling fans

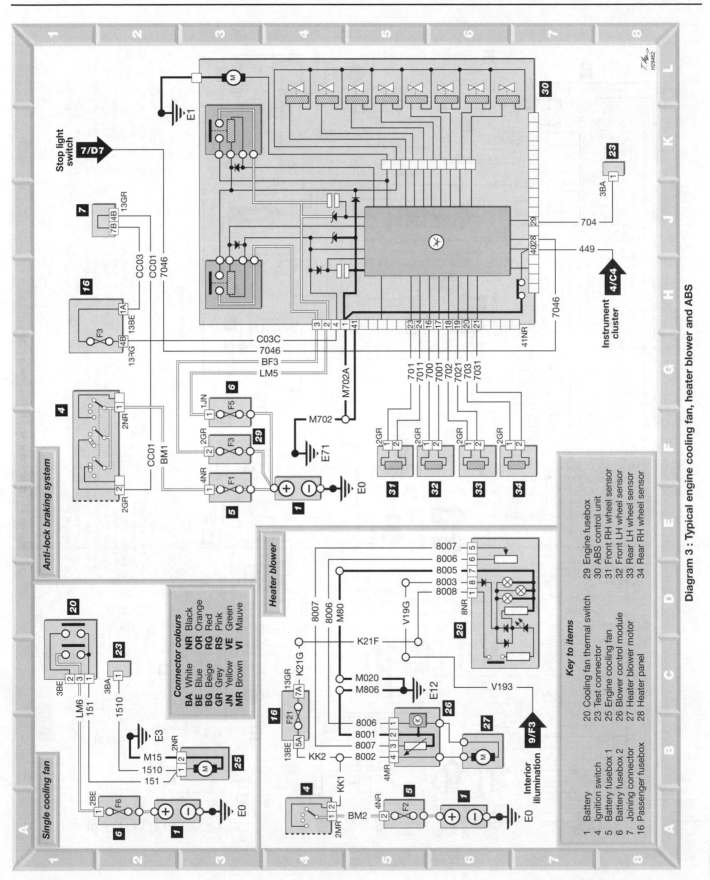

Diagram 3 : Typical engine cooling fan, heater blower and ABS

Stop light switch **7/D7**

Instrument cluster **4/C4**

Anti-lock braking system

Single cooling fan

Heater blower

Interior illumination **9/F3**

Connector colours

BA White	**NR** Black		
BE Blue	**OR** Orange		
BG Beige	**RG** Red		
GR Grey	**RS** Pink		
JN Yellow	**VE** Green		
MR Brown	**VI** Mauve		

Key to items

1 Battery
4 Ignition switch
6 Battery fusebox 1
7 Battery fusebox 2
7 Joining connector
16 Passenger fusebox

20 Cooling fan thermal switch
23 Test connector
25 Engine cooling fan
26 Blower control module
27 Heater blower motor
28 Heater panel

29 Engine fusebox
30 ABS control unit
31 Front RH wheel sensor
32 Front LH wheel sensor
33 Rear LH wheel sensor
34 Rear RH wheel sensor

12

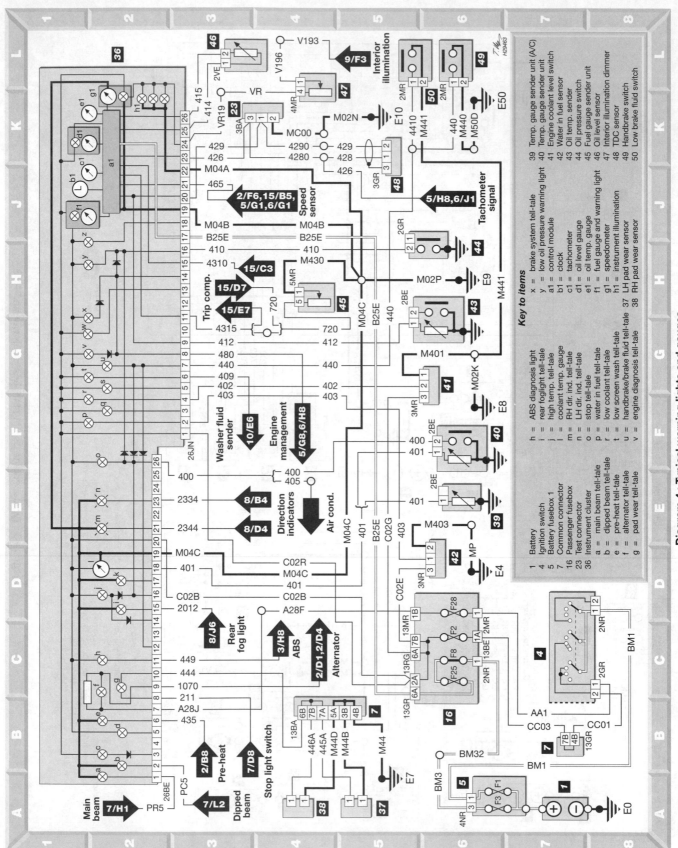

Diagram 4 : Typical warning lights and gauges

Key to items

1 = Battery
4 = Ignition switch
5 = Battery fusebox 1
16 = Passenger fusebox
23 = Test connector
36 = Instrument cluster

a = main beam tell-tale
b = dipped beam tell-tale
e = pre-heat tell-tale
f = alternator tell-tale
g = pad wear tell-tale

h = main beam tell-tale
i = rear foglight tell-tale
j = high temp. tell-tale
k = coolant temp. gauge
m = RH dir. ind. tell-tale
n = LH dir. ind. tell-tale
o = stop tell-tale
p = water in fuel tell-tale
r = low coolant tell-tale
t = low screen wash tell-tale
u = handbrake/brake fluid tell-tale 37 = LH pad wear sensor
v = engine diagnosis tell-tale 38 = RH pad wear sensor

x = brake system tell-tale
y = low oil pressure warning light
a1 = control module
b1 = clock
c1 = tachometer
d1 = oil level gauge
e1 = oil temp. gauge
f1 = fuel gauge and warning light
g1 = speedometer
h1 = instrument illumination

39 = Temp. gauge sender unit (A/C)
40 = Temp. gauge sender unit
41 = Engine coolant level switch
42 = Water in fuel sensor
43 = Oil temp. sender
44 = Oil pressure switch
45 = Fuel gauge sender unit
46 = Oil level sensor
47 = Interior illumination dimmer
48 = TDC sensor
49 = Handbrake switch
50 = Low brake fluid switch

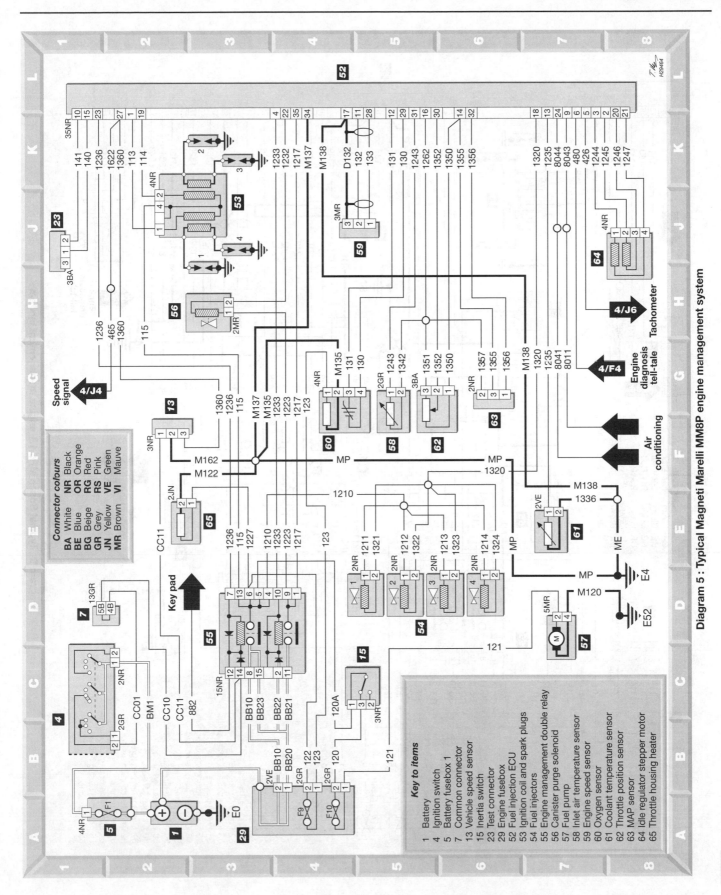

Diagram 5 : Typical Magneti Marelli MM8P engine management system

Connector colours

BA	White	NR	Black
BE	Blue	OR	Orange
BG	Beige	RG	Red
GR	Grey	RS	Pink
JN	Yellow	VE	Green
MR	Brown	VI	Mauve

Key to items

1 Battery
4 Ignition switch
5 Battery fusebox 1
7 Common connector
13 Vehicle speed sensor
15 Inertia switch
23 Test connector
29 Engine fusebox
52 Fuel injection ECU
53 Ignition coil and spark plugs
54 Fuel injectors
55 Engine management double relay
56 Canister purge solenoid
57 Fuel pump
58 Inlet air temperature sensor
59 Engine speed sensor
60 Oxygen sensor
61 Coolant temperature sensor
62 Throttle position sensor
63 MAP sensor
64 Idle regulator stepper motor
65 Throttle housing heater

Speed signal 4/J4

4/J6 Tachometer

4/F4 Engine diagnosis tell-tale

Air conditioning

12

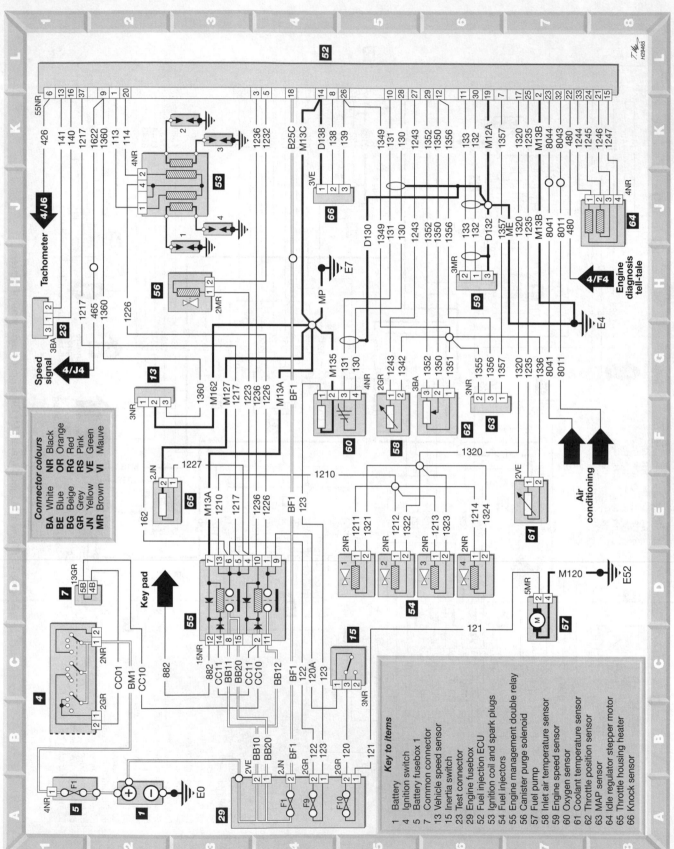

Diagram 6 : Typical Bosch MP5.1.1 engine management system

Connector colours
BA White   NR Black
BE Blue   OR Orange
BG Beige   RG Red
GR Grey   RS Pink
JN Yellow   VE Green
MR Brown   VI Mauve

Key to items
1 Battery
4 Ignition switch
5 Battery fusebox 1
7 Common connector
13 Vehicle speed sensor
15 Inertia switch
23 Test connector
29 Engine fusebox
52 Fuel injection ECU
53 Ignition coil and spark plugs
54 Fuel injectors
55 Engine management double relay
56 Canister purge solenoid
57 Fuel pump
58 Inlet air temperature sensor
59 Engine speed sensor
60 Oxygen sensor
61 Coolant temperature sensor
62 Throttle position sensor
63 MAP sensor
64 Idle regulator stepper motor
65 Throttle housing heater
66 Knock sensor

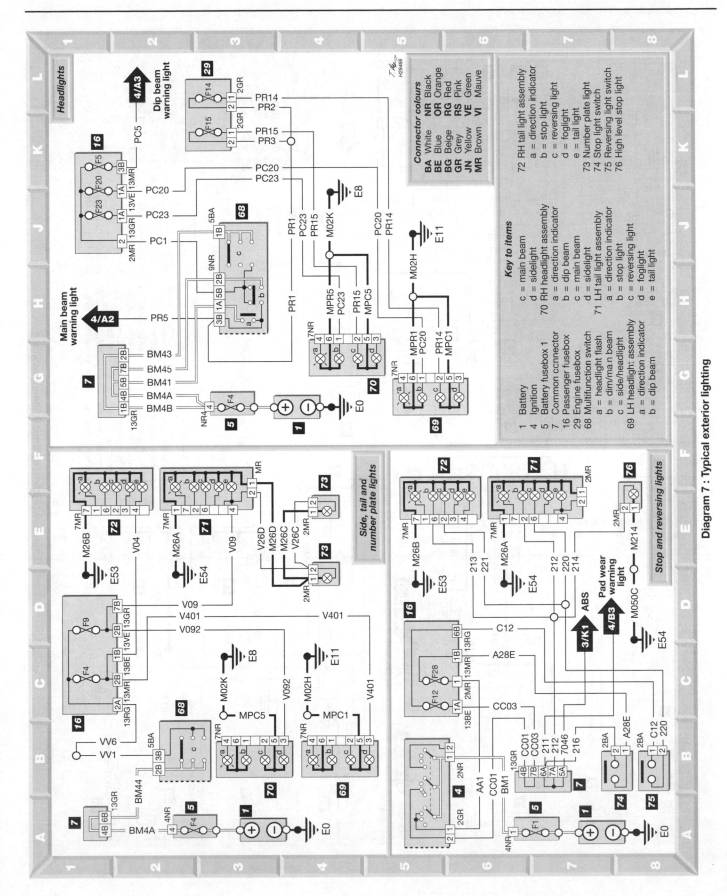

Diagram 7 : Typical exterior lighting

Key to items

1 Battery
5 Ignition
7 Common connector
16 Passenger fusebox
29 Engine fusebox
68 Multifunction switch
  a = headlight flash
  b = dim/man beam
  c = side/headlight
69 LH headlight assembly
  a = direction indicator
  b = dip beam

  c = main beam
  d = sidelight
70 RH headlight assembly
  a = direction indicator
  b = dip beam
  c = main beam
  d = sidelight
71 LH tail light assembly
  a = direction indicator
  b = stop light
  c = reversing light
  d = foglight
  e = tail light

72 RH tail light assembly
  a = direction indicator
  b = stop light
  c = reversing light
  d = foglight
  e = tail light
73 Number plate light
74 Stop light switch
75 Reversing light switch
76 High level stop light

Connector colours

BA	White	NR	Black
BE	Blue	OR	Orange
BG	Beige	RG	Red
GR	Grey	RS	Pink
JN	Yellow	VE	Green
MR	Brown	VI	Mauve

12

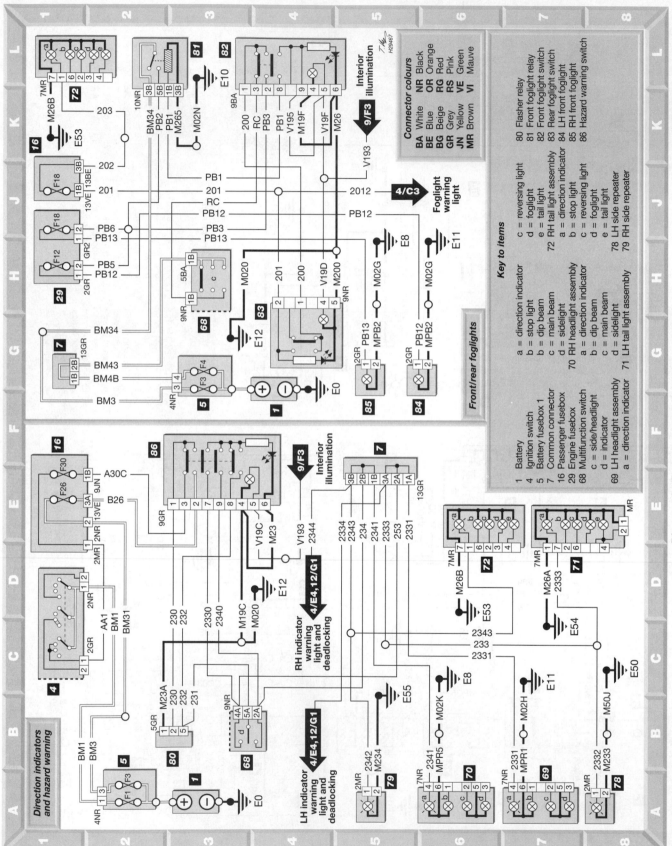

Diagram 8 : Typical exterior lighting continued

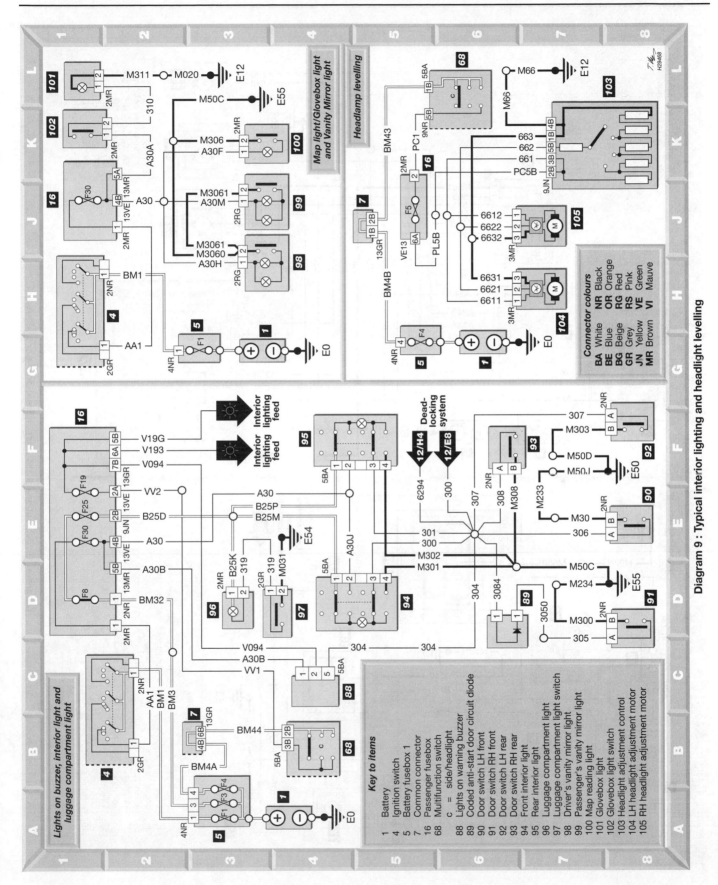

Diagram 9 : Typical interior lighting and headlight levelling

Map light/Glovebox light and Vanity Mirror light

Headlamp levelling

Lights on buzzer, interior light and luggage compartment light

Interior lighting feed

Interior lighting feed

Dead-locking system

Connector colours

BA	White	NR	Black
BE	Blue	OR	Orange
BG	Beige	RG	Red
GR	Grey	RS	Pink
JN	Yellow	VE	Green
MR	Brown	VI	Mauve

Key to items

1 Battery
4 Ignition switch
5 Battery fusebox 1
7 Passenger fusebox
16 Multifunction switch
c = side/headlight
68 Lights on warning buzzer
88 Coded anti-start door circuit diode
89 Door switch LH front
90 Door switch RH front
91 Door switch LH rear
92 Door switch RH rear
93 Front interior light
94 Rear interior light
95 Luggage compartment light
96 Luggage compartment light switch
97 Driver's vanity mirror light
98 Passenger's vanity mirror light
99 Map reading light
100 Glovebox light
101 Glovebox light switch
102 Headlight adjustment control
103 Headlight adjustment control
104 LH headlight adjustment motor
105 RH headlight adjustment motor

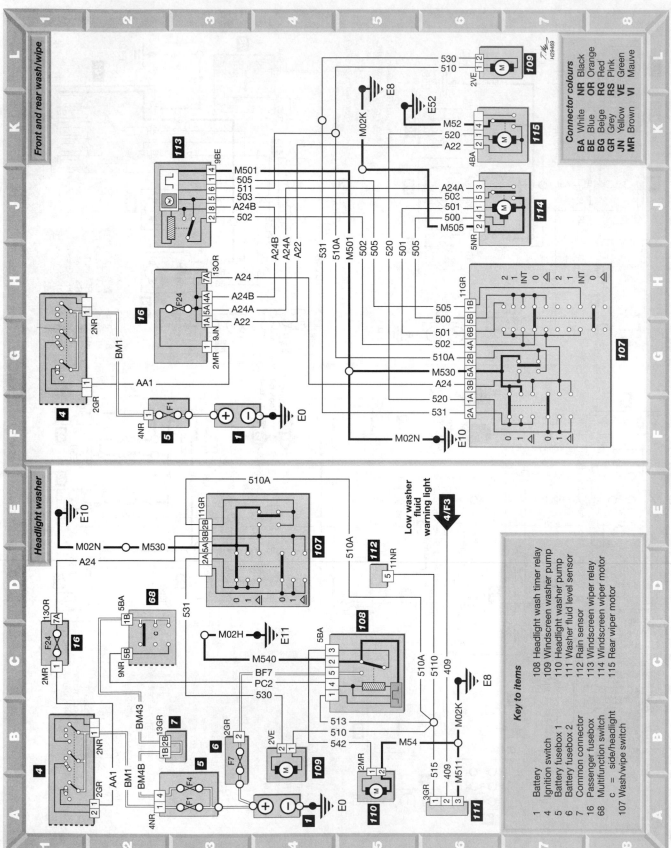

Diagram 10 : Typical headlight washer, front and rear wash/wipe

Front and rear wash/wipe

Headlight washer

Connector colours

BA White	**NR** Black		
BE Blue	**OR** Orange		
BG Beige	**RG** Red		
GR Grey	**RS** Pink		
JN Yellow	**VE** Green		
MR Brown	**VI** Mauve		

Low washer fluid warning light

Key to items

1	Battery	108	Headlight wash timer relay
4	Ignition switch	109	Windscreen washer pump
5	Battery fusebox 1	110	Headlight washer pump
6	Battery fusebox 2	111	Washer fluid level sensor
7	Common connector	112	Rain sensor
16	Passenger fusebox	113	Windscreen wiper relay
68	Multifunction switch	114	Windscreen wiper motor
107	c = side/headlight Wash/wipe switch	115	Rear wiper motor

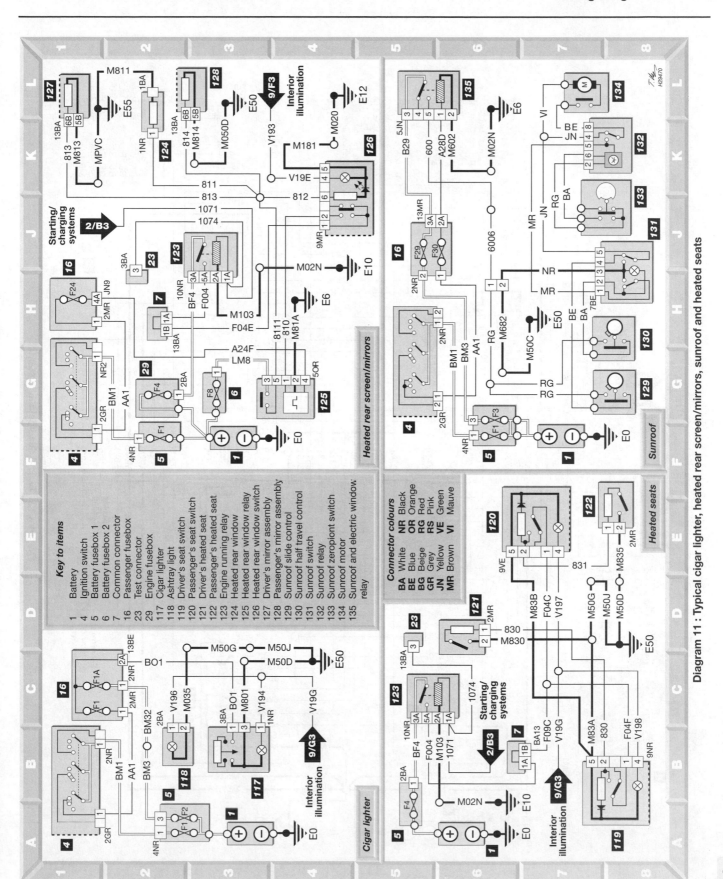

Diagram 11 : Typical cigar lighter, heated rear screen/mirrors, sunroof and heated seats

Key to items

1 Battery
4 Ignition switch
5 Battery fusebox 1
6 Battery fusebox 2
7 Common connector
16 Passenger fusebox
23 Test connector
29 Engine fusebox
117 Cigar lighter
118 Ashtray light
119 Driver's seat switch
120 Passenger's seat switch
121 Driver's heated seat
122 Passenger's heated seat
123 Engine running relay
124 Heated rear window
125 Heated rear window relay
126 Heated rear window switch
127 Driver's mirror assembly
128 Passenger's mirror assembly
129 Sunroof slide control
130 Sunroof half travel control
131 Sunroof switch
132 Sunroof zeropoint switch
133 Sunroof relay
134 Sunroof motor
135 Sunroof and electric window relay

Connector colours

BA White   NR Black
BE Blue   OR Orange
BG Beige   RG Red
GR Grey   RS Pink
JN Yellow   VE Green
MR Brown   VI Mauve

Heated rear screen/mirrors

Sunroof

Heated seats

Cigar lighter

12

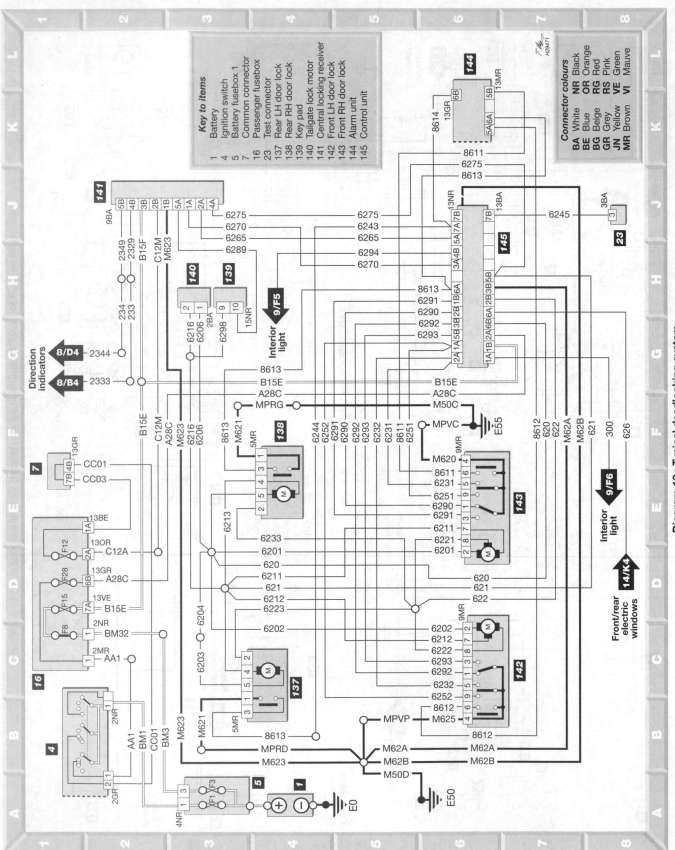

Diagram 12 : Typical deadlocking system

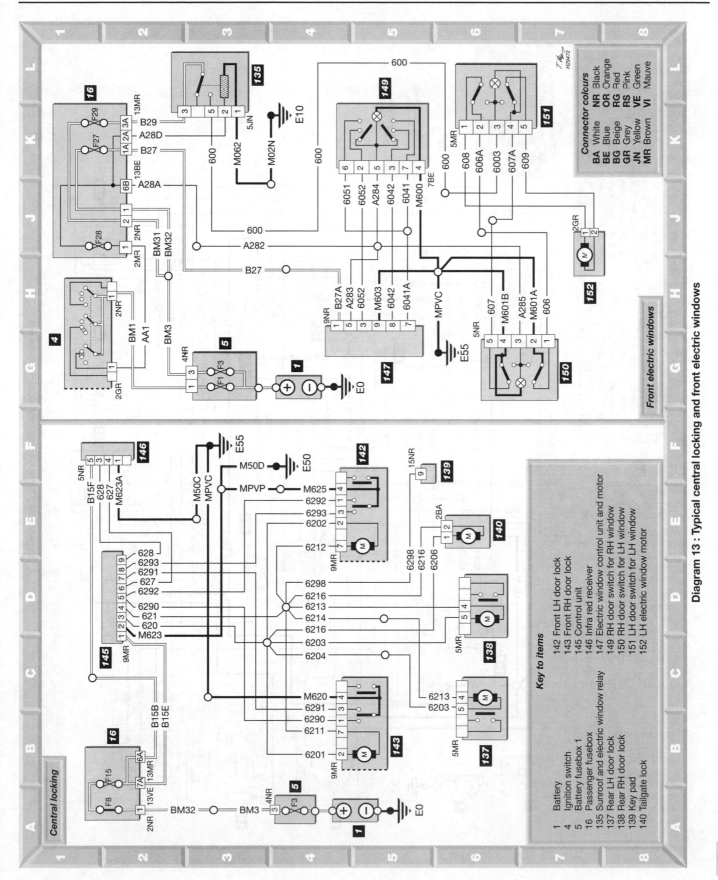

Diagram 13 : Typical central locking and front electric windows

Front electric windows

Central locking

Key to items

1 Battery
4 Ignition switch
5 Battery fusebox 1
16 Passenger fusebox
135 Sunroof and electric window relay
137 Rear LH door lock
138 Rear RH door lock
139 Key pad
140 Tailgate lock

142 Front LH door lock
143 Front RH door lock
145 Control unit
146 Infra red receiver
147 Electric window control unit and motor
149 RH door switch for RH window
150 RH door switch for LH window
151 LH door switch for LH window
152 LH electric window motor

Connector colours
BA White   NR Black
BE Blue   OR Orange
BG Beige   RG Red
GR Grey   RS Pink
JN Yellow   VE Green
MR Brown   VI Mauve

12

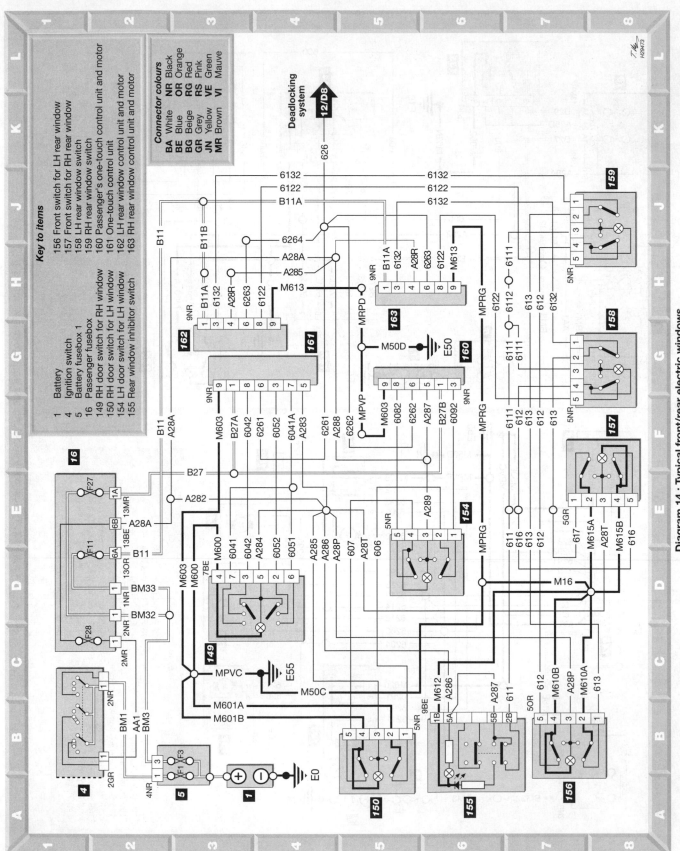

Diagram 14 : Typical front/rear electric windows

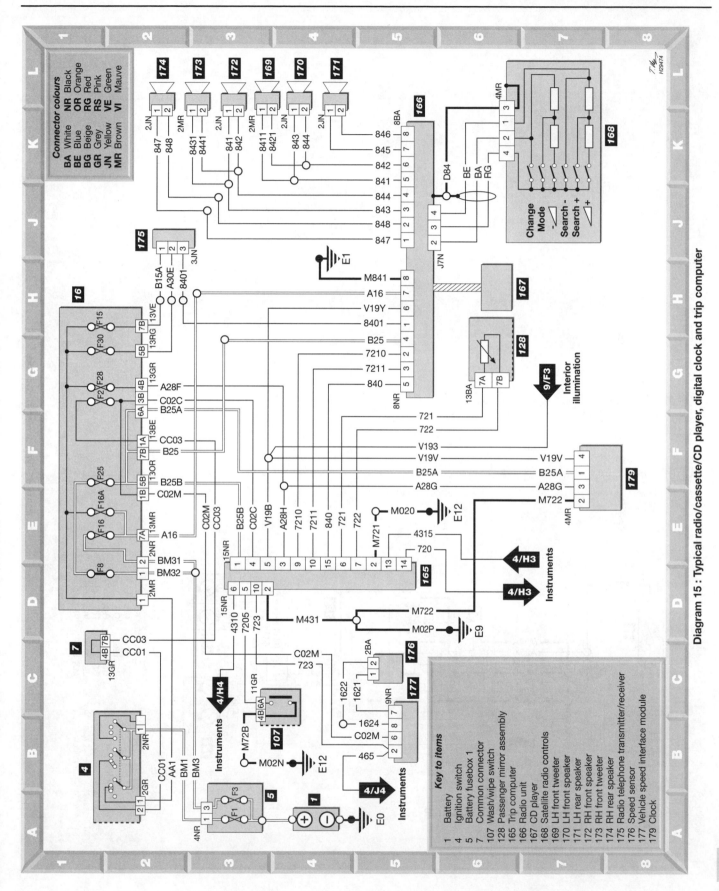

Diagram 15 : Typical radio/cassette/CD player, digital clock and trip computer

Connector colours

BA White	NR Black
BE Blue	OR Orange
BG Beige	RG Red
GR Grey	RS Pink
JN Yellow	VE Green
MR Brown	VI Mauve

Interior illumination

Change Mode

Search –

Search +

Key to items

1 Battery
4 Ignition switch
5 Battery fusebox 1
7 Common connector
107 Wash/wipe switch
128 Passenger mirror assembly
165 Trip computer
166 Radio unit
167 CD player
168 Satellite radio controls
169 LH front tweeter
170 LH front speaker
171 LH rear speaker
172 RH front speaker
173 RH front tweeter
174 RH rear speaker
175 Radio telephone transmitter/receiver
176 Speed sensor
177 Vehicle speed interface module
179 Clock

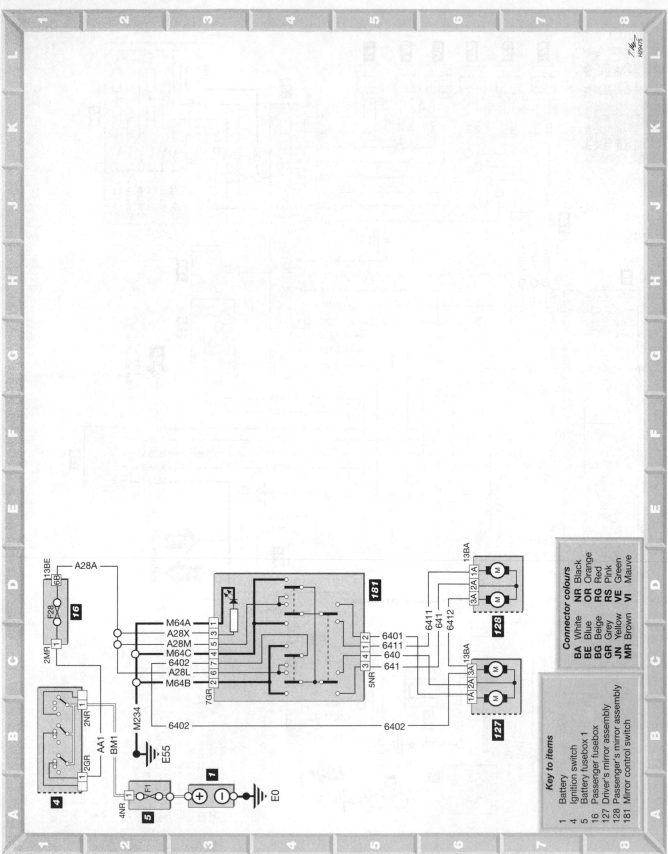

Diagram 16 : Typical electric mirrors

Connector colours

BA White	**NR** Black		
BE Blue	**OR** Orange		
BG Beige	**RG** Red		
GR Grey	**RS** Pink		
JN Yellow	**VE** Green		
MR Brown	**VI** Mauve		

Key to items

1	Battery
4	Ignition switch
5	Battery fusebox 1
16	Passenger fusebox
127	Driver's mirror assembly
128	Passenger's mirror assembly
181	Mirror control switch

Dimensions and weights

Note: *All figures are approximate, and may vary according to model. Refer to manufacturer's data for exact figures.*

Dimensions

Overall length:
  Saloon . . . . .4555 mm
  Estate . . . . .4715 mm
Overall width (excluding mirrors) . . . . .1760 mm
Overall height (unladen):
  Saloon . . . . .1396 mm
  Estate . . . . .1450 mm
Wheelbase . . . . .2700 mm

Weights

Kerb weight*:
  Saloon models:
    1.6 litre petrol . . . . .1240 kg
    1.8 litre petrol . . . . .1275 kg
    2.0 litre petrol . . . . .1315 kg*
    1.9 litre diesel . . . . .1300 kg
    2.1 litre diesel . . . . .1415 kg
  Estate models:
    1.8 litre petrol . . . . .1310 kg
    2.0 litre petrol . . . . .1378 kg*
    1.9 litre diesel . . . . .1389 kg
    2.1 litre diesel . . . . .1485 kg
Automatic transmission models add 50 kg

Maximum gross vehicle weight:
  Saloon models:
    1.6 litre petrol . . . . .1757 kg
    1.8 litre petrol . . . . .1807 kg
    2.0 litre petrol . . . . .1847 kg*
    1.9 litre diesel . . . . .1832 kg
    2.1 litre diesel . . . . .1947 kg
  Estate models:
    1.8 litre petrol . . . . .1805 kg
    2.0 litre petrol . . . . .1884 kg*
    1.9 litre diesel . . . . .1833 kg
    2.1 litre diesel . . . . .1949 kg
Automatic transmission models add 50 kg
Maximum towing weight (braked trailer):
  1.6 litre petrol models . . . . .1000 to 1300 kg
  All other models . . . . .1200 to 1500 kg
Maximum trailer nose weight:
  1.6 litre petrol models . . . . .65 kg
  All other models . . . . .80 kg

Conversion factors

Length (distance)

Inches (in)	x 25.4 = Millimetres (mm)	x 0.0394 = Inches (in)
Feet (ft)	x 0.305 = Metres (m)	x 3.281 = Feet (ft)
Miles	x 1.609 = Kilometres (km)	x 0.621 = Miles

Volume (capacity)

Cubic inches (cu in; in³)	x 16.387 = Cubic centimetres (cc; cm³)	x 0.061 = Cubic inches (cu in; in³)
Imperial pints (Imp pt)	x 0.568 = Litres (l)	x 1.76 = Imperial pints (Imp pt)
Imperial quarts (Imp qt)	x 1.137 = Litres (l)	x 0.88 = Imperial quarts (Imp qt)
Imperial quarts (Imp qt)	x 1.201 = US quarts (US qt)	x 0.833 = Imperial quarts (Imp qt)
US quarts (US qt)	x 0.946 = Litres (l)	x 1.057 = US quarts (US qt)
Imperial gallons (Imp gal)	x 4.546 = Litres (l)	x 0.22 = Imperial gallons (Imp gal)
Imperial gallons (Imp gal)	x 1.201 = US gallons (US gal)	x 0.833 = Imperial gallons (Imp gal)
US gallons (US gal)	x 3.785 = Litres (l)	x 0.264 = US gallons (US gal)

Mass (weight)

Ounces (oz)	x 28.35 = Grams (g)	x 0.035 = Ounces (oz)
Pounds (lb)	x 0.454 = Kilograms (kg)	x 2.205 = Pounds (lb)

Force

Ounces-force (ozf; oz)	x 0.278 = Newtons (N)	x 3.6 = Ounces-force (ozf; oz)
Pounds-force (lbf; lb)	x 4.448 = Newtons (N)	x 0.225 = Pounds-force (lbf; lb)
Newtons (N)	x 0.1 = Kilograms-force (kgf; kg)	x 9.81 = Newtons (N)

Pressure

Pounds-force per square inch (psi; lbf/in²; lb/in²)	x 0.070 = Kilograms-force per square centimetre (kgf/cm²; kg/cm²)	x 14.223 = Pounds-force per square inch (psi; lbf/in²; lb/in²)
Pounds-force per square inch (psi; lbf/in²; lb/in²)	x 0.068 = Atmospheres (atm)	x 14.696 = Pounds-force per square inch (psi; lbf/in²; lb/in²)
Pounds-force per square inch (psi; lbf/in²; lb/in²)	x 0.069 = Bars	x 14.5 = Pounds-force per square inch (psi; lbf/in²; lb/in²)
Pounds-force per square inch (psi; lbf/in²; lb/in²)	x 6.895 = Kilopascals (kPa)	x 0.145 = Pounds-force per square inch (psi; lbf/in²; lb/in²)
Kilopascals (kPa)	x 0.01 = Kilograms-force per square centimetre (kgf/cm²; kg/cm²)	x 98.1 = Kilopascals (kPa)
Millibar (mbar)	x 100 = Pascals (Pa)	x 0.01 = Millibar (mbar)
Millibar (mbar)	x 0.0145 = Pounds-force per square inch (psi; lbf/in²; lb/in²)	x 68.947 = Millibar (mbar)
Millibar (mbar)	x 0.75 = Millimetres of mercury (mmHg)	x 1.333 = Millibar (mbar)
Millibar (mbar)	x 0.401 = Inches of water (inH₂O)	x 2.491 = Millibar (mbar)
Millimetres of mercury (mmHg)	x 0.535 = Inches of water (inH₂O)	x 1.868 = Millimetres of mercury (mmHg)
Inches of water (inH₂O)	x 0.036 = Pounds-force per square inch (psi; lbf/in²; lb/in²)	x 27.68 = Inches of water (inH₂O)

Torque (moment of force)

Pounds-force inches (lbf in; lb in)	x 1.152 = Kilograms-force centimetre (kgf cm; kg cm)	x 0.868 = Pounds-force inches (lbf in; lb in)
Pounds-force inches (lbf in; lb in)	x 0.113 = Newton metres (Nm)	x 8.85 = Pounds-force inches (lbf in; lb in)
Pounds-force inches (lbf in; lb in)	x 0.083 = Pounds-force feet (lbf ft; lb ft)	x 12 = Pounds-force inches (lbf in; lb in)
Pounds-force feet (lbf ft; lb ft)	x 0.138 = Kilograms-force metres (kgf m; kg m)	x 7.233 = Pounds-force feet (lbf ft; lb ft)
Pounds-force feet (lbf ft; lb ft)	x 1.356 = Newton metres (Nm)	x 0.738 = Pounds-force feet (lbf ft; lb ft)
Newton metres (Nm)	x 0.102 = Kilograms-force metres (kgf m; kg m)	x 9.804 = Newton metres (Nm)

Power

Horsepower (hp)	x 745.7 = Watts (W)	x 0.0013 = Horsepower (hp)

Velocity (speed)

Miles per hour (miles/hr; mph)	x 1.609 = Kilometres per hour (km/hr; kph)	x 0.621 = Miles per hour (miles/hr; mph)

Fuel consumption*

Miles per gallon (mpg)	x 0.354 = Kilometres per litre (km/l)	x 2.825 = Miles per gallon (mpg)

Temperature

Degrees Fahrenheit = (°C x 1.8) + 32   Degrees Celsius (Degrees Centigrade; °C) = (°F - 32) x 0.56

It is common practice to convert from miles per gallon (mpg) to litres/100 kilometres (l/100km), where mpg x l/100 km = 282

Spare parts are available from many sources, including maker's appointed garages, accessory shops, and motor factors. To be sure of obtaining the correct parts, it will sometimes be necessary to quote the vehicle identification number. If possible, it can also be useful to take the old parts along for positive identification. Items such as starter motors and alternators may be available under a service exchange scheme - any parts returned should be clean.

Our advice regarding spare parts is as follows.

Officially appointed garages

This is the best source of parts which are peculiar to your car, and which are not otherwise generally available (eg, badges, interior trim, certain body panels, etc). It is also the only place at which you should buy parts if the vehicle is still under warranty.

Accessory shops

These are very good places to buy materials and components needed for the maintenance of your car (oil, air and fuel filters, light bulbs, drivebelts, greases, brake pads, touch-up paint, etc). Components of this nature sold by a reputable shop are usually of the same standard as those used by the car manufacturer.

Besides components, these shops also sell tools and general accessories, usually have convenient opening hours, charge lower prices, and can often be found close to home. Some accessory shops have parts counters where components needed for almost any repair job can be purchased or ordered.

Motor factors

Good factors will stock the more important components which wear out comparatively quickly, and can sometimes supply individual components needed for the overhaul of a larger assembly (eg, brake seals and hydraulic parts, bearing shells, pistons, valves). They may also handle work such as cylinder block reboring, crankshaft regrinding, etc.

Tyre and exhaust specialists

These outlets may be independent, or members of a local or national chain. They frequently offer competitive prices when compared with a main dealer or local garage, but it will pay to obtain several quotes before making a decision. When researching prices, also be sure to ask what "extras" may be added - for instance, fitting a new valve, balancing the wheel, and checking the tracking (front wheels) are all commonly charged on top of the price of a new tyre.

Other sources

Beware of parts or materials obtained from market stalls, car boot sales or similar outlets. Such items are not invariably sub-standard, but there is little chance of compensation if they do prove unsatisfactory. In the case of safety-critical components such as brake pads, there is the risk not only of financial loss, but also of an accident causing injury or death.

Second-hand components or assemblies obtained from a car breaker can be a good buy in some circumstances, but this sort of purchase is best made by the experienced DIY mechanic.

Vehicle identification

Modifications are a continuing and unpublicised process in vehicle manufacture, quite apart from major model changes. Spare parts manuals and lists are compiled upon a numerical basis, the individual vehicle identification numbers being essential to correct identification of the component concerned.

When ordering spare parts, always give as much information as possible. Quote the car model, year of manufacture and registration, chassis and engine numbers as appropriate.

The *Vehicle Identification Number (VIN)* plate is riveted to the right-hand end of the bonnet lock crossmember and is visible once the bonnet has been opened. The vehicle identification (chassis) number is also stamped onto the top of the right-hand side of the engine compartment bulkhead and is stamped on a plate attached to the top, left-hand end of the facia (visible through the windscreen) **(see illustrations)**. On certain models a *Homologation plate* is attached to the left-hand end of the bonnet locking crossmember.

The *engine number and code* can be found on the front of the cylinder block. On petrol engine models the number and code are stamped onto the cylinder block surface; on 1.6 and 1.8 litre models they can be found at the bottom, left-hand corner of the block, and on 2.0 litre models they are situated just to the left of the oil filter. On 1.9 litre diesel engine models the engine number and code are stamped onto a metal plate which is riveted to the centre of the block, directly behind the injection pump, and on 2.1 litre models the code and number are stamped on the centre of the cylinder block surface, just to the left of the oil filter **(see illustration)**.

The *paint code* is stamped onto the side of the left-hand front suspension strut mounting turret in the engine compartment.

The vehicle identification number (VIN) plate (arrowed) is riveted to the right-hand end of the bonnet lock crossmember

The chassis number (arrowed) is also stamped onto the top of the engine compartment bulkhead

The engine number and code can be found on the front of the cylinder block (2.0 litre petrol engine shown)

Whenever servicing, repair or overhaul work is carried out on the car or its components, it is necessary to observe the following procedures and instructions. This will assist in carrying out the operation efficiently and to a professional standard of workmanship.

Joint mating faces and gaskets

When separating components at their mating faces, never insert screwdrivers or similar implements into the joint between the faces in order to prise them apart. This can cause severe damage which results in oil leaks, coolant leaks, etc upon reassembly. Separation is usually achieved by tapping along the joint with a soft-faced hammer in order to break the seal. However, note that this method may not be suitable where dowels are used for component location.

Where a gasket is used between the mating faces of two components, ensure that it is renewed on reassembly, and fit it dry unless otherwise stated in the repair procedure. Make sure that the mating faces are clean and dry, with all traces of old gasket removed. When cleaning a joint face, use a tool which is not likely to score or damage the face, and remove any burrs or nicks with an oilstone or fine file.

Make sure that tapped holes are cleaned with a pipe cleaner, and keep them free of jointing compound, if this is being used, unless specifically instructed otherwise.

Ensure that all orifices, channels or pipes are clear, and blow through them, preferably using compressed air.

Oil seals

Oil seals can be removed by levering them out with a wide flat-bladed screwdriver or similar tool. Alternatively, a number of self-tapping screws may be screwed into the seal, and these used as a purchase for pliers or similar in order to pull the seal free.

Whenever an oil seal is removed from its working location, either individually or as part of an assembly, it should be renewed.

The very fine sealing lip of the seal is easily damaged, and will not seal if the surface it contacts is not completely clean and free from scratches, nicks or grooves. If the original sealing surface of the component cannot be restored, and the manufacturer has not made provision for slight relocation of the seal relative to the sealing surface, the component should be renewed.

Protect the lips of the seal from any surface which may damage them in the course of fitting. Use tape or a conical sleeve where possible. Lubricate the seal lips with oil before fitting and, on dual-lipped seals, fill the space between the lips with grease.

Unless otherwise stated, oil seals must be fitted with their sealing lips toward the lubricant to be sealed.

Use a tubular drift or block of wood of the appropriate size to install the seal and, if the seal housing is shouldered, drive the seal down to the shoulder. If the seal housing is unshouldered, the seal should be fitted with its face flush with the housing top face (unless otherwise instructed).

Screw threads and fastenings

Seized nuts, bolts and screws are quite a common occurrence where corrosion has set in, and the use of penetrating oil or releasing fluid will often overcome this problem if the offending item is soaked for a while before attempting to release it. The use of an impact driver may also provide a means of releasing such stubborn fastening devices, when used in conjunction with the appropriate screwdriver bit or socket. If none of these methods works, it may be necessary to resort to the careful application of heat, or the use of a hacksaw or nut splitter device.

Studs are usually removed by locking two nuts together on the threaded part, and then using a spanner on the lower nut to unscrew the stud. Studs or bolts which have broken off below the surface of the component in which they are mounted can sometimes be removed using a stud extractor. Always ensure that a blind tapped hole is completely free from oil, grease, water or other fluid before installing the bolt or stud. Failure to do this could cause the housing to crack due to the hydraulic action of the bolt or stud as it is screwed in.

When tightening a castellated nut to accept a split pin, tighten the nut to the specified torque, where applicable, and then tighten further to the next split pin hole. Never slacken the nut to align the split pin hole, unless stated in the repair procedure.

When checking or retightening a nut or bolt to a specified torque setting, slacken the nut or bolt by a quarter of a turn, and then retighten to the specified setting. However, this should not be attempted where angular tightening has been used.

For some screw fastenings, notably cylinder head bolts or nuts, torque wrench settings are no longer specified for the latter stages of tightening, "angle-tightening" being called up instead. Typically, a fairly low torque wrench setting will be applied to the bolts/nuts in the correct sequence, followed by one or more stages of tightening through specified angles.

Locknuts, locktabs and washers

Any fastening which will rotate against a component or housing during tightening should always have a washer between it and the relevant component or housing.

Spring or split washers should always be renewed when they are used to lock a critical component such as a big-end bearing retaining bolt or nut. Locktabs which are folded over to retain a nut or bolt should always be renewed.

Self-locking nuts can be re-used in non-critical areas, providing resistance can be felt when the locking portion passes over the bolt or stud thread. However, it should be noted that self-locking stiffnuts tend to lose their effectiveness after long periods of use, and should be renewed as a matter of course.

Split pins must always be replaced with new ones of the correct size for the hole.

When thread-locking compound is found on the threads of a fastener which is to be re-used, it should be cleaned off with a wire brush and solvent, and fresh compound applied on reassembly.

Special tools

Some repair procedures in this manual entail the use of special tools such as a press, two or three-legged pullers, spring compressors, etc. Wherever possible, suitable readily-available alternatives to the manufacturer's special tools are described, and are shown in use. In some instances, where no alternative is possible, it has been necessary to resort to the use of a manufacturer's tool, and this has been done for reasons of safety as well as the efficient completion of the repair operation. Unless you are highly-skilled and have a thorough understanding of the procedures described, never attempt to bypass the use of any special tool when the procedure described specifies its use. Not only is there a very great risk of personal injury, but expensive damage could be caused to the components involved.

Environmental considerations

When disposing of used engine oil, brake fluid, antifreeze, etc, give due consideration to any detrimental environmental effects. Do not, for instance, pour any of the above liquids down drains into the general sewage system, or onto the ground to soak away. Many local council refuse tips provide a facility for waste oil disposal, as do some garages. If none of these facilities are available, consult your local Environmental Health Department, or the National Rivers Authority, for further advice.

With the universal tightening-up of legislation regarding the emission of environmentally-harmful substances from motor vehicles, most current vehicles have tamperproof devices fitted to the main adjustment points of the fuel system. These devices are primarily designed to prevent unqualified persons from adjusting the fuel/air mixture, with the chance of a consequent increase in toxic emissions. If such devices are encountered during servicing or overhaul, they should, wherever possible, be renewed or refitted in accordance with the vehicle manufacturer's requirements or current legislation.

Note: It is antisocial and illegal to dump oil down the drain. To find the location of your local oil recycling bank, call this number free.

OIL CARE
FOLLOW THE CODE

OIL BANK LINE
0800 66 33 66

The jack supplied with the vehicle tool kit should only be used for changing the roadwheels - see *"Wheel changing"* at the front of this manual. When carrying out any other kind of work, raise the vehicle using a hydraulic (or "trolley") jack, and always supplement the jack with axle stands positioned under the vehicle jacking points.

To raise the front of the vehicle, position the jack head underneath the centre of the front suspension subframe. Lift the vehicle to the required height and support it on axle stands positioned underneath the vehicle jacking points on the sills **(see illustration)**.

To raise the rear of the vehicle, position the jack head underneath the rear suspension lower arm, directly beneath the coil spring. Lift the vehicle to the required height and support it on axle stands positioned underneath the vehicle jacking points on the sills **(see illustration)**.

The jack supplied with the vehicle locates with the jacking points on the sills. Ensure that the jack head is correctly engaged before attempting to raise the vehicle.

Never work under, around, or near a raised vehicle, unless it is adequately supported in at least two places.

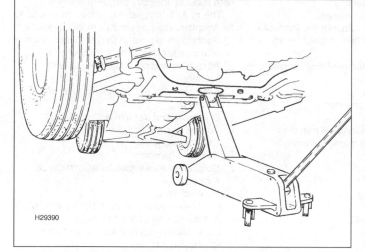

To raise the front of the vehicle, position the jack head underneath the centre of the subframe

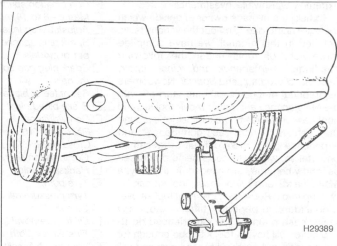

To raise the rear of the vehicle, position the jack head directly underneath one of the rear suspension coil springs

Radio/cassette unit anti-theft system - precaution

The radio/cassette/CD player/autochanger unit fitted as standard equipment by Peugeot is equipped with a built-in security code, to deter thieves. If the power source to the unit is cut, the anti-theft system will activate. Even if the power source is immediately reconnected, the radio/cassette unit will not function until the correct security code has been entered. Therefore if you do not know the correct security code for the unit, **do not** disconnect the battery negative lead, or remove the radio/cassette unit from the vehicle.

The procedure for reprogramming a unit that has been disconnected from its power supply varies from model to model - consult the handbook supplied with the unit for specific details or refer to your Peugeot dealer.

Introduction

A selection of good tools is a fundamental requirement for anyone contemplating the maintenance and repair of a motor vehicle. For the owner who does not possess any, their purchase will prove a considerable expense, offsetting some of the savings made by doing-it-yourself. However, provided that the tools purchased meet the relevant national safety standards and are of good quality, they will last for many years and prove an extremely worthwhile investment.

To help the average owner to decide which tools are needed to carry out the various tasks detailed in this manual, we have compiled three lists of tools under the following headings: *Maintenance and minor repair*, *Repair and overhaul*, and *Special*. Newcomers to practical mechanics should start off with the *Maintenance and minor repair* tool kit, and confine themselves to the simpler jobs around the vehicle. Then, as confidence and experience grow, more difficult tasks can be undertaken, with extra tools being purchased as, and when, they are needed. In this way, a *Maintenance and minor repair* tool kit can be built up into a *Repair and overhaul* tool kit over a considerable period of time, without any major cash outlays. The experienced do-it-yourselfer will have a tool kit good enough for most repair and overhaul procedures, and will add tools from the *Special* category when it is felt that the expense is justified by the amount of use to which these tools will be put.

Maintenance and minor repair tool kit

The tools given in this list should be considered as a minimum requirement if routine maintenance, servicing and minor repair operations are to be undertaken. We recommend the purchase of combination spanners (ring one end, open-ended the other); although more expensive than open-ended ones, they do give the advantages of both types of spanner.

☐ *Combination spanners:*
  Metric - 8 to 19 mm inclusive
☐ *Adjustable spanner - 35 mm jaw (approx.)*
☐ *Spark plug spanner (with rubber insert) - petrol models*
☐ *Spark plug gap adjustment tool - petrol models*
☐ *Set of feeler blades*
☐ *Brake bleed nipple spanner*
☐ *Screwdrivers:*
  Flat blade - 100 mm long x 6 mm dia
  Cross blade - 100 mm long x 6 mm dia
☐ *Combination pliers*
☐ *Hacksaw (junior)*
☐ *Tyre pump*
☐ *Tyre pressure gauge*
☐ *Oil can*
☐ *Oil filter removal tool*
☐ *Fine emery cloth*
☐ *Wire brush (small)*
☐ *Funnel (medium size)*

Repair and overhaul tool kit

These tools are virtually essential for anyone undertaking any major repairs to a motor vehicle, and are additional to those given in the *Maintenance and minor repair* list. Included in this list is a comprehensive set of sockets. Although these are expensive, they will be found invaluable as they are so versatile - particularly if various drives are included in the set. We recommend the half-inch square-drive type, as this can be used with most proprietary torque wrenches.

The tools in this list will sometimes need to be supplemented by tools from the *Special* list:

☐ *Sockets (or box spanners) to cover range in previous list (including Torx sockets)*
☐ *Reversible ratchet drive (for use with sockets)*
☐ *Extension piece, 250 mm (for use with sockets)*
☐ *Universal joint (for use with sockets)*
☐ *Torque wrench (for use with sockets)*
☐ *Self-locking grips*
☐ *Ball pein hammer*
☐ *Soft-faced mallet (plastic/aluminium or rubber)*
☐ *Screwdrivers:*
  Flat blade - long & sturdy, short (chubby), and narrow (electrician's) types
  Cross blade – Long & sturdy, and short (chubby) types
☐ *Pliers:*
  Long-nosed
  Side cutters (electrician's)
  Circlip (internal and external)
☐ *Cold chisel - 25 mm*
☐ *Scriber*
☐ *Scraper*
☐ *Centre-punch*
☐ *Pin punch*
☐ *Hacksaw*
☐ *Brake hose clamp*
☐ *Brake/clutch bleeding kit*
☐ *Selection of twist drills*
☐ *Steel rule/straight-edge*
☐ *Allen keys (inc. splined/Torx type)*
☐ *Selection of files*
☐ *Wire brush*
☐ *Axle stands*
☐ *Jack (strong trolley or hydraulic type)*
☐ *Light with extension lead*

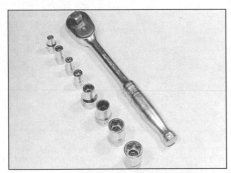

Sockets and reversible ratchet drive

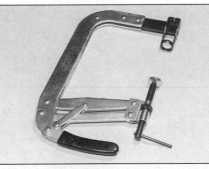

Valve spring compressor

Spline bit set

Piston ring compressor

Clutch plate alignment set

Special tools

The tools in this list are those which are not used regularly, are expensive to buy, or which need to be used in accordance with their manufacturers' instructions. Unless relatively difficult mechanical jobs are undertaken frequently, it will not be economic to buy many of these tools. Where this is the case, you could consider clubbing together with friends (or joining a motorists' club) to make a joint purchase, or borrowing the tools against a deposit from a local garage or tool hire specialist. It is worth noting that many of the larger DIY superstores now carry a large range of special tools for hire at modest rates.

The following list contains only those tools and instruments freely available to the public, and not those special tools produced by the vehicle manufacturer specifically for its dealer network. You will find occasional references to these manufacturers' special tools in the text of this manual. Generally, an alternative method of doing the job without the vehicle manufacturers' special tool is given. However, sometimes there is no alternative to using them. Where this is the case and the relevant tool cannot be bought or borrowed, you will have to entrust the work to a dealer.

- ☐ Valve spring compressor
- ☐ Valve grinding tool
- ☐ Piston ring compressor
- ☐ Piston ring removal/installation tool
- ☐ Cylinder bore hone
- ☐ Balljoint separator
- ☐ Coil spring compressors (where applicable)
- ☐ Two/three-legged hub and bearing puller
- ☐ Impact screwdriver
- ☐ Micrometer and/or vernier calipers
- ☐ Dial gauge
- ☐ Stroboscopic timing light
- ☐ Dwell angle meter/tachometer
- ☐ Universal electrical multi-meter
- ☐ Cylinder compression gauge
- ☐ Hand-operated vacuum pump and gauge
- ☐ Clutch plate alignment set
- ☐ Brake shoe steady spring cup removal tool
- ☐ Bush and bearing removal/installation set
- ☐ Stud extractors
- ☐ Tap and die set
- ☐ Lifting tackle
- ☐ Trolley jack

Buying tools

Reputable motor accessory shops and superstores often offer excellent quality tools at discount prices, so it pays to shop around.

Remember, you don't have to buy the most expensive items on the shelf, but it is always advisable to steer clear of the very cheap tools. Beware of 'bargains' offered on market stalls or at car boot sales. There are plenty of good tools around at reasonable prices, but always aim to purchase items which meet the relevant national safety standards. If in doubt, ask the proprietor or manager of the shop for advice before making a purchase.

Care and maintenance of tools

Having purchased a reasonable tool kit, it is necessary to keep the tools in a clean and serviceable condition. After use, always wipe off any dirt, grease and metal particles using a clean, dry cloth, before putting the tools away. Never leave them lying around after they have been used. A simple tool rack on the garage or workshop wall for items such as screwdrivers and pliers is a good idea. Store all normal spanners and sockets in a metal box. Any measuring instruments, gauges, meters, etc, must be carefully stored where they cannot be damaged or become rusty.

Take a little care when tools are used. Hammer heads inevitably become marked, and screwdrivers lose the keen edge on their blades from time to time. A little timely attention with emery cloth or a file will soon restore items like this to a good finish.

Working facilities

Not to be forgotten when discussing tools is the workshop itself. If anything more than routine maintenance is to be carried out, a suitable working area becomes essential.

It is appreciated that many an owner-mechanic is forced by circumstances to remove an engine or similar item without the benefit of a garage or workshop. Having done this, any repairs should always be done under the cover of a roof.

Wherever possible, any dismantling should be done on a clean, flat workbench or table at a suitable working height.

Any workbench needs a vice; one with a jaw opening of 100 mm is suitable for most jobs. As mentioned previously, some clean dry storage space is also required for tools, as well as for any lubricants, cleaning fluids, touch-up paints etc, which become necessary.

Another item which may be required, and which has a much more general usage, is an electric drill with a chuck capacity of at least 8 mm. This, together with a good range of twist drills, is virtually essential for fitting accessories.

Last, but not least, always keep a supply of old newspapers and clean, lint-free rags available, and try to keep any working area as clean as possible.

Micrometer set

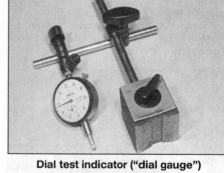

Dial test indicator ("dial gauge")

Stroboscopic timing light

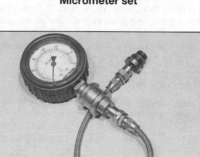

Compression tester

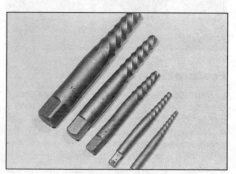

Stud extractor set

This is a guide to getting your vehicle through the MOT test. Obviously it will not be possible to examine the vehicle to the same standard as the professional MOT tester. However, working through the following checks will enable you to identify any problem areas before submitting the vehicle for the test.

Where a testable component is in borderline condition, the tester has discretion in deciding whether to pass or fail it. The basis of such discretion is whether the tester would be happy for a close relative or friend to use the vehicle with the component in that condition. If the vehicle presented is clean and evidently well cared for, the tester may be more inclined to pass a borderline component than if the vehicle is scruffy and apparently neglected.

It has only been possible to summarise the test requirements here, based on the regulations in force at the time of printing. Test standards are becoming increasingly stringent, although there are some exemptions for older vehicles. For full details obtain a copy of the Haynes publication Pass the MOT! (available from stockists of Haynes manuals).

An assistant will be needed to help carry out some of these checks.

The checks have been sub-divided into four categories, as follows:

1 Checks carried out **FROM THE DRIVER'S SEAT**

2 Checks carried out **WITH THE VEHICLE ON THE GROUND**

3 Checks carried out **WITH THE VEHICLE RAISED AND THE WHEELS FREE TO TURN**

4 Checks carried out on **YOUR VEHICLE'S EXHAUST EMISSION SYSTEM**

---

1 Checks carried out **FROM THE DRIVER'S SEAT**

Handbrake

☐ Test the operation of the handbrake. Excessive travel (too many clicks) indicates incorrect brake or cable adjustment.

☐ Check that the handbrake cannot be released by tapping the lever sideways. Check the security of the lever mountings.

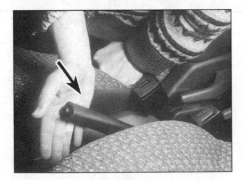

Footbrake

☐ Depress the brake pedal and check that it does not creep down to the floor, indicating a master cylinder fault. Release the pedal, wait a few seconds, then depress it again. If the pedal travels nearly to the floor before firm resistance is felt, brake adjustment or repair is necessary. If the pedal feels spongy, there is air in the hydraulic system which must be removed by bleeding.

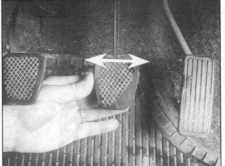

☐ Check that the brake pedal is secure and in good condition. Check also for signs of fluid leaks on the pedal, floor or carpets, which would indicate failed seals in the brake master cylinder.

☐ Check the servo unit (when applicable) by operating the brake pedal several times, then keeping the pedal depressed and starting the engine. As the engine starts, the pedal will move down slightly. If not, the vacuum hose or the servo itself may be faulty.

Steering wheel and column

☐ Examine the steering wheel for fractures or looseness of the hub, spokes or rim.

☐ Move the steering wheel from side to side and then up and down. Check that the steering wheel is not loose on the column, indicating wear or a loose retaining nut. Continue moving the steering wheel as before, but also turn it slightly from left to right.

☐ Check that the steering wheel is not loose on the column, and that there is no abnormal

movement of the steering wheel, indicating wear in the column support bearings or couplings.

Windscreen and mirrors

☐ The windscreen must be free of cracks or other significant damage within the driver's field of view. (Small stone chips are acceptable.) Rear view mirrors must be secure, intact, and capable of being adjusted.

Seat belts and seats

Note: *The following checks are applicable to all seat belts, front and rear.*

□ Examine the webbing of all the belts (including rear belts if fitted) for cuts, serious fraying or deterioration. Fasten and unfasten each belt to check the buckles. If applicable, check the retracting mechanism. Check the security of all seat belt mountings accessible from inside the vehicle.

□ The front seats themselves must be securely attached and the backrests must lock in the upright position.

Doors

□ Both front doors must be able to be opened and closed from outside and inside, and must latch securely when closed.

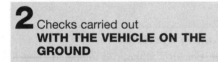

2 Checks carried out WITH THE VEHICLE ON THE GROUND

Vehicle identification

□ Number plates must be in good condition, secure and legible, with letters and numbers correctly spaced – spacing at (A) should be twice that at (B).

□ The VIN plate and/or homologation plate must be legible.

Electrical equipment

□ Switch on the ignition and check the operation of the horn.

□ Check the windscreen washers and wipers, examining the wiper blades; renew damaged or perished blades. Also check the operation of the stop-lights.

□ Check the operation of the sidelights and number plate lights. The lenses and reflectors must be secure, clean and undamaged.

□ Check the operation and alignment of the headlights. The headlight reflectors must not be tarnished and the lenses must be undamaged.

□ Switch on the ignition and check the operation of the direction indicators (including the instrument panel tell-tale) and the hazard warning lights. Operation of the sidelights and stop-lights must not affect the indicators - if it does, the cause is usually a bad earth at the rear light cluster.

□ Check the operation of the rear foglight(s), including the warning light on the instrument panel or in the switch.

Footbrake

□ Examine the master cylinder, brake pipes and servo unit for leaks, loose mountings, corrosion or other damage.

□ The fluid reservoir must be secure and the fluid level must be between the upper (A) and lower (B) markings.

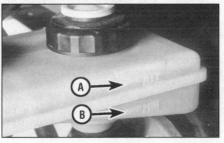

□ Inspect both front brake flexible hoses for cracks or deterioration of the rubber. Turn the steering from lock to lock, and ensure that the hoses do not contact the wheel, tyre, or any part of the steering or suspension mechanism. With the brake pedal firmly depressed, check the hoses for bulges or leaks under pressure.

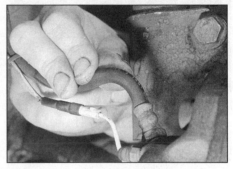

Steering and suspension

□ Have your assistant turn the steering wheel from side to side slightly, up to the point where the steering gear just begins to transmit this movement to the roadwheels. Check for excessive free play between the steering wheel and the steering gear, indicating wear or insecurity of the steering column joints, the column-to-steering gear coupling, or the steering gear itself.

□ Have your assistant turn the steering wheel more vigorously in each direction, so that the roadwheels just begin to turn. As this is done, examine all the steering joints, linkages, fittings and attachments. Renew any component that shows signs of wear or damage. On vehicles with power steering, check the security and condition of the steering pump, drivebelt and hoses.

□ Check that the vehicle is standing level, and at approximately the correct ride height.

Shock absorbers

□ Depress each corner of the vehicle in turn, then release it. The vehicle should rise and then settle in its normal position. If the vehicle continues to rise and fall, the shock absorber is defective. A shock absorber which has seized will also cause the vehicle to fail.

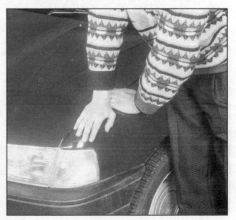

Exhaust system

☐ Start the engine. With your assistant holding a rag over the tailpipe, check the entire system for leaks. Repair or renew leaking sections.

3 Checks carried out
WITH THE VEHICLE RAISED AND THE WHEELS FREE TO TURN

Jack up the front and rear of the vehicle, and securely support it on axle stands. Position the stands clear of the suspension assemblies. Ensure that the wheels are clear of the ground and that the steering can be turned from lock to lock.

Steering mechanism

☐ Have your assistant turn the steering from lock to lock. Check that the steering turns smoothly, and that no part of the steering mechanism, including a wheel or tyre, fouls any brake hose or pipe or any part of the body structure.
☐ Examine the steering rack rubber gaiters for damage or insecurity of the retaining clips. If power steering is fitted, check for signs of damage or leakage of the fluid hoses, pipes or connections. Also check for excessive stiffness or binding of the steering, a missing split pin or locking device, or severe corrosion of the body structure within 30 cm of any steering component attachment point.

Front and rear suspension and wheel bearings

☐ Starting at the front right-hand side, grasp the roadwheel at the 3 o'clock and 9 o'clock positions and shake it vigorously. Check for free play or insecurity at the wheel bearings, suspension balljoints, or suspension mountings, pivots and attachments.
☐ Now grasp the wheel at the 12 o'clock and 6 o'clock positions and repeat the previous inspection. Spin the wheel, and check for roughness or tightness of the front wheel bearing.

☐ If excess free play is suspected at a component pivot point, this can be confirmed by using a large screwdriver or similar tool and levering between the mounting and the component attachment. This will confirm whether the wear is in the pivot bush, its retaining bolt, or in the mounting itself (the bolt holes can often become elongated).

☐ Carry out all the above checks at the other front wheel, and then at both rear wheels.

Springs and shock absorbers

☐ Examine the suspension struts (when applicable) for serious fluid leakage, corrosion, or damage to the casing. Also check the security of the mounting points.
☐ If coil springs are fitted, check that the spring ends locate in their seats, and that the spring is not corroded, cracked or broken.
☐ If leaf springs are fitted, check that all leaves are intact, that the axle is securely attached to each spring, and that there is no deterioration of the spring eye mountings, bushes, and shackles.

☐ The same general checks apply to vehicles fitted with other suspension types, such as torsion bars, hydraulic displacer units, etc. Ensure that all mountings and attachments are secure, that there are no signs of excessive wear, corrosion or damage, and (on hydraulic types) that there are no fluid leaks or damaged pipes.
☐ Inspect the shock absorbers for signs of serious fluid leakage. Check for wear of the mounting bushes or attachments, or damage to the body of the unit.

Driveshafts (fwd vehicles only)

☐ Rotate each front wheel in turn and inspect the constant velocity joint gaiters for splits or damage. Also check that each driveshaft is straight and undamaged.

Braking system

☐ If possible without dismantling, check brake pad wear and disc condition. Ensure that the friction lining material has not worn excessively, (A) and that the discs are not fractured, pitted, scored or badly worn (B).

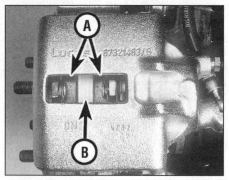

☐ Examine all the rigid brake pipes underneath the vehicle, and the flexible hose(s) at the rear. Look for corrosion, chafing or insecurity of the pipes, and for signs of bulging under pressure, chafing, splits or deterioration of the flexible hoses.
☐ Look for signs of fluid leaks at the brake calipers or on the brake backplates. Repair or renew leaking components.
☐ Slowly spin each wheel, while your assistant depresses and releases the footbrake. Ensure that each brake is operating and does not bind when the pedal is released.

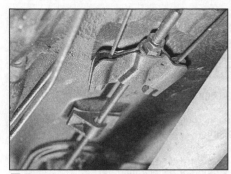

☐ Examine the handbrake mechanism, checking for frayed or broken cables, excessive corrosion, or wear or insecurity of the linkage. Check that the mechanism works on each relevant wheel, and releases fully, without binding.

☐ It is not possible to test brake efficiency without special equipment, but a road test can be carried out later to check that the vehicle pulls up in a straight line.

Fuel and exhaust systems

☐ Inspect the fuel tank (including the filler cap), fuel pipes, hoses and unions. All components must be secure and free from leaks.

☐ Examine the exhaust system over its entire length, checking for any damaged, broken or missing mountings, security of the retaining clamps and rust or corrosion.

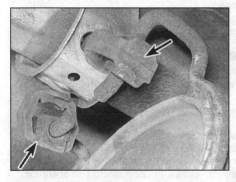

Wheels and tyres

☐ Examine the sidewalls and tread area of each tyre in turn. Check for cuts, tears, lumps, bulges, separation of the tread, and exposure of the ply or cord due to wear or damage. Check that the tyre bead is correctly seated on the wheel rim, that the valve is sound and

properly seated, and that the wheel is not distorted or damaged.

☐ Check that the tyres are of the correct size for the vehicle, that they are of the same size and type on each axle, and that the pressures are correct.

☐ Check the tyre tread depth. The legal minimum at the time of writing is 1.6 mm over at least three-quarters of the tread width. Abnormal tread wear may indicate incorrect front wheel alignment.

Body corrosion

☐ Check the condition of the entire vehicle structure for signs of corrosion in load-bearing areas. (These include chassis box sections, side sills, cross-members, pillars, and all suspension, steering, braking system and seat belt mountings and anchorages.) Any corrosion which has seriously reduced the thickness of a load-bearing area is likely to cause the vehicle to fail. In this case professional repairs are likely to be needed.

☐ Damage or corrosion which causes sharp or otherwise dangerous edges to be exposed will also cause the vehicle to fail.

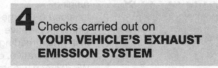

4 Checks carried out on YOUR VEHICLE'S EXHAUST EMISSION SYSTEM

Petrol models

☐ Have the engine at normal operating temperature, and make sure that it is in good tune (ignition system in good order, air filter element clean, etc).

☐ Before any measurements are carried out, raise the engine speed to around 2500 rpm, and hold it at this speed for 20 seconds. Allow

the engine speed to return to idle, and watch for smoke emissions from the exhaust tailpipe. If the idle speed is obviously much too high, or if dense blue or clearly-visible black smoke comes from the tailpipe for more than 5 seconds, the vehicle will fail. As a rule of thumb, blue smoke signifies oil being burnt (engine wear) while black smoke signifies unburnt fuel (dirty air cleaner element, or other carburettor or fuel system fault).

☐ An exhaust gas analyser capable of measuring carbon monoxide (CO) and hydrocarbons (HC) is now needed. If such an instrument cannot be hired or borrowed, a local garage may agree to perform the check for a small fee.

CO emissions (mixture)

☐ At the time of writing, the maximum CO level at idle is 3.5% for vehicles first used after August 1986 and 4.5% for older vehicles. From January 1996 a much tighter limit (around 0.5%) applies to catalyst-equipped vehicles first used from August 1992. If the CO level cannot be reduced far enough to pass the test (and the fuel and ignition systems are otherwise in good condition) then the carburettor is badly worn, or there is some problem in the fuel injection system or catalytic converter (as applicable).

HC emissions

☐ With the CO emissions within limits, HC emissions must be no more than 1200 ppm (parts per million). If the vehicle fails this test at idle, it can be re-tested at around 2000 rpm; if the HC level is then 1200 ppm or less, this counts as a pass.

☐ Excessive HC emissions can be caused by oil being burnt, but they are more likely to be due to unburnt fuel.

Diesel models

☐ The only emission test applicable to Diesel engines is the measuring of exhaust smoke density. The test involves accelerating the engine several times to its maximum unloaded speed.

Note: *It is of the utmost importance that the engine timing belt is in good condition before the test is carried out.*

☐ Excessive smoke can be caused by a dirty air cleaner element. Otherwise, professional advice may be needed to find the cause.

Engine 1
- ☐ Engine fails to rotate when attempting to start
- ☐ Engine rotates, but will not start
- ☐ Engine difficult to start when cold
- ☐ Engine difficult to start when hot
- ☐ Starter motor noisy or excessively-rough in engagement
- ☐ Engine starts, but stops immediately
- ☐ Engine idles erratically
- ☐ Engine misfires at idle speed
- ☐ Engine misfires throughout the driving speed range
- ☐ Engine hesitates on acceleration
- ☐ Engine stalls
- ☐ Engine lacks power
- ☐ Engine backfires
- ☐ Oil pressure warning light illuminated with engine running
- ☐ Engine runs-on after switching off
- ☐ Engine noises

Cooling system 2
- ☐ Overheating
- ☐ Overcooling
- ☐ External coolant leakage
- ☐ Internal coolant leakage
- ☐ Corrosion

Fuel and exhaust systems 3
- ☐ Excessive fuel consumption
- ☐ Fuel leakage and/or fuel odour
- ☐ Excessive noise or fumes from exhaust system

Clutch 4
- ☐ Pedal travels to floor - no pressure or very little resistance
- ☐ Clutch fails to disengage (unable to select gears)
- ☐ Clutch slips (engine speed increases, with no increase in vehicle speed)
- ☐ Judder as clutch is engaged
- ☐ Noise when depressing or releasing clutch pedal

Manual transmission 5
- ☐ Noisy in neutral with engine running
- ☐ Noisy in one particular gear
- ☐ Difficulty engaging gears
- ☐ Jumps out of gear
- ☐ Vibration
- ☐ Lubricant leaks

Automatic transmission 6
- ☐ Fluid leakage
- ☐ Transmission fluid brown, or has burned smell
- ☐ General gear selection problems
- ☐ Transmission will not downshift (kickdown) with accelerator pedal fully depressed
- ☐ Engine will not start in any gear, or starts in gears other than Park or Neutral
- ☐ Transmission slips, shifts roughly, is noisy, or has no drive in forward or reverse gears

Driveshafts 7
- ☐ Vibration when accelerating or decelerating
- ☐ Clicking or knocking noise on turns (at slow speed on full-lock)

Braking system 8
- ☐ Vehicle pulls to one side under braking
- ☐ Noise (grinding or high-pitched squeal) when brakes applied
- ☐ Excessive brake pedal travel
- ☐ Brake pedal feels spongy when depressed
- ☐ Excessive brake pedal effort required to stop vehicle
- ☐ Judder felt through brake pedal or steering wheel when braking
- ☐ Brakes binding
- ☐ Rear wheels locking under normal braking

Suspension and steering 9
- ☐ Vehicle pulls to one side
- ☐ Wheel wobble and vibration
- ☐ Excessive pitching and/or rolling around corners, or during braking
- ☐ Wandering or general instability
- ☐ Excessively-stiff steering
- ☐ Excessive play in steering
- ☐ Lack of power assistance
- ☐ Tyre wear excessive

Electrical system 10
- ☐ Battery will only hold a charge for a few days
- ☐ Ignition/no-charge warning light remains illuminated with engine running
- ☐ Ignition/no-charge warning light fails to come on
- ☐ Lights inoperative
- ☐ Instrument readings inaccurate or erratic
- ☐ Horn inoperative, or unsatisfactory in operation
- ☐ Windscreen wipers inoperative, or unsatisfactory in operation
- ☐ Windscreen washers inoperative, or unsatisfactory in operation
- ☐ Electric windows inoperative, or unsatisfactory in operation
- ☐ Central locking system inoperative, or unsatisfactory in operation

Introduction

The vehicle owner who does his or her own maintenance according to the recommended service schedules should not have to use this section of the manual very often. Modern component reliability is such that, provided those items subject to wear or deterioration are inspected or renewed at the specified intervals, sudden failure is comparatively rare. Faults do not usually just happen as a result of sudden failure, but develop over a period of time. Major mechanical failures in particular are usually preceded by characteristic symptoms over hundreds or even thousands of miles. Those components which do occasionally fail without warning are often small and easily carried in the vehicle.

With any fault-finding, the first step is to decide where to begin investigations. Sometimes this is obvious, but on other occasions, a little detective work will be necessary. The owner who makes half a dozen haphazard adjustments or replacements may be successful in curing a fault (or its symptoms), but will be none the wiser if the fault recurs, and ultimately may have spent more time and money than was necessary. A calm and logical approach will be found to be more satisfactory in the long run. Always take into account any warning signs or abnormalities that may have been noticed in the period preceding the fault - power loss, high or low gauge readings, unusual smells, etc - and remember that failure of components such as fuses or spark plugs may only be pointers to some underlying fault.

The pages which follow provide an easy-reference guide to the more common problems which may occur during the operation of the vehicle. These problems and their possible causes are grouped under headings denoting various components or systems, such as Engine, Cooling system, etc. The Chapter and/or Section which deals with the problem is also shown in brackets. Whatever the fault, certain basic principles apply. These are as follows:

Verify the fault. This is simply a matter of being sure that you know what the symptoms are before starting work. This is particularly important if you are investigating a fault for someone else, who may not have described it very accurately. *Don't overlook the obvious.* For example, if the vehicle won't start, is there fuel in the tank? (Don't take anyone else's word on this particular point, and don't trust the fuel gauge either!) If an electrical fault is indicated, look for loose or broken wires before digging out the test gear.

Cure the disease, not the symptom. Substituting a flat battery with a fully-charged one will get you off the hard shoulder, but if the underlying cause is not attended to, the new battery will go the same way. Similarly, changing oil-fouled spark plugs for a new set will get you moving again, but remember that the reason for the fouling (if it wasn't simply an incorrect grade of plug) will have to be established and corrected.

Don't take anything for granted. Particularly, don't forget that a "new" component may itself be defective (especially if it's been rattling around in the boot for months), and don't leave components out of a fault diagnosis sequence just because they are new or recently-fitted. When you do finally diagnose a difficult fault, you'll probably realise that all the evidence was there from the start.

1 Engine

Engine fails to rotate when attempting to start

☐ Battery terminal connections loose or corroded (see *"Weekly checks"*)
☐ Battery discharged or faulty (Chapter 5)
☐ Broken, loose or disconnected wiring in the starting circuit (Chapter 5)
☐ Defective starter solenoid or switch (Chapter 5)
☐ Defective starter motor (Chapter 5)
☐ Starter pinion or flywheel ring gear teeth loose or broken (Chapters 2 and 5)
☐ Engine earth strap broken or disconnected (Chapter 5)

Engine rotates, but will not start

☐ Fuel tank empty
☐ Battery discharged (engine rotates slowly) (Chapter 5)
☐ Battery terminal connections loose or corroded (*"Weekly checks"*)
☐ Ignition components damp or damaged - petrol models (Chapters 1 and 5)
☐ Broken, loose or disconnected wiring in the ignition circuit - petrol models (Chapters 1 and 5)
☐ Worn, faulty or incorrectly-gapped spark plugs - petrol models (Chapter 1)
☐ Preheating system faulty - diesel models (Chapter 5)
☐ Fuel injection system fault - petrol models (Chapter 4)
☐ Stop solenoid faulty - diesel models (Chapter 4)
☐ Air in fuel system - diesel models (Chapter 4)
☐ Major mechanical failure (eg camshaft drive) (Chapter 2)

Engine difficult to start when cold

☐ Battery discharged (Chapter 5)
☐ Battery terminal connections loose or corroded (see *"Weekly checks"*)
☐ Worn, faulty or incorrectly-gapped spark plugs - petrol models (Chapter 1)
☐ Preheating system faulty - diesel models (Chapter 5)
☐ Fuel injection system fault - petrol models (Chapter 4)
☐ Other ignition system fault - petrol models (Chapters 1 and 5)
☐ Low cylinder compressions (Chapter 2)

Engine difficult to start when hot

☐ Air filter element dirty or clogged (Chapter 1)
☐ Fuel injection system fault - petrol models (Chapter 4)
☐ Low cylinder compressions (Chapter 2)

Starter motor noisy or excessively-rough in engagement

☐ Starter pinion or flywheel ring gear teeth loose or broken (Chapters 2 and 5)
☐ Starter motor mounting bolts loose or missing (Chapter 5)
☐ Starter motor internal components worn or damaged (Chapter 5)

Engine starts, but stops immediately

☐ Loose or faulty electrical connections in the ignition circuit - petrol models (Chapters 1 and 5)
☐ Vacuum leak at the throttle body or inlet manifold - petrol models (Chapter 4)
☐ Blocked injector/fuel injection system fault - petrol models (Chapter 4)

Engine idles erratically

☐ Air filter element clogged (Chapter 1)
☐ Vacuum leak at the throttle body, inlet manifold or associated hoses - petrol models (Chapter 4)
☐ Worn, faulty or incorrectly-gapped spark plugs - petrol models (Chapter 1)
☐ Uneven or low cylinder compressions (Chapter 2)
☐ Camshaft lobes worn (Chapter 2)
☐ Timing belt incorrectly fitted (Chapter 2)
☐ Blocked injector/fuel injection system fault - petrol models (Chapter 4)
☐ Faulty injector(s) - diesel models (Chapter 4)

Engine misfires at idle speed

☐ Worn, faulty or incorrectly-gapped spark plugs - petrol models (Chapter 1)
☐ Faulty spark plug HT leads (where fitted) - petrol models (Chapter 1)
☐ Vacuum leak at the throttle body, inlet manifold or associated hoses - petrol models (Chapter 4)
☐ Blocked injector/fuel injection system fault - petrol models (Chapter 4)
☐ Faulty injector(s) - diesel models (Chapter 4)
☐ Distributor cap cracked or tracking internally - petrol models (where applicable) (Chapter 1).
☐ Uneven or low cylinder compressions (Chapter 2)
☐ Disconnected, leaking, or perished crankcase ventilation hoses (Chapter 4)

Engine misfires throughout the driving speed range

☐ Fuel filter choked (Chapter 1)
☐ Fuel pump faulty, or delivery pressure low (Chapter 4)
☐ Fuel tank vent blocked, or fuel pipes restricted (Chapter 4)
☐ Vacuum leak at the throttle body, inlet manifold or associated hoses - petrol models (Chapter 4)
☐ Worn, faulty or incorrectly-gapped spark plugs - petrol models (Chapter 1)
☐ Faulty spark plug HT leads (where fitted) - petrol models (Chapter 1)
☐ Faulty injector(s) - diesel models (Chapter 4)
☐ Distributor cap cracked or tracking internally - petrol models (where applicable) (Chapter 1)

1 Engine (continued)

Engine misfires throughout the driving speed range (continued)

☐ Faulty ignition coil - petrol models (Chapter 5)
☐ Uneven or low cylinder compressions (Chapter 2)
☐ Blocked injector/fuel injection system fault - petrol models (Chapter 4)

Engine hesitates on acceleration

☐ Worn, faulty or incorrectly-gapped spark plugs - petrol models (Chapter 1)
☐ Vacuum leak at the throttle body, inlet manifold or associated hoses (Chapter 4)
☐ Blocked injector/fuel injection system fault - petrol models (Chapter 4)
☐ Faulty injector(s) - diesel models (Chapter 4)

Engine stalls

☐ Vacuum leak at the throttle body, inlet manifold or associated hoses - petrol models (Chapter 4)
☐ Fuel filter choked (Chapter 1)
☐ Fuel pump faulty, or delivery pressure low - petrol models (Chapter 4)
☐ Fuel tank vent blocked, or fuel pipes restricted (Chapter 4)
☐ Blocked injector/fuel injection system fault - petrol models (Chapter 4)
☐ Faulty injector(s) - diesel models (Chapter 4)

Engine lacks power

☐ Timing belt incorrectly fitted (Chapter 2)
☐ Fuel filter choked (Chapter 1)
☐ Fuel pump faulty, or delivery pressure low (Chapter 4)
☐ Uneven or low cylinder compressions (Chapter 2)
☐ Worn, faulty or incorrectly-gapped spark plugs - petrol models (Chapter 1)
☐ Vacuum leak at the throttle body, inlet manifold or associated hoses - petrol models (Chapter 4)
☐ Blocked injector/fuel injection system fault - petrol models (Chapter 4)
☐ Faulty injector(s) - diesel models (Chapter 4)
☐ Injection pump timing incorrect - diesel models (Chapter 4)
☐ Brakes binding (Chapters 1 and 9)
☐ Clutch slipping (Chapter 6)

Engine backfires

☐ Timing belt incorrectly fitted (Chapter 2)
☐ Vacuum leak at the throttle body, inlet manifold or associated hoses - petrol models (Chapter 4)
☐ Blocked injector/fuel injection system fault - petrol models (Chapter 4)

Oil pressure warning light illuminated with engine running

☐ Low oil level, or incorrect oil grade ("Weekly checks")
☐ Faulty oil pressure sensor (Chapter 5)
☐ Worn engine bearings and/or oil pump (Chapter 2)
☐ High engine operating temperature (Chapter 3)
☐ Oil pressure relief valve defective (Chapter 2)
☐ Oil pick-up strainer clogged (Chapter 2)

Engine runs-on after switching off

☐ Excessive carbon build-up in engine (Chapter 2)
☐ High engine operating temperature (Chapter 3)
☐ Fuel injection system fault - petrol models (Chapter 4)
☐ Faulty stop solenoid - diesel models (Chapter 4)

Engine noises

Pre-ignition (pinking) or knocking during acceleration or under load

☐ Ignition timing incorrect/ignition system fault - petrol models (Chapters 1 and 5)
☐ Incorrect grade of spark plug - petrol models (Chapter 1)
☐ Incorrect grade of fuel (Chapter 1)
☐ Vacuum leak at the throttle body, inlet manifold or associated hoses - petrol models (Chapter 4)
☐ Excessive carbon build-up in engine (Chapter 2)
☐ Blocked injector/fuel injection system fault - petrol models (Chapter 4)

Whistling or wheezing noises

☐ Leaking inlet manifold or throttle body gasket - petrol models (Chapter 4)
☐ Leaking exhaust manifold gasket or pipe-to-manifold joint (Chapter 4)
☐ Leaking vacuum hose (Chapters 4, 5 and 9)
☐ Blowing cylinder head gasket (Chapter 2)

Tapping or rattling noises

☐ Worn valve gear or camshaft (Chapter 2)
☐ Ancillary component fault (coolant pump, alternator, etc) (Chapters 3, 5, etc)

Knocking or thumping noises

☐ Worn big-end bearings (regular heavy knocking, perhaps less under load) (Chapter 2)
☐ Worn main bearings (rumbling and knocking, perhaps worsening under load) (Chapter 2)
☐ Piston slap (most noticeable when cold) (Chapter 2)
☐ Ancillary component fault (coolant pump, alternator, etc) (Chapters 3, 5, etc)

2 Cooling system

Overheating

- ☐ Insufficient coolant in system (*"Weekly checks"*)
- ☐ Thermostat faulty (Chapter 3)
- ☐ Radiator core blocked, or grille restricted (Chapter 3)
- ☐ Cooling fan faulty (Chapter 3)
- ☐ Inaccurate temperature gauge sender unit (Chapter 3)
- ☐ Airlock in cooling system (Chapter 3)
- ☐ Pressure cap faulty (Chapter 3)

Overcooling

- ☐ Thermostat faulty (Chapter 3)
- ☐ Inaccurate temperature gauge sender unit (Chapter 3)
- ☐ Cooling fan faulty (Chapter 3)

External coolant leakage

- ☐ Deteriorated or damaged hoses or hose clips (Chapter 1)
- ☐ Radiator core or heater matrix leaking (Chapter 3)
- ☐ Pressure cap faulty (Chapter 3)
- ☐ Coolant pump internal seal leaking (Chapter 3)
- ☐ Coolant pump-to-block seal leaking (Chapter 3)
- ☐ Boiling due to overheating (Chapter 3)
- ☐ Core plug leaking (Chapter 2)

Internal coolant leakage

- ☐ Leaking cylinder head gasket (Chapter 2)
- ☐ Cracked cylinder head or cylinder block (Chapter 2)

Corrosion

- ☐ Infrequent draining and flushing (Chapter 1)
- ☐ Incorrect coolant mixture or inappropriate coolant type (Chapter 1)

3 Fuel and exhaust systems

Excessive fuel consumption

- ☐ Air filter element dirty or clogged (Chapter 1)
- ☐ Fuel injection system fault - petrol models (Chapter 4)
- ☐ Faulty injector(s) - diesel models (Chapter 4)
- ☐ Ignition timing incorrect/ignition system fault - petrol models (Chapters 1 and 5)
- ☐ Tyres under-inflated (*"Weekly checks"*)

Fuel leakage and/or fuel odour

- ☐ Damaged or corroded fuel tank, pipes or connections (Chapter 4)

Excessive noise or fumes from exhaust system

- ☐ Leaking exhaust system or manifold joints (Chapters 1 and 4)
- ☐ Leaking, corroded or damaged silencers or pipe (Chapters 1 and 4)
- ☐ Broken mountings causing body or suspension contact (Chapter 1)

4 Clutch

Pedal travels to floor - no pressure or very little resistance

- ☐ Broken clutch cable/adjuster mechanism - cable-operated clutch (Chapter 6)
- ☐ Faulty hydraulic release system - hydraulically-operated clutch (Chapter 6)
- ☐ Broken clutch release bearing or fork (Chapter 6)
- ☐ Broken diaphragm spring in clutch pressure plate (Chapter 6)

Clutch fails to disengage (unable to select gears.

- ☐ Faulty clutch cable/adjuster mechanism - cable-operated clutch (Chapter 6)
- ☐ Faulty hydraulic release system - hydraulically-operated clutch (Chapter 6)
- ☐ Clutch disc sticking on gearbox input shaft splines (Chapter 6)
- ☐ Clutch disc sticking to flywheel or pressure plate (Chapter 6)
- ☐ Faulty pressure plate assembly (Chapter 6)
- ☐ Clutch release mechanism worn or incorrectly assembled (Chapter 6)

Clutch slips (engine speed increases, with no increase in vehicle speed)

- ☐ Faulty clutch cable/adjuster mechanism - cable-operated clutch (Chapter 6)
- ☐ Faulty hydraulic release system - hydraulically-operated clutch (Chapter 6)
- ☐ Clutch disc linings excessively worn (Chapter 6)
- ☐ Clutch disc linings contaminated with oil or grease (Chapter 6)
- ☐ Faulty pressure plate or weak diaphragm spring (Chapter 6)

Judder as clutch is engaged

- ☐ Clutch disc linings contaminated with oil or grease (Chapter 6)
- ☐ Clutch disc linings excessively worn (Chapter 6)
- ☐ Faulty or distorted pressure plate or diaphragm spring (Chapter 6).
- ☐ Worn or loose engine or gearbox mountings (Chapter 2)
- ☐ Clutch disc hub or gearbox input shaft splines worn (Chapter 6)

Noise when depressing or releasing clutch pedal

- ☐ Worn clutch release bearing (Chapter 6)
- ☐ Worn or dry clutch pedal bushes (Chapter 6)
- ☐ Faulty pressure plate assembly (Chapter 6)
- ☐ Pressure plate diaphragm spring broken (Chapter 6)
- ☐ Broken clutch disc cushioning springs (Chapter 6)

5 Manual transmission

Noisy in neutral with engine running

☐ Input shaft bearings worn (noise apparent with clutch pedal released, but not when depressed) (Chapter 7)*
☐ Clutch release bearing worn (noise apparent with clutch pedal depressed, possibly less when released) (Chapter 6)

Noisy in one particular gear

☐ Worn, damaged or chipped gear teeth (Chapter 7)*

Difficulty engaging gears

☐ Clutch fault (Chapter 6)
☐ Worn or damaged gearchange linkage/cable (Chapter 7)
☐ Incorrectly-adjusted gearchange linkage/cable (Chapter 7)
☐ Worn synchroniser units (Chapter 7)*

Jumps out of gear

☐ Worn or damaged gearchange linkage/cable (Chapter 7)
☐ Incorrectly-adjusted gearchange linkage/cable (Chapter 7)
☐ Worn synchroniser units (Chapter 7)*
☐ Worn selector forks (Chapter 7)*

Vibration

☐ Lack of oil (Chapter 1)
☐ Worn bearings (Chapter 7)*

Lubricant leaks

☐ Leaking differential output oil seal (Chapter 7)
☐ Leaking housing joint (Chapter 7)*
☐ Leaking input shaft oil seal (Chapter 7)*

Although the corrective action necessary to remedy the symptoms described is beyond the scope of the home mechanic, the above information should be helpful in isolating the cause of the condition, so that the owner can communicate clearly with a professional mechanic.

6 Automatic transmission

Note: *Due to the complexity of the automatic transmission, it is difficult for the home mechanic to properly diagnose and service this unit. For problems other than the following, the vehicle should be taken to a dealer service department or automatic transmission specialist. Do not be too hasty in removing the transmission if a fault is suspected, as most of the testing is carried out with the unit still fitted.*

Fluid leakage

☐ Automatic transmission fluid is usually dark in colour. Fluid leaks should not be confused with engine oil, which can easily be blown onto the transmission by airflow.
☐ To determine the source of a leak, first remove all built-up dirt and grime from the transmission housing and surrounding areas using a degreasing agent, or by steam-cleaning. Drive the vehicle at low speed, so airflow will not blow the leak far from its source. Raise and support the vehicle, and determine where the leak is coming from. The following are common areas of leakage:

a) *Oil pan (Chapter 1 and 7)*
b) *Dipstick tube (Chapter 1 and 7)*
c) *Transmission-to-fluid cooler unions (Chapter 7)*

Transmission fluid brown, or has burned smell

☐ Transmission fluid level low (Chapter 1)

General gear selection problems

☐ Chapter 7B deals with checking the selector cable on automatic transmissions. The following are common problems which may be caused by a faulty cable:

a) *Engine starting in gears other than Park or Neutral.*
b) *Indicator panel indicating a gear other than the one actually being used.*
c) *Vehicle moves when in Park or Neutral.*
d) *Poor gear shift quality or erratic gear changes.*

Transmission will not downshift (kickdown) with accelerator pedal fully depressed

☐ Low transmission fluid level (Chapter 1)
☐ Incorrect selector cable adjustment (Chapter 7)

Engine will not start in any gear, or starts in gears other than Park or Neutral

☐ Incorrect starter/inhibitor (multi-function) switch adjustment (Chapter 7)
☐ Incorrect selector cable adjustment (Chapter 7)

Transmission slips, shifts roughly, is noisy, or has no drive in forward or reverse gears

☐ There are many probable causes for the above problems, but the home mechanic should be concerned with only one possibility - fluid level. Before taking the vehicle to a dealer or transmission specialist, check the fluid level and condition of the fluid as described in Chapter 1. Correct the fluid level as necessary, or change the fluid if needed. If the problem persists, professional help will be necessary.

7 Driveshafts

Vibration when accelerating or decelerating

☐ Worn inner constant velocity joint (Chapter 8)
☐ Bent or distorted driveshaft (Chapter 8)
☐ Worn intermediate bearing (Chapter 8)

Clicking or knocking noise on turns (at slow speed on full-lock)

☐ Worn outer constant velocity joint (Chapter 8)
☐ Lack of constant velocity joint lubricant, possibly due to damaged gaiter (Chapter 8)
☐ Worn intermediate bearing (Chapter 8)

8 Braking system

Note: *Before assuming that a brake problem exists, make sure that the tyres are in good condition and correctly inflated, that the front wheel alignment is correct, and that the vehicle is not loaded with weight in an unequal manner. Apart from checking the condition of all pipe and hose connections, any faults occurring on the anti-lock braking system should be referred to a Peugeot dealer for diagnosis.*

Vehicle pulls to one side under braking

- [ ] Worn, defective, damaged or contaminated brake pads/shoes on one side (Chapters 1 and 9)
- [ ] Seized or partially-seized brake caliper piston/wheel cylinder (Chapters 1 and 9)
- [ ] A mixture of brake pad/shoe lining materials fitted between sides (Chapters 1 and 9)
- [ ] Brake caliper/backplate mounting bolts loose (Chapter 9)
- [ ] Worn or damaged steering or suspension components (Chapters 1 and 10)

Noise (grinding or high-pitched squeal) when brakes applied

- [ ] Brake pad/shoe friction lining material worn down to metal backing (Chapters 1 and 9)
- [ ] Excessive corrosion of brake disc/drum (may be apparent after the vehicle has been standing for some time (Chapters 1 and 9)
- [ ] Foreign object (stone chipping, etc) trapped between brake disc and shield (Chapters 1 and 9)

Excessive brake pedal travel

- [ ] Faulty master cylinder (Chapter 9)
- [ ] Air in hydraulic system (Chapters 1 and 9)
- [ ] Faulty vacuum servo unit (Chapter 9)

Brake pedal feels spongy when depressed

- [ ] Air in hydraulic system (Chapters 1 and 9)
- [ ] Deteriorated flexible rubber brake hoses (Chapters 1 and 9)
- [ ] Master cylinder mounting nuts loose (Chapter 9)
- [ ] Faulty master cylinder (Chapter 9)

Excessive brake pedal effort required to stop vehicle

- [ ] Faulty vacuum servo unit (Chapter 9)
- [ ] Disconnected, damaged or insecure brake servo vacuum hose (Chapter 9)
- [ ] Primary or secondary hydraulic circuit failure (Chapter 9)
- [ ] Seized brake caliper/wheel cylinder piston (Chapter 9)
- [ ] Brake pads/shoes incorrectly fitted (Chapters 1 and 9)
- [ ] Incorrect grade of brake pads/shoes fitted (Chapters 1 and 9)
- [ ] Brake pad/shoe linings contaminated (Chapters 1 and 9)
- [ ] Faulty vacuum pump - diesel models (Chapter 9)

Judder felt through brake pedal or steering wheel when braking

- [ ] Excessive run-out or distortion of discs/drums (Chapters 1 and 9)
- [ ] Brake pad/shoe linings worn (Chapters 1 and 9)
- [ ] Brake caliper/backplate mounting bolts loose (Chapter 9)
- [ ] Wear in suspension or steering components or mountings (Chapters 1 and 10)

Brakes binding

- [ ] Seized brake caliper/wheel cylinder piston (Chapter 9)
- [ ] Incorrectly-adjusted handbrake mechanism (Chapter 9)
- [ ] Faulty master cylinder (Chapter 9)

Rear wheels locking under normal braking

- [ ] Rear brake pad/shoe linings contaminated (Chapters 1 and 9)
- [ ] Rear brake discs/drums warped (Chapters 1 and 9)

9 Suspension and steering

Note: *Before diagnosing suspension or steering faults, be sure the trouble is not due to tyre pressures, mixtures of tyre types, or binding brakes.*

Vehicle pulls to one side

- [ ] Defective tyre ("*Weekly checks*")
- [ ] Excessive wear in suspension or steering components (Chapters 1 and 10)
- [ ] Incorrect front wheel alignment (Chapter 10)
- [ ] Accident damage to steering or suspension components (Chapter 1)

Wheel wobble and vibration

- [ ] Front roadwheels out of balance (vibration felt mainly through the steering wheel) (Chapters 1 and 10)
- [ ] Rear roadwheels out of balance (vibration felt throughout the vehicle) (Chapters 1 and 10)
- [ ] Roadwheels damaged or distorted (Chapters 1 and 10)
- [ ] Faulty or damaged tyre ("*Weekly checks*")
- [ ] Worn steering or suspension joints, bushes or components (Chapters 1 and 10)
- [ ] Wheel bolts loose (Chapters 1 and 10)

Excessive pitching and/or rolling around corners, or during braking

- [ ] Defective shock absorbers (Chapters 1 and 10)
- [ ] Broken or weak spring and/or suspension component (Chapters 1 and 10)
- [ ] Worn or damaged anti-roll bar or mountings (Chapter 10)

Wandering or general instability

- [ ] Incorrect front wheel alignment (Chapter 10)
- [ ] Worn steering or suspension joints, bushes or components (Chapters 1 and 10)
- [ ] Roadwheels out of balance (Chapters 1 and 10)
- [ ] Faulty or damaged tyre ("*Weekly checks*")
- [ ] Wheel bolts loose (Chapters 1 and 10)
- [ ] Defective shock absorbers (Chapters 1 and 10)

Excessively-stiff steering

- [ ] Seized steering linkage balljoint or suspension balljoint (Chapters 1 and 10)
- [ ] Broken or incorrectly-adjusted auxiliary drivebelt (Chapter 1)
- [ ] Incorrect front wheel alignment (Chapter 10)
- [ ] Steering gear damaged (Chapter 10)

Excessive play in steering

- [ ] Worn steering column/intermediate shaft joints (Chapter 10)
- [ ] Worn track rod balljoints (Chapters 1 and 10)
- [ ] Worn steering gear (Chapter 10)
- [ ] Worn steering or suspension joints, bushes or components (Chapters 1 and 10)

9 Braking system (continued)

Lack of power assistance

- [ ] Broken or incorrectly-adjusted auxiliary drivebelt (Chapter 1)
- [ ] Incorrect power steering fluid level (*"Weekly checks"*)
- [ ] Restriction in power steering fluid hoses (Chapter 1)
- [ ] Faulty power steering pump (Chapter 10)
- [ ] Faulty steering gear (Chapter 10)

Tyre wear excessive

Tyres worn on inside or outside edges

- [ ] Tyres under-inflated (wear on both edges) (*"Weekly checks"*)
- [ ] Incorrect camber or castor angles (wear on one edge only) (Chapter 10)
- [ ] Worn steering or suspension joints, bushes or components (Chapters 1 and 10)
- [ ] Excessively-hard cornering
- [ ] Accident damage

Tyre treads exhibit feathered edges

- [ ] Incorrect toe setting (Chapter 10)

Tyres worn in centre of tread

- [ ] Tyres over-inflated (*"Weekly checks"*)

Tyres worn on inside and outside edges

- [ ] Tyres under-inflated (*"Weekly checks"*)

Tyres worn unevenly

- [ ] Tyres/wheels out of balance (Chapter 1)
- [ ] Excessive wheel or tyre run-out (Chapter 1)
- [ ] Worn shock absorbers (Chapters 1 and 10)
- [ ] Faulty tyre (*"Weekly checks"*)

10 Electrical system

Note: *For problems associated with the starting system, refer to the faults listed under "Engine" earlier in this Section.*

Battery will only hold a charge for a few days

- [ ] Battery defective internally (Chapter 5)
- [ ] Battery terminal connections loose or corroded (*"Weekly checks"*)
- [ ] Auxiliary drivebelt worn or incorrectly adjusted (Chapter 1)
- [ ] Alternator not charging at correct output (Chapter 5)
- [ ] Alternator or voltage regulator faulty (Chapter 5)
- [ ] Short-circuit causing continual battery drain (Chapters 5 and 12)

Ignition/no-charge warning light remains illuminated with engine running

- [ ] Auxiliary drivebelt broken, worn, or incorrectly adjusted (Chapter 1)
- [ ] Alternator brushes worn, sticking, or dirty (Chapter 5)
- [ ] Alternator brush springs weak or broken (Chapter 5)
- [ ] Internal fault in alternator or voltage regulator (Chapter 5)
- [ ] Broken, disconnected, or loose wiring in charging circuit (Chapter 5)

Ignition/no-charge warning light fails to come on

- [ ] Warning light bulb blown (Chapter 12)
- [ ] Broken, disconnected, or loose wiring in warning light circuit (Chapter 12)
- [ ] Alternator faulty (Chapter 5)

Lights inoperative

- [ ] Bulb blown (Chapter 12)
- [ ] Corrosion of bulb or bulbholder contacts (Chapter 12)
- [ ] Blown fuse (Chapter 12)
- [ ] Faulty relay (Chapter 12)
- [ ] Broken, loose, or disconnected wiring (Chapter 12)
- [ ] Faulty switch (Chapter 12)

Instrument readings inaccurate or erratic

Instrument readings increase with engine speed

- [ ] Faulty voltage regulator (Chapter 12)

Fuel or temperature gauges give no reading

- [ ] Faulty gauge sender unit (Chapters 3 and 4)
- [ ] Wiring open-circuit (Chapter 12)
- [ ] Faulty gauge (Chapter 12)

Fuel or temperature gauges give continuous maximum reading

- [ ] Faulty gauge sender unit (Chapters 3 and 4)
- [ ] Wiring short-circuit (Chapter 12)
- [ ] Faulty gauge (Chapter 12)

Horn inoperative, or unsatisfactory in operation

Horn operates all the time

- [ ] Horn push either earthed or stuck down (Chapter 12)
- [ ] Horn cable-to-horn push earthed (Chapter 12)

Horn fails to operate

- [ ] Blown fuse (Chapter 12)
- [ ] Cable or cable connections loose, broken or disconnected (Chapter 12)
- [ ] Faulty horn (Chapter 12)

Horn emits intermittent or unsatisfactory sound

- [ ] Cable connections loose (Chapter 12)
- [ ] Horn mountings loose (Chapter 12)
- [ ] Faulty horn (Chapter 12)

Windscreen wipers inoperative, or unsatisfactory in operation

Wipers fail to operate, or operate very slowly

- [ ] Wiper blades stuck to screen, or linkage seized or binding (Chapters 1 and 12)
- [ ] Blown fuse (Chapter 12)
- [ ] Cable or cable connections loose or disconnected (Chapter 12)
- [ ] Faulty relay (Chapter 12)
- [ ] Faulty wiper motor (Chapter 12)

Wiper blades sweep over too large or too small an area of the glass

- [ ] Wiper arms incorrectly positioned on spindles (Chapter 1)
- [ ] Excessive wear of wiper linkage (Chapter 12)
- [ ] Wiper motor or linkage mountings loose or insecure (Chapter 12)

Wiper blades fail to clean the glass effectively

- [ ] Wiper blade rubbers worn or perished (*"Weekly checks"*)
- [ ] Wiper arm tension springs broken, or arm pivots seized (Chapter 12)
- [ ] Insufficient windscreen washer additive to adequately remove road film (*"Weekly checks"*)

10 Electrical system (continued)

Windscreen washers inoperative, or unsatisfactory in operation

One or more washer jets inoperative

☐ Blocked washer jet (Chapter 1)
☐ Disconnected, kinked or restricted fluid hose (Chapter 12)
☐ Insufficient fluid in washer reservoir ("*Weekly checks*")

Washer pump fails to operate

☐ Broken or disconnected wiring or connections (Chapter 12)
☐ Blown fuse (Chapter 12)
☐ Faulty washer switch (Chapter 12)
☐ Faulty washer pump (Chapter 12)

Washer pump runs for some time before fluid is emitted from jets

☐ Faulty one-way valve in fluid supply hose (Chapter 12)

Electric windows inoperative, or unsatisfactory in operation

Window glass will only move in one direction

☐ Faulty switch (Chapter 12)

Window glass slow to move

☐ Regulator seized or damaged, or in need of lubrication (Chapter 11)
☐ Door internal components or trim fouling regulator (Chapter 11)
☐ Faulty motor (Chapter 11)

Window glass fails to move

☐ Blown fuse (Chapter 12)
☐ Faulty relay (Chapter 12)
☐ Broken or disconnected wiring or connections (Chapter 12)
☐ Faulty motor (Chapter 11)

Central locking system inoperative, or unsatisfactory in operation

Complete system failure

☐ Blown fuse (Chapter 12)
☐ Faulty relay (Chapter 12)
☐ Broken or disconnected wiring or connections (Chapter 12)
☐ Faulty motor (Chapter 11)

Latch locks but will not unlock, or unlocks but will not lock

☐ Faulty master switch (Chapter 12)
☐ Broken or disconnected latch operating rods or levers (Chapter 11)
☐ Faulty relay (Chapter 12)
☐ Faulty motor (Chapter 11)

One solenoid/motor fails to operate

☐ Broken or disconnected wiring or connections (Chapter 12)
☐ Faulty operating assembly (Chapter 11)
☐ Broken, binding or disconnected latch operating rods or levers (Chapter 11)
☐ Fault in door latch (Chapter 11)

A

ABS (Anti-lock brake system) A system, usually electronically controlled, that senses incipient wheel lockup during braking and relieves hydraulic pressure at wheels that are about to skid.

Air bag An inflatable bag hidden in the steering wheel (driver's side) or the dash or glovebox (passenger side). In a head-on collision, the bags inflate, preventing the driver and front passenger from being thrown forward into the steering wheel or windscreen.

Air cleaner A metal or plastic housing, containing a filter element, which removes dust and dirt from the air being drawn into the engine.

Air filter element The actual filter in an air cleaner system, usually manufactured from pleated paper and requiring renewal at regular intervals.

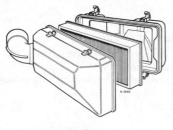

Air filter

Allen key A hexagonal wrench which fits into a recessed hexagonal hole.

Alligator clip A long-nosed spring-loaded metal clip with meshing teeth. Used to make temporary electrical connections.

Alternator A component in the electrical system which converts mechanical energy from a drivebelt into electrical energy to charge the battery and to operate the starting system, ignition system and electrical accessories.

Ampere (amp) A unit of measurement for the flow of electric current. One amp is the amount of current produced by one volt acting through a resistance of one ohm.

Anaerobic sealer A substance used to prevent bolts and screws from loosening. Anaerobic means that it does not require oxygen for activation. The Loctite brand is widely used.

Antifreeze A substance (usually ethylene glycol) mixed with water, and added to a vehicle's cooling system, to prevent freezing of the coolant in winter. Antifreeze also contains chemicals to inhibit corrosion and the formation of rust and other deposits that would tend to clog the radiator and coolant passages and reduce cooling efficiency.

Anti-seize compound A coating that reduces the risk of seizing on fasteners that are subjected to high temperatures, such as exhaust manifold bolts and nuts.

Asbestos A natural fibrous mineral with great heat resistance, commonly used in the composition of brake friction materials.

Asbestos is a health hazard and the dust created by brake systems should never be inhaled or ingested.

Axle A shaft on which a wheel revolves, or which revolves with a wheel. Also, a solid beam that connects the two wheels at one end of the vehicle. An axle which also transmits power to the wheels is known as a live axle.

Axleshaft A single rotating shaft, on either side of the differential, which delivers power from the final drive assembly to the drive wheels. Also called a driveshaft or a halfshaft.

B

Ball bearing An anti-friction bearing consisting of a hardened inner and outer race with hardened steel balls between two races.

Bearing The curved surface on a shaft or in a bore, or the part assembled into either, that permits relative motion between them with minimum wear and friction.

Bearing

Big-end bearing The bearing in the end of the connecting rod that's attached to the crankshaft.

Bleed nipple A valve on a brake wheel cylinder, caliper or other hydraulic component that is opened to purge the hydraulic system of air. Also called a bleed screw.

Brake bleeding Procedure for removing air from lines of a hydraulic brake system.

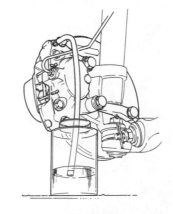

Brake bleeding

Brake disc The component of a disc brake that rotates with the wheels.

Brake drum The component of a drum brake that rotates with the wheels.

Brake linings The friction material which contacts the brake disc or drum to retard the vehicle's speed. The linings are bonded or riveted to the brake pads or shoes.

Brake pads The replaceable friction pads that pinch the brake disc when the brakes are applied. Brake pads consist of a friction material bonded or riveted to a rigid backing plate.

Brake shoe The crescent-shaped carrier to which the brake linings are mounted and which forces the lining against the rotating drum during braking.

Braking systems For more information on braking systems, consult the *Haynes Automotive Brake Manual*.

Breaker bar A long socket wrench handle providing greater leverage.

Bulkhead The insulated partition between the engine and the passenger compartment.

C

Caliper The non-rotating part of a disc-brake assembly that straddles the disc and carries the brake pads. The caliper also contains the hydraulic components that cause the pads to pinch the disc when the brakes are applied. A caliper is also a measuring tool that can be set to measure inside or outside dimensions of an object.

Camshaft A rotating shaft on which a series of cam lobes operate the valve mechanisms. The camshaft may be driven by gears, by sprockets and chain or by sprockets and a belt.

Canister A container in an evaporative emission control system; contains activated charcoal granules to trap vapours from the fuel system.

Canister

Carburettor A device which mixes fuel with air in the proper proportions to provide a desired power output from a spark ignition internal combustion engine.

Castellated Resembling the parapets along the top of a castle wall. For example, a castellated balljoint stud nut.

Castor In wheel alignment, the backward or forward tilt of the steering axis. Castor is positive when the steering axis is inclined rearward at the top.

Catalytic converter A silencer-like device in the exhaust system which converts certain pollutants in the exhaust gases into less harmful substances.

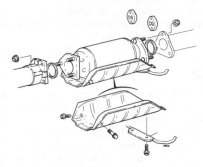

Catalytic converter

Circlip A ring-shaped clip used to prevent endwise movement of cylindrical parts and shafts. An internal circlip is installed in a groove in a housing; an external circlip fits into a groove on the outside of a cylindrical piece such as a shaft.

Clearance The amount of space between two parts. For example, between a piston and a cylinder, between a bearing and a journal, etc.

Coil spring A spiral of elastic steel found in various sizes throughout a vehicle, for example as a springing medium in the suspension and in the valve train.

Compression Reduction in volume, and increase in pressure and temperature, of a gas, caused by squeezing it into a smaller space.

Compression ratio The relationship between cylinder volume when the piston is at top dead centre and cylinder volume when the piston is at bottom dead centre.

Constant velocity (CV) joint A type of universal joint that cancels out vibrations caused by driving power being transmitted through an angle.

Core plug A disc or cup-shaped metal device inserted in a hole in a casting through which core was removed when the casting was formed. Also known as a freeze plug or expansion plug.

Crankcase The lower part of the engine block in which the crankshaft rotates.

Crankshaft The main rotating member, or shaft, running the length of the crankcase, with offset "throws" to which the connecting rods are attached.

Crankshaft assembly

Crocodile clip See Alligator clip

D

Diagnostic code Code numbers obtained by accessing the diagnostic mode of an engine management computer. This code can be used to determine the area in the system where a malfunction may be located.

Disc brake A brake design incorporating a rotating disc onto which brake pads are squeezed. The resulting friction converts the energy of a moving vehicle into heat.

Double-overhead cam (DOHC) An engine that uses two overhead camshafts, usually one for the intake valves and one for the exhaust valves.

Drivebelt(s) The belt(s) used to drive accessories such as the alternator, water pump, power steering pump, air conditioning compressor, etc. off the crankshaft pulley.

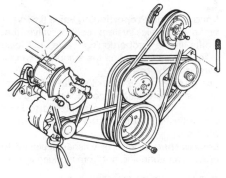

Accessory drivebelts

Driveshaft Any shaft used to transmit motion. Commonly used when referring to the axleshafts on a front wheel drive vehicle.

Drum brake A type of brake using a drum-shaped metal cylinder attached to the inner surface of the wheel. When the brake pedal is pressed, curved brake shoes with friction linings press against the inside of the drum to slow or stop the vehicle.

E

EGR valve A valve used to introduce exhaust gases into the intake air stream.

Electronic control unit (ECU) A computer which controls (for instance) ignition and fuel injection systems, or an anti-lock braking system. For more information refer to the *Haynes Automotive Electrical and Electronic Systems Manual.*

Electronic Fuel Injection (EFI) A computer controlled fuel system that distributes fuel through an injector located in each intake port of the engine.

Emergency brake A braking system, independent of the main hydraulic system, that can be used to slow or stop the vehicle if the primary brakes fail, or to hold the vehicle stationary even though the brake pedal isn't depressed. It usually consists of a hand lever that actuates either front or rear brakes mechanically through a series of cables and linkages. Also known as a handbrake or parking brake.

Endfloat The amount of lengthwise movement between two parts. As applied to a crankshaft, the distance that the crankshaft can move forward and back in the cylinder block.

Engine management system (EMS) A computer controlled system which manages the fuel injection and the ignition systems in an integrated fashion.

Exhaust manifold A part with several passages through which exhaust gases leave the engine combustion chambers and enter the exhaust pipe.

F

Fan clutch A viscous (fluid) drive coupling device which permits variable engine fan speeds in relation to engine speeds.

Feeler blade A thin strip or blade of hardened steel, ground to an exact thickness, used to check or measure clearances between parts.

Feeler blade

Firing order The order in which the engine cylinders fire, or deliver their power strokes, beginning with the number one cylinder.

Flywheel A heavy spinning wheel in which energy is absorbed and stored by means of momentum. On cars, the flywheel is attached to the crankshaft to smooth out firing impulses.

Free play The amount of travel before any action takes place. The "looseness" in a linkage, or an assembly of parts, between the initial application of force and actual movement. For example, the distance the brake pedal moves before the pistons in the master cylinder are actuated.

Fuse An electrical device which protects a circuit against accidental overload. The typical fuse contains a soft piece of metal which is calibrated to melt at a predetermined current flow (expressed as amps) and break the circuit.

Fusible link A circuit protection device consisting of a conductor surrounded by heat-resistant insulation. The conductor is smaller than the wire it protects, so it acts as the weakest link in the circuit. Unlike a blown fuse, a failed fusible link must frequently be cut from the wire for replacement.

G

Gap The distance the spark must travel in jumping from the centre electrode to the side electrode in a spark plug. Also refers to the spacing between the points in a contact breaker assembly in a conventional points-type ignition, or to the distance between the reluctor or rotor and the pickup coil in an electronic ignition.

Adjusting spark plug gap

Gasket Any thin, soft material - usually cork, cardboard, asbestos or soft metal - installed between two metal surfaces to ensure a good seal. For instance, the cylinder head gasket seals the joint between the block and the cylinder head.

Gasket

Gauge An instrument panel display used to monitor engine conditions. A gauge with a movable pointer on a dial or a fixed scale is an analogue gauge. A gauge with a numerical readout is called a digital gauge.

H

Halfshaft A rotating shaft that transmits power from the final drive unit to a drive wheel, usually when referring to a live rear axle.

Harmonic balancer A device designed to reduce torsion or twisting vibration in the crankshaft. May be incorporated in the crankshaft pulley. Also known as a vibration damper.

Hone An abrasive tool for correcting small irregularities or differences in diameter in an engine cylinder, brake cylinder, etc.

Hydraulic tappet A tappet that utilises hydraulic pressure from the engine's lubrication system to maintain zero clearance (constant contact with both camshaft and valve stem). Automatically adjusts to variation in valve stem length. Hydraulic tappets also reduce valve noise.

I

Ignition timing The moment at which the spark plug fires, usually expressed in the number of crankshaft degrees before the piston reaches the top of its stroke.

Inlet manifold A tube or housing with passages through which flows the air-fuel mixture (carburettor vehicles and vehicles with throttle body injection) or air only (port fuel-injected vehicles) to the port openings in the cylinder head.

J

Jump start Starting the engine of a vehicle with a discharged or weak battery by attaching jump leads from the weak battery to a charged or helper battery.

L

Load Sensing Proportioning Valve (LSPV) A brake hydraulic system control valve that works like a proportioning valve, but also takes into consideration the amount of weight carried by the rear axle.

Locknut A nut used to lock an adjustment nut, or other threaded component, in place. For example, a locknut is employed to keep the adjusting nut on the rocker arm in position.

Lockwasher A form of washer designed to prevent an attaching nut from working loose.

M

MacPherson strut A type of front suspension system devised by Earle MacPherson at Ford of England. In its original form, a simple lateral link with the anti-roll bar creates the lower control arm. A long strut - an integral coil spring and shock absorber - is mounted between the body and the steering knuckle. Many modern so-called MacPherson strut systems use a conventional lower A-arm and don't rely on the anti-roll bar for location.

Multimeter An electrical test instrument with the capability to measure voltage, current and resistance.

N

NOx Oxides of Nitrogen. A common toxic pollutant emitted by petrol and diesel engines at higher temperatures.

O

Ohm The unit of electrical resistance. One volt applied to a resistance of one ohm will produce a current of one amp.

Ohmmeter An instrument for measuring electrical resistance.

O-ring A type of sealing ring made of a special rubber-like material; in use, the O-ring is compressed into a groove to provide the sealing action.

Overhead cam (ohc) engine An engine with the camshaft(s) located on top of the cylinder head(s).

Overhead valve (ohv) engine An engine with the valves located in the cylinder head, but with the camshaft located in the engine block.

Oxygen sensor A device installed in the engine exhaust manifold, which senses the oxygen content in the exhaust and converts this information into an electric current. Also called a Lambda sensor.

P

Phillips screw A type of screw head having a cross instead of a slot for a corresponding type of screwdriver.

Plastigage A thin strip of plastic thread, available in different sizes, used for measuring clearances. For example, a strip of Plastigage is laid across a bearing journal. The parts are assembled and dismantled; the width of the crushed strip indicates the clearance between journal and bearing.

Plastigage

Propeller shaft The long hollow tube with universal joints at both ends that carries power from the transmission to the differential on front-engined rear wheel drive vehicles.

Proportioning valve A hydraulic control valve which limits the amount of pressure to the rear brakes during panic stops to prevent wheel lock-up.

R

Rack-and-pinion steering A steering system with a pinion gear on the end of the steering shaft that mates with a rack (think of a geared wheel opened up and laid flat). When the steering wheel is turned, the pinion turns, moving the rack to the left or right. This movement is transmitted through the track rods to the steering arms at the wheels.

Radiator A liquid-to-air heat transfer device designed to reduce the temperature of the coolant in an internal combustion engine cooling system.

Refrigerant Any substance used as a heat transfer agent in an air-conditioning system. R-12 has been the principle refrigerant for many years; recently, however, manufacturers have begun using R-134a, a non-CFC substance that is considered less harmful to the ozone in the upper atmosphere.

Rocker arm A lever arm that rocks on a shaft or pivots on a stud. In an overhead valve engine, the rocker arm converts the upward movement of the pushrod into a downward movement to open a valve.

Rotor In a distributor, the rotating device inside the cap that connects the centre electrode and the outer terminals as it turns, distributing the high voltage from the coil secondary winding to the proper spark plug. Also, that part of an alternator which rotates inside the stator. Also, the rotating assembly of a turbocharger, including the compressor wheel, shaft and turbine wheel.

Runout The amount of wobble (in-and-out movement) of a gear or wheel as it's rotated. The amount a shaft rotates "out-of-true." The out-of-round condition of a rotating part.

S

Sealant A liquid or paste used to prevent leakage at a joint. Sometimes used in conjunction with a gasket.

Sealed beam lamp An older headlight design which integrates the reflector, lens and filaments into a hermetically-sealed one-piece unit. When a filament burns out or the lens cracks, the entire unit is simply replaced.

Serpentine drivebelt A single, long, wide accessory drivebelt that's used on some newer vehicles to drive all the accessories, instead of a series of smaller, shorter belts. Serpentine drivebelts are usually tensioned by an automatic tensioner.

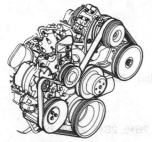

Serpentine drivebelt

Shim Thin spacer, commonly used to adjust the clearance or relative positions between two parts. For example, shims inserted into or under bucket tappets control valve clearances. Clearance is adjusted by changing the thickness of the shim.

Slide hammer A special puller that screws into or hooks onto a component such as a shaft or bearing; a heavy sliding handle on the shaft bottoms against the end of the shaft to knock the component free.

Sprocket A tooth or projection on the periphery of a wheel, shaped to engage with a chain or drivebelt. Commonly used to refer to the sprocket wheel itself.

Starter inhibitor switch On vehicles with an automatic transmission, a switch that prevents starting if the vehicle is not in Neutral or Park.

Strut See MacPherson strut.

T

Tappet A cylindrical component which transmits motion from the cam to the valve stem, either directly or via a pushrod and rocker arm. Also called a cam follower.

Thermostat A heat-controlled valve that regulates the flow of coolant between the cylinder block and the radiator, so maintaining optimum engine operating temperature. A thermostat is also used in some air cleaners in which the temperature is regulated.

Thrust bearing The bearing in the clutch assembly that is moved in to the release levers by clutch pedal action to disengage the clutch. Also referred to as a release bearing.

Timing belt A toothed belt which drives the camshaft. Serious engine damage may result if it breaks in service.

Timing chain A chain which drives the camshaft.

Toe-in The amount the front wheels are closer together at the front than at the rear. On rear wheel drive vehicles, a slight amount of toe-in is usually specified to keep the front wheels running parallel on the road by offsetting other forces that tend to spread the wheels apart.

Toe-out The amount the front wheels are closer together at the rear than at the front. On front wheel drive vehicles, a slight amount of toe-out is usually specified.

Tools For full information on choosing and using tools, refer to the *Haynes Automotive Tools Manual*.

Tracer A stripe of a second colour applied to a wire insulator to distinguish that wire from another one with the same colour insulator.

Tune-up A process of accurate and careful adjustments and parts replacement to obtain the best possible engine performance.

Turbocharger A centrifugal device, driven by exhaust gases, that pressurises the intake air. Normally used to increase the power output from a given engine displacement, but can also be used primarily to reduce exhaust emissions (as on VW's "Umwelt" Diesel engine).

U

Universal joint or U-joint A double-pivoted connection for transmitting power from a driving to a driven shaft through an angle. A U-joint consists of two Y-shaped yokes and a cross-shaped member called the spider.

V

Valve A device through which the flow of liquid, gas, vacuum, or loose material in bulk may be started, stopped, or regulated by a movable part that opens, shuts, or partially obstructs one or more ports or passageways. A valve is also the movable part of such a device.

Valve clearance The clearance between the valve tip (the end of the valve stem) and the rocker arm or tappet. The valve clearance is measured when the valve is closed.

Vernier caliper A precision measuring instrument that measures inside and outside dimensions. Not quite as accurate as a micrometer, but more convenient.

Viscosity The thickness of a liquid or its resistance to flow.

Volt A unit for expressing electrical "pressure" in a circuit. One volt that will produce a current of one ampere through a resistance of one ohm.

W

Welding Various processes used to join metal items by heating the areas to be joined to a molten state and fusing them together. For more information refer to the *Haynes Automotive Welding Manual*.

Wiring diagram A drawing portraying the components and wires in a vehicle's electrical system, using standardised symbols. For more information refer to the *Haynes Automotive Electrical and Electronic Systems Manual*.

Note: *References throughout this index are in the form - "Chapter number" • "page number"*

Haynes Manuals – The Complete List

Title	Book No.
ALFA ROMEO	
Alfa Romeo Alfasud/Sprint (74 - 88)	0292
Alfa Romeo Alfetta (73 - 87)	0531
AUDI	
Audi 80 (72 - Feb 79)	0207
Audi 80, 90 (79 - Oct 86) & Coupe (81 - Nov 88)	0605
Audi 80, 90 (Oct 86 - 90) & Coupe (Nov 88 - 90)	1491
Audi 100 (Oct 82 - 90) & 200 (Feb 84 - Oct 89)	0907
Audi 100 & A6 Petrol & Diesel (May 91 - May 97)	3504
AUSTIN	
Austin/MG/Rover Maestro 1.3 & 1.6 (83 - 95)	0922
Austin/MG Metro (80 - May 90)	0718
Austin/Rover Montego 1.3 & 1.6 (84 - 94)	1066
Austin/MG/Rover Montego 2.0 (84 - 95)	1067
Mini (59 - 69)	0527
Mini (69 - Oct 96)	0646
Austin/Rover 2.0 litre Diesel Engine (86 - 93)	1857
BEDFORD	
Bedford CF (69 - 87)	0163
Bedford/Vauxhall Rascal & Suzuki Supercarry (86 - Oct 94)	3015
BMW	
BMW 316, 320 & 320i (4-cyl) (75 - Feb 83)	0276
BMW 320, 320i, 323i & 325i (6-cyl) (Oct 77 - Sept 87)	0815
BMW 3-Series (Apr 91 - 96)	3210
BMW 3- & 5-Series (sohc) (81 - 91)	1948
BMW 520i & 525e (Oct 81 - June 88)	1560
BMW 525, 528 & 528i (73 - Sept 81)	0632
CITROEN	
Citroën 2CV, Ami & Dyane (67 - 90)	0196
Citroën AX Petrol & Diesel (87 - 97)	3014
Citroën BX (83 - 94)	0908
Citroën C15 Van Petrol & Diesel (89 - Oct 98)	3509
Citroën CX (75 - 88)	0528
Citroën Saxo Petrol & Diesel (96 - 98)	3506
Citroën Visa (79 - 88)	0620
Citroën Xantia Petrol & Diesel (93 - 98)	3082
Citroën XM Petrol & Diesel (89 - 98)	3451
Citroën ZX Diesel (91 - 93)	1922
Citroën ZX Petrol (91 - 94)	1881
Citroën 1.7 & 1.9 litre Diesel Engine (84 - 96)	1379
COLT	
Colt/Mitsubishi 1200, 1250 & 1400 (79 - May 84)	0600
FIAT	
Fiat 126 (73 - 87)	0305
Fiat 127 (71 - 83)	0193
Fiat 500 (57 - 73)	0090
Fiat Cinquecento (93 - 98)	3501
Fiat Panda (81 - 95)	0793
Fiat Punto Petrol & Diesel (94 - 99)	3251
Fiat Regata (84 - 88)	1167
Fiat Tipo (88 - 91)	1625
Fiat Uno (83 - 95)	0923
Fiat X1/9 (74 - 89)	0273

Title	Book No.
FORD	
Ford Capri II (& III) 1.6 & 2.0 (74 - 87)	0283
Ford Capri II (& III) 2.8 & 3.0 (74 - 87)	1309
Ford Cortina Mk IV (& V) 1.6 & 2.0 (76 - 83)	0343
Ford Escort (75 - Aug 80)	0280
Ford Escort (Sept 80 - Sept 90)	0686
Ford Escort & Orion (Sept 90 - 97)	1737
Ford Escort Mk II Mexico, RS 1600 & RS 2000 (75 - 80)	0735
Ford Fiesta (76 - Aug 83)	0334
Ford Fiesta (Aug 83 - Feb 89)	1030
Ford Fiesta (Feb 89 - Oct 95)	1595
Ford Fiesta Petrol & Diesel (Oct 95 - 97)	3397
Ford Granada (Sept 77 - Feb 85)	0481
Ford Granada & Scorpio (Mar 85 - 94)	1245
Ford Ka (96 - 99)	3570
Ford Mondeo Petrol (93 - 99)	1923
Ford Mondeo Diesel (93 - 96)	3465
Ford Orion (83 - Sept 90)	1009
Ford Sierra 4 cyl. (82 - 93)	0903
Ford Sierra V6 (82 - 91)	0904
Ford Transit Petrol (Mk 2) (78 - Jan 86)	0719
Ford Transit Petrol (Mk 3) (Feb 86 - 89)	1468
Ford Transit Diesel (Feb 86 - 99)	3019
Ford 1.6 & 1.8 litre Diesel Engine (84 - 96)	1172
Ford 2.1, 2.3 & 2.5 litre Diesel Engine (77 - 90)	1606
FREIGHT ROVER	
Freight Rover Sherpa (74 - 87)	0463
HILLMAN	
Hillman Avenger (70 - 82)	0037
HONDA	
Honda Accord (76 - Feb 84)	0351
Honda Accord (Feb 84 - Oct 85)	1177
Honda Civic (Feb 84 - Oct 87)	1226
Honda Civic (Nov 91 - 96)	3199
HYUNDAI	
Hyundai Pony (85 - 94)	3398
JAGUAR	
Jaguar E Type (61 - 72)	0140
Jaguar MkI & II, 240 & 340 (55 - 69)	0098
Jaguar XJ6, XJ & Sovereign; Daimler Sovereign (68 - Oct 86)	0242
Jaguar XJ6 & Sovereign (Oct 86 - Sept 94)	3261
Jaguar XJ12, XJS & Sovereign; Daimler Double Six (72 - 88)	0478
JEEP	
Jeep Cherokee Petrol (93 - 96)	1943
LADA	
Lada 1200, 1300, 1500 & 1600 (74 - 91)	0413
Lada Samara (87 - 91)	1610
LAND ROVER	
Land Rover 90, 110 & Defender Diesel (83 - 95)	3017
Land Rover Discovery Diesel (89 - 95)	3016
Land Rover Series IIA & III Diesel (58 - 85)	0529
Land Rover Series II, IIA & III Petrol (58 - 85)	0314
MAZDA	
Mazda 323 (Mar 81 - Oct 89)	1608
Mazda 323 (Oct 89 - 98)	3455

Title	Book No.
Mazda 626 (May 83 - Sept 87)	0929
Mazda B-1600, B-1800 & B-2000 Pick-up (72 - 88)	0267
MERCEDES-BENZ	
Mercedes-Benz 190, 190E & 190D Petrol & Diesel (83 - 93)	3450
Mercedes-Benz 200, 240, 300 Diesel (Oct 76 - 85)	1114
Mercedes-Benz 250 & 280 (68 - 72)	0346
Mercedes-Benz 250 & 280 (123 Series) (Oct 76 - 84)	0677
Mercedes-Benz 124 Series (85 - Aug 93)	3253
MG	
MGB (62 - 80)	0111
MG Midget & AH Sprite (58 - 80)	0265
MITSUBISHI	
Mitsubishi Shogun & L200 Pick-Ups (83 - 94)	1944
MORRIS	
Morris Ital 1.3 (80 - 84)	0705
Morris Minor 1000 (56 - 71)	0024
NISSAN	
Nissan Bluebird (May 84 - Mar 86)	1223
Nissan Bluebird (Mar 86 - 90)	1473
Nissan Cherry (Sept 82 - 86)	1031
Nissan Micra (83 - Jan 93)	0931
Nissan Micra (93 - 99)	3254
Nissan Primera (90 - Oct 96)	1851
Nissan Stanza (82 - 86)	0824
Nissan Sunny (May 82 - Oct 86)	0895
Nissan Sunny (Oct 86 - Mar 91)	1378
Nissan Sunny (Apr 91 - 95)	3219
OPEL	
Opel Ascona & Manta (B Series) (Sept 75 - 88)	0316
Opel Ascona (81 - 88) (Not available in UK see Vauxhall Cavalier 0812)	3215
Opel Astra (Oct 91 - Feb 98) (Not available in UK see Vauxhall Astra 1832)	3156
Opel Calibra (90 - 98) see Vauxhall/Opel Calibra Book No. 3502	
Opel Corsa (83 - Mar 93) (Not available in UK see Vauxhall Nova 0909)	3160
Opel Corsa (Mar 93 - 97) (Not available in UK see Vauxhall Corsa 1985)	3159
Opel Frontera Petrol & Diesel (91 - 98) see Vauxhall/Opel Frontera Book No. 3454	
Opel Kadett (Nov 79 - Oct 84)	0634
Opel Kadett (Oct 84 - Oct 91) (Not available in UK see Vauxhall Astra & Belmont 1136)	3196
Opel Omega & Senator (86 - 94) (Not available in UK see Vauxhall Carlton & Senator 1469)	3157
Opel Omega (94 - 99) (See Vauxhall/Opel Omega Book No. 3510)	
Opel Rekord (Feb 78 - Oct 86)	0543
Opel Vectra (Oct 88 - Oct 95) (Not available in UK see Vauxhall Cavalier 1570)	3158
Opel Vectra Petrol & Diesel (95 - 98) (Not available in UK see Vauxhall Vectra 3396)	3523

Title	Book No.
PEUGEOT	
Peugeot 106 Petrol & Diesel (91 - 98)	1882
Peugeot 205 (83 - 95)	0932
Peugeot 305 (78 - 89)	0538
Peugeot 306 Petrol & Diesel (93 - 99)	3073
Peugeot 309 (86 - 93)	1266
Peugeot 405 Petrol (88 - 96)	1559
Peugeot 405 Diesel (88 - 96)	3198
Peugeot 406 Petrol & Diesel (96 - 97)	3394
Peugeot 505 (79 - 89)	0762
Peugeot 1.7/1.8 & 1.9 litre Diesel Engine (82 - 96)	0950
Peugeot 2.0, 2.1, 2.3 & 2.5 litre Diesel Engines (74 - 90)	1607
PORSCHE	
Porsche 911 (65 - 85)	0264
Porsche 924 & 924 Turbo (76 - 85)	0397
PROTON	
Proton (89 - 97)	3255
RANGE ROVER	
Range Rover V8 (70 - Oct 92)	0606
RELIANT	
Reliant Robin & Kitten (73 - 83)	0436
RENAULT	
Renault 5 (Feb 85 - 96)	1219
Renault 9 & 11 (82 - 89)	0822
Renault 18 (79 - 86)	0598
Renault 19 Petrol (89 - 94)	1646
Renault 19 Diesel (89 - 95)	1946
Renault 21 (86 - 94)	1397
Renault 25 (84 - 92)	1228
Renault Clio Petrol (91 - May 98)	1853
Renault Clio Diesel (91 - June 96)	3031
Renault Espace Petrol & Diesel (85 - 96)	3197
Renault Laguna Petrol & Diesel (94 - 96)	3252
Renault Mégane & Scénic Petrol & Diesel (96 - 98)	3395
ROVER	
Rover 213 & 216 (84 - 89)	1116
Rover 214 & 414 (89 - 96)	1689
Rover 216 & 416 (89 - 96)	1830
Rover 211, 214, 216, 218 & 220 Petrol & Diesel (Dec 95 - 98)	3399
Rover 414, 416 & 420 Petrol & Diesel (May 95 - 98)	3453
Rover 618, 620 & 623 (93 - 97)	3257
Rover 820, 825 & 827 (86 - 95)	1380
Rover 3500 (76 - 87)	0365
Rover Metro, 111 & 114 (May 90 - 96)	1711
SAAB	
Saab 90, 99 & 900 (79 - Oct 93)	0765
Saab 900 (Oct 93 - 98)	3512
Saab 9000 (4-cyl) (85 - 95)	1686
SEAT	
Seat Ibiza & Cordoba Petrol & Diesel (Oct 93 - 99)	3571
Seat Ibiza & Malaga (85 - 92)	1609

Title	Book No.
SKODA	
Skoda Estelle (77 - 89)	0604
Skoda Favorit (89 - 96)	1801
Skoda Felicia Petrol & Diesel (95 - 99)	3505
SUBARU	
Subaru 1600 & 1800 (Nov 79 - 90)	0995
SUZUKI	
Suzuki SJ Series, Samurai & Vitara (4-cyl) (82 - 97)	1942
Suzuki Supercarry (86 - Oct 94)	3015
TALBOT	
Talbot Alpine, Solara, Minx & Rapier (75 - 86)	0337
Talbot Horizon (78 - 86)	0473
Talbot Samba (82 - 86)	0823
TOYOTA	
Toyota Carina E (May 92 - 97)	3256
Toyota Corolla (Sept 83 - Sept 87)	1024
Toyota Corolla (80 - 85)	0683
Toyota Corolla (Sept 87 - Aug 92)	1683
Toyota Corolla (Aug 92 - 97)	3259
Toyota Hi-Ace & Hi-Lux (69 - Oct 83)	0304
TRIUMPH	
Triumph Acclaim (81 - 84)	0792
Triumph GT6 & Vitesse (62 - 74)	0112
Triumph Spitfire (62 - 81)	0113
Triumph Stag (70 - 78)	0441
Triumph TR7 (75 - 82)	0322
VAUXHALL	
Vauxhall Astra (80 - Oct 84)	0635
Vauxhall Astra & Belmont (Oct 84 - Oct 91)	1136
Vauxhall Astra (Oct 91 - Feb 98)	1832
Vauxhall/Opel Calibra (90 - 98)	3502
Vauxhall Carlton (Oct 78 - Oct 86)	0480
Vauxhall Carlton & Senator (Nov 86 - 94)	1469
Vauxhall Cavalier 1600, 1900 & 2000 (75 - July 81)	0315
Vauxhall Cavalier (81 - Oct 88)	0812
Vauxhall Cavalier (Oct 88 - 95)	1570
Vauxhall Chevette (75 - 84)	0285
Vauxhall Corsa (Mar 93 - 97)	1985
Vauxhall/Opel Frontera Petrol & Diesel (91 - Sept 98)	3454
Vauxhall Nova (83 - 93)	0909
Vauxhall/Opel Omega (94 - 99)	3510
Vauxhall Vectra Petrol & Diesel (95 - 98)	3396
Vauxhall/Opel 1.5, 1.6 & 1.7 litre Diesel Engine (82 - 96)	1222
VOLKSWAGEN	
VW Beetle 1200 (54 - 77)	0036
VW Beetle 1300 & 1500 (65 - 75)	0039
VW Beetle 1302 & 1302S (70 - 72)	0110
VW Beetle 1303, 1303S & GT (72 - 75)	0159
VW Golf & Jetta Mk 1 1.1 & 1.3 (74 - 84)	0716
VW Golf, Jetta & Scirocco Mk 1 1.5, 1.6 & 1.8 (74 - 84)	0726
VW Golf & Jetta Mk 1 Diesel (78 - 84)	0451
VW Golf & Jetta Mk 2 (Mar 84 - Feb 92)	1081

Title	Book No.
VW Golf & Vento Petrol & Diesel (Feb 92 - 96)	3097
VW LT vans & light trucks (76 - 87)	0637
VW Passat & Santana (Sept 81 - May 88)	0814
VW Passat Petrol & Diesel (May 88 - 96)	3498
VW Polo & Derby (76 - Jan 82)	0335
VW Polo (82 - Oct 90)	0813
VW Polo (Nov 90 - Aug 94)	3245
VW Polo Hatchback Petrol & Diesel (94 - 98)	3500
VW Scirocco (82 - 90)	1224
VW Transporter 1600 (68 - 79)	0082
VW Transporter 1700, 1800 & 2000 (72 - 79)	0226
VW Transporter (air-cooled) (79 - 82)	0638
VW Transporter (water-cooled) (82 - 90)	3452
VOLVO	
Volvo 142, 144 & 145 (66 - 74)	0129
Volvo 240 Series (74 - 93)	0270
Volvo 262, 264 & 260/265 (75 - 85)	0400
Volvo 340, 343, 345 & 360 (76 - 91)	0715
Volvo 440, 460 & 480 (87 - 97)	1691
Volvo 740 & 760 (82 - 91)	1258
Volvo 850 (92 - 96)	3260
Volvo 940 (90 - 96)	3249
Volvo S40 & V40 (96 - 99)	3569
Volvo S70, C70 & V70 (96 - 99)	3573
YUGO/ZASTAVA	
Yugo/Zastava (81 - 90)	1453
AUTOMOTIVE TECHBOOKS	
Automotive Brake Manual	3050
Automotive Carburettor Manual	3288
Automotive Diagnostic Fault Codes Manual	3472
Automotive Diesel Engine Service Guide	3286
Automotive Disc Brake Manual	3542
Automotive Electrical and Electronic Systems Manual	3049
Automotive Engine Management and Fuel Injection Systems Manual	3344
Automotive Gearbox Overhaul Manual	3473
Automotive Service Summaries Manual	3475
Automotive Timing Belt Manual - Ford	3474
Automotive Timing Belts Manual - Austin/Rover	3549
Automotive Timing Belts Manual - Peugeot/Citroën	3568
Automotive Timing Belt Manual - Vauxhall/Opel	3577
Automotive Welding Manual	3053
In-Car Entertainment Manual (3rd Edition)	3363
OTHER TITLES	
Automotive Fuel Injection Systems	9755
Car Bodywork Repair Manual (2nd Edition)	9864
Caravan Manual (2nd Edition)	9894
Motorcaravan Manual, The	L7322
Small Engine Repair Manual	1755
SU Carburettors	0299
Weber Carburettors (to 79)	0393

CL08.09/99

All the products featured on this page are available through most motor accessory shops, cycle shops and book stores. Our policy of continuous updating and development means that titles are being constantly added to the range. For up-to-date information on our complete list of titles, please telephone: (UK) +44 1963 440635 • (USA) +1 805 498 6703 • (France) +33 1 47 78 50 50 • (Sweden) +46 18 124016 • (Australia) +61 3 9763 8100

Preserving Our Motoring Heritage

<
The Model J Duesenberg
Derham Tourster.
Only eight of these
magnificent cars were
ever built – this is the
only example to be found
outside the United
States of America

Almost every car you've ever loved, loathed or desired is gathered under one roof at the Haynes Motor Museum. Over 300 immaculately presented cars and motorbikes represent every aspect of our motoring heritage, from elegant reminders of bygone days, such as the superb Model J Duesenberg to curiosities like the bug-eyed BMW Isetta. There are also many old friends and flames. Perhaps you remember the 1959 Ford Popular that you did your courting in? The magnificent 'Red Collection' is a spectacle of classic sports cars including AC, Alfa Romeo, Austin Healey, Ferrari, Lamborghini, Maserati, MG, Riley, Porsche and Triumph.

A Perfect Day Out

Each and every vehicle at the Haynes Motor Museum has played its part in the history and culture of Motoring. Today, they make a wonderful spectacle and a great day out for all the family. Bring the kids, bring Mum and Dad, but above all bring your camera to capture those golden memories for ever. You will also find an impressive array of motoring memorabilia, a comfortable 70 seat video cinema and one of the most extensive transport book shops in Britain. The Pit Stop Cafe serves everything from a cup of tea to wholesome, home-made meals or, if you prefer, you can enjoy the large picnic area nestled in the beautiful rural surroundings of Somerset.

>
John Haynes O.B.E.,
Founder and
Chairman of the
museum at the wheel
of a Haynes Light 12.

<
Graham Hill's Lola
Cosworth Formula 1
car next to a 1934
Riley Sports.

Roscommon County Library Service

WITHDRAWN FROM STOCK

COUNTY LIBRARY SERVICE
ROSCOMMON

The Museum is situated on the A359 Yeovil to Frome road at Sparkford, just off the A303 in Somerset. It is about 40 miles south of Bristol, and 25 minutes drive from the M5 intersection at Taunton.
Open 9.30am - 5.30pm (10.00am - 4.00pm Winter) 7 days a week, except Christmas Day, Boxing Day and New Years Day
Special rates available for schools, coach parties and outings. Charitable Trust No. 292048